NEW ESSAYS ON THE A PRIORI

THE topics of a priori knowledge and a priori justification have long played a prominent part in epistemology and the theory of meaning. Recently there has been a surge of interest in the proper explication of these notions. These newly commissioned essays, by a distinguished, international group of philosophers, will have substantial influence on later work in this area. They discuss the relations of the a priori to meaning, justification, definition and ontology; they consider the role of the notion on Leibniz, Kant, Frege and Wittgenstein; and they address its role in recent discussions in the philosophy of mind. Particular attention is also paid to the a priori in logic, science and mathematics. The authors exhibit a wide variety of approaches, some remaining skeptical of the notion itself, some proposing that it receive a non-factualist treatment, and others proposing novel ways of explicating and defending it. The editors' Introduction provides a helpful route into the issues.

New Essays on the A Priori

Edited by

Paul Boghossian
and
Christopher Peacocke

CLARENDON PRESS · OXFORD
2000

OXFORD
UNIVERSITY PRESS

Great Clarendon Street, Oxford OX2 6DP

Oxford University Press is a department of the University of Oxford.
It furthers the University's objective of excellence in research, scholarship,
and education by publishing worldwide in

Oxford New York

Athens Auckland Bangkok Bogotá Buenos Aires Calcutta
Cape Town Chennai Dar es Salaam Delhi Florence Hong Kong Istanbul
Karachi Kuala Lumpur Madrid Melbourne Mexico City Mumbai
Nairobi Paris São Paulo Shanghai Singapore Taipei Tokyo Toronto Warsaw

with associated companies in Berlin Ibadan

Oxford is a registered trade mark of Oxford University Press
in the UK and in certain other countries

Published in the United States
by Oxford University Press Inc., New York

British Library Cataloguing in Publication Data

Data available

Library of Congress Cataloging in Publication Data

New essays on the a priori / edited by Paul Boghossian and Christopher Peacocke
p. cm.
Includes biographical references and index.
1. A priori. I. Boghossian, Paul Artin. II. Peacocke, Christopher.
BD181.3.N49 2000   121′3—dc21   00–057421

ISBN 0–19–924126–0
ISBN 0–19–924127–9 (pbk.)

1 3 5 7 9 10 8 6 4 2

Typeset in Times
by Cambrian Typesetters, Frimley, Surrey
Printed in Great Britain
on acid-free paper by
Biddles Ltd
Guildford & King's Lynn

Acknowledgements

We have been greatly helped in the preparation of this collection by the work of Jo Cartmell in Oxford. Christopher Peacocke once again thanks the Leverhulme Trust, and Paul Boghossian thanks the National Endowment for the Humanities, for time and research support. We are also especially grateful for the assistance of Matthew Soteriou in preparing the Index at exceptionally short notice.

Contents

Contents

Notes on Contributors

PAUL BOGHOSSIAN is Professor of Philosophy and Chair of Department at New York University. He previously taught at the University of Michigan at Ann Arbor. Amongst other topics, he has written about colour, self-knowledge, eliminativism, rule-following, naturalism, analytic truth, and the aesthetics of music.

BILL BREWER is Lecturer in Philosophy at Oxford University and Fellow of St Catherine's College. He has been a Visiting Professor at Brown and Berkeley, and is also on the Steering Committee of the British Academy project on Consciousness and Self-Consciousness. He is an editor of *Spatial Representation* (Oxford University Press, 1999), and author of *Perception and Reason* (Oxford University Press, 1999), along with various articles in epistemology and philosophy of mind.

TYLER BURGE is a Professor of Philosophy at the University of California, Los Angeles. He is the author of many articles in philosophy of mind, philosophy of language, philosophy of logic, epistemology, and history of philosophy. He has given numerous lecture series, including the Locke Lectures at Oxford in 1993 and the Whitehead Lectures at Harvard in 1994. He is a member of the American Academy of Arts and Sciences and a corresponding member of the British Academy.

QUASSIM CASSAM is Reader in Philosophy at Oxford University, and Fellow and Tutor in Philosophy at Wadham College, Oxford. He is the author of *Self and the World* (Oxford University Press, 1997) and editor of *Self-Knowledge* (Oxford University Press, 1994).

MARTIN DAVIES was a Lecturer and then Reader in Philosophy at Birkbeck College London, and subsequently the Wilde Reader in Mental Philosophy at Oxford. He is now Professor of Philosophy in the Research School of Social Sciences, Australian National University. He is the author of *Meaning, Quantification, Necessity: Themes in Philosophical Logic* and of papers in the philosophy of language, mind, and psychology. He is working on a book, *Knowing What Thought Requires*. He was one of the founding editor of the interdisciplinary journal *Mind and Language* and has edited collections on *Consciousness*, *Folk Psychology*, *Mental Stimulation*, and most recently, *Pathologies of Belief*.

HARTRY FIELD is Professor of Philosophy at New York University. He is the author of *Science Without Numbers*; *Realism, Mathematics and Modality*; and the forthcoming volume *Truth, Indeterminacy and Objectivity*.

MICHAEL FRIEDMAN is Ruth N. Halls Professor of Arts and Humanities, Professor of History and Philosophy of Science, and Professor of Philosophy at Indiana University. He is the author of *Foundations of Space-Time Theories: Relativistic Physics and Philosophy of Science* (Princeton, 1983), *Kant and the Exact Sciences* (Harvard, 1992), and *Reconsidering Logical Positivism* (Cambridge, 1999).

BOB HALE is Professor of Metaphysical Philosophy in the University of Glasgow. His research interests lie mainly in the philosophy of mathematics and the philosophy of logic and language. He is the author of *Abstract Object*.

PAUL HORWICH is Kornblith Professor of Philosophy at the Graduate Center of the City University of New York. He taught at MIT from 1973 until 1995, spent the next five years at University College London, and has just moved to New York. He is the author of *Probability and Evidence* (1982), *Assymetries in Time* (1987), *Truth* (1990: 2nd edn. 1998), and *Meaning* (1998).

FRANK JACKSON is Professor of Philosophy and Director of the Institute for Advanced Studies, Australian National University. His publications include *Perception, Conditionals, Philosophy of Mind and Cognition* (with David Braddon-Mitchell), *From Metaphysics to Ethics*, and *Mind, Method and Conditionals*. He gave the Locke lectures in Oxford in 1995.

PHILIP KITCHER is Professor of Philosophy at Columbia University. He has written books and articles on various topics in the philosophy of science, the philosophy of biology, and the philosophy of mathematics, including *The Nature of Mathematical Knowledge* (Oxford University Press, 1983).

PENELOPE MADDY is Professor and Chair of the Department of Logic and Philosophy of Science at the University of California at Irvine. She is the author of *Naturalism in Mathematics* (Oxford University Press, 1990), and a member of the American Academy of Arts and Sciences.

THOMAS NAGEL is Professor of Philosophy and Law at New York University. Among his books are *The View from Nowhere* and *The Last Word*.

CHRISTOPHER PEACOCKE is Professor of Philosophy at New York University. He is a Fellow of the British Academy. He was previously Waynflete Professor of Metaphysical Philosophy at Oxford University, and Stebbing Professor of

Philosophy at King's College London. He has been a Fellow of All Souls College, Oxford and of New College, Oxford, and has taught at Berkeley and UCLA. His books include *Sense and Content* (1983), *A Study of Concepts* (1992), and *Being Known* (1999).

PETER RAILTON is Nelson Professor of Philosophy at the University of Michigan, Ann Arbor. He has written on ethics and philosophy of science. This essay represents his first attempt to discuss the nature of the a priori.

STEWART SHAPIRO is Professor of Philosophy at the Ohio State University at Newark and Professorial Fellow at the University of St Andrews in Scotland. His major works include *Foundations without Foundationalism* (Oxford University Press, 1991), which is an articulation and defence of second-order logic; *Philosophy of Mathematics: Structures and Ontology* (Oxford University Press, 1997), a presentation of structuralism; and his recent text in the philosophy of mathematics, *Thinking about Mathematics* (Oxford University Press, 2000).

CRISPIN WRIGHT, FBA, FRSE, is Bishop Wardlaw Professor and Professor of Logic and Metaphysics at the University of St Andrews, and a regular Visiting Professor at Columbia Univeristy. He currently holds a Leverhulme Research Professorship. He is the author of *Wittgenstein on the Foundations of Mathematics* (1980), *Frege's Conception of Numbers as Objects* (1983), *Realism, Meaning and Truth* (1987), *Truth and Objectivity* (1992), and, with Bob Hale, is co-author of their forthcoming anthology *The Reason's Proper Study*.

STEPHEN YABLO works mainly in metaphysics, he has strong side interests in logic, epistemology, semantics, and philosophy of mind. His latest interest is the problem that metaphor creates for the project of ontology. He lives in Cambridge, Massachusetts, and is Professor of Philosophy in the Department of Linguistics and Philosophy at Massachusetts Institute of Technology.

1

Introduction

Paul Boghossian and Christopher Peacocke

1. IDENTIFYING THE A PRIORI

An a priori proposition is one which can be known to be true without any justification from the character of the subject's experience. This is a brief, pre-theoretical characterization that needs some refinement; but it captures the core of what many philosophers have meant by the notion. Under this intuitive characterization, propositions which are plausibly a priori include the following: the axioms, inference rules, and theorems of logic; the axioms and theorems of arithmetic, and likewise the axioms and theorems of other parts of mathematics and other sciences of the abstract; the principles of the probability calculus; principles of colour incompatibility and implication; some definitions; and perhaps some truths of philosophy itself.

To say that something can be known without any justification from the character of the subject's experience is to say that there is a way of coming to know it which does not rely on any such justification. When we are considering issues about the a priori, it can often help to focus on ways of coming to know and their distinctive properties. Suppose you see someone across a restaurant, and you thereby come to believe and know 'That's the cellist Yo-Yo Ma.' The way in which you come to know this may involve the following: you have a memory image of a photograph of Yo-Yo Ma; you believe that the face you see across the restaurant is an older version of that remembered face; and you accept the content of your current perception. The memory, the belief, and your current experience are all causally influential in producing your knowledge; and taken jointly, they entitle you to your belief 'That's the cellist Yo-Yo Ma.' A specification of the way in which something comes to be known will include at least a tree-structure of events and states which are causes of the knowledge, together with some specification of why the thinker makes the transitions it involves.

Now consider someone who comes to know a logical truth, $(p{\supset}q)v(q{\supset}p)$ say, by reading a proof of it. His seeing the lines of the proof, and his seeing the citations of the rules used at each step, cause his belief that $(p{\supset}q)v(q{\supset}p)$. We must, however, distinguish sharply between the relation of causation and the relation of entitlement. The thinker is entitled to his belief that (p⊃q)v(q⊃p) because he has an outright proof of it, resting on no assumptions. The proof itself provides an entitlement to belief in its last line. Perception of the written proof gives access to that entitlement, but is not itself part of that entitlement.

By contrast, in the case of seeing Yo-Yo Ma, the occurrence of the visual experience of Yo-Yo Ma across the restaurant is part of the entitlement to the belief 'That's Yo-Yo Ma.' It is not as if the visual experience merely gives access to something else which provides the entitlement. There is no further thing to which the visual experience gives access. Rather, the visual experience itself is, in the circumstances, entitling.

On this approach, an a priori proposition is one such that there is a way of coming to know it under which the thinker's entitlement to accept the proposition does not involve the character of the thinker's experience. An a posteriori proposition is one such that any way of coming to know it will involve an entitlement which does concern the character of the thinker's experience. In the same spirit, we may say that an a priori justification is a justification which does not involve the character of the thinker's experience. Similarly, a person comes to know something a priori if the entitlement which makes his belief knowledge does not involve the character of his experience. Amongst ways of coming to know which sustain a priori status, some rationalists, including Frege, have distinguished certain ways as philosophically more fundamental, or canonical, in an account of justification. Some ways of coming to know may be a priori, but rather indirect, as in certain proofs by *reductio ad absurdum*. The distinction between canonical and non-canonical ways of coming to know is not, however, employed by everyone who has used the notion of the a priori.

In the case of a priori propositions, much experience, perhaps of a specific character, may be required to grasp the concepts implicated in the proposition or to access the entitlement to believe it; but conditions of grasp and of access remain distinct from the nature of the entitlement. This is in accord with the traditional rationalist position from Leibniz onwards. Experience may be a precondition of coming to know a prior truths, but those truths nevertheless have a justification, and can also be justified for the thinker, independently of experience.

There are several variant notions of the a priori, of varying degrees of strength. Each variant notion is generated by a different construal of 'experience' as it occurs in the characterization of the a priori. The strictest construal of 'experience' takes it to mean perceptual experience of the world beyond the thinker's body. An intermediate construal takes it to apply to any perceptual experience, whether of the external world, or of the thinker's own bodily states and events. The most general construal takes it to apply to any conscious state or event, whether perception or conscious thinking, wishing, or imagining. If we use the strictest construal of 'experience' in characterizing the a priori, then 'I am in pain' will be counted as a priori, when the thinker judges it because he is in pain. His belief that he is in pain is not justified by the character of any experience of the world beyond his own body. On the intermediate construal, 'I am thinking about which city to visit', when the thinker judges it because he is so thinking, will be counted as a priori. On the most general construal of 'experience', none of these self-ascriptions will be a priori.

Different variants of the notion of the a priori may each be important for different theoretical purposes. The paradigm case of the a posteriori is that of perceptual judgement. One should not, however, simply take it for granted that any judgement in whose etiology a conscious state plays a justifying or entitling role will also be a posteriori. That would be to beg the question against any updated version of Kant's view on geometry. In his essay, Tyler Burge emphasizes that for Kant, the conscious states of pure intuition, a species of imagination, are states which entitle a subject to make judgements of geometrical principles, and provide a justification which is independent of perceptual experience. Burge contrasts the role played by particular intuitions in this Kantian conception with the insistence on derivability from purely general laws in Frege's philosophical explication of the a priori in *The Foundations of Arithmetic*.[1] Any modern elaboration of a neo-Kantian view must of course abandon the commitment to specifically Euclidean geometry; and it is likely to be better received when detached from Kant's transcendental idealism. Some room may remain for a neo-Kantian conception meeting these conditions.

Being a priori is to be sharply distinguished from being necessary, from being true purely in virtue of meaning, and from being knowable infallibly. Examples, and reflection on the nature of the properties, both show that there are a priori propositions which are not necessary. Kripke and Kaplan supplied conclusive examples: 'If something is uniquely F, then the actual F is F' is a priori but not necessary; so, more generally, is anything of the form 'If *p*, then actually *p*.'[2] Reflection on the nature of the properties should also suggest that their extensions may be distinct. For a proposition to be knowably true a priori in the actual world requires only that there be some non-empirical route to its justifiability; but that is very different from its being necessary. Conversely, in the presence of examples of the necessary a posteriori, it is clear that a proposition's being necessary does not ensure that it is a priori.

These preliminary remarks do not conflict with the classical rationalist view, which has received further elaboration in recent work, that all necessity can be

---

[1] G. Frege, *The Foundations of Arithmetic*, tr. J. L. Austin (Oxford: Blackwell, 2nd edn., 1953): last paragraph of section 3.

[2] S. Kripke, *Naming and Necessity* (Oxford: Blackwell, 1980); David Kaplan argues the same for 'I am here now', in 'Demonstratives: An Essay on the Semantics, Logic, Metaphysics, and Epistemology of Demonstratives and Other Indexicals', in *Themes From Kaplan*, ed. J. Almog, J. Perry, and H. Wettstein (New York: Oxford University Press, 1989). Further discussion of the issue would have to address the question of whether in the indexical case a priori status is predicated of something linguistic.

traced back ultimately to the a priori.[3] The non-coincidence of the a priori and the necessary serves just to emphasize how much work any contemporary development of that rationalist view has to do in explaining its notion of the source of necessity.

To say that a proposition is a priori is also not to be committed to the view that it is true purely in virtue of meaning. Something can be both knowable in a way which is justificationally independent of experience, whilst also being true in virtue of its truth condition holding, just like any other truth. Our own view is that Quine decisively refuted the idea that anything could be true purely in virtue of meaning.[4] (The arguments Quine used were quite free of his behaviourist inclinations.) But to refute a bad theory of the nature of the a priori is not to show that the phenomenon of the a priori does not exist. A major challenge for a contemporary theorist of the a priori is to do better in explaining the links between meaning and a priori knowledge, without reverting to the discredited idea of truth purely in virtue of meaning.

A priori justification is not infallible justification. Just as one may be justified in believing an ordinary empirical proposition that is subsequently revealed on empirical grounds to be false, so one may be justified (non-conclusively) in believing an a priori proposition that is subsequently revealed on a priori grounds to be false.

For all that, it may still seem that a priori propositions cannot be defeated by wholly empirical information; that is, that they may still be experientially indefeasible. It may be natural to wonder: if something is empirically defeasible, how can it be known justificationally independently of experience?

Certainly, much of the controversy surrounding the a priori has centred on the question of whether there are principles, such as those of logic or Euclidean geometry, which are immune to empirical disconfirmation. There is, however, nothing contrary to reason in the idea of an a priori warrant which is empirically defeasible. There are general reasons for thinking that there must be some such cases; and there are examples of it. One humble illustration is that of inference to a universal quantification from finitely many instances, so-called enumerative induction. The existence of this particular illustration of the non-conclusive a priori is, philosophically speaking, relatively unproblematic. It is so because it is

---

[3] Some varieties of this general type: G. W. Leibniz, *New Essays on Human Understanding*, tr. and ed. P. Remnant and J. Bennett (Cambridge: Cambridge University Press, 1981); B. van Fraassen, 'The Only Necessity if Verbal Necessity', *Journal of Philosophy* 74 (1977): 71–85, and his *Laws and Symmetry* (Oxford: Oxford University Press, 1989); G. Forbes, *The Metaphysics of Modality* (Oxford: Oxford University Press, 1985); C. Peacocke, *Being Known* (Oxford: Oxford University Press, 1999): ch.4.

[4] 'Truth by Convention' and 'Carnap and Logical Truth', both repr. in W. Quine, *The Ways of Paradox and Other Essays* (Cambridge, Mass.: Harvard University Press, 1976, 2nd edn.). For further discussion, see Paul Boghossian, 'Analyticity', in Bob Hale and Crispin Wright (eds.), *A Companion to the Philosophy of Language* (Oxford: Blackwell, 1998).

an example in which the premises of the transition ensures, a priori, the holding of some but not all of what is required for the truth of its conclusion.

Other apparent instances of non-conclusive a priori justification or entitlement are philosophically much more challenging. Many philosophers have held that a person is a priori, but non-conclusively, entitled to take the representational content of her perceptual experiences, and her memories, and the utterances of other persons, at face value.[5] It seems that no such entitlement could ever emerge solely from experience itself. Experience can lead to new entitlements only if the subject is already entitled to take at least some experiences at face value. The same seems to apply to memory and to testimony. If it is sound, this type of reasoning shows that such instances of non-conclusive and empirically defeasible entitlement must be a priori.

It is, though, one thing to know that these non-conclusive transitions must be a priori, and quite another to know how and why they are so. Though there are various approaches to this issue in the philosophical literature, it remains a major task to give a full explanation of these non-conclusive entitlements, and to unify them with other instances of the a priori.

A further task is that of elucidating the relations of the epistemic notion of the a prior to a closely related concept which emerges in modal semantics. In two-dimensional modal semantics, we consider a range of models in which different worlds are labelled as the actual world. This framework allows characterization of the property of some propositions of being true in the actual world, whichever world is labelled as the actual world. Instances of the form 'If p, then actually p' have this property. The property is a special case of being a logical truth in the framework of Kaplan's logic of demonstratives; or of having, in Robert Stalnaker's framework a 'diagonal proposition' which is always true; or of holding 'Fixedly' in the apparatus of Martin Davies and Lloyd Humberstone.[6] The property seems to be sufficient for being a priori, and it merits further investigation why this is so. The issue is of particular interest, because in these models it is clear that accepting that a proposition has the property is in no way restricting the range of possibilities, and hence does not correspond to any kind of epistemic

---

[5] C. A. J. Coady, *Testimony: A Philosophical Study* (Oxford: Oxford University Press, 1992); T. Burge, 'Content Preservation', *Philosophical Review* 102 (1993): 457–88; L. BonJour, *In Defense of Pure Reason* (Cambridge: Cambridge University Press, 1998); B. Brewer, *Perception and Reason* (Oxford: Oxford University Press, 1999). For a historic statement claiming a parallelism between perception and testimony, see T. Reid, *An Inquiry*, repr. in T. Reid, *Inquiry and Essays*, ed. R. Beanblossom and K. Lehrer (Indianapolis: Hackett, 1983): esp. 87–103.

[6] See D. Kaplan, 'Demonstratives', *Themes from Kaplan*; R. Stalnaker, 'Assertion', repr. in his *Context and Content* (Oxford: Oxford University Press, 1999), esp. his discussion of 'propositional concepts' and the diagonal proposition they determine at 12-16 of his Introduction; and M. Davies and L. Humberston, 'Two Notions of Necessity', *Philosophical Studies* 38 (1980): 1–30. As Stalnaker notes, the earliest investigations of two-dimensional operators seem to have been those of Frank Vlach and Hans Kamp at UCLA.

arrogance. Rather, the possibilities are given in advance; it is just that whichever world turns out to be actual, a proposition with this property will be true with respect to it. Some theorists will find this a tempting model for certain kinds of a priori proposition.

Finally, whilst we are still on the topic of identifying the a priori, we emphasize that, for all the rationalists' insistence on the existence of a priori truths, one should not automatically classify anyone who believes in a priori truth as a rationalist. In his contribution to this collection, Quassim Cassam notes that many self-declared empiricists, including A. J. Ayer, have certainly believed in the existence of a priori truths. Cassam suggests that we obtain a much better understanding of the distinction between rationalist and empiricist positions if we look not to the question of whether there exist a priori truths, but rather to the different explanations which those respective positions offer for the existence of such truths. It is to that issue of explanation which we now turn.

2. EXPLAINING THE A PRIORI

Within the USA, philosophical thought in the second half of the twentieth century has been marked by a profound scepticism about the existence of a priori truths, a scepticism that has been fuelled not so much by the intuitive appearances but by argument. (The British and the Europeans have not exhibited the same scepticism.) While no philosopher denies that there appear to be propositions that are justificationally independent of experience, many have been persuaded by considerations of a theoretical nature that there could not in fact be any.

These considerations may be seen as falling into one of three general types: those which view apriority as being equivalent to, or entailing, a property—such as non-defeasibility—that no proposition could have; those that purport to show that there can be no satisfactory explanation of how any proposition could be known independently of experience; and those that argue that the correct account of the growth of scientific knowledge refutes the suggestion that there are a priori truths. In the present collection, Philip Kitcher's contribution is an instance of the first sort of consideration, and Penelope Maddy's an instance of the third. Quine, whose own scepticism about the a priori has dominated discussion of the subject, deployed a version of each.

Quine may, in rough outline, be represented as having reasoned as follows. Unless we are to resort to postulating occult faculties of knowledge, a priori knowledge will be explicable only if grasp of meaning—understanding—is somehow sufficient for knowledge of truth. Understanding will only suffice for knowledge of truth, however, if there are sentences that are true purely by virtue of their meaning. But there can be no such sentences, and so a priori knowledge is not explicable. In any event, the correct account of the growth of scientific knowledge—as articulated in the famous web-of-belief model—refutes the suggestion that there are sentences whose justification is a priori.

Subsequent discussions have involved the development of a variety of approaches to the a priori which are very different from Quine's, each with their own responses to his arguments. First, and as the contributions of Hartry Field, Paul Horwich, Peter Railton, and Stephen Yablo illustrate, there are several non-meaning-based approaches to explaining the possibility of a priori knowledge. Field's idea is that we can demystify the apriority of certain propositions and rules if we adopt a 'non-factualist' view of justification itself. Peter Railton explores a position in the same spirit as Field's. Railton suggests that we regard apparently a priori principles as rules, regulative of certain practices. He compares the use of rules with a workman's use of a ruler or a carpenter's square—something which serves as a norm, needed for practical purposes, but which is also defeasible. Railton notes the links between his views and those of Wittgenstein in the first part of his *Philosophical Investigations*. Horwich, after mounting a critique of meaning-based approaches to a priori justification, enter-tains the suggestion that apriority might be explicable in terms of innateness and psychological indispensability. Yablo, for his part, explores the suggestion that the apriority of existence claims within the abstract sciences might be attributable to their metaphorical nature. While it is, of course, an open question whether these theories succeed in reconstructing the full-blooded phenomenon of experi-ence-independent knowledge, they show that the theory of understanding is by no means the only epistemological resource open to a proponent of the a priori.

As for Quine's second claim, that any meaning-based approach to the a priori would be committed to the existence of sentences that are true by virtue of mean-ing alone, this too is now faced with developing alternatives. There are a number of different models for the way in which grasp of meaning might contribute to the explanation of a thinker's entitlement to a particular type of transition or belief that make no play whatsoever with the bizarre idea of a metaphysically analytic truth. Paul Boghossian's essay explores one such model for the case of logic, a model that is based on the idea that the logical constants are implicitly defined by certain of the axioms and inference rules in which they are involved. Christopher Peacocke considers more generally how we should conceive of the relations between understanding and the a priori, and suggests a programme for moderate rationalists. Bob Hale and Crispin Wright defend and develop the model of implicit definition, in particular, as one capable of explaining some cases of a priori knowledge. Frank Jackson argues quite generally that anyone who agrees that sentences have representational content and who is not a sceptic should accept that there are a priori truths which outrun the logical truths.

Finally, Quine's claim that the history of science cannot be told correctly in the presence of a commitment to the a priori seems to get matters exactly the wrong way round. In the first place, there is the implausibility of the claim that our acceptance of (say) a truth of arithmetic, whether obvious or unobvious, is justified only by its role in wider empirical theories, let alone total science. It certainly seems that someone can know a truth of arithmetic even if that truth has not played, either for her or for anyone else, any role in empirical science. Moreover, when arithmetic does play a role in some empirical science and empirical reasoning, and is used in predicting the outcome of some experiment, we do not regard the experiment as a test of arithmetic. The scientist who finds an experimental result not in accordance with her theory and auxiliary hypotheses is not entitled to revise current arithmetic in attempting to explain the discrepancy. No particle accelerator, however powerful, can refute the proposition that $7 + 5 = 12$. Any good theory of the a priori, even the most sceptically inclined, must either explain or explain away this phenomenon.

The second salient point is an elaboration of the general consideration we noted earlier, in support of the existence of empirically defeasible a priori warrants. When a thinker reasons to an empirical conclusion from certain premises, it seems that some of the principles of reasoning or belief-formation which he employs must be a priori if the process of reasoning is to be knowledgeable. In their respective contributions to this volume, Stewart Shapiro, Hartry Field, and Michael Friedman investigate the way in which various principles must have an a priori status if the process of empirical confirmation is to make sense. Shapiro focuses on the basic principles of logic, Field on logic and the fundamental epistemic norms, and Friedman on the principles that are constitutive of the spatio-temporal framework within which a particular scientific theory is formulated.

3. THE SCOPE OF THE A PRIORI

Explaining the possibility of a priori knowledge, then, is one of the major challenges faced by a theorist of the a priori; a second challenge, only slightly less important, is to demarcate its proper boundaries. How much, exactly, can we know a priori?

If we adopt the most permissive available reading of 'independent from experience', according to which a priori knowledge just is non-empirical knowledge, then, as noted above, we seem to have intuitively clear instances of a priori knowledge of the principles of logic, arithmetic, geometry, probability, of the principles of colour incompatibility and implication, of some definitions, perhaps of some truths of philosophy itself—and also, given the permissive reading, of the contents of some of our own mental states.

Now, one difficulty that has exercised a number of recent writers is that, when putative instances of a priori knowledge are combined, they seem to lead to an even greater capacity for a priori knowledge than anyone can sensibly claim. For example, it appears to be a truth established by philosophy that many of our concepts have anti-individualist possession conditions: for a thinker to possess one of these concepts it is necessary for him to have been in a certain sort of environment. A much discussed case concerns the concept *water*: to possess this concept, it is said, a chemically indifferent thinker must at some point either have interacted with water, or come into contact with others who have interacted with water.[7]

However, if we combine this putative item of a priori philosophical knowledge with a priori access to the contents of our own propositional attitudes, we seem forced to say that we can know a priori that we have interacted with water. For under the appropriate conditions, instances of the following argument template now seem available a priori:

1. I believe that water is wet.
2. If I believe that water is wet, then someone has interacted with water. Therefore,
3. Someone has interacted with water.

Yet the suggestion that anyone could know the conclusion in question a priori seems absurd. What is to be done?

One obvious strategy is to reject the apriority of one or another of the premises involved. But it is not very appealing: if we can be *that* wrong about what is knowable a priori, how could we be confident about the other claimed instances?

In their respective contributions to this volume, Martin Davies and Bill Brewer explore an alternative way out of this puzzle, one that turns on denying that instances of the argument template are capable of yielding items of genuine a priori knowledge. Brewer argues that empirical knowledge of water is required for a thinker to possess the concept *water* in the first place, so this knowledge cannot be said to be derived a priori by means of the argument. Davies explores the suggestion that there are certain limitations on the transmission of warrant across known a priori entailments, limitations that instances of the argument template necessarily flout.

In a different way, Thomas Nagel, too, is concerned with resisting what he regards as potentially inflated claims to a prior knowledge. The problem that interests Nagel is the role of a priori reasoning in the context of the mind-body problem. A priori reflection on the concepts of mental and physical properties seems to show that mental state and event types could not be identical with physical state and event types. Nagel wishes to block the conclusion that it really does show this because he finds the resultant property dualism profoundly unsatisfactory.

Of course, as Kripke argued in *Naming and Necessity*, the mere inconceivability of a particular property identity need not preclude its truth. Sounds have

---

[7] It is controversial exactly how specific this necessary condition on possession of concepts like water must be, on externalist views. What does seem clear is that, in a significant range of cases, it will be specific enough to raise the problem addressed in the text.

been empirically discovered to be vibrations in the air even though mere reflection on the ingredient concepts might have made that identity appear absurd. So why is it not enough simply to point to this observation?

The answer, as Kripke himself argued, is that a refusal to take an appearance of impossibility (inconceivability) as grounds for a judgement of genuine impossibility must be susceptible of explanation: it must be possible to explain why in this particular case the appearance is held to be misleading. Kripke went on to maintain, however, that in the case of identities involving mental and physical properties, such an explanation would not be available. In his essay, Nagel takes up Kripke's challenge and attempts to reconcile the conceptual appearance of impossibility with the possible identity of mental and physical properties.[8]

---

[8] We thank the referee for Oxford University Press for comments on an earlier draft of this Introduction.

2

Frege on Apriority

Tyler Burge

Frege's logicism incorporated both a set of purported proofs in mathematical logic and an investigation into the epistemology of arithmetic. The epistemological investigation was for him the motivating one. He saw his project as revealing 'the springs of knowledge' and the nature of arithmetical justification. Frege maintained a sophisticated version of the Euclidean position that knowledge of the axioms and theorems of logic, geometry, and arithmetic rests on the *self-evidence* of the axioms, definitions, and rules of inference.[1] The account combines the traditional rationalist view that beliefs that seem obvious are fallible and understanding is hard to come by, with his original insistence that understanding depends not primarily on immediate insight but on a web of inferential capacities.

Central to Frege's rationalism is his view that knowledge of logic and mathematics is fundamentally apriori. In fact, near the end of *The Foundations of Arithmetic* he states that the purpose of the book is to make it probable that 'the laws of arithmetic are analytic judgements and consequently apriori.'[2] In this essay I want to discuss Frege's conception of apriority, with particular reference to its roots in the conceptions of apriority advanced by Leibniz and Kant.

Frege advertised his notion of apriority as a 'clarification' of Kant's notion. It is well known that Frege did not read Kant with serious historical intent. But even

---

I gave a shorter version of this paper at a conference on Frege in Bonn, Germany, in October 1998. I am indebted to John Carriero, Wolfgang Kunne, Christopher Peacocke, Rainer Stuhlmann-Laisz, and Christian Wenzel for comments that led to improvements. In the text I use 'apriori' and 'aposteriori' as single English words. In quotations from Frege, Kant, and Leibniz, I use the Latin phrases 'a priori' and 'a posteriori'. I use 'apriority' instead of the barbaric 'aprioricity'. The latter is the misbegotten result of drawing a mistaken parallel to 'analyticity'. It would be appropriate to the form 'aprioric' which of course has no use. 'Apriority' bears no natural relation to 'apriori'. Quine pointed this out to me several years back.

[1] Burge (1998*a*).

[2] Frege (1884: sect. 87). (Translations are mine. I have consulted Austin's free but often elegant renderings. I will henceforth cite this book by section under the abbreviation "FA" in the text.) Frege's view of analyticity has been more often discussed than his view of apriority. Essentially he takes a proposition to be analytic if it is an axiom of logic or derivable from axioms of logic together with definitions. He rejects conceptions of analyticity that would tie it to containment or to emptiness of substantive content.

allowing for this fact, his advertisement seems to me interestingly misleading. I believe that his notion is in important respects very different from Kant's and more indebted to Leibniz.

I

Frege's only extensive explication of his conception of apriority occurs early in *The Foundations of Arithmetic*. He begins by emphasizing that his conception concerns the ultimate canonical justification associated with a judgement, not the content of truths:

These distinctions between a priori and a posteriori, synthetic and analytic, concern, as I see it,* not the content of the judgement but the justification for the judgement-pronounce-ment [*Urteilsfällung*]. Where there is no such justification, the possibility of drawing the distinctions vanishes. An a priori error is thus just as much a non-entity [*Unding*] as a blue concept. When a proposition is called a posteriori or analytic in my sense, this is not a judgement about the conditions, psychological, physiological, and physical, which have made it possible to form the content of the proposition in our consciousness; nor is it a judgement about the way in which another has come, perhaps erroneously, to believe it true; rather, it is a judgement about the deepest ground upon which rests the justification for holding it to be true.
*(Frege's footnote): By this I do not, of course, want to assign a new sense but only meet [*treffen*] what earlier writers, particularly Kant, have meant. (*FA*, sect. 3)

Frege writes here of apriori judgements. But afterwards he writes of apriori propositions and then apriori truths, and eventually (*FA*, sect. 87, cf. note 1) apriori laws. These differences are, I think, not deeply significant. Judgements in Frege's sense are idealized abstractions, commitments of logic or other sciences, not the acts of individuals. Individuals can instantiate these judgements through their acts of judgement, but the abstract judgements themselves seem to be independent of individual mental acts. Truths and judgements are, of course, different for Frege. But the difference in Frege's logic concerns only their role in the logical structure. Some truths (true antecedents in conditionals) are not judged. They are not marked by the assertion sign. But everything that is judged is true.[3]

---

[3] This doctrine is of a piece with Frege's view that (in logic) inferences can be drawn only from truths. Here he means not that individuals cannot infer things from falsehoods, but rather that the idealized inferences treated in logic proceed only from true axioms. Inferences for Frege are steps in proof that constitute ideal, correct justifications that exhibit the natural justificatory order of truths. Michael Dummett seems to me to get backwards Frege's motivations for the view that proofs have to start from true premises and that one should not derive a theorem by starting with a supposition. Dummett claims that Frege believed that a complete justification is possible *because* of his rejection of inference from reductio or from other suppositions. Cf. Dummett (1991: 25–6). It seems clear that Frege rejected such inference because he thought of proofs as deductive arguments that reveal natural justificatory order. I do not see that this view

Only truths or veridical judgements can be apriori for Frege. He writes that an apriori error is as impossible as a blue concept. Frege justifies his claim that only truths can be apriori by claiming that apriority concerns the nature of the justification for a judgement. Of course, some ordinary judgements can be justified without being true. But Frege seems to be focused on justifications—deductive proofs from self-evident propositions—that cannot lead judgement into error. Here Frege signals his concern with canonical, ideal, rational justifications, for which the truth-guaranteeing principles and proofs of mathematics and logic provide the paradigm.

In predicating apriority of truths and judgements, understood as canonical commitments of logic and mathematics, Frege is following Leibniz.[4] Leibniz gave the first modern explication of apriority. He maintained that a truth is apriori if it is knowable independent of experience.[5] Since Leibniz explicitly indicates that one might depend psychologically on sense experience in order to come to know any truth, he means that a truth is apriori if the justificational force involved in the knowledge's justification is independent of experience.

Like Leibniz, Frege conceives of apriority as applying primarily to abstract intentional structures. Leibniz applied the notion not only to truths but to proofs, conceived as abstract sequences of truths.[6] Frege assumes that all justifications are proofs, indeed deductive proofs. The apriority of a justification (a series of truths constituting a deductive argument) resides in the character of the premises and rules of inference—in the 'deepest ground [justification, reason, *Grund*] on which a judgement rests'. Like Leibniz, Frege thinks that there is a natural order of justification, which consists in a natural justificatory order among truths.

Frege's definitional explication of apriority continues directly from the passage quoted above:

Thus the question is removed from the sphere of psychology and referred, if the truth concerned is a mathematical one, to the sphere of mathematics. It comes down to finding

---

is incompatible with allowing 'proofs' *in the modern sense* that proceed without axioms, by natural deduction. Frege's conception of proof is very different from the modern one. It is concerned with an ideal, natural order of justification. Leibniz also thought of reductios as second-class proofs because they do not reveal the fundamental order of justification. Cf. Leibniz (1705, 1765, 1989: III, iii, 15); also Adams (1994: 109–110). I believe that Dummett may be right in holding that Frege's actual mathematical practice may have been hampered by too strict a focus on the justificatory ideal.

[4] Frege makes explicit his dependence on Leibniz on these matters in Frege (1884: sect. 17): 'we are concerned here not with the mode of discovery but with the ground of proof; or as Leibniz says, "the question here is not about the history of our discoveries, which differs in different men, but about the connection and natural order of truths, which is always the same." ' Frege draws his quotation of Leibniz from Leibniz (1705, 1765, 1989: IV, vii, 9).

[5] Cf. Leibniz (1705, 1765, 1989: IV, ix, 1, 434); Leibniz (1989: 'Primary Truths', 31); Leibniz (1989: 'On Freedom', 97).

[6] Cf. Leibniz (1989: 'First Truths') and Leibniz (1714: sect. 45). There are also occasional attributions of apriority to knowledge or acquaintance. But Leibniz is fairly constant in attributing apriority primarily to truths and proofs.

the proof and following it back to the primitive truths. If on this path one comes only upon general logical laws and on definitions, one has an analytic truth, bearing in mind that one must take account also of all propositions upon which the admissibility of a definition depends. If, however, it is impossible to carry out the proof without making use of truths which are not of a general logical nature, but refer to the sphere of a special science, then the proposition is a synthetic one. For a truth to be a posteriori, it must be that its proof will not work out [*auskommen*] without reference to facts, i.e. to unprovable truths which are not general [*ohne Allgemeinheit*], and which contain assertions about determinate objects [*bestimmte Gegenstände*]. If, on the contrary, it is possible to derive the proof purely from general laws, which themselves neither need nor admit of proof, then the truth is a priori. (*FA*, sect. 3)[7]

Several points about this famous passage need to be made at the outset. Frege distinguishes apriori from analytic truths. Analytic truths derive from general *logical* truths together perhaps with definitions. Apriori truths derive from general laws, regardless of whether they are logical, which neither need nor admit of proof. It is clear that Frege regards all analytic truths as apriori. The relevant logical truths are laws. It is also clear that Frege regards some apriori truths as not analytic. Truths of geometry are synthetic apriori, thus not analytic.

Although Frege uses the language of giving a sufficient condition in explaining 'analytic', 'synthetic', and 'apriori', he uses the language of giving a necessary condition in the case of 'aposteriori'. But Frege elsewhere (e.g. *FA*: sect. 63) uses 'if' when he clearly means 'if and only'. And I believe on a variety of grounds that Frege sees himself as giving necessary and sufficient conditions, probably even definitions, for all four notions. I will mention some of these grounds.

In the passage from section 3 that precedes this passage, and which I quoted above, Frege states that judgements concerning all four categories are judgements about 'the deepest ground upon which rests the justification for holding [the relevant proposition] to be true'. This is a characterization of the nature and content of the judgement, not merely a characterization of a necessary or a sufficient condition. The subsequent individual characterizations of the four categories characterize the nature of the deepest grounds for a predication of each category. Thus they seem to be characterizing the nature of the judgements predicating the categories ('analytic', 'apriori', and so on), not merely one or another condition on their truth.

Frege's characterization of analytic judgements is clearly intended to provide necessary as well as sufficient conditions. His characterization is traditional and may be seen as a gloss on Leibniz's view of analyticity. The parallel in language

---

[7] Austin's translation mistakenly speaks of giving or constructing a proof, which might suggest that the definition concerns what is possible for a human being to do. In fact, Frege's language is abstract and impersonal. His account concerns the nature of the mathematical structures, not human capacities. Austin translates 'bestimmte Gegenstände' as 'particular objects'. In this, I think that he is capturing Frege's intent, but I prefer the more literal translation.

between the characterization of analytic judgements and the characterization of apriori judgements counts towards regarding both as necessary and sufficient. As we shall see, the characterization of apriori judgements is one that Leibniz held to be necessary and sufficient, at least for finite minds. This was known to Frege. If he had meant to be less committal than Leibniz on the matter, it would have been natural for him to have said so.

In the fifth sentence of section 13 of *Foundations*, Frege tries to reconcile his account of intuition as singular with the view that the laws of geometry are general. Frege believed that the laws of geometry are general, that they are about a special domain of (spatial) objects, and that they do not need or admit of proof. He is assuming that arithmetic and geometry are both apriori, but that they differ in that geometry rests on intuition and is synthetic. I think that Frege is attempting to deal with the worry that since geometrical laws rest on intuition, they must rest on particular facts. This would not be a worry unless Frege regarded it as a necessary as well as sufficient condition on the apriority of geometry that its proofs rest on general laws that neither need nor admit of proof.

Frege's solution is roughly that intuition in geometry does not make reference to particular objects, and the geometric proofs begin with self-evident general principles, though they rest in some way, not well articulated (and which we shall discuss later), on the 'not really particular' intuition. Frege is clearly trying to explicate intuition's role in geometry in a way that leaves that role compatible with taking geometrical proofs to be grounded purely in general geometrical laws. Presumably intuition is meant to be part and parcel of the self-evidence of the general laws.

I do not think that Frege quite solves the problem, particularly inasmuch as he intends to agree with Kant. As I shall later argue, Frege is trying to marry a Leibnizian conception of apriority with Kant's account of synthetic apriority in geometry while siding with Leibniz about the analyticity of arithmetic. The marriage is not a complete success.

There is, of course, a parallel worry that runs as an undercurrent through Frege's mature work. The worry is that the attempt to derive arithmetic from general logical laws (which is required for it to be analytic apriori) is incompatible with the particularity of the numbers. How does one derive particularity from generality in arithmetic? The issue is signalled at the end of *Foundations*, sect. 13. This worry centres ultimately on Law V, which is the bridge in Frege's mature theory from generality to particularity. Again, this issue is naturally seen in the light of the demand that in being analytic apriori, arithmetic must derive ultimately from logical laws that are purely general.

For these and other reasons, I shall assume that Frege's characterization of apriority in *Foundations*, sect. 3 is intended as a necessary and sufficient condition. In fact, I think he views it as a definition.

The notion of a fact about a determinate object in Frege's explication of aposteriori truth in the passage from section 3 is reminiscent of Leibniz's identification of

aposteriori truths with truths of 'fact', as contrasted with truths of reason.[8] Frege
and Leibniz agree in not seeing truths of reason as any less 'factual' than truths
of fact. The point is not that they are not factual, but that they are not 'merely'
factual, not merely contingent happenstance. They are principles that are fundamental or necessary to the very nature of things. The point that apriori truths are
general is basic to the Leibniz-Frege conception of apriority. I will return to this
point.

Frege departed from Leibniz in thinking that apriori truths include both truths
of reason and synthetic apriori truths that involve a combination of reason and
geometrical spatial intuition. In this, of course, Frege follows Kant. I believe,
however, that Frege's departure from Leibniz on this point is not as fully Kantian
as it might first appear. I shall return to this point as well.

Mill had claimed that all justification ultimately rests on induction.[9] Turning
Mill virtually on his head, Frege holds that empirical inductive justification is a
species of deductive proof, which contains singular statements together with
some general principle of induction as premises (*FA*: sect. 3). He does not make
clear what he considers the form of the deduction to be. And he does not indicate
in his definition of aposteriori truths how he thinks singular judgements about
'facts' are justified. Presumably he thinks the justification depends in some way
on sense experience. It seems likely that he regarded sense-perceptual observations of facts as primitively justified aposteriori. For our purposes, it is enough
that Frege thought that justifications relevant to apriori truths are either deductive
proofs or self-evident truths. Such justifications have to start with premises that
are self-evident and general.

Frege assumed that all apriori truths, other than basic ones, are provable within
a comprehensive deductive system. Goedel's incompleteness theorems undermine this assumption. But insofar as one conceives of proof informally as an epistemic ordering among truths, one can perhaps see Frege's vision of an epistemic
ordering as worth developing, with appropriate adjustments, despite this problem.[10]

Frege writes that the axioms 'neither need nor admit of proof'. This phrase is
indicative of Frege's view of proof as a canonical justificational ordering of
truths, or ideal judgements, that is independent of individual minds or theories.
Any truth can be 'proved' within some logical theory, in the usual modern sense
of the word 'prove'. But Frege conceived of proof in terms of natural or canonical justification. He saw some truths as fundamental 'unprovable' truths, axioms,
or canonical starting points in a system of ideal canonical justification. Such

---

[8] Cf. e.g. Leibniz (1705, 1765, 1989: IV, vii, 9, 412; IV, ix, 1, 434).

[9] Mill (1843: II, VI, 1).

[10] Michael Dummett (1991: 29–30), in effect makes this point. Dummett errs, however, in
thinking that Frege is concerned with what is knowable by *us* (cf. *ibid*. 24, 26, 28–9). There is
no such parameter in Frege's account. The natural order of justification among truths is
conceived as a matter that is independent of whether *we* can follow it.

primitive truths do not need proof in that they are self-evident or self-justifying. And they cannot be justified through derivation from other truths, because no other truths are justificationally more basic. Thus they do not admit of proof in his sense. The formula of basic truths and axioms neither needing nor admitting of proof can be found *verbatim* in Leibniz, from whom Frege surely got it.[11]

In introducing his conception of apriority, Frege follows the traditional rationalist practice of indicating the *compatibility* of apriority with various sorts of dependence on experience. In particular, Frege notes that a truth can be apriori even though being able to think it, and learning that it is true, might each depend on having sense experience of facts.[12] Whether a truth is apriori depends on the nature of its canonical justification. Thus one could need to see symbols or diagrams in order to learn a logical or mathematical truth. One could need sense experience—perhaps in interlocution or simply in observing various stable objects in the world—in order to be able to think with certain logical or mathematical concepts. Perhaps, for example, to count or to use a quantifier, one needs to be able to track physical objects. But these facts about learning or psychological development do not show that the propositions that one thinks, once one has undergone the relevant development, are not apriori. Whether they are apriori depends on the nature of their justification. Frege thinks that such justification in logic and mathematics is independent of how the concepts are acquired, and independent of how individuals come to recognize the truths as true.

In his discussion of Mill's empiricism, Frege reiterates the point:

If one calls a proposition empirical because we have to have made observations in order to become conscious of its content, one does not use the word 'empirical' in the sense in which it is opposed to 'a priori'. One is then making a psychological statement, which concerns only the content of the proposition; whether the proposition is true is not touched. (*FA*: sect. 8)[13]

The key element in the rationalist approach is this distinction between questions

---

[11] Leibniz (1705, 1765, 1989: e.g. IV, ix, 2; 434). The formula also occurs in Lotze. Perhaps Frege got the phrase from Leibniz through Lotze. Cf. Lotze (1880, 1888: sect. 200). Frege seems, however, to have read Leibniz's *New Essays*. I discuss this notion of proof and Frege's view of axioms in some detail in Burge (1998a).

[12] Cf. this section of the passage quoted above: 'When a proposition is called a posteriori . . . in my sense, this is not a judgement about the conditions, psychological, physiological, and physical, which have made it possible to form the content of the proposition in our consciousness; nor is it a judgement about the way in which another man has come, perhaps erroneously, to believe it true; rather, it is a judgement about the deepest ground upon which rests the justification for holding it to be true.'

[13] Frege fixes here on truth, not justification. I think that he is assuming that one learns something about the nature of apriori truths by understanding the proof structure in which they are embedded; and this proof structure constitutes their canonical justification. Cf. Frege (1884: sect. 105).

Substantially the same distinction between the nature of a truth (and ultimately its justification) and the ways we come to understand the relevant proposition or to realize its truth is made by Leibniz (1705, 1765, 1989: Preface, 48-9; IV, vii, 9); and by Kant (1781, 1787: A1, B1).

about the psychology of acquisition or learning and normative questions regarding the nature of the justification of the propositions or capacities thus learned.

I say 'propositions or capacities'. Frege follows Leibniz in predicating apriority of propositions, or more particularly, truths, or sequences of truths—*not* capacities, or mental states, or justifications associated with types of propositional attitudes. Apriority ultimately concerns justification. But Leibniz and Frege share the view that apriority is a feature of an ideal or canonical way of justifying a proposition. For them, a proposition is either apriori or aposteriori, but not both, depending on the nature of the ideal or canonical justification associated with it.[14]

In this, Leibniz and Frege diverge from one distinctive aspect of Kant's thinking about apriority. Like Leibniz and Frege, Kant predicates apriority in a variety of ways—to intuitions, concepts, truths, cognition, constructions, principles, judgements. But whereas Leibniz and Frege predicate apriority primarily of truths (or more fundamentally, proofs of truths), Kant predicates apriority primarily of cognition and the employment of representations. For him apriori cognition is cognition that is justificationally independent of sense experience, and of 'all impressions of the senses'.[15] Apriori cognition is for Kant cognition whose justificational resources derive purely from the function of cognitive capacities in contributing to cognition. Apriori employment of concepts (or other representations) is employment that carries a warrant that is independent of sensory experiences. Aposteriori cognition is cognition which is justificationally derivative, in part, from sense experiences.

Both conceptions are ultimately epistemic. Frege very clearly states that his classification concerns 'the ultimate ground on which the justification for taking [a truth] to be true depends' (*FA*: sect. 3). Both sharply distinguish epistemic questions from questions of actual human psychology. Both take apriority to hinge on the source or method of warrant.

One might think that the main difference lies in the fact that Kant acknowledges more types of warrant as sources of apriority. Leibniz and Frege allow self-evidence and proof. Kant allows, in addition, constructions that rest on pure intuition and reflection on the nature of cognitive faculties.

I think, however, that this difference is associated with a fundamentally different orientation towards apriority. Frege and Leibniz explicate the nature of apriority in terms of a deduction from general basic self-evident truths. All that matters to apriority is encoded in the eternal, agent-independent truths themselves. For

---

[14] Some modern philosophers who take apriority to be predicated primarily of propositions call a proposition apriori if it *can* be justified apriori. Apriori justification is then explained in some non-circular way. Cf. Kripke (1972: 34). This formulation avoids commitment to that way's being canonical or ideal. But it also leaves out a serious commitment of such rationalists as Leibniz and Frege. For them, apriori justification is the best and most fundamental sort of justification. When something can be known or justified apriori, that is the canonical way.

[15] Kant (1781, 1787: B2–3).

deductive proof turns entirely on such contents. An individual's being apriori justified consists just in thinking through the deductive sequence with under-standing.

For Kant, the apriority of mathematics depends on possible constructions involving a faculty, pure intuition, that does not directly contribute components of truths, the conceptual components of propositions or thoughts. According to Kant, the proofs in arithmetic and geometry are not purely sequences of proposi-tions. The justifications, both in believing axioms and in drawing inferences from them, must lean on imaginative constructions in pure intuition, which cannot be reduced to a sequence of truths. The intuitive faculty contributes singular images in apriori imagination. Not only are these not part of an eternal order of concep-tual contents. The proof themselves essentially involve mental activity and make essential reference, through intuition, to particulars. For Kant these particulars are aspects of the mind. So the structure of a mathematical proof makes essential reference to possible mental particulars. It is not an eternal sequence of truths that are fundamentally independent of particulars.

Kant's conception of synthetic apriori cognition thus depends on an activity, a type of synthesis involved in the making of intuitive constructions in pure imag-ination. It is significant that, unlike Leibniz and Frege, he makes no appeal to self-evidence. That is, he does not claim that the evidence for believing the basic truths of geometry and arithmetic is encoded in the truths. In arithmetic he does not even think that axiomatic proof is the basis of arithmetical practice.[16]

This orientation helps explain Kant's tendency to predicate apriority of cogni-tion rather than truths. It is also at the root of his concentration, in his investiga-tion of apriori warrant, on the functions and operations of cognitive capacities, not on the nature of conceptual content and the relations among truths. The orien-tation makes the question of what it is to *have* a justification much more complex and interesting than it is on the Leibniz–Frege conception. And it ties that ques-tion more closely to what an apriori warrant is.

Kant's shift in his understanding of apriority from the content of truth and of proof-sequences of propositions to the character of cognitive procedures opens considerably more possibilities for understanding sources of apriority, and for seeing its nature in capacities and their functions, or even in specific acts or mental occurrences, rather than purely in propositional forms. Kant's account does not depend on empirical psychology, but it does centre on a transcendental psychology of the cognitive capacities of any rational agent.[17]

---

[16] Kant (1781, 1787: A164/B205).

[17] The relation between the two approaches is complex and needs further exploration. But it is worth remarking that Kant's approach has this advantage of flexibility. For Leibniz and Frege, a truth is either apriori or aposteriori. It is apriori if its canonical or ideal mode of justification is apriori. Its canonical mode of justification is apriori if it is situated in a natural proof struc-ture either as a primitive truth—which does 'not need or admit of proof'—or as a deductive consequence from primitive truths and rules of inference. On Kant's conception, a truth can be

A second way in which Frege diverges from Kant is that his explanation of apriority in *The Foundations of Arithmetic*, section 3 makes no mention of sense experience. Instead he characterizes it in terms of the generality of the premises of its proof.[18] Both Leibniz and Kant characterize apriority directly in terms of justificational independence of experience. Unlike Leibniz, Kant consistently takes experience to be *sense* experience. Since any modern notion of apriority seems necessarily tied somehow with justificational independence of experience, Frege's omission is, strictly speaking, a mischaracterization of the notion of apriority.[19]

From one point of view, this omission is not of great importance. Frege evidently took his notion of apriority to be equivalent with justificational independence of

known or justifiably believed either apriori or aposteriori, depending on what form of justificational procedure supports it for the individual. For on this conception, apriority is predicated not primarily of truths but of modes of justification, or even states of cognition. Kant did not make use of this flexibility. Its possibility is, however, implicit in his conception.

Michael Dummett (1991: 27) writes 'it is natural to take Frege as meaning that an a priori proposition may be known a posteriori: otherwise the status of the proposition would be determined by any *correct* justification that could be given for it.' He goes on to discuss whether there are any propositions that can be known only apriori. I have no quarrel with Dummett's substantive discussion. But his historical reasoning is off the mark. Frege's characterization takes apriority to apply to truths or idealized judgements. There is no relativization to particular ways of knowing those truths. A truth or judgement-type is either apriori or not. A truth or judgement is apriori if its best or canonical justification proceeds as a deductive proof from general principles that neither need nor admit of proof. Dummett fails to notice that there is no clear meaning within Frege's terminology for a question whether a truth can be known both apriori and aposteriori. That question can be better investigated by shifting to a Kantian conception of apriority. Dummett slides between the two conceptions. Frege could certainly have understood and accepted the Kantian conception; but he did not use it or propose it.

Dummett's reasoning to his interpretation is unsound. Suppose for the sake of argument that we reject the view that an apriori proposition can be known aposteriori. (I myself would resist such a rejection.) We might allow that there are empirical justifications for something weaker than knowledge for all propositions. For example, we might strictly maintain the Leibniz-Frege conception and insist that apriori truths can be known only apriori. Then it simply does not follow that the status of the proposition would be determined by any correct justification that could be given for it. The status would still be determined by the best justification that could be given for it. Oddly, Dummett clearly sees that this is Frege's conception elsewhere—Dummett (1991: 23).

[18] As Dummett notes, Frege's definition of 'apriori' is cast in such a way that the premisses of apriori proofs are counted neither apriori nor aposteriori (1991: 24). I think that Dummett is correct in thinking this an oversight of no great significance. It would be easy and appropriate to count the primitive truths and rules of inference apriori.

[19] There are differences between Leibniz's and Kant's accounts on this point that are relevant, but which I intend to discuss elsewhere. Leibniz often characterizes apriority in terms of justificational independence of experience. Leibniz sometimes allows intellectual apprehension of intellectual events to count as 'experience'. Kant firmly characterizes apriority in terms of justificational independence of *sense* experience. Kant's specification has important consequences, and makes his view in this respect the more modern one. It was taken up by Mill, the positivists, and most other twentieth-century empiricists. For purposes of epistemological discussion, 'experience' has come to mean *sense experience*.

sense experience. His discussion of Millian empiricism follows his definition of apriority by a few pages. In those sections he repeatedly writes of 'observed facts', apparently picking up on the notion of fact that appears in his definition of aposteriority (*FA*: sects. 7–9). He seems to assume that mere 'facts'—unprovable truths that are not general—can enter into justifications only through observation.[20] So a proof's depending on particular facts would make it rest on sense experience. Moreover, his criticism of Mill explicitly takes 'empirical' to be opposed to 'apriori' (*FA*: sect. 8).

In *Foundations of Arithmetic*, section 11, Frege infers from a proof's not depending on examples to its independence of 'evidence of the senses'. The inference suggests that he thought that a proof from general truths necessarily is justificationally independent of sense experience. At the beginning of *The Basic Laws of Arithmetic* he states the purpose of *The Foundations of Arithmetic* as having been to make it plausible that arithmetic is a branch of logic and 'need not borrow any ground of proof whatever from either experience or intuition.'[21] Here also Frege assumes that a proof's proceeding from general logical principles entails its justificational independence from experience or intuition. Frege commonly accepts the Kantian association of intuition (in humans) with sensibility, so here again it is plausible that he meant by 'experience' 'sense experience'.

In very late work, forty years after the statement of his definition, Frege divides sources of knowledge into three categories: sense perception, the logical source of knowledge, and the geometrical source of knowledge. He infers in this passage from a source's not being that of sense perception that it is apriori.[22]

So Frege took his definition of apriority in terms of derivation from general truths to be equivalent to a more normal definition that would characterize apriority in terms of justificational independence from sense experience. Still, the non-standardness (incorrectness) of Frege's definition is interesting on at least two counts. First, its focus on generality rather than independence from sense experience reveals ways in which Frege is following out Leibnizian themes but in a distinctively Fregean form. Second, the definition is backed by a presupposition, shared with Leibniz, that there is a necessary equivalence between justifications, at least for finite minds, that start from general principles and justifications that are justificationally independent of sense experience. It is of some interest, I think, to raise questions about this presupposition.

---

[20] Precisely the same inference can be found in Leibniz (1705, 1765, 1989: Preface 49–50).

[21] Frege (1893*a*,*b*, 1902,*a*,*b*: sect. 0). Compare this characterization of the earlier book's purpose with the one quoted from Frege (1884: sect. 87; cf. note 1 above). It is possible that the latter characterization constitutes a correction of the mischaracterization of apriority in Frege (1884: sect. 3).

[22] Frege (1979: 267 ff., 276–7); Frege (1983: 286 ff., 296–7).

II

Let us start with the first point of interest. Leibniz and Frege both see apriori truth as fundamentally general. Apriori truths are derivable from general, universally quantified, truths. Both, as we have seen, contrast apriori truths with mere truths of fact. Leibniz held that mere truths of fact are contingent, and that apriori truths are necessary. He took necessary truths to be either general or derivable from general logical principles together with definitional analyses and logical rules of inference. So for Leibniz the apriori–aposteriori distinction lines up with the necessary–contingent distinction, and both are closely associated with Leibniz's conception of a distinction between general truths and particular truths.[23]

It is tempting to regard Frege in the same light. As we have seen, Frege even defines apriority in terms of derivability from general truths and aposteriority in terms of derivability from particular truths. But there is little evidence that Frege associated apriority or generality with necessity. In fact, modal categories are strikingly absent from Frege's discussion.

We can gain a more refined understanding of Frege's differences from both Leibniz and Kant by contrasting his terminology with Kant's. Kant's conception of apriority, as we have seen, is explicitly defined in terms of a cognition's independence for its transcendental or epistemological genesis and its justification from sense experience. But he cites two other properties as marks (*Merkmale*) or sure indications (*sichere Kennzeichen*) of apriority. One is necessity. The other is strict generality (or universality) (*strenge Allgemeinheit*).[24]

---

[23] Leibniz (1705, 1765, 1989: Preface 49–50; IV, vii, 2-10, 408–13; IV, xi, 13, 445–6). The characterization of Leibniz's view that I use in this section, which brings it very close to Frege's, depends on laying aside Leibniz's views of God's cognition. The characterization seems to me true for Leibniz's view of finite, human cognition, but less obviously true of his view of divine cognition. Leibniz thought that God could have apriori knowledge of contingent truths through infinite analysis. By analysing the infinitely complex individual concepts of contingently existing individuals, God could know all truths about them. Cf. 'Necessary and Contingent Truths' in *Leibniz: Logical Papers*, Parkinson trans. and ed. (Oxford, Clarendon Press, 1966): 97 ff. In discussing God's infinite analyses, Leibniz lays no explicit weight on the generality of the apriori truths. It is not clear that Leibniz thought that for God apriority is ultimately general. What Leibniz emphasizes is analysis of contents in such a way as to resolve them into identities. There is little discussion of the nature of the contents, where they come from, how they are determined. Whether these truths, which are knowable apriori through formal analysis by God, are ultimately singular is open to question. On the other hand, Leibniz thought that even individuals are reflections of a plan of God's. It therefore seems possible that contingent singular identities, on Leibniz's view, are ultimately instantiations of some general rational plan, which might have the status of a general law. Cf. *Discourse on Metaphysics*, sect. 6. Leibniz sees singular identities in logic and mathematics as resolvable into identities that instantiate general necessary truths. These are truths that are knowable apriori by finite minds. In this Leibniz and Frege are one. Regardless of whether he thought that a generalization lay at the bottom of infinite analysis of contingent truth, Leibniz is also kin to Frege in his emphasis on the idea that apriority lies in formal structure. I am indebted for these qualifications to John Carriero.

[24] Kant (1781, 1787: B3–4; cf. A2; A91–2/B124). The same point is made in Kant (1790:

There are two points to be noted about these remarks. One is that Kant provides these marks or indications not as elements in the definition of apriority, but as signs, which according to his theory are necessarily associated with apriority. In fact, in providing these signs, he takes them to be sufficient for apriority. He does not, in these famous passages, claim that they are necessary conditions.[25] The reason why on his view apriori judgements are associated with necessity and strict generality, is not that these associations follow from his definition or conception of apriority. The associations derive from further commitments in Kant's system.

Kant explains strict generality itself in terms of modality. Kant contrasts strict generality with comparative or assumed generality. Comparative generality holds only as far as we have observed.[26] A judgement thought in strict generality 'permits no possible exception'. Kant infers from this that such a thought is taken as holding absolutely apriori.

Neither Kant nor Leibniz gives any hint of defining apriority in terms of generality. Both appeal, however, to generality in their elucidations of apriority. Frege's use of generality (*Allgemeinheit*) in his definition is surely inherited from them.

---

sect. 7; *Akademie Ausgabe* V, 213). There Kant calls comparative generality 'only general' (*nur generale*), and strict generality 'universal' (*universale*). Compare Leibniz (1705, 1765, 1989: IV, ix, 14, 446): 'The distinction you draw [between particular and general propositions] appears to amount to mine, between "propositions of fact" and "propositions of reason". Propositions of fact can also become general, in a way; but that is by induction or observation, so that what we have is only a multitude of similar facts . . . This is not perfect generality, since we cannot see its necessity. General propositions of reason are necessary.'

[25] I think that Kant believed that necessity was (necessarily) necessary as well as sufficient for the apriority of a judgement. He clearly believed that being, or being derivable from, a strictly general proposition is sufficient for the apriority of a judgement. Kant surely believed that all apriori judgements are true without any possible exceptions. Whether he believed that all apriori judgements have to be derivable from judgements that are in the form of universal generalizations is more doubtful. I shall discuss this matter below. Whether strict generality was only a sufficient condition (a mark) of apriority, not a necessary one—or whether it was both necessary and sufficient, but understood in such a way as not to entail the logical form of a generalization—is a complex question that I shall leave open. What is certain is that Kant's views on the relation between apriority and both necessity and strict generality depend not merely on his definition or conception of apriority, but on other elements in his system. I believe that rejecting Kant's positions on these relations is compatible with maintaining his conception of apriority.

[26] Cf. n. 24. Strictly speaking comparative generality and strict generality do not seem to be exhaustive categories. It would appear that there are propositions that are comparatively general but which are not true accidental generalizations (there is a counter-instance that simply has not been found); yet true accidental generalizations are not necessary truths. This is because it is possible for there to be true accidental generalizations which have no counter-instances yet observed. (I leave open whether there are also empirical laws which are general but which are not strictly general, in Kant's sense.) It is possible, of course, that Kant means the 'we' in 'what we have so far observed' in a loose and highly idealized sense. It is conceivable that he intended comparative generality to include all possible actual observations by 'us'. Given his idealism, he would take this as equivalent to the empirical truth of the generalization. This is a matter that could bear more investigation.

Like them he believed that apriority is deeply connected with some form of generality of application, or universal validity. But he interpreted and used his notion of generality differently. He departs from both Leibniz and Kant in *defining* apriority in terms of generality. He departs from both in saying little about the relation between apriority and necessity. Indeed, his conception of generality differs from both in that he does not connect it to modal notions, seen as independent notions, at all.

Frege does comment on the relation between generality and necessity very briefly in *Begriffsschrift*. He associates generality with the logical form of the contents of judgements. He claims that apodictic judgements differentiate themselves from merely assertoric ones in that they suggest the existence of general judgements from which the proposition can be inferred. He then writes:

When I designate a proposition as necessary, I thereby give a hint about the grounds of my judgement. But since the conceptual content of the judgement is not thereby touched, the form of the apodictic judgement has no significance for us.[27]

Frege seems to think that necessity is not represented in logical form, but is to be explained in terms of a pragmatic suggestion regarding the epistemic grounds for a judgement. Generality for Frege (in the sense relevant to this context) is simply universal quantification. What makes a truth a priori is that its ultimate grounds are universally quantified. So Frege seems to explicate necessity in terms of apriority. Apriority is the notion that Frege attaches in *Foundations of Arithmetic* to the condition he envisages here in the *Begriffsschrift* of a judgement's having its ground in general propositions. If anything, Frege explains necessity in terms of the (ordinary) generality of the grounds of the proposition. This contrasts with Kant's explaining (strict) generality in terms of necessity.

I think that Frege was trying to get the effect of the difference between accidental generalizations and empirical laws, on the one hand, and necessary generalizations, on the other, while avoiding explicit introduction of independent modal notions. His notion of generality is the simple one of universal quantification. Not just any general truth is apriori, however. Only general truths that are self-evident axioms, or first-truths, or which are derivable from self-evident axioms, or first-truths, are apriori. Apriori generalizations are generalizations whose *ultimate justification* does not rest on particular truths.

Frege does use the notion of law in his characterization of apriority: 'If … it is possible to derive the proof purely from general laws, which themselves neither need nor admit of proof, then the truth is apriori' (*FA*: sect. 3).[28] Empirical laws need and admit of 'proof', in that they need justification from statements of observation about particulars. It is common to hold that the notion of law contains

---

[27] Frege (1879: sect. 4). The issue is discussed briefly by Gabriel (1996).

[28] I believe that Frege's use of 'possible' in this remark is dispensable. It is possible to derive the proof in his sense if and only if there is a proof.

or implies modal notions. That may well be. But I believe that Frege thought of laws in terms of basic principles in a system of scientific propositions—either an empirical science or a deductive science—not (at least not officially) in terms of any modal or counterfactual element. Empirical laws are basic principles of idealized empirical scientific systems of true, grounded propositions. But they are not basic in the order of justification: singular observational statements (along with an apriori principle of induction) are supposed to be justificationally prior. Apriori laws differ in just this respect.

So the key idea in distinguishing empirical laws and accidental generalizations from apriori truths is taking apriority to be justificational derivation from general truths, which themselves are self-evident and do not need or admit of proof. Frege's notion of *generality* is fundamentally less modal than Kant's notion of strict generality or universality. It is simply that of universal quantification, where quantification is understood to be unqualifiedly general—to range over *everyzthing*. Apriority is understood in terms of the priority of generality in justification.[29]

I have no doubt that Frege worked with an intuitive notion of logical validity. This enters his formulation of rules of inference. But the universal validity of *logical* laws is supposed to lie in their applicability to *everything*—which includes mathematical and geometrical objects and functions. The mathematical objects provide a sufficiently large and strict subject matter to enable true quantifications in logic and mathematics to have some of the force and effect of necessary truths that purport to quantify over possible objects or possible worlds. This force and effect seems to suffice for Frege's purposes. Frege seems to avoid invocation of an independent notion of modality and of merely possible objects, in epistemology, metaphysics, and logic.

Leibniz took all truths to be deducible in principle from truths of logic. On his view, it is a mere weakness of the finite human intellect that requires it to invoke empirical experience to arrive at ordinary truths about the physical world. Frege joined the rest of mankind in regarding Leibniz's view as overblown (*FA*: sect. 15). Of course, he agreed with Leibniz in holding that arithmetic is derivable from logic. Logic is naturally seen as a canon of general principles associated with valid inference. Here Frege sided with Leibniz against Kant in holding that one can derive truths about particular, determinate objects—the numbers—from purely general logical principles. Frege specifically states his opposition to Kant's view that without sensibility, no object would be given to us (*FA*: sect. 89). He argues that he can derive the existence of numbers from purely general logical laws. In this, of course, he failed. But the Leibnizian idea of obtaining truths about particular determinate objects from general, logical, apriori principles is fundamental to his logicist project.

---

[29] Frege has another concept of 'generality', of course, by which he distinguishes arithmetic and logic, which are completely general in their domain of applicability, from geometry, which applies only to space.

It seems to me likely that Frege's opposition to iterative set theory partly derives from the same philosophical picture.[30] Iterative set theory naturally takes objects, the ur-elements which are the members of sets, as primitive. They may be numbers or unspecified ur-elements, but they are naturally taken as given. Frege thought that an apriori discipline has to start from general principles. And it would be natural for him to ask where the ur-elements of set theory come from. If they were empirical objects, they would not be given apriori. He regarded the null set as an indefensible entity from the point of view of iterative set theory. It collects nothing. He thought a null entity (a null extension) is derivable only as the extension of an empty concept. If one took the numbers as primitive, one would not only be giving up logicism. One would be assuming particular objects without deriving their existence and character from general principles—thus controverting Frege's view of the nature of an apriori subject. If one could derive the existence of numbers from logical concepts, one would not need set theory to explain number theory or, Frege thought, for any other good purpose. Thus it would have been natural for him to see set theory as raising an epistemic puzzle about how its existence claims could be apriori, inasmuch as they appear to take statements about particulars as primitive or given.

Leibniz actually *characterizes* reason as the faculty for apprehending apriori, necessary truths. These include for him all mathematical truths. As I have noted, Leibniz regards all necessary truths as ultimately instances of, or derivative from, *general* logical principles together with definitional analyses and logical rules of inference.[31] Generality for Leibniz is a hallmark of human reason. Principles of identity and non-contradiction underlie and provide the logical basis for proof of mathematical truths. As noted, Frege agrees that arithmetic is thus derivative from general logical principles. He takes arithmetic to be an expression of pure reason, and its objects given directly to reason through logical principles (*FA*: sect. 105).

Kant famously separates apriority and necessity from pure reason in the sense that he holds that some apriori, necessary truths, the synthetic ones, can be known only by supplementing reason with the products of a non-rational faculty for producing singular representations—intuition. For Kant intuition is essentially a faculty for producing *singular* representations. It is part of his view that synthetic cognition of objects, including synthetic apriori cognition in arithmetic and geometry, must partly rest its justification on the deliverances of intuition. Hence the justification must rest partly on singular representations, and perhaps propositions or thoughts in singular form as well.

---

[30] Frege (1884: sects. 46-54; 1893,*a,b,* 1902*a*: 30; 1893, 1902*b*: I, 2–3; 1984: 114, 209, 228; 1967: 104–5, 209–10). The latter passage especially seems to find the problem in the assumption of single things at the base of set theory. The idea that concepts are general and objects must be derivative from principles governing concepts guided his opposition.

[31] Leibniz (1705, 1765, 1989: Preface 49–50; I, i, 19, 83; IV, vii, 2–10, 408–13; IV, vii, 19, 424; IV, xi, 13, 445–6). On these matters, see Margaret Wilson, 'Leibniz and Locke on First Truths', *Journal of History of Ideas* 28 (1967): 347–66. Cf. n. 23.

Of course, Frege disagrees with Kant about arithmetic. He holds that arithmetic is not synthetic, but analytic—at least in the sense that it is derivative from general logical principles without any need to appeal to intuition. But Frege purports to agree with Kant about geometry (*FA*: sect. 89). He agrees that it is synthetic apriori. It is synthetic in that it is not derivable from logic. The logical coherence of non-Euclidean geometries seemed to confirm its synthetic character. Frege also purports to agree that geometry rests on pure apriori intuition.[32] He agrees with Kant in counting intuition a faculty different from the faculty of thought (e.g. *FA*: 26, 90). Frege's agreement with Kant that apriori truths of geometry rest on intuition, a faculty for producing singular representations, puts some pressure on Frege's view that apriori truths must rest on fundamentally general laws. As we shall see, there is some reason to think that Frege's relation to Kant on this matter is not as straightforwardly one of agreement as he represents it to be.

III

Let us now consider the second point of interest in Frege's characterization of apriority. This is his presumption that his characterization of apriority in terms of the primacy of generalizations in proof is equivalent with the usual post-Kantian characterization in terms of justificational independence from sense experience.

There are at least three areas where both the general characterization and Frege's assumption of equivalence can be challenged. One has to do with certain types of self-knowledge, and perhaps more broadly, certain context-dependent truths. One has to do with geometry. One has to do with arithmetic. I will not go into these issues in depth. But I hope that broaching them will be of both historical and substantive value.

Frege exhibits no interest in *cogito* judgements: judgements like the judgement that I am now thinking. But his characterization of apriority immediately rules them aposteriori, in view of the singularity of their form and their underivability from general laws. Now the question of whether *cogito* judgements are in fact aposteriori is a complex one.

Leibniz is in accord with Frege in counting them aposteriori. He counts them primitive, self-evident truths which nevertheless depend on 'experience'.[33] What Leibniz means by 'experience' is not very clear. His view suffers by comparison to Kant's in its vastly less developed conception of cognitive faculties and of the

---

[32] Unlike Kant, Frege gives no clear evidence of believing that all synthetic apriori principles rest on intuition. He holds that the principle underlying (non-mathematical) induction is synthetic apriori, but he gives no reason to think that it rests on intuition. This point is made by Michael Dummett (1982: 240).

[33] Leibniz (1705, 1765, 1989: IV, vii, 7, 411; IV, ix, 3, 434; cf. IV, ii, 1, 367).

nature of experience. Sometimes Leibniz associates experience with sense experience. But it appears that he sometimes uses a very broad conception of experience that would include any direct awareness of an object or event, whether or not this awareness proceeds through one of the senses. Thus 'experience' for Leibniz, at least at times, seems to include not only what we would count sense experience but intellectual 'experience' as well. A conception of apriority as independence from experience in this broad sense would be defensible. Its counting instances of the *cogito* 'aposteriori' would also be defensible.

Frege consistently associates experience with *sense experience*. If he were to relax this association, it would be open to him to side with Leibniz (or one side of Leibniz) here against Kant in counting non-sensory intellectual awareness of particular intellectual events as experience.[34] Such a conception would, however, sever the connection between apriority and independence of the experience of the senses. Frege seems to accept this connection. It has dominated conceptions of apriority since Kant. What seems to me thoroughly doubtful is that our cognition of instances of the *cogito* (and perhaps other indexical thoughts such as *I am here now* or *I exist*) is justificationally dependent on sense experience. Such cognition seems to depend only on intellectual understanding of the thought content in an instance of thinking it. Contingent, singular truths seem to be apriori in the sense that our warrant to accept them is justificationally independent of sense experience.

If these points are sound, they raise interesting questions about the relation between apriority, reason, and generality. It seems to me natural—at least as a working conjecture—still to regard reason (with Leibniz and Kant) as essentially involved in supplying general principles and rules of inference. A warrant can, however, be justificationally independent of sense experience if it gains its force from either reason or understanding. And understanding essentially involves singular elements. The view is fundamentally Kantian: Reason is essentially general. Understanding, because of its interdependence with non-rational capacities, is sometimes understanding of truths in singular form that cannot be proved from general truths. Warrant can be apriori if it derives from reason or from understanding, if it does not depend on sense experience for any of the force of its epistemic warrant.

I believe that Kant was mistaken, however, in holding that understanding can yield non-logical cognition only if it applies to the form or deliverances of sensory capacities (and non-logical apriori cognition only if it applies to their form). I believe that understanding is capable of yielding non-empirical and non-

---

[34] Kant also thought that instances of the *cogito* produce no 'apriori' cognition. But this view cannot be directly derived from his characterization of apriority alone, as it can be from Leibniz's characterization. Rather Kant's view depends on his very complex (and I think mistaken) theory of the justification dependence of cognition of one's thoughts in time on inner sense, which ultimately depends, albeit indirectly, for its justificational force on outer sense. I shall not discuss this Kantian view here.

sensible cognition of thoughts in singular form that are not derivable from general ones. One can, for example, know by intellection and understanding alone that certain of one's intellectual mental events are occurring (or have occurred), or that one is thinking. No invocation of sensible intuition or the form of one's sensory capacities is needed for the justification that underwrites the relevant knowledge. It seems to me plausible that our understanding sometimes applies to intentional contents that are tokens, instances of indexicals, in singular form.[35]

Perhaps to account for the apriority of our warrant for believing such instances, the warrant must be seen as deriving *partly or in some way* from something general. For example, to understand the self-evidence of an instance of *I am now thinking*, one must understand *I* according to the general rule that it applies to whomever is the author of the thought that contains its instantiation. One must understand a similar general rule for *now*. Thinking according to such rules, one can realize that any instance of *I am now thinking* will be true. This is an entirely general insight. It seems to me plausible to consider a logic for the *forms* of such indexicals as an expression for reason. Here the generality of reason would not reside in the form of the propositional content (which is singular), but in the generality of the rules governing its application. The semantical rule is in general form.[36]

But the realization of the truth of an *instance* of the *cogito* cannot be derived purely from these generalities. It cannot be derived purely from a logic of indexicals or from anything purely general. It must involve an awareness in understanding of an actual event of thinking and a recognition of its content. Thus the warrant cannot rest purely on an inference from general principles. There is something irreducibly singular in the application of the understanding. The warrant depends essentially for its force on the exercise of this singular application. Although the truth—the instance of the *cogito*—would count as aposteriori on Leibniz's conception and on Frege's conception, it is plausibly apriori on the Kantian conception: The warrant for an instance of thinking it is justificationally independent of sense experience. The warrant depends for its force purely on intellectual understanding applied to a singular instance of a *cogito* thought (cf. n. 34).

IV

I turn now to Frege's application of his characterization of apriority to geometry. Frege accepted Kant's doctrine that Euclidean geometry is synthetic apriori. Frege meant by 'synthetic' here *not derivable from logic*. Frege also maintains with Kant that geometry rests on sensible geometrical spatial intuition. With

---

[35] Cf. Burge (1996; 1998*b*).
[36] For an example of a logic of such singular indexicals, see Kaplan (1989).

Kant, Frege held the now discredited view that Euclidean geometry is both apriori and apriori-applicable to physical space. It is now tenable to hold that Euclidean geometry is apriori only if one considers it a pure mathematical discipline
whose proper application, or applicability, to physical space is a separate and
empirical question. I want, however, to discuss the issue of the epistemic status
of Euclidean geometry from Frege's perspective.

What did Frege mean by his agreement with Kant about the epistemology of
Euclidean geometry? There is no firm evidence that Frege accepted Kant's idealist conception of physical space. Frege's whole philosophy, especially in his
mature period, seems out of sympathy with the explanation of apriority in terms
of the mind's imposing its structure on the physical or mathematical worlds.[37]
Frege articulated his agreement with Kant by agreeing that geometry is based on,
or has its 'ground' in, pure intuition (*FA*: sects.12, 89).[38]

For Kant, pure intuition is both a faculty and one product of the faculty. Intuition is a faculty for singular, immediate representations. It represents singular
elements of (or in) space or time without being mediated by any further representations that apply to the same semantical values or referents. Pure intuition is
the faculty itself, considered independent of any passively received, sensational
content. For Kant intuition could be either an intellectual faculty (in which case
its exercises would always be pure), or a sensible one.[39] We humans have, according to Kant, only sensible intuition. Pure sensible intuition is the structure of the
faculty which is constant regardless of what sensational contents one receives in
sense-perceptual experience or produces in empirical imagination.

Kant also believed that pure sensible intuition could itself yield pure representations as product—pure formal intuitions.[40] Such representations are representations of elements in the structure of space and time. Given his idealism, these
elements were supposed to be features of the structure of the faculty of sensible
intuition. Intuitions of all sorts are characterized by Kant as being objective representations that are both immediate and singular.[41]

---

[37] For an elaboration of some aspects of this theme, see Burge (1998*a*).

[38] Cf. also 'On a Geometrical Representation of Imaginary Forms in the Plane' in Frege
(1984: 1; or 1967: 1); 'Methods of Calculation based on an Extension of the Concept of Quantity' in Frege (1984: 56; or 1967: 50).

[39] Frege shows a certain superficiality in his reading of Kant in Frege (1884: sect. 12). There
he first notes that in his *Logic* Kant defines an intuition as a singular representation, noting that
there is no mention there of any connection with sensibility. He further notes that in the Transcendental Aesthetic part of *Critique of Pure Reason* the connection is added (*hinzugedacht*),
and must be added to serve as a principle of our cognition of synthetic a priori judgements. He
concludes that the sense of the word 'intuition' is wider in the *Logic* than in the *Critique*. But it
is not wider. In both books intuition is characterized in terms of singularity (and in the *Critique*
sometimes in terms of immediacy as well). Cf. Kant (1800: sect. I.1; 1781, 1787:
A320/B376–7). Kant intentionally leaves sensibility out of the characterization of the notion in
both books because he takes intellectual (non-sensible) intuition to be one possible type of intuition—possible in principle, though not for humans.

[40] Kant (1781, 1787: B160).   [41] Kant (ibid.: A320/B377).

If one strips this view of its idealist elements, one can regard pure sensible intuition as a faculty for intuiting the pure structure (not of the faculty itself but) of mind-independent space and time. Frege shows no interest in pure temporal intuition. Of course, in his mature period he rejects Kant's view that arithmetic rests on pure temporal intuition, or intuition of any sort. He believed however, that we have a capacity for pure spatial intuition. He believed that Euclidean geometry is in some way grounded in exercises of this capacity. Like Kant, Frege associates the capacity for pure intuition (in humans at least) with sensibility—the capacity for having sense experiences. He distinguishes it from a capacity for conceptual thought (*FA*: sect. 14).

What interests me is Frege's understanding of the singularity of pure intuition and its relation to his characterization of apriori truths as following from general principles that do not need or admit of proof. He cites and does not reject Kant's conception of intuitions as individual representations (*FA*: sect. 12). He regards the axioms and theorems of Euclidean geometry as apriori. So he thought that they are, or follow from, general principles that do not need or admit of proof. The proof must work out without reference to unprovable truths which are not general and which contain assertions about determinate objects (*bestimmte Gegendstaende*). Kant takes intuitions to play a role in the warrant of some geometrical axioms and rules of inference. What is the epistemic role in Frege's view of pure intuitions—which for Kant are certainly singular, not general—in warranting the axioms of geometry?

Frege is aware of this question. He speaks to it in section 13 of *The Foundations of Arithmetic*. He writes,

One geometrical point, considered in itself, is not to be distinguished any way from any other; the same applies to lines and planes. Only if more points, lines, planes are comprehended at the same time in an intuition, does one distinguish them. From this it is explicable that in geometry general propositions are derived from intuition: the intuited points, lines, planes are really not particular (*besondern*) at all, and thus they can count as representatives of the whole of their kind. But with numbers it is different: each has its own particularity (*Eigentumlichkeit*).[42]

Frege does not use language in this passage that connects precisely with the language of his characterization of apriority.[43] Perhaps he simply believed that since the relevant objects of intuitions are not 'particular' (*besondern*), they are

---

[42] Frege does not make it clear why it matters that one can distinguish the objects of intuition from one another only if they are comprehended in a complex intuition, or why this fact shows that the objects are not really particular at all.

[43] In a paper on Hilbert, Frege seems to sympathize with the idea that axioms assert basic facts about intuition. But he is focused on Hilbert's view that axioms both assert and define things. Frege's main point is that axioms cannot do both; he clearly believes that they assert something. There is little in the passage to help us with his attitudes towards the singularity of intuitions or their precise role in the epistemology of geometry. Cf. Frege (1984: 275–7; 1967: 264–6).

not 'determinate objects' (*bestimmte Gengenstaende*). (Cf. the definition of 'aposteriority'.) Or perhaps he believed that pure intuition's contribution to the justification of general truths lies not in its representation of determinate objects (the individual lines and planes that it represents), but of aspects of them that are not particular to those objects. He may have thought that although we must be presented with particulars in pure intuition, the warranting power of the intuition lies *only* in geometrical properties that are invariant under Euclidean transformations. In either case, Frege does not give a precise explanation of how intuition helps 'ground' (*FA*: section 12) our knowledge. Hence Frege gives no precise explanation of how his view of the apriority of geometry is compatible with his view of its depending on pure intuition—a faculty for singular representation.

Nevertheless, the main thrust of the passage seems to be to downgrade the role of the particularity of the geometrical objects, and of the singularity of thoughts about them, in the 'derivation' of general truths. In fact, Frege says that the objects of pure intuition in geometrical imagination are not genuinely particular. He seems to see the lines that he regards as objects of intuition as types. So they can serve as representatives whose characteristics that are shareable with relevantly similar objects are all that matter for arriving at general propositions. It is difficult to see here how Frege's view relates to Kant's, even bracketing the fact that Frege does not advocate Kantian idealism.

Let us approach this question by first comparing the just quoted passage from Frege with a passage in Leibniz. Leibniz writes:

> But I do not agree with what seems to be your view, that this kind of general certainty is provided in mathematics by 'particular demonstrations' concerning the diagram that has been drawn. You must understand that geometers do not derive their proofs from diagrams, although the expository approach makes it seem so. The cogency of the demonstration is independent of the diagram, whose only role is to make it easier to understand what is meant and to fix one's attention. It is universal propositions, i.e. definitions and axioms and theorems which have already been demonstrated, that make up the reasoning, and they would sustain it even if there were no diagram.[44]

Leibniz holds that the singular elements introduced through reliance on a diagram are inessential to a proof or derivation of the general propositions of geometry. Frege's passage does not squarely advocate Leibniz's position. But Frege seems to be explaining away the elements of singularity in his conception of pure intuition in order to avoid acknowledging that the general truths of geometry are derivative in any way from singular elements in intuition. This direction of thought about (pure) geometry seems to me reasonable and plausible. But it is questionable whether Frege's view is really compatible with Kant's.

Kant sees himself as fundamentally at odds with Leibniz about geometry. He takes the role of pure intuition in geometry to be to produce an irreducibly singular element into mathematical understanding, reasoning, and justification. The

---

[44] Leibniz (1705, 1765, 1989: IV, i, 360–1).

problem for making these comparisons cleanly is that Kant's own view, though developed in great detail and subtlety, is not entirely clear or agreed upon.

I shall, however, sketch my view of it. Kant takes pure intuition in geometry to be intuitions of determinate objects. The objects of intuition are particulars, such as line-drawings, or even possible line-drawings, in pure geometrical intuition—pure imagination. (They can also be intuised in empirical intuition, on paper; but only non-empirical formal aspects of the empirical intuition play any role in mathematical understanding, reasoning, and justification.) From these objects one abstracts objects of a more general kind—'the triangle', for example—which are the objects of mathematical reasoning.[45] These latter objects are forms within the structure of space or time—on Kant's idealist view, forms of spatio-temporal intuition itself.

Theoretical cognition for Kant is fundamentally cognition of objects. Kant thought that pure mathematics has objects, and that those objects are not contingent, empirical objects.[46] 'Determination' (*Bestimmung*) is a fundamental term in Kant's epistemology. Objects of successful theoretical cognition—the sort yielded in geometry—are necessarily determinate, or objects of determinate concepts, specific, non-vague concepts. They are abstracted from determinate particulars that are referents of pure intuition. The abstracted objects are determinate formal objects—spatial shapes, like triangles, and lines, planes, volumes. They form the subject matter of Euclidean geometry. The principles of geometry are about these objects. And thoughts about them are supported and guided by pure intuition about particular instances of these determinate objects. The role of intuition, hence the role of representation of *particulars*, is ineliminable from Kant's account of our understanding and warrant for pure geometry.

A passage in Kant that is comparable to the passages in Frege and Leibniz that we have just quoted is as follows:

Mathematical cognition [is reason-cognition out of] the construction of concepts. To construct a concept means to exhibit the intuition corresponding to it. For construction of a concept therefore a non-empirical intuition is required, which consequently as intuition is a single object (*einzelnes Objekt*), but nonetheless, as the construction of a concept (of a general representation), it [the intuition] must express in the representation general [or universal] validity (*Allgemeingultigkeit*) for all possible intuitions, which belong under the same concept. Thus I construct a triangle by exhibiting the object corresponding to this concept, either through mere imagination in pure intuition, or in accordance therewith also on paper through empirical intuition, but in both cases purely a priori, without having had to borrow the pattern for it from any experience. The single drawn figure is empirical, yet it serves to express the concept without impairing its universality (*Allgemeinheit*); for in

---

[45] Kant (1781, 1787: A713–4/B741–2; A723/B751).

[46] The point is denied in Friedman (1992: chs. 1 and 2). There are, however, numerous passages in which Kant makes it clear that he believes that pure mathematics has objects which are *not* the empirical objects experienced in space and time. For one such passage, see Kant (1781, 1787: A723/B751). I will develop these points in some detail in future work on Kant.

the case of this empirical intuition we look only at the action of the construction of the concept, to which [concept] many determinations [*Bestimmungen*]—for example, the magnitude of the sides and angles—are completely indifferent, and therefore we abstract from these differences, which do not alter the concept of triangle. . . . mathematical cognition [considers] the general in the particular [*Besonderen*), in fact even in the individual (*Einzelnen*), although still a priori and by means of reason, so that just as this individual is determined under certain general conditions of construction, the object of the concept, to which this individual corresponds only as its schema, must be thought as universally (*allgemein*) determined.[47]

Frege's claim that 'the intuited points, lines, planes are really not particular (*besondern*) at all' is definitely not compatible with Kant's view. Kant maintains that the referents of intuition are always particular or singular.[48] He takes the singularity of the intuition to be essential to the normative, justificational account of mathematical cognition. He takes abstraction from certain particularities inherent in the single object presented in pure intuition (or even in empirical intuition) to be necessary to understanding the mathematical concept (the general concept, triangle) and to doing pure geometry. But the singularity of the intuition is irreducibly part of the justification of mathematical cognition.

Frege explains the general validity of geometrical truths by maintaining that the particularity of pure intuition is only apparent. They can therefore 'count as representatives of the whole of their kind'. Like Kant, he sees the particulars as serving as representatives or stand-ins for more general features. He does not explain what role the singular aspects of intuition play in the process. But unlike Kant, he appears to be committed to thinking that they play no role in mathematical justification. This would explain his departure from Kantian doctrine in his claim that the intuited lines and so forth are not really particular at all. Unlike Kant, Frege is not interested in the particularity of mental acts in his explanation; this is a sign of his lack of commitment to Kantian idealism. He sees intuition as presenting typical geometrical structures which have no intrinsic individuality.

Kant explains the general validity of geometrical truths by maintaining that the particularity is genuine and ineliminable but is *used* as a schema. One abstracts from particular elements of the objects of intuition in forming a general object of the geometrical concept (and geometrical principle).

Like Frege, Kant does not make completely clear the role of the particular in warranting and guiding universal principles and inferential transitions. He seems to think that the particularistic elements in mathematical reasoning ground it in

---

[47] Kant (1781, 1787: A713-4/B741–2). The translation 'we look at' and 'we abstract from' is necessary for smooth rendering in English but the German uses an impersonal passive construction in both cases.

[48] Actually for Kant the immediate referents of intuitions are property instances or mark-instances had by particular objects. And objects include parts of space and time as well as physical objects. But these are subtleties that we need not go into here.

particular elements of space and time that reveal mathematical structures with maximum concreteness, and thus safeguard mathematical reasoning from the dangers that even transcendental philosophy is faced with. Kant seemed to think that mathematics' concern with particularity helps explain its certainty. But it *is* clear that he thought that the role of the particular is not to be explained away or seen as merely apparent. It is hard to escape the view that for Kant, in contrast to Frege, synthetic apriori propositions in geometry are grounded not in general propositions but in possible or actual particularistic judgements that are guided and supported by intuitions about particular, determinate objects of pure geometrical intuition. Although there are ways of understanding Frege's own view so as to render it internally consistent, and even perhaps sound, it is doubtful that it is consistent with Kant's.

Frege is aware of a need to discount the role of the particular, individual, or singular in geometrical warrant. If the general propositions rested, justificationally, on singular propositions, they could not be apriori in his sense.

Kant holds that the principles of geometry are strictly general or universally valid. He thinks that the basic principles are in the form of generalizations. But he does not hold that the root of geometrical warrant—the apriority of geometry—lies in generality. The synthetic apriori axioms—and the inferential transitions—in pure geometry rest on non-general representations, pure intuitions. His examples of pure intuition supplementing our conceptions to yield warranted belief commonly involve propositions used singularly about particular geometrical constructions in Euclidean space.[49]

Kant claims that the successive synthesis of the productive imagination in the generation of figures—a process of singular representation—is the basis of axioms and inferences in Euclidean geometry. Although the axioms are general, their warrant does not rest on general propositions or general thoughts alone.[50]

There is a way of construing Frege's introduction of the notion of apriority that would reconcile his view with Kant's. Recall that Frege writes: 'If . . . it is possible to derive the proof purely from general laws, which themselves neither need

---

[49] Kant (1781, 1787: A220–1/B267–8; A234/B287).

[50] Of course, in his theory of arithmetic, Kant denies that arithmetical propositions are derivable from axioms—hence from anything general—at all. He seems to regard the singular arithmetical operations and equations as basic. Cf. Kant (1781, 1787: A164–6/B204–6). Frege effectively criticized this extreme rejection of the role of axioms and proof in arithmetic. Frege (1884: sect. 5). He is of course right in rejecting Kant's view that intuition enters into the justification of *inferences* in geometry and arithmetic. The issue of whether particularity is basic to mathematical justification is independent of whether justification of mathematical propositions (commonly) involves proof, and even of whether particularity enters the justification through non-conceptual intuition or directly from understanding. For a fine discussion of Kant's view of the role of intuition in inferences, see Friedman (1992: chs. 1 and 2). I believe that in supporting his sound view that Kant believed that intuition is necessary to mathematical inference, Friedman underplays the role of intuition in providing a basis for at least some of the axioms of Euclidean geometry. I think that Kant thought that intuitive constructions are as much a part of geometrical warrant and practice as commitment to the axioms is. Indeed the two go together.

nor admit of proof, then the truth is a priori' (*FA*: sect. 3). Geometrical proof, in the modern sense of 'proof', starts with geometrical axioms. These are general. Thus for Frege 'proof' in geometry rests on general truths, axioms. One might hold that Kant realized as well as anyone that geometrical proof begins with the axioms. On his own view, the axioms are general (universally quantified). Thus interpreted, there is no disagreement.

What makes this resolution unsatisfying to me is that neither Frege nor Kant utilized precisely this modern notion of proof. For Frege, proof is canonical justification. The axioms are, on his view, general, self-evident, and in need of no warrant from anything further. For Kant the axioms and proofs in geometry are warranted through their relations to actual or possible line-drawings in pure intuition—thus through their relation to singular representations.[51] These representations must (to represent their objects at all) be conceptualized and backed by propositions or judgements in singular form.

So, Frege's notion of proof is one of canonical justification, not merely deductive sequences of thoughts. And on Kant's view axioms and proofs in geometry require warrant from pure intuition, which is essentially a faculty of singular representation. Unlike Frege, Kant is not wedded to a view of apriority that takes it to be founded in generality.[52] For Kant, synthetic apriori cognition is cognition that is grounded in the particular. For Kant the use of pure intuition is an integral part of geometrical practice and the mathematical understanding of the axioms and inferences themselves. Thus insofar as it is possible to compare like to like—Frege's epistemological conception of proof with Kant's conception of justificational reasoning within geometry—the views of the two epistemologies appear quite different.

As I have emphasized, Frege leaves it unclear exactly what role intuition plays. But he implicitly denies a basic Kantian doctrine in holding that the objects of intuition are either not particular, or not fundamental to warrant in geometry. His picture of the role of particular elements in intuition seems in this respect to be more Leibnizian than Kantian. There is no evident room on his view to give intuition (as a singular representation) a warranting role.

I believe that Frege's verbal agreement with Kant about geometry is thus misleading. Frege accepts the language of Kant's doctrine of pure intuition—as applied to geometry. But it is doubtful that he can consistently accept all that Kant

---

[51] Ultimately for Kant the warrant presupposes the point that space is a form of our intuition of physical objects. Cf. Kant (1781, 1787: A46–8/B64–6; B147). Hence the warrant for geometry (and indeed all of mathematics) depends on the alleged fact that its applicability to the world of experience is guaranteed through its having as its subject matter the forms of our experience. This is part of Kant's 'transcendental deduction' of the objectivity of mathematics. I have little sympathy for this side of Kant's view, which in large part depends on his transcendental idealism.

[52] In fact, he contrasts apriori cognition in mathematics with apriori cognition in philosophy by insisting on the central role of particularity in the justification of mathematical cognition. Cf. Kant (1781, 1787: A164/B204; A713–5/B741–3).

intends by this doctrine, and maintain the centrality of generality in his conception of apriority. Frege's Leibnizian conception of apriority takes generality of justificational starting point to be fundamental. He uses Kant's terminology of pure intuition, but he divests it of any commitment to referential singularity or reference to particulars, at least in its role in grounding geometrical principles. He retains Kant's view that intuition is essentially a non-rational (non-logical) faculty, thus appealing to intuition in order to explain his non-logicist, non-Leibnizian view of geometry. In this way he holds together a Leibnizian conception of apriority with a Kantian rejection of logicism about geometry. The fact that Frege provides a less detailed account of geometry, and less full explication of his term 'intuition' than Kant does, is explained by Frege's preoccupation with the mathematics of number.

There is a further aspect of Frege's account of intuition in geometry that renders it very different from Kant's. Kant takes intuition to be a type of *objective* representation.[53] Frege holds that intuition is not objective. In fact, he explains objectivity partly in terms of independence from intuition, which he regards as essentially subjective (*FA*: sect. 26). In this passage, Frege makes his notorious claim that what is intuitable is not communicable. He sets out the thought experiment according to which what one being intuits as a plane another intuits as a point. He holds that since they can agree on geometrical principles (despite their subjective differences), their agreement is about something objective—about spatial structures that are subject to laws. Here again, it appears that particularistic aspects of intuition play no substantive role in Frege's account of the warrant for believing geometrical principles.

This doctrine of the subjectivity of spatial intuition is certainly not Kantian. Indeed, Kant characterizes intuition as an objective representation, in explicit contrast with subjective representations (sensations).[54] It is true that from a transcendental point of view, Kant regards space itself and hence pure apriori intuition as a form of our 'subjective' constitution.[55] This is part of Kant's transcendental deduction of the objectivity of geometry. Kant thinks that only because, from the transcendental point of view, space, geometry, and apriori intuition are *all* to be construed idealistically as forms of the subject, can one account for the objectivity of apriori principles—and indeed the objectivity of pure intuition—in geometry about space. From the 'empirical point of view'—the point of view of the practice of ordinary science and mathematics—, apriori intuition, geometrical principles, and space itself are all objectively valid and in no way confined to individuals' subjectivity.

Frege appears to have thought that the ability of mathematicians to produce logically coherent non-standard geometries shows that one can conceive (though not imagine or intuit) the falsity of Euclidean geometry. He thought that our grasp

---

[53] Kant (1781, 1787: A320/B376–7).
[54] Ibid.: A320/B377.   [55] Ibid.: A48/B65.

of the self-evidence of the axioms of Euclidean geometry depends on some non-rational, or at least non-logical, capacity that he termed 'intuition'. The elements intuited that are captured by the axioms are common to all—and in fact can be grasped in thought even by subjects whose subjective intuitions differ from ours.[56] So particularistic aspects of the intuitions seem to play no role in their warranting the axioms.

Frege calls Euclidean axioms self-evident. This view is in some tension with his appeal to intuition as grounds for the axioms. The warrant ('evidence') for believing the axioms seems not to rest purely in the senses of the axioms themselves. At least, one can apparently conceive of them as being false if one abstracts from spatial intuition. So the notion of self-evidence must be understood to include support from capacities whose deliverances is not entirely assimilated into the senses of the axioms themselves, or at least provides a support for them that is needed as supplement to any conceptual grasp of them that would abstract from such support.[57] Perhaps general features associated with what mathematicians intuit, but *only* general features, play a role in warranting the axioms.

Both Kant and Frege held that Euclidean geometry yields apriori knowledge of physical space. As noted, this view is now untenable. What remains philosophically interesting is the epistemology of *pure* geometry. Warrant for mathematicians' belief in pure geometry seems to be apriori. Understanding the axioms seems sufficient to believe them. But what does such understanding consist in? Geometrical concepts appear to depend in some way on a spatial ability. Although one can translate geometrical propositions into algebraic ones and produce equivalent models, the meaning of the geometrical propositions seems to me to be thereby lost. Pure geometry has some spatial content, even if it involves abstraction from the exact empirical structure of physical space. Perhaps there is something in common to all legitimate spatial notions that any pure geometry makes use of. Whether the role for a spatial ability in our warrant for believing them is particularistic and non-conceptual—as Kant claims—or fully general and

---

[56] This explication is well expressed by Dummett (1982: 250). I believe also that Dummett is correct in arguing that there is substantial evidence against the view that Frege accepted Kantian idealism about space. For an excellent, general discussion of Frege's views on geometry, see Tappenden (1995).

[57] It is not entirely clear to me what Frege, in his mature *post-Foundations* work, thought the relation between intuition and the senses of geometrical propositions is. The subjective elements in intuition are surely not part of the senses. Whether he thought that in conceiving non-Euclidean geometries and regarding them as logically consistent yet incompatible with Euclidean geometry, we give different senses to the key terms ('straight') or give the same sense but somehow abstract from intuitive support is not clear to me. Frege seems to have thought that sometimes intuitions are used in symbolic ways, as representations of something other than what is intuited, in geometrical reasoning. For example, in discussing generalizations of geometry beyond Euclidean space to a space of four dimensions, Frege says that intuition is not taken for what it is but as symbolic for something else (Frege 1884: sect. 14). He may have seen the same sort of process as involved in conceiving Euclidean geometry false in the context of reasoning within non-Euclidean geometry. This is a matter that invites further investigation.

conceptual—as Leibniz, and seemingly Frege, believe—seems to me to invite further investigation.

I believe that Kant is likely to be right about the dependence of our understanding of pure geometries on our representation of spatial properties through sensory, non-rational capacities. Frege appears to have sided with Kant on this matter. I think that Kant is probably wrong in holding that a non-conceptual capacity, pure intuition, plays a warranting role in geometrical understanding much less geometrical inference. Leibniz's view of warrant as deduction from basic (conceptually) understood truths of pure geometry seems closer to a sound modern mathematical epistemology. Like Kant, Frege appears to give pure intuition a role in warranting at least belief in the axioms of geometry. (I know of no evidence that Frege agreed with Kant that intuition is essential to warranting geometrical inference.) But Frege gives pure intuition a role in geometrical warrant only after removing the key Kantian feature of singularity of reference from this role. Moreover, Frege's view of the relation between the role of intuition in geometrical warrant and the alleged subjective character of intuition is left unclear.

It seems to me that conceptual understanding of the axioms of the various pure geometries suffices to warrant one in believing those axioms, as propositions in pure mathematics. Intuition in the Kantian sense seems to play a role in the fixing of geometrical content, but not in the warrant for believing the axioms or rules of inference.

V

I turn finally to the application of Frege's account of apriority to arithmetic. It is, of course, central to Frege's logicist project that truths about the numbers—which Frege certainly regarded as particular, determinate, formal objects (e.g. *FA*: sects. 13, 18)—are derivative from general logical truths. The attempt to extract the existence and properties of particular objects from general principles centres, unfortunately, in Frege's defective Axiom V. There is a wide range of difficult issues here, and I cannot engage them seriously in this essay. But I want to broach, very briefly, some further points regarding Frege's characterization of apriority.

Suppose that Frege is mistaken, and arithmetic is not derivable in an epistemically fruitful way from purely general truths. Suppose that arithmetic has the form that it appears to have—a form that includes primitive singular intentional contents or propositions. For example, in the Peano axiomatization, arithmetic seems primitively to involve the thought that 0 is a number. And in normal arithmetical thinking we seem to know intentional contents that have singular form ($0 + 1 = 1$, for example) without deriving them from general ones. If some such knowledge is primitive—underived from general principles—, then it counts as aposterior on Frege's characterization. This would surely be a defect of the characterization. The knowledge does not seem to rest on anything other than arithmetic understanding. This seems to be intellectual understanding. The justification of the knowledge does not involve sense experience in any way. Even though the knowledge does not seem to rest on pure sensible intuition, or on anything having essentially to do with perceptual capacities, it may be irreducibly singular.[58] Indeed it seems to be irreducibly singular from an epistemic point of view, regardless of whether it concerns (as it appears to) abstract but particular objects. At any rate, the failure of Frege's logicism gives one reason to worry whether apriority and generality coincide, even in the case of arithmetic. It seems to me, even after a century of reductive attempts, that we need a deeper investigation into the epistemology of arithmetic.

I think that from an epistemological perspective, arithmetic should be distinguished from set theory, second-order logic, and various other parts of logic and mathematics. The enormous mathematical interest of the logicist project, and other reductive enterprises that have dominated the twentieth century, should not be allowed to obscure the fact that our understanding and hence our mode of knowing these other theories is different from our understanding of arithmetic. It seems to me even that the typical Peano formulation of arithmetic in terms of the successor function is epistemologically different from the formulation in terms of Arabic numerals on a base ten, which most of us learned first. Mathematical equivalence does not entail sameness of sense (in Frege's sense), and hence sameness of cognitive mode of presentation.

VI

It is time to summarize. Frege's characterization of apriority in terms of generality is a mischaracterization. Apriority bears an essential connection to justificational independence from experience. In modern times, 'experience' has come to mean *sense* experience. But Frege's characterization raises fundamental questions about the relation between apriority and generality. Frege followed a Leibnizian conception that assumed a close coincidence between the two notions.

If one thinks of experience sufficiently broadly (so as to include 'intellectual experience' not just sense experience), some of the pressure against the coincidence can be dissipated. Such a conception may have been one of Leibniz's conceptions of experience, and the associated conception of apriority may there-

[58] In fact, our knowledge of set theory, while apriori, also seems to make primitive reference to particular sets, as noted earlier. Whereas Frege blamed set theory, rejecting it altogether, I am inclined to fault Frege's conception of apriority.

fore have been Leibnizian as well. Such a conception could treat the instances of the *cogito* and other token, indexically based, self-evident truths as aposteriori. This is because the conception construes apriority in a way that excludes from the apriori even justificational dependence on purely intellectual 'experience'. Given a Kantian conception of apriority, which is more in line with the dominant modern conception, self-knowledge and knowledge of certain other indexical-involving truths can be apriori. For warrant seems to derive purely from intellectual understanding. It in no way rests on sense perception.

Problems with geometry and arithmetic remain. Leibniz, Kant, and Frege all maintained that geometry and arithmetic are apriori. If the position is carefully confined to pure geometry, it seems highly plausible. I believe, however, that we do not understand very well the role of spatial abilities in the content and justification of pure geometries. So I think that it is not fully clear whether justification in pure geometry rests on purely general propositions, although it seems to me likely that it does. The case of arithmetic is, I think, more serious as a possible counter-example to the claim of a coincidence between apriority and the primacy of generalizations in canonical justification. For arithmetic is apparently committed to basic truths in singular form, in its most natural and straightforward formulations.

I think that Frege is right to reject Kant's claim that the deliverances of a non-conceptual faculty, pure intuition, are *justificationally* basic in the warrant for arithmetic. But Kant may nevertheless have been right to hold that although cognition of arithmetic is apriori, cognition (or propositions) in singular form can be justificationally basic. One's justification derives from an understanding that encompasses singular intentional contents. On such a view, some apriority would be non-logical, and would not derive purely from *general* principles of pure reason. In arithmetic apriori knowledge would derive from intellectual, non-sense-perceptual understanding of necessary, non-context-dependent, singular intentional contents. I think that we should investigate in more depth the innovation that Kant offered: apriority that does not rest on logical or other general principles. I recommend doing so without assuming that apriori theoretical cognition must be constrained, as Kant insisted, by relation to sensibility. I recommend doing so without presuming that we must invoke Kant's notion of pure sensible intuition. I believe that we can follow Leibniz and Frege in avoiding essential reliance on pure intuition in arithmetic, without following them in insisting that generality lies at the base of all apriori warrant. Kant's conception of underived, singular understanding which is nevertheless apriori seems to be worth pursuing.

References

Adams, R. M. (1994), *Leibniz: Determinist, Theist, Idealist* (Oxford: Oxford University Press).
Burge, T. (1992), 'Frege on Knowing the Third World', *Mind* 101: 633–50.

Burge, T. (1996), 'Our Entitlement to Self-Knowledge', *Proceedings of the Aristotelian Society* 96: 91–116.

—— (1998*a*), 'Frege on Knowing the Foundation', *Mind* 107: 305–47.

—— (1998*b*), 'Memory and Self-Knowledge', *Externalism and Self-Knowledge*, P. Ludlow and N. Martin (eds.). (Stanford: CSLI Publications).

Dummett, M. (1982), 'Frege and Kant on Geometry', *Inquiry* 25: 233–54.

—— (1991), *Frege: Philosophy of Mathematics* (Cambridge, Mass.: Harvard University Press).

Frege, G. (1879), *Begriffsschrift.*

—— (1884), *The Foundations of Arithmetic.*

—— (1893a), (1902), *The Basic Laws of Arithmetic.*

—— (1893b), (1902b),*Grundgesetze der Arithmetik.*

—— (1967), *Kleine Schriften*, ed. I. Angelelli (Hildesheim: Georg Olms).

—— (1979), *Posthumous Writings*, H. Hermes, F. Kambartel, and F. Kaulbach (eds.) (Chicago: University of Chicago Press).

—— (1983), *Nachgelassene Schriften* (Hamburg: Felix Meiner).

—— (1984), *Collected Papers*, ed. B. McGuinness (Oxford: Blackwell).

Friedman, M. (1992), *Kant and the Exact Sciences* (Cambridge, Mass.: Harvard University Press).

Gabriel, G. (1996), 'Frege's "Epistemology in Disguise"', in *Frege: Importance and Legacy*, ed. M. Schirn (Berlin: Walter de Gruyter).

Kant, I. (1781), (1787), *The Critique of Pure Reason.*

—— (1790), *The Critique of Judgment.*

—— (1800), *Jäsche Logic.*

Kaplan, D. (1989), 'A Logic of Demonstratives', in *Themes from Kaplan*, J. Almog, J. Perry, and H. Wettstein eds. (New York: Oxford University Press).

Kripke, S. (1972), *Naming and Necessity* (Cambridge, Mass.: Harvard University Press).

Leibniz, G. W. (1966), *Leibniz: Logical Papers*, trans. and ed. By G. H. R. Parkinson (Oxford: Clarendon Press).

—— (1714), 'Monadology', in *Philosophical Essays* (1989).

—— (1705), (1765), (1989), *New Essays on Human Understanding* (New York: Cambridge University Press).

—— (1989), *Philosophical Essays*, R. Ariew and D. Garber (eds.) (Indianapolis: Hackett Publishing Co.).

Lotze, R. H. (1880), *Logik* (Leipzig).

—— (1888), *Logic*, trans. B. Bosanquet (Oxford 1888; repr. New York 1980).

Mill, J. S. (1843), *System of Logic* (New York: Harper & Bros., 1893).

Schirn, M. (ed). (1996), *Frege: Importance and Legacy* (Berlin: Walter de Gruyter).

Tappenden, J. (1995), 'Geometry and Generality in Frege's Philosophy of Arithmetic', *Synthese* 102: 319–61.

Wilson, Margaret (1967), 'Leibniz and Locke on "First Truths"', *Journal of the History of Ideas* 28: 347–66.

3

Rationalism, Empiricism, and the A Priori

Quassim Cassam

I

How is the distinction between 'rationalist' and 'empiricist' theories of a priori knowledge to be understood? Those who organize their accounts of a priori knowledge around this distinction are not committed to regarding it as sharp or straightforward, but it is nevertheless widely assumed that there are distinctive core elements or principles by reference to which most theories of a priori knowledge can usefully be classified either as 'rationalist' or as 'empiricist'. Is this assumption correct? If so, what are the core elements of each doctrine?

In answering the second of these questions, it would be inappropriate to ignore historical considerations. For example, one should be extremely reluctant to accept any answer to it which results in the classification of Leibniz as an 'empiricist' or A. J. Ayer as a 'rationalist'. Equally, the fact that someone such as Ayer is deemed to be a paradigm empiricist should not be taken to imply that every element of his position is a core element of empiricism about the a priori. The key is to be able to distinguish, among the principles held by some paradigmatic historical figure, between those without which he would fail to qualify as, say, an 'empiricist', and those which are peculiar to his particular brand of empiricism. There is, no doubt, some element of arbitrariness in this distinction, just because the boundaries of concepts such as those of 'empiricism' and 'rationalism' are neither precise nor uncontroversial. To concede this much is, however, not to concede that no distinction can be drawn between the fundamental tenets of these doctrines and the idiosyncratic commitments of a particular philosopher.

As it turns out, these fundamental tenets are surprisingly hard to identify. There is no shortage of principles by reference to which theories of a priori knowledge have traditionally been classified as either 'rationalist' or 'empiricist', but a good many of these principles are obscure and ambiguous. Some of them appear to have been held both by paradigm rationalists and paradigm empiricists, and it remains to be seen whether it is possible to account for this by referring to the idiosyncrasies of particular historical figures or to differences in interpretation. In other cases, the problem is that the intelligibility of allegedly core principles is open to question. Quine's conclusion is, in effect, that 'rationalism' and 'empiricism' are 'pseudo-doctrines' between which 'there is no real difference' (Quine 1976: 113).[1] I agree with Quine, at least to the extent that some of the most popular and influential accounts of the dispute between these doctrines are, in my view, untenable. However, instead of rejecting the traditional classification outright, I will conclude by proposing my own alternative account of what is at issue between 'rationalism' and 'empiricism'.

II

According to the standard account, one area of disagreement between rationalism and empiricism concerns the source of a priori knowledge. Suppose that a proposition p is said to be known a priori as long as p is true and one's justification or warrant for believing it is independent of experience. Rationalism is then said to be committed to the principle that the source of some or all of our a priori knowledge is what is variously described as 'rational intuition', 'clear and distinct perception', or 'rational insight'. For one's knowledge of p to count as a priori, one's justification for believing this proposition must be a priori, and the rationalist claims that rational intuition or one of its variants is the source of one's a priori justification.[2] In contrast, the empiricist is characterized as rejecting this account on the grounds that it requires us to posit a mysterious faculty of intuition which cannot be properly explained.[3] For some empiricists, the moral of this 'argument from queerness'[4] against the notion of rational intuition is that the very

---

[1] There is no explicit mention of 'rationalism' and 'empiricism' at this point in Quine's discussion. The doctrines between which he claims there to be no real difference are the linguistic doctrine of elementary logical truth—the doctrine that such truths are true purely by virtue of language—and the doctrine of 'ultimate and inexplicable insight into obvious traits of reality' (1976: 113). The linguistic doctrine is a core element of 'logical' empiricism, and talk of insight into obvious traits of reality is characteristic of rationalist accounts of a priori knowledge. This is the basis of my suggestion that Quine's discussion has a direct bearing on the dispute between 'rationalism' and 'empiricism'.

[2] See BonJour (1998) for a defence of this claim.

[3] This is the basis of Paul Boghossian's criticism of the view that the source of our a priori knowledge is 'a special evidence-gathering faculty of *intuition*, distinct from the standard five senses, which allows us to arrive at justified beliefs about necessary properties of the world' (1997: 334). His objection is that this special faculty 'has never been described in satisfactory terms' (1997: 334). In his discussion, A. J. Ayer claims that 'the fundamental tenet of rationalism is that thought is an independent source of knowledge' (1946: 98). He objects that rationalism requires us to 'accept it as a mysterious inexplicable fact that thought has [the] power to reveal to us authoritatively the nature of objects which we have never observed' (1946: 98).

[4] This is J. L. Mackie's expression. He uses it to describe an argument against moral realism which is very similar to some empiricist arguments against the idea that 'rational intuition' could be a source of a priori knowledge. According to the epistemological component of

idea of a priori knowledge is problematic. For others, it is that while it might be appropriate to describe some of our knowledge as 'a priori' the possibility of such knowledge can and should be accounted for without appealing to occult faculties of the kind which the rationalist invokes.

A second point at issue between rationalism and empiricism is said to concern the scope of a priori knowledge. This is the area of disagreement which Ayer emphasizes in his classic discussion of these matters in *Language, Truth and Logic*. According to Ayer, rationalism is the view that 'there are some truths about the world which we can know independently of experience' (1946: 98). In contrast, empiricism is committed to the principle that 'there can be no a priori knowledge of reality' (1946: 115). On one reading, to say that there can be no a priori knowledge of 'reality' would be to say that there can be no a priori knowledge. This is not the version of empiricism which Ayer himself favours. His version of empiricism allows that a priori knowledge of some necessary truths is possible, but denies that the truths in question are 'about the world'. His way of making this point is to restrict a priori knowledge to analytic propositions, defined as ones which are true solely in virtue of the meaning of their constituent symbols, and to argue that analytic truths are 'entirely devoid of factual content' (Ayer 1946: 105).

Here, then, are two fundamental issues over which there are apparently straightforward disagreements between 'rationalism' and 'empiricism'. To summarize, the standard account maintains that to be a 'rationalist' one must believe that:

(R1) Rational intuition is the source of some or all of our a priori knowledge

and

(R2) A priori knowledge of reality is possible.

To count as an 'empiricist', one must believe that:

(E1) Rational intuition is the source of none of our a priori knowledge[5]

and

(E2) A priori knowledge of reality is not possible.

Given this account of what is supposed to be at issue between rationalism and empiricism about the a priori, the next questions which need to be addressed are these:

Mackie's argument, if we were aware of objective moral values, 'it would have to be by some special faculty of moral perception or intuition, utterly different from our ordinary ways of knowing everything else' (Mackie 1977: 38).

[5] This should not be read as committing empiricism to the view that a priori knowledge is possible for us. In BonJour's terminology, an empiricist who denies the existence of a priori knowledge is 'radical' rather than 'moderate'. In my discussion, however, I will focus on 'moderate' versions of 'empiricism', which accept that we have some a priori knowledge but deny that rational intuition is the source of our a priori knowledge. For more on the distinction between 'radical' and 'moderate' empiricism, see BonJour (1998: 18–19).

(Q1) how is the notion of 'rational intuition' to be understood?

(Q2) what would it be for a piece of a priori knowledge to count as a priori
       knowledge of 'reality'?

A popular answer to (Q1) is that rational intuition is what Laurence BonJour
calls 'intuitive insight into necessity' (1998: 18). To say that rational intuition is
the source of my a priori knowledge of some proposition is therefore to say that
'when I carefully and reflectively consider the proposition (. . .) in question, I am
able to see or grasp or apprehend that the proposition is *necessary*' (ibid. 106).
With regard to (Q2), Ayer's discussion suggests that a priori knowledge of reality
would have to be a priori knowledge of the truth of propositions which are 'about
the world' (Ayer 1946: 98). I take it that for a proposition to be 'about the world',
its truth must, as Quine puts it, 'hinge on reality' (1970: 10); it must be true by
virtue of 'traits of reality' (Quine 1976: 113). It remains to be seen what all this
talk of 'reality' amounts to, and also how the phrase 'true by virtue of' is to be
understood.

One way of undermining the standard account of the dispute between 'rationalism' and 'empiricism' would be to show that 'empiricism' is not committed
(E1) and is therefore not committed to denying (R1). Another possibility would
be to show that 'empiricism' is not committed to (E2) and is therefore not
committed to disputing (R2). These are not the only possibilities, but they are the
ones which I will focus on to begin with. Clearly, anyone who tries to argue that
(R1) and (R2) are compatible with 'empiricism' needs to explain how a position
which accepts these theses can still count as 'empiricist'. On one view, the only
basis for the continued use of such labels is tradition, and if it is the case that (R1)
and (R2) are compatible with what would generally be regarded as prominent
examples of 'empiricism', then this only goes to show that Quine's scepticism
about the traditional classification is entirely justified. For those who do not share
Quine's scepticism, the lesson would have to be that there are other ways of drawing the distinction between rationalism and empiricism, or that what really counts
in the present context is not one's acceptance or rejection of (R1) and (R2), but
rather one's interpretation of these theses or one's specific grounds for accepting
or rejecting them. The suggestion, in other words, is that the agreement over (R1)
and (R2) may turn out to be comparatively superficial.

How might an empiricist be brought to accept (R1), and hence to abandon
(E1), given the argument from queerness? If the very idea of 'rational intuition'
is dismissed as queer or occult, how can one possibly agree that rational intuition
is the source of any of our a priori knowledge? Perhaps the best way of talking an
empiricist out of his opposition to (R1) would be to persuade him that an appeal
to rational intuition is required to account for our a priori knowledge of analytic
truths.[6] An argument along these lines would not cut much ice with someone who

---

[6] This is BonJour's response to 'moderate' empiricism. He criticizes moderate empiricists
for claiming that 'the a priori justification of analytic propositions (or 'statements') can be

is sceptical about analytic-synthetic distinction, but it ought to carry considerable weight with those empiricists who take it for granted that there is such a distinction and that a priori knowledge of analytic truths is possible. If, as many empiricists concede, we have a priori knowledge of some analytic truths, and if rational intuition is a necessary condition of such knowledge, then the idea of rational intuition should not be dismissed as queer.

This attempt to demystify the concept of rational intuition is a 'transcendental' argument in something like Kant's sense.[7] It attempts to legitimate a concept which empiricists have called into question by showing that an appeal to this concept is required to explain how a cognitive achievement which many empiricists regard as actual—a priori knowledge of analytic truths—is possible. I will refer to this transcendental argument for (R1) as the *argument for rational intuition* (ARI).

As with other transcendental arguments, there are basically two ways of attempting to undermine ARI. The first would be to deny that the cognitive achievement from which it sets out is actual. It would need to be claimed, in other words, that we do not have a priori knowledge of analytic truths, or what I will refer to from now on as analytic a priori knowledge. I will not pursue this option here. The second option would be to show that what ARI identifies as a necessary condition of the cognitive achievement from which it sets out is not in fact necessary, and that this achievement can be counted for in other ways. What this amounts to is the proposal that rational intuition is not a necessary condition of the possibility of analytic a priori knowledge. Critics of ARI who endorse this proposal are under an obligation to provide an alternative explanation of how a priori knowledge of analytic propositions is possible, one which does not appeal to 'rational intuition'. The range of genuine alternatives will, in turn, depend on one's answer to (Q1). Intuitively, the broader one's conception of rational intuition, the harder it will be to explain analytic a priori knowledge without appealing to the possibility of 'rational intuition'.

With regard to (R2), one way of defending this thesis would be to argue that (i) a priori knowledge of some synthetic truths is possible, and that (ii) synthetic truths are 'about the world'. The problem with this argument is that there are no uncontroversial examples of synthetic truths which can be known a priori, and that the rejection of the possibility of synthetic a priori knowledge is arguably a fundamental tenet of 'empiricism'. In general, those who regard themselves as empiricists have responded to examples of supposedly synthetic a priori judgements either by denying that they are synthetic or by denying that they are a

---

understood epistemologically in a way that does not require the sort of allegedly mysterious intuitive capacity advocated by rationalism' (1998: 29).

[7] In the words of Gary Hatfield, 'transcendental argument starts from some given body of knowledge, or some cognitive achievement, and asks how it is possible. If it can be shown that the cognitive achievement in question is possible in only one way, then, given that the achievement is actual, the only possible means for its possibility must be actual, too' (1990: 79).

priori. While rationalist critics of (E2) have not always found these responses persuasive, the fact that there are so many different ways of understanding the analytic–synthetic distinction has meant that the debate over the possibility of synthetic a priori knowledge has more or less ground to a halt.[8]

A more promising argument for (R2), one which stands a better chance of persuading an empiricist to give up (E2), is this: (i)* analytic a priori knowledge is possible; (ii)* analytic truths are 'about the world'; therefore, (R2) a priori knowledge of reality is possible. From an empiricist perspective, a major attraction of this argument is that it does not require one to accept that synthetic a priori knowledge is possible. If empiricists can be brought to accept that even judgements which are straightforwardly and unquestionably analytic by their lights are not devoid of factual content, then they should no longer be committed to (E2) and opposed to (R2). I will call it, this argument for (R2), the *argument for factual content* (AFC).

III

To begin with ARI, what is the case for saying that rational intuition is a necessary condition of analytic a priori knowledge? According to one version of ARI, the case is this: for one's knowledge of a proposition to be a priori, one's justification for believing it must be a priori. Suppose, next, that an analytic truth is, as Ayer maintains, one which is necessarily true purely in virtue of its meaning. This suggests that one's justification for believing an analytic truth will be a priori or independent of experience as long as one understands the proposition in question, and sees or recognizes, in virtue of one's grasp of its meaning, that the proposition is necessarily true. In the words of Crispin Wright:

> The real motivation for thinking of necessity as truth in virtue of meaning derives from the fact that, in simple cases at least, we want to describe ourselves as reflecting on the content of a sentence and *thereby* coming to see that it cannot but be true. In such cases, necessity is recognized by *the light of* understanding. (1980: 353–4)

How does this show that *rational intuition* is a necessary condition of analytic a priori knowledge? It shows this because, according to ARI, seeing 'by the light of understanding' that a proposition is necessary is exactly the same thing as rationally intuiting its necessity. Where the present version of ARI speaks of 'seeing' that certain propositions are necessarily true, rationalists speak of an 'intuitive' or 'rational' insight into the necessity of propositions which one has carefully and reflectively considered, but these ways of putting things appear to be equivalent. The rationalist overtones of Wright's formulation are, after all, unmistakable. So

---

[8] Cf. BonJour (1998: 30).

if 'seeing' by 'the light of understanding' that analytic truths are necessarily true is a necessary condition of a priori knowledge of such truths, then it follows that rational intuition is a necessary condition of analytic a priori knowledge.

There are at least two things which those who are sceptical abut the notion of rational intuition can say in response to this argument. They can object that (a) 'seeing by the light of understanding' that an analytic proposition is necessarily true is not a necessary condition of a priori knowledge of that proposition, or that (b) 'seeing by the light of understanding' that a proposition is necessarily true is not the same thing as rationally intuiting its necessity. Consider, in the light of these options, the following passage from Ayer's *Language, Truth and Logic*:

The contention . . . which we reject is that the propositions of logic and mathematics have the same status as empirical hypotheses; that their validity is determined in the same way. We maintain that they are independent of experience in the sense that they do not owe their validity to empirical verification. We may come to discover them through an inductive process; but once we have apprehended them we see that they are necessarily true, that they hold good for every conceivable position. (1946: 100)

This passage suggests that (a) could not have been Ayer's response to ARI. He explicitly refers to our ability to 'see' that logical and mathematical propositions are necessarily true, and this insight into their necessity is clearly supposed to be the result of one's understanding of these propositions. In both of these respects, Ayer's approach is strikingly similar to some rationalist approaches to the a priori.

The same paradoxical conclusion is suggested by Christopher Peacocke's recent characterization of rationalism in the context of an account of what it is to possess a concept. Peacocke describes his own view as having 'the distinctive flavour of a classical rationalist position' (1998: 78) on the grounds that it endorses six principles which were held by 'that paradigm rationalist Leibniz'. The principles are that (1) the evidentness of particular axioms is grounded in the understanding of the terms they contain, (2) finding an axiom evident, when this is properly grounded in the understanding, is a way of coming to know the Thought expressed by the axiom, (3) logical axioms can be known a priori, (4) logical axioms are necessary, (5) reflection is needed to discover the axioms of logic, and (6) there is an important distinction to be drawn between clear ideas and distinct ideas. Yet, with the possible exception of (6), there seems no reason why these principles could not also be accepted by that paradigm empiricist Ayer. Where Peacocke's rationalist speaks of finding a logical axiom 'evident', Ayer speaks of 'seeing' that logical truths are necessarily true. For Ayer, as for the rationalist, this 'seeing' is, in Peacocke's terminology, 'understanding-based' and a source of knowledge. In addition, logical axioms are both necessary and knowable a priori. As for (5), Ayer's emphasis on 'the power of logic and mathematics to surprise us' (1946: 114) implies that we may need to reflect in order to discover them. Are we therefore to fly in the face of tradition and conclude that Ayer's view also has the flavour of a classical rationalist position?

This paradoxical conclusion would only follow if what Ayer describes as 'seeing' that a proposition is necessarily true is the same thing as 'rationally intuiting' its necessity.[9] This is what (b) disputes. Before examining the case for (b), it would be worth pointing out that even if *Ayer's* approach turns out to be 'entirely' indiscernible from that of the rationalist' (BonJour 1998: 39),[10] it is a further question whether this vindicates the Quinean view that there is no real difference between 'empiricism' and 'rationalism'. I said that one should be very reluctant to accept any account of the distinction between these doctrines which has Ayer coming out as some kind of rationalist, but I added that it is also necessary to distinguish between the idiosyncratic commitments of a particular philosopher and the fundamental tenets of 'rationalism' or 'empiricism'. Ayer's talk of 'seeing' that analytic propositions are necessarily true certainly commits him to what might be called an 'intuitionist' conception of our a priori knowledge of such propositions, and this is the basis of the charge that his view has at least the flavour of a classical rationalist position.[11] But quite apart from the question of whether Ayer's intuitionism is the same as the intuitionism of those who endorse (R1), it is also possible that his intuitionism is an idiosyncratic feature of his brand of empiricism rather than a crucial element of 'empiricism' as such, or even a crucial element of his own approach to the a priori. To the extent that 'empiricism' in the strict sense is opposed to intuitionism, it is not entirely discernible from 'rationalism', and the moral is that (a) *should* have been Ayer's response to ARI, whether or not it would have been his response.

I will come back to this suggestion below. First, I need to complete my discussion of (b). If there is a distinction between the sense in which empiricists such as Ayer think that 'seeing' that a proposition is necessarily true is required for a priori knowledge of that proposition and the sense in which rationalists think that intuitions of necessity are necessary for a priori knowledge, then there

---

[9] BonJour takes it for granted that anyone who thinks that 'one who understands an a priori proposition can see or grasp that it is necessary' (1998: 40) is thereby committed to rationalism about the a priori. This is the basis of his charge that so-called 'moderate empiricists' such as C. I. Lewis are *de facto* rationalists when it comes to explaining our a priori knowledge of analytic truths. But this charge fails to take into account the possibility that, as (b) suggests, moderate empiricism and rationalism have very different conceptions of what is involved in seeing that a proposition is necessary. As BonJour himself acknowledges, the rationalist's 'intuitive insight' is supposed to be rational insight into 'the nature of reality' (1998: 18). For many moderate empiricists, intuitive insight 'extends only to propositions that reflect relations among our concepts or meanings or linguistic conventions, rather than to those that make claims about the character of the extra-conceptual world' (1998: 18). This distinction is hard to reconcile with the claim that Lewis's view is 'entirely indiscernible from that of the rationalist' (1998: 39).

[10] BonJour makes this comment about C. I. Lewis's version of moderate empiricism, but he would presumably want to say the same thing about Ayer's position.

[11] I take 'intuitionism' to be the view that our a priori knowledge of some proposition P rests upon our ability to 'see' that P is necessarily true. See Ayers (1991: i. 264–8) for a recent defence of 'a qualified form of intuitionism'. In Ayers' version of intuitionism, a priori knowledge of P involves not just the knowledge *that* P is necessarily true, but also the ability to 'see' *why* it is true.

is no need to conclude that empiricism as such and intuitionism are incompatible. A familiar argument for (b) is that the intuitions of necessity which are referred to by Ayer and Wright are *linguistic*, whereas what the rationalist calls 'intuitions of reason' are not on the same level as 'merely linguistic intuitions' (Ayers 1991: i, 293).[12] So when empiricists say that the ability is 'see' that analytic propositions are necessarily true is a necessary condition of analytic a priori knowledge, they are *not* saying, in effect, that rational intuition is a necessary condition of analytic a prior knowledge. Far from committing him to (R1), or to giving up (E1), Ayer's 'linguistic' intuitionism can be seen as a threat to ARI and as leaving the argument from queerness intact. It is a threat to ARI because, assuming that (b) is correct, its explanation of how analytic a priori knowledge is possible is an alternative to the explanation offered by the rationalist's transcendental argument. And it is compatible with the argument from queerness because, given (b), it does not follow from the fact that the notion of 'rational intuition' is unacceptably mysterious that the notion of a merely linguistic intuition is unacceptably mysterious.

All of this assumes that the notion of a merely linguistic intuition is coherent in its own right, and that there is a genuine distinction between merely linguistic intuitions of necessity and so-called 'intuitions of reason'. Are these assumptions defensible? To begin with the notion of a linguistic intuition, this can be understood in either a narrow or a broad sense. Linguistic intuitions in the narrow sense are syntactic intuitions. To borrow an example from Chomsky, a sentence such as 'sincerity frighten may the boy' is a 'violation of purely syntactic rules' (Chomsky 1965: 76), and our recognition of its deviance might, in virtue of this fact, be described as involving the exercise of 'linguistic intuition' in the narrow sense. In contrast, the deviance of 'oculists are generally better trained than eye doctors' is semantic rather than syntactic. Intuitions of semantic deviance might be described as 'linguistic' in the broad sense.[13]

As I have already pointed out, Ayer characterizes an analytic proposition as one which is true solely in virtue of the meaning of its constituent symbols. His view is that 'seeing' that an analytic proposition is necessarily true is an immediate, non-derivative product of a proper grasp of its meaning. To say this is, in effect, to say that our intuitions of necessity are 'understanding-based', since understanding a proposition and grasping its meaning come to the same thing. An understanding-based intuition cannot, however, be characterized as purely syntactic. Rather, to the extent that 'seeing', in the empiricist's sense, that an analytic proposition is necessary is the product of one's grasp of its meaning, one would have to regard this 'seeing' as involving the exercise of semantic rather than merely syntactic intuition. This means that for (b) to be defensible, it would

---

[12] See Ayers (1991: i. 289–300) for an interesting discussion of a version of this argument.

[13] This discussion should not be taken to imply that syntactic and semantic considerations can always be sharply distinguished. See Chomsky (1964: 75–9), and Ayers (1991: i, 289–300), for further discussion of this important qualification.

have to be the case that so-called 'intuitions of reason' are *not* semantic, or, at any rate, not merely semantic.

On one reading, to say that intuitions of reason are not semantic would be to say that language-mastery is not a necessary condition of the ability to recognize the necessity of analytic propositions.[14] This claim is extremely implausible. In order to recognize the necessity of a proposition such as 'all bachelors are unmarried', one must be able to understand it, and it is difficult to see how this would be possible without mastery of a language. Perhaps, then, the point of (b) is that language-mastery is a sufficient condition for seeing by 'the light of understanding' that analytic propositions are necessarily true, but not sufficient for the rational intuition of necessity. This claim is, on the face of it, also implausible. Once it is granted that analytically necessary propositions are necessarily true purely in virtue of meaning, how can it be supposed that grasp of their necessity in either sense requires anything more than the 'ability to know what we mean by the expressions which we use, and to discern the implications of meaning them in such-and-such ways' (Wright 1980: 343)? Possession of these abilities is, however, just what 'reflective language-mastery' (ibid.) consists in, so it seems that reflective language-mastery is, as the linguistic intuitionist claims, not just necessary but also sufficient for one's intuitive insight into the necessity of analytic propositions. It is not as if 'reason' is not involved in one's mastery of a language, or that it can be sharply distinguished from what the linguistic intuitionist calls 'understanding', so the attempt to distinguish sharply between 'intuitions of reason' and 'linguistic intuitions' is bound to be problematic.[15]

An objection to this line of argument is that it accepts the assumption that those propositions whose necessity we can intuit are necessarily true purely in virtue of meaning. To accept that analytic propositions are true purely by virtue of meaning is, in Paul Boghossian's terminology, to endorse a 'metaphysical' conception of analyticity.[16] *Once granted* that an analytic proposition is true solely in virtue of the meaning of its constituent symbols, the proposal that intuitive insight into its necessity requires anything other than the exercise of semantic intuition may seem mysterious, but perhaps the rationalist's point is to deny that 'intuitions of reason' pertain to propositions which are metaphysically analytic. An alternative proposal would be that 'the world' is responsible for the truth of propositions whose necessity we can rationally intuit, and that rational intuition is therefore to be regarded as 'intuitive insight into the nature of reality' (BonJour 1998: 18). As long as one is willing to admit that analytic propositions are 'about the world', this proposal is

---

[14] BonJour claims that 'there are some a priori knowable propositions that do not depend on language at all' (1998: 57).

[15] As Michael Ayers remarks, it is a good idea when thinking about the relationship between reason and language, to 'reflect on the role of rationality, or, less portentously, of general intelligence in the acquisition and employment of language' (1991: i. 290).

[16] A statement is metaphysically analytic 'provided that, in some appropriate sense, it *owes its truth-value completely to its meaning*, and not at all to "the facts"' (Boghossian 1997: 334).

compatible with the thesis that the propositions whose necessity we can intuit are analytically necessary. To say that analytic propositions are 'about the world' is, however, to deny that they are 'metaphysically' analytic. A different conception of analyticity is required, one which does not imply that analytic propositions are true purely by virtue of meaning.[17]

In contrast, linguistic intuitionists think that our intuitions of necessity are merely linguistic because they think that necessity itself is merely linguistic. Our intuitions of necessity are therefore linguistic both in origin and in scope. They originate exclusively in a general capacity of reflective language-mastery, and only 'enlighten us by illustrating the way in which we use certain symbols' (Ayer 1946: 106). Since, by Ayer's lights, the 'world' is not responsible for the necessary truth of analytic propositions, seeing by the light of understanding that an analytic proposition is necessarily true does not amount to intuitive insight into necessary properties of reality. In this crucial aspect, his intuitionism is, as (b) claims, fundamentally different from the rationalist's intuitionism. This means that, as anticipated above, the fact that an empiricist is a *linguistic* intuitionist does not commit him to (R1), or to abandoning (E1).

This defence of (b) provides 'empiricism' in Ayer's sense with the resources to challenge the conclusion of ARI, but only at a price. For it now appears that for empiricists who are also intuitionists to be in a position to resist the charge that their position is indistinguishable from rationalism, they must insist that necessary truths are metaphysically analytic and devoid of factual content. These are not claims with which all those who regard themselves as 'empiricists' would wish to be saddled.[18] If the notion of metaphysically analyticity is incoherent, or if analytic propositions are 'about the world', this would strengthen the case for (a), for the view that 'empiricism' should have nothing to do with intuitionism in any form. Since demonstrating that analytic propositions have factual content is the business of the argument for factual content (AFC), it is now time to examine this argument.

IV

For a proposition to be 'about the world' is for it to be true by virtue of 'traits of reality'. Suppose that analytic propositions are true by virtue of traits of reality and therefore, as (ii)* claims, 'about the world'. According to AFC, this would

---

[17] Boghossian, who is no rationalist, also questions the coherence of the metaphysical concept of analyticity. The alternative is to think of analyticity as an 'overtly *epistemological* notion' (1997: 334). A statement is epistemologically analytic 'provided that grasp of its meaning alone suffices for justified belief in its truth' (1997: 334). The question raised by this proposal is whether it is possible to separate the metaphysical and epistemological notions in the way that Boghossian suggests. I have my doubts about this, but will not attempt to spell them out here.

[18] See Boghossian (1997) for a broadly 'empiricist' conception of a priori knowledge which repudiates both claims.

mean that analytic a priori knowledge is a priori knowledge of 'reality'. This is the basis of AFC's defence of (R2). The conclusion which ARI draws from the supposition that analytic propositions have factual content is that intuitive insight into their necessity is intuitive insight into necessary traits of reality. This is the basis of ARI's defence of (R1).

This account of the use which rationalists can try to make of (ii)* raises the following questions:

(Q3) what does 'reality' mean in the claim that analytic propositions are 'true by virtue of reality'?

(Q4) what is the case for saying that analytic propositions are true by virtue of traits of reality?

With regard to the first of these questions, 'naturalism' is the view that 'reality' is identical with nature, with what exists in space or time. Platonism is the view that 'reality' includes universals or abstract objects, which do not exist in nature. A naturalistic argument for the thesis that analytic propositions are devoid of factual content would therefore be that 'every truth must be a truth about the natural world' (Strawson 1997: 62) and that analytic propositions are not about the natural world. Because analytic propositions are not true by virtue of traits of nature, they 'say nothing' (Ayer 1946: 106). By the same token, a Platonist argument for the view that analytic propositions are not devoid of factual content would be to allow that there are truths which are about the world without being about the natural world, and to insist that 'we speak of the non-natural relations that hold between universals, or abstract entities, themselves. . . . whenever we speak of conceptual (or logical or analytic or semantic) necessities' (Strawson 1997: 61). From a Platonist perspective, Ayer's assertion that analytic propositions say nothing is based on an answer to (Q3) which is far too restrictive.

Is a commitment to Platonism the only possible basis for a defence of (ii)*? While many rationalists are Platonists, (ii)* has also been endorsed by writers on a priori knowledge who would not describe themselves as Platonists. The question which this raises is whether it is possible to argue for (ii)* without committing oneself to Platonism. One such argument, which is broadly Quinean in inspiration, is this: (A) 'no sentence is true but reality makes it so' (Quine 1970: 10); (B) analytic propositions or sentences are true; therefore (C) analytic truths are true by virtue of reality.

Both 'empiricists' in Ayer's sense, and rationalists accept (B). Ayer maintains that analytic propositions 'can be true and useful and surprising' (1946: 97), but he does not take this to be equivalent to the assertion that they have factual content.[19] The sense in which they are true and useful is that they illustrate the

---

[19] In his discussion of 'logical Conventionalism', Boghossian identifies the view that the sentences of logic are factual with the view that 'they can express truths' (1997: 349). Ayer rejects this identification.

way in which we use certain symbols. They lack factual content because they are true purely by virtue of meaning rather than by virtue of traits of reality. It is this thesis which is at odds with (A). The point of (A) is, firstly, that (Ai) there is no such thing as a true statement which does not owe its truth to the 'world' or to the 'facts', and, secondly, that (Aii) there are therefore no true propositions which are true purely by virtue of meaning. In other words, there are no metaphysically analytic statements or propositions.[20] It follows from this that analytic propositions cannot both be true and lack factual content. If they are literally 'true', it is the world which makes them so, and this means that they have factual content.

What is the argument for (Ai)? Quine's argument is that when the truth predicate is attached to a sentence, it always 'serves, as it were, to point through the sentence to reality' (1970: 11). Just as 'the sentence "Snow is white" is true, as Tarski has taught us, if and only if real snow is really white' (1970: 10), so the sentence 'All bachelors are unmarried' is true if and only if all bachelors are unmarried. In both cases, sentences are mentioned but 'reality is still the whole point' (1970:11). It makes no difference that the second sentence would be classified by most rationalists and empiricists as 'analytic', though Quine himself is sceptical about the notion of analyticity. Crucially, there is apparently no suggestion in any of this that the reality which is responsible for the truth of 'All bachelors are unmarried' is abstract. Quine is no Platonist. So here is an argument for (Ai) which does not presuppose the truth of Platonism. On the assumption that the notions 'true by virtue of traits of reality' and 'true purely by virtue of meaning' are mutually exclusive, it is also an argument for (Aii), for the claim that there are no metaphysically analytic propositions.[21]

These arguments undoubtedly pose a serious threat to Ayer's version of empiricism, but is there any reason why 'empiricism' as such should want to resist them? If not, then this would strengthen the case for regarding Ayer's empiricism as idiosyncratic. It would also add weight to the suggestion that the standard account of the dispute between 'rationalism' and 'empiricism' is inadequate. If empiricism as such can agree that analytic truths are true by virtue of traits of reality, then it can also agree that analytic a priori knowledge is a priori knowledge of reality, and that intuitive insight into the necessary truth of analytic propositions is intuitive insight into necessary traits of reality. In that case, (R1) and (R2) fail to distinguish between empiricism and rationalism. For there to be a genuine difference between these two doctrines, rationalism would need to insist on the possibility of a priori knowledge of synthetic truths, or empiricism would need to reject *all* forms of intuitionism. Once empiricists go along with the idea that intuitive insight into necessity is the source of a priori justification, the Quinean argument for (ii)*

---

[20] See Boghossian (1997) for a defence of (Ai) and (Aii).

[21] It is not beyond dispute that these notions are mutually exclusive. See Ewing (1939–40; 231–2) for a contrary view.

makes it extremely difficult to hold the line between empiricism and rationalism by distinguishing between different forms of intuitionism. Perhaps the lesson is, as (a) implies, that the difference between rationalism and empiricism is simply the difference between a conception of a priori justification which is intuitionist and one which is not. Alternatively, it may be the thesis that so-called 'necessary truths' are literally true which empiricism needs to dispute.

Before endorsing either of these alternatives, however, it would be worth asking whether the Quinean case for (ii)* is really all that compelling or one which even non-idiosyncratic empiricists can or should accept. The first point to note is that Quine himself puts forward an argument which apparently undermines the notion that analytic truths are true by virtue of traits of reality. The argument is this:

How, given certain circumstances and a certain true sentence, might we hope to show that the sentence was true by virtue of those circumstances? If we could show that the sentence was logically implied by sentences describing those circumstances, could more be asked? But any sentence logically implies the logical truths. Trivially, then, the logical truths are true by virtue of any circumstances you care to name—language, the world, anything (1970: 96).

This argument trades on the paradox of strict implication, the paradox that a necessary proposition is strictly implied by any proposition. Since analytic truths are necessary, this means they too are strictly implied by any proposition. In that case, they are also true by virtue of any circumstances you care to name. They are true by virtue of traits of reality only in the trivial sense that they are 'true by virtue of anything and everything' (1970: 97). To ask whether analytic truths are true by virtue of linguistic meaning or by virtue of the way the world is is therefore to ask an empty question.

This argument suggests that the case for saying that a necessary truth is made true by reality is different from the case for saying that a contingent truth is made true by reality, since a contingent truth is not made true by any circumstances one cares to name. Instead of saying that the difference between necessary and contingent truths is the difference between propositions which are, and those which are not devoid of factual content, Ayer's empiricist can now say that it is the difference between propositions which are factual only in the sense that they are true by virtue of anything and everything and propositions which are factual in a less vacuous sense. While it would still be inappropriate and misleading to describe analytically necessary truths as true purely by virtue of meaning, Quine's reading of the phrase 'true by virtue of' suggests that it would be equally inappropriate and misleading to describe such truths as true by virtue of reality.

Supporters of (ii)* are unlikely to be impressed by this argument. They will object that the most that it shows is that Quine's position is not wholly consistent, and that the fact that a necessary proposition is strictly implied by any proposition shows that the phrase 'true by virtue of' should not be read in the way that Quine reads it. On a different reading, the point of the claim that there is no such thing as a true statement which does not owe its truth to the 'world' or to the 'facts' is simply that 'any true sentence is true in virtue of the holding of its disquotational truth condition' (Peacocke 1993: 187), and this is all that is required to sustain the thesis that analytically necessary propositions are factual.[22] As for whether there are any true propositions which are true purely by virtue of meaning, the problem is not just that a sentence which is true in virtue of the holding of its disquotational truth condition cannot be said to be true purely in virtue of its meaning. The problem is that it is incoherent to suppose that linguistic meaning can, by itself, generate truth or that there is 'a better answer to the quesion: What is responsible for generating the truth of a given class of statements? than something bland like "the world" or "the facts" ' (Boghossian 1997: 336).

These considerations reopen the question of whether the world which is responsible for generating the truth of necessary truths can be the natural world. The Platonist's question is whether it would be coherent to regard conceptual truths as true by virtue of anything other non-natural relations between universals or abstract objects, and the fact that Quine is no Platonist does not settle this question. I will not have anything more to say about this issue here since most empiricists are not Platonists.

From an empiricist perspective, the important contrast is not that between propositions which are true by virtue of natural reality and those which are true by virtue of abstract reality. It is, rather, the contrast between what is true by virtue of natural reality and what is true by virtue of what might be called 'social or conventional reality' (Tully 1980: 13). While many empiricists share Quine's scepticism about Platonism, one does not have to be a Platonist to take the view that an undifferentiated notion of 'reality' cannot account for the fundamental difference between the sense in which 'reality' is responsible for the truth of, say, 'January has thirty-one days'[23] or 'All bachelors are unmarried', and the sense in which it is responsible for the truth of propositions which owe their validity to empirical verification. Thus, instead of continuing to insist that analytic propositions are devoid of factual content, perhaps empiricists should maintain that the 'reality' to which many such propositions pertain is conventional, and that this is the 'reality' into which 'intuitive insight' is possible for us. 'Rationalism' can then be distinguished from empiricism on the basis that it does not accept this restriction on the scope of our a priori knowledge. So the next question which needs to be considered, with a view to determining the accuracy and significance of the principle that no sentence is true but reality makes it so, is the question of whether the distinction between 'natural' and 'conventional' reality is coherent.

---

[22] Peacocke adds that this view of truth 'does not preclude further substantive elaboration of the characteristics of the truth predicate in different areas of discourse' (1993: 187).

[23] This is Michael Dummett's example. See Dummett 1973: 601.

V

The distinction between natural and conventional reality is, as James Tully has pointed out, one which does important work in Locke's theory of knowledge and ideas. According to Locke, as Tully reads him, general ideas of substances are 'ectype' ideas. They are called 'ectypes' (copies) because 'they are intended to stand for an archetype existing independent of our knowledge *in rerum natura*' (Tully 1980: 12). The conclusion which Locke draws from this is that our ideas of substances are 'inadequate'. Adequate ideas are ones which perfectly represent their archetypes, but our ideas of substance do not and cannot 'exactly, and fully, contain all that is to be found in their Archetypes' (II. xxxi. 8).[24] The reason for this is that substances are natural rather than man-made, and Locke assumes that our knowledge of what we do not make ourselves is bound to be limited and inadequate.

In contrast, general ideas of 'modes' and relations are 'archetype' ideas.[25] They comprise ideas of sorts of things which 'are, in some sense, constructed by man as opposed to substances, which are constructed by nature' (Tully 1980: 9).[26] Ideas of modes and relations cannot but be adequate because they are not copies, "or made after the Pattern of any real Existence"(II. xxxi. 14). They refer to social or conventional reality and define their objects. Whereas the adequacy of our knowledge of substances is judged by comparing the idea to its object, knowledge of social or conventional reality is just the opposite, since 'conventional things are judged for their adequacy by comparing the "object" to its idea' (Tully 1980: 12). Archetype ideas are, in this sense, 'normative', and our knowledge of conventional things is an example of what has sometimes been referred to as 'maker's knowledge', the knowledge of what we ourselves have made or brought about.[27]

Locke illustrates the normativeness of archetype ideas by means of the following example: Adam observes that Lamech is troubled, and assumes that the cause of his unhappiness is jealousy of his wife's adultery. So Adam invents the Hebrew words *kinneah* (jealousy) and *niouph* (adultery) to enable him to discuss the matter with Eve. It subsequently transpires that Lamech was worrying about something else, but this does not undermine the ideas of *kinneah* and *niouph*,

---

[24] All references in this form are to Locke 1975.

[25] Modes are defined by Locke as complex ideas which 'contain not in them the supposition of subsisting by themselves, but are considered as Dependences on, or Affections of Substances; such are the *Ideas* signified by the Words *Triangle, Gratitude, Murther*, etc.' (II. xii. 4).

[26] Archetype ideas include those of 'products, actions, institutions, practices, social relations, and so on' (Tully 1980: 22).

[27] As Tully points out, 'it is not the making or doing which gives a person special knowledge but, rather, knowing the archetype in accordance with which what is done is done' (1980: 23). For further discussion of the notion of maker's knowledge, see Craig (1987: 232–43), and Hintikka (1974).

which 'remain archetypes of what jealousy and adultery are' (Tully 1980: 13). Similarly, the necessity of necessary propositions such as 'suicide is the taking of one's life' consists for Locke 'not in the fact that they are derived from reality but, rather, that reality is judged in accordance with them. It is the conventionalist thesis that an archetype idea tells us what kind of object any non-natural thing is' (Tully 1980: 14).

What is the significance of these considerations for the suggestion that there is no better answer to the question: What is responsible for generating the truth of a given class of statements? than something bland like 'the world' or 'the facts'? What they suggest is that there is a better answer to this question. To be sure, a better answer would not be one which rejects the principle that no sentence is true but reality makes it so. Rather, a better answer would be one which, as anticipated above, does not operate with an undifferentiated notion of 'reality'. Just as the sentence 'Snow is white' is true if and only if snow is white, so the sentence 'Suicide is the taking of one's life' is true if and only if suicide is the taking of one's life. Each of these sentences is true in virtue of the holding of its disquotational truth condition, but 'Suicide is the taking of one's life' is normative or constitutive in a way that 'Snow is white' is not. The occurrence of suicides is, like the existence of bachelors, but unlike the existence of snow, a social fact, and the world to which 'Suicide is the taking of one's life' is answerable is the social world.

Why does this distinction matter? It matters because 'Suicide is the taking of one's life' would widely be regarded as an analytically necessary proposition, and the Lockean account of its necessity brings out the limitations of (ii)*. On one view, the Quinean principle that no sentence is true but reality makes it so implies that 'the notions "true purely by virtue of convention", or "true purely in virtue of meaning" do not apply to any sentences or contents' (Peacocke 1993: 187), but if it makes sense to speak of 'conventional objects' or 'conventional reality', then it is not clear that this implication holds. For sentences such as 'Suicide is the taking of one's life' or 'January has thirty-one days' can now be seen *both* as true by virtue of the (conventional) reality which they help to constitute *and* as 'conventional in character' (Dummett 1973: 621). Whether the sense in which such sentences are conventional in character implies that they are true purely in virtue of meaning is a further question, but the important point for present purposes is that there are at least some sentences whose necessity it would not be inappropriate to regard as broadly 'conventional', despite the fact that they are 'about the world'.

This is not to say that the distinction between 'natural' and 'conventional' reality is entirely clear or clear-cut. In the case of the notorious 'Nothing can be red and green all over at the same time', there does not seem to be a straightforward answer to the question whether it is nature or convention to which it owes its necessary truth. As D. F. P. Pears remarks, 'perhaps the emphasis on either side is a mistake; perhaps the culprit is neither convention alone nor nature alone'

(1973: 113). Despite the existence of such cases, the fact remains that something like the distinction 'natural' and 'conventional' reality does appear to be along the right lines, and that the blank insistence that no sentence is true but reality makes it so fails to address any of the important metaphysical and epistemological questions which Locke's distinction brings into focus. I want to conclude by saying a little more about these questions, and developing the suggestion that Locke's approach enables one to see the dispute between 'rationalist' and 'empiricist' theories of a priori knowledge in an entirely new light.

VI

Let me summarize the position so far: I began by taking (R1) and (R2) to be the key theses of 'rationalism', and (E1) and (E2) to be the key theses of 'empiricism'. On this reading, the argument for factual content results in an easy victory for rationalism. In order to undermine the claim that there can be no a priori knowledge of reality, it only needs to be pointed out that analytic a priori knowledge is possible, and that analytic propositions are 'about the world'. The case for saying that they are about the world is that they are true, and that no sentence is true but reality makes it so. And once it is granted that analytic propositions are factual, then it would surely be quite legitimate to regard what the empiricist himself characterizes as our ability to 'see' that analytic propositions are necessarily true as amounting to some form of intuitive insight into the reality to which these propositions pertain. This, in essence, is the argument for rational intuition.

I represented Ayer's empiricist as protesting that analytic propositions cannot be factual because they are true purely in virtue of meaning. The intuitions of necessity to which analytic propositions give rise are therefore merely semantic, and do not have any bearing on the structure of reality. On a Quinean view, however, even analytic sentences are true in virtue of the holding of their disquotational truth conditions, and it makes no sense to suppose that linguistic meaning alone can generate truth. This led to the suggestion that Ayer's version of 'empiricism' is idiosyncratic, and that the moral of Quine's argument is that empiricism should have nothing to do with intuitionism in any form. According to one version of this suggestion, an empiricist should say that a factual statement is analytic 'provided that grasp of its meaning along suffices for justified belief in its truth' (Boghossian 1997: 334). What the empiricist should refrain from saying is that analytic propositions are devoid of factual content and true purely in virtue of meaning. Since this account does not represent intuitive insight into the necessity of analytic propositions as the source of a priori justification, it does not face awkward questions about the relationship between this form of insight and what the rationalist calls 'rational intuition'.

The attractions of this non-intuitionist approach to a priori justification are obvious, but it has now emerged it is not the only option for empiricism in the face of AFC and ARI. Another option would be for non-idiosyncratic empiricists to allow that a priori knowledge of 'reality' is possible but to insist that most, if not all, of our a priori knowledge is of aspects of reality which are conventional in character. By the same token, these are the aspects of reality into which it would be appropriate to describe ourselves as having some form of 'intuitive insight'. For example, we can know the truth of 'January has thirty-one days' a priori because the calendar is a human artefact. And we can know the truth of 'All bachelors are unmarried' a priori because the idea of a bachelor is not the idea of something which exists in nature, prior to our conceptualization. On this reading, a priori knowledge might be described as a form of self-knowledge, to the extent that it is knowledge of the content of our own archetype ideas. This is the sense in which our recognition of necessity is furnished by our ability to know what we mean by the expressions which we use, and in which our intuitions of necessity are 'semantic'. Accordingly, the real point of (E2) is only to deny that a priori knowledge of natural reality is possible for us. This form of knowledge is not possible for us because, to put it crudely, we are not responsible for the structure or order of nature.

Kant's idealist response to empiricism is to agree that 'we can know a priori of things only what we ourselves have put into them' (Bxviii),[28] but to argue that 'the understanding is itself the source of the laws of nature' (A127). Like Locke, Kant sees a priori knowledge as maker's knowledge, but he disagrees with Locke over the scope of a priori knowledge because he has a broader conception of what the human mind is responsible for. In effect, Kant applies Locke's conception of our knowledge of modes and relations to our knowledge of certain aspects of nature, namely, just those aspects which are made by the mind.

Like Kant, the rationalist wants to keep open the possibility of a priori knowledge of nature, but his underlying metaphysical outlook is very different. The rationalist does not think that a priori knowledge of nature is possible because he thinks that nature is a human artefact. He thinks that a priori knowledge of nature is possible because he does not think that our a priori knowledge is confined to human artefacts or to the products of our conceptualization. In defence of his position, he can point out that we have a priori knowledge of many propositions which cannot plausibly be viewed merely as descriptions of conventional or social reality. One example of such a proposition is 'Nothing can be red and green all over at the same time.' Other examples arguably include basic logical laws and the truths of mathematics. Indeed, in the case of mathematical propositions, rationalists are likely to want to maintain that the reality to which they pertain is neither conventional nor natural, but abstract. As Dummett remarks, while we might be prepared to treat 'January has thirty-one days' as 'the object of a conventional

---

[28] All references in this form are to Kant 1929. Hintikka (1974) rightly interprets such passages as placing Kant squarely within the 'maker's knowledge' tradition.

stipulation' (1973: 621), the same cannot be said for 'many problematic propositions of the kind discussed by philosophers' (1973: 620). So if a priori knowledge
of the truth of such propositions is possible at all, then it cannot be accounted for
by the supposition that it is a priori knowledge of merely conventional or social
reality.

The full force of this objection may be brought out by returning to Quine's
discussion of the ground of logical truth. Quine rejects the idea that while 'Tom
is mortal or Tom is not mortal' is about sentences, 'Tom is mortal' and 'Tom is
Tom' are about Tom. In Quine's view, 'all three are about Tom' (1970: 11). It is
scarcely intelligible, however, that the truth of 'Tom is Tom' is something for
which 'we' are responsible. So if 'Tom is Tom' is knowable a priori, then this
would be a clear-cut case of a piece of a priori knowledge which cannot plausibly be regarded as a form of maker's knowledge. The lesson is that Locke and
Kant cannot easily account for our a priori knowledge of elementary logical truths
in the way that Tully's Locke accounts for the fact that 'Suicide is the taking of
one's life' is knowable a priori. Interestingly, Locke's own response to 'purely
identical' propositions such as 'Obligation is obligation' is to describe them as
'trifling', and to insist that they fail to convey 'instructive *real Knowledge*' (IV.
viii. 8).[29] Perhaps the suggestion here is that purely identical propositions are not,
strictly speaking, objects of 'knowledge'. This would save Locke from having to
claim that we have a priori knowledge of such propositions, and hence that this
knowledge is a priori knowledge of aspects of reality for which we are in some
way responsible. On the other hand, the suggestion that purely identical propositions are not objects of knowledge is difficult to reconcile with the thesis that they
have factual content.

It is no part of my present purpose to settle the dispute between rationalism,
empiricism, and idealism. My aim is the more modest one of trying to understand
what is at issue in this dispute. Although the questions raised by Locke's account
of purely identical propositions are important in their own right, they do not affect
the central point of the present discussion. The fact remains that although the
principle that 'no sentence is true but reality makes it so' brings out the inadequacy of Ayer's account of the dispute between rationalism and empiricism as a
dispute over the possibility of a priori knowledge of reality, it would be wrong to
conclude that rationalism and empiricism are pseudo-doctrines between which
there is no real difference. The right conclusion is that the differences between
these doctrines are more subtle than Ayer's account suggests, and that Quine's
principle is too blunt an instrument to constitute the basis of a good account of
what rationalists and empiricists have been arguing about. The fundamental question is whether it is true, as Kant claims, that 'reason only has insight into that
which it produces after a plan of its own' (Bxiii), and there is no way of answer-

---

[29] Locke defines 'identical propositions' as ones 'wherein the same Term importing the same
Idea, is affirmed of it self' (IV. viii. 3).

ing this question without distinguishing between those aspects of 'reality' for which reason is responsible and those aspects with respect to which our knowledge is not archetypal.

For it to be plausible that there is really no difference between rationalism and empiricism, it would have to be plausible that there is no difference between natural and conventional or social reality, and that Quine's principle says all there is to say about what is responsible for generating the truth of a given class of statements. In effect, I have explained the distinction between conventional and natural reality in terms of Locke's distinction between constituents of the 'world' which are 'concept-relative' (Ayers 1991: ii. 113) and those which are not, but, according to an extreme form of conceptualism, there is nothing in the 'world' which is not concept-relative.[30] If one were persuaded by this view, which is certainly Quinean in spirit, then it would indeed be mysterious how the differences between 'rationalism' and 'empiricism' could be anything other than notational. Extreme conceptualism is, however, even more incredible than the thesis that all that separates 'empiricism' about the a priori from 'rationalism' is a difference in notation.[31] The terms in which Locke and Kant think about the problem of a priori knowledge are not unproblematic, but they remain indispensable for a proper understanding of the dispute between these doctrines.

References

Ayer, A. J. (1946), *Language, Truth and Logic*, 2nd edn. (Harmondsworth: Penguin).

Ayers, M. R. (1991), *Locke*, 2 vols. (London: Routledge).

Boghossian, P. A. (1997), 'Analyticity', in B. Hale and C. Wright (eds.), *A Companion to the Philosophy of Language* (Oxford: Blackwell).

BonJour, L. (1998), *In Defence of Pure Reason* (Cambridge: Cambridge University Press).

Chomsky, N. (1965), *Aspects of the Theory of Syntax* (Cambridge, Mass.: MIT Press).

Craig, E. J. (1987), *The Mind of God and the Works of Man* (Oxford: Clarendon Press).

Dummett, M. (1973), *Frege: Philosophy of Language* (London: Duckworth).

Ewing, A. C. (1939–40), 'The Linguistic Theory of *A Priori* Propositions', *Proceedings of the Aristotelian Society*, 40.

Hatfield, G. (1990), *The Natural and the Normative: Theories of Spatial Perception from Kant to Helmholtz* (Cambridge, Mass.: MIT Press).

Hintikka, J. (1974), 'Kant's "New Method of Thought" and his Theory of Mathematics', in *Knowledge and the Known: Historical Perspectives in Epistemology* (Dordrecht: Reidel).

Kant, I. (1929), *Critique of Pure Reason*, trans. Norman Kemp Smith (London: Macmillan).

Locke, J. (1975), *An Essay Concerning Human Understanding*, edited by P. H. Nidditch (Oxford: Clarendon Press).

---

[30] See Ayers (1991: ii. 113) for an account of the distinction between 'conceptualism' and 'realism'.

[31] There is a powerful attack on extreme conceptualism in Ayers (1991: ii. 110–28).

Mackie, J. L. (1977), *Ethics: Inventing Right and Wrong* (Harmondsworth: Penguin).

Peacocke, C. (1993), 'How Are *A Priori* Truths Possible?', *European Journal of Philosophy*, 1.

——— (1998), 'Implicit Conceptions, Understanding, and Rationality', in E. Villanueva (ed.) *Philosophical Issues, 8: Concepts* (Atascadero, Calif.: Ridgeview).

Pears, D. F. (1973), 'Incompatibilities of Colours', in A. G. N. Flew (ed.), *Logic and Language*, 2nd series (Oxford: Blackwell).

Quine, W. V. (1970), *Philosophy of Logic* (Englewood Cliffs, NJ: Prentice Hall).

——— (1976), 'Carnap and Logical Truth', in *The Ways of Paradox* (Cambridge, Mass.: Harvard University Press).

Strawson, P. F. (1997), 'Universals', in *Entity and Identity and Other Essays* (Oxford: Clarendon Press).

Tully, J. (1980), *A Discourse on Property: John Locke and His Adversaries* (Cambridge: Cambridge University Press).

Wright, C. (1980), *Wittgenstein on the Foundations of Mathematics* (London: Duckworth).

4

A Priori Knowledge Revisited

Philip Kitcher

Some years ago, I offered an account of a priori knowledge.[1] My aim in doing so was to prepare for inquiring if mathematical knowledge is, or can be, a priori. Since I ended up defending an unpopular answer to this question—'No'—it's hardly surprising that people have scrutinized the account, or that many have concluded that I stacked the deck in the first place.[2] Of course, this was not my view of the matter. My own judgement was that I'd uncovered the tacit commitments of mathematical apriorists and that the widespread acceptance of mathematical apriorism rested on failure to ask what was needed for knowledge to be a priori. Nevertheless, my critics have raised important challenges, and have offered rival conceptions that are less demanding.[3] I want to examine their objections to my explication of a priori knowledge, and to explore whether the weaker alternatives succeed in preserving traditional philosophical claims. What follows is a mixture of penitence and intransigence.

Let me start by reviewing some features of my account and adding connections

I am grateful to the many people who have thought hard about my previous work on a priori knowledge, and particularly to Charles Parsons and Albert Casullo for their formulation of important objections. The original stimulus for writing this essay was an excellent commentary on some of Casullo's views about apriority, presented by Kadri Vihvelin. The final version has been greatly improved by penetrating suggestions of Paul Boghossian and Christopher Peacocke.

[1] In 'A Priori Knowledge', *Philosophical Review* 89: 3–23.

[2] My case for the negative answer was mounted in *The Nature of Mathematical Knowledge* (New York: Oxford University Press, 1983). Criticisms have been offered by Charles Parsons (Review of *The Nature of Mathematical Knowledge, Philosophical Review* 95 (1986). 129–37; Donna Summerfield, Albert Casullo, and Christopher Peacocke, 'The Origins of the A Priori' (in Paolo Parrini (ed.), *Kant and Contemporary Epistemology* (Dordrecht: Kluwer, 1994: 47–72). Perhaps the most trenchant formulation is William Harper's suggestion that a particular a priori warrant might 'even approach the outrageously high standards set out by Philip Kitchen in his attempt to explicate a priori knowledge' ('The A Priori and Material Necessary' in Robert E. Butts (ed.), *Kant's Philosophy of Physical Science* (Dordrecht: Kluwer, 1986: 239–72; note 8, 268).

[3] See e.g. Peacocke, 'The Origins of the A Priori'; Tyler Burge, 'Content Preservation' (*Philosophical Review*, 102, (1993): 457–88; Hartry Field, 'The Aprioricity of Logic' (*Proceedings of the Aristotelian Society* (1996): 359–79), and Michael Friedman, 'Naturalism' (*Proceedings and Addresses of the American Philosophical Association* 71(2): 7–21.

with other important notions, only some of which I've noted before. First, I take 'a priori' to be an epistemological predicate, one that applies primarily to items of knowledge, so that the notion of a priori truth is derivative: a priori truths are those propositions that could be known a priori. It seems to me that analyses that begin with the conception of a priori truth run the risk of conflating apriority with something quite different—the property of being a logical truth, or a proposition whose truth can be explained by features of concepts, for example.[4]

The account of a priori knowledge is embedded within a general approach to knowledge (the *psychologistic* approach) according to which whether or not a state of true belief counts as a state of knowledge depends on the causal process that generated that state. If a state is produced by the right kind of causal process, so that it is a state of knowledge, then I say that the process is a *warrant* for the belief. My general understanding of warrants is a version of reliabilism (of which more later): warrants are processes belonging to types that regularly and reliably produce true belief.[5] One condition that I *don't* require of a warrant is that it involve reasons that the knower could cite in justification of the belief. This idea would prove important were we to consider if denying the apriority of logic and mathematics commits one to scepticism.

A priori knowledge is knowledge produced by special types of processes, a priori *warrants*. The classical way of introducing the notion of a priori knowledge is to take it to be knowledge that is independent of experience. However, most apriorists have allowed for the possibility that we could have a priori knowledge of propositions containing concepts that could only be garnered from experience.[6] Hence I explicate a priori knowledge by reference to the notion of an experience's being *sufficiently rich for p*, that is someone who had that experience could acquire the concepts needed to entertain p. Now we can't say that X knows a priori that p just in case X knows that p, and, for any e sufficiently rich for p, X could have had e and known that p, because this formulation would collapse the distinction between a priori knowledge and empirical knowledge of propositions that could have been known a priori. To arrive at an appropriate definition, we need to insist that the subject could have known the proposition in the same way,

---

[4] The latter is a rough characterization of Peacocke's sophisticated proposal. Although he struggles valiantly to recapture the distinctive epistemological import of apriority, Peacocke ends up with a divorce between the features that determine apriority in his sense and those that pertain to our knowledge.

[5] The *locus classicus* of reliabilism is Alvin Goldman, *Epistemology and Cognition* (Harvard University Press, 1986). Fortunately, the full details of Goldman's theory are not needed for the present discussion.

[6] This point is explicit in Kant who distinguishes between those items of a priori knowledge that contain only 'pure' concepts and those that involve concepts for whose acquisition experience is needed. It is especially evident in those authors who suppose that a priori kowledge is generated from the knower's 'grasp' of the appropriate concepts—see e.g. Peacocke, 'The Origins of the A Priori'; Burge, 'Content Preservation', and Boghossian, 'Analyticity Reconsidered', *Noûs* 30 (1996): 360–91.

given any sufficiently rich experience, and this leads us to the idea of an a priori warrant, a process that could have produced the knowledge against the background of any sufficiently rich experience.

So, finally, the account:

> X knows a priori that p iff X knows that p and X's knowledge that p was produced by α process that is an a priori warrant for p.
> α is an an a priori warrant for X's belief that p just in case α is a process such that for any sequence of experiences sufficiently rich for X for p
> (a) some process of the same type could produce in X a belief that p;
> (b) if a process of the same type were to produce in X a belief that p, then it would warrant X in believing that p;
> (c) if a process of the same type were to produce in X a belief that p, then p.

The explication of a priori knowledge in terms of a priori warrants is only likely to be controversial among those who object to the background psychologistic framework. I won't repeat the arguments that have been offered in support of this framework;[7] instead, I'll focus on criticisms of my conditions on a priori warrants.

Of these, (a) is the least controversial. The motivation for (a) draws on the traditional idea that a priori knowledge must be independent of experience: surely, if the process that undergirds one's knowledge would not have been available, given a different sufficiently rich experience, then that knowledge can't count as independent of experience. Nonetheless there's an important objection. After all, might it not be the case that, in some worlds, while I'm able to grasp the concepts pertinent to a proposition, I lack the intellectual acumen to formulate the proof that I actually construct; or perhaps my memory lets me down, and I don't discover a complicated, tree-structured, justification?[8] It seems plausible to suppose that these possibilities don't undermine the status of the proof as an a priori warrant in the actual world. This line of criticism reveals that we must be quite careful in interpreting (a).

To assess the credentials of an actual process α as an a priori warrant for my belief that p, we're asked to consider possible worlds in which I have different experiences that are sufficiently rich for me for p. Let e be one such sequence of experiences. Then there's a set of worlds, $W(e)$, in which e is exactly my sequence of experiences. To say that some process of the same type as α would be available given e is to maintain that there's *some* world in $W(e)$ in which I produce a process of that type. That's quite compatible with supposing that in many worlds in $W(e)$ I

---

[7] See Gilbert Harman, *Thought* (Princeton: Princeton University Press, 1973): ch. 2; Hilary Kornblith, 'Beyond Foundationalism and the Coherence Theory', *Journal of Philosophy* 77 (1980): 597–612; Alvin Goldman, *Epistemology and Cognition*.

[8] I'm grateful to Paul Boghossian and Christopher Peacocke for a trenchant formulation of this objection.

am appallingly dull, or have a memory like a sieve, or am simply never interested enough to seek out the pertinent type of process. Indeed, it seems that $W(e)$ will contain a world very similar to the actual one, in which my faculties are much as they are in the actual world but my actual stream of experience is replaced by e, and in which I undergo a process of the same type as α (construct the same proof). Condition (a) thus allows actual processes to survive the envisaged possibilities.

There is, nonetheless, a deeper point to the criticism. Isn't it possible that the proof of p might require concepts beyond those occurring in p, and that, consequently, some experiences sufficiently rich for me for p might not be sufficiently rich for the formulation of the proof of p? Specifically, let p contain the concepts in C and suppose that the concepts in C^+ ($C \subset C^+$) are required to formulate the proof. Let e now be an experience that suffices for my acquisition of all of the concepts in C but not for all those in C^+. There's now *no* world in $W(e)$ in which I undergo a process of the same type as the proof. Hence (a) rules out the actual proof as an a priori warrant.

I offer two possible reactions to this point. First, one might declare that this is just as it should be. Behind this declaration is the thought that the classical conception of apriority supposes that experiences that would suffice for entertaining a proposition are also enough to allow a thinker who is astute to generate the conceptual resources for the proof of that proposition—if that can't be done, then the alleged proof isn't an a priori warrant but a process that depends on special features of the person's experience to supply the needed concepts. In case that response seems too blunt, one can accommodate the example by a slight amendment to my account. Instead of supposing that the crucial notion for recognizing the role of experience in a priori knowledge in the supplying of concepts is that of a life sufficient for X for p, where p is the proposition known, we can replace that notion with that of *a life sufficient for X for α^** (where α^* is the type to which α belongs). Obviously this substitution rules out the worrying possibility that some lives wouldn't allow for the formulation of the proof, since, for any sufficiently rich life e, $W(e)$ now contains worlds in which the knower has all the pertinent concepts. I won't try to decide between these alternatives, but will leave it to the friends of the a priori to decide which more adequately captures the venerable idea that experience may be needed for people to have the conceptual resources to gain a priori knowledge.

I conclude that condition (a), either in its original form or slightly amended, is unproblematic. Conditions (b) and (c), on the other hand, have aroused objections that require much more lengthy discussion. Many of my critics have wanted to adopt an account of a priori knowledge that makes a priori warrants fallible or defeasible. So, in the ensuing sections, I'll want to compare two conceptions of a priori knowledge: the *Strong Conception* that requires (a)–(c), and the *Weak Conception* that demands only (a).[9] The strategy will be to examine the concep-

---

[9] This discussion between the two conceptions is very close to that drawn by Hartry Field

tions in relation to traditional thinking about apriority, looking both at general theses about links to other philosophical notions and at the particular types of knowledge that are classified as a priori. I'll start with the former.

II

In a classic discussion,[10] Saul Kripke revealed deep problems with the thesis

(1) It is possible to know *a priori* that *p* iff it's necessary that *p*.

Given either the Weak or the Strong conception, (1) fails in both directions. For there are plenty of necessary truths that we are unable to express, let alone know a priori; conversely, each of us can know a priori that he/she exists and that he/she is actual; the latter knowledge can be used to generate Kripke-style examples of contingent a priori knowledge.[11]

Next, consider

(2) It is possible to know a priori that *p* iff *p* is known innately.

On the Strong conception, (2) fails in both directions. First, note that the relativization to lives sufficiently rich for *p* already allows for a priori knowledge that isn't innate; conversely, even though one could know that *p* on the basis of *no* experience, it doesn't follow that one could know that *p* on the basis of any sufficiently rich experience; we might, for example, have innate knowledge of some principle of universal grammar, but later acquire empirical evidence for the existence of a language spoken by a fellow human (or humanoid) that violated that principle; whatever process originally warranted our belief would not be able to discharge its warranting function against this experiential background (condition (b) would fail). The Weak conception rejects (2) on the grounds that not all a priori knowledge is innate, but it does preserve the traditional idea that innate knowledge is a priori. On this score, then, the Weak conception seems closer to the tradition.

Matters are similar with respect to

(3) It is possible to know a priori that *p* just in case *p* is analytic.

'Apriority of Logic'. Field's use of it to defend the (weak) apriority of logic will be considered below (sect. VII). I should note that, for the remainder of this essay, I'll focus on the original formulation of the availability requirement (a); I don't think that the amendment involving lives sufficiently rich for α^* would make a difference to the arguments.

[10] See *Naming and Necessity* (Cambridge Mass.: Harvard University Press, 1980).

[11] I argued this point in some detail in 'Apriority and Necessity', *Australasian Journal of Philosophy* 58 (1980): 89–101.

The Strong conception takes this to fail in both directions. On the one hand, it allows that 'I exist' can be known a priori by each of us, but in none of our mouths is this analytic; on the other, if we think of analytic truths as those which can be known on the basis of our grasp of pertinent concepts, there is an old point, traceable to Mill and Kant, that experience can call into question our right to employ concepts and thus undermine the warranting power of a process that stems from our grasp of concepts;[12] consequently processes that elaborate our grasp of concepts don't meet condition (b) on a priori warrants in all instances (perhaps not even in many). The Weak conception agrees with the Strong conception about the first type of failure of (3), concluding that not all propositions that are knowable a priori are analytic, but, because it allows for defeasible a priori warrants and rejects my condition (b), it treats the Mill–Kant point differently, supposing that, when experience doesn't undermine the use of the pertinent concepts, our grasp of those concepts can serve to generate an a priori warrant for analytic truths. Thus, the Weak conception retains one of the most central ideas of traditional thinking about apriority, the thesis that grasp of concepts will typically yield a priori knowledge.

The Strong conception can manage, at best, a restricted version of this thesis, for propositions whose constituent concepts could never be undermined by experience. With a nod to Kant, let's call these a priori concepts. An obvious explication is

> C is an a priori concept just in case, for any sufficiently rich experience e, X would be warranted in believing that C was apt for the description of experience.

(Here I assume a form of epistemic democracy—what is an a priori concept for one is an a priori concept for all.) Now it does follow that if there are a priori concepts, then analytic propositions containing only such concepts (provided there are any) can be known a priori. It seems to me that one of Kant's great insights was the point that analyticity isn't a solution to the problem of a priori knowledge except in very special cases.

However, Kant (and some of his successors) have often conflated the notion of

---

[12] Mill makes this point in *A System of Logic (Collected Works of John Stuart Mill*, edited by John Robson) (Toronto: University of Toronto Press, 1963–91): vol. VII; see, in particular, 143–52; for Kant's appreciation of it, see H. E. Allison (ed.), *The Kant-Eberhard Controversy* (Baltimore: Johns Hopkins University Press, 1973): 175; and *Critique of Pure Reason*, note *a* to A 242, and A252–4, B 308–10. The argument becomes fully developed in W. V. Quine's writings, particularly in 'Truth by Convention', in *The Ways of Paradox* (New York: Random House, 1966) and in the final section of 'Two Dogmas of Empiricism', in *From a Logical Point of View* (New York: Harper & Row, 1963). I have discussed this line of objection in its historical context in 'How Kant Almost Wrote "Two Dogmas of Empiricism" (And Why He Didn't)', *Philosophical Topics* 12 (1981): 217–49, and in 'Mill, Mathematics, and the Naturalist Tradition', in John Skorupski (ed.), *The Cambridge Companion to Mill* (Cambridge: Cambridge University Press, 1998): 57–111.

an a priori concept with a related, but distinct, idea. Let's say that a *conceptual precondition* for experience (or knowledge) is a concept that a person must use in judgements if that person is to have experience (or knowledge). Assuming epistemic democracy, again, we can inquire if the Strong conception supports the thesis

(4) *C* is a conceptual precondition of experience (knowledge) just in case *C* is an a priori concept.

It doesn't. For, even though we might have to deploy a concept in order to have experience (knowledge), it doesn't follow that our belief that that concept was apt for the description of experience would have to be warranted against the background of any sufficiently rich experience. There are surely experiences that could dupe us into thinking that this is wrong, since finding the conceptual preconditions of experience (knowledge) has been a hotly contested business in the history of philosophy. Conversely, even though we could know that a concept was apt for the description of experience against the background of any sufficiently rich experience, it would not follow that that concept was a precondition of experience (knowledge). Perhaps recondite mathematical concepts are such that we would always be warranted in believing of them that they are apt for the description of experience, but we don't have to employ them to have experience (knowledge). Indeed, this may even be true of the simplest mathematical concepts.

In similar fashion, we can consider *propositional preconditions of experience* where

p is a propositional precondition of experience (knowledge) just in case we have to believe that *p* in order to have experience (knowledge).

The Strong conception rejects

(5) *p* is a propositional precondition of experience (knowledge) just in case *p* can be known a priori.

If there are any propositions that we have to believe in order to have experience (knowledge), it's an entirely separate issue whether there are processes that would warrant them given any sufficiently rich experience. This means that there are experiences, given which we'd be warranted in not believing propositions that are required for us to have experience (knowledge), and that, of course, sounds rather dire. As we shall see, however, this doesn't mean that we couldn't continue to have something rather like experience (knowledge). The failure of (5) in the opposite direction is more straightforward, since there are surely pieces of a priori knowledge that we don't have to believe in order to have experience—to use an earlier example, each of us can know a priori that he/she is actual, but I find it highly dubious that we have to believe this to have experience (knowledge).

The score so far is heavily in favour of the Weak conception. Not only does it preserve the classical ideas that innate knowledge and knowledge based on grasp of concepts are both a priori, but the Strong conception appears at odds with influential attempts to preserve residues of the latter theme. Hence, at least at first sight, the Strong conception appears vulnerable to complaints that it stacks the deck against the a priori.

III

So what can be said in its favour? When I originally developed my account of a priori knowledge, I claimed that conditions (b) and (c) were an important part of the idea that a priori knowledge is independent of experience. In fact, it seems to me that we can simplify the task of appraising the Strong conception by focusing just on (b), since, if (b) were accepted, it would be hard to resist (c).

Here's why. Suppose that there were processes satisfying (a) and (b) but not (c). Then there could be experiences sufficient for p such that, given those experiences, one might be warranted in believing that p, even though p were false. Let e be any such experience, and consider the following extension of e, e^*: the next phase of one's life consists in an encounter with an oracle who demonstrates power to answer vast numbers of significant questions, who testifies to the falsity of p, and who offers whatever can be done to show directly that p is false. e^* is sufficient for p, so, by assumption, the process is available given e^* and its warranting power is unaffected. But, in order to believe that p, one must override extremely strong evidence to the contrary. How can the process give one a licence to override when one would have been epistemically better off not overriding? Intuitively, the person who overrides the performance of the oracle is being dogmatic in insisting on the belief generated by the process, and the belief is no longer warranted. Hence it seems to me that the process cannot satisfy (b) unless it also satisfies (c).

One might try to avoid this argument by finding a proposition p and a belief-generating process such that the falsity of p and the existence of the process are incompatible with the assumptions used in the extension of e to e^*. But I have not been able to think of a convincing case in which this is so. I conclude that (c) is, in fact, a consequence of my other conditions on a priori knowledge. Thus, if there were a cogent defence of (b), it would provide a rationale for the Strong conception.

I used to believe that there was a relatively simple argument that would do the trick. After all, the heart of the classical view of apriority is that a priori knowledge is knowledge independent of experience. But it seems that one can hardly claim that an a priori warrant is independent of experience if its production of true belief and its warranting power could be subverted in worlds where one had different experiences. In various places, I tried to support this idea along the following lines:

[I]f alternative experiences could undermine one's knowledge then there are features of one's current experience which are relevant to the knowledge, namely those features whose *absence* would change the current experience into the subversive experience. The idea of the support lent by kindly experience is the obverse of the idea of the defeat brought by uncooperative experience.[13]

But this argument is bad. As several people have pointed out, there are important, epistemologically relevant, differences between the roles played by subversive experiences and those played in normal cases by the absence of those conditions. To take an example of Charles Parsons's, the fact that under imaginable circumstances I could have grounds for believing that my perceptual experience isn't veridical doesn't entail that the absence of those experiences are now playing a causal role in generating or sustaining my perceptual beliefs—I don't have to convince myself that I'm not the dupe of a Cartesian demon every time I observe objects in my vicinity.[14]

Indeed (I blush to admit) nobody who advocates a reliabilist approach to knowledge ought to be at all tempted by the reasoning just rehearsed. Without going very far into the details of the position, we can characterize reliabilism as the claim that the processes that generate and sustain those beliefs that count as knowledge are processes that regularly (though not invariably) generate true belief in the class of relevant alternatives to the actual situation. In introducing the position, Alvin Goldman explicitly considered ordinary perception in a variety of contexts.[15] On most occasions, when people drive through the countryside and observe a barn, they come to know that there's a barn in the vicinity. This is because the process that generates the belief that there's a barn over there belongs to a type that regularly generates true beliefs across relevant alternatives. If, however, this particular region is used as a movie set (perhaps for films based on Hardy's novels) and is full of barn-facsimiles, then, even if the particular object in the line of vision is a genuine barn, the tourist doesn't know that it's a barn, precisely because, in this instance, the class of relevant alternatives includes those occasions in which his eyes were pointed towards barn facsimiles. The crucial point here is that to appraise a candidate process as a warrant one must consider whether processes of the type would regularly generate true beliefs across the class of relevant alternatives, and that class varies according to the facts about the world (as in the presence of barn facsimiles) and according to facts about the person (as when someone has, incorrectly, told him that this region is full of barn facsimiles). This has direct significance for claims about a priori warrants. Provided that background conditions are benign, the class of alternatives is restricted and a type of process might well succeed in regularly generating true

---

[13] *The Nature of Mathematical Knowledge*: 89.

[14] Parsons makes this point in his review of *The Nature of Mathematical Knowledge*. Similar observations have been made by Albert Casullo.

[15] See 'Discrimination and Perceptual Knowledge', *Journal of Philosophy* 72 (1976): 771–91.

beliefs across this class, even though, were experience to be recalcitrant, a wider class of alternatives would be relevant, across which that type of process would fail the test of regularly generating true belief. Reliabilism thus develops the point that Parsons lucidly made against the Strong conception, and supports the thought that a process available given any sufficiently rich life might warrant belief under actual circumstances even though its warranting power could be defeated by some possible streams of experience, the thought that is central to the Weak conception.

Indeed, the idea of defeasible a priori warrants for mathematical knowledge can be developed quite plausibly on the basis of reliabilism. Consider two different versions of the thesis that mathematical knowledge is a priori. The first concentrates on the knowledge of new mathematical principles by the great mathematicians who discover (introduce?) them—we envisage Gauss or Dedekind or Cantor coming to a priori knowledge that nobody has had before on the basis of some kind of process (call it 'intuition'). In response to the challenge that there are circumstances under which the mathematician in question might have had reasons to worry about the reliability of the intuition, reliabilism notes that, under the actual circumstances, defeating such doubts may not be relevant, so that the intuition serves as an a priori warrant. The second version focuses on the elementary arithmetical knowledge possessed by everyone, claiming that once the basic concepts of arithmetic have been acquired each of us knows such things as that $2 + 1 = 3$ on the basis of our grasp of the pertinent concepts. Faced with the Mill–Kant point that experience might reveal that the employment of a concept (or family of concepts) isn't warranted, reliabilism concedes that, given certain kinds of experiences, the process of warrant by grasp of concepts would be defeated, but maintains that, for all of us virtually all of the time, there's no reason to worry about the concepts we've acquired, so that alternatives in which we face experiential challenges to our conceptual framework aren't relevant, and the process thus succeeds in warranting belief under actual circumstances.

I conclude that my earlier defence of the Strong conception and the attempts to refute the apriority of mathematics both fail. Nonetheless, I think that matters are more complicated than they've so far appeared. The Weak conception has a somewhat problematic relation to classical views of the a priori, and it will be important to draw out some of its epistemological consequences. In the next section, I'll take up some preliminary points. Sections V and VI will take up further issues that I view as more fundamental.

IV

I'll start with one of the substantive views of a priori mathematical knowledge envisaged in the last section. We imagine people like Cantor or Dedekind or Gauss introducing new principles on the basis of some special apprehension of mathematical truth (of course, there's a well-known puzzle of Paul Benacerraf's about how this could possibly work, but that's not my main concern here).[16] Now the most obvious difference between this and ordinary perception is that the ability is very rare indeed. Further, because it's rare, it's very difficult to get other people to check on whether or not you have done it well. Lastly, the exercise of this alleged ability has a highly chequered history—it's not just the Frege–Cantor disaster with naïve set theory that ought to concern us, but the long sequence of mathematicians who announced principles about continuity, limits, infinity and similar notions, whose ideas were, more or less quickly, repudiated.[17] Worries about ordinary empirical knowledge arise only in special circumstances, but that's because each of us has ample background reinforcement from others. By contrast, appeals to elusive processes of a priori reason ought always to be accompanied by doubts about whether one has carried out the process correctly, and whether, in this instance, the deliverances are true. Hence it appears that when we consider the kinds of processes that might have given a priori warrants for major innovations in mathematics the class of relevant alternatives over which those processes should regularly produce true belief is considerably expanded, including many instances in which the mathematician engages in beguiling procedures that lead to error. The power to warrant belief in the actual situation would thus be undermined—and indeed, we might claim that one couldn't satisfy the Weak conception unless the Strong conception were also satisfied.[18]

My critics could reasonably reply that I've stacked the deck by picking out the least plausible candidates for a priori warrants—Gödelian intuitions and kindred processes. The second substantive apriorist conception of the last section, they may insist, is free of the troubles I've canvassed. We acquire the basic arithmetical concepts at teacher's knee, and from then on carry within us the ability to apprehend such things as that $2 + 1 = 3$. Unlike the cloudy deliverances of mathematical intuition, this mundane grounding of arithmetical knowledge in our grasp of concepts has an auspicious track record—as good, in fact, as that of ordinary perceptual experience. In consequence, there's no threatening expansion of

---

[16] Paul Benacerraf, 'Mathematical Truth', *Journal of Philosophy* 70 (1973): 661–79.

[17] Perhaps one might respond that the career of ordinary perceptual knowledge is just as problematic. But that seems to me to ignore the fact that we've been able to arrive at a clear specification of the conditions under which perception is troublesome. By contrast, as far as the kinds of processes that are supposed to generate new axioms are concerned, we lack any such inventory of predicaments to be avoided.

[18] The minimal point is that, in this instance, the Weak conception seems to do no better at preserving the apriority of the mathematical knowledge than the Strong conception. To argue rigorously the more ambitious claim that the Weak conception is satisfiable only if the Strong conception is as well, I'd have to specify the class of relevant alternatives and show that regular generation of truth in that class requires the power to defeat the contrary suggestions of any sufficiently rich experience. I don't think it's impossible that that could be done, but, for the present, I offer the more ambitious claim as a conjecture.

the class of relevant alternatives and no intensification of the demand that the warranting process be reliable.

But what are we to say about the innovators who fashioned the framework of concepts on which later a priori knowledge is to draw? It seems to me that there are three possibilities. First, one can propose that the innovators' knowledge was grounded in some a priori intuition, precisely the view I've been trying to undermine. Second, in line with the view that a priori knowledge stems from grasp of concepts, it's possible to claim that the process of fashioning the concepts automatically yields a priori knowledge. That suggestion is vulnerable to an argument exactly parallel to the critique of intuition: the history of mathematics is full of unfruitful, even incoherent, specifications of mathematical concepts, so that, for the aspiring innovator, it's always relevant to determine how the novel definition serves the purposes of the pertinent branch of mathematics. As Dedekind (to cite just one example) saw so clearly, his definition of continuity had to be supported by a detailed exploration of its consequences.[19] Once again, the expansion of the class of relevant alternatives undermines the claim that the pertinent process—in this instance, conceptual innovation—provides a priori warrant, even on the Weak conception. The third, and most plausible, possibility is to declare that the knowledge of the innovators isn't a priori: they are warranted in proposing new concepts and principles through an often lengthy process of demonstrating that their new ideas play a fruitful role within inquiry. But now we arrive at a curious picture: a particular framework of concepts is available to us because of the history of constructing those concepts and showing the experiential fruitfulness of the framework; those who played crucial roles in this history did not have a priori knowledge, but, we, their lucky successors, are able to do better. The Weak conception claims that it doesn't matter that our current processes of generating belief are dependent on their endeavours. Note, however, that we might reasonably view our—allegedly a priori—knowledge as dependent on experience, the experience that warranted adoption of the conceptual framework on which we now draw.

This is only a first look at a crucial issue that will occupy us in Section VI, the question of tradition-dependence. I want to close the present section by taking up the second point advertised above, a point that charges the Weak conception with reducing an apparently important distinction to insignificance.

There are lots of distinctions that could be drawn among various kinds of knowledge, based upon the character of the processes that generated the pertinent beliefs. We could—and we do—distinguish knowledge obtained through testimony from knowledge we acquire for ourselves, knowledge based on current perception from knowledge through memory, knowledge deriving from the use of our eyes from knowledge obtained by using our ears. Dividing items of knowledge

---

[19] See the monograph *Continuity and Irrational Numbers* in W. Beman (ed.), *Dedekind's Essays on the Theory of Numbers* (New York: Dover, 1901).

according to the causal factors that generated the knowledge might be useful for a number of philosophical and psychological purposes, but none of the divisions I've mentioned attributes any special role to a kind of knowledge, a unique function that it can fulfil in our activities as knowers. Historically, the a priori–a posteriori distinction has had functional significance in that items of a priori knowledge aren't just supposed to be generated in a special way but, once they are in place, to be deployed differently from their empirical counterparts. Indeed, for philosophers like Kant and Frege, the ways in which a priori knowledge is generated are of interest precisely because of the functional significance of the a priori.[20]

The guiding thought is, of course, that a priori principles can be taken for granted in our future empirical investigations. Our scientific hypotheses are revisable—we have to be on the lookout for possible experiences that call them into question—but with respect to our a prior knowledge we don't have to harbour such worries. Hence the a priori–a posteriori distinction has seemed much more fundamental than the distinction between knowledge based on memory and knowledge not so based, or that between knowledge based on touch and knowledge based on smell. Notice, however, that the Weak conception would effectively make the a priori–a posteriori distinction just like these: we'd have another separation of items of knowledge produced by fallible processes, according to the particular faculties that were the source of those processes. We would have abandoned the traditional thought that a priori knowledge can prescribe to experience, that when we know something a priori we don't have to be concerned about what future experiences may be bring. Here then is a short argument for the conformity of the Strong conception to the philosophical tradition: the tradition ascribes to a priori knowledge the functional significance of being in a position to prescribe to future experience; knowledge that prescribes to future experience is irrefutable by future experience; any warrant whose warranting power would survive any possible future experience must be a process that would be able to warrant belief given any life sufficiently rich for the pertinent proposition; hence any analysis of apriority that endorses the traditional function of a priori knowledge must satisfy condition (b).

I've been suggesting that the Weak conception is not entirely consonant with traditional thinking about apriority because it abandons parts of the idea that a priori knowledge is independent of experience. The next section will reinforce the complaint by arguing that the Weak conception radically enlarges the scope of our a priori knowledge.

---

[20] As we'll see in Section VII, contemporary philosophers like Hartry Field and Michael Friedman attempt to show how the Weak conception can fulfil something like the traditional function if the propositions in question have a further special property (that of being 'constitutive' of evidence, or of experience).

V

Many contemporary apriorists want to use the Weak conception to support the possibility that we can have a priori knowledge generated from our grasp of concepts. But they need to be on guard that the Weak conception doesn't bring them more than they had bargained for. For it seems that all kinds of procedures routinely employed in educational exercises that motivate students to accept various kinds of scientific claims could be transformed into processes that generate a priori knowledge. Let's start with a very simple example.

Imagine a cube on whose faces are inscribed signs for the numbers 1–6, and suppose that this cube is made of some homogeneous material. The cube is rolled once. What is the chance that the uppermost face will show a 6? Well, one of the faces will show, and the situation is completely symmetrical. Thus there's no reason why one face should be more likely to show than another. Hence the probability that the uppermost face will show a 6 is 1/6.

Of course, most philosophers have heard this little piece of reasoning many times, and may well have offered it to students who are beginning to think about probabilities. Does it provide those who undergo it with a priori knowledge? Specifically, does it enable people to know a priori that a cubical die made out of uniform material has a chance of 1/6 of showing 6?

If you think that the answer is 'No', then the Weak conception of a priori knowledge runs into fairly immediate trouble. For the process that generates the belief is available given any sufficiently rich life, and the only question is whether that process warrants belief. In fact, given the way the world works, processes of viewing symmetry as a guide to chance regularly generate true beliefs—most dice made of uniform materials conform to this probability. So if we consider the relevant type of process to be the class of thought-experiments in which one employs considerations of symmetry to conclude that the chance that an n-sided die made of uniform materials will land on any particular face will be $1/n$, then it seems that, in the relevant alternatives, cases in which such processes are used to generate beliefs in worlds very like ours, the processes will regularly yield true beliefs. So the symmetry reasoning meets the reliabilist criterion and it should count as a warrant for belief, and, according to the Weak conception, an a priori warrant.

Champions of the Weak conception might try to resist this result by claiming that the pertinent class of processes, or the class of relevant alternatives, are not as I've characterized them. Maybe they propose that we have to consider symmetry arguments in general and to focus on worlds in which such arguments usually fail. The first point to note is that it will be a dangerous and delicate strategy to conjoin this proposal with the claims about a priori knowledge based on grasp of concepts—for it will be important to preserve the easygoing approach that allows us to go along with the concepts we inherit from our teachers without worrying about their scientific utility in our world (or in other worlds). But even if we concede that something like this can be achieved, perhaps because our accumulated wisdom about the use of symmetry arguments casts doubt on their reliability (a move that depends crucially on treating as relevant symmetry arguments that don't take the form of simple reflections on uniform dice), the Weak conception has to recognize that this feature of our tradition is thoroughly contingent.

Let's envisage a world very like our own, one in which the course of nature runs just the same but in which the history of inquiry and the socialization of inquirers are rather different. In this world, the first few phenomena for which people develop symmetry arguments happen to be ones for which such arguments work well, and, in consequence, young investigators are trained to trust the outcome of such arguments—just in the way our tradition sanctions beliefs generated from grasp of concepts. Even if we can't know a priori that a homogeneous cubical die has a probability of 1/6 of showing 6, our counterparts in the other world can, and this reveals something rather counter-intuitive about the Weak conception of a priori knowledge: what is knowable a priori depends on the history of inquiry and the conditions of socialization.

But perhaps the champions of the Weak conception have another option, that of supposing we *can* know a priori the probability of a uniform die's showing 6. The obvious danger is that this will set the Weak conception at variance with the classical view of the bounds of apriority—if it delivers this result, then it cheapens the notion. But, almost as obviously, there are two replies: one that seeks to assimilate what is known to what traditional apriorists have thought we could know a priori, and one that contends that there's more a priori knowledge than has been dreamed of in previous rationalist philosophy.

The former starts by asking what is meant by the claim that the die is made out of *uniform* material. If our everyday standards for testing uniformity are being employed, then, of course, the claim that the die has probability 1/6 of showing 6 looks synthetic and the classical boundaries of a priori knowledge seem to be outrun. However, it may be suggested that this is the wrong interpretation of what's going on. In fact, the argument works because the standards for uniformity are inflated, so that, in effect, a cube could only be uniform if there was no process that could introduce asymmetries, or, in other words, a die that didn't have probability 1/6 of showing 6 would be, *ipso facto*, non-uniform. Hence, the story goes, what is known a priori is analytic.

This interpretation of how the process of reasoning works strikes me as implausible: after all, the point of the reasoning is to induce people to form beliefs about the probabilities of events involving ordinary objects, objects that they can test for uniformity in familiar ways. The result isn't only counter-intuitive but also seems to make no sense of the ways in which scientists actually devise experiments to test claims. Instead of checking on the probabilities generated from particular set-ups, what should really be sought are demonstrations that those set-ups accord with the symmetries and invariances posited in the principles that are known a priori. So, in investigating dice, we ought to be exploring whether there are any features of their composition that can be exploited asymmetrically by physical forces.

The last alternative for the Weak conception is to admit that arguments that appeal to symmetries and invariances do warrant belief in substantial claims about nature, and to claim all this shows is that the classical view of the scope of apriority was a little too narrow. But now we can envisage a smooth transition from my humble example all the way up to claims about sex-ratios in populations, the invariance of laws in frames of reference, even the existence of particles that fill particular places in a mathematical scheme. In all of these instances, people have appealed to symmetry arguments and other non-empirical motivating suggestions to generate conclusions, and these appeals often figure in classroom 'demonstrations' for students of the pertinent fields. Unless the proponent of the Weak conception can draw a boundary between the simple probabilistic cases and the thought-experiments of physicists, biologists, and economists, there will be no minor addendum to the classical bounding of apriority but a tremendous explosion of 'a priori' knowledge. The celebration of apriority will outrun the scope of a priori knowledge, even for the most ambitious rationalists.

VI

At this point, we come to the last, and, I think, the deepest reason for concern about the Weak conception. In my discussion of mathematical knowledge, I introduce a conception of knowledge that is at odds with central features of the epistemological tradition, although, at the time, I did not see clearly how radical the break was. On my *socio-historical* conception of knowledge, the knowledge we have today isn't simply a matter of what we have experienced or thought during the course of our lives, but is dependent on the historical tradition in which we stand and on the social institutions that it has bequeathed to us.[21] Each of us acquires in childhood both a stock of beliefs, the lore that our elders pass on, and a training that prompts us to undergo certain sorts of belief-forming processes and to trust those processes as reliable guides to truth. During our lives we modify those beliefs, typically in idiosyncratic and ephemeral ways, occasionally by introducing or discarding beliefs that belong to the transmitted corpus. In the special case of mathematics, I proposed that our knowledge starts with the vast amount of instruction we are given, by teachers who effectively sum up two millennia of accomplishment. The creative mathematicians of our generation will

---

[21] In *The Nature of Mathematical Knowledge*, I employed this conception without much explicit reflection on its departures from standard epistemology. I have been more candid in some subsequent work, especially in 'The Naturalists Return', *Philosophical Review* 101 (1992): 53–114 and in 'Knowledge, Society, and History', *Canadian Journal of Philosophy* 23 (1993): 155–78.

show how some of the assumptions they have acquired generate, in ways governed by the rules they have learned, new, and maybe surprising, conclusions. Maybe a very few of them will introduce some new basic assumption that will be passed on to the next generation. If so, that assumption will be accepted because it fits well with the mathematics that had already been developed beforehand.

I doubt if any figure in the history of epistemology, from Descartes on, has doubted that something like this is the way in which most people actually acquire and modify their beliefs. Yet, ever since Descartes, philosophers have been beguiled by the idea that this isn't the way *knowledge* should be. Descartes was quite explicit about the ideal of retreating from the beliefs and practices one had acquired, subjecting them to scrutiny, and building them up anew.[22] Even philosophers who don't subscribe to his standards for the reconstructive work still contemplate the possibility of some sort of synchronic justification of belief. Like Descartes, they contrast the ordinary ways in which we come to believe what we do with an epistemological ideal, a synchronic reconstruction of an individual's body of beliefs that shows how and to what extent that person is justified. My radical break with the tradition consists in abandoning this ideal, in saying, if you like, that the socio-historical process is all there is.

Let us say that a person's knowledge is independent of socio-historical tradition just in case that person could have had the knowledge, even given socialization in a different tradition, provided only that the socialization made it possible to entertain the propositions known. More formally:

> X's knowledge that p is tradition-independent just in case for any tradition adequate to enable X to entertain p X could have had the sequence of experiences X actually has and known that p.

For many, perhaps almost all, of the alternative traditions envisaged here, X may know what he knows in ways quite different from the ways he actually knows things. The point of insisting on the tradition-independence of knowledge is to suppose that, together, X's experiences and powers of thought would provide warrants for belief that do not depend in any way on the particularities of what X has absorbed from the past. Some versions of the idea would go further than I've done, supposing that the concepts required to entertain the propositions someone knows can usually be gleaned from experience or (perhaps) are innate, so that the clause that restricts traditions to those that suffice for entertaining the pertinent propositions makes no difference and can be omitted.

A thesis shared by most epistemologists from Descartes to the present is that our knowledge is tradition-independent, and one of the primary tasks of epistemology is to reveal the 'structure' of knowledge by making that clear. So, one imagines an idealized subject, retreating from society, considering all the propositions she accepts and appealing to a mixture of experience and reason to warrant

---

[22] See the first of Descartes' *Meditations.*

them for herself. This has been most evident in discussions of empirical knowledge, where, in their different ways, foundationalists and coherence theorists have offered synchronic reconstructions of a subject's beliefs. Now I think that all these proposals are flawed because we cannot escape from our socio-historical tradition: we need a vocabulary for describing our experiences and we need guidance for assessing what kinds of processes reliably induce true belief. Given any suggested way of reconstructing our empirical knowledge, it's possible to imagine an alternative socio-historical tradition that would commend alternative ways of describing experience and would insist that the knowledge-generating processes be reliable against a different background of alternatives. The idea of showing the tradition-independence of empirical knowledge fails.

Of course, my main concern here isn't with empirical knowledge. Rather I want to emphasize the importance of the idea of the tradition-independence of a priori knowledge in the philosophy of mathematics. Consider the famous passages in which Frege introduces the notions of a priori and a posteriori as he understands them; these notions, he tells us, concern 'the justification for making the judgement'.[23] In introducing the notions in this way, and in posing the problem of the foundations of mathematics as he does, Frege envisages a route to the propositions of mathematics (primarily arithmetic) that is tradition-independent, and those who debate the foundations of mathematics after him follow him in this. Suppose that the conception of a priori knowledge employed in these discussions were just the Weak conception. Then there are possible lives, given which processes that would normally warrant belief in various mathematical propositions would fail to do so. Now imagine a historical tradition whose members have such experiences in the generation that precedes ours. There are two possibilities: in socializing us they either respond to the subversive experiences by explicitly identifying certain processes as unreliable (in the way that we've learned to mark off certain kinds of perceptual situations as unreliable) or they do not. If they do, then we are not warranted in believing parts of mathematics on the basis of the processes, any more than someone who has been told about mirages is warranted by his perceptions in believing that there is an oasis in the distance (even though there may be one there). If they do not, then we are still not warranted, for our epistemic situation is akin to that of people reared in a community of dedicated clairvoyants who ignore evidence that their chosen methods are unreliable. Either way, we who live in this hypothetical tradition are not warranted by processes that, as things stand (at least, so the foundationalist story goes) warrant us in our mathematical beliefs. Hence, the reconstruction of our knowledge turns out to be tradition-dependent.

On the other hand, if the Strong conception is adopted, then not only is this argument blocked but we see why Frege and his successors can suppose that they

---

[23] G. Frege, *The Foundations of Arithmetic*, trans. J. L. Austin (Oxford: Blackwell, 1950): sect. 4.

are offering a reconstruction of our mathematical knowledge that is independent of the social and historical circumstances of its genesis.[24] They envisage displaying the structure of processes that would be available and which would warrant belief whatever our past experiences and whatever the past experiences of those who socialized us—any concerns about the reliability of these processes can be overridden by us, that is the point of (b). As I noted earlier, failure to insist on (b) results in the historical contingency of a priori knowledge.

Perhaps you may think that giving up the tradition-independence of a priori knowledge is not too bad. I claim, however, that this diverges from the classical idea of apriority in important ways.

Let me offer you my preferred story about mathematical knowledge. I think that mathematical knowledge began with simple experiences of manipulating objects in the world.[25] Over two millennia ago, some of our intellectual ancestors systematized the scraps of knowledge previously obtained by introducing postulates and definitions. Then, in the Renaissance, with the rise of early modern science, the community of inquirers instituted a division of labour. Some members of the community were to work on developing new mathematical concepts and principles, on the basis of what had already been achieved; others were to draw from the languages provided by the first group, formulating hypotheses about nature and devising experiments to test them. The institutionalization of that division has bequeathed to the language-makers of our day, who typically inhabit mathematics departments, a power to propose concepts and principles and to articulate those concepts, so long as they follow the rules of mathematical methodology, extending the mathematical traditions in which they have been schooled. They do not make observations or do experiments; they think and scribble. Their peers sometimes count what they produce as additions to knowledge, and such additions become available to their colleagues who do grub around in the world (or in the artificial world of the laboratory). Given the institutional backdrop, given the processes of socialization that have provided them with their starting points, their thoughts lead them to mathematical knowledge. I see no reason to doubt that the processes that warrant their beliefs often satisfy condition (a). But, of course, the warranting power is tradition-dependent.

The dependence on tradition connects contemporary mathematical knowledge

---

[24] In effect, I'm arguing that some important facets of classical epistemology, particularly in the Rationalist tradition and in the philosophy of mathematics, are best understood by supposing that the notion of apriority under discussions conforms to the Strong conception. But, as I'll admit in the text below, the history of philosophy in this area is extremely complex, and almost anyone can quote scripture to his or her purpose. The aim, then, isn't to show that the Strong conception articulates what the Great Dead Philosophers had in mind, or even that it's the best bet for doing so, but rather that the Weak conception makes some of their claims and arguments unintelligible. All this is prelude to recognizing that the notion of the a priori is a complicated mess—and to transcending it.

[25] Here I offer a highly condensed version of the account I give in chs. 7–10 of *The Nature of Mathematical Knowledge*.

with experience in two distinct ways. First, there is the obvious point that the ultimate starting points lie in those scattered perceptions that began the whole show
(and, as I've noted elsewhere, there may be other places where experience enters
in the subsequent development of mathematics). Second, and less evident, the
warranting power of the contemporary processes depends on the division of
labour and the long sequence of experiences that have warranted our ancestors,
and now us, in making that division. We have learned, *from experience*, that
having a group of people who think and scribble, who proceed to extend and
articulate mathematical languages in the ways that mathematicians find fruitful[26]
and who provide resources for empirical science is a good thing, that creating this
role promotes our inquiry.

The tradition-dependence of contemporary mathematical knowledge indicates
an important kind of dependence on experience. Philosophers beguiled by the
obvious fact that mathematicians generate a lot of knowledge without any
recourse to observation and experiment, and concerned to save the apriority of
mathematical knowledge by weakening the conception so that it only demands
(a), have failed to see that the warranting power of the processes of thought they
take to underlie mathematical knowledge depends on the *experiences of those
who came before us in the mathematical tradition*. Champions of the Weak
conception save the apriority of mathematics by proposing, for example, that our
current grasp of arithmetical concepts gives us a warrant for belief in the elementary truths of arithmetic, a warrant that is available given any sufficiently rich
experience, but which, they concede, is defeasible. In emphasizing the tradition-
dependence of such warrants, I've tried to transcend the inadequate individualistic epistemology that demands that we offer a synchronic reconstruction of
human knowledge in which every item of knowledge is either categorized as
empirical (grounded in the knower's own experiences) or a priori; if those were
our options, then, I agree, classifying the knowledge as a priori would be preferable.[27] But we ought to reject the individualistic framework, recognizing explicitly that our knowledge is dependent on the tradition in which we stand, and that
our a priori knowledge, in the Weak sense, depends on the experiences of historical figures who have played important roles in past inquiry. Once we see this,

[26] Here I simply gesture at a methodology of mathematics, parts of which I tried to sketch in
the later chapters of *The Nature of Mathematical Knowledge*, but which remains woefully
underdeveloped.

[27] In his interesting and sensitive essay on tradition and a priori knowledge, 'Content Preservation', Tyler Burge both seems to recognize the importance of tradition in all our knowledge
and to want to apply the a priori-aposteriori distinction which is, I think, a residue of the desire
for synchronic (tradition-independent) reconstruction. If one were forced to answer the question
'Do people have a priori or empirical entitlements to trust those who socialize them?', the better
answer would surely favour apriority (as Burge's does), because the alternative threatens either
regress or paradox. But a much better approach is to reject the question as based on an illegitimate presupposition and to see all knowledge as dependent on processes that extend far beyond
the individual knower.

we'll recognize that the issue isn't one of apriorism versus empiricism, but of apriorism versus historicism, and here the interesting question is whether one can find, for logic, mathematics, or anything else, some tradition-independent warrant, something that will meet the requirements that Descartes and Frege hoped to satisfy—in short, something that will answer to the Strong conception. Those who settle for the Weak conception have preserved the label 'a priori', but, to adapt a nice phrase of Michael Devitt's, they have offered us fig-leaf apriorism.[28]

I don't offer this as a claim that the Strong conception captures what epistemologists have always understood about apriority. It seems to me that the discussions of the past decades have made clear how intricate and complex the classical notion of the a priori is, and that *neither* the Strong conception *nor* the Weak conception (nor anything else) can provide a coherent explication. In the end, it doesn't matter much whether we declare that mathematics isn't a priori (cleaving to the Strong conception) or whether we argue that mathematics is a priori (on the basis of the Weak conception). The important point is to understand the tradition-dependence of our mathematical knowledge and the complex mix of theoretical reasoning and empirical evidence that has figured in the historical process on which current mathematical knowledge is based.

VII

I want to extend these points by looking at two perceptive recent discussions of classical claims about the a priori. Both Hartry Field and Michael Friedman have offered defences of the apriority of types of propositions traditionally favoured with this status, defences that seem to take into account many of the points I've been urging. Field is concerned with the apriority (or 'aprioricity' as he calls it) of classical logic.[29] Friedman wants to argue for the apriority of mathematics.[30] In both instances, the defence takes the same form, in that beliefs in the pertinent propositions are supposed to be needed for people to perform certain kinds of cognitive tasks—engage in any assessment of evidence (Field), or formulate and assess the kinds of theories that we take to represent the pinnacle of our empirical knowledge (Friedman). I think this represents a confusion of the sort indicated in Section I, between apriority and a quite different idea, the notion of a propositional precondition, and that the confusion makes the Weak conception seem more attractive than it actually is.

Field starts by formulating the issue in terms of *evidential systems*. Roughly, an epistemic system for a person is a system of rules that idealize that person's

---

[28] In *Realism and Truth* (Princeton: Princeton University Press, 1984): 15, Michael Devitt describes a position he calls 'fig-leaf realism'.
[29] See 'The Aprioricity of Logic'.
[30] See 'Naturalism'.

belief-forming and belief-retaining behaviour: as I understand it, the rules are supposed to embody the person's own conception of evidence. A proposition *p* is weakly a priori for a person just in case the evidential system licenses belief even in the absence of any particular sensory inputs and strongly a priori if, in addition, the rules don't license retraction of belief on the basis of any sensory inputs. The difference between these conceptions is parallel to the difference between the Weak conception and the Strong conception, although Field wants to rule out certain kinds of sensory inputs as not pertinent to questions about apriority. (These include the sorts of experiences I've invoked to discredit the apriority of mathematics, so it will be important, later on, to come to terms with his efforts at restriction.) So far the account of the a priori is highly subjectivist, since we can envisage people using all sorts of evidential systems and, having, in consequence, quite different sets of a priori propositions. Field is explicit about this, and proposes that the question is 'whether or not it is a good thing to have an evidential system that licenses the beliefs in a (weakly or strongly) a priori fashion'.[31] Once he has posed the issue in this way, he can defend the apriority of logic in two steps, first by showing that our evidential system does license belief in logic without regard to sensory input, and second by arguing that our evidential system is a good thing.

If the aim is simply to establish the weak apriority of logic, then the first step seems trivial, for, if we understand evidential systems as Field does, then surely our evidential system does license endorsement of the principles of classical logic in the absence of any particular sensory inputs. In pursuing a stronger conclusion, Field points out that we have no idea how to make sense of evidential relations involving the proposed rivals to classical logic, and that all the well-known reconstructions of measures of empirical evidence license our acceptance of classical logic, come what may. In my terminology, classical logic (or at least, its most central tenets) consists of propositional preconditions for our assessing empirical evidence in the way we do.

Turning now to the second step, Field doesn't make what seems to me a rather obvious point, namely that confidence in the progressiveness of inquiry ought to incline us to think that our evidential system is a good one. As we reflect on the history of science, it does appear that we've learned a lot about the world and we've learned a lot about how to learn about the world, and, while admitting our fallibility on all counts, we ought to endorse the view that we have a good evidential system. Field does, however, offer a related, forward-looking, point, noting that the possibility of a future system that would be superior to ours doesn't undermine the claim that our system is a good one. An important part of his case here is that evidential systems aren't correct or incorrect, so that we can't insist that the apriority of logic turns on whether our belief in classical logic is licensed by *the right* evidential system.

---

[31] Field 'The Aprioricity of Logic': 364.

I'm more inclined to factualism in epistemology than Field is, but, for present purposes, I'm going to sidestep those thorny questions. The main point on which I want to insist is Field's divorce between strong apriority (in his sense) and the possibility of a priori knowledge (in the Strong sense). Assume that it's true that logic is weakly a priori and that logic is a set of propositional preconditions for the assessment of evidence. What does that show about our knowledge of the laws of classical logic?

Nothing. I believe the laws of classical logic, in part because I was taught them, and in part because I think I see how those laws are used in assessing evidence. But my belief could easily be undermined by experience. Perhaps I could be shown that the laws I've accepted really don't reconstruct the inferences that are made in the parts of our knowledge we esteem most (as Frege and Russell argued that classical Aristotelian logic was inadequate to reconstruct mathematical proofs); although my evidential system really does license the laws, it doesn't follow that I have to recognize this, or that I couldn't be brought to think that my system ought to be reconstructed by favouring different laws. In the history of inquiry human practice has often been at odds with the theoretical principles that people take to govern the reasoning in which they engage, and, even if that's not true of us, there are lots of ways in which our identification of logic might be disturbed.

Second, as Field acknowledges, we might modify our practice (although, as he points out, it's not easy to give substance to this idea). It's conceivable that future investigators may discover a new way to think about evidence and inference that transforms our approaches to these concepts even more radically than the modifications achieved in the wake of modern mathematical logic. There are two versions of this scenario, one in which our principles of logic turn out not to be correct (perhaps they involve faulty conceptualizations that our successors transcend) and one in which we are seduced into believing that they are incorrect by the apparent successes of a rival community of investigators (these investigators convince us to adopt a different evidential system that is not actually as good as our own, despite appearances). Neither way of articulating the scenario is at odds with the claims that our evidential system licenses the laws of classical logic, irrespective of sensory input, and that our evidential system is a good one. Weak apriority of logic is sustained.

But it's easy to see how either scenario would affect the view that we know the laws of logic a priori in the sense of the Strong conception. Imagine a community that lives through one of the envisaged transitions. After the presentation of the powerful, or apparently powerful, rival system, the community splits. Most become converted to the new way of doing things, and they no longer believe the laws of our logic, but a small group of traditionalists persist in the old ways. Notice that they believe the laws, they endorse an evidential system that licenses the belief, and their system is a good one. Nonetheless, their beliefs are based on ignoring or misevaluating the apparent advantages of the revisionist way of doing things. Under these conditions, we can't see them as anything other than blind dogmatists, and, in consequence, we shouldn't view their beliefs as warranted. So, even though classical logic may contain (even comprise) propositional preconditions of experience (or evidence), it's not the case that classical logic can be known Strongly a priori.

Now it may quite reasonably be suspected that my argument against Field depends crucially on ignoring a distinction he makes quite early on in his discussion, the distinction between primary and secondary undermining evidence. The latter 'does not primarily go against the claim being undermined but against the claim that we knew it a priori',[32] and Field proposes that strong apriority doesn't require the ability to survive secondary undermining evidence. Field might contend that the only debunking scenarios involve secondary evidence.

When we probe this contention, we see that the distinction is much less clear than it initially appears. Consider a standard undermining story. Our descendants come across a group of inquirers who seem, by all our lights, extraordinarily successful: their predictions even of complex phenomena are quite staggering. They try to teach us their evidential system and we find it very hard to understand (perhaps in much the way some students find logic alien and tough going), but some of us are able to follow their recommendations about inference and those people obtain apparently wonderful results. Maybe they offer us 'proofs' of difficulties within our own system. These might be more complex versions of the 'proofs' that $1 = 2$ that sometimes baffle schoolchildren, and, I'll assume, diagnosing the trouble is beyond our abilities. Does this hypothetical sequence of experiences furnish us with primary or secondary undermining evidence? If it's primary, then Field's distinction is unavailing with this sort of case. If, on the other hand, it's secondary, then one has to restrict the notion of primary evidence quite narrowly. After all, we might say that there's indirect primary evidence against the truth of our logical principles and that this is furnished by the demonstration of success of a group of people who proceed in ways that support the idea that they are using different principles, as well as by the (presumably fallacious) 'proofs'. If one denies that there ever can be primary evidence where the testimony of others is involved, then we have extraordinarily little primary evidence for anything—that's the lesson of the socio-historical view of knowledge. I think that Field's distinction is influenced, at bottom, by the notion that there is a sort of evidence that is available to individuals independently of their training and of the history of the society in which they live. Once we understand how little (if anything) would qualify for that role, then I don't think one can exclude the debunking scenarios without robbing the notion of primary evidence of any interest.

Although Field is much less friendly to apriorism than Friedman, there's a striking convergence in their recent strategies. In a penetrating recent discussion

---

[32] Field 'The Apriority of Logic': 362.

of philosophical naturalism, Friedman follows Reichenbach in distinguishing two notions of the a prior: 'necessary and unrevisable, fixed for all time, on the one hand, "constitutive of the object of [scientific] knowledge", on the other.'[33] The real hero of the story is Carnap, who 'brought this new, relativized and dynamical conception of the a priori to its most precise expression.'[34] According to Carnap, our formulations of hypotheses and our assessment of them presuppose a mathematico-logico-linguistic framework, and, within any such framework, the mathematical principles play a constitutive role, so that they cannot be questioned while we remain with the framework. Of course, as Carnap took pains to point out, we can change frameworks, inscribing a different set of principles in our practice of formulating and testing empirical hypotheses. In changes of framework, however, we appeal not only to empirical evidence but also to specifically mathematical and even philosophical considerations. Instead of the holistic vision of evidence familiar from Quine, Friedman offers an alternative

[T]he picture of a dynamical system of beliefs, concepts, and principles that can be analyzed, for present purposes, into three main components: an evolving system of empirical natural scientific concepts and principles, an evolving system of mathematical concepts and principles which frame those of empirical science and make their rigorous formulation and precise experimental testing possible, and an evolving system of philosophical concepts and principles which serve, especially in periods of conceptual revolution, as a source of suggestions and guidance in choosing one scientific framework rather than another. All of these systems are in continual dynamical evolution, and it is indeed the case that no concept or principle is forever immune to revision. Yet we can nonetheless clearly distinguish the radically different functions, levels, and roles of the differing component systems. In particular, although the three component systems are certainly in perpetual interaction, they nonetheless evolve according to their own characteristic dynamics.[35]

There is much here with which I agree. What puzzles me most is why this should be thought of as any kind of rehabilitation of apriority.

For present purposes I'm going to ignore one of Friedman's component systems (the body of philosophical lore, whose role in his argument is much less clearly delineated) and consider the image of the interplay between mathematics and natural science that he offers us. Mathematicians supply some of the ingredients out of which frameworks are constructed, and scientists draw on their offerings to formulate successors to previous empirical theories in the light of observations and experiments. Now there are two quite distinct ways to think about the way in which the mathematical tools are fashioned, or, in Friedman's idiom about the dynamics according to which this component system evolves.

According to one of these, mathematical knowledge grows by the kinds of processes I've discussed in the later chapters of *The Nature of Mathematical Knowledge*: mathematicians try to devise ways of responding to unanswered

---

[33] Friedman, 'Naturalism': 13.   [34] Ibid.   [35] Ibid. 19.

questions, they develop generalizations of methods and concepts that have previously been introduced, they attempt to find rigorous replacements for forms of reasoning that appear to yield correct conclusions but do not accord with prevailing standards—and, in doing all this, they propose definitions and axioms that systematize previous mathematics. The ultimate roots of their practice lie in experience, and, from time to time, connections with the empirical sciences are reforged, and particular parts of mathematics are inspired by the needs of particular lines of investigation into natural (or social) phenomena. Hence, there is genuine co-evolution between mathematics and science. Yet, above all, the entire strategy of licensing a group of people to develop languages and principles in this way—essentially by thinking about what has been achieved in the past and how to generalize and systematize it further—rests on our appreciation of its fruitfulness for inquiry. The knowledge of contemporary mathematicians may be proximally produced by their reflections on what they have absorbed from the past, reflections that do not depend on any specific sensory input, but it is ultimately dependent on the collective experiences of the tradition in which they stand.

If this is Friedman's picture, then he and I are in fundamental accord. We can even agree to call mathematical knowledge '*relatively* a priori', or, as I would prefer, '*proximally* a priori', so long as we are clear that this Weak conception diverges from traditional ideas about a priori mathematical knowledge. For the tradition sees the dynamic of the mathematical subsystem in very different terms. Mathematicians are supposed to have ways of warranting their beliefs that stand outside the historical process, that are independent of tradition. It would be possible to try to articulate Friedman's vision by adopting this idea, insisting that mathematical knowledge is a priori in the sense of the Strong conception, although I think that that would be at odds with his point about the Carnap–Reichenbach insight. Any such programme would return mathematical epistemology to the venture of seeking processes that can serve as tradition-independent warrants—a venture I believe to be fruitless. Field's efforts to secure the apriority of logic seem to me to be an ingenious last-ditch attempt to bind the relativized notion of apriority (the Carnap–Reichenbach, 'constitutive', conception) to the more traditional notion, by arguing that the framework-constituting principles are immune to empirical evidence. I've argued that those efforts fail. The proximal a priori is the best one can hope for.

Let me set this in the context of my main point. Traditionally apriorism has been opposed to radical empiricism, and, in my earlier discussions of the issues, I tended to endorse that opposition. But it now seems to me that apriorism and empiricism are both best understood as rival versions of attempts to give a tradition-independent conception of human knowledge. The most fundamental feature of my attack on apriority is my attempt to debunk tradition-independence. If I interpret them correctly, Field thinks he can deploy the notion of a propositional precondition of experience to defend the tradition-independence of our knowledge of logic, while Friedman thinks that this notion will retain the significance of classical theses about apriority, even when we admit the 'relative' (tradition-dependent) character of apriority. In my judgement, neither of these last-ditch efforts succeeds. I recommend declaring a truce on the apriorism–empiricism debate on the grounds that logic, mathematics, and (as Section V suggested) whole chunks of other disciplines count as a priori in the Weak sense. That truce should be coupled with a clear understanding of the places in which the Weak conception departs from classical lore about apriority, agreement on the tradition-dependence of our logical and mathematical knowledge, and a resolve to explore the complex ways in which experience has figured in the genesis of our current logical and mathematical knowledge.

5

Naturalism and the A Priori

Penelope Maddy

The naturalism I aim to practise is a descendant of Quine's.[1] My goal here is to place this naturalism in what I hope to be an illuminating historical context, to trace the status of the a priori through its various twists and turns, and eventually to draw some tentative conclusions about the naturalistic status of the a priori. To do this, I first return to Kant. While it's surely no surprise that an examination of the a priori should start from Kant, perhaps his relevance to naturalism is less obvious. Let me begin, then, with an introductory word on that connection.

Though my naturalism differs from Quine's in a couple of significant ways, these disagreements won't matter until the very end, so we can begin with Quine's leading idea: the 'abandonment of the goal of a first philosophy' (Quine 1975: 72). The interconnections between Quine and Carnap will take centre stage later, but for now we need only note that the bare rejection of first philosophy can be seen as evolving out of Carnap's classification of many traditional metaphysical claims as 'pseudo-statement[s] without cognitive content' (Carnap 1950: 250). Carnap's idea is that legitimate scientific questions, 'theoretical questions', are asked within the linguistic framework of scientific language, with its associated principles of evidence; in contrast, metaphysical pseudo-questions are posed outside of all linguistic frameworks; perhaps as preamble to the adoption of a linguistic framework, as such, they are asked without the backing of associated evidential rules that would make them answerable, and indeed, that would give them sense.

Now Kant also had a keen nose for the pseudo-question:

To know what questions may reasonably be asked is already a great and necessary proof of sagacity and insight. For if a question is absurd in itself and calls for an answer where

I would like to thank Lara Denis, Ruth Marcus, Sally Sedwick, and Martin Schwab for their help and patience during my struggles with Kant, the Departments of Philosophy at OSU (and Kurt Mosser), UC Riverside, and the University of Iowa for lively discussions, and Denis, Marcus, and Sedgwick for comments on earlier drafts.

[1] For details, see my (1997).

none is required, it not only brings shame on the propounder of the question, but may betray an incautious listener into absurd answers, thus presenting, as the ancients said, the ludicrous spectacle of one man milking a he-goat and the other holding a sieve underneath. (A58/B82–3)

Kant is particularly concerned to warn against applying concepts outside their proper range:

[I]t is very tempting to use these pure modes of knowledge of the understanding and these principles by themselves, and even beyond the limits of experience, which alone can yield the matter . . . to which those pure concepts of understanding can be applied. (A63/B87–8)

Or, more poetically,

The light dove, cleaving the air in her free flight, and feeling its resistance, might imagine that its flight would be still easier in empty space. (A5/B8)

Kant's goal is to warn against this 'transcendental illusion', to 'expose the false, illusory character of these groundless pretensions' (A63–4/B88). Thus I think it is no stretch to suppose that an understanding of Kant's critical philosophy and its fortunes might shed light on the sources of naturalism.

Admittedly, Kant's critical philosophy is not the sort of thing at which it's easy to take a brief look. If I've learned anything from my foray into the secondary literature, it is that the game of isolating the correct interpretation of Kant is not one a novice like myself can profitably play. What I propose to do instead is to sketch two well-known interpretations of transcendental idealism that lie at opposite extremes. My hope is that this contrast will provide some useful tools for our advance into the twentieth century.

For all the customary focus on Hume in discussions of Kant, our story begins with Locke and Berkeley. 'The celebrated Locke', as Kant calls him (A86/B119), held a representative theory of perception: we are directly aware of our sensory experiences; some features of those sensory experiences match actual properties of external things—these are the primary qualities, like shape—while other features of sensory experiences are merely the result of the actions of those external things on our sensory apparatus—these are the secondary qualities, like colour. This sort of theory immediately gives rise to sceptical worries, as Locke himself realized:

It is evident the mind knows not things immediately, but only by the intervention of the ideas it has of them. Our knowledge, therefore, is real only so far as there is a *conformity* between our ideas and the reality of things. . . . How shall the mind, when it perceives nothing but its own ideas, know that they agree with things themselves? (Locke 1690: IV. iv. 3)

As we might put it: how are we to infer the properties of external things from the properties of our sensations?

Unfortunately, Locke's attempts to answer this question were less than satisfactory.[2] The good Bishop Berkeley then solved the sceptical problem by 'the simple, but extraordinarily dramatic expedient' (Pitcher 1971: 92) of eliminating the extra-mental world altogether and identifying objects with collections of sensations:

By sight I have the ideas of light and colours, with their several degrees and variations. By touch I perceive hard and soft, heat and cold, motion and resistance . . . Smelling furnishes me with odours; the palate with tastes; and hearing conveys sounds to the mind in all their variety of tone and composition. . . . And as several of these are observed to accompany each other, they come to be marked by one name, and so to be reputed as one *thing*. Thus, for example, a certain colour, taste, smell, figure and consistence having been observed to go together, are accounted one distinct thing, signified by the name apple. (Berkeley 1710: '1)

There is no difficulty as to how we know about apples, so characterized, as our sensations are precisely the things of which we are directly aware.

With this backdrop in place, let me sketch the first of the two promised interpretations of transcendental idealism; this might be called the 'harsh reading'.[3] The general outlines of Kant's Copernican revolution are undisputed: as space and time are the forms of our human intuition and the categories are the conditions of any discursive intellect, all possible human experience will conform to them; as a result, we can know a priori various mathematical and scientific facts about the world as it is experienced. The harsh reading continues from here by concentrating on the distinction between the appearance, phenomenon, or representation on the one hand, and the thing in itself, noumenon or the transcendental object on the other.[4] That these are distinct items is shown by Kant's insistence that the former are spatio-temporal while the later are not:

Space does not represent any property of things in themselves . . . Space is nothing but the form of all appearances of outer sense. (A26/B42) . . . we are here speaking only of an appearance in space and time, which are not determinations of things in themselves but only of our sensibility. (A493/B522)

This spatio-temporality, enjoyed by appearances, but not by things in themselves, is purely ideal:

[T]his space and this time, and with them all appearances . . . are nothing but representations, and cannot exist outside our mind. (A492/B520)

These appearances are the only objects of our knowledge, but the extra-mental transcendental objects are somehow responsible for them:

[2] Bennett (1971: 65–7) gives a summary.
[3] Prominent variations on the harsh reading can be found in Prichard (1909), Strawson (1966), and Guyer (1987).
[4] Considerable subtlety is lost by ignoring the differences in Kant's uses of the alternative terms on either side of this dichotomy (see e.g. Bird (1962): 76–80); Allison (1983): 242–6), but it would take us too far afield to attend to them here.

How things may be in themselves, apart from the representations through which they affect us, is entirely outside our sphere of knowledge. (A190/B235) The non-sensible cause of these representations is completely unknown to us. (A494/B522)

Things in themselves are unknown, but they affect our senses to produce appearances, which we can and do know.

The result of this analysis is a mixed and unsavoury stew. Appearances are experiences, strictly mental—essentially Berkeleian congeries of ideas. Things in themselves are like Locke's external objects, except that even the properties Locke counted as primary—extension, figure—are now taken to be secondary, so that nothing in our experience corresponds to their actual features:

Long before Locke's time, and assuredly since him, it has been generally assumed and granted without detriment to the actual existence of external things that many of their predicates may be said to belong, not to the things in themselves, but to their appearances, and to have no proper existence outside our representation. Heat, colour, and taste, for instance, are of this kind. Now, . . . I go farther and, for weighty reasons, rank as mere appearances the remaining qualities of bodies, also, which are called primary—such as extension, place, and, in general, space, with all that which belongs to it (impenetrability or materiality, shape, etc.). (Kant 1783: 13, Remark II)

We are left with a combination of Berkeleian idealism with a Lockian representative theory, a combination which seems to preserve the bitter of Berkeley—his idealism—without the sweet—his reply to scepticism. A supporter of this interpretation remarks that 'Kant . . . is closer to Berkeley than he acknowledges' (Strawson 1966: 22), and a detractor concludes that 'Kant is seen as a . . . skeptic malgré lui' (Allison 1983: 5–6).

Now even the staunch opponents[5] of the harsh reading admit that there is much in Kant that might seem to support it; e.g. one writes, '[i]t would be foolish to deny that Kant can be interpreted in this way' (Matthews 1969: 205).[6] In response, they point to passages in which Kant rejects Berkeleian idealism (B69–71, B274–5) and the representative theory of perception (B332), and defends himself against the charge of scepticism (B333–4). The trick is to interpret these and similar passages in such a way as to suggest reinterpretations of the passages most supportive of the harsh reading. I will try to do this in the course of sketching out the second promised interpretation of transcendental idealism, which I'll call the 'benign reading'.

The first point to notice is that Kant's appearances are not mere sensations:

That in appearance which corresponds to sensation I term its *matter*; but that which so determines the manifold of appearance that it allows of being ordered in certain relations, I term the *form* of appearance. That in which alone the sensations can be posited and

---

[5] For a sampling, see Bird (1962) in reply to Prichard (1909); Matthews (1969), Bird (1982), and Allison (1983) in reply to Strawson (1966).

[6] Cf. Bird (1962:3): 'it is also true that some things which Kant says appear quite strongly to support Prichard's interpretation'.

ordered in a certain form, cannot itself be sensation; and therefore, while the matter of all appearance is given to us *a posteriori* only, its form must lie ready for the sensations *a priori* in the mind. (A20/B34)

These necessary forms of appearances include space and time, so appearances are spatio-temporal, external to us.[7] But,

When I say that the intuition of outer objects . . . represent[s] the objects . . . in space and in time, as they affect our sense, that is, as they appear, I do not mean to say that these objects are a mere illusion. . . . when I maintain that the quality of space and of time, in conformity with which, as a condition of their existence, I posit . . . bodies . . ., lies in my mode of intuition and not in those objects in themselves, I am not saying that the bodies merely *seem* to be outside me. (B69–70)

The key to understanding this perplexing position lies in the distinction between two perspectives: the empirical and the transcendental.

The central idea here is that questions about appearance and reality are ambiguous: they can be posed, considered, and answered either empirically or transcendentally. At the empirical level, we draw a distinction between the real and the illusory:

The rainbow in a sunny shower may be called a mere appearance, and the rain the thing in itself. This is correct, if the latter concept be taken in a merely physical [empirical] sense. (A45/B63)

The rainbow is an optical phenomenon while the rain itself is real. But, if we now inquire into the reality of the rain at the transcendental level,

We then realise that not only are the drops of rain mere appearances, but that even their round shape, nay even the space in which they fall, are nothing in themselves, but merely modifications or fundamental forms of our sensible intuition, and that the transcendental object remains unknown to us. (A46/B63)

In short, the rain drops are empirically real, but (to a large extent)[8] transcendentally ideal.

Once this distinction is drawn, we see that the appearance and the thing in itself are not two separate objects, but a single thing regarded in different ways:

[W]e can . . . have no knowledge of any object as thing in itself, but only in so far as it is an object of sensible intuition, that is, an appearance. (B xxvi)

The object as appearance is subject to our human forms of sensibility—space and time—and the categories of the discursive understanding—like substance and causation; it is spatio-temporal, external to our minds, and subject to causal laws. Thus Kant is an empirical realist, as opposed to Berkeley's empirical idealist

---

[7] I am speaking, here and in what follows, of objects of outer sense. Objects of inner sense are another story, one I will not pursue.

[8] The 'matter' of the appearance is not transcendentally ideal.

(who holds, e.g. that objects of experience only appear to be extra-mental). On the other hand, the object as it is in itself is not subject to our forms and categories; spatio-temporality and the categories are impositions of our minds, necessary for the object to be experienced, not features of the thing in itself. This is transcendental idealism, as opposed to Locke's transcendental realism (which holds, e.g. that things in themselves are spatio-temporal). Because we are discursive intellects, that is, because all our knowledge arises from the application of concepts to the products of intuition—appearances—we can know nothing of the things in themselves.

This reading goes a long way towards interpreting passages favoured by the harsh theorists, passages in which Kant refers to 'mere appearances' or objects 'in the mind': he is to be read as speaking transcendentally, not empirically. And there is considerable textual support for this distinction:

Our exposition therefore establishes the *reality*, that is, the objective validity, of space in respect of whatever can be presented to us outwardly as object, but also at the same time, the *ideality* of space in respect of things when they are considered in themselves through reason, that is, without regard to the constitution of our sensibility. We assert, then, the *empirical reality* of space, as regards all possible outer experience; and yet at the same time we assert its *transcendental ideality*—in other words, that it is nothing at all, immediately we withdraw the above condition, namely, its limitation to possible experience, and so look upon it as something that underlies things in themselves. (A28/B44)

This reading clearly undermines the harsh interpretation of Kant's appearances as similar to Berkeley's congeries of ideas.

What about the second component of the harsh reading: the representative theory of perception with things in themselves somehow producing appearances by their action on our senses? Though the two-object interpretation has been abandoned, we could still imagine that the way things are in themselves affects us so as to produce the way things appear. First, notice that from the empirical point of view, something very like a Lockian analysis is possible: objects, in the empirical realm of appearances, cause certain responses in the sensory organs of human beings, again regarded empirically, some of these responses produce veridical beliefs, others illusions; these facts can be described and explained scientifically (see, e.g. A28; (Allison 1983: 249)). It's important to realize that Kant's transcendental inquiry does not compromise or even affect the ordinary practice of empirical science (e.g. A39/B56, A393, A30/B45).[9]

But back to the transcendental perspective: do things as they are in themselves affect us to produce appearances? The various Kantian passages that suggest an affirmative answer to this question raise two of the oldest problems for his interpreters: how can we know that things in themselves do this when we can know nothing about them?, and how can things in themselves 'affect' us or 'cause'

---

[9] I come back to this point in a moment.

appearances when causation is a category of the understanding, and as such, only applicable to the world of phenomena? Harsh theorists tend to cite these passages as evidence of deep inconsistencies in Kant, while their opponents give other readings.

To see how one of these other readings might go, consider the following continuation of a passage quoted a moment ago:

The non-sensible cause of these representations is completely unknown to us, and cannot therefore be intuited by us as object. For such an object would have to be represented as neither in space nor in time . . ., and apart from such conditions, we cannot think any intuition. We may, however, entitle the purely intelligible cause of appearances in general the transcendental object, but merely in order to have something corresponding to sensibility viewed as receptivity. (A494/B522)

The picture is this: sensibility is a capacity to be affected in a certain manner; the affecting agent provides the matter for the resulting appearance; this matter becomes an appearance only after being submitted to the forms of intuition. Under these conditions, what can the affecting agent be? Not an appearance, which is already imbued with spatio-temporal form, but something as yet unaffected by that intuitive processing, in other words, a thing as it is in itself. But to say this is not to gain any contentful knowledge of things in themselves, but only to follow out the concepts involved.[10] To speak of the transcendental object is a harmless way of alluding to the receptive character of sensibility.[11]

The third and final feature of the harsh interpretation is the accusation of scepticism: Kant admits that we can only know appearances, not things as they are in themselves. To this objection, Kant gives a direct reply:

If by the complaints—*that we have no insight whatsoever into the inner [nature] of things*—it be meant that we cannot conceive by pure understanding what the things which appear to us may be in themselves, they are entirely illegitimate and unreasonable. For what is demanded is that we should be able to know things, and therefore to intuit them, without senses, and therefore that we should have a faculty of knowledge altogether different from the human, and this not only in degree but as regards intuition likewise in kind— in other words, that we should be not men but beings of whom we are unable to say whether they are even possible, much less how they are constituted. (A277–8/B333–4)

The important point is that Kant takes our knowledge of external, spatio-temporal objects to be direct; there is no scepticism here. By contrast, to ask to know

---

[10] In other words, the claim is merely analytic. See Allison (1983: 247–54). Allison (1976) gives a similar reply to another puzzle which I won't discuss, namely: how we can know that the thing in itself is not spatio-temporal (as opposed to the agnostic position that we can't know whether it is or isn't)? See also Allison (1983: 27, 104–14). For a spirited reply, see Guyer (1987: 336–42).

[11] Another benign reading would be to understand the idea (or Idea) of the transcendental object as operating in a regulative, rather than factual sense: to say that the transcendental object causes appearances is to commit ourselves to an unending pursuit of deeper and deeper causal factors. See also Bird (1962: 68–9, 78–9).

what things are like in themselves is to ask to know what things are like when they are not known. To reject this demand is good judgement, not scepticism.

In sum, then, the benign interpretation goes like this: two levels of discourse must be distinguished—empirical and transcendental; from the empirical perspective, appearances are perfectly real, contrasted with sensory illusions; from the transcendental perspective, they are (partly) ideal, contrasted with things as they are in themselves; neither appearances nor things in themselves are Berkeleian congeries of ideas and neither is a Lockian object inscrutable behind its veil of perception. Kant's notions of thing in itself, noumenon, and transcendental object have various uses, but never to give us contentful knowledge of matters beyond the world of experience. The empirical world is the world, and we have direct knowledge of it.

Leaving aside the question of how Kant is best interpreted, I think most of us would find the benign view a more attractive piece of philosophy than the harsh, so let's press on a bit further. At the empirical level, the appearance–reality distinction remains robust—we give the usual account of sensory illusions—but at the transcendental level, we find the transcendental companion to appearances an increasingly empty notion;[12] the thing in itself is not a separate entity, but a sort of empty placeholder[13] that calls attention to the receptivity of our senses, to the role of the forms of intuition and the categories in our knowledge, perhaps to certain methodological principles.[14] In fact, Kant sometimes says that our inquiries at the transcendental level, our critique of pure reason, gives us no knowledge at all, properly speaking:

Its utility, in speculation, ought properly to be only negative, not to extend, but only to clarify our reason, and keep it free from errors—which is already a very great gain. (A11/B25)[15]

Now, given the wide range of transcendental claims that pepper the *Critique*, a rank outsider like myself is tempted to wonder at their status. They certainly sound like knowledge claims: e.g. there are two forms of human sensibility; human knowledge is discursive; or one of my personal favourites

The transcendental unity of apperception is that unity through which all the manifold given in an intuition is united in a concept of the object. (B139)

If these are not knowledge claims, we need some general instruction on how they should be read; if they are knowledge claims, we need to know how they can be

---

[12] See A255/B310: 'the domain that lies out beyond the sphere of appearances is for us empty.'

[13] See A104: 'we have to deal only with our representations . . . that x (the object) which corresponds to them is nothing to us.'

[14] See n. 11.

[15] See also A12/B26: 'It is upon this enquiry, which should be entitled not a doctrine, but only a transcendental critique, that we are now engaged. Its purpose is not to extend knowledge, but only to correct it.'

fitted into Kant's own account of human knowledge: are concepts being applied to intuitions, as is required of all human (i.e. discursive) knowledge? are the claims analytic or synthetic, a priori or a posteriori?

Questions of this sort have led even a sympathetic commentator like Lewis White Beck to a less than satisfying 'meta-critique of pure reason'; he writes:

Not only is it [the claim that 'the only intuition available to us is sensible'] not proved, it is not even a well-formed judgment under the rubrics allowed in the *Critique*, for it is neither analytic nor a posterior, and if it is synthetic yet known a priori, none of the arguments so painfully mounted in the *Critique* to show that such knowledge is possible has anything to do with how we know this (if indeed we do know it). (Beck 1976: 24)

H. E. Matthews, a leading benign theorist,[16] discusses another such claim:[17]

The statement . . . can certainly not be given any factual content, since the conditions for the empirical application of the concept . . . cannot be met. But the statement is not self-contradictory, and may well have a function, that of expressing the limitations of our experience, which gives it some kind of meaning. The difficulty which is met here is one which arises whenever one tries to talk about the limits of human knowledge . . . The only way in which one can really present the limits of human thought is by showing the confusions and contradictions that arise when one tries to overstep the limits (as Kant does in the Antinomies). But if one does try to *state* the limits (rather than just *showing* them), then the statement, despite its factual appearance, should be interpreted as having a different function. (Matthews 1969: 218–19)

The implicit appeal to Wittgenstein's position in the Tractatus is made explicit in Matthew's discussion.

Given the inherent difficulties associated with these discussions at the transcendental level, the rank outsider might go on to wonder whether the gains are worth the costs, to wonder, that is, what would be lost by resting content with empirical realism neat? Of course, the Kantian opus provides various fascinating and much debated answers to this question—e.g. the role of transcendental idealism in his solutions to the cosmological antinomies and in the transition to his moral philosophy—but the most fundamental role is the one that takes centre stage here:

This transcendental consideration is a duty from which nobody who wishes to make any *a priori* judgments about things can claim exemption. (A263/B319)

Only from the transcendental perspective can we identify conditions on human experience that are not merely empirical, psychological, and only transcendentally necessary conditions of this sort can deliver a priori knowledge of the world.[18] So the transcendental perspective is essential if we are 'to supply a

---

[16] See Ameriks (1982) for a slightly dated, but still useful survey of the literature.

[17] This one concerns the purely intuitive intellect, with which Kant contrasts our human discursive intellect.

[18] Psychological conditions, if they could be isolated, would be part of our empirical theory

touchstone of the value, or lack of value, of all *a priori* knowledge' (A12/B26).

Armed with this thumbnail account of Kant's project and theory, let's now move forward in time and consider the impact of scientific developments since his day. Notice that on the harsh reading, it is hard to see how our empirical knowledge could ever extend beyond what we actually perceive (as in Berkeley) or, perhaps, beyond what we could possibly perceive (as in phenomenalism), and predictably, there are passages that suggest this interpretation:

[F]rom the perception of the attracted iron filings we know of the existence of a magnetic matter pervading all bodies, although the constitution of our organs cuts us off from all immediate perception of this medium. For in accordance with the laws of sensibility and the context of our perceptions, we should, were our senses more refined, come also in an experience upon the immediate empirical intution of it. (A226/B373)

This may sound like phenomenalism, but the benign theorist[19] takes the counterfactual suggestion to be inessential, because Kant also writes:

[T]he knowledge of things as *actual* does not, indeed, demand immediate perception . . . of the object whose existence is to be known. What we do, however, require is the connection of the object with some actual perception, in accordance with the analogies of experience, which define all real connection in an experience in general. (A225/B272)

The key phrase is 'in accordance with the analogies of experience', which include, e.g. the law of causality. Thus, even Newton's findings result from 'the empirical employment of the understanding' (A257/B313), and an early twentieth-century Kant could grant empirical reality to, say, atoms, despite our inability to perceive them, because they are suitably connected to what we can perceive by the postulates of empirical thought.[20]

So far so good. Unfortunately, as is well known, further developments in twentieth-century physics cannot be so easily incorporated into the Kantian account. The theory of relativity, for example, denies the objectivity of Kant's time sequence (that is, its observer-independence), replaces his a priori forms of intuition—space and time—with a new conception of space-time, and most famously, forgoes his a priori Euclidean geometry in favour of an a posteriori non-Euclidean geometry. These problems are confined to the forms of intuition, but with the development of quantum mechanics, difficulties spread to the categories of pure understanding; there the law of universal causation is undermined and even the category of substance may be called into question.[21]

---

of ourselves as knowers. What we would learn would be how we are bound to regard objects, not how they really are; part of the payoff of the theory would be to help us better understand how they really are. Transcendental conditions, on the other hand, tell us how the things we experience must be, a priori.

[19] See Allison (1983: 32–3).

[20] This should help explain how considerations at the transcendental level have no effect on the practice of empirical science.

[21] See e.g. Reichenbach (1949), or Körner (1955: 87–9).

Though we have seen that extrapolation using the analogies can carry us to knowledge of matters beyond what is perceived or even perceptible, it is quite another matter to come to know things that conflict with the necessary conditions of experience. There is no particularly Kantian way of dealing with this problem. One reaction would be to suppose that modern physics has taken us beyond the world of appearances—saddled as they are with Kant's forms and categories—and closer to the things in themselves.[22] Another would be to admit that Kant's preferred principles are not necessary after all, that they can, and sometimes should be, revised. Either way, propositions once taken to be true will come to be modified, and the grounds for these modifications will be empirical.[23] At this point, the very distinction Kant's transcendental idealism was designed to found—the distinction between a priori and a posteriori truths about the world—emerges as a distinction without a difference.[24] Once again, pure empirical realism, without the transcendental perspective, presents itself as an alternative worth considering.[25]

My use of the phrase 'distinction without a difference' is meant to recall Quine's critique of Carnap. What I want to suggest now is that this echo is not misplaced, that it is illuminating to view Carnap's position on the a priori and Quine's reaction to it as a variation on the rise and fall of Kantianism as just rehearsed. Perhaps this is not implausible, given that Carnap began his career as a neo-Kantian. In any case, by the early 1930s, Carnap had produced his theory of logical syntax, which the historian Alberto Coffa describes as 'the first genuine alternative . . .'[26] to Kant's conception of the a priori' (Coffa 1991: 259).

---

[22] See e.g. Gödel (1946/9: 240, 244–6, 257–9).

[23] Körner (1970: 19) attempts what he calls a 'relativized' version of Kant's synthetic a priori principles. But in the end, he admits that philosophical argumentation has had and can have no evidential influence on changes in these principles (see 69–74). Presumably, then, these changes are made on empirical grounds.

[24] The historian Alberto Coffa (1991: ch. 10) describes the reluctant progress of twentieth-century neo-Kantians to this conclusion. See also Friedman (1983: ch. 1).

[25] This seems a fair description of one strain of Reichenbach's thinking. 'The development of science . . . has led away from Kantian metaphysics. . . . the synthetic principles of knowledge which Kant has regarded as a priori were recognized as a posteriori, as verifiable through experience only and as valid in the restricted sense of empirical hypotheses' (Reichenbach 1949: 307). According to Reichenbach, though Kant claimed to be giving an analysis of pure reason, his methods actually led to an account of (the conceptual underpinnings of) the scientific knowledge of his time (see M. Reichenbach 1965: p. xix). Reichenbach aimed to do the same job for Einsteinian physics (Reichenbach 1949: 310). Finally, on the methods available, he writes, 'modern science . . . has refused the authority of the philosopher who claims to know the truth from intuition, from insight into a world of ideas or into the nature of reason or the principles of being, or from whatever super-empirical source. There is no separate entrance to truth for philosophers. The path of the philosopher is indicated by that of the scientist.' (ibid. 310). This is clearly a version of proto-naturalism.

[26] The full quotation says that Wittgenstein's and Carnap's 'theories of philosophical grammar and of logical syntax may well be regarded as the first genuine alternatives to Kant's conception of the a priori.' The two 'trains of thought were largely independent of each other' (1991: 260).

As indicated earlier, the leading idea of Carnap's position is the linguistic framework. Consider, for example, a linguistic framework for talking about observable things and events in space and time, what Carnap calls 'the thing language' (Carnap 1950: 242–4). Such a language would include the usual logical apparatus–variables, predicates letters, function symbols, names—some logical axioms, and evidential rules specifying what counts as evidence for what. It would be part of this linguistic framework that, for example, certain sensory experiences would count as evidence for certain physical object claims. For speakers of this language, then, it is fairly easy to resolve the truth or falsity of a statement like 'there is a tree outside my window', and from this statement it will follow by pure logic—part of the language—that there are physical objects.

But this is not the resolution philosophers have in mind when they ask whether or not there are physical objects. What the philosopher wants answered is not a question asked inside the thing language—what Carnap calls an 'internal question'—but a question asked outside the thing language, perhaps prior to a decision on whether or not we are justified in speaking the thing language at all. The prior philosopher's question Carnap calls an 'external question'; he writes:

Realists give an affirmative answer, subjective idealists a negative one, and the controversy goes on for centuries without being resolved. And it cannot be solved because it is framed in a wrong way. To be real in the scientific sense means to be an element of the system [i.e. the linguistic framework]; hence this concept cannot be meaningfully applied to the system itself. (Carnap 1950: 243)

In other words, the evidential rules for resolving reality claims about things are to be found inside the thing language; to ask a reality question outside that framework is to pose a pseudo-question.

There is, however, a perfectly reasonable question that can be asked outside the thing language, and that is: should we adopt the thing language?[27] The philosopher imagines that there is a right or wrong answer to this question, based on the prior external question, but Carnap considers it a matter for purely conventional decision in which there is no issue of truth or falsity and tolerance should reign:

In logic, there are no morals. Everyone is at liberty to build up his own logic, i.e. his own form of language, as he wishes. All that is required of him is that, if he wishes to discuss it, he must state his methods clearly, and give syntactic rules instead of philosophical arguments. (Carnap 1934: 52)

Naturally, our reasons for choosing one linguistic framework over another will involve various factual considerations—its effectiveness, fruitfulness, simplicity—

---

[27] Carnap recognizes that the question is odd in the case of this particular linguistic framework because 'there is usually no deliberate choice because we all have accepted the thing language early in our lives as a matter of course' (1950: 243). But this isn't so for other frameworks e.g. the atom framework (see below).

but these are pragmatic reasons in favour of adopting the new framework, not theoretical evidence of its correctness. In Carnap's words:

[I]t would be wrong to describe this situation by saying: 'The fact of the efficiency of the thing language is confirming evidence for the reality of the thing world'; we should rather say instead: 'This fact makes it advisable to accept the thing language.' (Carnap 1950: 244)

To see how this bears on the question of a priority, suppose we've adopted the thing language, and we are considering whether or not to add a new linguistic framework that combines the thing language with something new, the number language. This would mean adding relation symbols for things and numbers, number-theoretic names, predicates symbols, function symbols, axioms (say, first-order Peano Arithmetic), plus evidential rules that would allow us to make assertions like 'there are three apples on the table.' We can well imagine that pragmatic considerations would prompt us to adopt these new conventions.

Now compare the grounds on which our new linguistic framework allows us to make various knowledge claims: if we have experiences so-and-so, we can combine those with the relevant evidential rule and conclude that 'there is a tree outside my window'; if we form a numerical term 5 (SSSS0), we can combine it with '0 is a number' and 'for all x, if x is a number, then Sx is a number' to conclude that '5 is a number.' To justifiably assert that there is a tree outside my window, I need to have certain experiences, but to justifiably assert that 5 is a number, I need nothing beyond the linguistic framework itself. In other words, '5 is a number' is true by virtue of our linguistic conventions; it is, in Carnap's sense, analytic. Thus, '5 is a number' is a priori, and 'there is a tree outside my window' is not. (Notice also that the evidential rule that allows me to infer from my experiences to the assertion about the tree is part of the linguistic framework, and hence a priori.) This is Carnap's new account of a priority.

To the extent that it makes sense to ask questions about Carnap's view in terms borrowed from Kant's, I think it is fair to say that this new account of the a priori does not deliver synthetic truths, but purely linguistic ones. And, obviously, Carnap's a priori truths are not absolute or necessary; they are dependent on conventional choices. Still, there is an important structural similarity between the two positions: in both cases, we have to distinguish two perspectives from which a question can be asked. For Kant, these are the empirical and transcendental perspectives, which deliver different answers to a question like 'is the rain real?': empirically real, transcendentally (at least partly) ideal. For Carnap, these are the internal and external perspectives, which deliver different answers to a question like 'do physical objects exist?': internal to the thing language, the existence of physical objects follows logically from the fact that there are, e.g. trees; external to the thing language, the question is a pragmatic one about the advisability of adopting certain conventions. And for both philosophers, there is a danger of confusion at the higher level: for Kant, we must not be led into thinking that we are gaining knowledge of transcendental objects, or things in themselves; for

Carnap, we must not confuse reasons for adopting a linguistic framework with reasons for believing that its objects really exist, in some external sense. So there is a strong analogy between the old and the new.

In fact, the analogy carries over into some of the difficulties associated with the higher level of inquiry. For Kant, the nature and status of transcendental knowledge proved a mystery. For Carnap, a similar question arises about the status of our meditations on linguistic frameworks: where do these take place? Inside another linguistic framework? If not, we need an account of the non-conventional meta-language; if so, we need to understand why we should adopt the views Carnap espouses over various alternative meta-languages. For example, why should we adopt a linguistic framework that includes the principle of tolerance? What is it to be tolerant about tolerance? As in the case of Kant, these meta-questions are disputed by interpreters of Carnap.[28] Once again, we might well wonder about the tenability of the higher perspective.

Let me leave that problem for now and turn to Quine's criticism of Carnap; I hope to isolate one particular strand from their debate. To see how, consider: when it comes to judging linguistic frameworks, Carnap tells us that 'The purposes for which the language is intended to be used . . . will determine which factors are relevant for the decision' (Carnap 1950: 244).

So the factors involved in choosing linguistic frameworks will be as varied as the goals those frameworks are intended to serve. Our focus, however, is on linguistic frameworks intended for scientific uses; presumably the thing language is the first such language. Carnap tells us that its purpose is 'communicating factual knowledge', that it is judged by such factors as its 'efficiency, fruitfulness and simplicity of use' (ibid.).

Now suppose that we have adopted a scientific framework—complete with logical and evidential rules—and we are considering, internally, a new scientific hypothesis. What sorts of considerations will be raised? Quine suggests that the virtues of such hypotheses are roughly these: simplicity, familiarity of principle, scope, fecundity, and consistency with experiment (see Quine 1955). There may be a subtle trading off of one virtue against another, but an hypothesis that is successful by these criteria is considered well confirmed.

Now suppose, by way of contrast, that we have adopted a scientific framework, and we are considering, not the confirmation of an internal hypothesis, but a move to another, more inclusive linguistic framework; this time, we are considering what Carnap calls an 'ontological question', that is, the addition of syntactic apparatus and evidential rules for a new sort of entities, like atoms, or sets. What sorts of considerations will be raised? Quine's suggestion is that the very same theoretical virtues will be relevant this time around:

[28] See Coffa (1991: ch. 17) for the view that 'behind the first level semantic conventionalism there is a second level semantic factualism' (ibid. 322). For an opposing perspective, see Goldfarb (OAC).

Our acceptance of an ontology is, I think, similar in principle to our acceptance of a scientific theory, say a system of physics: we adopt, at least insofar as we are reasonable, the simplest conceptual scheme into which the disordered fragments of raw experience can be fitted and arranged. Our ontology is determined once we have fixed upon the over-all conceptual scheme which is to accommodate science in the broadest sense; and the considerations which determine a reasonable construction of any part of that conceptual scheme, for example, the biological or the physical part, are not different in kind from the considerations which determine a reasonable construction of the whole. To whatever extent the adoption of any system of scientific theory may be said to be a matter of language, the same—but no more—may be said of the adoption of an ontology. (Quine 1948: 16–17)

In other words, the methods used to evaluate ordinary scientific hypotheses are the same as those used to decide Carnap's ontological questions.[29] Thus, Quine argues, there is no methological basis for the distinction Carnap draws.[30]

The parallel with the Kantian saga so recently rehearsed is obvious. The problem for the twentieth-century Kantian is that the criteria for modifying our intuitive and categorical principles are indistinguishable from those for modifying our scientific beliefs generally. This Quinean objection to Carnap is that the criteria for adopting linguistic frameworks are indistinguishable from the criteria for adopting scientific hypotheses generally. In both cases, the cherished distinction seems groundless.

Quine's response to this situation is analogous to the response that tempted us in the Kantian case: forgo the transcendental level; fall back on empirical realism neat. In the more recent context, this is Quinean naturalism: 'the recognition that it is within science itself, and not in some prior philosophy, that reality is to be identified and described' (Quine 1981a: 21) Carnap's external pseudo-questions—'are there physical objects?' or 'are there numbers?'—are actually ordinary scientific questions: 'Ontological questions, under this view, are on a par with questions of natural science' (Quine 1951a: 45).

Epistemological questions are also to be addressed from within science:

Naturalism does not repudiate epistemology, but assimilates it to empirical psychology. Science itself tells us that our information about the world is limited to irritations of our surfaces, and then the epistemological question is in turn a question within science: the question how we human animals can have managed to arrive at science from such limited information. (Quine 1975: 72)

[29] Carnap sometimes argues that the methods are different because the question of whether or not to adopt a linguistic framework is based on considerations that are a matter of degree, while the question of the truth of a scientific claim is all or nothing: 'these questions [as to the pragmatic virtues of the thing language] cannot be identified with the question of realism. They are not yes-no questions, but questions of degree' (Carnap 1950: 244). But the comparison is faulty: the considerations that lead us to adopt a scientific claim are also matters of degree.

[30] At least, insofar as it applies to scientific frameworks. If we imagine a framework with a very different goal, say to generate sentences with particular aesthetic qualities, then the internal criteria for deciding which sentence to 'assert' might be very different from the external criteria for deciding which such framework to adopt.

To describe naturalistic philosophy in general, Quine appeals to a favourite image:

Neurath has likened science to a boat which, if we are to rebuild it, we must rebuild plank by plank while staying afloat in it. (Quine 1960: 3) The naturalistic philosopher begins his reasoning within the inherited world theory as a going concern. He tentatively believes all of it, but believes also that some unidentified portions are wrong. He tries to improve, clarify, and understand the system from within. He is the busy sailor adrift on Neurath's boat. (Quine 1975: 72)

For the naturalist, there is no higher perspective, where transcendental or other extra-scientific considerations hold sway. The naturalist operates 'from the point of view of our own science, which is the only point of view I can offer' (Quine 1981b: 181).

A similar rejection of the transcendental level is found in Arthur Fine's 'natural ontological attitude', or NOA.[31] The context here is the realism-anti-realism debates of the late 1970s and early 1980s, exemplified, for example, by Putnam's attack on 'metaphysical realism'[32] and van Fraassen's agnosticism about unobservables.[33] As Fine understands it, the impulse towards realism is actually based in 'homely' beliefs, which, he says

I will put it in the first person. I certainly trust the evidence of my senses, on the whole, with regard to the existence and features of everyday objects. And I have similar confidence in the system of 'check, double-check, check, triple-check' of scientific investigation, as well as the other safeguards built into the institutions of science. So, if the scientists tell me that there really are molecules, and atoms, and y/J particles, and, who knows, maybe even quarks, then so be it.[34] (Fine 1986: 126–7)

From this point of view, we can ask after the relations between humans, as described in psychology, physiology, linguistics, etc., and the world, as described in physics, chemistry, geology, etc., and draw conclusions about the relations between sentences and the world, an investigation that may result in a correspondence theory of truth or a deflationary theory of truth or some other theory of truth or no theory of truth at all, depending how things go.[35] But however they go, this theory will be just one part of our overall scientific theory of the world.

---

[31] See Fine (1986 and 1996a). In the latter (1996a: 176–7), Fine allies NOA with Quinean naturalism while rejecting some of its descendants. Much as I applaud the general outlines of NOA, I fear I must also distance myself from some of Fine's further views (e.g. see Fine 1996b).

[32] See e.g. Putnam (1981).

[33] See van Fraassen (1980).

[34] This quotation may suggest that NOA eschews the normative, but this isn't so (see Fine 1996a: 177–8). Whatever Fine's precise views on the subject, Quine explicitly locates the norms of science within science (see Quine 1981b: 181), and I follow him in this see my (1977: III.3).

[35] I take this to be the debate that began with Field (1972) and Leeds (1978). Horwich (1990) presents a recent summary. By taking this to be a scientific question on which the jury is still out, I find myself in disagreement with Quine (see Quine 1970: 10–13), and perhaps also with Fine (cf. Fine 1986: 130 and 134; 1996a: 184; and 1996b).

On these matters, Putnam and van Fraassen agree with the NOAer, but they don't stop here; each, in his own way, goes beyond science, to a higher level. There Putnam distinguishes metaphysical realism, which adds to NOA's core an extra-scientific correspondence theory of truth, and internal realism, which adds to the same core a Peircean analysis of truth as warranted assertability in the ideal limit.[36] Focused on the problem of ontology rather than truth, van Fraassen adds an extra level of epistemological analysis where we must abstain from belief in molecules and atoms and electrons, despite our acceptance of these same entities for scientific purposes. Here the holder of our homely beliefs will be tempted to object that atoms *really* do exist, thus embodying Kant's 'incautious listener', faced with 'a question . . . absurd in itself', who then gives 'an answer where none is required' (A58/B82–3): he wants to insist on the reality of atoms, but all the genuine scientific evidence, though accepted at the lower level, has been ruled out of bounds at the higher level; the frustrated Scientific Realist ends by stomping his foot. Fine's proposal is that we rest with the natural ontological attitude and resist the temptation to engage in extra-scientific debate.

To subject our naturalism to the same challenge put to both Kant and Carnap, we should ask: is naturalism itself a scientific thesis? I think the right answer to this question is that naturalism is not a thesis at all, but an approach. The naturalistic philosopher is the Neurathian sailor, working within science to understand, clarify, and improve science; she will treat philosophical questions on a par with other scientific questions, insofar as this is possible; faced with first philosophical demands—that is, questions and solutions that require extra-scientific methods—she will respond with befuddlement, for she knows no such methods; from her scientific perspective, she is sceptical that there are such methods, but she has no a priori argument that there are such methods, but she has no a priori argument that there are none; until such methods are explained and justified, she will simply set aside the challenges of first philosophy and get on with her naturalistic business. Naturalism contrasts with both Kantianism and Carnapianism in forgoing any 'higher-level' considerations.

Now while I am in hearty agreement with these naturalistic sentiments, I find myself less comfortable with the Quinean argument that got us here: the time has come for me to own up to my departures from Quinean orthodoxy. These are several,[37] but the one relevant here concerns the thoroughgoing pragmatism that

---

[36] There is some irony in Putnam's move to the extra scientific perspective, given that he was once a devout naturalist: 'it is silly to agree that a reason for believing that p warrants accepting p in all scientific circumstances, and then to add "but even so it is not *good enough*". Such a judgment could only be made if one accepted a tran-scientific method as superior to the scientific method; but this philosopher, at least, has no interest in doing *that*' (1971: 356).

[37] My (1997) describes additional disagreements over the force of indispensability arguments and the treatment of pure mathematics.

underlies the objection to Carnap we've been considering.[38] I've told this story in some detail elsewhere (1997: II.6), so I will be as brief as possible here.

Consider, for illustration, the case of atomic theory. Attention to the historical details of the debate over atoms, as it stood at the turn of the century, reveals some surprising features. First, by any account of confirmation that depends on an enumeration of general theoretical virtues (like Quine's), atomic theory was extremely well confirmed; it was central to chemistry in all theories of composition and combination and to physics in the wide-ranging kinetic theory. Second, despite this, there was still scepticism among respectable scientists for respectable reasons about the existence of atoms. In 1905, Einstein set out to provide the theoretical grounds for a proof of atomic reality, and soon thereafter, Perrin produced experimental results. Only then did the scientific community as a whole embrace atoms. The moral of the story is that no amount of general theoretical support was enough; the new unobservables had to be 'detected' by a sufficiently direct procedure.

Now consider this case from the perspective of the debate between Carnap and Quine. For Carnap, the question 'are there atoms?' is prime example of an external ontological question, just the sort of thing that van Fraassen and the foot-stomping Scientific Realist would vigorously debate. Carnap would replace this external pseudo-question with a legitimate one—should we adopt the atoms language?—and this question he would answer on pragmatic grounds. Quine, regarding the original ontological question as an ordinary scientific question, would decide it on the same pragmatic grounds. But historical analysis reveals that the question of atoms, however interpreted, was not, in fact, decided on such grounds. Atoms were still considered problematic after they had passed every pragmatic test imaginable.

Now consider, for contrast, another example, one not so neatly comprised in a single historical episode, but I think no less compelling for that. In the beginning, the motion of a medium-sized physical object was represented by a table: at time t, the object is at position x, at t', position x', and so on. Eventually, this crude approach gave way to our current notion of a function from real numbers to real numbers—with the independent variable representing time and the dependent variable representing position—which allowed the powerful methods of the calculus to be applied. Nowadays, space and time have been replaced by space-time, and ordinary calculus by more elaborate analysis, but the principle of using continuum mathematics for such purposes has remained the same. The success of this way of doing things can hardly be exaggerated.

Notice that this account of motion depends on a strong assumption about the

---

[38] This is not Quine's only objection; e.g. in his (1951*b*), Quine argues that Carnap's distinction between external and internal questions rests on a prior distinction between 'category questions' and 'subclass questions', which he dismisses as 'a distinction which is not invariant under logically irrelevant changes of typography' (ibid. 210).

structure of physical reality, namely that space-time is continuous, that it is, or is isomorphic to, a continuous manifold. Despite this, physicists still consider the question of the continuity of time and space to be open. On the face of it, this case parallels the case of atomic theory: the pragmatic success of a theory is not enough to fully confirm it. But, in fact, or so I would claim, there are striking disanalogies. On the one hand, the continuity of time and space have not been a subject of debate in the same sense that atoms were before Einstein and Perrin: no one worries over this use of continuum mathematics, no one demands experimental confirmation, no one demands reform.[39] On the other hand, the success of the structural assumption that space-time is continuous has not counted in favour of its truth: despite the overall confirmation of the theory, physicists consider the question to be wide open. In cases like these, it's hard to avoid the conclusion that these assumptions are not being treated on the same epistemic terms as other scientific hypotheses, that the conditions for adoption are not as stringent and the confirmatory benefits of their success are negligible. Indeed, it seems that scientists feel free to use whatever mathematical apparatus they find convenient and effective, without regard for the abstract ontology required, and more to the point, without regard for the physical structural assumptions presupposed.

Of course, I can't be considered to have argued for this claim here,[40] but supposing it is correct, then there is a distinction to be drawn, within science, between hypotheses that are subjected to the full range of empirical testing and available for full confirmation, and those that are not; indeed, hypotheses in the second category might well be described as having been adopted on pragmatic, conventional grounds. Essentially, what I am objecting to is Quine's blanket pragmatic account of the method of science; it seems to me that the practice of actual science is much more varied that any such general account allows. And, in particular, there does seem to be room for the sort of methodological distinction on which Carnap rests his two-level picture. The line between the conventional and the ordinary scientific hypotheses doesn't fall quite where Carnap would have it—the embrace of atoms was not a pragmatic linguistic change but an internal, scientific one—but there remains room to classify such hypotheses as the continuity of space-time as conventional/pragmatic, and for so distinguishing it from theoretical/empirical hypotheses like the existence of atoms. Given the centrality of the two-level model to Carnap's account of the a priori and given that Quine's views lead him to reject the distinction between a priori and a posteriori entirely,

---

[39] I am ignoring the fact that anomalies in quantum field theory, anomalies with roots as far back as classical electrodynamics, have led some physicists to question the small-scale continuity of space-time. (See my 1997: II.6, for discussion.) For our purposes, it is enough to notice that another sort of objection was advanced against atoms before Einstein and Perrin: that their existence was too theoretical, that it hadn't been sufficiently verified. No such objection has been raised to continuous space-time.

[40] Again, my (1997: II.6) contains some more detail.

we should take a moment to reconsider: could a viable two-level account of the a priori be based on this methodological distinction?[41]

As I've said, I myself favour a one-level view, a version of naturalism, largely because I don't believe in a perspective outside of science from which science, or even scientific language, is evaluated. The nagging difficulties that arise when we try to characterize the methods of that higher level of inquiry are symptoms of the disorientation that sets in when we imagine ourselves to be operating outside of science. In the case of Carnap, or rather, the neo-Carnap we're imagining, I think the interplay between conventional/pragmatic and the theoretical/empirical is too involved and too important to permit the two to be segregated as the two-level picture requires. By the time I'm done here, I hope to have made this claim plausible.

That said, let me suspend (for the moment) this question about the two-level neo-Carnapian to consider one last approach to the a priori. Quine, as we've noted, rejects the distinction when he moves to his naturalistic web of belief, explaining away our impression that some truths are a priori as an illusion of a difference in kind created by a difference in degree. But given that we've departed from Quine's uniform vision of scientific methods, perhaps this conclusion comes too quickly for us. We wonder: does the rejection of a two-level view, by itself, doom prospects for the a priori? To put it another way: can our naturalist give an account of the a priori without appeal to a 'higher level' of inquiry?

For the record, Quine figures that the external–internal distinction is not essential to Carnap's account:

No more than the distinction between *analytic* and *synthetic* is needed in support of Carnap's doctrine that statements commonly thought of as ontological . . .[[42]] are analytic or contradictory given the language. No more than the distinction between analytic and synthetic is needed in support of his doctrine that the statements commonly thought of as ontological are proper matters of contention only in the form of linguistic proposals. (Quine 1951*b*: 210)

Without the higher level, such an account will lack some of the virtues of Carnap's two-level version, simply because the two-level view allows us to ask after the status of a given statement in two distinct ways: at the higher level, we consider various options and plump for one on conventional/pragmatic grounds,

---

[41] I do not assume that a neo-Carnapian could, in fact, draw a workable distinction between the empirical and the conventional based on the methodological observations rehearsed here, but I will extend the benefit of the doubt for the sake of argument.

[42] In this hiatus, Quine gives examples: 'statements such as "There are physical objects", "There are classes", "There are numbers". The first of these seems to me problematic. On my understanding of the thing language, it is the evidential rules that are analytic—such-and-such counts as evidence that there is a tree outside my window—and it takes experiential input to draw the conclusion that the tree exists. 'There are physical objects' then follows from the existence of the tree, but this conclusion does not follow from features of the linguistic framework alone; it is not analytic.

but once we'd adopted the winning linguistic framework and begun to work within it, as long as we continue to speak that language, the framework principles are analytic and unrevisable. In other words, a statement that's optional and revisable when viewed at the higher level is necessary and unrevisable when viewed from the lower level, and thus, robustly a priori at that lower level. When the naturalist drops the higher level, all these considerations are placed side-by-side; the statement in question is recognized as the revisable result of a conventional/pragmatic decision.

What might be salvaged—and this is what Quine has in mind—is a distinction between revisions that are changes in theory and revisions that are changes in language, and it is this distinction that Carnap never gave up:

> I should make a distinction between two kinds of readjustment in the case of a conflict with experience, namely, between a change in the language, and a mere change in or addition of, a truth-value ascribed to an indeterminate statement . . . A change of the first kind constitutes a radical alteration, sometimes a revolution, and it occurs only at certain historically decisive points in the development of science. On the other hand, changes of the second kind occur every minute. (Carnap 1963: 921)

If this distinction can be drawn, then even the one-level naturalist can say that an analytic statement is unrevisable *short of a change in language*, and in that sense, might be considered a priori.

Quine's reaction to this possibility, famously, is to reject the distinction between analytic and synthetic. Whatever we think of his arguments, even if a scientific inquiry into the semantics of natural language, within linguistic theory, were to conclude that 'Bachelors are unmarried' is true by virtue of the meanings of the terms involved, I sincerely doubt that any such inquiry would generate the outcome that 'continuous manifold' is part of the meaning of the term 'space', or that the axiom of replacement is part of the meaning of the term 'set'. So I will follow Quine in rejecting this as a viable account of the a priori.[43] But our methodological inquiries—part of our scientific study of science itself—suggest that the conventional/pragmatic vs. theoretical/empirical distinction, which Quine also rejects, might be revived without appeal to an external level of analysis. So perhaps there is room for the a priori on a one-level view, after all, making use of this methodological distinction.[44]

To see the trouble with this approach, consider the notion of knowledge. On the two-level model, the conventional/pragmatic considerations are raised externally, where knowledge is not an issue; once we adopt the linguistic framework, we have a scientific account of what counts as knowledge, and the elements of the

---

[43] I mean 'viable' in the Kantian tradition of delivering some (seemingly) contentful scientific or mathematical claims (like the examples in the text, the sort of thing Kant might count as synthetic) as a priori. (Notice that none of this discussion concerns the status of elementary logic.)

[44] See n. 41.

linguistic framework count as a priori knowledge by that standard. On the one-level approach, the conventional/pragmatic considerations and the theoretical/empirical considerations are both raised internally; we recognize internally that some hypotheses are adopted as a result of full empirical testing and confirmation, while others are adopted for other reasons. Given our scientific account of knowledge, it seems unavoidable that the former hypotheses will count as knowledge, while the latter will not. Our discussion of the continuity of space-time brings this point into high relief: it would seem odd to say that scientists know space-time to be continuous. Space-time is so represented, but the question of its actual continuity remains open. Finally, if we don't know something, we can't be said to know it a priori. So it seems a neo-Carnapian defence of the distinction between changes of meaning and changes of theory that rests on the methodological distinction between the conventional/pragmatic and the theoretical/empirical elements of our theory will not support a viable notion of a priori knowledge.

This leaves the one-level theorist with the brute fact of this methodological distinction. As naturalistic philosophers of science, we will try to understand and explain this phenomenon of scientific practice, even if we can't use it to construct a notion of a priority: to say that some hypotheses are adopted for conventional/pragmatic reasons is only the barest beginning of an account of how such hypotheses function. In particular cases, a range of deep and important methodological questions arise. Sometimes, we are unsure whether or not a given hypothesis is, in fact, conventional/pragmatic (e.g. physical geometry, and careful analysis is required.[45] Sometimes, conventional/pragmatic hypotheses are adopted even when they are known to be false, like the hypothesis that matter is continuous in fluid dynamics; in such cases, we need to ask what it is about the world that is reflected in that idealization, what it is about the world that supports the effectiveness of that idealization.[46] Sometimes, the status of a conventional/pragmatic hypothesis is unknown, like the hypothesis of continuous space-time. (In fact, I suspect we are willing to adopt hypotheses like continuous space-time in the spirit we do because we are confident that even if they should turn out to be false, they will remain good idealizations for many purposes.) In such cases, we need to ask whether the hypothesis is amenable to further testing: if not, why not?, and if so, how? These are among the important naturalistic

---

[45] e.g. consider Friedman's debate with the proto-naturalist Reichenbach on the status of geometry: Friedman aims to show that empirically equivalent theories with alternative geometries are not equally valid, as Reichenbach claims, but rather, that 'there are methodological principles or criteria . . . that are capable of singling out one theory from a class of empirically equivalent theories' (Friedman 1983: 268). Friedman insists that 'These criteria can be justified only by showing that they tend to produce true hypotheses in actual scientific practice in the real world . . . Hence, any justification of our actual inductive methods must itself be empirical' (ibid. 273). For these two, the debate over the conventional or empirical status of geometry takes place within a scientific (i.e. naturalistic) study of science.

[46] I am grateful to Mark Wilson for making the importance of these issues clear to me.

inquiries that emerge out of our foiled pursuit of a one-level account of the a priori.

Finally, let me double back to the two-level neo-Carnapian account of the a priori that we left hanging a moment ago. At the time, I suggested that the interplay between conventional/pragmatic and the theoretical/empirical is too involved and too important to permit the two to be segregated as the two-level picture requires. We can now see more clearly what I had in mind. If the conventional/pragmatic is forcibly separated from the theoretical/empirical, if the decision on scientific language must be made before scientific inquiry begins, then the differences between hypotheses of these two sorts cannot be studied side-by-side, using scientific methods. This means that the important naturalistic inquiries just sketched cannot find a home: from the external perspective, we are not doing science, but pragmatics, so questions of literal truth or falsehood cannot be raised; from the internal perspective, the linguistic framework is a given, known a priori, not subject to further debate. In other words, because the pragmatic considerations arise at the higher level, their interactions with internal facts cannot be discussed internally. So the trade-off is between a two-level view that provides an account of the a priori, but blocks a certain style of scientific inquiry into science, and a one-level view that fails to underwrite the a priori–a posteriori distinction, but encourages this style of inquiry into science. For my money, there is no contest.

Let me sum up. I have traced the role of an extra-scientific level of analysis in the Kantian and the Carnapian accounts of a priori knowledge, and I have suggested that such accounts suffer from two serious difficulties: how to explain the status of this extra-scientific analysis, and how to differentiate revisions in the purportedly a priori claims from ordinary scientific progress. In my opinion, these difficulties are symptoms of a more basic error, an error to be avoided by adopting a one-level, naturalistic approach, that is, by adopting the methods and results of science and working from within to understand, clarify, and improve them. Any discussion of naturalism these days is—overtly or covertly—an attempt to define the term; I've tried to locate the fundamental naturalistic impulse in a stubborn scepticism about any of the recurring two-level philosophies, about any philosophy that posits an extra-scientific perspective from which to view science. I've suggested that naturalism of this sort turns up a methodological contrast within science between hypotheses subjected to the full range of empirical testing and potentially confirmed thereby and hypotheses adopted for conventional, pragmatic reasons. A neo-Carnapian might hope to revive a two-level or a one-level account of the a priori based on this distinction, and I've explained why I think the one is not advisable and the other not viable. But while naturalism may doom the time-honoured notion of a priori knowledge, it also highlights new methodological questions about the detail of scientific practice, a trade-off that I for one am quite willing to accept.

References

Allison, Henry (1976), 'The non-spatiality of things in themselves for Kant', *Journal of the History of Philosophy* 14: 313–21.

—— (1983), *Kant's Transcendental Idealism* (New Haven, Conn.: Yale University Press).

Ameriks, Karl (1982), 'Recent work on Kant's theoretical philosophy', *American Philosophical Quarterly* 19: 1–24.

Beck, Lewis White (1976), 'Toward a meta-critique of pure reason', repr. in his *Essays on Kant and Hume* (New Haven, Conn.: Yale University Press, 1978): 20–37.

Bennett, Jonathan (1971), *Locke, Berkeley, Hume* (Oxford: Oxford University Press).

Berkeley, George (1710), *Principles of Human Knowledge*, repr. in D. Armstrong (ed.), *Berkeley's Philosophical Writings* (New York: Macmillan, 1965).

Bird, Graham (1962), *Kant's Theory of Knowledge* (New York: Routledge & Kegan Paul).

—— (1982), 'Kant's transcendental idealism', in G. Vesey (ed.), *Idealism Past and Present* (Cambridge: Cambridge University Press): 71-92.

Carnap, Rudolf (1934), *Logical Syntax of Language*, trans. A. Smeaton (London: Routledge & Kegan Paul, 1937).

—— (1950), 'Empiricism, semantics and ontology', repr. in P. Benacerraf and H. Putnam (eds.), *Philosophy of Mathematics*, 2nd edn. (Cambridge: Cambridge University Press, 1983): 241–57.

—— (1963), 'Replies and systematic expositions', in P. Schilpp (ed.), *The Philosophy of Rudolf Carnap* (La Salle, Ill.: Open Court): 859–1013.

Coffa, Alberto (1991), *The Semantic Tradition from Kant to Carnap: to the Vienna Station*, L. Wessels (ed.) (Cambridge: Cambridge University Press).

Field, Hartry (1972), 'Tarski's theory of truth', *Journal of Philosophy* 69, pp. 347–75.

Fine, Arthur (1986), *The Shaky Game* (Chicago: University of Chicago Press).

—— (1996a), 'Afterword', in 2nd edn. (1986): 173–-201.

—— (1996b), 'Science made up: constructivist sociology of scientific knowledge', in P. Galison and D. Stump (eds.), *The Disunity of Science* (Stanford: Stanford University Press): 231–54.

Friedman, Michael (1983), *Foundations of Space-time Theories* (Princeton: Princeton University Press).

Goldfarb, Warren (OAC), 'On Alberto Coffa's *The Semantic Tradition from Kant to Carnap*' unpublished.

Gödel, Kurt (1946/9), 'Some observations about the relationship between theory of relativity and Kantian philosophy', in his *Collected Works*, iii, S. Feferman *et al.* (eds.) (Oxford: Oxford University Press, 1995): 230–59.

Guyer, Paul (1987), *Kant and the Claims of Knowledge* (Cambridge: Cambridge University Press).

Horwich, Paul (1990), *Truth* (Oxford: Blackwell).

Kant, Immanuel (1781/7), *Critique of Pure Reason*, trans. Norman Kemp Smith (New York: St Martin's Press, 1965). (References to the Critique in the text are given in the customary style: the page number in the first (A) edition followed by the page number in the second (B) edition.)

—— (1783), *Prolegomena to Any Future Metaphysics*, trans. L. W. Beck (Indianapolis: Bobbs-Merrill, 1950).

Körner, Stephan (1955), *Kant* (London: Penguin Books).

Körner, Stephan (1970), *Categorial Frameworks* (Oxford: Blackwell).

Leeds, Stephen (1978), 'Theories of reference and truth', *Erkenntnis* 13: 111–29.

Locke, John (1690), *An Essay Concerning Human Understanding* (New York: Dover, 1959).

Maddy, Penelope (1997), *Naturalism in Mathematics* (Oxford: Oxford University Press).

Matthews, H. E. (1969), 'Strawson on transcendental idealism', *Philosophical Quarterly* 19: 204–20.

Pitcher, George (1977), *Berkeley* (London: Routledge & Kegan Paul).

Prichard, H. A. (1909), *Kant's Theory of Knowledge* (Oxford: Oxford University Press).

Putnam, Hilary (1971), 'Philosophy of Logic', repr. in his *Philosophical Papers*, ii, 2nd edn. (Cambridge: Cambridge University Press, 1979): 323–57.

—— (1981), *Reason, Truth and History* (Cambridge: Cambridge University Press).

Quine, W. V. (1948), 'On what there is', repr. in his (1980): 1–19.

—— (1951*a*), 'Two dogmas of empiricism', repr. in his (1980): 20–46.

—— (1951*b*), 'Carnap's view on ontology', repr. in his (1976): 203–11.

—— (1955), 'Posits and reality', repr. in his (1976): 246–57.

—— (1960), *Word and Object* (Cambridge, Mass.: MIT Press).

—— (1970), *Philosophy of Logic* (Englewood Cliffs, NJ: Prentice-Hall).

—— (1975), 'Five milestones of empiricism', repr. in *Theories and Things* (Cambridge, Mass.: Harvard University Press): 67–72.

—— (1976), *The Ways of Paradox*, revised edn. (Cambridge, Mass.: Harvard University Press).

—— (1980), *From a Logical Point of View*, 2nd edn. (Cambridge, Mass: Harvard University Press).

—— (1981*a*), 'Things and their place in theories', in (1981b) 1–23.

—— (1981*b*), *Theories and Things* (Cambridge, Mass: Harvard University Press).

Reichenbach, Hans (1920), *The Theory of Relativity and A Priori Knowledge*, trans. M. Reichenbach (Berkeley and Los Angeles: University of California Press, 1965).

—— (1949), 'The Philosophical significance of the theory of relativity', in P. A. Schilpp (ed.), *Albert Einstein: Philosopher-Scientist* (La Salle, Ill.: Open Court): 287–311.

Reichenbach, Maria (1965), 'Introduction to Reichenbach' (1920): pp. xi–xliv.

Strawson, P. F. (1966), *The Bounds of Sense* (London: Methuen).

Van Fraassen, Bas (1980), *The Scientific Image* (Oxford: Oxford University Press).

6

Apriority as an Evaluative Notion

Hartry Field

A priori justification is often thought mysterious or out of keeping with a naturalistic view of the world; strong forms of a priori justification that involve empirical indefeasibility are often thought especially mysterious. While this is no doubt correct for *excessive* claims of a priority—for instance, claims to a priori access to features of the physical world—I will argue that it is incorrect if intended as a claim about the existence of any apriority at all.[1] What is mysterious in most forms of (non-excessive) apriorism isn't the apriorism itself but the background assumptions about epistemology. But in questioning these background assumptions, I will be producing an account of apriority that few apriorists will like.

1. THE CONCEPT OF APRIORITY

Let's define a *weakly a priori* proposition as one that can be reasonably believed without empirical evidence;[2] an *empirically indefeasible* proposition as one that admits no empirical evidence against it;[3] and an *a priori* proposition as one that is both weakly a priori and empirically indefeasible. Some writers use 'a priori' in a way that imposes no empirical indefeasibility requirement, but it seems to me that that removes the main philosophical interest of apriority: traditional debates about the apriority of logic and Euclidean geometry have largely concerned the issue of whether any empirical evidence could count against them. Another reason for keeping an indefeasibility requirement will be given later in this section.

Thanks to Ned Block, Paul Boghossian, Stephen Schiffer, and Nick Zangwill for extremely helpful discussions.

[1] The mystery that excessive claims to apriority would create is briefly discussed in n. 19. I believe that there is no analogous mystery for apriorism about logic, or for apriorism about the basic features of scientific method.

[2] Here and throughout, 'reasonable' will mean 'epistemically reasonable': crassly pragmatic motivations for and against believing are not to be taken into account.

[3] 'Empirically indefeasible' may be too weak a term for what I've just defined: the term suggests only that there can never be *sufficient* empirical evidence against it to outweigh any initial plausibility it might have. But it isn't easy to find examples that meet the weaker condition but not the stronger, and I will continue to use the term in the stronger sense.

The empirical indefeasibility requirement does need to be either restricted or interpreted delicately if it is not to immediately rule out a priori knowledge. As a first illustration (emphasized in Kitcher 1983), the credibility of any proposition could be diminished by evidence that well-regarded experts don't accept it. This first illustration doesn't seem to me very interesting: perhaps it shows that we must impose a slight restriction on empirical indefeasibility to allow for defeasibility by the opinions of others,[4] but surely it doesn't suggest that we should give up an indefeasibility requirement entirely (so that we could reasonably regard a proposition of logic as a priori while at the same time granting that experimental results in quantum mechanics could tell against it).

But there is a more interesting argument against an empirical indefeasibility requirement. The argument has two steps. First, empirical indefeasibility seems equivalent to *empirical unaugmentability*: the condition that there can be no empirical evidence *for* the proposition. Their equivalence follows from the hard-to-contest principle that an experience counts as evidence for a proposition only if some contrary experience would count as evidence against it and vice versa. But second, as has often been noted, complex and unobvious logical truths can admit empirical justification without diminishing their claims to a priori status. For instance, a proposition of form $((p \supset q) \supset p) \supset p$ is obviously entailed by p, so someone who didn't realize it was a logical truth might empirically justify it by empirically justifying p. So a proposition that should be an extremely plausible candidate for apriority seems empirically augmentable and therefore (given the equivalence) empirically defeasible.

The best way to deal with this argument, is to distinguish empirical justification and empirical evidence: evidence involves something like *ideal* justification, ideal in that limitations of computational capacity are ignored. The idea is that reflection on the logical facts reveals that the evidence for p doesn't raise the 'ideal credibility' of the logical truth $((p \supset q) \supset p) \supset p$: for ideally that would have been fully credible to begin with. If an observation doesn't raise the *ideal* credibility of the claim, it shouldn't count as evidence for it. Similarly, an observation must lower the *ideal* credibility of a claim to count as evidence against it. A nice thing about this resolution of the second argument against an empirical indefeasibility requirement is that it could be employed in the Kitcher example too: while the non-ideal credibility of, say, a complex logical truth can certainly be lowered by empirical evidence that well-respected logicians didn't accept it, ideal credibility can't be lowered in this way; for that reason, the evidence about the opinions of logicians really isn't *evidence* against the logical truth. Whether the Kitcher examples are to be handled this way or by a slight restriction on the empirical indefeasibility requirement is something I leave to the reader.

I want to say a bit more about my proposed definition of apriority, but first it would be well to generalize: it is important to consider not only the apriority of

---

[4] One restriction that would have this effect was suggested in Field (1996).

propositions, but the apriority of methodologies or rules for forming and revising beliefs. For the moment, we can take as examples of such methodologies (classical) *deductive inference*, (your favourite version of) *inductive inference*, and (your favourite rules of) *perceptual belief formation*, i.e. of the formation of perceptual beliefs on the basis of experience. In analogy to the above, I will call such a methodology or rule *weakly a priori* iff it can be reasonably employed without empirical evidence; *empirically indefeasible* if no empirical evidence could undermine the reasonableness of its employment; and *a priori* if it meets both conditions. Again, I think the most interesting component of apriority is empirical indefeasibility.

Note that I have not required that an a priori proposition can only be reasonably believed by someone who has a non-empirical justification for it: not only would that conflict with the examples above of a priori propositions reasonably believed entirely because of empirical justifications, it would also conflict with the possibility of a priori propositions reasonably believed without any justification at all. ('Default reasonable' propositions.) Similarly in the case of rules. I think that we ought to allow for the possibility of default reasonable propositions and rules;[5] more on this shortly. My definition classifies default reasonable propositions and rules as, trivially, *weakly* a priori; so that they are a priori if and only if they are empirically indefeasible. If one were to hold that a priori justification is required for reasonable belief in an a priori proposition and for reasonable employment of an a priori rule, then default reasonable propositions and rules could never count as a priori. That would be most undesirable: surely among the most plausible examples of default reasonable propositions and rules are simple logical truths like 'If snow is white then snow is white' and basic deductive rules like modus ponens and 'and'-elimination. It would be odd to exclude these from the ranks of the a priori merely because of their being default reasonable.[6]

---

[5] One must be careful not to be led into ruling them out by pun on the word 'justified'. In one sense, a justified belief is simply a reasonable belief; in another, it is a belief that has a justification. If it is assumed that these senses are equivalent, the exclusion of default reasonableness is automatic; but in fact their equivalence needs argument. (Note that if their equivalence is not assumed, there is no reason not to suppose that 'unjustified' beliefs in the second sense can be essential ingredients in the justification of other beliefs.)

[6] The problem of default reasonable propositions and rules is curiously overlooked in discussions of how the notion of a priori proposition and/or a priori justification is to be defined. For instance, the discussion of a priori justification in Bonjour 1998 assumes throughout that for a belief to be reasonable it must have some justification or other, if not empirical then a priori. Presumably Bonjour thinks that there are no default reasonable propositions. However, the obvious way to retain that position is to allow for circularity in the justificatory process (see the next section), and Bonjour makes a point of disallowing such circularity: that is the basis on which he argues that for induction to be reasonable it must be possible to give a justification of it that doesn't use induction. He thinks that such a non-circular justification of induction is possible; I will not discuss this, but unless he also thinks that a non-circular justification of deduction is possible, then the exclusion of circularity would seem to make the recognition of default-reasonable rules of deduction mandatory if deductive scepticism is to be avoided. (I suspect that

If our concept of apriority were simply weak apriority we would have the oppo-site problem: default reasonable propositions would automatically count as a priori. But there is no obvious reason why propositions such as 'People usually tell the truth' shouldn't count as default reasonable, and it would be odd to count such propositions a priori. Empirical indefeasibility seems the obvious way to distin-guish those default reasonable propositions that are a priori and those that aren't.

There is another possibility worth considering: I have argued against saying that a priori propositions and rules are those that *require* non-empirical justifica-tion to be reasonably believed, but why not say that they are those that *admit* non-empirical justification? The answer is that this too might exclude simple logical truths, or rules like modus ponens and 'and'-elimination. For the only obvious way to try to give 'a priori justifications' for them is by appeal to the truth-table for 'and'. But as has often been pointed out, 'justification' of 'and'-elimination by the truth-table for 'and' requires the use of 'and'-elimination (or some equiv-alent principle) at the meta-level: one must pass from '"A" and "B" are both true' to '"A" is true'. If this counts as a justification it is a circular one,[7] and it is not obvious that 'circular justification' makes sense. I'll soon discuss that issue more fully, but at least we can say that the alternative approach to defining a priority contemplated at the start of this paragraph requires the acceptance of circular justification.[8]

I close this section by noting that it is not built into the definitions that an a priori proposition be true or an a priori methodology reliable; much less, that its truth or reliability is somehow *guaranteed* by some non-empirical justification of it. We do have strong *reason to think* that a prior propositions are true and a priori methodologies reliable: if we didn't have reasons to think these things, it wouldn't be reasonable to believe the propositions or employ the methodologies, so they couldn't be a priori.[9]

2. *DEFAULT* REASONABLENESS

There is a familiar argument for the default reasonableness of certain methodolo-gies, including deductive reasoning, inductive reasoning, forming beliefs as a

Bonjour would say that rather than being default reasonable, the basic rules of logic are justi-fied by acts of a priori insight. But this seems like just an obscurantist redescription; in any case the only argument for it seems to rest on defining a priori justification in a way that ignores the possibility of default reasonableness.)

[7] 'Circular' here is taken to include 'rule-circular': the relevant sort of circularity is where we justify *the claim that a rule is truth-preserving* by use of that very rule.

[8] Relative to principles of justification which allow for circular justification, the alternative definition of apriority contemplated in this paragraph may be equivalent to the one I proposed.

[9] A further point worth mentioning: I do not assume that it is a failure of rationality to believe of a proposition that is not a priori that it is a priori, or to believe of one that is a priori that it is not.

result of observation or testimony or memory-impression, and so forth. (Recall that if they are default reasonable then they are at least *weakly* a priori.) The argument is that no justification for anything could be given without using some of these forms of reasoning.[10] So if justifications are assumed to be non-circular, and if we exclude the totally sceptical possibility that no methodology for forming and revising beliefs is reasonable, then some methodologies must be reasonable without justification: they must be 'default reasonable'.[11]

Should we exclude all circular 'justifications' of methodological rules from being genuine *justifications*? A number of authors have argued against such an exclusion (Black 1958; Dummett 1978; Friedman 1979; van Cleve 1984), on what appear at first glance to be reasonable grounds. Indeed, at least part of what Dummett and Friedman say seems incontestable: a deductive justification of deduction does give us some kind of rational explanation of why we should value our deductive practice more highly than alternative deductive practices we consider defective. This is doubtless of importance—more on this later. But it is not obvious that its providing this sort of explanation of our valuing the practice means that it should count as a justification. To be sure, Dummett and Friedman grant that such circular explanations are not the sort of justifications that would persuade a committed proponent of alternative methods; but I take the issue of whether they count as justifications not to be that, but rather, whether they should add to the credibility we attach to the mode of reasoning in question. In my view, the explanations can have this justificatory value only if they aren't too easy to come by: only if there was a prima-facie risk of it being impossible to explain our valuing the method,[12] so that the actual providing of the explanation can justify the method by showing that the risk is not genuine. I think that in the case of deduction and induction and perception there is reason to doubt that there is a significant prima-facie risk, in which case it is hard to see why the circular 'justifications' should count as justifications at all. (More about this in the inductive and perceptual cases in Section 4.)

Even if we concede that such circular 'justifications' have justificatory value,

---

[10] Admittedly, this might not be so if 'acts of a priori insight' are both possible and count as justifications; but let's agree to put obscurantism aside.

[11] This is compatible with 'externalist' views about reasonableness (as well as with 'internalist' views). The externalist holds that a necessary condition on the reasonable employment of inductive procedures or perceptual procedures is that those procedures in fact be 'reliable' or 'truth-conductive' or whatever (where the 'whatever' covers any other intuitively 'externalist' condition that might be imposed). This is compatible with certain procedures being default reasonable: it just implies (i) that what procedures are default reasonable depends on which ones satisfy the appropriate externalist conditions; and (ii) that *evidence in favour of* the satisfaction of those conditions isn't also necessary for the procedures to be reasonably employed. (I doubt that the contrast between internalist and externalist conditions is altogether clear, but I will not be making much of the contrast. In fact, I will eventually argue that even if that distinction is clear, the distinction between internalism and externalism rests on a false assumption.)

[12] Indeed, only if there was a prima-facie risk that in using our methods we will come to the conclusion that the methods do not have the properties we value.

there is a case for certain deductive, inductive, and perceptual rules being 'default reasonable'. Indeed, the case for default reasonableness is explicit in most of the works just cited: the authors argue that what makes the rule-circular justifications of certain rules count as justifications is that those rules already have a kind of initial credibility. (They think that use of initially credible rules to argue for the reliability or truth-preservingness of the rules adds to this initial credibility.) Their 'initial credibility' is my 'default reasonableness'.

It is, however, not out of the question to hold that without circular justifications there is no reasonableness at all. That is the view of a certain kind of coherence theorist. This coherence theorist holds that simple deductive, inductive and perceptual rules don't count as 'reasonable to employ' until the users of those procedures have argued (using some combination of deduction, induction, and perception, the combination varying from one case to the next) that those rules are reliable. But once the rules have been used to support themselves to a sufficient degree, the rules become reasonable to employ.

But I doubt that this way of avoiding the default-reasonableness of certain inferential rules has any substance. Presumably not any set of procedures that are self-supporting (i.e. which can be used in arguments for their own reliability) count as reasonable to employ: consider various sorts of counter-deductive and counter-inductive methods. What differentiates those which are reasonable (e.g. ours) from those which aren't? The natural answer is that our methods have a certain proto-reasonableness, independent of empirical evidence in their favour, that counter-deductive and counter-inductive methods lack. This proto-reasonableness might be due entirely or in part to factors like truth-preservingness or reliability; or it might be just due to the fact that we find these procedures natural to employ. Either way, once we use our method to reach the conclusion that that method is reliable, the proto-reasonableness is converted to full reasonableness; counter-deductive and counter-inductive methods don't have proto-reasonableness to begin with, so they don't become reasonable upon self-support. That, I submit, is the most straightforward way for a coherence theorist to differentiate the reasonable from the unreasonable self-supporting methods.

But then it is transparent that the view is basically just a notational variant of the view that there is default reasonableness; it just calls it proto-reasonableness. Of course, 'default reasonable' is supposed to imply 'reasonable', whereas 'proto-reasonable' is supposed not to imply it (and indeed, to imply that something else is needed before reasonableness is achieved); but my point is that the advocates of this view do ascribe a positive value to what they call proto-reasonableness, it's just that they adopt a higher threshold for the value that must be obtained to deserve to be called 'reasonable'.

There are two considerations that favour the lower (non-coherentist) threshold. First, if as I have suggested there is less than meets the eye to deductive justifications of deduction and inductive justifications of induction, the point of elevating the standard of reasonableness in the way the coherentist proposes is obviously diminished. I'll say no more about this now. Second, I think that at least in the case of induction, it is impossible even using the rules in question to argue for crucial features of the reliability of the rules; this means that it is hard to motivate a higher (coherentist) threshold without motivating one so high that it is unattainable. Arguing this is a bit outside the main thrust of the paper, so I leave it to a footnote.[13]

Despite these considerations, the decision on 'threshold of reasonableness' is partly verbal, and this partly verbal decision affects the scope of weak apriority as I've defined it. Consider inductive and perceptual rules (good ones; this presumably includes the ones *we* use). On the lower (non-coherentist) threshold, such rules come out default reasonable and therefore weakly a priori. But on the higher (coherentist) threshold according to which good inductive and perceptual rules are merely proto-reasonable, then those rules don't count as weakly a priori unless they can be given non-empirical justifications; and this is most unlikely

---

[13] Here is the argument that empirical evidence for the reliability of relevant features of our inductive procedures is simply unavailable. Suppose we have developed a comprehensive and appealing physical theory T that the evidence at our disposal strongly supports. We can always invent bizarre alternatives that no one would take seriously, but which the available evidence equally accords with: for instance,

(T*) T holds at all times until the year 2000, at which time U holds

(where U is some detailed development of a totally discredited theory, say Aristotelian physics). The reason for saying that the available evidence accords with T* just as well as it accords with T is that the available evidence all concerns what happens at times before 2000, and T and T* agree completely about that. Despite this, we would of course all base predictions on T rather than on T*: it is part of our empirical methodology to do so, and surely doing so is reasonable. But it is hard to see that we have any evidence favouring this methodology over an alternative one which favours T* over T.

Someone might claim that we do have such evidence: the abundant evidence in our possession that the laws of physics haven't changed in the past. But this is a mistake: if the laws had changed in the past, that would be incompatible with both T and T*, so it wouldn't favour either over the other, and so evidence against it also doesn't favour one over the other. To make this clearer, let's look at two more theories besides T and T*:

V*: The current laws of physics are T; but the laws have changed every 100 years, and will continue to do so.

V: The current laws of physics are T; but the laws have changed every 100 years in the past. However, the laws won't change in 2000 or thereafter.

There is little doubt that if the laws had changed in the years 100, 200, ..., 1900, that would be pretty good inductive evidence that they would also change in 2000; and that the fact that they didn't change then is evidence that they won't change in 2000. The reason is that our methodology gives a strong a priori bias to V* over V and to T over T*. Evidence that the laws have changed in the past would rule out T and T* but leave V* and V as consistent with the evidence; given the a priori bias, V would be dismissed as highly implausible, leaving V*, which entails a change in the year 2000. Similarly, evidence that the laws haven't changed rules out V and V*, leaving T and T* as consistent with the evidence; but this time the a priori bias leads us to dismiss T* as hopelessly implausible. But at no point is the bias for T over T* or for V* over V ever supported by evidence. (At least, it is never supported prior to 2000; and it is only prior to 2000 that the bias is important to us.)

even allowing circular 'justifications', since the premises of an inductive 'justification' of inductive or an inductive-perceptual 'justification' of perceptual rules are empirical. So the issue of the weak apriority of inductive and perceptual rules is largely a verbal issue about the threshold of reasonableness. For the reasons above, I prefer the lower, non-coherentist threshold, on which good inductive and perceptual rules count as weakly a priori. The question of their full apriority then reduces to the question of whether they are empirically indefeasible. I will have something to say in support of the empirical indefeasibility of certain inductive and perceptual rules later, though we'll eventually see that this question too has a quasi-terminological component.

3. DEFAULT *REASONABLENESS* AND THE EVALUATIVIST APPROACH TO APRIORITY

So far the discussion of default reasonableness has been focused more on the 'default' than on the 'reasonableness'. To call a proposition or rule default *reasonable* is to hold that it is *reasonable* to believe or employ it without first adducing evidence or arguments in its favour. Or in other words, that it is *reasonable* to adhere to it as a 'default belief' or 'default rule' (a belief or rule that is accepted or employed without adducing considerations in its favour). The previous section argued (with a slight qualification) that if one is going to have very many beliefs at all one must have default rules; but to get from this to the conclusion that some rules are default *reasonable* and hence weakly a priori, one needs to assume that it is possible to have a sufficient array of reasonable beliefs; and to get to the conclusion that some of the rules *we employ* are default reasonable and hence weakly a priori, one needs to assume that some of our own beliefs are reasonable.

What is it for a default rule (or any other rule) to be reasonable? My main discussion of this will come later, in Section 5, but it will help to give a brief preview now.

One approach to explaining reasonableness (I'll call it 'naturalistic reductionism') has it that the reasonableness of a rule is entirely a matter of how good the rule is at producing truth, avoiding falsehood, and so forth. In the case of deductive rules, we think that ours are objectively correct in that they have complete and non-contingent reliability; and naturalistic reductionism simply identifies this objective correctness with their reasonableness. In the case of inductive and perceptual rules it is less easy to make sense of objective correctness, but we do apparently think that the ones we employ are as a matter of contingent fact reliable, and so are good at arriving at the truth, and naturalistic reductionism simply identifies the reasonableness of the rule with some combination of these and similar 'truth-oriented' characteristics.

In my view, this approach is thoroughly implausible, on numerous grounds. Here is a partial list:

(1) In the case of deductive rules, the notion of reliability is quite clear: and correct rules do have complete and non-contingent reliability while incorrect ones don't. So in this case, the question of whether reliabilism gives the right answer about reasonableness is equivalent to the question of whether it is always reasonable to believe correct logical rules and unreasonable to believe incorrect ones. But I would have thought the answer to be 'no': even if the correct logic for dealing with vagueness or the semantic paradoxes is a non-classical logic (perhaps one that no one has yet formulated), we who do not realize the virtues of such a revision of logic, or even know how to formulate the logic, are not unreasonable in trying to cope with vagueness or the semantic paradoxes in the context of classical logic. We are unreliable but not unreasonable.

(2) The standard 'internalist' criticism: it is implausible to hold that our methods (assuming them reliable in the actual world) would be straightforwardly unreasonable in a 'demon world' (a world designed to make those methods unreliable, but undetectably so).

(3) It isn't easy for a reductionist to satisfactorily explain why a method is unreasonable if it simply builds in an a priori belief in whatever physical theory is in fact correct. (The obvious reductionist approach to explaining that is to require that the method work in certain possible worlds other than our own as well as in our own world; but specifying which other possible worlds are relevant and which aren't, and doing so in a way that isn't grossly *ad hoc*, seems to me extremely difficult.)

(4) The application of the notion of reliability to our basic inductive methods is crucially unclear, for reasons to be given at the end of Section 4; and it is hard to supply a clear replacement for the demand that our basic inductive methods be reliable that isn't either too weak to exclude obviously unreasonable methods or so strong as to further accentuate the problems in (2).

(5) The motivation for reliabilism is suspect: the motivation for wanting our beliefs to be true is clear, and this might motivate an interest in the reliability of a rule as evidence of the truth of beliefs formed by the rule, but it doesn't motivate the stronger role that the reliabilist gives to reliability. More fully: there are lots of classes to which a given belief B belongs such that the proportion of truth to falsehood in that class would have an evidential bearing on the truth of B. If our interest is in the truth of B, we thus have an indirect interest in the proportion of truth to falsehood in many such classes. But the reliabilist, in trying to reduce reasonableness to a precisely defined notion of reliability, wants to single out one particular such class as having a more-than-evidential interest: it's what constitutes the reasonableness of B. Why think that this has any interest?

(6) 'Reliability' is certainly not the only thing we want in an inductive rule: *completely* reliable methods are available, e.g. the method of believing nothing whatever the evidence, or believing only logical truths; but we don't value them, and value instead other methods that are obviously not perfectly reliable, because of their other characteristics. And reliability itself subdivides into many different

notions: for instance, short term vs. long term; yielding a high probability of exact truth vs. yielding a high probability of approximate truth; reliability in the actual world vs. reliability over a range of 'nearby' possible worlds; etc. When one thinks about the different more precise characteristics we value, and the fact that they tend to be in competition with each other, it is hard to imagine how they could be combinable into a package that could plausibly be held to constitute reasonableness.

(7) Familiar worries about naturalistic reductionism in ethics carry over to the epistemological case. For instance, (i) identifying reasonableness with a natural property seems to strip it of its normative force; (ii) in cases of fundamental disagreement about *what* natural property is coextensive with reasonableness, it is difficult to take seriously the idea that one party to the debate is right and the others wrong. (Indeed, that idea seems to presuppose a non-natural property of reasonableness, whose extension is up for grabs.)[14] The naturalist can avoid this by supposing that those in fundamental disagreement about what is reasonable are using the term for *different* natural properties; but this relativist conclusion has the consequence that they aren't really disagreeing, which seems incredible.[15]

Despite all this, I don't think naturalistic reductionism wholly misguided: I hope to provide an attractive picture that captures its insights.

If naturalistic reductionism is rejected, what is to take its place? Another approach is to take our own rules as completely reasonably by fiat, and to regard other people's rules as reasonable to the extent that they are similar to ours. I'll call this 'the egocentric approach'. It too strikes me as hopelessly implausible, this time because it chauvinistically takes our own rules as sacrosanct quite independent of any properties they might have.

What alternatives remain? One could try to combine features of the above approaches, taking reasonableness to be a combination of reliability (and related characteristics) and similarity to ones own methods; but this wouldn't be much better than the egocentric approach as regards chauvinism, and wouldn't help with the main problems with the naturalistic approach either.

---

[14] This parenthetical point would need to be stated with care, so as not to run afoul of the fact that there are genuinely controversial property-identities (e.g. between being in pain and being in a certain psychofunctional state), and that controversies about them does not necessarily have to be understood in terms of higher-order properties associated with the two terms of the identity, but can be explained in terms of the differing conceptual roles of the terms. But I don't think that the analogy of controversial judgements about reasonableness to controversial judgements about pain does much to raise the plausibility of evaluative naturalism. For one thing, there is a physical property centrally involved in causing our pain judgements, and it seems a fairly straightforward factual question what this is. There seems to be no such straightforward factual question in the case of reasonableness.

[15] Of course, the relativist can admit that the parties disagree in attitude, but in the context of naturalism (or any sort of fully factualist view of reasonableness) this seems *ad hoc*: the natural notion of disagreement for a naturalist (or any sort of factualist) is factual disagreement, and on this notion the parties do not disagree.

A third approach ('non-naturalism') is to regard reasonableness as a primitive property of rules or methods, not explainable in terms of anything non-normative (hence presumably undetectable by ordinary perceptual processes). But what reason would there be to suppose that any rules or methods have this strange property? And even if we assume that *some* have it, what reason would there be to suppose that the rules or methods *we employ* have it? If reasonableness consists in the possession of such a curious property, shouldn't we believe that our rules and methods (and any alternative rules and methods) are unreasonable?

It seems to me that we need another option. The options above had one thing in common: they assumed that reasonableness was a straightforwardly factual property. My proposal is that it is an evaluative property, in a way incompatible with its being straightforwardly factual.[16] We do, I think, evaluate rules and methods in part on the basis of our judgements as to whether using them will be good at leading to true beliefs and avoiding error. We also favour our own method over other quite dissimilar ones. These two strands in our evaluation procedure are inseparable: for (I will argue) we *inevitably* believe that our own methods will be better than the dissimilar methods at leading to truths and avoiding errors. One shouldn't ask whether it is the conduciveness to truth or the similarity to our methods in which the reasonableness consists, for reasonableness doesn't *consist in* anything: it is not a factual property.

The approach I'm recommending ('evaluativism') shares with non-naturalism the conviction that it is quite misguided to try to reduce epistemological properties like reasonableness to other terms. But it is very different from non-naturalism when it comes to the question of scepticism. A sensible evaluativist will think that there are no non-natural properties, or anyway none that is ever instantiated; so that if scepticism were defined as the failure to believe that any rules and methods have such a non-natural property, then the sensible evaluativist is a 'sceptic'. But the evaluativist should say that this is a totally perverse definition of scepticism. On a more reasonable definition, a sceptic is someone who positively evaluates abstention from all belief; scepticism in that sense is idiotic, and surely doesn't follow from the non-instantiation of mysterious properties.

The meta-epistemological views just sketched are important to the interpretation of default reasonableness, and of weak apriority more generally. One kind of

---

[16] The conception of evaluative properties as 'not fully factual' has been spelled out in different ways. My favourites are Gibbard (1990) and Field (1994). One feature of these views is that they employ a general notion of disagreement that incorporates disagreement in both attitudes and values. When straightforwardly factual matters are at issue, disagreement reduces to factual disagreement. In typical normative disagreement, it is a combination of facts and values that are in dispute. In certain cases of fundamental normative disagreement, no facts are relevant to the disagreement, only values. In this case, the disagreement is of attitudes. But note that this invocation of disagreement in attitudes is very different from the factualist's (n. 15): on a factualist view it is factual disagreement that should be primarily important, so invoking disagreement in attitude seems *ad hoc*; whereas on Gibbard's or my evaluativism, there is only one notion of disagreement, and disagreement in attitude is simply a special case of it.

question about these characteristics is: in virtue of what does a given proposition or method have them? In virtue of what is it reasonable to use modus ponens on no evidence?[17] The difficulty of providing an answer to this question is one of the main reasons that apriority has seemed mysterious. The meta-epistemology I've suggested requires that this question be recast: the proper question is, why value a methodology that allows the use of modus ponens on no evidence? Well, one needs some methodology, so the question can only be why favour this methodology over alternatives, and the answer will depend on what alternative methodologies are possible. The alternatives to a methodology that allows use of modus ponens on no evidence divide between those that license its use on certain empirical evidence (maybe on the evidence that snow is white?) and those that don't license its use at all (but license no deductive inference at all, or license only some particular weak logic that doesn't include it). The question then reduces to showing what is wrong with particular methodologies of each type. I don't want to get into a substantive discussion of what is wrong with particular methodologies of each of these types; my point is only that that is what is involved in defending the weak apriority of modus ponens, once one adopts the evaluativist perspective. This seems to me a substantially different perspective on a priority than one gets from more fully 'factualist' meta-epistemologies, and this different perspective does a great deal to remove the mystery from weak apriority.

It isn't just issues about weak apriority that evaluativism recasts; issues about empirical indefeasibility are recast as well. For an evaluativist, defending the empirical indefeasibility of modus ponens is a matter of arguing that a methodology that takes it as empirically indefeasible is preferable to methodologies that allow it to be empirically defeated by particular kinds of evidence. If an anti-apriorist charges that it would be dogmatic for a system of rules to license the use of modus ponens *on any evidence whatever*, the response should be 'This is better than their licensing its revision on inappropriate evidence (say, the discovery of a new kind of virus); give me a plausible example of possible evidence that would make it *appropriate* to abandon modus ponens! And if the possible evidence you cite isn't *obviously* appropriate for this purpose, then give me at least a sketch of a theory of evidence on which the evidence *is* appropriate!' Without even a sketch of an answer, it is hard to see why we should take empiricism about modus ponens seriously. I don't say that we ought to rule out the possibility that someone could come up with an example of possible evidence that would seem to make it appropriate to give up modus ponens (were the evidence actual), and of a possible theory of evidence that explained why this was evidence against the adequacy of modus ponens. But ruling out that possibility is something no a

---

[17] If default reasonableness rather than weak a priority is in question, I should say 'on no evidence *or argument*'. But presumably we attach little importance to the difference between a methodology that takes modus ponens to be default reasonable and one that takes it to be weakly a priori because derivable from disjunctive syllogism which is in turn taken as default reasonable.

priorist should try to do: however apriorist we are about logic, we ought to be fallibilist enough to recognize the possibility that new conceptual developments will undermine our apriorism.[18]

Incidentally, the failure to distinguish apriorism from infallibism about apriorism seems to underlie the widespread belief that Quine has provided an alternative to apriorism about logic. Quine's view is that one should evaluate alternative logics in combination with theories of the rest of the world: given a theory of everything, including a logic, one uses the logic in the theory to generate the theory's consequences. Then we choose a theory, including a logic, on such grounds as overall simplicity and conservativeness and agreement with observations. But this description of the methodology is so vague that it is not in the least clear that it dictates that modus ponens or any other part of logic should be revisable on empirical evidence. Whether it so dictates depends on the standards of simplicity and conservativeness of overall theories: it depends on whether the decrease of simplicity and conservativeness that results from modifying the logic could be compensated by increased simplicity and conservativeness in other parts of the theory (holding the observational predictions fixed). It is *conceivable* that the standards of simplicity we use, or attractive alternative standards, will be such as to say that there are possible observations that would lead to favouring a theory that includes an alternative to our logic over ours. That is enough to undermine infallibilism about apriority, but to undermine a priority one must show that there actually are attractive standards of simplicity under which possible observations would lead to an alternative logic, and Quine has given no clue as to what those standards of simplicity might be. (Indeed there is reason for scepticism about the existence of standards that would let possible observations undermine modus ponens. For one is likely to need modus ponens in the background logic in which one reasons about what follows from each theory-plus-logic and how well it accords with observations; and it is hard to imagine that a person using this background logic could rationally come to favour a theory-plus-logic in which the logic conflicted with the background logic.)

I don't pretend that this discussion settles the case for a priorism about logic: it is intended only to illustrate how evaluativism supplies a perspective for answering the question that does not turn on rational insight into the nature of non-natural epistemological properties.[19]

---

[18] More on this and some of the other claims in this paragraph and the next is to be found in Sections 2 and 4 of Field (1998*b*).

[19] One of the important issues not addressed is whether Benacerraf's (1973) puzzle about how a priori mathematical knowledge is possible extends to other alleged cases of a priori knowledge. I think Benacerraf's argument does work against many claims to apriority. (Including claims of a priori access to mathematical entities *as these are conceived by most Platonists*. For a discussion of which Platonist views might survive the argument, see Field (1998*a*).) For instance, the reasons for negatively evaluating a system of rules that would allow us to adhere *whatever the evidence* to a particular physical theory that we hold true have to do with the fact

4. AN EPISTEMOLOGICAL PUZZLE

I turn next to the question of whether our inductive and perceptual methodologies are best viewed as empirically indefeasible; this will lead into further discussion of reliabilism and evaluativism. A good way into these issues is by way of an epistemological puzzle.[20] It comes in two parts.

Part One starts with the idea that we want our empirical methods to be reliable: to lead to a fairly high proportion of true beliefs. In particular, we want them to be reliable in present and future applications. But we can empirically investigate whether they have been reliable in past applications; and it is surely possible that we will discover that one of our empirical methods hasn't been reliable, and that some alternative to it has been. Alternatively, we might discover that our method has been *fairly* reliable, but that some alternative method has done much better. If we did discover one of these things, then since we take the past to be the best guide to the future we should conclude that our method will continue to be less reliable than the alternative. But surely if we think that one of our own empirical methods will be less reliable than an alternative, then we ought to switch from our method to the other. All of this would seem to apply not only to our 'non-basic methods'— our rules of thumb (like 'Believe what the *NY Times* says') that are evaluated using more basic methods (like induction); it would seem to apply to our most basic inductive method itself. That is, it would seem that we want our most basic inductive method to be reliable, and can investigate empirically whether it has been, and we will stop using it if we find that it has not. But in this case, the investigation of the most basic method can't be by another method, for by hypothesis none is more basic. Rather, the investigation of our most basic method uses that very method. So in the case where we empirically discover that method unreliable, the decision not to use the method would be based on that very method.[21]

that doing so would clearly make our belief causally and counterfactually independent of the facts; and such independence from the facts would defeat the epistemological value of the considerations on which the belief was based. (I think that is what a Benacerrafian argument against apriority about physics would amount to.) It might seem that this would apply equally well to apriority about logic. The idea would be that a priori belief in logic makes logical beliefs similarly independent of the facts, and that this is equally bad. But I think that in the logical case one simply can't make sense of the question of whether logical beliefs depend on the logical facts; so we can't make sense of the claim that is supposed to defeat the evidential value of the considerations on which the belief was based, and so the logical beliefs remain undefeated. For more details, see Field (1996: sect. V) or Field (1998*b*: sect. 5).

[20] The puzzle is implicit in many epistemological writings; probably its most explicit presentation is as the argument against 'norm externalism' in Pollock (1987) (though it is close to explicit in Putnam (1963) and Lewis (1971).) My resolution is not too far from Pollock's, though Pollock's view is closer to what I've called the egocentric approach than to the evaluativism I recommend.

[21] It has been suggested to me in conversation that our basic method is the meta-method 'employ whatever first-order method is most reliable'; and that this meta-method couldn't fail

Part Two of the puzzle says that the conclusion of Part One is incoherent. How can our method, in combination with evidence E (in this case, evidence of its own unreliability), tell us not to follow that very method? Our method presumably already tells us something about what is legitimate to belief and what is illegitimate to believe when our evidence includes E (say, when it consists of E&F).[22] These instructions might be empty: they might allow us to believe what we like. Or they might tell us to stop believing. Or they might tell us any of numerous other things. But whatever they tell us it's legitimate to believe on E&F, that's what we must do if we are to follow the method. Now if the method tells me that E undermines the method, it must tell me not to always do what the method tells me to do; in other words, it must tell me to do something different, on some evidence E&F, from what it tells me to do on E&F. In other words it must offer me inconsistent instructions. It would seem that only an inconsistent empirical method can allow itself to be undermined by empirical evidence of its own past unreliability; to suppose that good empirical methods must allow themselves to be empirically undermined in this way is then to suppose that good methods must be inconsistent, which seems absurd.

To summarize: Part Two is an argument that we can't possibly treat our basic empirical methods as empirically defeasible, whereas Part One is an argument that we must do so; where to take a method *as* empirically defeasible is to adopt standards on which empirical evidence could count against it. Obviously something is wrong, but what?

A superficially plausible diagnosis is that the key error was the presupposition that there is such a thing as 'our basic empirical method': that is, in the supposition that we employ a method that can't be undermined by any of our other methods. One might argue that this supposition is incorrect, that in fact we employ many different methods, each of which can be assessed using the others. I think myself that the assumption of a basic inductive method is defensible if properly understood, but I will save that issue for an appendix. What I want to do now is argue that the issue of whether there is a basic method isn't central to the puzzle, because there is a more straightforward error in the argument in Part One.

In investigating this, it helps to be a bit more concrete: instead of talking about 'our basic empirical method' let's instead talk about a specific inductive rule. For simplicity I'll pick an extremely simple-minded rule, but one which I think will have crucial features in common with any inductive rule that might plausibly be regarded as part of our basic inductive method. The rule I'll pick for illustration is the following:

---

to be reliable. But in fact the proposed meta-method is not an employable method. To make it into one, we would need to recast it as something like 'employ whatever first-order method you believe to be most reliable', or 'employ whatever first-order method your first-order methods tell you to believe most reliable'; and these *can* certainly fail to be reliable.

[22] Our method may take into account factors other than the available evidence—for instance, it may take account of which theories have been thought of—but as far as I can see, such additional factors won't matter to the argument that follows.

(R) If in the past you have observed n ravens, and m of them have been black, you should believe to degree $(m+j)/(n+k)$ of any raven not yet observed that it is black,

where j and k are fixed real numbers, $0<j<k$.[23] The idea of the rule is that j/k is your initial degree of belief that a raven will be black; as observations of raven colour accumulate, that initial degree of belief gradually becomes swamped by the observed frequency. (This happens slowly if k is large, quickly if k is small.) This is of course a thoroughly implausible rule: among other defects, (i) it takes no account of any evidence other than observations of raven colour; (ii) it takes no account of any regularities in the *ordering* of black and non-black among the ravens observed; and (iii) it takes no account of how the ravens were selected for observation. When I say that the rule is implausible, part of what I mean is that our own basic inductive rule does not have these limitations. But let's pretend that we do employ this rule, and let's ask how if at all empirical evidence (e.g. of the past unreliability of the rule) could lead us to rationally revise it.

Since the rule is one for degrees of belief rather than for all-or-nothing belief, talk of reliability or unreliability may not be strictly appropriate; but clearly the analog of a discovery of past unreliability in the rule is the discovery that the actual proportion of blackness among ravens observed in the past has been substantially different from j/k. The argument of Part One suggests that were we to discover this, then those observations would provide evidence against the rule. But this is mistaken. There is of course no doubt that if j/k is small, then the observation of many ravens with a high proportion of blackness among them should lead us to revise the probability of blackness for an unobserved raven upwards (barring special additional information anyway). But this doesn't mean that we should modify the rule: our observation of a high proportion of blackness among ravens is something that the rule takes into account. Suppose our initial bias was j = 1, k = 10, so that the degree of belief assigned to a given raven being black was only 0.1. And suppose we observe 20 ravens, of which 19 are black. Then the rule tells us to believe to degree 0.667 (20/30) of an unobserved raven that it is black. The rule has in a sense told us to modify our biases. In another sense, though, the biases go unchanged: the initial bias, represented by the pair <j,k> from which we started, is still there producing the new degree of belief. Of course, the initial bias produces that new degree of belief only with the accumulated evidence, and *the effect of using the initial bias with the accumulated evidence is in a sense equivalent to altering the bias:* it is equivalent to altering the initial bias to j = 21 and k = 25, *and then dropping the observation of the first 20 ravens from our evidence.* (It would be double counting to let it alter the bias

[23] The rule is to be generalized to apply to other pairs of predicates besides 'raven' and 'black', though as the 'grue' paradox makes vivid, using the rule for some pairs requires not using it for certain others. The rule given is in effect an instance of Carnap's λ-continuum (at least when k/j is an integer ≥ 2): it results from taking $\lambda=k$ and the number of kinds as k/j.

and then *in addition* let it count as evidence with the new bias.) In a sense then our rule is 'self-correcting': with accumulating evidence the old rule behaves like an altered rule would *without* the added evidence. Because it is 'self-correcting' in this way, there is no need for it to be revised when evidence of its unreliability in previous applications is accumulated.

Of course there *are* ways that a rule like (R) might be inductively challenged. (R) was supposed to be a rule for ravens; and if we had a great deal of experience with other birds showing that a high degree of concentration in colour tends to prevail within each species, that would give us grounds for lowering the correction factor (lowering the j and the k while keeping their ratio constant) in the raven rule. But that simply shows that the original rule isn't a serious candidate for a basic inductive rule. Any serious candidate for a basic inductive rule will allow 'cross-inductions': it will allow for evidence about other birds to affect our conclusions about ravens.[24] Were we not to employ a rule that allows cross-inductions, we wouldn't regard the evidence about other species as relevant to ravens, and so would not see such evidence as providing any reason to lower the correction factor in (R).

So the point is that we use a more complicated inductive rule than (R) (one that 'self-corrects' to a greater extent than R does); using the more complicated rule, we can inductively conclude that our future practice should not accord with the more simple-minded rule. But if we had used the more simple-minded rule in doing the assessment, we wouldn't be able to conclude that our practice should no longer accord with that simple-minded rule; similarly, I suggest, if we tried to assess the more complicated rule using the more complicated rule, we couldn't ever recognize anything as evidence for the conclusion that we shouldn't use it. We could recognize evidence that our rule hadn't worked well in the past, but this would simply be evidence to be fed into the rule that would affect its future applications; we would not regard it as evidence undermining the rule. (Some apparent objections to this are discussed in the appendix.)

What I have said suggests that if indeed some inductive rule is basic for us, in the sense that we never assess it using any rules other than itself, then it must be one that we treat as empirically indefeasible (hence as fully a priori, given that it will surely have default status). So in the puzzle, the error in reasoning must have come in Part One. Moreover, it is now clear just where in Part One the error was: the error was in supposing that because the rule had been unreliable in the past it was likely to be unreliable in the future. What the discussion shows is that *there is no reason to extrapolate from the past in this way: for the future employment of the rule takes account of the unreliability of the past employments, in a way that makes the future applications qualitatively different from the past employments.* That's so in the case of rule (R), and it will also be so in the case of any

---

[24] Kemeny and Carnap investigated how to expand Carnap's λ-continuum to include a new parameter that allows for such cross-inductions: see Kemeny (1963: 732-3) and Carnap (1963: 977). The resulting formulation of an inductive method is still quite simplistic, but a step in the right direction.

sufficiently general inductive rule that anyone would be tempted to employ. So to resolve the puzzle there is no need to deny the existence of basic rules, we must merely recognize that any plausible candidate for a person's basic rule will have the same 'self-correcting' character as (R).[25]

I have been discussing whether we could empirically overturn a most basic inductive rule, and concluded that we could not. If so, this also calls into question the idea that we could ever rationally accept anything as empirically *supporting* these rules: for it is hard to see how there could be possible observations that support the rules without possible alternative observations that undermine them. The idea that our most basic inductive rules could get inductive support has been much discussed in the context of the justification of induction. It has often been dismissed on the ground that an inductive justification of induction is circular, though as noted earlier a number of authors have argued that the sort of circularity involved here (rule-circularity) is not vicious. I agree with these authors that the kinds of arguments that are offered as rule-circular justifications are of interest; but their worth *as justifications* turns on the idea that they remove a prima-facie risk, a risk that reasoning with the rule will lead to the rule's invalidation. In the case of inductive justifications of induction, what they turn on is the idea that the basic inductive rule might be inductively undermined; and that, I am suggesting, is impossible. It is that, not rule-circularity in itself, that is the real reason why the inductive justification of induction is an illusion. (Something similar holds of deductive justifications of deduction, I believe.)

Before drawing further morals, it will be helpful to consider another illustration, this time involving a perceptual rule. It is natural to suppose that rules of perception can be empirically overturned. Suppose we are initially disposed to regard things that look a certain way 'red'. (I'll pretend here that how things look to us is independent of our tendencies to judge their colour: it won't affect the point.) We then discover that in certain lighting, things that look that way often aren't red; and using this information, we revise our practice of making colour judgements. So it looks like our initial 'rule of perceptual judgement'

    (P) Believe things red if they look red

has been overturned. But that, I submit, is misleading: the right thing to say rather is that our initial practice was sensitive to inductive considerations that weren't built into (P), so that (P) isn't the most basic rule we were following (even before the information about the lighting). After all, if it had been the most basic rule we were following, it is hard to see how the information about the lighting could have influenced us.

---

[25] Less inductively sophisticated creatures doubtless employ simpler inductive methods that are not 'self-correcting' in this way. Such creatures could either never have evidence for the past unreliability of their methods, or could never think to extrapolate it, or would continue reasoning as before despite the belief that their methods would be unreliable. But they aren't us.

One way to think about what's going on in this case concedes that we do employ (P), but only as a default rule. The more basic rule is a meta-rule that says: use (P) unless it is inductively shown unreliable in certain circumstances; if that happens, stop using it in those circumstances. The meta-rule allows (P) to be inductively overturned, but it's hard to see how the meta-rule itself can be inductively overturned: we treat the meta-rule as empirically indefeasible (indeed, as a priori).

We don't really need the 'default rule'—'meta-rule' contrast, we can build everything into the ground level rule, by taking that rule not to be (P) but rather something more like

> (P*) Believe a thing red if it looks red, unless there are circumstances C that you believe you're in such that you have inductive evidence that looking red is misleading in those circumstances

or

> (P**) The extent to which you should believe a thing red should be such and such a function of (i) how it looks to you; (ii) your evidence about the perceptual circumstances; (iii) your background evidence about how the way that things look depends on the perceptual circumstances; and (iv) your background evidence about what colour it actually is.

Here the point is that inductive evidence that the rule has failed in the past feeds into the rule, in a way that alters the results of applying the rule in the future: for instance, in (P**) the evidence does this by affecting our beliefs of type (iii), on which the degree of belief that the thing is red depends. We have the same situation as with the inductive rule (R): the relevance of evidence of the past unreliability of the rule isn't to undermine the rule; rather, the evidence is something *that the rule will itself take account of, and that will substantially modify the future applications of the rule (in a way that might be expected to make those future applications more reliable than the past ones).* Of course, not every conceivable rule will 'self-correct' (in this sense) on the basis of evidence of its past unreliability; but those rules that we in fact take seriously do.[26] Such general rules are never really put to risk in inductive assessment; all that is put to risk is the particular manner in which they've been employed. And again, that means that the idea

---

[26] So even if we had been unlucky enough, or evolutionary maladapted enough, to employ rules which gave initial weight to our purported telepathic experiences in addition to our perceptual experiences, then as long as those rules were analogous to (P*) or (P**) rather than the cruder (P), we would have long since discounted telepathy. (This is in response to Goldman (1980: 42); although Goldman's formulation, and the surrounding discussion, seems to depend on (i) his temporarily assuming that we *choose* our basic inductive and perceptual rules, and (ii) his assuming that what we are after is finding *the uniquely correct* epistemological rules. I want no part of either assumption.)

of inductive justification of the rules, which requires the rules themselves to be put to risk but to survive the challenge, doesn't get off the ground.

The bearing of all this on the apriority (or empirical indefeasibility) of inductive and perceptual rules is not entirely direct. For one thing, the discussion has been premissed on the supposition that some inductive rule is basic for us. Whether that is so is a matter I discuss in the appendix: I argue that the question has a quasi-terminological component, but that there are considerations that favour a positive answer. But even given a positive answer to this, what I have argued hasn't been that our most basic rules are a priori or empirically indefeasible; it has been that we *treat them as* empirically indefeasible and indeed a priori: we *don't regard* anything as evidence against them. For a non-evaluativist, this distinction is crucial. For instance, a non-naturalist will say that the non-natural evidence relation may well hold between some evidence and an alternative to one of our basic rules, even though we could never be persuaded to adopt such an alternative on the basis of that evidence by principles of evidence we accept; and a reliabilist will say something analogous. From an evaluativist perspective, though, the distinction is rather academic: the only question is whether we should accept any possible evidence as undermining our rule, and since the rule itself is employed in making the evaluation of what we should do, there is no chance of a positive answer. More on this perspective in the next section.

The examples of (R) and (P*) or (P**) have an importance beyond their bearing on the empirical indefeasibility of our empirical methodology: they also create a problem of interpretation for many versions of naturalistic reductionism. According to naturalistic reductionism, the reasonableness of an epistemological rule *consists in* its having a certain combination of truth-oriented properties, and most advocates of naturalistic reductionism place 'reliability' high on the list of the properties that a reasonable rule must have. But as applied to 'self-correcting' rules like (R) and (P*) or (P**), it is not entirely clear what 'reliability' comes to (even if the reliability of a rule is assessed relative to the specific circumstances of application within a possible world, rather than assessed in the possible world as a whole).[27]

---

[27] Goldman (1988) offers a substantial reason for *not* relativizing to circumstances within a possible world in assessing reliability: if one is allowed to do so, what is to keep one from so narrowing the circumstances that they apply only to one instance? (That would mean that whenever the rule yields a truth, however accidentally, it would come out reliable, and so following it on that occasion would count as reasonable according to reliabilist lights.) Perhaps there are ways to block carving the circumstances so finely, but it isn't in the least clear how to do so without gross ad-hocness; and so Goldman adopts for not allowing any relativization to circumstances within a world. (Indeed, he argues that even consideration of reliability within a possible world as a whole is too narrow: one must consider reliability with respect to a class of similar worlds. The motivation for doing this is so that a rule that 'happens' to yield truths about a particular world independent of evidence won't count as reliable. At this point one might raise the question of how to carve out the relevant class of worlds without gross ad-hocness, but I will not press the matter.)

We can see this in the case of (R) by imagining that there was a fairly strong initial bias (moderately large k), and the initial degree of belief j/k differed drastically from the actual frequency of blackness among ravens: perhaps j/k is quite small whereas the proportion of blackness among ravens is very high. (For simplicity I will confine my attention to the case where that proportion is fairly stable from one epoch to another and one region to another.) And suppose that (R) is applied long enough for the initial bias to become largely swamped by the observations. On the question of whether the use of the rule counts as reliable, there seem to be three options:

(i) We can say that the rule was not reliable in its early uses (prior to the swamping), but became so later (after the swamping); after all, the degrees of belief produced by late uses of the rule closely reflected the actual frequencies, but degrees of belief produced by early uses were wildly at variance with actual frequencies. (Of course the swamping is gradual, so the shift from unreliability to reliability is gradual.)

(ii) We can say that the rule was not reliable in early or late uses: the fact that it initially produces degrees of belief wildly at odds with frequencies shows that it simply isn't a reliable rule, but merely gives results in its later uses that closely match the results given by reliable rules (those with a more optimal ratio j/k).

(iii) We could say that it was reliable in both: that the apparent unreliability in early uses results from taking too short-term a perspective.

Which option should a reliabilist adopt? Given reliabilism, (ii) would make reasonableness hard to come by: a faulty bias would doom us to unreasonableness forever (barring a shift in inductive policy that is not evidence-driven). I think that (i) accords best with the normal use of 'reliable'. However, given reliabilism, (i) requires that the use of the rule was unreasonable at first but became reasonable as the rule was used more and more; this strikes me as somewhat counter-intuitive, and it is contrary to the doctrines of at least one prominent reliabilist: see note 27. Some reliabilists might then prefer the long-run perspective implicit in (iii): even early uses of the rule count as reliable, because the rule would yield good results if applied in the long run. If 'long run' here means *really* long run, this would be even more counter-intuitive than (i): 'dogmatic' versions of (R) with exceptionally large k that would take millions of observations to significantly swamp would count as reliable and hence reasonable. It would also blunt the force of reliabilism, in that very few rules would be declared unreliable. But a reliabilist could avoid this by adopting (iii) for the case under discussion, where k is moderately large, and adopting view (i) or (ii) in the case of exceptionally large k where it would take a very long time for swamping to occur; in effect this is to use an intermediate length of reliability as a criterion of reasonableness for the early uses of the rule. This combination gives the most intuitively appealing results about reasonableness. But it is not clear that this is in keeping with the spirit of reliabilism: for it is now a priori (relative anyway to the assumption of stability in proportions) that *all* versions of (R) where k is not too large are reliable from the start, whatever the value of j (greater than 0 and less than k); the idea that the facts about the actual world determine an inductive method uniquely or close to uniquely (see Goldman 1980) is completely abandoned.

Something similar holds for perceptual rules like (P*) or (P**). Imagine a world where deceptive appearances are common enough so that in the initial stages of use the rule leads to error a quite substantial per cent of the time, but not so common as to prevent the rule from ultimately 'self-correcting' if appropriate observations are made. We can again ask whether uses of the rule are 'reliable' and hence reasonable before such a 'self-correction' and whether they are reliable and hence reasonable afterwards. (Actually there are two important differences between this case and the induction case: first, it is likely to take much longer for the rule to self-correct; second, the self-correction is not automatic, in that whether a self-correction is ever made is likely to depend on accidents of which observations are made and which theories are thought of. I think that both of these factors diminish the chance that a reasonable long-term perspective on reliability could rule the early uses of the rule 'reasonable'.) In this case too it is unclear what a reliabilist can say that keeps the spirit of reliabilism without making reasonableness implausibly hard to come by.

5. MORE ON EPISTEMOLOGICAL EVALUATIVISM

I propose an alternative to reliabilism, more in line with 'non-factualist' views about normative discourse. The alternative is that reasonableness doesn't consist in reliability or anything else: it's not a 'factual property'. In calling a rule reasonable we are evaluating it, and all that makes sense to ask about is what we value. So the relevance of the reliability of a rule to its reasonableness is simply that we place a high value on our inductive and perceptual rules leading to truth in the circumstances in which we apply them; more or less equivalently, we place a high value on a given rule to the extent that we *believe* it will be reliable in the circumstances in which we apply it. We saw earlier that one will inevitably believe our most basic rules to be reliable in the circumstances in which we intend to apply them.[28] If so, we will inevitably place a high value on our own inductive and perceptual rules.

Is this an 'externalist' view or an 'internalist' view? The answer is that that distinction as normally drawn (for instance in Goldman (1980)) rests on a false presupposition. The presupposition is that epistemological properties like reasonableness are factual. If they are factual, it makes sense to ask whether the factual

---

[28] More accurately, our rules license us to so believe.

property involved includes 'external' elements.[29] On an evaluativist view, it is hard to draw a distinction between externalism and internalism that doesn't collapse. Any sensible evaluativist view will be 'externalist' in that one of the things we value in our rules is (some restricted version of) reliability. A sensible view will also be 'internalist' in that we also place a high value on our own rules: indeed, those are the rules we will use in determining the reliability of any rules we are evaluating. Which is primary, the high valuation of *our own* rules or the high valuation of *reliable* rules? It is hard to give clear content to this question, since (by the previous section) we inevitably ought to regard our own rules as likely to be reliable in the circumstances in which we intend to apply them.[30]

A view like this raises the spectre of extreme relativism. For mightn't it be the case that different people have different basic standards of evaluation? If so, aren't I saying that there is no fact of the matter as to which standard of evaluation is correct? And doesn't that mean that no standard is better than any other, so that those who 'justify' their belief in reincarnation on the basis of standards that positively evaluate just those beliefs that they think will make them feel good about their cultural origins are no worse epistemologically than those with a more 'scientific bias'? That of course would be a totally unacceptable conclusion.

But nothing I have said implies that no standards are better than others. Indeed, some clearly are better: they lead both to more truth and to less falsehood. Of course, in saying that that makes them 'better' I am presupposing a goal that is being rejected by the imaginary 'feel gooders', but so what? All evaluations presuppose goals, and of course it is my own goals that I presuppose in making evaluations. (To paraphrase David Lewis: Better I should use someone else's goals?)

Not only must I presuppose my own goals in saying that my standards are better than others, I must presuppose my own beliefs. This is most easily seen by contrasting my own standards not to 'feel good' standards but to the standards of those who are interested in the truth but have bizarre views about what best achieves it (e.g. they accept counter-inductive methods, or believe whatever the Reverend Moon tells them). If one were to apply the methods such people accept, one would be led to the conclusion that their methods are better than scientific methods. But again, so what? What makes scientific methods better isn't that *they say that* they will lead to more truth and less falsehood than these other methods,

---

[29] I assume for present purposes that the contrast between external and internal elements is clear.

[30] One could hope to make sense of it by considering conditional evaluations: we ask people to evaluate certain rules *on the supposition that* they are reliable, or unreliable. For instance, we consider the possibility of a world where our methods are unreliable and methods we find bizarre are reliable, and ask whether our method or the bizarre method is 'reasonable' in that world. But it seems to me that when asked this question we are torn: the two strands in our evaluation procedure come apart, and what to say is simply a matter of uninteresting verbal legislation.

it is that *they do* lead to more truth and less falsehood than these other methods. In saying that they do this I am presupposing the methods I accept, but that should go without saying: that's what accepting a method involves.

Of course, this is circular. ('Rule-circular', anyway). Earlier I objected that in using a methodology to evaluate itself, a positive evaluation isn't worth much *as a justification* of the methodology unless there was a prima-facie risk that the evaluation would have turned out negative; and that with our most basic rules there is no such risk. But I conceded that rule-circular 'justifications' of our methods have another role: they serve to explain why we value our methods over competing ones. It is that point I am stressing here, and it is enough for the point at hand; for the point at hand was that it is not part of the evaluativist view in question that all methods are equally good. (I'm not now addressing the sceptical issue: to what extent are we *reasonable* in thinking that our methods are better than others. I'll address that soon.)

Returning to the 'argument' for extreme relativism, I think we should concede that different people have slightly different basic epistemological standards: for one thing, any serious attempt to formalize inductive methods always invokes a number of variable parameters ('caution parameters' and the like), and there seems no motivation whatever for supposing that these are the same for all people. I doubt that there are many people with *radically* different basic epistemological standards, though there may be some: in the case of the Moonies it is hard to know what epistemological standards might have been used in producing their beliefs. But the extent of variation is a sociological issue on which I do not want to rest my views: whatever the extent of the actual variation in basic epistemological standards, there might have been such variation—even radical variation. Given that there is possible variation in basic standards (whether moderate or radical), should we suppose that some standards are *correct* and others *incorrect*? I doubt that any clear sense could be given to the notion of 'correctness' here. If there were a justificatory fluid that squirts from evidence to conclusions, we could say that correct standards were those that licensed beliefs in proportion to the fluid they receive from available evidence; but absent that, it is hard to see what can make standards correct or incorrect. What we *can* say is that some standards are better than others in achieving certain goals; and to the extent that one adopts those goals, one can simply say that some standards are better than others. Even given the goals, talk of 'correct' standards is probably inappropriate: for if it means 'best' there may be no best (there could be incomparabilities or ties; and for each there could be a better); and if it means 'sufficiently good', then it blurs relevant differences (two methods over the threshold would count as both correct even if one were better than the other).[31] We need a goal-relative notion of better

---

[31] One way to see the importance of this is to suppose that standards improve over time, and that a certain belief B counts as reasonable on the evidence E available at t using the quite good standards S in use at t, but counts as unreasonable on the same evidence using slightly better

standards, not a notion of correct standards. The argument for extreme relativism failed primarily in the slide from 'there are no correct standards' to 'all standards are equally good.'

The position I'm advocating does allow for a sort of moderate relativism. For in evaluating systems of epistemological rules, we can recognize that certain small modifications would produce results which have certain advantages (as well as certain disadvantages) over the results ours produce. For instance, we recognize that a system slightly more stringent in its requirements for belief is more reliable but less powerful. So we recognize that a slight modification of our goals—an increase in the relative value of reliability over power—would lead to a preference for the other system, and we regard the alternative goals as well within the bounds of acceptability. Consequently we make no very strong claims for the preferability of our system over the alternative: the alternative is slightly less good than ours given our precise goals, but slightly better on alternative goals that are by no means beyond the pale. 'Relativism' in this weak sense seems to me an eminently attractive position.

(Pollock (1987: sect. 4) tries to avoid even this weak form of relativism, by proposing that each person's concepts are so shaped by the system of epistemological rules that he or she employs that there can be no genuine conflict between the beliefs of people with different such systems; as a result, the systems themselves cannot be regarded as in conflict in any interesting sense. But this view is wholly implausible. I grant that there's a sense in which someone with even slightly different inductive rules inevitably has a slightly different concept of *raven* than I have, but it is not a sense that licenses us to say that his belief 'The next raven will be black' doesn't conflict with my belief 'The next raven will not be black.' It seems hard to deny that there would be a conflict between these raven beliefs, and if so, the systems of rules give genuinely conflicting instructions.)[32]

A complaint about evaluativism that has sometimes been made to me in conversation is that it places no constraints on what one's epistemological goals ought to be: nothing makes it *wrong* for a person not to care about achieving truth and avoiding falsehood, but care only about adopting beliefs that will make him feel good about his cultural origins. But I'm not sure what sort of ought (or what sort of wrongness) is supposed to be involved. If it's a moral ought that's at issue,

standards S' that only become available later (but which might in turn, for all we know, eventually be superceded). Any attempt to describe this situation in the language of 'correct standards' loses something important.

[32] Pollock's view is that it is our object level concepts like *raven* that are determined by our system of rules. A slightly more plausible view is that our epistemological concepts like *reasonable* are so determined: 'reasonable' just means 'reasonable according to our (the assessor's) rules'. But that view wouldn't serve Pollock's purposes: the advocates of alternative systems of rules would still be in genuine conflict about ravens, and each could raise sceptical worries about whether it mightn't be better to shift from the system that is reasonable in their own sense (viz. their own system) to the system that is reasonable in the other person's sense (viz. the other's system).

fine: I'm not opposing moral standards on which one ought to aim for the truth. But I assume that what was intended was not a moral ought, but some sort of epistemological ought. And that gives rise to a perplexity: on the usual understanding of 'epistemological oughts' they govern beliefs, not goals, and I have no idea what the sort of epistemological ought that governs goals could amount to.

As for 'constraints' on epistemological goals, again I don't think that the intended sense of 'constraint' is intelligible. If McRoss's main goal in forming beliefs is making himself feel good about his cultural origins, well, I don't approve, and I might try to browbeat him out of it if I thought I could and thought it worth the trouble. If I thought that my telling him he OUGHT not have such goals would influence him, I'd tell him that. Is this saying there are 'constraints' on his goals? Nothing is constraining him unless he takes my social pressure as a constraint. But if the question is whether there are constraints in some metaphysical sense, I don't think the metaphysical sense is intelligible. We don't need to believe in metaphysical constraints to believe that he's got lousy goals. (And if calling the goals lousy is evaluative rather than factual, so what?)

Perhaps talk of 'metaphysical constraints' on goals is supposed to mean only that McRoss's goals shouldn't count as 'epistemological'. Or alternatively, that the so-called 'beliefs' arrived at by a system motivated by the satisfaction of such goals shouldn't count as genuine beliefs. I have nothing against 'metaphysical constraints' in one of these senses, though they might better be called 'semantic constraints': they are simply stipulations about the meaning of 'epistemological goal' or 'belief', and of course one may stipulate as one likes. Such stipulations do nothing to constrain McRoss in any interesting way: if he has goals that don't satisfy my constraints, why should he care whether I call his goals 'epistemological' or his mental states 'beliefs'? Nor is it clear what other useful purpose such stipulations might serve.

As I've said, I doubt that there are many people with such radically different epistemological (or schmepistemological) goals for forming beliefs (or schmeliefs). But their non-existence has nothing to do with 'metaphysical constraints': as Richard Jeffrey once remarked, 'The fact that it is legal to wear chain mail on city buses has not filled them with clanking multitudes' (Jeffrey 1983: 145).

Let's now turn to a different complaint about evaluativism: this time not about the lack of objectivity in the goals, but about the lack of objectivity in the beliefs even when the goals are fixed. One way to press the complaint is to make an unfavourable contrast between evaluativism in epistemology and evaluativism in moral theory. In the moral case, an evaluativist might stress the possibility of variation in moral goals (e.g. with regard to the respective weights given to human pleasure and animal pain), but agree that relative to a choice of moral goals some moral codes are objectively better than others, and that we can make useful evaluations as to which ones are better given the goals. Such evaluations are in no way circular: in evaluating how well a given moral code satisfies certain goals, one may need to employ factual beliefs (for instance, about the extent of animal suffering), but such factual beliefs can be arrived at without use of a moral code. In the epistemological case, however, the evaluation has the sort of circularity that has cropped up several times already in this paper: in assessing how well a system of inductive or perceptual rules satisfies goals such as reliability, one needs to use factual beliefs, which in turn are arrived at only using inductive or perceptual rules. And this circularity might be thought to somehow undermine evaluativism—either directly, or by leading to a sceptical conclusion that makes the evaluativism pointless.

The circularity is undeniable: it might be called the fundamental fact of epistemological life, and was the basis for the puzzle in Section 4. But it doesn't directly undermine evaluativism, it leads only to the conclusion that our basic system of inductive rules (if indeed we have a basic system) is in Lewis's phrase 'immodest': it positively evaluates itself over its competitors (Lewis 1971: 1974). Nor is scepticism the outcome: true, systems of rules that we don't accept lead to different evaluations than ours do, but why should that undermine the evaluations provided by the rules that we do accept?

I concede that in dealing with people who use different standards of evaluation from ours, we typically don't just insist on our standards: we have several techniques of negotiation, the most important of which is to evaluate on neutral grounds. And to some extent we can do this with epistemological rules. For instance, the respective users of two inductive rules A and B that differ only in the value of a 'caution parameter' can agree that Rule A is more reliable but less powerful than Rule B; as a result, each realizes that a small shift in the relative value of reliability and power could lead to a preference for the other. In fact, the process of negotiating with people whose standards of evaluation differ from ours sometimes leads to a shift in our own standards (though of course such a shift is not evidence-driven). But though we sometimes negotiate or even shift standards in this way, we don't always: in dealing with a follower of the Reverend Moon, we may find that too little is shared for a neutral evaluation of anything to be possible, and we may have no interest in the evaluations that the Moonie gives. The fact that he gives them then provides no impetus whatever to revise our own evaluations, so the sceptical argument has no force from an evaluativist perspective.

Indeed, a main virtue of evaluativism is that it removes the force of most sceptical arguments. Most sceptical arguments depend on assuming that reasonableness is a factual property of beliefs or of rules, and on the understandable resistance to stripping away the normative nature of reasonableness by identifying it with a natural property like reliability (for rules; or being arrived at by reliable rules, for beliefs). Given the assumption and the understandable resistance to naturalistic reductionism, there is no alternative when faced with two radically different systems that positively evaluate themselves beyond (i) declaring them equally reasonable, (ii) postulating some mysterious non-natural property by which they differ, and (iii) saying that one is better simply by being mine (or more similar to mine). The second position seems crazy, and raises epistemological questions about how we could ever have reason to believe that a particular system has this property; the third position seems to strip away the normative force of reasonableness much as naturalistic reductionism did (indeed it could be regarded as a version of naturalistic reductionism, but one that uses chauvinistic natural properties); and this leaves only the sceptical alternative (i). Not a bad argument for scepticism, *if* one assumes that reasonableness is a factual property. Evaluativism provides the way out.

APPENDIX

Rules and Basic Rules

In the text I have tried to remain neutral as to whether a person's behaviour is governed by 'basic rules', but here I would like to argue that there is something to be said for supposing that this is so.

First a clarification: when I speak of someone 'following' a rule, what I mean is (i) that the person's behaviour by and large accords with the rule, and there is reason to expect that this would continue under a decent range of other circumstances; and (ii) that the person tends to positively assess behaviour that accords with the rule and to negatively assess behaviour that violates the rule. (In the case of epistemic rules, the 'behaviour' is of course the formation, retention, or revision of beliefs.) This is fairly vague, and the vagueness means that there is likely to be considerable indeterminacy involved in ascribing epistemic or other rules to a person: to ascribe a rule to a person is to idealize his actual behaviour, and idealizations needn't be unique. (I will discuss the significance of this shortly.) In any case, when I speak of rule-following I *don't* mean to suggest that the person has the rule 'written into his head'. There may be rules 'written into the head', but for those to be of use some part of the brain has to read them, and reading them is done by following rules; obviously these ones needn't be written in the head, on pain of regress.

In particular, when I imagined as a simple-minded illustration that we follow inductive rule (R) and that no evidence could lead us to change it, I certainly didn't mean to suggest that a person has something like my formulation of (R) 'written into his head', never to be altered by evidence. Even if some sort of formulation of the rule is explicitly written into the head, it might be very different from formulation (R). For instance, it might be that at a given time t what is written is not (R) but instead

(R) If after t you have observed s_t ravens, and r_t of them have been black, you should believe to degree $(r_t+b_t)/(s_t+c_t)$ of any raven not yet observed that it is black, where b_t and c_t are parameters representing the current bias, which changes over time. Following this sequence of rules is equivalent to following (R).[33] (If q_t is the number of ravens observed by time t and p_t is the number of them that have been black, then b_t and c_t are $j+p_t$ and $k+q_t$ respectively; since r_t and s_t are just $m-p_t$ and $n-q_t$ respectively, the equivalence is transparent.) 'Following this sequence of rules' might better be described as following the meta-rule (R*)

> Act in accordance with (R_t), *where the parameters b_t and c_t are obtained from earlier parameters by such and such updating process.*

But a psychological model could allow (R*) to be followed without being written into the head: the system is simply built to act in accordance with (R*), and to make assessments in accordance with it also. Again, no unchanging rule-formulation need be 'written into the head'.

A second clarification: not only don't I mean to suggest that the rule-formulations written into the head can't change over time, I don't mean to suggest that *the rules themselves* can't change as a result of observations: only that a person for whom that rule is fundamental can't recognize any observations as *evidence* undermining the rules. There are plenty of ways that the rules might change over time as a result of observations in a non-evidential way. Besides obviously non-rational changes (e.g. those produced by traumatic observations, or by computational errors), we might imagine changes made for computational convenience. Imagine a rule-formulation in the style of (R_t), where new evidence revises some parameters, but where the agent stores rounded off versions of the new values.[34] Over time, the values produced might start to vary considerably from what they would have been if the system had never rounded off. Here the rule-formulation changes to a *non-equivalent* rule formulation, on the impact of evidence; the rule itself changes. But this isn't a case where the accumulated observations serve as evidence against the old rule and for the new. (If we had started with a more

---

[33] As a model of what might be 'written into the head', the sequence of (R_t)s is far more plausible than (R): if (R) were what was written in it would require the agent to keep track of all the relevant evidence accumulated since birth, which is grossly implausible, in part because the computational requirements for storage and access would be immense. Still more plausible as a model is something 'in between' (R_t) than (R), where the agent doesn't need to remember all the evidence, but does remember some of it and retains a sense of what judgements he would make if something of the remembered evidence weren't in. (Indeed, something more like this is probably needed to handle assessments of our past inductive behaviour.)

[34] One might ask, why represent the meta-rule that the agent was following as the original (R*), rather than as a meta-rule that explicitly tells us to round off? I don't think this modified description of the agent would be incorrect, but neither do I think that a description of the agent as following the original (R*) would be incorrect: describing an agent as following a rule involves idealization of the agent's practices (especially when that rule is not explicitly represented in the agent, as it almost certainly wouldn't be for these meta-rules), and it's just a question of the extent to which one idealizes. Obviously, as the element of idealization of the agent's actual practices at revising beliefs lessens, the scope for arguing that the practices of revising beliefs can change lessens correspondingly.

complicated inductive rule than (R), there would have been more interesting ways for observations to lead to non-evidential changes in rules for purposes of computational simplicity.)

A less trivial example of how rules might change due to observations but not based on evidence arises when the rules are valued as a means of meeting certain goals (perhaps truth-oriented goals like achieving truth and avoiding falsehood). For there are various ways in which observations might cause a shift in goals (e.g. bad experiences might lead us to increase the weight given to avoiding falsehood over achieving truth), and thus lead to shifts in the rules for evaluating beliefs. But here too the shift in rules for believing isn't evidence-based, it is due to a change in goals. (It could also be argued that the basic rule in this example isn't the goal-dependent rule, but the rule about how beliefs depend on evidence *and* goals. This rule doesn't even change in the example described, let alone change as a result of evidence.)

Perhaps more important are cases where observations lead us to think up new methodological rules that had never occurred to us, and we are then led to use them on the basis of their intrinsic appeal. (Or maybe we observe others using them, and are led to use them out of a desire for conformity.) Here too it is transparent that the shift of rules is not due primarily to evidence against the old rules. Of course, on the basis of the new rules we might find that there is evidence against the old. But if the old rules didn't agree that it was evidence against them (and our resolution of the puzzle in Section 4 of the text says that they won't agree, if the rules are basic), then the decision to count the alleged evidence as evidence depends on an independent shift in the rule.

A third clarification: to assert that a person's inductive behaviour is governed by a basic rule is not to assert that there is a uniquely best candidate for what this basic rule is. To attribute a rule of inductive behaviour to someone is to give an idealized description of how the person forms and alters beliefs. For a variety of reasons, there need be no best idealized description. (The most important reason is that there are different levels of idealization: for instance, some idealizations take more account of memory limitations or computational limitations than do others. Also though I think less important, there can be multiple good idealized descriptions with the same level of idealization, especially when that level of idealization is high: since a description at a given highly idealized level only connects loosely with the actual facts, there is no reason to think it uniquely determined by the facts.) So there are multiple good candidates for the best idealization of our total inductive behaviour. Any such idealization counts any factors it doesn't take into account as non-rational. Insofar as the idealization is a good one, it is *appropriate* to take the factors it doesn't take into account as non-rational. The lack of a uniquely best candidate for one's basic rule is largely due to a lack of a uniquely best division between rational and non-rational factors.

With these clarifications in mind, let's turn to the issue of whether there are basic inductive rules. Since in attributing rules one is idealizing, really the only sensible issue is whether a good idealization will postulate a basic inductive rule (which might vary from one good idealization to the next). The alternative is an idealization that postulates multiple rules, each assessable using the others. But there is an obvious weakness in an idealization of the latter sort: it is completely uninformative about what the agent does when the rules conflict. There is in fact some process that the agent will use to deal with such conflicts. Because this conflict-breaking process is such an important part of how the agent operates, it is natural to consider it a rule that the agent is following. If so, it would seem to be a basic rule, with the 'multiple rules' really just default rules that operate only when they don't come into conflict with other default rules. Of course, this basic rule needn't be deterministic; and as stressed before, there need be no uniquely best candidate for what the higher rule that governs conflict-resolution is. But what seems to be the case is that idealizations that posit a basic rule are more informative than those that don't.

According to the discussion of the epistemological puzzle in Section 4, no rule can be empirically undermined by following that rule.[35] But if there are multiple candidates for one's basic inductive rule, it may well happen that each candidate C for one's basic inductive rule can be 'empirically undermined' by other candidates for one's basic inductive rule; that is, consistently adhering to a candidate other than C could lead (on certain observations) to a departure from the rule C. There's good reason to put 'empirically undermined' in quotes, though: 'undermining' C via C* only counts as genuine undermining to the extent that C* rather than C is taken as the basic inductive rule. To the extent that C is regarded as the basic inductive rule, it has not been empirically undermined.

I've said that the most important reason for the existence of multiple candidates for a person's basic inductive rule is that we can idealize the person's inductive practices at different levels. At the highest level, perhaps, we might give a simple Bayesian description, with real-number degrees of belief that are coherent (i.e. obey the laws of probability). At a lower level of idealization, we might give a more sophisticated Bayesian description, allowing for interval-valued degrees of belief and/or failures of coherence due to failures of logical omniscience. At a still lower level we might abandon anything recognizably Bayesian, in order to more accurately accommodate the agent's computational limitations. Eventually we might get to a really low level of idealization, in terms of an accurate map of

---

[35] That argument did not depend on an assumption that (candidates for) our basic inductive rules be deterministic. Suppose that our most basic rules dictate that in certain circumstances a 'mental coin-flip' is to be made, and that what policies one employs in the future is to depend upon its outcome. One can describe what is going on in such a case along the lines of (R) or (R*)—unchanging indeterministic rules, simply a new policy. In that case, obviously there is no change in the basic rules based on evidence, because there is no change in basic rules at all. Alternatively, one can describe what is going on along the lines of (R$_t$): the rules themselves have changed. But in this case, the indeterministic nature of the change would if anything *lessen* the grounds for calling the change evidence-based.

the agent's system of interconnected neurons, but using an idealization of neuron functioning. And of course there are a lot of levels of idealization in between. The rules of any one of these levels allow criticism of the rules of any other level as imperfectly rational: higher levels would be criticized for taking insufficient account of computational limitations, lower levels for having hardware that only imperfectly realizes the appropriate rules. But again, insofar as you somewhat arbitrarily pick one level as the 'level of rationality', then one's rules at 'the level of rationality' can't allow there to be empirical reasons for revising what is at that level one's basic inductive rule.[36]

References

Benacerraf, Paul (1973), 'Mathematical truth', *Journal of Philosophy* 70: 661–80.

Black, Max (1958), 'Self-supporting inductive arguments', *Journal of Philosophy* 55: 718–25.

Bonjour, Laurence (1998), *In Defense of Pure Reason* (Cambridge: Cambridge University Press).

Carnap, Rudolph (1963), 'An axiom system for inductive logic', in *The Philosophy of Rudolph Carnap*, ed. Paul Schilpp (La Salle: Open Court): 973–9.

Dummett, Michael (1978), 'The justification of deduction' in his *Truth and Other Enigmas* (Cambridge, Mass.: Harvard University Press).

Field, Hartry (1994), 'Disquotational Truth and Factually Defective Discourse', *Philosophical Review* 103: 405–52.

—— (1996), 'The a prioricity of logic', *Proceedings of the Aristotelian Society* 96: 359–79.

—— (1998*a*), 'Mathematical objectivity and mathematical objects', in Stephen Laurence and Cynthia MacDonald (eds.), *Contemporary Readings in the Foundations of Metaphysics* (Oxford: Blackwell): 387–403.

—— (1998*b*), 'Epistemological Nonfactualism and the A Prioricity of Logic', *Philosophical Studies* 92: 1–24.

Friedman, Michael (1979), 'Truth and confirmation', *Journal of Philosophy* 76: 361–82.

Gibbard, Alan (1990), *Wise Choices, Apt Feelings* (Cambridge, Mass.: Harvard University Press).

Goldman, Alvin (1980), 'The internalist conception of justification', in *Midwest Studies in Philosophy*, v. 5, ed. Peter French, Theodore Uehling, and Howard Wettstein, (Minneapolis: University of Minnesota): 27–51.

—— (1988), 'Strong and weak justification', *Philosophical Perspectives* 2: 51–69.

Jeffrey, Richard (1983) 'Bayesianism with a human face', in *Testing Scientific Theories*, ed. John Earman (Minneapolis: University of Minnesota): 133–56.

---

[36] Presumably the rules at the very low levels in the hierarchy just described are in any reasonable sense beyond our control, whereas the higher-level rules should count as somehow 'in our control' (despite the fact that any changes made in the higher-level rules are due to the operation of the lower-level rules). One might want to stipulate that 'the level of rationality' is the lowest level of rules in our control. But 'in our control' is itself extremely vague, so this would do little to pin down a unique 'level of rationality'.

Kemeny, John (1963), 'Carnap's theory of probability and induction', in *The Philosophy of Rudolph Carnap*, ed. Paul Schilpp, (La Salle: Open Court): 711–38.

Kitcher, Philip (1983), *The Nature of Mathematical Knowledge* (Oxford: Oxford University Press).

Lewis, David (1971), 'Immodest inductive methods', *Philosophy of Science* 38: 54–63.

—— (1974), 'Lewis and Spielman on inductive immodesty', *Philosophy of Science* 41: 84–85.

Pollock, John (1987), 'Epistemic norms', *Synthese* 79: 61–95.

Putnam, Hilary (1963), '"Degree of confirmation" and inductive logic' in *The Philosophy of Rudolph Carnap*, ed. Paul Schlipp (La Salle: Open Court): 761–83.

Van Cleve, James (1984), 'Reliability, Justification, and the Problem of Induction' in *Midwest Studies in Philosophy*, v. 9, ed. Peter French, Theodore Uehling, and Howard Wettstein (Minneapolis: University of Minnesota): 555-67.

7

Stipulation, Meaning, and Apriority

Paul Horwich

1. INTRODUCTION

Is there such a thing as a priori knowledge and, if there is, where does it come from? More specifically, could a belief be rational yet not help at all to accommodate experience?[1] And if so, how? I think that the answer to the first question is yes: some of our justified beliefs are indeed a priori. And I will eventually say a little to support this claim and to explain the existence of a priori knowledge. But to begin with—in fact this will be my predominant concern here—I want to look at a popular account of apriority that I *don't* believe in.

The view I wish to challenge is that fundamental (i.e. underived) a priori knowledge—and, in particular, our knowledge of the basic principles of logic and arithmetic—is engendered by our understanding of words or by our grasp of concepts. Here is a familiar way of implementing this idea:- certain postulates are implicit definitions of some of their constituent terms; that is to say, our deciding to mean what we do by those terms guarantees the truth of the postulates; consequently, our knowledge of these truths derives merely from our understanding of them; hence this knowledge is independent of experience. In particular, it is not implausible that the basic laws of classical logic fix the meanings of logical terms, including 'or', 'not', and 'every'; and that Hume's Principle ('The number of fs equals the number of gs if and only if the fs and gs can be put into one-to-one correspondence with one another') determines the meaning of 'The number of _s'. And the view I'm going to criticize has it that we can on this basis explain our a priori knowledge within logic and arithmetic.

I would like to thank Ned Block, Paul Boghossian, Harty Field, Marcus Giaquinto, and Michael Williams for their helpful comments on an earlier draft of this paper.

[1] I am ignoring issues, not relevant here, regarding *precisely* how the a priori/a posteriori distinction should be drawn. For an illuminating discussion of these issues see Hartry Field's 'Apriority as an Evaluative Notion', in the present volume.

This idea—which I'll call 'semantogenic apriority'—was developed by the positivists and logical empiricists. But you certainly don't have to be a card-carrying positivist in order to sympathize with it. Witness such contemporary figures as Paul Boghossian, Bob Hale, Christopher Peacocke, and Crispin Wright, who have offered accounts of a priori knowledge very much along these lines, as we shall see.[2]

2. SEMANTOGENIC APRIORITY

Let me begin by giving a simple formulation of the strategy of semantogenic apriority. We are entirely free to decide what our terms will mean; consequently we are entitled to stipulate that a given word, 'f', will mean whatever would make true a certain conjunction of sentences, '#f', that contain this word;[3] if we do so, then it will be known a priori that 'f' has that meaning; therefore—since its having that meaning entails the truth of the sentences—it will be known a priori that those sentences are true. That is to say

> (1) I am entitled to mean what I want by 'f'.
> ∴ (2) I stipulate (perhaps implicitly) that 'f' means what will make '#f' true.
> ∴ (3) I am entitled to hold a priori that 'f' means what will make '#f' true.
> ∴ (4) I infer that '#f' is true.
> ∴ (5) I infer that #f.
> ∴ (6) I am entitled to hold a priori that #f.
> ∴ (7) My belief that #f is justified and a priori.

In order to clarify and assess this explanatory model (and certain variants of it) several various interrelated questions will need to be addressed:

(a) In what conditions is it possible to *stipulate* that something is to be a certain way (e.g. that the walls of this room are to be painted white). And, what particular form do these conditions take in the special case of *semantic* stipulation—for example, in the case where we stipulate that 'f' is to have the meaning that will make '#f' come out true?

(b) How are we to determine *which* of the sentences containing a term comprise its definition? In other words, to which instances of 'f' and '#f' does the

---

[2] Boghossian (in 'Analyticity Reconsidered', *Nous* 30(3): 1996) calls the view 'the analytic theory of the a priori'; Peacocke's term (in 'How Are A Priori Truths Possible?', *European Journal of Philosophy*, August 1993) is 'the metasemantic account'; and Hale and Wright (in 'Implicit Definition and the A Priori', the present volume) speak of 'the traditional connection' between implicit definition and a priori knowledge.

[3] In some cases the stipulation will take a slightly different form: namely that a given word is to mean whatever would make *truth-preserving* a certain set of *inference-rules* containing it.

model apply? Can we really use it to explain the meanings of logical and arithmetical terms and our a priori knowledge in logic and arithmetic?

(c) From the fact that a certain proposition is *stipulated* to be true, may we really infer that it known a priori? Or that it is known at all? Or even that it is true?

(d) Does the model really explain, as advertised, how a priori commitments are *engendered* by knowledge of meaning, rather than merely showing that knowledge of meaning presupposes a priori commitments?

(e) Can our entitlement to mean a certain thing by a word really provide an epistemic reason (sufficient for knowledge) to make those commitments (e.g. accept those sentences) that will constitute the word's having that meaning?

Let us start by looking at the notion of stipulation.

3. STIPULATION

To stipulate that something be the case is, in a sense, to 'command' that is to be so—to state that it shall be so with the expectation of being able thereby to bring it about that it is so. Thus a teacher might stipulate which questions the students are to answer correctly in order to pass his course; a dictator might stipulate who her successor will be; the owner of a dog might stipulate what it should be called; and we might for convenience introduce a new term, 'autofanticide', under the stipulation that it is to mean 'the killing by a time-traveller of his infant self'.

Some stipulations are successful and others are not. That is, some actually bring about the 'commanded' state of affairs and others do not. For example, perhaps NN is stipulated to be the next leader, but then dies before the stipulation can take effect. Now one might be tempted to respond that *genuine* stipulations *must* succeed, and to say that I was speaking loosely—oversimplifying—in characterizing the content of the dictator's stipulation in the way I did, as the stipulation that NN will be the next leader. Was its content not, somewhat more accurately, that NN will be the next leader *unless this is prevented by his death, the destruction of the state, ..., and so on*? However, on this alternative way of conceiving of stipulation, it would often be very hard, and perhaps impossible, to specify exactly what is stipulated. Nor, on reflection, does it seem at all deviant to say of a stipulation that it was not realized. Thus it is both less problematic and more natural to continue to suppose, as I did initially, that stipulations need not succeed; they may or may not be frustrated.

Thus S can stipulate that p, yet, because of infelicitous circumstances, not be successful in bringing it about that p. However, S cannot stipulate that p unless he believes he is able thereby to bring it about that p. Therefore he cannot, at the time of stipulation, be aware of circumstances that that will evidently prevent it coming about that p. For example, I cannot stipulate that I will be the next King of England, or that 'Giorgione' will stand for the largest prime number, because I know that I don't qualify for that office and that there is no such number.

4. SEMANTIC STIPULATION

For any successful stipulation one can raise the question of how it was implemented. Often the answer is fairly obvious. One of the conditions of a person's authority over others is that they follow his instructions; he is then in a position to stipulate that certain things be done. But there are cases in which it is more obscure how a stipulation works — and these more problematic cases include *semantic* stipulations. No doubt I *can* stipulate what 'autofanticide' is to mean in my idiolect, or that my puppy's name is to be 'Pooch', but *how*? How does it come about that my 'commanding' these things will result in their being so? The main difficulty we have in answering this question is not hard to identify. We are not clear enough about *what it is* for two expressions to have the same meaning, or for a certain word to be the name of a certain thing. We aren't clear about which underlying facts would *constitute* those semantic facts. Consequently we don't fully understand how our stipulations can bring such semantic relations into being. Note that this is so even when all one wishes to stipulate are the meanings and referents of words in one's own idiolect.

A virtue of the *use* theory of meaning is that it can help us to address this problem in a plausible way and can thereby contribute to a reasonable explanation of the phenomena of semantic stipulation. Suppose that for two expressions to mean the same thing is for them to have the same use. Of course, a proper account and defence of this proposal would require a specification of just what is meant by 'use' in this context.[4] But for present purposes we can leave this matter somewhat vague. The important thing is that we can see how I can 'command' myself—i.e. decide— to use 'autofanticide' in the same way that I already use 'the killing by a time-traveller of his infant self'. I might for example do it by following the rules of inference

$$\frac{\pounds(\text{the killing} \ldots \text{etc.})}{\therefore \ \pounds(\text{autofanticide})} \qquad \frac{\pounds(\text{autofanticide})}{\therefore \ \pounds(\text{the killing} \ldots \text{etc.})}$$

(where '$\pounds$' may include intensional contexts). Thus we can begin to understand how it is possible to stipulate the meaning of a word.

In addition, the character of *naming*—i.e. reference stipulation—is illuminated by the use theory of meaning. For my holding true

This (ostended) puppy is Pooch

---

[4] For an articulation and defence of the use theory of meaning, see my *Meaning* (Oxford University Press, 1998).

establishes my using the word 'Pooch' in a particular way, and this use provides the word 'Pooch' with the meaning it has. Now in general

w means **N** $\rightarrow$ (x)(w refers to x $\leftrightarrow$ x = n),

(where **N** is the singular concept expressed by the name 'n'). And in particular

w means **POOCH** $\rightarrow$ (x)(w refers to x $\leftrightarrow$ x = Pooch).

Therefore, in using the word as I do, and thereby meaning by it what I do, I make it the case that

(x)('Pooch' refers to x $\leftrightarrow$ x = Pooch)

and, in particular (letting x be this puppy) that

'Pooch' refers to this puppy $\leftrightarrow$ (this puppy = Pooch).

Therefore, given the fact of identity, I bring it about that

'Pooch' refers to this puppy.

Notice that my stipulation (that this puppy is to be named 'Pooch') is put into effect by a combination of facts—one of which is entirely up to me (i.e. that I hold true the sentence 'This puppy is Pooch') and some of which are not (e.g. the non-linguistic fact that this puppy *is* Pooch).[5]

Let us now move on to the particular sort of stipulation deployed within the strategy of semantogenic apriority—namely stipulations of the form: that the word 'f' is to have whatever meaning will make true some conjunction of postulates, '#f', containing that word. In investigating this idea we must bear in mind two morals from the discussion so far: first, that the decision to give a word a meaning is effected by giving it a use; and second, that an act of stipulation requires the belief that it could help to bring about the stipulated state of affairs. So we must consider whether there is any way in which I might use the new term 'f' that, I can plausibly believe, will result in its possessing a meaning relative to which '#f' will be true.

Well, one thing I might do with the term 'f' in order to effect this stipulation is to accept the sentence '#f'. That use would provide 'f' with a meaning. Moreover, in accepting '#f' I would be taking it to be true. Thus I would indeed believe that I am giving 'f' a meaning relative to which '#f' is true.

Note, however, that a crucial condition must be satisfied for this stipulation to be possible. I must be *able* to use 'f' in the necessary way—namely to regard '#f'

---

[5] One might be tempted to think that even this puppy's being Pooch results, at least in part, from my linguistic decision. But this would be a mistake. In the first place, necessary identities (another example is that Hesperus = Phosphorus) are not susceptible to explanation—and, a fortiori, are not the results our cognitive activity. In the second place, it is no more natural to think that we make Pooch into this puppy than that we give Pooch four legs. And to accept that sort of thing is to endorse a radical and highly implausible ('world-making') form of anti-realism.

as true. And this is a substantial concern, since that use of 'f' could well be ruled out by the pre-existing meanings of the words that make up '#–', together with my pre-existing epistemic attitudes to certain sentences formed from those words. For example, given the current meanings of the symbols '&' and '→', I cannot stipulate that 'tonk' will have a meaning relative to which all instances of the schema, '[(p tonk q) → q] & [p → (p tonk q)]', are true, because I would have to accept all those instances and therefore be prepared, via trivial deductions, to accept every single sentence; but this is impossible since it would violate the very concept of acceptance.[6] Similarly, insofar as I am not willing to abandon certain convictions or to alter current meanings, I cannot now stipulate that 'glub' is to have a meaning relative to which 'Mars is glub and harbours life' is true. The impossibility of this stipulation does not depend on my taking 'Mars harbours life' to be certainly false; it suffices that I do not presently accept it.

In general, suppose, for some sentence, u, I am aware (a) that it is a logical consequence of '#f', (b) that it is formulated merely in terms of the vocabulary of '#–', and (c) that I do not accept it. In that case I can see that whether there is, or is not, a fact described by u, is not up to me to decide; it is already determined by what u means and by the nature of the world; therefore I am not free to stipulate the truth of '#f'. Thus I can stipulate the truth of '#f' only if I already believe that every 'f'-free sentence entailed by '#f' is true. But every 'f'-free consequence of '#f' is entailed by '∃(x(#x)'—which is itself 'f'-free. Therefore I can stipulate the truth of '#f' only if I already believe in the truth of '∃x(#x)'.

Notice that even if the *possibility* of a certain stipulation is not precluded by the meaning of '#–' and by previous beliefs, it by no means follows that the stipulation will be *successful*. It may well be that, in virtue of the meaning of '#–', the sentence '#f' has logical consequences that are false, even though I believed them to be true when I made the stipulation. For example, someone might design a new formulation of an established physical theory—one he is convinced is correct. And he might stipulate that the new theoretical terms are to mean whatever will make his theory-formulation true. But if some of the theory's observable consequences are in fact false, then the stipulation will not be successful.

5. CONDITIONAL SEMANTIC STIPULATION

It might be thought that in such cases—where either it is not possible to stipulate that 'f' will mean whatever will make '#f' true, or where there is some prospect that such a stipulation would be unsuccessful—one might avoid both these potential difficulties by instead stipulating merely the *conditional*: that *if* 'f' has any

---

[6] It is plausibly an essential characteristic of *acceptance* that the sentences we accept are relied upon in deliberation leading to action. But this characteristic is inconsistent with our accepting *every* sentence, since such a profligate acceptance practice would prevent any particular action from being selected over its alternatives.

meaning, it has whatever meaning would make '#f' true.[7] This, one might contend, is a stipulation that certainly can be made and certainly will be success-ful. But, as before, in order to determine whether these contentions are really correct, we have to consider how the suggested stipulation could possibly be implemented. And this turns out to be problematic.

Suppose, for example, my plan for implementing it is to hold true '#f'. The trouble with this plan, as we have just seen, is that being able to carry it out is *not* guaranteed: it is subject to the constraints implied by the already established mean-ing of '#–'. Moreover, even if these constraints are satisfied, so that I do in fact accept '#f' and thereby give 'f' a meaning, it might well be, as I mentioned, that '#f' is nonetheless false; so the stipulation will fail. Thus, if holding true '#f' is how I aim to effect my conditional stipulation, then that stipulation stands no better chance of being feasible or successful that did the original, unconditional one!

So is there anything else I might try in order to effect that conditional stipula-tion? How about holding true

If 'f' is meaningful, then its meaning renders '#f' true.

But how would I do this? Given the use theory of meaning, it would have to be done by my holding true

If 'f' has a use, then that use makes '#f' true.

But clearly, whether or not I can hold true this conditional depends on what I do with 'f'—on whether or not I give it a meaning-constituting use. If I *don't* give it a use, then I can indeed be confident (trivially, by falsity of antecedent) that the stipulation is both possible and successful. But if I *do* give 'f' a use, then I can hold true the conditional only by accepting its consequent—i.e. by holding true '#f'. But then, we are back exactly where we were before: the prospects of (a) not being *able* to make the stipulation, and (b) failing to make a *successful* stipula-tion, have not been diminished. Moving to Boghossian's conditional form of stip-ulation does not help us to avoid these hazards; so let us resume consideration of the standard form.

6. PURELY MEANING-CONSTITUTING STIPULATION

Suppose I stipulate that 'f' is to mean what will make '#f' true, and, to that end, I decide to regard '#f' as true. In doing so I am also committing myself to the logical consequences of '#f'. However, amongst these consequences, it may be that some do not involve the term 'f'. And, surely, my holding true *such* consequences cannot be necessary for 'f''s meaning what it does.

For example, someone's acceptance of the conjunction of Euclidean geometry and phlogiston theory might suffice to fix the meanings of his words 'point' and 'line'; but the commitment to phlogiston theory is plainly irrelevant.

Therefore, let us say that the stipulation that 'f' is to mean whatever will make '#f' true is *'purely* meaning-constituting' only if '#f' cannot be factored in this way into conjuncts such that holding true only one of them suffices to fix 'f''s meaning.

The question then arises, in regard to any particular theory-formulation that we accept, as to whether our decision to accept it is purely meaning-constituting, or whether it is perhaps the product of two decisions—only one of them purely meaning-constituting, and the other one motivated in some other way (e.g. by empirical considerations).

Consider for example the case of a physical theory. Here (following Russell, Carnap, Ramsey, and Lewis)[8] it is plausible to regard the theory-formulation '#f' as the conjunction of two components

$$(S) \quad \exists x(\#x)$$

and

$$(M) \quad \exists x(\#x) \Rightarrow \#f,$$

the first of which captures the theory's substance—its empirical content—and the second of which pertains to the meaning of 'f'.[9] This two-way factorization explains how people can disagree as to whether '#f' is correct, yet nonetheless agree on what 'f' means: for they may disagree about (S) yet agree on (M). It also explains something we observed in Section 4: that it is possible to stipulate the truth of a substantive theory, '#f', in order to fix 'f''s meaning, if and only if one already believes in the truth of '$\exists x(\#x)$'. Thus the stipulation that 'f' shall mean whatever is needed for '#f' to be true is *not* purely meaning constituting; rather, our commitment to the conditional, '$\exists x(\#x) \Rightarrow \#f$', is what provides 'f' with its meaning.

What about the case of arithmetic? Consider the stipulation that the

---

[8] See B. Russell, *The Analysis of Matter* (London: Allen & Unwin, 1927); R. Carnap, *Der Logische Aufbau der Welt* (Berlin: Schlachtensee Weltkreis-Verlag, 1928); F. Ramsey, 'Theories', 1929, repr. in his *Foundations*, ed. H. D. Mellor (London: Routledge & Kegan Paul, 1978); and D. Lewis, 'How to Define Theoretical Terms', *Journal of Philosophy*, 57 (July 1970): 427–66.

[9] Note that (M) cannot be a *material* conditional; for the conditional commitment we want to express cannot come merely from regarding its antecedent as false. Note also that (M) must not be confused with Boghossian's conditional, 'If "f" has a meaning, then "f"'s meaning makes "#f" true.' As we saw in sect. 5, the latter can be regarded as true only if either 'f' has *no* use, or if the unconditional theory-formulation, '#f', is regarded as true. And note finally that our Carnapian 'two factor' approach requires ontological commitment to *properties*. Indeed the virtues of the approach might be taken to provide an argument in favour of such a commitment.

expression, 'The number of _s', is to mean whatever will make true Hume's Principle[10]

> The number of fs = the number of gs *iff* the fs and the gs can be put into one-to-one correspondence.

As in the case of a physical theory, Hume's Principle can be divided into two parts. First there is

(HS) $(\exists\%)$ (f) (g) $(\%f = \%g \leftrightarrow f{\sim}g)$,

(where '%' stands for a variable ranging over functions from properties to objects, and 'f~g' means 'the fs and the gs can be put into one-to-one correspondence'), which asserts that there is *some* function from properties to objects that satisfies Hume's Principle. Second there is the conditional

(HM) $(\exists\%)$ (f) (g) $(\%f = \%g \leftrightarrow f{\sim}g) \Rightarrow$
(f) (g) (the number of fs = the number of gs iff f~g).

And surely it is no less plausible here than it is in the case of a physical theory to suppose that it is our acceptance only of this conditional, (HM), that is required for 'the number of _s' to mean what it does. After all, scepticism about the existence of numbers does appear to be possible; and does not seem to carry with it an inability to mean what we non-sceptics mean by arithmetical terms. This sceptical position would be expressed by someone who denied (HS) but accepted (HM). That acceptance will suffice to assign 'the number of _s' the potential theoretical role, or use, that constitutes it meaning. Thus what is *purely* meaning-constituting here is that 'the number of _s' shall mean whatever will make (HM) true. Our acceptance of (HS) is an *additional* commitment—one which might well be a priori, but which is not required for 'the number of _s' to mean what it does.

I see little reason not to treat logic analogously. An intuitionist might reject our classical logic. But we need not suppose that he is thereby prevented from appreciating what we mean by our logical terms. In order to keep things clear he could well employ different symbols to express his intuitionistic concepts, and he could then use our logical words unambiguously—attaching the same meanings to them that we do. Thus, in order to give classical meanings to these symbols, it is not necessary to deploy them in classical reasoning. What is needed, rather, is something along the above lines: a conditional commitment that one would be prepared so to deploy them *if* one were to accept classical reasoning.

Granted, it might not be easy to *formulate* this conditional commitment. One problem would be the need to quantify into the positions of logical constants.

---

[10] For a defence of the view that Hume's Principle is a priori because it implicitly defines 'the number of _s', see Crispin Wright's *Frege's Conception of Numbers as Objects* (Aberdeen, Aberdeen University Press, 1980); Bob Hale's, 'Grundlagen $64', *Proceedings of the Aristotelean Society*, 1996–7; and their joint paper, 'Implicit Definition and the A priori', in the present volume.

Another would be the need for a kind of conditional commitment that can be accepted by both intuitionistic and classical logicians. However, the technical difficulty of articulating the position in logically precise terms should not be allowed to obscure its intuitive plausibility. Why shouldn't even a *logical* practice be factored into the substantive epistemic commitments it embodies, and the decision about how to express them?

For surely *any* belief or inferential move may be expressed in a variety of different ways. Thus in English one says 'The proposition that snow is white is true if and only if snow is white', and in Italian 'La proposizione che la neve e bianca e vero se e solo se la neve e bianca'; in German one infers from 'p und q' to 'p', whereas in French it's from 'p et q' to 'p'; and so on. Thus, whether in science, mathematics, or logic, there is always a difference between, on the one hand, an epistemic commitment and, on the other hand, the linguistic decision to express that commitment in one way rather than another. There is a difference between the commitment to accept, for some term 'x', something of the form '#x', and the decision that *if* one makes that commitment one will fulfil it by accepting '#f'— that is, by having 'f' be the particular term one uses to discharge it. Thus, although it may sometimes be unclear just how this pair of factors should be articulated, their existence and distinctness can hardly be doubted—even in the case of logic.

7. IMPLICIT PURELY MEANING-CONSTITUTING STIPULATION

I have been suggesting that a certain complication arises in the attempt to apply the strategy of semantogenic apriority to the theories to which we are most inclined to apply it. The difficulty is that when a term is introduced by regarding as true a *substantive* theory-formulation that contains the term, then only one component of that decision is necessary for providing the term with its meaning. And we shall soon be emphasizing the disappointing epistemological consequences of this fact. But in the meanwhile it is important to note a further complication. Obviously, most of the theories whose possible aprioricity we are investigating (e.g. arithmetic and classical logic) were not, at some specific moment in time, suddenly accepted by way of explicitly stipulating the meanings of constituent terms ('and', 'not', 'plus', etc.). Therefore, if the strategy of semantogenic aprioricity is to have any application to those theories, it will have to be shown that they nevertheless involve semantic stipulations of a certain sort— namely *implicit* stipulations—and that these can have the same semantic and epistemological potential as explicit ones.[11]

---

[11] If one didn't mind courting confusion, one might speak of '*implicit* implicit definition'— the second 'implicit' indicating that the defining sentence does not have the form 'x is f ≡ . . . x . . .', and the first one conveying that 'f' was not introduced by an overt decision to accept that sentence.

Let us see how these things can indeed be shown. To stipulate that p is to 'command' that p in the expectation of thereby bringing it about that p. So we must explain how this could happen when the 'commanding' and expecting are not overt. In the semantic case, the 'commands' and subsequent decisions concern the uses of words: our further use of 'f' is to proceed from our accepting such-and-such theory-formulation. So we might well suppose that, even in the absence of an *articulated* commitment of this sort, the mere *practice* of using a word as we do could manifest an *implicit* decision to base its use on the acceptance of certain sentences containing it. In order to identify *which* sentences these are—i.e. in order to identify *which* stipulation is implicit in our practice with a word—we have to find out (by inference to the best explanation) which sentences are such that their acceptance provides the most plausible basis for everything else that we do with the word. We can then say that the word's meaning is given by the implicit stipulation that it is to mean whatever would make those sentences true. Thus, to decide which of the many 'f'-sentences that are held true are so held as a matter of implicit purely meaning-constituting stipulation, we need to determine which acceptance-facts are explanatorily fundamental with respect to 'f''s overall usage.

This strategy might not always work. We might find, for a given word, that the explanatorily basic fact about it is *not* that certain sentences or rules of inference containing it are accepted, but rather that the basic fact is some complex conditional decision that is not characterizable as 'true' or 'truth-preserving' or 'correct' (in any truth-theoretic sense). In such cases we will not be able to say that we stipulate that the word is given whatever meaning is needed for the decision to be correct; but we can nonetheless say that the word's meaning is assigned—implicitly defined—by that decision.

8. APRIORITY

Now, at long last, we are ready for a priori *justification*; we are finally in a position to examine the relations between this notion and the notions of *stipulation* and *meaning*. To begin with, it is evident that S may stipulate that p without believing a priori that p. Remember the stipulation that NN will be the next leader. The dictator's presuppositions—including her assumption that NN will not die before she does—obviously need not be held a priori. Similarly, if I have stipulated that 'f' is to mean whatever will make '#f' true, my view that 'f' now has such a meaning might well not be a priori. For, as we have seen, I may be perfectly aware that 'f' can have such a meaning only because an *empirical* condition, '$\exists x(\#x)$', is satisfied.

But suppose we restrict our attention to stipulations that are *purely* meaning-constituting. Are these bound to be a priori? Here I believe the answer is yes. The decision to endorse

$$\exists x(\#x) \Rightarrow \#f$$

does no more that attach a word to a concept, and makes no commitment to whether that concept is to be deployed. And so it cannot rest on empirical beliefs. Therefore one can stipulate that 'f' is to have the meaning that will make true this conditional; and one can do so without needing to make any empirical assumptions.

However, as we have seen, the contents of our purely meaning-constituting stipulations regarding the terms of arithmetic and logic are *not* that these terms are to have the meanings that make correct our substantive arithmetical and logical theories. So we cannot conclude, from the fact that the meanings of these symbols are (implicitly) stipulated, that those substantive theories are a priori. What can be identified as a priori are nothing more than the Carnapian *conditional* commitments discussed in section 6.[12]

Moreover, even though the object of a purely meaning-constituting stipulation seems bound to be held a priori, we cannot conclude that its being so held *results from* its being meaning-constituting. On the contrary, the actual explanatory direction would seem to be precisely the opposite. To begin with, we decide, on non-empirical grounds, to hold true '$\exists x(\#x) \Rightarrow \#f$'. In other words, that conditional is held a priori. And this fact is responsible for 'f' meaning what it does. Therefore it is certainly not *because* our acceptance of that sentence engenders 'f''s meaning that this acceptance is non-empirical.

This point concerns the question of why a purely meaning-constituting sentence *is* accepted. But there is a more important question: why *should* it be accepted? Are we *justified* in accepting it, and if so how? Unless the semantogenic perspective can provide an answer to this normative question, it cannot pretend to be an account of a priori *knowledge*. But it is not clear that an adequate semantogenic answer is available.

One conceivable strategy is to cite our *right* to mean what we want, and to argue that this amounts to a right to hold true the appropriate meaning-constituting sentences. But can we suppose that such a right, or entitlement, provides the sort of justification required for knowledge? It implies perhaps that no epistemic requirement would be infringed if we were to accept the purely meaning-constituting sentences. But that does not entail that we *ought* to accept them—i.e. that we have a positive epistemic *obligation* to accept them.

A second way of trying to show that purely meaning-constituting sentences are a priori justified is to argue that they must be true, and to argue that our epistemic reason to accept them resides in this fact. To this end it might be claimed

---

[12] As indicated at the end of sect. 7, it can be argued, and with some plausibility, that meanings are not always constituted by the acceptance of sentences or rules of inference, but sometimes by a complex conditional decision that is not susceptible to truth-theoretic characterization. However, given our concerns here, it does not matter whether this is so. Either way, the provision of meaning will be independent of our substantive commitments.

that the meaning given to a word by its implicit definition can only be the meaning that would make that sentence true. And from this it indeed follows that any purely meaning-constituting sentence is true. But why should we agree with the claim that a sentence containing 'f' must actually be true in order for our acceptance of it to give 'f' a meaning? In stipulating that the sentence be true—and stipulating that 'f' have the meaning that will make it true—we no doubt feel certain that the sentence is true and that 'f' has that meaning. But whether these convictions are actually *correct* is a further matter. The stipulation will not be successful if they are not correct; but insofar as a use for 'f' has been established, a meaning for it will have been assigned. Thus one cannot show that our acceptance of meaning–constituting sentences is justified by arguing that they must be true.

The discussion so far points to three defects in the strategy of semantogenic apriority:

First: our a priori commitment to certain sentences containing a word is not really *explained* by our knowledge of its meaning. Rather, it is the other way around. We accept a priori that certain sentences containing the word are true, and we thereby provide it with meaning—we assume that it means, as we have stipulated, whatever will make true those sentences. Thus, although what we stipulate here is indeed held a priori, its being held a priori is not semantogenic.

Second: it is one thing to believe something a priori and another for this belief to be epistemically *justified*. The latter is required for a priori knowledge. But it is not clear how, on the semantogenic view, that justification can exist.

Third: the theory-formulations we employ as implicit definitions do not express the substantive theories whose apriority we hoped to establish and explain. For a theory-formulation whose acceptance *suffices* to fix the meaning of one of its constituent terms may not be one whose acceptance is *necessary* for understanding that term. And, if it is not, then our entitlement to mean whatever we want does not enable us to stipulate that the term means whatever is required for the theory-formulation to be true. For that stipulation would be hostage to the truth of that part of the theory-formulation whose acceptance is *not* required for the term's meaning what it does. Thus a stipulation of the form

'f' is to mean whatever is needed for '#f' to be true

can be meaning-constituting only if the acceptance of '#f' is necessary, as well as sufficient, for 'f' to mean what it does. But it is by no means obvious that logical or mathematical theories can meet this condition. Even though it may be plausible that the acceptance of such a theory suffices to fix the meanings of some of the terms in which it is formulated, it is not so plausible that its acceptance is necessary for those terms to mean what they do. For it is not obvious that we cannot factor such commitments into independent components, such that only one of them is needed for the terms to mean what they do. Evidence for the division of such a mathematical or logical practice into meaning-constituting and non-meaning-constituting parts comes from the possibility of *rejecting* the practice as a whole whilst nevertheless understanding its terms in the same way as those who engage in it.

9. BOGHOSSIAN AND PEACOCKE

In order to clarify these criticisms of semantogenic aprioricity, and to show their relevance to current thinking in the area, let me apply them to the versions of the approach that have been proposed by Paul Boghossian and Christopher Peacocke. The essence of Boghossian's account is as follows.[13] We can know a priori that

> *If* 'f' has a meaning, then '#f' is true

since this follows from our (perhaps implicit) stipulation that 'f' is to have the meaning (if there is such a meaning) that will make '#f' true. And we can know a priori that

> 'f' has a meaning

(at least in certain cases). Moreover the argument from these premises to the conclusion, '#f' is true, is valid. Therefore '#f' is known a priori.

However this line of thought is susceptible to our three-pronged critique. In the first place our a priori acceptance of the conclusion is being explained in part by the fact that

> If 'f' has a meaning, then its meaning will make '#f' true

is *stipulated* to hold. But, as we saw in Section 5, implementation of this sort of stipulation requires two things: first, for the sake on non-triviality, 'f' must be given some use; and second, for the sake of the truth of the conditional, 'f''s use must be thought to render '#f' true—and all one can do to try to ensure this is to accept '#f'. But clearly, if that acceptance is not itself a priori, then the conditional cannot be held a priori either. Thus although the conditional is stipulated, its apriority *depends on* the aprioricity of '#f'. Therefore it would be getting things the wrong way round to attempt to explain our a priori acceptance of '#f' in terms of the stipulation that 'f' is to mean, if anything, whatever would make true '#f'. Consider, for example, the case of Hume's Principle and the meaning of 'The number of _s'. In order to stipulate that this expression is to mean, if anything, something that will make Hume's Principle true (and assuming we do mean something by the expression), we must accept Hume's Principle. But a precondition for the object of this stipulation to be accepted a priori is that Hume's Principle be accepted a priori.

---

[13] I am here criticizing the account that Boghossian gives in his 'Analyticity Reconsidered' and 'Analyticity'. The view of fundamental a priori knowledge offered in his 'Reasons and Our Knowledge of Logic', in the present volume, escapes some of this criticism. See n. 16 below.

In the second place, the *justification* we have for accepting '#f' is supposed to consist in the fact that '#f' is deducible from other things that we know a priori: first, that *if* 'f' has a meaning then it means something that will render '#f' true; and second, that 'f' does have a meaning. But how can the first premiss—the conditional—be justified? Boghossian's answer is that our justification resides in the fact that the truth of this conditional is *stipulated*. But, as we have seen, a stipulation can perfectly well be meaning-constituting without being successful.

And in the third place, it is questionable whether the proposed stipulation can be purely meaning-constituting when '#f' is a substantive theory (e.g. a logical, arithmetic, or scientific theory). For suppose '#f' entails '$f', but not vice versa. And suppose our acceptance of '$f' is both necessary and sufficient for 'f' to mean what it does. Then it would seem that our purely meaning-constituting stipulation is really that

If 'f' has a meaning, then its meaning will render '$f' true

rather than

If 'f' has a meaning, then its meaning will render '#f' true.

So, in order to show that our logical or arithmetical commitments are purely meaning-constituting it would have to be shown that no weaker commitments will do that job. But given the fact, discussed above, that one can coherently reject any logical or arithmetical theory, it seems that weaker meaning-constituting commitments will indeed exist.

Peacocke's account of a priori knowledge is conducted at the level of *thought* rather than at the level of *language*; but it is also a version of the semantogenic strategy.[14] He has argued that it may be a condition of possessing a certain concept **F** (where **F** is the concept expressed by the English term 'f') that one be fundamentally committed to certain propositions which contain it. In other words, it may be constitutive of the identity of concept **F** that it plays a specific role in the cognitive economy of those who possess it—a role that includes believing (as 'primitively compelling') the proposition that #f. This idea is intimately related to the idea that the term 'f' is implicitly defined by our underived acceptance of '#f', and I have no quarrel with it. However, Peacocke claims, in addition, that this phenomenon provides an explanation of our a priori knowledge in various areas, including logic. And this runs up against versions of the three difficulties I have been emphasizing.

In the first place, a priori adoption of the belief that #f, would seem to consist in the fact that this belief is *basic* (i.e. 'primitively compelling', i.e. not inferred and not contingent on experience)—a fact which also happens to constitute the nature of the concept **F**. Thus although a priori commitment is indeed *entailed* by our grasp of concepts, it is not *explained* by that grasp.

---

[14] See his *A Study of Concepts* (Cambridge, Mass.: MIT Press, 1992); and 'How Are A Priori Truths Possible?'

In the second place, there is the problem of justification. Why *ought* we to adopt those primitively compelling beliefs that are concept-constituting? Peacocke's answer is to claim that beliefs can be concept-constituting only when they are true. And this claim is based on his distinctive view of how the nature of a concept *determines* the referent (semantic value) of that concept:

> (DT) The referent of a concept is that which will make true the primitively compelling beliefs that provide its possession condition.

But I have two objections to this way of trying to account for the justification for our primitively compelling, concept-constituting beliefs:

(1) Peacocke's 'determination theory', (DT), is highly questionable. One may grant that if concepts **F** and **G** have the same possession condition, then they must have the same referent (if any). In this sense of 'determine', the nature of a concept uncontroversially determines its referent. But this is not sufficient to motivate (DT). Moreover, consider a cluster of primitively compelling beliefs that cannot be made true by any judicious selection of referent for some common component of them. It is hard to see on what grounds one could deny that that this component is nonetheless a concept — a concept whose identity is given by those beliefs.[15]

(2) Suppose the 'determination theory', (DT), were correct. Our justification for supposing that a given body of primitively compelling beliefs is true would rest on our justification for supposing that they are concept-constituting. But no account is given of how the latter supposition (which, as Peacocke allows, will sometimes be false) can ever be justified.

The final component of my three-pronged critique of semantogenic apriority also applies to Peacocke's version of the strategy. That is, it is doubtful whether possession conditions involve *substantial* commitments. In particular, it is doubtful whether the possession conditions for our logical concepts involve the commitment to substantive logical principles (i.e. rules of inference). For example, why should we suppose that the possession condition for **AND** is to infer <p and q> from <p> and <q>, and vice versa? Can we not separate the commitment to there *existing* a higher-order entity satisfying those inferential principles, from the commitment to identify that entity with *conjunction*? And in that case, is it not plausibly just the second of these commitments that provides the concept's possession condition? Thus, it would seem that our concept-constituting commitments are not the substantive theories in logic and arithmetic whose justification has generally been the object of the strategy of semantogenic apriority.

---

[15] For further discussion of Peacocke's 'determination theory', see my 'Meaning, Use, and Truth' (*Mind*, April 1995), where I argue that DT is affiliated with inflationism about truth.

10. QUINE'S REVISABILITY ARGUMENT

I think we must conclude that the idea of semantogenic apriority cannot be sustained. But if interesting a priori knowledge is not engendered by meaning or by the nature of concepts, where might it come from? I'm not going to attempt anything like a full answer to this question. But I'm afraid someone might maintain that the strategy of semantogenic apriority must be more or less correct since there is no alternative to it. So I want to indicate the lines along which I think that an alternative approach might be developed.

To begin with, let me quickly defend the presupposition that there is such a thing as substantive a priori knowledge. To that end it is necessary to address the main basis for scepticism: namely Quine's epistemological holism and its implication that every belief is revisable in light of experience. In brief, the Quinean line of thought goes like this

(1) According to the web-of-belief model, our set of scientific beliefs evolves through time subject to constraints of empirical adequacy, overall simplicity, and conservativism.

(2) This model is highly plausible both in light of the history of science and in light of our conception of rationality.

(3) It implies that any scientific hypothesis—including a logical principle— might be abandoned on empirical grounds; for doing so might bring about an overall gain in simplicity.

(4) Therefore, none of our scientific beliefs is a priori.

Given this argument, how is it possible to hang on to the possibility of a priori knowledge?

The answer is simple. Science is only one of the many assertoric practices in which we engage. In other words, not everything we maintain is a scientific hypothesis. Therefore, not everything we believe is subject to the pressures of empirical adequacy and global simplicity. Thus Quine's argument provides no reason to doubt the existence of a priori knowledge *outside the domain of science*. Consider some of the standard alleged examples of what is known a priori:

Spinsters are not married.

If London is larger than Paris, then Paris is not larger than London.

If John persuaded Mary to go, then Mary intended to go.

The belief that snow is white is true if snow is white.

The chess bishop moves diagonally.

One ought to have some concern for the welfare of other people.

Nothing can be both red and green (all over).

Since these are not scientific hypotheses, we need not suppose that their credibility is hostage to empirical considerations. But, in that case, how could they be credible? Let me briefly indicate various possibilities.

11. SEMANTIC, PRAGMATIC, AND GENETIC ORIGINS OF APRIORITY

We are dealing with beliefs that are taken to qualify as knowledge—and taken therefore to be epistemically justified—despite the absence of any empirical or argumentative support for them. So there would be a confusion in hoping that we might be clever enough to find some argument to rationalize that way of treating such beliefs. After all, if we ought to believe *that we ought to believe that p*, then we simply ought to believe that p. Therefore any argument that would justify our regarding a certain belief as justified would yield an argument justifying that belief. Consequently, insofar as our epistemic practice is to designate certain beliefs as rational despite the absence of any supporting rationale for them, there can be no argument justifying that practice. The most we can aspire to is some *explanation* of it—including some account of *which* beliefs are given this special status, and *why*.

Bearing this point in mind, we should look again at the semantogenic idea. Ought we perhaps to regard it—not as purporting to show how an a priori belief may be given a justification—but as aiming to circumscribe the circumstances in which an unsupported a priori belief is nonetheless justified?[16] It seems to me that this is indeed the best gloss one can put on the semantogenic view of a priori knowledge. However, we have seen that purely meaning-constituting commitments can be nothing stronger than Carnap conditionals. They cannot be principles of arithmetic or logic, the a priori knowledge of which is our main concern. So, besides the condition, 'belonging to the category of purely meaning-constituting postulates', there must be other conditions in which an unsupported sentence is rational for us to accept a priori. What might those conditions be?

One promising answer is that suggested by the later Carnap: namely that some beliefs are motivated by purely *pragmatic* considerations and not at all by *epistemological* considerations, and these are a priori.[17] Where Carnap went wrong was in ignoring his 1920's insight into the factorizability of theories (which I emphasized in Section 6) and attempting to draw the pragmatic–epistemological distinction *within* the domain of substantive scientific hypotheses. But no such distinction can be drawn. For the allegedly *pragmatic* rationale for adopting

[16] In his essay, 'Reasons and our Knowledge of Logic', in the present volume, Paul Boghossian develops the semantogenic strategy along something like these lines.

[17] See R. Carnap, 'Empiricism, Semantics and Ontology' (1950) in his *Meaning and Necessity*, 2nd edn. (Chicago: University of Chicago Press, 1956).

certain hypotheses—namely, convenience—derives from considerations of simplicity. But standard *epistemological* considerations—namely our conviction that simple theories are more likely to be true—will perfectly well suffice to explain our adoption of simple hypotheses. Thus there can be no good reason for claiming that a particular scientific hypothesis is merely pragmatically motivated; it will always be more economical and hence more plausible to invoke the epistemological motivations that are already known to be at work in the scientific domain. However this objection to the possibility of pragmatically motivated acceptance has no force if we are concerned with a domain of discourse whose purpose is *not* to construct the simplest overall account of what we observe. In any such domain it should be possible to find beliefs whose motivation is wholly pragmatic.

Note that to characterize such beliefs as a priori is not to deny that they are revisable. The point is that they are not revisable for empirical reasons, but only for pragmatic reasons. Note also that my claim here is not that pragmatic reasons can constitute epistemic support. As we have seen, there can be no coherent prospect of giving support in the case of underived a priori beliefs. The point is merely to help delineate the class of beliefs that can qualify as epistemically justified in the absence of supporting epistemic reasons.

A further potential source of a priori knowledge is the innate structure of our minds. Suppose that each human being is born with, and stuck with, a simple language of thought (i.e. mentalese) containing, amongst other things, certain symbols whose intrinsic nature is such that the principles of classical logic are obeyed. In that case we would have an a priori commitment to classical logic. For this commitment would neither derive from experience nor be revisable in light of it. Of course, the a priori *justification* of a belief does not consist merely in how it is actually engendered, but is a matter of the conditions in which it *ought* to be adopted and maintained. To say that a proposition is known a priori is to make a normative claim about it, not a descriptive claim. However, norms are constrained by possibilities: ought implies can. In particular, if it is the case that certain beliefs are innate and irremovable, then we can understand why they would be amongst those beliefs that we treat as unconditionally rational.

Where does this leave logic, arithmetic, and geometry—which are deployed both inside and outside science? My own inclination is to say that within science such beliefs are subject to Quine's empirical revisability argument: quantum logic may turn out to be needed in the best overall theory; so the logic, arithmetic, and geometry of science are justified a posteriori. However, regardless of what science comes up with, it is a safe bet that in ordinary life, in moral and legal contexts, in game-playing, and other non-scientific areas, we will continue to rely on classical logic, on standard arithmetic, and on Euclidean geometry. It is possible that these commitments are innate, and hence rational. Thus we might end up with two logics: an a priori one involving our familiar logical concepts, and an a posteriori one deploying technical versions of 'and', 'not', 'every', etc.

12. CONCLUSION

To summarize: my main concern in this paper has been to argue that our a priori knowledge of logic and mathematics can derive neither from the meanings of words nor from the nature of concepts. For someone may possess whatever meanings and concepts are needed to articulate our logical and mathematical convictions, and yet disagree with us about them. Moreover, understanding is itself based on a priori commitment. And finally, semantogenic attempts to demonstrate the *justification* for such meaning-constituting commitments are (and must be) unsuccessful. Nonetheless our logical and mathematical beliefs *are* both a priori and rational— at least to the extent that they are deployed outside science and therefore escape the reach of Quine's holistic revisability considerations. So there is a need for some account of how this can be so. My suggestion is that although our practice of designating certain basic a priori beliefs as justified cannot be given epistemic support, it can be described and explained. To that end we can identify three classes to which such beliefs belong: (a) the purely meaning-constituting, (b) the purely pragmatically motivated, and (c) the innate and irremovable.

8

A Priori Rules: Wittgenstein on the Normativity of Logic

Peter Railton

INTRODUCTION

Like many, I have long been uneasy with the category of the a priori. Perhaps my uneasiness rests upon a misunderstanding? The way things have looked to me, asserting a claim or principle as a priori is tantamount to claiming that we are justified in ruling out some alternatives in advance, no matter what the future course of experience might hold. And I could not discover in myself any feeling of the authority required to make such an assertion, or even any clear idea of where to look for guidance. Defenders of the a priori tell me that my uneasiness is misplaced, since wherever there is genuine a priori knowledge, no genuinely possible 'future course of experience' would or could be excluded—my worry really reduces to a purely epistemic concern not to be mistaken in making a claim to a priori knowledge, and so does not touch the question of the existence of such knowledge as such. Confusedly, I wonder aloud whether a priori isn't meant precisely to be an epistemic category. It is indeed such a category, a 'special status' in inquiry, I am told, but I'm still not getting it.

This seems promising, until my interlocutor begins to cite examples of 'propositions true a priori', for they tend to reawaken rather than still my anxiety. I feel the cold shadow of history. Claims like 'the excluded middle is a priori' and 'the attribution of rationality is a priori in intentional explanation' keep sounding, to my ears, as if they echo 'the Euclidean geometry of space is a priori' or 'the principle of sufficient reason is a priori in physical explanation'. And those echoes prompt just sort of the worry that initially unsettled me, that I would pronounce myself satisfied that certain claims, at least, were immune from the threat of

I am much in debted to Paul Boghossian, Hartry Field, James Joyce, Allan Gibbard, and Christopher Peacocke for discussion of many of the issues canvassed here. I owe special thanks to Hartry Field, whose paper 'Apriority as an Evaluative Notion' was presented at Michigan in 1998. His evaluative approach differs from that pursued here, but it has been an important source of insight and encouragement for me. Research for this paper was partially supported by the National Endowment for the Humanities (Grant FA–35357–99).

contrary experience, just on the eve of developments in our ongoing view of the world that would lead a sensible person to want to reopen the question. So I would emerge looking like the (perhaps apocryphal) fellow who claimed, in the wake of the great inventions of the nineteenth century, that the US Patent Office could now be closed, since all the genuinely new ideas had already been used up.

But where's the real problem? It sounds as if I have just reverted once again to a worry about being wrong, about picking the wrong 'propositions true a priori' to settle upon. And we often enough find ourselves in the wrong – sometimes, embarrassingly, just when we have expressed supreme confidence. Why should this impugn any particular class of knowledge claims? Indeed, isn't there something epistemically reassuring about the possibility of such embarrassment? Since we can hardly suppose that humans came onto the scene already fully equipped to comprehend the most intricate secrets of the world, if we were to find an utter fixedness of human thought or its categories throughout the history of inquiry, that would be rather too suggestive of a mental straightjacket. Of course, mere fluctuation of opinion or method, akin to the parade of styles seen in fashion, would hardly be reassuring. But if we instead see a pattern of conceptual change integrated with an active process of enlarging and diversifying the range of human experience and our capacity to predict and control natural phenomena—well, this is what we would have hoped to see if we humans possess an adaptive intelligence hard at work.

So *there's* the problem: adaptiveness. The notion of the a priori seems to stand between me and this reassuring picture. For the a priori is not as such just one more *area* of inquiry, like physics, mathematics, biology, or psychology. In all of these areas, history has led us to expect significant evolution of the categories and fundamental presuppositions of inquiry.[1] The a priori is rather a special *standing* in the process of inquiry, which by its nature seems to rule out such change in advance. The distinctive content of a claim of apriority is not a matter of being right, or justified, or certain—such claims can coherently be made a posteriori. To claim a priori standing for a proposition or principle, it would seem, is to commit oneself to an epistemic imperative: one is to treat all testimony of experience—

---

[1] If we think of *logic* as an area of inquiry, say, as a part of mathematics, rather than as 'the most general principles of thought', then a similar question might arise. Although I am no historian of logic, it would seem to me that changes in the treatment of universal quantification in an empty universe, or the discernment of a hierarchy of infinities or types, or changes in conceptions of proof and its scope (including changing norms in proof theory and the acknowledgement of incompleteness and non-computability), among others, are at least candidates for being considered conceptual revisions or innovations in logic. For they seem to fit a pattern in which an anomalous result within an existing scheme—such as inconsistency, paradox, or a truth-value gap—precipitates a discontinuous revision of the scheme itself, altering conceptions of the 'full range of possibilities'. This may be like other potential cases of 'conceptual revision' in 'non-empirical' domains, e.g., the introduction of infinitesimals in mathematics. (For further discussion of potential 'conceptual revision' in logic, and of the distinction between propositional logic and 'general rules of thought', see below.)

whether it be favourable or unfavourable to the way we currently think—as bearing *elsewhere* on our scheme. When would one take it to be rational or justified, in advance of inquiry, to make such a commitment? And on what basis? Surely no mere feeling of certainty, or sense that one cannot think of clear alternatives, would suffice.

Of course, if some propositions or principles by their nature make no claims about the actual course of experience, then an a priori stance towards them would appear to require no peculiar foresight on our part. Unfolding experience could neither confirm nor disconfirm them, simply because it would be irrelevant to them. We would be in a position to accord them a priori standing in virtue of possessing nothing more extraordinary than a grasp of their meaning or content. This answer should be especially encouraging for a philosopher suffering from epistemic anxiety. For although we philosophers do not carry out real experiments and can seldom strictly prove our conclusions, we do specialize in analysing meaning and its implications. So perhaps we have the right sort of qualifications to make reasonable claims to a priori knowledge after all?

A BAYESIAN SIMULATION OF THE A PRIORI

However, one might wonder whether appeal to meaning could rescue the a priori if we, as philosophers, insist that meaning is the sort of thing entirely susceptible to analytic methods. For this makes it look as if we could establish *analytically* that a certain epistemic imperative is in force. And any such action- or thought-guiding imperative, Kant would remind us, must be synthetic. Let us consider what happens if we try to develop a model of issuing ourselves an epistemic imperative to treat experience as 'bearing elsewhere', and see whether it does not end up a more substantive epistemic stance than we thought. Consider what I will call a *Bayesian simulacrum* of the a priori.

On an orthodox Bayesian scheme, rationality in belief consists in rigorously following Bayes's Rule to modify our existing degrees of belief, our *prior probabilities*, in the light of new evidence. Within this scheme, propositions identified as purely logical or purely analytic are automatically assigned prior probability 1 or 0 at the outset. This nicely simulates the feature of the a priori we needed: since the application of Bayes's Rule will never alter prior probabilities of 1 or 0, by following it we would always treat experience, whatever its character, as bearing elsewhere on our system of beliefs.

But now look what we have done to ourselves as inquirers. So long as we remain committed Bayesians in belief revision, never permitting ourselves any exceptions to the application of Bayes's Rule e.g. no 'spontaneous' or discontinuous (i.e. not Bayes's-Rule-governed) reassessments of prior probabilities—we will in effect treat these purported purely logical and analytic propositions (a supposition about their semantic character) as if our propositional attitude towards them were forever *certain* and *unrevisable* (an epistemic status). Any inquirer who introduced conceptual innovations or revisions that required 'spontaneous' reallocation of prior probabilities—say, who introduced the idea of the curvature of space, such that 'Two lines on a plane either intersect at one point or at none' goes from being assigned prior probability 1 to having no determinate prior probability, because an incomplete proposition could not be following Bayes's Rule, and would have to be counted an epistemic outlaw, a violator of the demands of epistemic rationality. But suppose we have encountered persistent strains and paradoxes—Kuhnian 'anomalies'[2]—in applying our existing conceptual scheme. Mightn't the 'outlaw' behaviour of conceptual revision be more rational than an iron resolve never to depart from the iterated application of Bayes's Rule using the old predicate system (or conceptually conservative 'logical constructions' therefrom)? Must we apply a mental straightjacket of our own making?

Now I might be accused of an elementary conflation of *epistemic* with *semantic* or *conceptual possibility*, but we do understand a priori to be an epistemic category. We cannot appeal 'over the head of' epistemology directly to semantic or conceptual possibility to map out its boundaries. True, the Bayesian simulacrum, however vivid it helps to make my concern, might or might not be a good model of what philosophers have had in mind in speaking of a priori knowledge. But we must find some way, I think, to make room for the thought that the particular conceptual scheme we inherit may not be adequate—even via 'logical extensions'—to express the whole truth about the world. We will want to license adverse experience to bring recognizably epistemic pressure to bear on us a posteriori for more or less radical conceptual innovation.

UNREVISABILITY

There is another, more Kantian way of expressing this appropriate humility. If we suppose that somehow or other, thought *must* be adequate to the world—perhaps because 'the world' itself must be 'thought' in order to have any role in inquiry and deliberation—then we should simply admit that we are thereby engaged in a substantive commitment, licensing ourselves to make claims with existential import. If it is a priori, it is *synthetic* a priori, and not to be established by meaning alone. A more transcendental style of argument is called for. On the Bayesian simulacrum, the orthodox Rule-follower is in effect treating *his* scheme of thought as if it were adequate to the world. Now Kant concedes that any such idea

[2] T. S. Kuhn, *The Structure of Scientific Revolutions*, 2nd edn. (Chicago: University of Chicago Press, 1970): ch. 6.

must be treated as a substantive *postulate* of reason. By contrast, the Bayesian in our example seems to have adopted what is functionally a synthetic, substantive a priori commitment solely on the strength of taking certain propositions as definitionally true. We should recall Wittgenstein's warning to philosophers that sometimes, 'We predicate of the thing what lies in the method of representing it' (*PI* 46).[3]

'But surely', it will be replied, 'there *are* limits to conceptual revision. A priori knowledge is about those limits. Indeed, for there even to be such a thing as 'the bearing of experience on our belief scheme' there must be *inferential connections* within the scheme that are not simply up for grabs in experience. That is, logical relations are *presupposed* whenever we speak of 'adverse experience', of the 'incompatibility' of belief that *p* and observation that ~*p*.'

There is something to this reply. Consider the case of 'quantum logic', meant as a conceptual revision of 'classical logic' rather than a special-purpose supplement to it. When quantum logicians ask us to revise our logical framework in light of the a posteriori 'contradictions' or 'anomalies' we have encountered in applying our existing conceptual scheme to quantum phenomena, we are entitled to raise an eyebrow. As Saul Kripke has observed, if quantum logicians use classical logic to derive the 'contradictions' of our present scheme in fitting observation, and then go on to deploy a classical meta-language to define new 'quantum connectives' or rules of inference, and to 'draw the implications', we don't really have before us a proposal to revise our logic after all—quantum logicians are simply assuming classical logic's good standing and universal applicability.[4] But if they do not do this, and instead formulate their evidence, introduce their new connectives or rules, and make their arguments using inferences or definitions that *violate* our antecendently understood logic, then their proposals will simply be unintelligible to us, and present us with no motivation for change. Why, for example, should the fact that someone could use inferential rules we do not accept to derive what he calls 'contradictions' in our present theories or beliefs have any tendency to convince us that we are in deep epistemic difficulty and need to be rescued by accepting some novel inferential scheme that we deem invalid? So the very idea of 'revising our logic' begins to look fishy.

Should we now comfort ourselves that we have an a priori refutation of 'alternative logics'? It might be well, however, to bring the Bayesian simulacrum back to mind and ask exactly what we seem to have talked ourselves into. I myself have no idea how we arrived at our current understanding of 'classical logic' and its rules, or whether a historian of logic would claim that our current understanding can properly be seen as a continuous extension of the understanding of logic that prevailed in (say) Aristotlean or pre-Aristotlean times. But somehow it seems to

---

[3] All page references in the text are to Ludwig Wittgenstein, *Philosophical Investigations*, 3rd edn., trans. by G. E. M. Anscombe (London: Macmillan, 1953), hereinafter abbreviated as *PI*.

[4] I am indebted here to a seminar on quantum logic taught by Saul Kripke at Princeton University in 1977. I do not know whether he would accept the view attributed to him here.

me unlikely that we will find an evolution of thought and language from prehistoric human verbal exchange to contemporary propositional logic, such that, at each step of the way, the earlier conceptual structure was definite and rich enough to express by some conservative extension the meanings or connections necessary for motivating and defining the later. 'Classical logic' is not self-defining and self-interpreting, rather, it must be introduced and interpreted using our background natural language as a metalanguage.

But what now prevents our general openness on the question of the expressive adequacy and epistemic standing of our current conceptual repertoire (or our self-understanding of it) from encompassing those very elements of our language with which we introduce and debate logical rules and constants? Ongoing controversies among mathematicians, logicians, and philosophers over various parts of logic and their interpretation—intuitionist logics, criteria of proof and computability, the boundary between logic proper and set theory or 'strengthened' logic, etc.—suggest that there are genuine 'open questions' concerning *which* rules and constants to adopt as authoritative, even in logic. Yet we seem to have been able to construct and make much good use of the classical propositional calculus without resolving all these questions. As Wittgenstein noted:

120. When I talk about language (words, sentences, etc.) I must speak the language of every day. Is this language somehow too coarse and material for what we want to say? *Then how is another one to be constructed?*—And how strange that we should be able to do anything at all with the one we have! (*PI* 49)

A PRIORI RULES

Once we recognize that if we treat classical propositional logic as giving the limits of real possibility and real thought we are engaged in a substantive, synthetic commitment, should we then simply understand logic as a set of substantive, quasi-metaphysical claims about 'the fundamental structure of the world' rather than merely formal, analytic truths? This might be more forthright, but perhaps another response would be better. After all, a set of substantive claims about the world sounds like a set of *propositions*, and to give a complete account of logic we need to encompass as well the notion of a *rule* of logic. But rules, unlike propositions, do not strictly speaking make claims capable of truth or falsity. Moreover, if our account is supposed to capture the purportedly a priori status of logic, then it must explain the notion of 'a rule with a priori standing'.

Furthermore, recently the thought has become current that meaning (or content) is *normative*,[5] since it *guides* but does not merely describe or predict use.

---

[5] See Paul Boghossian, 'The Status of Content', *The Philosophical Review* 99 (1990): 157–84.

The sense in which meaning is thought to govern or regulate use cannot be that in which we speak of a law of nature as governing or regulating the movement of a particle. For if an individual particle is credibly observed to move in a way that would violate a law of nature, this tends to disconfirm the law, whereas it is quite compatible with an account of the meaning of a word or thought that there be uses that unquestionably violate it—in such cases, it is the use, not the meaning claim, that is deemed 'incorrect'. We could understand this if meanings were like *rules for use* rather than empirical generalizations about use. For rules can 'hold' or be 'in force' in those particular instances in which they are violated as well as those in which they are followed—that is, indeed, something like their special office. And, if meaning, like logic, is a priori, then, again, we have encountered the notion of an a priori rule.

How are we to understand this notion? Most recent philosophical discussion of a priority with which I am familiar has focused on a priori (or a priori justifiable) propositions. Fortunately, we get a clue from the feature of rules just mentioned: rules can indicate, in advance of use, how we are to 'go on', and yet their 'holding' is compatible with our *failing* to go on in this way. This is a kind of a priori standing: unlike empirical generalizations, rules are not vulnerable to a posteriori disconfirmation by the occurrence of particular instances in which they are violated. By the same token, a rule is not confirmed a posteriori by instances of rule-conforming use: when, struggling, I manage to use a phrase correctly in French, this may somewhat enhance my credibility as a French-speaker, but it does not strengthen the credibility of the rules of French grammar. One might say that the very possibility of my use being either correct or incorrect presupposes the 'holding' of a relevant rule as a condition, and so my particular verbal (or mental) conduct can neither confirm nor disconfirm it.

A rule, then, can be thought of as a priori *regulative* of practice, in the sense just described. Could it, or our acknowledgement of it, also be spoken of as a priori *justified*? If rules do not owe their standing to something like confirmation by the course of experience, where does their standing come from? When is a rule genuine or applicable? This is not a question about how to establish the truth of 'This community thinks and acts as if rule *R* holds', which presumably can be confirmed or disconfirmed in familiar a posteriori ways. Rather, it is a question about how to establish a genuinely regulative claim that rule *R* holds—that usage in accord with *R* would be correct, not simply taken to be correct.

Can we deploy the notion of an a priori justified *proposition* to explain that of a priori justified regulative claim? Perhaps an a priori justified regulative claim could owe its special standing to the a priori justifiability of an 'associated proposition'. For example, the a priori status of logic could be defended on the grounds that the definitions of the logical constants determine that certain patterns of inference are valid. Thus, the Rule of the Excluded Middle might be deemed a justified a priori regulative claim concerning deductive inference since the 'associated proposition', '$p \vee \sim p$', is true in virtue of the definitions of 'v' and '~' alone. In the case of induction, Bayes's Rule might be deemed a justified a priori regulative claim concerning belief revision because the 'associated proposition', Bayes's Theorem, is provable within the axioms of the probability calculus (which are said to 'implicitly define' 'probability'), given a standard definition of conditional probability. To accept such an approach as explanatory, however, we would have to convince ourselves that it involves no circularity or regress.

Circularity threatens when we try to spell out what we mean by 'true in virtue of the definitions alone': for we are bound to speak not just of definitions or stipulations, but of their *logical consequences*. Thus we will already have assumed the a priori justified regulative standing of the rules of logic in accepting our explanation.

Regress threatens because of Lewis Carroll's 'Achilles and the Tortoise' argument.[6] Suppose we were to say, 'No, the rules do not hover outside or behind the inferences, they are themselves premisses of it, always admissable because they are *immediately* true by definition or stipulation.' Yet now the Tortoise patiently shows us that if we treat a rule of inference as an additional, propositional premise in an inference, we generate the need for another premiss, and another, and . . .. Rules seem to be distinctive in their *function*.

For example, orthodox Bayesians and non-Bayesians may be in full agreement that Bayes's Theorem is provably true, and they share a core understanding of 'probability' as 'partially interpreted' by the Kolmogorov axioms. Moreover, they may accept the same definition of 'conditional probability', and agree that conditional probabilities bear precisely the structural relationship Bayes's Theorem displays. Yet one group deploys this relationship as a generalized regulative guide in belief revision and the other does not. What does this difference consist in? For the Bayesian, the Theorem gives a *model* or *pattern* for rational belief revision, an inductive principle or 'rule of reason'. Our degrees of credence, as they evolve in response to evidence, are to be 'normed' to fit this pattern of conditional probabilities if they are to be rational. This claim is a priori in the sense discussed above: it specifies in advance of inquiry how we are to 'go on' in response to new evidence, and those actual individuals who fail to go on in this way do not 'disconfirm' Bayes's Rule, but only show a defect of rationality in their beliefs. By contrast, Non-Bayesians need not treat the probabilistic relationship displayed in the Theorem as an a priori gauge of rationality in credence. For example, they might not think it a condition of rationality that one's beliefs be representable probabilistically, or 'normed by' a probabilistic scheme. The Bayesian will of course dispute this, and claim that unless our beliefs are representable probabilistically, various ills may befall us—such as the Dutch Book. But the non-Bayesian will counter that

---

[6] Lewis Carroll, 'What the Tortoise said to Achilles', *Mind* 4 (1895): 278–80.

if we attempt to pattern our beliefs on classical probabilities and rigorously norm them to Bayes's Theorem, various other ills may befall us—as the Bayesian simulacrum suggests. This is a substantive debate about how to 'go on' in belief, about which rules have rational authority in epistemology, if any. It is plainly not a dispute that is resolved even if we all settle upon the analytic or provable status of Bayes's Theorem.

Another example, drawn from the classic literature on the synthetic a priori, might help here. Consider the proposition of *Universal Causality*, 'All events have sufficient cause', which is associated with the purported 'rule of reason' known as the *Principle of Sufficient Reason*. The proposition of Universal Causality receives increased a posteriori confirmation when we find sufficient cause for a previously unexplained type of event, and its degree of confirmation is correspondingly reduced to the extent that intense efforts to accomplish this continue to fail. On the other hand, in the Principle of Sufficient Reason, we in effect treat Universal Causality normatively—as a pattern for guiding how to 'go on' in rational inquiry—and so treat it as synthetic a priori. When a search for sufficient cause comes up short, as in various quantum-mechanical phenomena, we do not say the 'rule of reason' is discredited, but that 'We simply lack an adequate rational explanation of these phenomena', and thereby urge further inquiry or conceptual development to promote greater understanding. In effect, we withhold from irreducibly probabilistic accounts of these phenomena the designation 'explanation' or 'full understanding', saying instead 'We still do not understand *the reason why* this occurs as it does'. Were we to depart from the Principle, and say, 'No, we do have a complete understanding of this probabilistic phenomenon', this would be deemed a partial abandonment of our commitment to rational empirical inquiry. Indeed, it might be thought to undermine not only our engagement as inquirers on behalf of giving 'reasons why something occurred', but also to weaken our notion of giving 'reasons for belief', since a fundamentally probabilistic law linking a system's state S with a subsequent outcome O is compatible with both the occurrence and the non-occurrence of O in any given instance.

By contrast, those who reject the Principle of Sufficient Reason as a rule of reason, may hold that quantum mechanics offers ample a posteriori evidence that Universal Causality is false, and that in a world including fundamental chance processes, we can be fully responsive to the *reasons why* things occur in the world and to the *reasons for* belief, only if we accept irreducibly probabilistic explanation and confirmation relations. For this group, there need be nothing at all 'second class' or 'imperfectly rational' about such relations, or our acceptance of them.

We have, then, a distinctive idea of what it is (at least in part) for a principle to function normatively in a practice: there is, in the sense illustrated above, an a priori commitment to the principle as affording a regulative standard of comparison to guide the practice.

NORMA, REGULA, ESTANDARD OF CORRECTNESS

In a famous passage, Wittgenstein writes:

81. F. P. Ramsey once emphasized in conversation with me that logic was a 'normative science'. I do not know exactly what he had in mind, but it was doubtless closely related to what only dawned on me later: namely, that in philosophy we often *compare* the use of words with games and calculi which have fixed rules, but cannot say that someone who is using language *must* be playing such a game. (*PI* 38)

Later, he treats this notion of comparison in a remarkably concrete way:

131. For we can avoid ineptness or emptiness in our assertions only by presenting the model [e.g. a calculus with 'fixed rules'] as what it is, an object of comparison—as, so to speak, a measuring-rod [*Masstab*]; not as preconceived idea to which reality *must* correspond. (The dogmatism into which we fall so easily in doing philosophy.) (*PI* 50–1)

The nature of these epithets—the 'inept', 'empty', 'dogmatic' figure who cannot escape his preconceptions is a familiar object of ridicule—encourages us to listen attentively to what Wittgenstein might be hinting at, and to prepare ourselves to have certain fond pretensions deflated. To try to avoid the fate of this ridiculous figure, who cannot see things for what they really are, let us try to stick to the concrete and everyday. And let us also try to keep in mind Wittgenstein's claim that the way he sees things:

To obey a rule, to make a report, to give an order, to play a game of chess, are *customs* (uses, institutions).
    To understand a sentence means to understand a language. To understand a language means to be master of a technique. (*PI* 81)

Happily as it turns out, our talk of *rules*, of the *normative*, and of *standards of correctness*, for all its seeming abstractness, has reassuringly concrete and 'customary technique'-based origins. Indeed, just the sort of origin that seems to have informed Wittgenstein's images of the use of 'objects of comparison' or 'measuring rods' to guide an everyday practice.

    'Rule' descends from *regula*, a ruler or straight-edge (Wittgenstein's word, *Masstab*, is translated here as 'measuring-rod', and elsewhere in the *Investigations* simply as 'ruler' (cf. *PI* 128)). 'Normative' and 'norm' descend from *norma*, a mason's or carpenter's square. 'Standard' descends from *estandard*, a banner or device that served, e.g. in combat ('a battle standard' or 'regimental standard'), to help lead individuals in a common direction or otherwise direct and coordinate their movements. And 'correctness' descends from *corrigere*, which in turn derives from *kom-* + *reg-*, to bring into alignment with a straight line.[7] The *regula*, *norma*, and

---

[7] The derivations for 'rule' and 'norm' go via Latin and seem to be well attested. The derivation for 'standard' goes via Frankish, and is more uncertain. Tracing *regula* further back, we get

estandard are tools or devices used to accomplish vital purposes, such as making things, or movements, *corrigere*. Let us then begin by looking into the builder's toolkit, where we find the ubiquitous *norma* and *regula*. How are they normally used, and why they usually are the first tools acquired after the saw or chisel and hammer?

The mason or carpenter initially confronts rough workpieces—lumber or stone—to be cut to size for their place in the construction to be made. Prior to making a cut, the workman places the *norma* or *regula* against a workpiece as a guide, and scribes a line for his cut to follow. He then cuts to the line, and afterwards reapplies the *norma* or *regula* to test the cut for squareness or straightness. If there are gaps between tool and workpiece, the cut will be 'brought into line' or 'corrected' (*corrigere*) using a saw, chisel, rasp, or plane, until the fit is tight. Only in Chaplin comedies will the *norma* or *regula* itself be 'corrected' to match a crooked cut by filing away at the tool until it fits.

Thus, the typical role of the *norma* or *regula* in building is, like the role of rules discussed in the previous section, to be a priori regulative of the carpenter's or mason's practice. Prior to the cut, the *norma* or *regula* are used to indicate how to 'go on', and if an actual cut fails to conform to the *norma* or *regula*, it is the cut that is corrected, not the tool. Thus the *norma* or *regula* are not vulnerable a posteriori to 'disconfirmation' by actual practice that fails to conform, but neither are they 'confirmed' by practice that does conform.

How does the notion of an *estandard* of correctness get into this process? Each *norma* purports to give a standard for a right angle, each *regula* a standard for a straight line or unit of length (a 'yardstick'). But if builders are working together on a construction site, or a worker or group of workers is preparing materials ahead of time for later assembly, how do they know that the pieces they make will fit together and fit well in the final assembly or construction? The various measuring tools in their individual toolkits cannot reliably guide them in making finished pieces that will fit together (other than by chance) unless their tools share a common pattern. The final fit will not be good—the walls will not be vertical and stable, the floors and building surfaces not horizontal and smooth, the seams and corners not tight—unless these tools embody shapes with certain systematic characteristics and relations, right angles, straight lines, etc. They need, in short, each to have in their kits tools that can be taken in the hand as instantiations of common *estandards* of particular geometric forms, to provide regular guidance to

the purported Indo-European root *reg-*, for movement in a straight line; tracing *norma* further back we find involvement of the purported Indo-European *gno-*, for knowing (hence, a tool for knowing when something is straight, just as the Greek *gnomon* was a device for telling the time by casting a shadow on a sundial); tracing *estandar* further back we get the purported Indo-European *sta-* + *kar-*, to stand fast (or 'stand hard'). (Etymologies and purported Indo-European roots from: *The American Heritage Dictionary*, 3rd edn. (Boston: Houghton Mifflin, 1997)). Apologies in advance to readers of my paper, 'Normative Force and Normative Freedom: Hume and Kant—but *not* Hume vs. Kant', *Ratio* 12 (1999): 320–53, which also discusses these etymologies and the examples they support.

their cutting. The geometry of building can vary—round forms, rectilinear, etc. So there are various tools that, if replicated and distributed among carpenters and masons, could have the desired effect, depending especially on the kind of building to be created and the needs it is to meet. Surely one of the simplest and most practical solutions, given materials such as wood or stone, is the rectilinear one, and for this the *norma* and *regula* serve admirably as *estandards* of correctness (co-alignment). Each individual worker in the division of labour, or in a distribution of labour over time, will possess a reliable guide for 'going on' in such a way that his contribution will fit in the whole and play its role. So evident has this been to carpenters and masons through the ages that their guilds and unions often feature the *norma* or *regula* on their banners—their symbolic as well as practical *estandards*.

So far we have spoken of a priori regulative uses of tools, akin to rules. What of the other side of the contrast, a posteriori correctible empirical claims? Have builders no need for this? Contrast another tool, the contour gauge. Looking like an oversized comb with teeth that can slide in or out, a contour gauge is pressed against a shape to record its profile. If a mason or carpenter applies a contour gauge to a surface and finds there are gaps, then it is the gauge that is to be 'corrected', brought into alignment, not the surface. Depending upon the thickness of the teeth, the contour gauge can give a more or less faithful or fine-grained *representation* of the original shape. Contour gauges are ordinarily equipped with a set-screw or friction device to lock the representation of the profile into place. Such uses of the gauge are a posteriori, as more or less fine-grained empirical records. Alternatively, a builder may keep the contour gauge in active use, tracing its 'locked' profile with a scribe to guide the shaping of new workpieces. Here the gauge functions a priori, in much the same way as a *norma* or *regula*, though with a capacity to impose more complex, non-rectilinear *estandards*. One can readily see why the carpenter's and mason's toolkits typically contain both rigid measuring tools like the *norma* or *regula* and 'open-ended' or adjustable measuring tools, like the contour gauge.

The case of the contour gauge helps us resist an impression that the tools themselves regulate use as if by some inherent power. The physical *norma* and *regula* could be used, if inefficiently, to replicate complex, curvilinear shapes—simply proceed in the Chaplinesque manner of cutting away at the tool until it matches the shape. This is not to deny that the inherent features of a tool impose some limits on how it might effectively be used. Rulers are finite in length; carpenter's squares cannot resist gravitational forces that vary with orientation in space; a contour gauge can record the geometric profile of a surface, but its reading will not, except by accident, reliably represent the surface's colour, reflectivity, composition, etc. These relatively *limited* and *form-related* (formal) characteristics of such tools are at once their strength and their limitation. They can be used repeatedly, on materials of many kinds, by builders deploying a wide variety of cutting techniques and tools for indefinitely many objects. This is a dimension of (what one might call) *generality* of application. At the same time, they do not enable us to assess or control for many of variables relevant to construction, such as uniformity of surface colour, or strength and appropriateness of materials. They are not, then, all-purpose guides, despite their general usefulness as 'standards of comparison'. We must know when to use or follow them, for what purposes, and when not.

Wittgenstein writes:

430. 'Put a ruler against this body; it does not say that the body is of such-and-such a length. Rather is it in itself—I should like to say—dead, and achieves nothing of what thought achieves,'—It is as if we had imagined that the essential thing about a living man was the outward form. Then we made a block of wood in that form, and were abashed to see the stupid block, which hadn't even any similarity to a living being. . . .
432. Every sign *by itself* seems dead. *What* gives it life?—In use it is *alive*. Is life breathed into it then? Or is the *use* its life? (*PI* 128)

It is of particular importance for our purposes here that we notice what *normae*, *regulae*, and contour gauges do not 'say'. Any tool in itself is mute, but in our hands, in a practice, it can be a guide or a record or a standard. This does not represent these tools as possessing magical powers, but it does show something: though the *norma* and *regula* lack 'inherent power' to guide, we nonetheless can, by disciplining ourselves to use them as guides, enlarge our powers. We can, for example, achieve a degree of precision, uniformity, accuracy (in communicating or replicating a shape), an independence from distracting interests or compromises, that would be virtually unattainable without their assistance.

If they are not taken as all-purpose guides, and if their use depends upon us and our purposes, are they therefore somehow 'hypothetical' measures or standards? Hardly. A *norma* or *regula* affords, in use, a standard of squareness or straightness that is utterly indifferent to our particular purposes, interests, or wishes. The square or straight-edge is a demanding master indeed when one is working with a recalcitrant material—and it knows of no concession in rigour to accommodate us. My square shows me no fear or favour, but fits (or doesn't fit) my cuts just as it would yours. And if I don't care whether the square fits, that is not a way of making it fit. The *norma* and *regula* enable us to categorize cuts as square or straight, independently of our desires or interests—this sort of fit is in no way 'up to us'—and so they are more properly seen as *non-hypothetical* or *categorical* standards.

NORMA AND SUPER-NORMA

Non-hypotheticalness or categoricalness need to be distinguished, however, from (what might be called) *unconditional* or *intrinsic* action-guidingness. Though 'normative', *norma* and *regula* do not tell us 'how we *ought* to cut' a given workpiece.[8] Perhaps, given its use in the finished structure we're creating, a workpiece ought to be cut round or curved rather than straight and square. A wooden ship, for example, contains thousands of pieces of wood, almost none straight and square on all sides. Shipwrights make relatively little use of the *norma*, and certainly would never place it on their guild's or union's banner. And although firewood could without loss of functionality be nicely squared on its ends, this would be without particular point. So woodcutters can rely on their hands and eyes to make their cuts roughly square, and do not go into the forest with *norma* in hand. Even a fine-finish carpenter often sets his *norma* aside to shape a piece that is cleverly curved or angled to 'look straight' when in fact it is not.

So a *norma* or *regula* issues no unconditionally action-guiding command. No tool in the kit does so—and a good thing, too, since once taken up, it would leave us unfree to depart from its guidance (except perhaps through fatigue or weakness). We would be guided as if by rails to follow it with or without a seconding evaluation on our part. This sort of super-*norma* is not a good model of any familiar sort of *normative regulation*; it would be experienced more like the force of effective coercion or a trance. As Wittgenstein writes, when we follow rules in everyday life, it is not as if we had 'at every step . . . a feeling of being guided by the rules as by a spell' (*PI* 87). One might think at first that imperfect craftsmen like me could be made better builders of handymen if only one could put into their hands a super-*norma* that would not permit straying from the line or second-guessing of it. But given the varying and sometimes unpredictable needs of building, as well as the continuing evolution of building materials and techniques, we would in fact be poorer builders—closer in capacity to machine tools that need external reprogramming than to adaptive general builders and effectively improvising handymen.[9]

A programmable computer might encounter the following sequence of unconditional command lines:

(1) Display 'I obey' on the screen and go to (2).
(2) Go to (1).

These commands, once 'understood' (compiled and read in from memory) and sent to 'execute', would be carried out competently, without condition, reluctance, or distraction. But also without point. The computer would loop forever between (1) and (2), the screen displaying a neatly arranged and uninterrupted stream of 'I obey's, until the power fails or the circuits roast.

Well, perhaps it will be said that any *genuine* super-*norma* would or could not

---

[8] As we will later see, treating the rules of propositional logic as 'normative' in Wittgenstein's sense does not mean taking them to tell us 'how we *ought* to think'.

[9] For further discussion of the normative as a domain of freedom, see P. Railton, 'Normative Force and Normative Freedom'.

fail to anticipate all needs and situations, and all innovations in building materials or techniques. Unless it provided a strict, general-purpose algorithm that somehow gave no justifiable role to evaluation or improvisation in shaping the pattern of its application, it would be no more than a run-of-the-mill *norma*, and not super. But if arithmetic is undecidable, what chance is there for building? Better to recognize that we have no more idea of what it would take to have an all-purpose super-*norma* for builders than, according to Wittgenstein, we have an idea of how a meaning could give us a super-rule for the 'whole use of the word' in thought and language:

192. You have no model of this superlative fact, but you are seduced into using a super-expression. (It might be called a philosophical superlative.) (*PI* 77)

'Objects of comparison', unlike unconditional action-guiding commands, can be picked up, tried out, put down until they serve a purpose. They furnish us models or patterns that enable us to tell how things are, but do not of themselves tell us how things must be or ought to be. Recall Wittgenstein's reminder to:

131. . . . present [. . .] the model as what it is, as an object of comparison—as, so to speak, a measuring-rod; not as a preconceived idea to which reality *must* correspond. (The dogmatism into which we fall so easily in doing philosophy.) (*PI* 51)

We can use the *norma*, *regula*, and *estandard* as prosaic illustrations of the role that Wittgenstein imagines for logic when he calls it a 'normative science', or of the role of Bayes's Theorem or the proposition of Universal Causality when we speak of using them regulatively in inductive practice.

Return to the 'normative science' of the ultra-orthodox Bayesian. His rule is Bayes's Rule, his standard of rationality in belief revision is rigorous modelling of his degrees of 'subjective probability' or 'credence' upon it, whatever experience might bring. Suppose him to be a member of a scientific community whose dominant theory is facing a rising tide of anomalies, and where an alternative theory has begun to emerge that employs a conceptual scheme not wholly definable in terms of the dominant theory. Shifting to this alternative theory would thus involve a discontinuous revaluation of priors, one not 'driven' or licensed by evidence via Bayes's Rule. Suppose that, nonetheless, this alternative theory is making headway, gaining adherents as scientists use it to report novel, reproducible phenomena and improve our capacity to predict or control familiar phenomena—though perhaps under different descriptions. The orthodox Bayesian will keep his head down in all the fuss, refusing to be distracted from his scrupulous conditionalization on his prior probabilities in obedience to Bayes's Rule.

Now in so doing, he will no doubt respond to critics by invoking Good's Theorem, to the effect that inquirers starting with different priors but religiously conditionalizing on new evidence, will in the limit converge in their posterior probabilities, and indeed converge upon a hypothesis that accurately represents the underlying relative frequencies in the actual sample population.[10] 'So I'll continue to keep my head down,' the orthodox Bayesian concludes, satisfied he is missing nothing worth seeing. Unfortunately, this conclusion overlooks a *condition* of Good's Theorem: that the correct hypothesis is among (or is expressible in terms of) the set of hypotheses to which some finite initial prior probability was assigned. If this condition is not met—if, say, unanticipated conceptual innovation is called for—then conditionalization will not generate the novel hypotheses needed to get things convergent or correct.[11] If Bayes's Rule were somehow unconditionally action-guiding, such that once we understood it we could not but follow it, we would, like the orthodox Bayesian, be launched into future experience upon rails, and could do little but hope that our initial hypothesis set will be sufficient.

Bayes's Theorem, then, might more profitably be thought of as a *norma* than as a super-*norma*. We can use it with great epistemic profit as a tool for regulating and checking how we reshape our beliefs in response to new evidence, but only if we also are alert to whether certain appropriate conditions are met: that the beliefs in question can effectively be represented as quasi-probabilistic degrees of credence in propositional contents, that fundamental conceptual revision does not appear to be called for, and so on. We can use it to keep ourselves honest, to avoid certain forms of incoherence or self-defeating conduct, to escape 'base rate' fallacies, and to promote evidence-driven convergence among inquirers with disparate starting points who nonetheless agree in using the theorem as an *estandard,* thus permitting an epistemic division of labour. In so doing we discipline ourselves to treat the Theorem as a categorical *norma*, not allowing personal preferences or interests to enter into its application.

But we had better not discipline ourselves to treat the Theorem as an unconditional super-*norma*, sticking to the Rule religiously, come what may, and insisting that beliefs we cannot represent as quasi-probabilistic degrees of credence in propositional contents are without epistemic relevance. Not, that is, unless we are prepared to treat *ourselves*, or rather, that *part* of our scheme of beliefs and

[10] See I. J. Good, 'Weight of Evidence, Corroboration, Explanatory Power, Information, and the Utility of Experiments', *Journal of the Royal Statistical Society* B 22 (1960): 319–31 and 30 (1968): 203; and 'On the Principle of Total Evidence', *British Journal for the Philosophy of Science* 17 (1967): 319–21. For some discussion of the implicit assumptions of Good's results, see Paul R. Graves, 'The Total Evidence Theorem for Probability Kinematics', *Philosophy of Science* 56 (1989): 317–24. For Good's own reservations about Bayesianism, see his 'Explicativity, Corroboration, and the Relative Odds of Hypotheses' [with comments and a reply], *Synthese* 30 (1975): 39–93.

[11] Similarly, the philosopher who claims to 'demonstrate' that his purported a priori truth would hold no matter what the course of experience might turn out to be, must assume that no possibilities have been omitted in the conditions or premisses of his demonstration, and that nothing 'made true by' these conditions and premisses has been overlooked. These would appear to be very strong assumptions, in light of incompleteness results and the general limits on in-principle computability (not to mention the limitations of actual human thought processes).

concepts which meets the conditions of application for the Rule, as authoritative about the bounds of real possibility.

A Kantian might insist that we have no choice but to attribute to ourselves such authority, at least at the most basic level of understanding. A transcendental argument for this is possible because reasons for belief must be reasons for any rational being, so universally communicable in content; therefore, in particular, empirical reasons for belief must be intelligible to the empirical understanding as such—which by its nature is limited to certain categories. Still, as we urged earlier, the Kantian will frankly admit that this seemingly super-*norma*-like status is a sheer, synthetic postulate of thought-guiding authority, not an 'a priori truth' guaranteed by meaning or concepts.

Similarly in Kantian practical reason. Even the Categorical Imperative has conditions, without which we cannot guarantee the practical rationality of rigorously applying it as a *norma* or test to guide our deliberation and actions: we must have free will; virtue must be rewarded—at least, in an afterlife—with happiness; the maxim of our action must in some sense be available to us; and so on.[12] For Kant, we have no real alternative but to take it as an article of faith that these conditions are met, while rejecting any idea that we can learn how we *ought* to act from a sheer grasp of concepts.

In reality, I think, there is an alternative to transcendental, unrevisable postulation. For subsequent developments in geometry, science, psychology, and philosophy suggest that there were possibilities not entertained in Kant's own 'hypothesis set', and that some of the categories he took to be fixed limits of understanding—and the associated 'antinomies' he identified—might be overcome with theoretical and conceptual revision. (Much as nineteenth-century work on infinitesimals helped overcome the 'antinomies' of calculus.) But this revision could only happen if our initial conceptual categories were not forever taken as unconditionally and intrinsically 'thought-guiding', i.e. were not *treated* as super-*normae*-like.

Postulates may, at any point in a practice, be more or less contextually unavoidable. A carpenter in her daily work takes her *norma* to embody a genuine right angle, and her *regula* to be genuinely straight, often having no better standard of squareness or rightness to test them against. There would be no point in hiring a carpenter if, before relying on her *norma* or *regula*, she always had to check it against a standard measure, and that against yet another standard, and . . . Nonetheless, the postulated accuracy of the tools in her kit is not an irrevocable status. If, for example, following them closely as possible, she finds that joints and corners still do not fully touch, she will have them checked. Squares and

---

[12] Strictly speaking, we should distinguish the 'test of the maxim of our will' contained within the Categorical Imperative, which is, in effect, the *norma*, from the Categorical Imperative proper, which is a rule to the effect that we should always act so that our will's maxim can pass this test (or fit this *norma*).

straight-edges that have become warped are said to be 'out of true', and to need 'truing' against a more reliable standard lest they cease to serve well their ordinary functions. As Wittgenstein observes in a related context:

125. . . . The fundamental fact there is that we lay down rules, a technique, for a game, and then when we follow the rules, things do not work out as we had assumed. That we are therefore as it were entangled in our own rules. (*PI* 50)

If any actual *norma* ever came to be treated as a super-*norma*, to be followed however much the anomalies of application suggest that it might be warped or inadequate, our entanglement would be complete and irremediable, much as Kant infamously says a rational man would not violate the categorical imperative and lie, even to save a friend from a murderer or a nation from a tyrant.[13]

DIRECTIONS OF FIT

Thus we see in these normative uses not just one, but several 'directions of fit'. With respect to a given cut, the worker attempts to bring the workpiece into line with the *norma* or *regula*, not vice versa. With respect to a given *norma* or *regula*, a repairman or tool-maker attempts to bring it into 'trueness' with a square angle or straight line. It is because the actual tools in circulation and use as *normae* and *regulae* correspond reasonably well to these objective standards that workers can count on them as a shared and effective *estandard* in building projects. Yet we can always ask, of a given *norma* or *regula*, does it really embody the standard it purports to?

Moreover, we can ask a further question: Is this the relevant standard to be following? Given the building task before us—the site, the materials at hand, the planned or likely use, the tools we have to work with—do square corners, vertical walls, and straight edges 'fit' the task? Are we making a simple house, a ship, an arch? The question whether, or how much—in which dimensions, say—to follow *norma* or *regula*, and the related question whether, or how much, to use some other tool as a guide, is another aspect of 'fit'.

Like the question of the tool's 'trueness', these are not questions we can ask the tool itself to answer. We can unreflectively go on following the *norma* or *regula* even when that is not what we should be doing—when it is pointless, or counterproductive, or dangerous. A mason who insists on squaring off the springer stones of an arch, checking carefully with his *norma*, is creating not a superior structure, but an unstable hazard.

Not all hazard is physical, nor does it always lie in instability. If we were to

---

[13] For a more sympathetic discussion of how Kant arrived at these views, see P. Railton, 'Normative Force and Normative Freedom'.

watch an ultra-Bayesian Newtonian physicist meticulously updating his beliefs by conditionalization, refusing to be distracted from 'staying the course' by all the excitement surrounding relativistic space-time, we might think it uncharitable to accuse him of irrationality or epistemic irresponsibility. But there is a kind of failure of fit between his avowed goal of being fully responsive to new evidence in the assessment of scientific hypotheses and the 'epistemic rigour' he claims for his practice. Similarly for the adherent of the Principle of Sufficient Reason, who continues to reject quantum theory as a priori unacceptable, despite its spectacular successes, out of concern that he be responsive only to 'bona fide scientific reasons for belief'. In both these cases, a very robust stability has become an epistemic hazard.

WITTGENSTEIN ON THE STATUS OF LOGIC

Tool kit in hand, let us now return to Wittgenstein on logic. We began this discussion of *normae, regulae,* and *estandards* of correctness as an effort to make sense of Wittgenstein's intriguing invocation of Ramsey's remark that logic is a 'normative science', used as an 'object of comparison' in the way a 'measuring-rod' is used.

When I first encountered Wittgenstein's seeming endorsement of a normative conception of logic, I was deeply puzzled. The only 'normative science' I had associated with logic was the sort of thing that had gone under the label 'Principles of Right Reasoning' or 'Rules of Mental Hygiene', and I had been taught that this sort of enterprise was to be distinguished sharply from logic proper. Logic is not about mental states or how we *ought* to think, I was told, but about formal, structural relations among propositions (or even the uninterpreted elements of a calculus). Mental states were for psychology to study; and ideals of mental hygiene, I supposed, were for tutors and preachers to espouse.

Now Wittgenstein does distinguish his conception of logic from an empirical, merely a posteriori science:

81. [L]ogic does not treat of language—or of thought—in the sense in which a natural science treats of a natural phenomenon. . . .
108. . . . We are talking about the spatial and temporal phenomenon of language, not about some non-spatial, non-temporal phantasm. [Note in the margin: Only it is possible to be interested in a phenomenon in a variety of ways.] But we talk about it as we do about the pieces in chess when we are stating the rules of the game, not describing their physical properties. (*PI* 38, 47)

This might suggest a contrast: chess pieces as obeying laws of physics vs. pieces as obeying rules that define legitimate moves. Is logic, then, an ideal set of rules that determines the *limits* of thought and language—just as 'playing chess' without following the rules to a high approximation would not be playing chess at all?

Yet Wittgenstein wishes to distance his conception of logic as a normative science from this idea, too:

81. . . . [we] cannot say that someone who is using language *must* be playing such a game [a 'calculus with fixed rules'].
. . . [I]f you say that our languages only *approximate* to such calculi you are standing on the very brink of a misunderstanding. . . . [T]he most that can be said is that we *construct* ideal languages. But here the word 'ideal' is liable to mislead, for its sounds as if these languages were better, more perfect, than our everyday language: and as if it took the logician to shew people at last what a proper sentence looked like. (*PI* 38)

Logic does involve idealization, the creation of 'crystalline' models. But the function of these models is not to give us an ideal for all thought and language, an image of how the content of our thinking would be structured if all were right with us.

If logic is not normative in the sense of supplying an ideal that must be followed, in what sense could it be normative?—in the sense that a *norma* is. Consider:

130. Our clear and simple language games are not preparatory studies for a future regularization of language . . . The language games are rather set up as *objects of comparison* which are meant to throw light on the facts of our language by way not only of similarities, but also of dissimilarities. (*PI* 50)

The *norma* and *regula* were said to function regulatively for us as builders a priori—standards we require our cuts to meet, and correct them to fit. This normative function was distinguished from an a posteriori claim based on investigative work concerning how our cuts actually are made. Wittgenstein says of logic: 'the crystalline purity of logic was, of course, not a *result of investigation*: it was a requirement' (*PI* 46).

But what sort of requirement? One sense might be a *logico-metaphysical requirement*:

89. These considerations bring us up to the problem: In what sense is logic sublime?
For there seemed to pertain to logic a peculiar depth—a universal significance. Logic lay, it seemed, at the bottom of all the sciences. . . .
97. Thought is surrounded by a halo.—Its essence, logic, presents an order, in fact the a priori order of the world: that is, the order of *possibilities*, which must be common to both world and thought. But this order, it seems, must be *utterly simple*. It is *prior to* all experience, must run through all experience; no empirical cloudiness or uncertainty can be allowed to affect it—It must rather be of purest crystal. (*PI* 42, 44)

This logico-metaphysical conception—for an example of which Wittgenstein cites his own *Tractatus*—and the associated idea that 'the answer to [our] questions is to be given once for all; and independently of any future experience' (*PI* 43) is what he has now come to reject:

101. We want to say that there can't be any vagueness in logic. The idea now absorbs us,

that the ideal '*must*' be found in reality. Meanwhile, we do not as yet see *how* it occurs there, nor do we understand the nature of this 'must'. We think it must be in reality; for we think we already see it there.

102. The strict and clear rules of the logical structure of propositions appear to us as something in the background—hidden in the medium of the understanding. I already see them (even though through a medium): for I understand the propositional sign, I use it to say something.

103. The ideal, as we think of it, is unshakeable. You can never get outside it; you must always turn back. There is no outside; outside you cannot breathe.—Where does this idea come from? It is like a pair of glasses on our nose which we see whatever we look at. It never occurs to us to take them off. . . .

114. (*Tractatus Logico-Philosophicus*, 4.5): 'The general form of a proposition is: This is how things are.'—That is the kind of proposition one repeats to oneself countless times. One thinks that one is tracing the outline of the thing's nature over and over again, and one is merely tracing round the frame through which we look at it. (*PI* 45–8)

In this logico-metaphysical conception, we find the problem of the a priori status of logic as often posed by philosophers: logical possibility delineates the whole domain of possibility, and does so a priori—it is possibility in the widest sense, encompassing all possible worlds.

But there is an alternative conception of the sense of 'requirement' in which the 'crystalline purity' of logic might be a requirement of investigation in the sense in which use of a *norma* or *regula* is a requirement in building. We require this of ourselves, not because it is inherent in the material, but because we have needs that square and straight lumber and stone can meet.

108. . . . The *preconceived idea* of crystalline purity can only be removed by turning our whole examination round. (One might say: the axis of our examination must be rotated, but about the fixed point of our real need.) (*PI* 46)

Following the *norma* or *regula* is something we can advantageously require of ourselves, once we have made these tools. Deploying rigorous propositional reasoning is also something we can profitably require of ourselves, once we have used our existing language to construct such an ideal language with its fixed rules and its powerful capacity to express and assess relations among truth-functional propositions. This of course would not be true were the rules of logic as arbitrarily related to enduring expressive, cognitive, and practical needs as the rules of a board game. A propositional structure may be a 'medium', a 'method of representing the thing', or a 'frame through which look', but this no more makes it 'subjective' in its character or arbitrary in its capacities than is the builder's *norma* and *regula*. The objective, precise, rule-governed features of a propositional structure suit it well for a wide range of representational and deliberative purposes, even though it does not capture all of the content and structure that underlies thought and reality.

For what is the *propositional structure* of phenomenal experience? Of *de se* attribution?[14] Of the similarities and dissimiliarities of images (including 'family resemblances'), or of the looks, sounds, feels, smells, and tastes that tell us 'what something is like', and guide so much of our thought, judgement, and communication?

107. The more narrowly we examine actual language, the sharper becomes the conflict between it and our requirement [of 'crystalline purity']. . . .
108. We see that what we call 'sentence' and 'language' has not the formal unity I imagined, but is the family of structures more or less related to one another. (*PI* 46)

Propositionality may not be essential for thought (lest we claim that primates and prelinguistic infants cannot think) any more than geometric measuring tools are essential for building shelter (lest we say a rude hut cannot be a house). But a practice of thought equipped with means to represent propositions, and therefore of disciplining itself to some significant extent by explicit rules of logic, has vastly greater representative and epistemic power than one that cannot, just as a building practice equipped with geometric measuring tools can create edifices of vastly greater size, complexity, and functionality.

A worry jumps out at us. If our capacity to think is more than a system of propositions, governed by logic, doesn't logic become *too optional*? Something we might pick it up, or put it down—decide on its applicability? Continuing with Wittgenstein:

108. . . . But what becomes of logic now? Its rigour seems to be giving way here. But in that case doesn't logic altogether disappear?—For how can it lose its rigour? Of course not by our bargaining any of its rigour out of it. (*PI* 46)

We do not 'bargain' the rigour out of a *norma* when we set it aside in order to cut an angled block for an arch, nor can we by this act 'decide' that it does not apply to the block—the *norma* will apply and would show the gap whether we actually apply it or not, and whether we welcome this gap or not. If someone attempted to make a *norma* using a material so flexible that it would uncomplainingly fit the angle of arch stone, it would be less functional as a *norma* for carpenters and masons—they need a *rigorous* (from *rigere*, 'to be stiff') standard of squareness. So there is no desire to diminish the *norma*'s rigour, or make the *norma* 'disappear', even as we realize that it is not an all-purpose guide, and that it is able to guide us as reliably and truly as it does precisely because it does not 'accommodate' to all cutting tasks, including those are better done by making something unsquare.

Similarly, the 'tool assortment' propositional logic offers us includes the pattern of the truth-table used to define the material conditional. Thanks to this truth-table, we have a rigorous check for the validity of inferences, given no more than the truth-functions of the component parts and their structural relations. In

---

[14] See David Lewis, 'Attitudes *De Dicto* and *De Se*', in his *Philosophical Papers*, i (New York: Oxford University Press, 1983).

doing many kinds of reasoning, from proof in mathematics to spotting fallacies and unacknowledged commitments in ordinary deliberation, we desperately need to be able to carry out this sort of rigorous check of correctness in an inference. So we would be ill-advised to 'bargain' this rigour out of the material conditional. Compare Wittgenstein's example of 'taking one's inspiration' from a formula, but *not* following a rule:

237. Imagine someone using a line as a rule in the following way: he holds a pair of compasses, and carries one of its points along the line that is the 'rule', while the other one draws the line that follows the rule. And while he moves along the ruling line he alters the opening of the compasses, apparently with great precision, looking at the rule the whole time as if it determined what he did. And watching him we see no kind of regularity in the opening and shutting of the compasses. We cannot learn his way of following the line from it. Here perhaps one really would say: 'The original seems to *intimate* to him which way he is to go. But it is not a rule.' (*PI* 67)

We would be ill-advised to trade in the material conditional for a non-truth-functional conditional we could 'adjust' by inspiration, or by the whisperings of an intuitive sense (cf. *PI* 86). But we would also be ill-advised to assess all 'if . . . then . . .' reasoning in actual life by applying the norma of the material conditional, 'correcting' all conditional reasoning until it meets this truth-functional standard. Without access to 'strong conditionals', and to different standards for assessing them, we would assign the same truth-value to, for example, 'If Wittgenstein were reading this, he'd be outraged' and 'If Wittgenstein were reading this, he'd be delighted.' That would diminish, not enhance, our deliberative capacity and the expressive power of language and thought—especially since a chief function of deliberation is to consider hypothetical (i.e. non-actual) circumstances. Disciplined in our reasoning by sheer truth-functionality, we would be less rather than more rational in thought and action. If, that is, 'rational' means anything like 'capable of responding to reasons'.

Propositional logic as *norma* does not 'disappear' or lose rigour when we engage in non-truth-functional inference. On the contrary, we may rely upon its rigour in such cases precisely to discover and understand *dissimilarities* as well as similarities (compare Wittgenstein's remark about 'similarities' and 'dissimilarities', quoted above and at *PI* 50). Who among us has not taught undergraduates the non-truth-functional character of ordinary 'if . . . then . . .' inference precisely by showing how it does not fit the *norma* of the material conditional's truth-table?

Thus, if propositional logic really determined the bounds of thought, we would be much less thoughtful in many ways. We could not reason using non-propositional image-evaluation or image-comparison ('What is the criterion for the sameness of two images?', *PI* 117), could not be guided in reflection and choice by the felt character of various imagined situations ('What is the criterion for the redness of an image?', *PI* 117), could not hypothesize *reductios*, could not follow a chain of merely associative resemblance which cannot be distilled into propositional form, and could not identify the analogies that help us understand themes in music:

527. Understanding a sentence is much more akin to understanding a theme in music than one might think. . . . One would like to say '[I understand a musical theme] Because I know what it's all about.' But what is it all about? I should not be able to say. In order to 'explain' I could only compare it with something else which has the same rhythm (I mean the same pattern). (One says 'Don't you see, this is as if a conclusion were being drawn' . . .).
528. It would be possible to imagine people who had something not quite unlike a language: a play of sounds, without vocabulary or grammar. . . .
529. 'But what would the meaning of the sounds be in such a case?'—What is it in music? (*PI* 143)

Indeed, neurological evidence increasingly suggests that the processes underlying even our propositional reasoning are themselves associative and non-computational, drawing upon a probabilistic mental architecture cobbled from many interactive components rather obeying a unifying master algorithm.

We should no more tax these alternative forms of cognition, communication, and understanding with 'failure to fit' the *norma* of propositional logic than we should tax a builder's square for failure to fit arch stones or to help us regulate surface colour. Nor should we 'bargain away' the simplicity and purity of propositional logic in an effort to accommodate all such mental activity, any more than we should seek to develop a super-*norma* to replace our familiar box of non-super tools. We should instead see that categorical, strict *normae* for assessing truth-functional consistency and validity are valuable assets in our mental toolkit. For they are crucial to making good use of a representational system such as is afforded by propositions, where the *estandard* of correctness (alignment or co-alignment) is truth, and the *estandard* of equivalence or inclusion therefore truth-functional.

136. . . . to say that a proposition is whatever can be true or false amounts to saying: we call something a proposition when *in our language* we apply the calculus of truth functions to it. (*PI* 52)

It is no mere accident that we have disciplined elements of language in this way. It would be difficult to imagine, for example, how scientific inquiry and the resulting theoretical understanding of natural phenomena could have reached anything like its current state of development, determinacy, and dispersion through the thought, experience, experimentation, and technological activity of so many distinct individuals and groups without a shared representational scheme disciplined in this way. But this does not show that the propositional system is adequate to express everything that might exist or be imagined, or that it could ever serve as an autonomous replacement for our ordinary language, thought, and ways of being guided by experience—even the experience that empirical science must draw upon.

'But don't we, in the final analysis, use logical reasoning in order to decide whether to use this supposed 'tool' you are calling 'logic'? So isn't logic at the bottom of thought, at the limits of reasoning, after all?' We do indeed use logic in such decisions. We also use purposes, capacities to recognize and compare formal patterns and sensory experiences, non-truth-functional inferences, analogical reasoning, and more. And we need an antecedently-understood metalanguage— ordinary language and thought—with which to introduce and interpret the propositional calculus and its fixed rules. To repeat an earlier passage:

120. When I talk about language (words, sentences, etc.) I must speak the language of every day. Is this language somehow too coarse and material for what we want to say? *Then how is another one to be constructed?*—And how strange that we should be able to do anything at all with the one we have! (*PI* 49)

THE NEED FOR THE A PRIORI

Initially suspicious of the a priori, I have come to see that we need it. We need it in part because we need to be able to regulate our practices by *normae* that fit various purposes and can be used as standards for our often actual imperfect performance, that do not simply bend to fit that performance a posteriori, as empirical generalizations must if they are to be correct. Depending upon the purposes, these *normae* will have different characteristics. Some in particular will correspond to well-defined formal features and exhibit high rigidity and wide range in application—like a carpenter's square or mason's straight-edge, or the propositional calculus. Others may be more open-ended and flexible, adjusting *here* to achieve further application *there*—like a contour gauge, or some (but not all) concepts in language.

Thinking of logic as such a *norma* does not, however, require us to think it is unconditional in application or inherently thought-guiding—some of our thought has non-propositional content (which does not satisfy the conditions for logic's application), and *all* of our thought, considered as a mental phenomenon, lies outside of logic's proper realm. At the same time, nothing about our ways of thought could exempt whatever propositional content it does have from the rules of propositional logic. Thus logic can be used as a non-hypothetical or categorical *norma* (or set of *normae*), even though it is not inherently and unconditionally action- or thought-guiding. The question becomes: How are we able, given our all-too-human nature, capable of disciplining our thought and practices by such categorical *normae* to the extent that we do? The answer seems to lie in our capacity to deploy in our practices *estandards* that correspond to objective relations and magnitudes, and that permit 'measurements' that will not be partisan or to reflect our particular wishes.

240. Disputes do not break out (among mathematicians, say) over whether a rule has been obeyed or not. People don't come to blows over it, for example. That is part of the framework on which the working of our language is based. . . .

241. If language is to be a means of communication there must be agreement not only on definitions but also (queer as this may sound) in judgements. This seems to abolish logic, but it does not do so.—It is one thing to describe methods of measurement, and another to obtain and state results of measurement. But what we call 'measuring' is partly determined by a certain constancy in results of measurement. (*PI* 88)

As a result, the a priori character of propositional logic can be part of a shared language that enhances our expressive power and reach, and need not stand between us and the empirical, conceptual, and practical innovations we will need to make if we are to adapt our thinking to a world not of our making. This particular rigid discipline can be part of our overall intellectual adaptiveness. Of course, we might decide that the only *normae* or *regulae* of reasoning properly called 'logic' are those determined by the familiar constants of the classical propositional calculus. But that might not be a barrier to conceptual innovation or innovation even in reasoning itself; it means only that we will use another term—e.g. 'analogical reasoning' as opposed to 'logical reasoning'—as we label the items in our toolkit, and debate which ones, if any, to use in a given application.

However much we need propositional logic as *normae*, it had better not be treated as a super-*norma*. If all meaningful thought or language required propositional expression—and therefore had propositional logic as its *estandard*—to the exclusion of other types of representation and reasoning, then thought and language would indeed force us onto rigid rails. We would be confined to these rails, come what may, until our mental energy were spent, whatever richer understanding we would thus railroad by. As in the Bayesian simulacrum, experience, however surprising, would never count for us as justifying 'leaving the rails', for a posteriori rethinking or discontinuously altering the structure of the scheme of representation itself. It would, of course, be absurd to ask logic to provide us with a rule permitting its own discontinuous alteration. Either the alteration would be permitted, and hence within the rules after all, or it would be discontinuous, and hence not rule-permitted. This kind of instruction or learning is not something we can sensibly ask of a *norma* or *regula*. What is Wittgenstein's alternative?

144. What do I mean when I say 'the pupil's capacity to learn may come to an end here?' ... Well, I should like you to say: 'Yes, it's true, you can imagine that too, that might happen too!'—But was I trying to draw someone's attention to the fact that he is capable of imagining that?—I wanted to put that picture before him, and his *acceptance* of the picture consists in his now being inclined to regard a given case differently: that is, to compare it with *this* rather than *that* set of pictures. I have changed his *way of looking at things*. (*PI* 57)

If a scheme of representation had to be entirely truth-functional or propositional in order to function meaningfully, and if our maxim in all reasoning were to 'norm' its content and extension to the scope and rules of propositional logic—if this were the limit of the possibility of thinking and rethinking, learning and communicating—then it would be unclear that there could be any thoughtful process that amounted to giving or accepting *pictures*, or to gesturing at *this* rather than *that* way of looking at things. As a result, schemes of representation would be much less useful things.[15] And thought and language themselves would much less effective as sources of humankind's vaulted adaptiveness to the world.

[15] If I understand Wittgenstein's overall argument about rules, then things would be a good deal worse than this. For our very capacity to be guided by non-hypothetical *normae* or rules—or by concepts and definitions—depends upon abilities that are not themselves rule-based and not entirely representable by relations expressible within propositional logic. For example, the 'fit' of a thought process with a maxim or rule is not a simple propositional relation, yet the 'role' of words such as 'fit' and 'being able to' 'is what we need to understand in order to resolve philosophical paradoxes' (*PI* 73).

Haven't we already been all the way around the barn with the idea of logic as a set of tools, and decided that this view cannot explain how logic could afford any 'standards of correctness' for arguments, since tools cannot be 'correct' or 'incorrect', but only more or less useful? — Yes, we have. But we picked the wrong tools for understanding the analogy. Hammers may not function as 'standards of correctness' for building, but tools like *normae* and *regulae* function precisely as *estandards* of correctness (*corrigere*) or comparison, as Wittgenstein knew in speaking of rulers and measuring-rods.

9

Apriority and Existence

Stephen Yablo

1. A PARADOX

Fifty years ago, something big happened in ontology. W. V. O. Quine convinced everyone who cared that the argument for abstract objects, if there were going to be one, would have to be a posteriori in nature. And it would have to an a posteriori argument of a particular sort: an *indispensability* argument representing numbers, to use that example, as entities that 'total science' cannot do without.[1]

This is not to say that a priori arguments are no longer attempted. They are, for instance by Alvin Plantinga in *The Ontological Argument*, and Crispin Wright in *Frege and the Conception of Numbers as Objects*. These arguments are put forward, however, with a palpable sense of daring, as though a rabbit were about to be pulled out of a hat. Nobody supposes that there are *easy* proofs, from a priori or empirically obvious premises, of the existence of abstracta.[2] (The only easy existence proof we know of in philosophy is Descartes' *cogito ergo sum*.)

The paradox is that, if we are to go by what philosophers say in other contexts, this bashfulness about what can be shown a priori is quite unnecessary. Abstract objects are a priori deducible from assumptions that nobody would deny.

Example (i). As everyone knows, an argument is valid iff every model of its

This paper is a revised and expanded version of 'A Paradox of Existence', to appear in a CSLI volume on ontology an fiction. David Hills, Ken Walton, Mark Crimmins, Ralph Wedgwood, Ned Hall, John Hawthorne, Peter van Inwagen, Stephen Schiffer, David Chalmers, Kent Bach, Laura Shroeter, Sol Feferman, Thomas Hofweber, David Velleman, Peter Railton—thanks for your comments and advice. Related papers were read at Southern Methodist University, University of Colorado, Brandeis University, Harvard University, Brown University, University of Connecticut, Syracuse University, CSLI, Notre Dame University, and Columbia University.

[1] The classic formulation is Hilary Putnam's: 'quantification over mathematical entities is indispensable for science . . ., therefore we should accept such quantification; but this commits us to accepting the existence of the mathematical entities in question' (1971: 57).

[2] A possible exception is Arthur Prior in 'Entities', who comments: 'This is very elementary stuff—I am almost tempted to apply the mystic word 'tautological'—and I apologise for so solemnly putting it forward in a learned journal. But I do not think it can be denied that these things need to be said. For there are people who do not agree with them' (1976:26).

premises is a model of its conclusions. I have never seen empirical evidence offered for this equivalence so I assume the knowledge is a priori. On the other hand, it is *also* (often) known a priori that such and such an argument is invalid. From these two pieces of a priori knowledge it follows by elementary logic that there exist certain abstract objects, viz. models.

Example (ii). It is a priori, I assume, since observational evidence is never given, that there are as many *F*s and *G*s iff there is a one to one function from the *F*s to the *G*s. It is also known, a posteriori this time, that I have as many left shoes as right. From these two pieces of information it again follows by logic that certain abstract objects exist, viz. functions.

2. PLATONIC OBJECTS

So far, so bad. But matters can be made even worse. This is because objects that are *not* abstract, or not obviously so, can be similarly 'deduced' on the basis of a priori-looking bridge principles. I have in mind principles like 'it is possible that *B* iff there is a *B*-world', and 'Jones buttered the toast *F*-ly iff there was a buttering of the toast by Jones and it was *F*', and 'Jones is human iff being human is one of Jones's properties.' That non-abstract (or not obviously abstract) objects appear also to admit of overeasy proof shows that we still have not got an exact bead on the problem.

Suppose we try again. There's a tradition in philosophy of finding 'unexpected objects' in truth-conditions—of detecting whatsits in the truth-conditions of statements that are not on the face of it *about* whatsits. So,

the truth-value of	*is held to turn on*
'argument *A* is valid'	the existence of *countermodels*
'it is possible that *B*'	the existence of *worlds*
'there are as many *C*s as *D*s'	the existence of 1–1 *functions*
'there are over five *E*s'	the number of *E*s exceeding five
'they did it *F*ly'	the *event* of their doing it being *F*
'there are *G*s which BLAH'	there being a *set* of *G*s which BLAH
'she is *H*'	her relation to the *property H*-ness

Objects with a tendency to turn up unexpected in truth-conditions like this can be called *platonic*. Models, worlds, properties, and so on, are platonic, relative to the areas of discourse on the left, because the sentences on the left aren't intuitively *about* models, worlds, and properties. (If an example of non-platonicness is wanted, consider people in relation to population discourse. That the truth about which regions are populated should hinge on where the people are does not make anything platonic, because people are what population-discourse is visibly and unsurprisingly all about.)

Objects are platonic relative to an area of discourse due to the combination of something positive—the discourse depends for its truth-value on how objects like that behave—with something negative—the discourse is not *about* objects like that. It appears to be this combination, truth-dependence without aboutness, that makes for the paradoxical result. It appears, in other words, that with *all* platonic objects, abstract or not, there is going to be the possibility of an overeasy existence proof. Just as functions are deducible from my having as many left shoes as right ones, events can be conjured a priori out of the fact that Jones buttered the toast slowly, and worlds out of the fact that she could have done it quickly.

3. QUINE'S WAY OR THE HIGHWAY

Our paradox is now shaping up as follows. Let X be whatever sort of platonic object you like: numbers, properties, worlds, sets, it doesn't matter. Then on the one hand we've got

> *Quineanism:* to establish the existence of Xs takes a holistic a posteriori indispensability argument;

while on the other hand we've got

> *Rationalism:* the existence of Xs follows by 'truths of reason'—a priori bridge principles—from a priori and/or empirical banalities.

The reason this is a paradox and not merely a disagreement is that Quineanism is received opinion in philosophy, while Rationalism is a straightforward *consequence* of received opinion: the opinion that we are capable in some cases of a priori insight into truth-conditions, and can a priori 'see' that an argument is valid iff it has no countermodels, that it is possible that S iff there is an S-world, and so on.

What is to be done? One option of course is to embrace Rationalism and admit that the proof of numbers and the rest is easier than anyone had imagined. I am going to assume without argument that such a course is out of the question. Our feeling of hocus-pocus about the 'easy' proof of numbers (etc.) is really very strong and has got to be respected. If that is right, then only one option remains: we have to renounce our claim to knowing the bridge principles a priori. Perhaps the principles are *false*, as John Etchemendy maintains about the Tarskian validity principle.[3] Or perhaps it is just that our justification is not a priori; the Tarski principle owes its plausibility to the prior hypothesis that there are sets, and the argument for *them* is experiential and holistic. The point either way is that we have to stop carrying on as though it is known independently of experience that, e.g. the valid arguments are the ones without countermodels.

---

[3] Etchemendy (1990).

If only it were that easy! The trouble is that our rights of access to the bridge principles do not *seem* to be hostage to empirical fortune in the way suggested; our practice with the principles does not *feel* like it is 'hanging by a thread' until the empirical situation sorts itself out. This shows up in a couple of ways, one having to do with our actual attitudes, one having to do with the attitudes we would have had in certain counterfactual situations.

Actual: Many or most of us using the Tarski biconditional *have no particular view* about abstract ontology. Certainly we are not committed Platonists. If the biconditional (as employed by us) truly presupposed such an ontology, then we *ought* to feel as though we were walking on very thin ice indeed. I don't know about you, but I have never, not once, heard anxieties expressed on this score.

Counterfactual: Also testifying to our (surprising) lack of concern about the true ontological situation is the 'hypothetical' fact that if someone were to *turn up* with evidence that abstract objects did not exist, our use of models to figure validity would not be altered one iota. Burgess and Rosen begin their book *A Subject with No Object* with a relevant fable:

Finally, after years of waiting, it is your turn to put a question to the Oracle of Philosophy . . . you humbly approach and ask the question that has been consuming you for as long as you can remember: 'Tell me, O Oracle, what there is. What sorts of things exist?' To this the Oracle responds: 'What? You want the whole list? . . . I will tell you this: everything there is is concrete; nothing there is is abstract.' (1997: 3)

Suppose we continue the fable a little. Impressed with what the Oracle has told you, you return to civilization to spread the concrete gospel. Your first stop is at—plug in here the name of your favourite department of mathematics or logic—where researchers are confidently reckoning validity by way of calculations on models. You demand that the practice be stopped at once. It's true that the Oracle has been known to speak in riddles; but there is now a well-enough justified *worry* about the existence of models that all theoretical reliance on them should cease. They of course tell you to bug off and amscray. Which come to think of it is exactly what you yourself would do, if the situation were reversed.

4. IMPATIENCE

Our question really boils down to this. What is the source of the *impatience* we feel with the meddling ontologist—the one who insists that the practice of judging validity by use of Tarski be put on hold until the all-important matter is settled of whether models really exist?

One explanation can be ruled out immediately: we think the principles would still hold (literally) true whether the objects existed or not.[4] That would be to think that if, contrary to what we perhaps suppose, there are no models, then every argument is valid! It would be to think that if the models were found to peter out above a certain finite cardinality—not for deep conceptual reasons, mind you, but as a matter of brute empirical fact—then a whole lot of statements we now regard as logically contingent, such as 'there are fifty zillion objects', are in fact logically false. It seems as clear as anything that we are not in the market for this sort of result. And so we can draw the following moral:

> *Ontology Matters to Truth*: Our complacency about the bridge principles is *not* due to a belief that they hold literally true regardless of the ontological facts. (It can't be, since we have no such belief.)

A second explanation of our impatience seems equally misguided: we are confident that the negative empirical findings will never be made. It may be that we *are* confident of this; it is not as though any great number of ontological controversies have been resolved by empirical means in the past. Even if it is granted, though, that we do not expect evidence to turn up that casts doubt on the existence of models, why should that prevent us from having a view about what to say if it did? I take it that we are also confident that it will never be discovered that there are no people. Nevertheless, it seems clearly true that *if* the Oracle convinces us that all the so-called people are no more than clever illusions, we will conclude via the population principle that no region is populated; and clearly false that if the Oracle convinces us that there are no models, we will conclude via Tarski's principle that all arguments are valid. The point is that

> *Experience Matters to Ontology*: Our complacency about the bridge principles is not due to a belief that the trouble-making empirical facts will never come to light. That belief may be there, but our complacency runs deeper than it can explain.

But then it does not really solve the paradox to say that Quineanism wins out over Rationalism. If experience matters to ontology, and ontology matters to truth, then *experience ought to matter to truth* as well. How is it then that the bridge principles are treated, and apparently rightly treated, as experience-independent?

---

[4] Compare the non-platonic bridge principle

(R) a region is populated iff it contains people.

Should it be discovered that there are no people—everyone but you is a holographic projection, and you are a deluded angel—we would willingly conclude, on the basis of (R), that no regions are populated. This is (one of many reasons) why friends of the population principle do not stay up late at night worrying about the existence of people.

What accounts for the a priori-like deference we pay to them? How can we feel justified in *ignoring* a kind of evidence that would, by our own lights, exhibit our belief as false?[5]

5. PLATONISM AS THE PRICE OF ACCESS

Here is the only way out I can see: What entitles us to our indifference about evidence that would exhibit the principles as false is that *we were never committed in the first place to their truth.*[6] Our attitude towards them is attitude *A*, and attitude *A* leaves it open whether the alluded-to objects really exist.

Now that, you may say, is just crazy. Our everyday reliance on the principles surely presupposes a belief in their truth. Take again Tarski's validity principle

    (V) an argument is valid iff it has no countermodels.

The point of the 'iff' is to give us licence to infer back and forth between (V)'s left- and right-hand sides, and their negations. If these inferences require us to regard (V) as true, then that is a powerful reason so to regard it.

Humour me for a minute while I state the case a little more guardedly: The back and forth inferences give us reason to regard (V) as true *if* they are inferences that people actually perform.

Well, aren't they? You find a countermodel, you conclude that the argument is invalid. You show that there are no countermodels, you conclude that the argument is valid.

I wonder whether that is a fair description of what really goes on. If you're anything like me, the activity you call 'finding a countermodel' *really* just consists in describing to yourself what the countermodel would have to be like; it consists in laying out a blueprint for a structure of the appropriate sort. The issue of whether anything indeed *answers* to the blueprint is not taken up and seems rather beside the point.

As for the other direction, where countermodels cannot be found and we judge the argument to be valid, again, the activity of 'finding that there are no countermodels' is misdescribed. The fact that one is *really* relying on in judging validity is not that countermodels fail to exist—*that* you could have learned from the Oracle, and it would not have altered your validity-judgements one bit—but that there is something in the very notion of a countermodel to argument *A* that prevents there from being such a thing. A consistent blueprint can't be drawn up

---

[5] Here is the problem stated a little more carefully: On the one hand, we feel entitled to the bridge principles regardless of the empirical facts (experience doesn't matter to truth), on the other hand, we think that the empirical facts are highly relevant to whether the mentioned objects exist (experience does matter to ontology); on the third hand, we think the bridge principles are false if the objects do not exist (ontology matters to truth).

[6] To their literal truth, that is; see below.

because the conditions such a model would have to meet are directly at odds with each other. Once again, the issue of whether models do or do not really exist is not broached and seems of no genuine relevance.

So: if you look at the way the Tarski biconditional is actually used, any larger issue of the existence of models 'in general' is bracketed. It's almost as though we were understanding (V) as

> (V*) an argument *A* is valid iff—ontological worries to the side, that is, *assuming that models in general exist*—*A* has no countermodels.[7]

The idea that (V) is in practice understood along the lines of (V*) has the added virtue of explaining our impatience with the ontologist's meddling. If the issue is whether there are countermodels *assuming models*, it doesn't *matter* whether models exist. Of course, the question will be raised of why someone would utter (V) when what they really literally meant was (V*). Suffice it for now to say that linguistic indirection of this sort is not unknown; we'll come back to this later. Meanwhile we need to look at some other reasons why a literal interpretation of the bridge principles might seem unavoidable. (Readers in a hurry should go straight to Section 9, or even 10.)

6. PLATONISM AS THE KEY TO CLARITY

A great goal of analytic philosophy is to make our ideas clear. Of course, the goal is not often achieved to everyone's satisfaction, but in a few instances there has been undeniable progress. Everyone will agree, I think, that our notions of limit and of continuity are clearer thanks to Weierstrass's epsilon-delta story; that our notion of cardinality (especially infinite cardinality) was made clearer by Cantor's explanation in terms of 1–1 functions; that the notion of inductive definability was clarified by the device of quantifying over all sets meeting appropriate closure conditions; and, to return to our favourite example, that our notion of validity was clarified by the appeal to models. This gives us a second reason for insisting on the reality of platonic objects. If we have to quantify over functions, models, sets, etc. to clarify our ideas, and clarification of ideas is a principal goal of analytic philosophy, how can we be expected to reject such quantification and the ontological commitment it carries?

An example will help us to sort the issue out. Recall the controversy sparked by C. I. Lewis's work in modal logic. What Lewis did was to distinguish a number of modal systems: S_1, S_2, S_3, and so on. These systems, at least the ones that attracted most of the attention, differed in their attitude towards formulae like

---

[7] Cf. Field in a critical response to Wright: 'the conceptual truth is [not 'the number of *A*s = the number of *B*s iff there are as many *A*s as *B*s' but] rather '*if numbers exist, then* . . .' (Field 1989: 169).

(a) $\Box P \to \Box\Box P$,
(b) $\Diamond\Box P \to \Box P$, and
(c) $\Diamond S \to \Box\Diamond S$.

One response to Lewis's menu of options was to argue about which of the systems was really 'correct'. But many philosophers preferred to see disputes about which system was best as stemming from subtly different ideas of necessity and possibility. The problem was to identify a *kind* of variation in ideas of necessity that would predict the observed differences in modal intuition.

Then came possible worlds semantics. Acceptance of (a) could now be linked with a transitive conception of relative possibility: a world w' that *would* have been possible, had possible world w obtained, *is* possible. (Likewise, *mutatis mutandis*, for (b) and (c).) The benefits were and remain substantial: fewer spurious ('merely verbal') disagreements, improved semantical self-understanding, fewer fallacies of equivocation, a clearer picture of why modal principles fall into natural packages, and so on.

The platonist now argues as follows. If the clarification that confers these benefits requires us to treat modal operators as (disguised) quantifiers over worlds, then that is how we have to treat them; and that means believing in the worlds.

Isn't there something strange about this line of argument? Clarification is more of a cognitive notion than an ontological one; my goal as a clarifier is to elucidate the content of an idea so that it will be easier to tell apart from other ideas with which it might otherwise get confused. But then, how well I have succeeded ought not to depend on ontological matters *except* to the extent that the content of my idea exhibits a similar dependence.

With some ideas—'externalist' ideas—this condition is perhaps satisfied. There may be no way for me to make my idea of water, or of Hillary Clinton, fully clear without bringing in actual water, or actual Hillary.[8] But my ideas of validity and possibility do not *appear* to be externalist in this way. It is strange then to suppose that actual models and worlds would have to be brought in to make them fully clear.

Where does this leave us? The clarificatory powers of platonic objects are not to be doubted. But they do not depend on the objects' actually being there. I can do just as good a job of elucidating my modal concepts by saying

> supposing for the moment that necessity is truth at all worlds possible-from-here, *my* concept is one that calls for relative possibility to be transitive,

as I can by saying

---

[8] Some would argue that unless there is water, my idea of water cannot *be* fully clear.

my concept of necessity has it that necessity *is* truth at all relatively possible worlds, where relative possibility *is* transitive.

Along one dimension, indeed, I can do a better job. Suppose I were to explain my concept of possibility in the second, realistic, way. Then it becomes a conceptual truth that if (contra Lewis) ours is the one and only world, whatever is actually the case is necessarily the case. But this is just *false* of my concept, and I venture to guess of yours as well. An explication that gets a concept's extension-under-a-supposition wrong—that makes mistakes about what goes into the extension on that supposition—does *less* justice to the concept than an explication that avoids the mistakes.

7. PLATONISM AS NEEDED FOR PROOF AND EXPLANATION

Another place principle (V) is appealed to is in metalogical proofs. Classical validity is widely agreed to be monotonic: if $P_1 \ldots P_n/C$ is valid, then so is $P_1 . \ldots P_n P_{n+1}/C$. If we want to prove this result, and/or explain why it holds, we have to quantify over models.[9]

(i) An argument is valid iff every model of its premises satisfies its conclusion, (This is (V).)

(ii) If every model of $P_1 \ldots P_n$ satisfies C then every model of $P_1 \ldots P_n P_{n+1}$ satisfies C. (By logic and definitions.)

(iii) If $P_1 \ldots P_n/C$ is valid, then $P_1 \ldots P_n P_{n+1}/C$ is valid. (From (i) and (ii).)

Proofs like this are of course often given. But the reason for giving them is not so clear. It can't be to show *that* monotonicity holds, since on the one hand, no one ever doubted it, while on the other, the Tarskian analysis of validity has been doubted. Nor does the proof do a very good job of explaining *why* monotonicity holds. The fact allegedly being explained—that adding more premises can't make a valid argument invalid—seems on the face of it to lie at a *deeper* level than the facts called in to explain it, that is, the facts stated in (i) and (ii). One might as well try to 'explain' the fact that sisters are siblings by pointing out that a set containing all siblings thereby contains all sisters.

What a proof like the above *does* come close to showing is that monotonicity

---

[9] I am grateful here to Peter van Inwagen, and, for the idea that models are called on to explain validity-facts, to Kent Bach.

holds as a conceptual matter; it is implicit in the classical concept of validity.[10] The argument is in two steps. It flows from the classical concept of validity that an argument is valid iff it lacks-countermodels-assuming-models. And it flows from our concept of a model that any countermodel to the 'expanded' argument is a countermodel to the original argument as well. Explicitly:

> (1) An argument is valid iff, assuming models, models of its premises satisfy its conclusion. (This is (V*), a conceptual truth about validity.)
>
> (2) Assuming models, if models of $P_1 \ldots P_n$ satisfy C, then models of $P_1 \ldots P_n P_{n+1}$ satisfy C. (A conceptual truth about models.)

Now, let it be that $P_1 \ldots P_n/C$ is valid, i.e. that assuming models, models of $P_1 \ldots P_n$ satisfy C. Then from (2) we see that, again assuming models, models of $P_1 \ldots P_n P_{n+1}$ satisfy C as well. (The principle used here is that if the members of $\{A, \text{if } A \text{ then } B\}$ are true-assuming-models, then B too is true-assuming-models.) So by (1), $P_1 \ldots P_n P_{n+1}/C$ is valid.

> (3) $P_1 \ldots P_n/C$ is valid only if $P_1 \ldots P_n P_{n+1}/C$ is valid. (From (1) and (2).)

Note that an argument like this is *not* automatically available to someone whose concept of validity is non-classical. Suppose that Smith is working with a version of the 'circumscriptive' concept, whereby an argument is valid iff minimal models of its premises are models of its conclusion. Her version of (1)-(3) would start like this:

> (1') An argument is valid iff, assuming models, *minimal* models of its premises satisfy its conclusion.
>
> (2') Assuming models, minimal models of $P_1 \ldots P_n$ satisfy C only if minimal models of $P_1 \ldots P_n P_{n+1}$ satisfy C.

But now wait. $P_1 \ldots P_n$'s minimal models may or may not include the minimal models of $P_1 \ldots P_n P_{n+1}$, so (2') is just false.[11] This illustrates how one can use (1)–(3)-style arguments to tease out the content of a quantificationally explicated concept, without for a moment supposing that the quantified-over entities constitute the real grounds of the concept's application.

A second example where platonic objects fail to play their advertised role is this. Equinumerosity is symmetrical: if there are exactly as many Fs as Gs, then there are exactly as many Gs as Fs. The usual proof of this result appeals to the fact that inverting a bijection yields another bijection. Do we want to see the proof as *demonstrating*—say, to someone who didn't already believe it—that exactly-as-many-as is symmetrical? Probably not; that as many Fs as Gs means as many

---

[10] As opposed to, say, the various alternative concepts discussed in the literature on nonmonotonic logic.

[11] e.g. let $P_1 = Fa$, $P_2 = Gb$, and $P_3 = \neg Fb$. Then minimal models of $\{P_1, P_2, P_3\}$ have two elements each, while those of $\{P_1, P_2\}$ have just one.

*G*s as *F*s seems prima facie at least as obvious as the invertibility of bijections. Nor does the proof appear to show *why* equinumerosity is symmetrical. If bijections exist, there are going to be lots of them. But then, rather than grounding my fingers' equinumerosity with my toes in the fact that there are all these bijections, it would seem better to explain the bijections—their possibility, at least—in terms of the prior fact that I have as many fingers as toes. That way we explain many facts in terms of one, rather than one in terms of many.

The proof motive for positing platonic objects is not without merit. Platonic argumentation can be enormously instructive.[12] Once we get clearer, though, on what the arguments actually show—not that weakening holds, or that equinumerosity is symmetrical, but that these results are implicit in concepts open to a certain sort of elucidation—then the case for actually *believing* in the objects is tremendously weakened. Once again, we gain as much purchase on the concept by aligning it with a condition on assumed objects as we would by treating the objects as real.

8. PLATONISM AS A CHECK ON PRIMITIVE IDEOLOGY

Everywhere in philosophy we are faced with 'ideology–ontology' trade-offs. Roderick Chisholm trades primitive adverbial modification off against sense data; the adverbs win. Donald Davidson trades primitive adverbs off against events; this time the adverbs lose. Arthur Prior has primitive non-nominal quantifiers trading off against properties and propositions. David Lewis pits primitive metaphysical possibility against concrete worlds, conceived as possibility-exemplifiers. Hartry Field does the same, except that his modality is a logical one and the exemplifiers are Tarskian models.

If the examples do nothing else, they remind us that how these trade-offs are carried out is a matter of taste. Some philosophers (e.g. Lewis) want to minimize semantic primitives at the expense of a bigger than expected ontology. Other philosophers (e.g. Field) want to minimize ontology at the expense of a bigger than expected lexicon. About the only thing people seem to agree on is that an *infinite* number of semantic primitives would be too many. Thus Davidson:

When we can regard the meaning of each sentence as a function of a finite number of features of the sentence, we have an insight not only into what there is to be learned [in learning a language]; we also understand how an infinite aptitude can be encompassed by finite accomplishments. For suppose that a language lacks this feature; then no matter how many sentences a would-be speaker learns to produce and understand, there will be others whose meanings are not given by the rules already mastered. It is natural to say that such

---

[12] I should stress that we are not talking about the use of, say, models, to prove results explicitly about models. Our interest is in discourses with respect to which the given objects are platonic.

a language is *unlearnable*. . . . we may state the condition under discussion by saying: a learnable language has a finite number of semantical primitives (1984: 8–9).[13]

The relevance of this to the ontology–ideology issue is that oftentimes the only way of keeping the number of semantic primitives down is to postulate a certain kind of object. Davidson's showcase example, which he wants to make the basis of a new 'method of truth in metaphysics', has already been mentioned; we have to countenance events, he thinks, to get a tractable semantics for adverbs:

[I]t takes an ontology to make [the device] work: an ontology including people for 'Someone fell down and broke his crown', an ontology of events . . . for 'Jones nicked his cheek in the bathroom on Saturday.' It is mildly ironic that in recent philosophy it has become a popular manoeuvre to try to *avoid* ontological problems by treating certain phrases as adverbial. One such suggestion is that we can abjure sense-data if we render a sentence like 'The mountain appears blue to Smith' as 'The mountain appears bluely to Smith.' Another is that we can do without an ontology of intensional objects by thinking of sentences about propositional attitudes as essentially adverbial: 'Galileo said that the earth moves' would then come out, 'Galileo spoke in-a-that-the-earth-moves-fashion'. There is little chance, I think, that such adverbial clauses can be given a systematic semantical analysis without ontological entanglements (1984: 212–13).

If speakers' competence with adverbs is thought of as grounded (potentially, anyway) in a mechanism that derives '*S* VERBED *G*ly' from a deep structure along the lines of 'there was a VERBing with agent *S* which was *G*', then there will be no need to learn separate inference rules for each action-verb VERB and adverb *G*. Both turn into predicates and so their inferential powers are already given by the rules of first-order logic.

The trouble with this as an *ontological* argument is that nowhere in Davidson's account is use made of the fact that the events are actually *there*. At most the conclusion is that we, or pertinent subpersonal systems, are set up to *suppose* they are there. Couldn't the supposition be just that: a supposition? Maybe 'the adverb mechanism' derives '*S* VERBed *G*ly' not from

   (i) 'there was a VERBing with agent *S* which was *G*,' but
   (ii) 'doubts about events aside, there was a VERBing which etc.'

Or maybe it derives '*S* VERBed *G*ly' from (i), but a token of (i) inscribed not in the speaker's 'belief box' but her 'suppose box'. At any rate it is very hard to see how the existence-out-there of real VERBings could lend any help to the speaker trying to acquire a language; whatever it is that events are supposed to contribute to the language-acquisition task would seem to be equally contributed by merely supposed events. This is not to say that there are no events—just that one needs a better reason to believe in them than the help they provide with language-learning.

---

[13] Davidson sees violations of the learnability requirement in the work of Tarski on quotation marks, Church on sense and denotation, Scheffler on indirect discourse, and Quine on belief attributions.

9. PLATONISM AS A PROP FOR REALISM

One more try: why would anyone want (V), or any other bridge principle, to be literally true, so that the platonic objects it quantifies over were really there?

One can think of this as a query about the relations between *ontology*, the study of what is, and *alethiology*, the study of what is the case. A lot of people find it plausible and desirable that what is the case should be controlled as far as possible by what is, and what it is like—that, in Lewis's phrase,[14] *truth should supervene on being*. This is a view that Lewis himself accepts, in the following form: truth is supervenient on what things there are and which perfectly natural properties they instantiate.[15] Since the properties things instantiate are themselves in a broad sense 'things', the view is really that *truth is supervenient on what things there are and their interactions, e.g. which instantiate which.*

Although Lewis maintains supervenience about truth quite generally, it is more common to find it maintained of truth in a particular area of discourse; the usual claim is that truth supervenes on being not *globally* but *locally*. It is very often said that what is wrong, or at least different, about evaluative discourse is that there are no moral/aesthetic *properties* out there to settle the truth-value of evaluative utterances. And it is common to hear anti-realism about *F*-discourse identified with the thesis that there is no such property as *F*ness.[16]

This linking of anti-realism with the lack of an associated property is only one symptom of a broader tendency of thought. When truth in an area of discourse is controlled by the existence and behaviour of objects, that is felt to *boost the discourse's credentials* as fact-stating or objective. The more truth can be pinned to the way a bunch of objects comport themselves, the more *objective* the discourse appears. Talk about possibility feels more objective if its truth-value is controlled by which possible worlds exist. Talk about what happened yesterday, or what will happen tomorrow, feels more objective if its truth-value is controlled by a still somehow lingering past, or a future out there lying in wait for us.[17] And to return to our original example, talk about validity feels more objective if its truth-value is controlled by the existence or not of countermodels.

Why should objects appear to contribute to objectivity in this way? A little more grandiosely, why should *realism*—which holds that an area of discourse is objective—seem to be bolstered by *platonism*—which points to a special ensemble of objects as determining the distribution of truth values?

Realism à la Dummett says that once you get a sentence's meaning sufficiently clear and precise, its truth-value is settled. The question is, settled by what? As long as this question is left hanging, there's room for the anti-realist suspicion that we who employ the sentence are exercising an unwholesome influence.

---

[14] Borrowed from John Bigelow. See Lewis (1992).   [15] Lewis (1992).
[16] This is a particular theme of Paul Boghossian's paper 'Status of Content'.
[17] Cf. McDowell on yesterday's rainstorm.

How is the question to be closed? Well, we've got to point to *another* part of reality that *monopolizes* the influence on truth-value, leaving no way that we by our attitudinalizing could be playing a role. This is where platonism comes in. The existence of objects, especially external objects, is the paradigm of an issue that's *out of our hands*. Either worlds with flying pigs are there, or they're not. Either tomorrow's sea battle awaits us, or it doesn't. Either the countermodels exist, or they don't.

10. A DILEMMA

So—there is a strategy, or tendency of thought, that links *realism* in an area of discourse to *platonism*: belief in a special range of objects whose existence and behaviour settles the question of truth. What are we to make of this strategy? I find it deeply suspicious. The added confidence that the objects are supposed to give us about the objectivity of the discourse strikes me as unearned, or unneeded, or both. To see the problem, look again at what the ontologist is telling us:

> You may be right that models aren't needed to settle the truth value of *particular* 'A has a countermodel' claims. These we can read as short for 'assuming models, A has a counter-model.' What you need the models for is the objectivity of the form of speech of which 'A has a countermodel' is an example. If there really are models, then there's an objective fact of the matter about which arguments have countermodels. Take the models away, and all you've got left is the human practice of developing and swapping around model-descriptions. And this practice, not to say it isn't highly disciplined, doesn't provide as objective a basis for validity-talk as bona fide models would.

The reason I find this suspicious can be put in the form of a dilemma. Logicians speak of 'the space of models,' the space that allegedly functions via (V) to make discourse about validity especially objective. Do we have a determinate grasp of this space or not? By a determinate grasp, I mean

> A grasp sufficient to determine a definite truth-value for each instance of 'assuming models, there is a countermodel to argument A'.

Does our grasp go fatally blurry, for instance, when it comes to models with very large finite cardinalities? Or is it precise enough to settle the existence of countermodels in every case?

Suppose that it's precise enough; we have a determinate grasp in the specified sense. That by itself ensures that there's a determinate fact of the matter about which arguments have-countermodels-assuming-the-space-of-models.[18]

---

[18] Contrast the population principle: region R is populated iff there are people in it. A determinate conception of people isn't itself enough to make for an objective fact of the matter about which regions are populated.

So the models are not needed; you've got your determinate truth-values without them.

Suppose next that we *lack* a determinate conception of the space of models; our grasp *fails* to determine an appropriate truth-value for each instance of 'assuming the space of models, there is a countermodel to argument *A*'. How is it that we nevertheless manage to pick out the right class of mathematical objects as models?

The answer has got to be that the world meets us half way. The intended objects somehow jump out and announce themselves, saying: over here, *we're* the ones you must have had in mind. A particularly attractive form of this is as follows: look, we're the only remotely plausible candidates for the job that even *exist*. The idea either way is that we understand the space of models as whatever out there best corresponds to our otherwise indeterminate intentions.

But this reintroduces the hostage-to-fortune problem. An argument's validity-status would seem to be a conceptually necessary fact about it. Surely we don't want the validity of arguments to be held hostage to a brute logical contingency like what model-like entities happen to exist!

So Tarski's principle (considered now as objectively-bolstering) is faced with a dilemma. If we are clear enough about what we *mean* by it, then the principle isn't *needed* for objectivity; (V*) would do just as well. And if we aren't clear what we mean, then it isn't going to *help*. It isn't even going to be tolerable, because an argument's status as valid is going to blow with the ontological winds in a way that no one could want.

10. CRIME OF THE CENTURY?

It begins to look as if the objectivity argument does not really work. The objects would only be needed if they 'stiffened the discourse's spine'—if they had consequences for truth-values over and above anything determined already by our *conception* of the objects. But by that fact alone, we wouldn't trust them to deliver the right results.

The reason this matters is that as far as I can see, the objectivity argument is the *only* one that argues for a truth-link with actual objects. The other principal motives for accepting platonic objects are served just as well by *pretended* or *assumed* ones.

Which suggests a wild idea. Could it be that sets, functions, properties, worlds, and the like, are one and all put-up jobs, meaning, only pretended or assumed to exist? Call this the say-hypothesis, because what it essentially does is construe talk of platonic objects as following on an unspoken 'say there are models (or whatever)' prefix.

How to evaluate the hypothesis? Bertrand Russell said that postulation of convenient objects has 'all the advantages of theft over honest toil'. This might seem to apply to the say-hypothesis as well. For the suggestion in a way is that an enormous intellectual *crime* has been committed; an entire species of much-beloved and frequently deferred-to entities has been stolen away, leaving behind only persistent appearances.

Suppose we discuss the theft of the platonic objects the way we would any other crime. Means, motive, opportunity—are all these elements present?

The question of means is: how would a job like this be pulled off, where objects appear to be in play but really aren't? The question of motive is: why would anyone *want* to fabricate these objects in the first place? The question of opportunity is: how could a job this big be pulled off without anyone noticing?

12. MEANS

How might it happen that, of the things that regularly crop up in people's *apparently* descriptive utterances, not all really exist, or are even believed to exist by the speaker?

Before addressing this question, we need to acknowledge how nervous it makes us. A certain automatic indignation about people who 'refuse to own up to the commitments of their own speech' has become hugely fashionable. The attitude goes back at least to *Word and Object*, where Quine misses no opportunity to deplore the 'philosophical double talk, which would repudiate an ontology while simultaneously enjoying its benefits' (1960: 242).

But rhetoric aside, the practice of associating oneself with sentences that don't, as literally understood, express one's true meaning is extraordinarily familiar and common. The usual name for it is (not lying or hypocrisy but) but *figurative speech*. I say 'that's not such a great idea' not to call your idea less-than-great—leaving it open, as it were, that it might be very good—but to call your idea bad. The figure in this case is meiosis or understatement. But the point could equally have been made with, say, hyperbole ('they are inseparable'), metonymy ('the White House is angry over allegations that . . .'), or metaphor ('I lost my head'). Not one of the sentences mentioned has a true literal meaning: the first because it exaggerates, the second because it conflates, the third for reasons still to be explored. But it would be insane to associate the speaker with these failings, because the sentences' literal content (if any) is not what the speaker believes, or what she is trying to get across.

The most important example for us is metaphor. What exactly is that? No one quite knows; but the most useful account for our purposes is Kendall Walton's in terms of prop oriented make-believe:

Where in Italy is the town of Crotone? I ask. You explain that it is on the arch of the Italian boot. 'See that thundercloud over there—the big, angry face near the horizon,' you say; 'it is headed this way.' . . . We speak of the saddle of a mountain and the shoulder of a highway . . . All of these cases are linked to make-believe. We think of Italy and the thundercloud as something like pictures. Italy . . . depicts a boot. The cloud is a prop which makes it fictional that there is an angry face . . . The saddle of a mountain is, fictionally, a horse's saddle. But . . . it is not for the sake of games of make-believe that we regard these things as props . . . [The make-believe] is useful for articulating, remembering, and communicating facts about the props—about the geography of Italy, or the identity of the storm cloud . . . or mountain topography. It is by thinking of Italy or the thundercloud . . . as potential if not actual props that I understand where Crotone is, which cloud is the one being talked about.[19]

A metaphor on this view is an utterance that represents its objects as being *like so*: the way that they would need to be to make it pretence-worthy—or, more neutrally, sayable—in a game that the utterance itself suggests. Sayability here is a function of (a) the rules of the game, and (b) the way of the world. But the two factors play very different roles. The game and its rules are treated as given; they function as medium rather than message. The point of the utterance is to call attention to factor (b), the world. It's to say that *the world has held up its end of the bargain.*

When people talk about metaphor, the examples that come to mind are of metaphorical *descriptions* of everyday objects. A hat is divine; a person is green with envy, or beside herself with excitement. Predicative expressions, though, are far from the only ones we use metaphorically. There is hardly a word in the language—be it an adverb, preposition, conjunction, or what have you—that is devoid of metaphorical potential.

The case of interest to us is *referring phrases*: names, definite descriptions, and quantifiers. An appendix to the *Metaphors Dictionary*[20] lists 450 examples of what it calls 'common metaphors'. Approximately one-half contain referential elements. Some examples drawn just from the beginning of the list:

he fell into *an abyss* of despair, he is tied to *her apron strings*, she has *an axe* to grind, let's put that on *the back burner*, those figures are in *the ballpark*, you're beating *a dead horse*, he's bit off *more than he can chew*, don't hide *your lamp* under *a bushel*, let's go by *the book*, don't blow *a fuse*, I have *a bone* to pick with you, I've burned *my bridges*, I hate to burst *your bubble*, you hit *the bull's-eye*, I have *butterflies* in my stomach, I'm going to lay *my cards* on *the table*, you're building *castles in the air*, we will be under *a cloud* until we settle *this thing*, he claimed *his pound of flesh*, she blew *her cool*, he threw me *a curve*, their work is on *the cutting edge*

Some additional examples not from the *Dictionary*; with some of them you have to rub your eyes and blink twice before the non-literal aspects shine through:

---

[19] Walton (1993: 40–1).
[20] Sommer and Weiss (1996).

They put *a lot of hurdles* in your path, there's *a lot* that could be said about that, there's *no precedent* for that, *something* tells me you're right, *there are some things* better left unsaid, *there is something* I forgot to tell you, viz. how to operate the lock, *nothing* gets *my goat* as much as chewing gum in class, *a lot* you can do for me, let's roll out *the red carpet, the last thing I want* is to ..., their people have been rising in *my esteem*, I took her into *my confidence, my patience* is nearly exhausted, I'll take *my chances*, there's *a trace of sadness* in your eyes, *a growing number* of these leaks can be traced to Starr's office, she's got *a lot of smarts*, let's pull out *all the stops*; let's proceed along *the lines suggested above.*

Now, the *last* thing I want to do with these examples is to start a bidding war over who can best accommodate our classificatory intuitions. The one unbreakable rule in the world of metaphor is that there is no consensus on how big that world is: on what should be counted a metaphor and what should not. What I do want to suggest is that the same semantical mechanisms that underlie *paradigmatic* metaphors like 'that hat is divine' seem also to be at work with phrases that for whatever reason— too familiar, insufficiently picturesque, too boring—strike us as hardly figurative at all. If that is right, then it does little harm, I think, to *stipulate* that any phrases that turn a non-committal 'say for argument's sake that BLAH' to descriptive advantage are to be seen as just as much metaphorical as the old campaigners.

Pulling these threads together, I contend that the *means* by which platonic objects are simulated is *existential metaphor*—metaphor making play with a special sort of object to which the speaker is not committed (not by the metaphorical utterance, anyway) and to which she adverts only for the light it sheds on other matters. Rather as 'smarts' are conjured up as metaphorical carriers of intelligence, 'numbers' are conjured up as metaphorical measures of cardinality. More on this below; first there are the questions of motive and opportunity to deal with.

13. MOTIVE

What is the *motive* for simulating platonic objects in this way? The answer is that lots of metaphors, and in particular lots of existential metaphors, are *essential*. They have no literal paraphrases: or no readily available ones; or none with equally happy cognitive effects. To see why, we need to elaborate our picture of metaphor a little.

A metaphor has in addition to its literal content—given by the conditions under which it is true and to that extent belief-worthy—a metaphorical content given by the conditions under which it is 'sayable' in the relevant game. If we help ourselves (in a purely heuristic spirit)[21] to the device of possible worlds, the claim is that

---

[21] Yablo (1996) maintains that worlds are metaphorical. So I am using a metaphor to explain metaphor. Derrida (1982) suggests this is unavoidable. It would be fine by me if he were right.

$$S\text{'s} \left\{ \begin{array}{l} \text{literal} \\ \text{metaphorical} \end{array} \right\} \text{content} = \text{the set of worlds making } S \left\{ \begin{array}{l} \text{true} \\ \text{sayable} \end{array} \right\}$$

The role of say-games on this approach is to bend the lines of semantic projection, so as to reshape the region a sentence defines in logical space (Fig. 9.1)[22] The straight lines on the left are projected by the ordinary, conventional meaning of 'Jimi's on fire'; they pick out the worlds which make 'Jimi's on fire' literally true. The bent lines on the right show what happens when worlds are selected according to whether they make the very same sentence sayable in the relevant game.

The question of motive can now be put like this: granted these metaphorical contents—these ensembles of worlds picked out by their shared property of legitimating an attitude of acceptance-within-the-game—what is the reason for accessing them metaphorically?

One obvious reason would be *lack of an alternative*: the language might have no more to offer in the way of a unifying principle for the worlds in a given content than that *they* are the ones making the relevant sentence sayable. It seems at least an open question, for instance, whether the clouds we call *angry* are the ones that are literally *F*, for any *F* other than 'such that it would be natural and proper to regard them as angry if one were going to attribute emotions to clouds.' Nor does a literal criterion immediately suggest itself for the pieces of computer code called *viruses*, the markings on a page called *tangled* or *loopy*, the vistas called *sweeping*, the glances called *piercing*, or the topographical features called *basins, funnels,* and *brows*.

The topic being ontology, though, let's try to illustrate with an *existential*

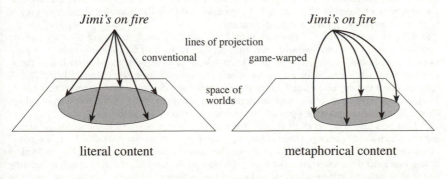

FIG. 9.1

---

[22] A lot of metaphors are (literally understood) impossible: 'I am a rock.' Assuming we want a non-degenerate region on the left, the space of worlds should take in all 'ways for things to be', not just the 'ways things could have been'. The distinction is from Salmon (1989).

metaphor. An example much beloved of philosophers is *the average so-and-so*.[23]
When a cosmologist tells us that

(*S*) The average star has 2.4 planets,

she is not entirely serious; she is making as if to describe an (extraordinary) entity
called 'the average star' as a way of really talking about what the (ordinary) stars
are like on average. True, this *particular* metaphor can be paraphrased away, as
follows:

(*T*) The number of planets divided by the number of stars is 2.4.

But the numbers in *T* are from an intuitive perspective just as remote from the
cosmologist's intended subject matter as the average star in *S*. And this ought to
make us, or the more nominalistic among us, suspicious. Wasn't it Quine who
stressed the possibility of unacknowledged myth-making in even the most familiar constructions? The nominalist therefore proposes that *T* is metaphorical too; it
provides us with access to a content more literally expressed by

(*U*) There are 12 planets and 5 stars or 24 planets and 10 stars or . . .[24]

And now here is the rub. The rules of English do not allow infinitely long
sentences; so the most literal route of access *in English* to the desired content is
T, and *T* according to the nominalist is not to be taken literally. It is only by
making *as if* to countenance numbers that one can give expression in English to
a fact having nothing to do with numbers, a fact about stars and planets and how
they are numerically proportioned.[25]

---

[23] I am indebted to Melia (1995). As always I am using 'metaphor' in a very broad sense. The
term will cover anything exploiting the same basic semantic mechanisms as standard 'Juliet is
the sun'-type metaphors, no matter how banal and unpoetic. (Several people have told me that
the semantics of 'average F' is much more complicated than I'm allowing. I am sure they're
right, and I apologize for the oversimplification.)

[24] Why not a primitive '2.4-times-as-many' predicate? Because 2.4 is not the only ratio in
which quantities can stand; 'we will never find the time to learn all the infinitely many [*q*-times-
as-many] predicates', with *q* a schematic letter taking rational substituends, much less the *r*-
times-as-long predicates, with *r* ranging schematically over the reals (Melia 1995: 228). A
fundamental attraction of existential metaphor is its promise of ontology-free semantic produc-
tivity. How real the promise is—how much metaphor can do to get us off the ontology-ideology
treadmill—strikes me as wide open and very much in need of discussion.

[25] Compare Quine on states of affairs: 'the particular range of possible physiological states,
each of which would count as a case of [the cat] wanting to get on that particular roof, is a gerrymandered range of states that could surely not be encapsulated in any manageable anatomical
description even if we knew all about cats . . . Relations to states of affairs. . . . such as wanting
and fearing, afford some very special and seemingly indispensable ways of grouping events in
the natural world' (Quine 1966: 147). Quine sees here an argument for counting states of affairs
into his ontology. But the passage reads better as an argument that the metaphor of states of
affairs allows us access to theoretically important contents unapproachable in any other way.
See also Lewis on counterfactuals: 'It's the character of our world that makes the counterfactual
true—in which case why bring the other worlds into the story at all? . . . it is only by bringing

Whether you buy the example or not, it gives a good indication of what it would be like for a metaphor to be 'representationally essential,' that is, unparaphrasable at the level of content; we begin to see how the description a speaker wants to offer of his *intended* objects might be inexpressible until *unintended* objects are dragged in as representational aids.

Hooking us up to the right propositional contents, however, is only one of the services that metaphor has to offer. There is also the fact that a metaphor (with any degree of life at all) 'makes us see one thing as another'; it 'organizes our view' of its subject matter; it lends a special 'perspective' and makes for 'framing-effects'.[26] An example of Dick Moran's:

To call someone a tail-wagging lapdog of privilege is not simply to make an assertion of his enthusiastic submissiveness. Even a pat metaphor deserves better than this . . . the comprehension of the metaphor involves *seeing* this person as a lapdog, and . . . experiencing his dogginess.[27]

The point here is not especially about seeing-as, though, and it is not only conventionally 'picturesque' metaphors that pack the intended sort of cognitive punch. Let me illustrate with a continuation of the example started above.

Suppose I am wrong and 'the average star has 2.4 planets' is representationally *accidental*; the infinite disjunction 'there are five stars and twelve planets etc.' turns out to be perfect English.[28] The formulation in terms of the average star is still on the whole hugely to be preferred—for its easier visualizability, yes, but also its greater suggestiveness ('then how many electrons does the average atom have?'), the way it lends itself to comparison with other data ('2.4 again? Well, what do you know?'), and so on.[29]

A second example has to do with the programme of 'first-orderizing' entailment relations.[30] Davidson in 'The Logical Form of Action Sentences' says that a key reason for rendering 'Jones VERBed *G*ly' as 'there was a VERBing done by Jones which was *G*' is that the argument from 'Jones VERBed *G*ly' to 'Jones VERBed' now becomes quantificationally valid. Of course, similar claims are often made on behalf of the possible worlds account of modality; unless you want the inference from 'possibly *S*' to 'possibly *S*-or-*T*' to be primitive and unanalyzable, you'd better understand 'possibly *S*' as 'there is a world making *S* true.' Any number of authors have made this sort of plea on behalf of propositions; how without quantifying over them can you hope to first-orderize the

the other worlds into the story that we can say in any concise way what character it takes to make the counterfactual true' (Lewis 1986: 22).

[26] Davidson (1978); Max Black in Ortony (1993); Moran (1989: 108).

[27] Moran (1989: 90).

[28] As maintained, for example, in Langendoen and Postal (1984).

[29] Similarly with Quine's cat example: the gerrymandered anatomical description *even if available* could never do the cognitive work of 'What Tabby wants is that she gets onto the roof.'

[30] See Davidson and Harman (1975). The underlying motivation had to do less with entailment than constructing axiomatic truth theories for natural language.

inference from 'I believe whatever the Pope believes' and 'the Pope believes abortion is wrong'?

The claim these authors make is not that the relevant contents are *inexpressible* without quantifying over events, or worlds, or what have you; that would be untrue, since we can use sentences like 'she did it skilfully' and 'possibly BLAH'. It's rather that the logical *relations* among these contents become much more tractable if we represent them quantificationally; the contents so represented wear (at least to a first-order-savvy audience like the community of philosophers) their logical potential on their sleeve.[31]

Along with its representational content, then, we need to consider a metaphor's 'presentational force'. Just as it can make all the difference in the world whether I grasp a proposition under the heading '*my* pants are on fire', grasping it as the retroimage of 'Crotone is in the arch of the boot' or 'the average star has 2.4 planets' or 'there is a world with blue swans' can be psychologically important too. To think of Crotone's location as the place it would *need* to be to put it in the arch of Italy imagined as a boot, or of the stars and planets as proportioned the way they would need to be for the average star to come out with 2.4 planets, is to be affected in ways going well beyond the proposition expressed. That some of these ways are cognitively advantageous gives us a second reason for accessing contents metaphorically.

14. OPPORTUNITY

Now for the question of opportunity. How are these metaphors slipped in without anyone's noticing?

The first thing that has to be said is that figurative elements in our speech are very *often* unconscious, and resistant to being brought to consciousness. To hear 'that wasn't very smart' (understatement) or 'a fine friend she turned out to be' (irony) or 'spring is just around the corner' (metaphor) as meaning what they literally say takes a surprising amount of effort. A tempting analogy is with the effort involved in making out the intrinsic colour of the paint in some section of a representational painting. As the painting analogy suggests, a too-vivid appreciation of literal meaning can even *interfere* with our understanding of the speaker's message. Wittgenstein tells of an art-lover leaning up to the bloodshot eyes in a Rembrandt painting and saying '*that's* the colour I want for my bathroom curtains.' Such a person is not—not at that moment, anyway—in tune with

---

[31] A question rarely addressed is why this presentational advantage should seem to argue for the *truth* of the quantificational rendering, as opposed to just its naturalness and helpfulness vis-à-vis audiences like ourselves. Is it that the naturalness and helpfulness would be a miracle if there were nothing out there to answer to the platonic quantifiers? I would like to see an argument for this. I suspect that there are very few putative object-types, however otherwise disreputable, that couldn't be 'legimated' by such a manoeuvre.

the painting's representational ambitions. Just so, overzealous attention to what a 'gutsy idea' would be like, or what it would really be to 'keep your eyes peeled', or 'pour your heart out' to your beloved, prevents any real appreciation of the intended message.[32]

If you're with me this far, consider now statements like 'there's something Jones is that Smith isn't: happy' or 'another way to get there is via Tegucigalpa'? Taken at face value, these sentences do indeed commit themselves to entities called 'happy' and 'via Tegucigalpa'. But overmuch attention to the fact is likelier to distract from the speaker's intended meaning than to illuminate it; what on earth could *via Tegucigalpa* be? Likewise someone who says that 'the number of Democrats is on the rise' wants the focus to be on the Democrats, not 'their number', whatever that might be. Their number is called in just to provide a measure of the Democrats' changing cardinality; it's expected to perform that service in the most inconspicuous way and then hustle itself off the stage before people start asking the inevitable awkward questions. (Which number is it? 50 million? Is 50 million really on the rise?)

A deeper reason for the unobtrusiveness of existential metaphors is this. Earlier we distinguished two qualities for which a metaphor might be valued: its representational content, and its presentational force. But that can't be the whole story. For we are still conceiving of the speaker as someone with a definite *message* to get across, and the insistence on a message settled in advance is apt to seem heavy-handed. Davidson says that 'the central error about metaphor' is the idea that

associated with [each] metaphor is a cognitive content that its author wishes to convey and that the interpreter must grasp if he is to get the message. ... It should make us suspect the theory that it is so hard to decide, even in the case of the simplest metaphors, exactly what the content is supposed to be.[33]

Whether or not all metaphors are like this, one can certainly agree that a lot are: perhaps because, as Davidson says, their 'interpretation reflects as much on the interpreter as on the originator';[34] perhaps because their interpretation reflects ongoing real-world developments that neither party feels in a position to prejudge. Either way, one can easily bring this third, *opportunistic*, grade of metaphorical involvement under the same conceptual umbrella as the other two:

> Someone who utters *S* in a metaphorical vein is recommending the project of (i) looking for games in which *S* is a promising move, and (ii) accepting the propositions that are *S*'s inverse images in those games under the modes of presentation that they provide.

[32] Thanks here to Peter Railton.
[33] Davidson (1978: 44).
[34] Ibid. 29. Davidson would have no use for even the unsettled sort of metaphorical content about to be proposed.

The overriding imperative here is to *make the most of it*;[35] we are to construe the utterance in terms of the game or games that retromap it onto the most plausible and instructive contents in the most satisfying ways. Should it happen that the speaker has definite ideas about the best game to be playing with *S*, I myself see no objection to saying that she intended to convey a certain metaphorical message—the first grade of metaphorical involvement—perhaps under a certain metaphorical mode of presentation—the second grade.[36] So it is, usually, with 'He lost his cool (head, nerve, marbles, etc.).'

The reason for the third grade of metaphorical involvement is that one can imagine other cases, in which the speaker's sense of the potential metaphorical truthfulness of a form of words outruns her sense of the particular truth(s) being expressed. Consider, for instance, the *pregnant* metaphor, which yields up indefinite numbers of contents on continued interrogation.[37] Consider the *prophetic* metaphor, which expresses a single content whose identity, however, takes time to emerge.[38] Consider, finally, the *patient* metaphor, which hovers indefinitely above competing interpretations, as though waiting to be told where its advantage really lies.

Strange as it may seem, it is this third grade of metaphorical involvement, supposedly at the furthest remove from the literal, that can be hardest to tell apart from the literal. The reason is that *one* of the contents that my utterance may be up for, when I launch *S* into the world in the opportunistic spirit described above, is its *literal* content. I want to be understood as meaning what I literally say if my statement is literally true (count me a player of the 'null game', if you like) and meaning whatever my statement projects onto via the right sort of 'non-null' game if my statement is literally false. It is thus indeterminate from my point of view whether I am advancing *S*'s literal content or not.[39]

Isn't this in fact our common condition? When people say that the number of apostles is twelve, that rainbows are due to refraction, that Karl Marx had some influential ideas, or that Richard Nixon had a stunted superego, they are far more

---

[35] David Hill's phrase, and idea.

[36] This of course marks a difference with Davidson.

[37] Thus, each in its own way, 'Juliet is the sun' and 'The state is an organism.'

[38] Examples: An apparition assures Macbeth that 'none of woman born' shall harm him; the phrase's meaning hangs in the air until Macduff, explaining that he was 'from his mother's womb untimely ripped', plunges in the knife. Martin Luther King said that 'The arc of the moral universe is long, but it bends towards justice'; Cohen (1997) shows how specific a content can be attached to these words. A growing literature on verisimilitude testifies to the belief that 'close to the truth' admits of a best interpretation albeit one it takes work to find.

[39] Indeterminacy is also possible about whether I am advancing a content at all, as opposed to articulating the rules of some game relative to which contents are figured. An example suggested by David Hills is 'there are continuum many spatio-temporal positions', uttered by one undecided as between the substantival and relational theories of spacetime. One might speak here of a fifth grade of metaphorical involvement, which—much as the third grade leaves it open *what* content is being expressed—takes no definite stand on whether the utterance *has* a content.

certain that S is getting at *something* right than that the thing it is getting at is the proposition that S, as some literalist might construe it. If numbers exist, then yes, we are content to regard ourselves as having spoken literally. If not, then the claim was that there were twelve apostles.[40] If Freud was right, then yes, Nixon had a superego and it really was stunted. If not, then the claim was (more or less) that Nixon had trouble telling when a proposed course of action was morally wrong.

An important special case of the patient metaphor, then, is (what we can call) the *maybe*-metaphor. That platonic metaphors are so often maybe-metaphors— that I *could* for all anyone knows be speaking literally—goes a long way towards explaining their inconspicuousness. If a literal interpretation is always and forever in the offing, then the fact that a metaphorical interpretation is also always and forever possible is liable to escape our notice.

15. . . . LOST?

Of all the reasons people give for thinking that platonic metaphors couldn't have slipped in unnoticed, the most common is probably this. I speak metaphorically only if I speak in a way that is guided by, but somehow at odds with, my notion of what would be involved in a literal deployment of the same sentence.[41] This immediately suggests a negative test. If, as Fowler puts it, metaphors are 'offered and accepted with a consciousness of their nature as substitutes,' then in the absence of any such consciousness—in the absence of a literal meaning the speaker can point to as exploited where it might instead have been expressed— one cannot be speaking metaphorically.

Call this the 'felt distance' test for metaphoricality. It appears to rule that my utterance of, say, 'twelve is the number of apostles' cannot possibly be metaphorical. Were I speaking metaphoricaly, I would experience myself as guided by meanings of 'number' or 'twelve' that I am at the same time disrespecting or making play with. The fact is, though, that I am not aware of being guided by any such disrespected meanings. I do not even have a conception of what those disrespected meanings could be; it hardly seems possible to use the words 'number' and 'twelve' more literally than I already do.

---

[40] 'When it was reported that Hemingway's plane had been sighted, wrecked, in Africa, the New York *Mirror* ran a headline saying, "Hemingway Lost in Africa", the word "lost" being used to suggest he was dead. When it turned out he was alive, the *Mirror* left the headline to be taken literally' (Davidson 1978). I suspect that something like this happens more often than we suppose, with the difference that there is no conscious equivocation and that it is the metaphorical content that we fall back on.

[41] The intuition here comes out particularly clearly in connection with Walton's account of metaphor; I need first to understand what S literally means, if I am to pretend that that meaning obtains in hopes of calling attention to the conditions that legitimate the pretence.

I have two responses, one which accepts the felt distance test for the sake of argument, one which finds the test unreliable. The first response goes like this. Why do you assume that the words being used metaphorically in 'twelve is the number of apostles' are 'number' and 'twelve'? By a 'number' we mean, roughly: entity of a kind that is suited by its intrinsic nature to providing a measure of cardinality (the number of BLAHs serves as a mark or measure of how many BLAHs there are) and that has not a whole lot more to its intrinsic nature than that. The literal meaning of 'twelve' is: number that provides a measure, cardinality-wise, of the BLAHs just in case there are twelve BLAHs. These are exactly the meanings with which 'number' and 'twelve' are used in 'twelve is the number of apostles'. So it should not be supposed that the metaphoricality of 'twelve is the number of apostles' hinges on a metaphorical usage of those two words.

Now, though, the objector will want to know which word *is* being used metaphorically.[42] A plausible candidate is not hard to find. There is a non-negligible chance that numbers do not exist, i.e. that nothing exists whose intrinsic nature is exhausted by the considerations mentioned. Someone who says that 'twelve is the number of apostles' is not really concerned about that, however; they are taking numbers for granted in order to call attention to their real subject matter, viz. how many apostles there are. How can someone unconcerned about the existence of Xs maintain with full confidence that 'So and so is the X which Fs,' that is, that 'there is at least one X which Fs and all such Xs are identical to so and so'? The answer is that they are using the definite article 'the', or rather the existential quantifier it implicitly contains, non-literally. Nothing else explains how they can subscribe in full confidence to 'there is an X which Fs' despite being unconvinced of, or at least unconcerned about, the existence of Xs. The reason this matters is that the existential quantifier *passes* the felt-distance test. When I assume for metaphorical purposes that numbers exist, I am guided by, but at the same time (running the risk of) disrespecting, the literal meaning of 'exists'—for using 'exists' literally, numbers may well *not* exist, in which case 'twelve is the number of apostles', i.e. 'there is an x such that a thing is x iff it numbers the apostles and x is twelve', is literally false.

Anyway, though, the felt-distance test is wrong. It is true that if I am to use a sentence S metaphorically, there had better be conditions under which S is pretence-worthy, or sayable, and conditions under which it is not. But as we know from the example of fiction, this does not require S to possess a literal meaning, as opposed to fictionally possessing one in the story or game. Flann O'Brien in *The Third Policeman* tells of a substance called 'gravid liquid', the tiniest drop of which weighs many tons, and whose subtle dissemination through the parts of material objects is all that prevents them from floating away. When I pretend, in discussions of that book, that gravid liquid cannot be held in a test tube, since it

---

[42] I do not see why the weight of a sentence's metaphoricality should always be borne by particular words. But let's not get into that here.

would break through the bottom, I am guided by my idea of what 'gravid' is *supposed in the game* to mean. I have no concern at all about what it means in English, and for all I know it is not even an English word.[43]

An example more to the present point is this. 'Smart' in my dictionary is an adjective, not a noun. How is it that we can say 'she has a lot of smarts' and be understood? Well, it is part of the relevant game that there are these entities called 'smarts' that are somehow the carriers of intelligence; the more of them you have, the smarter you are. The as-if meaning of 'smart' as a noun is of course informed by its literal meaning as an adjective. Why should it not be the same with 'twelve'? The meaning it is pretended (or said) to have *qua* noun is informed by its literal meaning *qua* adjective. Much as we're to say that someone has a lot of smarts (noun) just when they're very smart (adjective), we're to say that the number of *F*s is twelve (noun) just when there are twelve (adjective) *F*s.

I don't know which of the two responses to prefer, but let me call attention to a point of agreement between them. A metaphor for us is a supposition adverted to not because it is true but because it marks a place where truths are thought to lie. It is compatible with this that certain words might be used more often in a metaphorical vein than a literal one; it is compatible with it even that certain words should *always* be used metaphorically because they lack literal meaning. This points to a third reason why platonic metaphors do not call attention to themselves.

'Literal' is partly a folk notion, partly a theoretical one. The theoretical idea is that to understand the full range of speech activity, we should employ a divide-and-conquer strategy. Our first step is to set out words' 'primary' powers: what they are in the first instance *supposed* to do. Then we will take on the more multifarious task of accounting for words' 'secondary' powers: their ability to be used in ways not specifically provided for by the primary semantics. A certain kind of Davidsonian, for example, lays great weight on the notion of 'first meaning', constrained by the requirement of slotting into a recursive truth-theory for the full language. Speech is literal if it is produced with intentions lining up in an appropriate way with first meanings; otherwise we have irony, implicature, or metaphor.

Now, to the extent that literality is a theorist's notion, it comes as no great surprise that speakers occasionally misapply it. If we ask the person in the street whether she is using a word literally—using it to do what it is 'supposed' to do— her thoughts are not likely to turn to recursive semantics. More likely she will interpret us as asking about *standard* or *ordinary* usage. (All the more so when an expression has no literal use with which the standard use can be contrasted!) Since platonic metaphors are nothing if not standard, it would be only natural for them to be misconstrued as literal. One doesn't notice that talk of superegos is

---

[43] Apparently it is; my dictionary gives it the meaning 'pregnant'. Still my use of 'gravid' in the game owes nothing to this meaning or any other, or even to 'gravid''s being a word.

maybe-metaphorical until one reflects that 'Nixon had a stunted superego' would not be withdrawn even in the proven absence of mental entities with the relevant properties. One doesn't notice that talk of numbers is maybe-metaphorical until one reflects on our (otherwise very peculiar!) insouciance about the existence or not of its apparent objects.

16. SUGGESTIVE SIMILARITIES

The bulk of this paper has been an argument that it is less absurd than may initially appear to think that everyday talk of platonic objects is not to be taken literally. If someone believes that the objects are not really there—that, to revert to the crime analogy, they have been 'stolen away'—it seems like means, motive, and opportunity for the alleged caper are not at all that hard to make out.

Of course, it is one thing to argue that a metaphorical construal is not out of the question, another to provide evidence that such a construal would actually be correct. The best I can do here is list a series of *similarities* between platonic objects, on the one hand, and creatures of metaphorical make-believe, on the other, that strike me as being, well, suggestive. Not all of the features to be mentioned are new. Not all of them are universal among POs—platonic objects— or MBs—creatures of metaphorical make-believe. Not one of them is so striking as to show decisively that the relevant POs are just MBs. But the cumulative effect is, I think, nothing to sneeze at.

Of course we should not forget one final piece of evidence for the as-if nature of

PARAPHRASABILITY

MBs are often paraphrasable away with no felt loss of subject matter. 'That was her first encounter with the green-eyed monster' goes to 'that was her first time feeling jealous.' 'That really gets my goat' goes to 'that really irritates me.'

POs are often paraphrasable away with no felt loss of subject matter 'There is a possible world with furry donkeys' goes to 'furry donkeys are possible.' 'She did it in one way or another' goes to 'she did it somehow.' Etc.

IMPATIENCE

One is impatient with the meddling literalist who wants us to get worried about the fact that an MB may not exist. 'Well, say people *do* store up patience in internal reservoirs; then *my* patience is nearly exhausted.'

One is impatient with the meddling ontologist who wants us to get worried about whether a PO, or type of PO, really exists. 'Well, say there *are* models; then *this* argument has a countermodel.'

TRANSLUCENCY

It's hard to hear 'what if there is no green-eyed monster?' as meaning what it literally says; one 'sees through' to the (bizarre) suggestion that no one is ever truly jealous, as opposed say to envious.

It is hard to hear 'what if there are no other possible worlds?' as meaning what it literally says; one 'sees through' to the (bizarre) suggestion that whatever is, is necessary.

INSUBSTANTIALITY

MBs tend to have not much more to them than what flows from our conception of them. The green-eyed monster has no 'hidden substantial nature'; neither do the real-estate bug, the blue meanies, the chip on my shoulder, etc.

POs often have no more to them than what flows from our conception of them. All the really important facts about the numbers follow from (2nd order) Peano's Axioms. Likewise for sets, functions etc.

INDETERMINACY

MBs can be 'indeterminately identical'. There is no fact of the matter as to the identity relations between the fuse I blew last week and the one I blew today, or my keister and my wazoo ('I've had it up to the keister/wazoo with this paperwork'). The relevant game(s) leave it undecided what is to count as identical to what.[44]

POs can be 'indeterminately identical'. There is no fact of the matter as to the identity relations between the pos. integers and the Zermelo numbers, or worlds and maximal consistent sets of propositions, or events and property-instantiations. It is left (partly) undecided what is to count as identical to what.

SILLINESS

MBs invite 'silly questions' probing areas the make-believe does not address, e.g. we know how big the average star is, where is it located? You say you lost your nerve, has it been turned in? Do you plan to *drop*-forge the uncreated conscience of your race in the smithy of your soul?

POs invite questions that seem similarly silly.[45] What are the intrinsic properties of the empty set? Is the event of the water's boiling itself hot? Are universals wholly present in each of their instances? Do relations lead a divided existence, parcelled out among their relata?

---

[44] 'Keister' does in some idiolects have an identifiable anatomical referent; 'wazoo' as far as I've been able to determine does not. The text addresses itself to idiolects (mine included) in which 'keister' shares in 'wazoo''s unspecificity.

[45] Notwithstanding an increasing willingness in recent years to consider them with a straight face. Prior, 'Entities', deserves a lot of the credit for this: 'what we might call Bosanquetterie sprawls over the face of Philosophy like a monstrous tumour, and on the whole the person who

EXPRESSIVENESS

MBs show a heartening tendency to boost the language's power to express facts about other, more ordinary, entities. 'The average taxpayer saves more than the average homeowner.'

POs show a strong tendency to boost the language's power to express facts about other, more ordinary, entities. 'The area of a circle—any circle—is π times the square of its radius.'

IRRELEVANCE

MBs are called in to 'explain' phenomena that would not on reflection suffer by their absence. 'Why did I curse the HMO? Because I've had it up to the wazoo with this paperwork.' Take away the wazoos, and people are still going to curse their HMOs.

POs are called in to 'explain' phenomena that would not, on reflection, suffer bytheir absence. Suppose that all the one–one functions were killed off today; there would still be as many left shoes in my closet as right.

DISCONNECTEDNESS

MBs have a tendency not to do much other than expressive work. As a result, perhaps, of not really existing, they tend not to push things around.

POs have a tendency not to do much other than expressive work; numbers *et al.* are famous for their causal inertness.

AVAILABILITY

MBs' lack of naturalistic connections might seem to threaten epistemic access—until we remember that 'their properties' are projected rather than detected.

POs' lack of naturalistic connections might seem to threaten epistemic access—until we recognize that 'their properties' are projected too.

platonic objects. This is the fact that an *as-if interpretation of POs solves our original paradox.* Our reluctance to infer the existence of models from the Tarski equivalences is just what you'd expect if the inference goes through only on a literal interpretation, and Tarski's equation of invalidity with the existence of a countermodel is not in the end taken literally.

maintains that virtue is not square must count himself among the heretics. The current dodge or 'gambit' is to say that the question whether virtue is or is not square just doesn't arise, and it is astonishing what a number of questions modern philosophers have been able to dispose of by saying that they just don't arise. Indeed it is hardly too much to say that the whole of traditional philosophy has disappeared in this way, for among questions that don't arise are those which, as it is said, nobody but a philosopher would ask' (1976: 26).

References

Alston, W. (1958), 'Ontological Commitment', *Philosophical Studies*, (1): 8-17.

Boghossian, P. (1990), 'The Status of Content', *Philosophical Review* 99(2): 157–84.

Burgess, J., and G. Rosen (1997), *A Subject With No Object* (Oxford: Clarendon Press).

Cohen, J. (1997), 'The Arc of the Moral Universe', *Philosophy and Public Affairs* 26, (2): 91–134.

Davidson, D. (1980), *Essays on Actions and Events* (Oxford: Oxford University Press).

—— (1984), *Inquiries into Truth and Interpretation* (Oxford: Oxford University Press).

—— (1978), 'What Metaphors Mean', in Sacks 1979.

—— and G. Harman (1975), *The Logic of Grammar* (Encino: Dickenson).

Davies, M. and L. Humberstone (1980), 'Two Notions of Necessity', *Philosophical Studies* 38: 1–30.

Derrida, J. (1982), 'White Mythology: Metaphor in the Text of Philosophy', in *Margins of Philosophy* (Chicago: University of Chicago Press).

Etchemendy, J. (1990), *The Concept of Logical Consequence* (Cambridge, Mass.: Harvard University Press).

Field, H. (1989), 'Platonism for Cheap? Crispin Wright on Frege's Context Principle', in *Realism, Mathematics and Modality* (Oxford: Blackwell).

Hahn, L. and P. Schilpp (eds.) (1986), *The Philosophy of W. V. Quine* (La Salle, Ill.: Open Court).

Hills, D. (1988), 'Aptness and Truth in Metaphorical Utterance', *Philosophical Review* 88: 565–89.

Kaplan, D. (1989), 'Demonstratives', in J. Almog, J. Perry, and H. Wettstein (ed.), *Themes from Kaplan* (New York: Oxford University Press).

Langendoen, D. and P. Postal (1984), *The Vastness of Natural Languages* (Oxford: Blackwell).

Lewis, D. (1986), *On the Plurality of Worlds* (New York: Blackwell).

—— (1992), 'Critical Notice of D. M. Armstrong, *A Combinatorial Theory of Possibility*', *Australasian Journal of Philosophy* 70: 211–24.

Maddy, P. (1997), *Naturalism in Mathematics* (Oxford: Clarendon Press).

McGee, V. (1997), 'How We Learn Mathematical Language', *Philosophical Review* 106: 35–68.

Melia, J. (1995), 'On what there's not', *Analysis* 55 (4): 223–9.

Moran, R. (1989), 'Seeing and Believing: Metaphor, Image, and Force', *Critical Inquiry* 16: 87-112.

Ortony, A. (1993), *Metaphor and Thought*, 2nd edn. (Cambridge: Cambridge University Press).

Plantinga, A. (ed.) (1965), *The Ontological Argument* (Garden City, NY: Doubleday).

Prior, A. (1976), *Papers in Logic and Ethics* (Amherst: University of Massachusetts Press).

Putnam, H. (1971), *Philosophy of Logic* (New York: Harper & Row).

Quine, W. V. (1948), 'On What There Is', *Review of Metaphysics* 2(5), repr. in Quine 1953.

—— (1953), *From a Logical Point of View* (Cambridge, Mass.: Harvard University Press).

—— (1960), *Word and Object* (Cambridge, Mass.: MIT Press).

—— (1966), 'Propositional Objects', in *Ontological Relativity and Other Essays* (New York: Columbia University Press).

—— (1978), 'A Postscript on Metaphor', in Sacks (1978).

Quine, W. V. (1986), 'Reply to Parsons', in Hahn and Schilpp (1986).

Sacks, S. (ed.) (1978), *On Metaphor* (Chicago: University of Chicago Press).

Salmon, N. (1989), 'The Logic of What Might Have Been', *Philosophical Review* 98: 3–34.

Sommer, E. and D. Weiss (1996), *Metaphors Dictionary* (New York: Visible Ink Press).

Walton, K. (1993), 'Metaphor and Prop Oriented Make-Believe', *European Journal of Philosophy* 1: 39–57.

Wright, C. (1983), *Frege's Conception of Numbers as Objects* (Aberdeen: Aberdeen University Press).

Yablo, S. (1996), 'How in the World?' *Philosophical Topics* 24: 255–86.

—— (1998), 'Does Ontology Rest on a Mistake?' *Proceedings of the Aristotelian Society* supp. Vol. 72: 229–62.

—— (MS), 'Mathematics as Gameskeeping'.

10

Knowledge of Logic

Paul Boghossian

Is it possible for us to know the fundamental truths of logic a priori? This question presupposes another: is it possible for us to know them at all, a priori or a posteriori? In the case of the fundamental truths of logic, there has always seemed to be a difficulty about this, one that may be vaguely glossed as follows (more below): since logic will inevitably be involved in any account of how we might be justified in believing it, how is it possible for us to be justified in our fundamental logical beliefs?

In this essay, I aim to explain how we might be justified in our fundamental logical beliefs. If the explanation works, it will explain not merely how we might know logic, but how we might know it a priori.

THE PROBLEM STATED

To keep matters as simple as possible, let us restrict ourselves to propositional logic and let us suppose that we are working within a system in which modus ponens (MPP) is the only underived rule of inference. My question is this: is it so much as *possible* for us to be justified in supposing that MPP is a valid rule of inference, necessarily truth-preserving in all its applications?[1] I am not at the moment concerned with how we are *actually* justified, but only with whether it makes sense to suppose that we could be.

We need to begin with certain distinctions. Suppose it is a fact about S that, whenever he believes that p and believes that 'if p, then q', he is disposed either to believe q or to reject one of the other propositions. Whenever this is so, and

I am grateful to audiences at the University of Massachussetts/Amherst, Stirling, Princeton, Dalhousie, Harvard, NYU and especially to Stephen Schiffer, Crispin Wright, Christopher Peacocke, Ned Block, and Paul Horwich for comments on earlier versions of this paper.

[1] Some philosophers distinguish between the *activity* of giving a justification and the *property* of being justified. My question involves the latter, more basic, notion: Is it possible for our logical beliefs to have the property of being justified?

putting many subtleties to one side, I shall say that S is disposed to *reason accord-ing to the rule modus ponens*. In addition to this disposition to reason in a certain way, it can also be a fact about S that he has the full-blown *belief* that MPP is necessarily truth-preserving: he believes, that is, that if p is true and if 'if p, then q' is true, then q has to be true. As a number of considerations reveal, S's dispo-sition to reason in accordance with MPP and his belief that MPP is truth-preserv-ing are distinct kinds of state.[2]

Just as we need to distinguish between the disposition to reason and the belief, so we need to distinguish between the epistemic status of the disposition and that of the belief. I want to ask initially here about whether it is possible for us to be *justified* in holding the belief that MPP is valid. I will ask later about whether it is possible for us to be *entitled* to the disposition to reason according to MPP and about the relation between that question and the corresponding question about belief. (As my choice of language implies, I shall reserve the term 'justification' for the sort of warrant that a belief might have, and the term 'entitlement' for the sort of warrant that an employment of a rule might have.)[3]

Turning, then, to the question of the justifiability of the belief that MPP is truth-preserving, the space of available answers seems relatively clear: it is perspicuously represented by a flowchart (Fig. 10.1). When we look at the avail-able options, it is very tempting to say 'No' to the question about justification, that it is not possible for us to be justified in believing something as basic as modus ponens. For in what could such a justification consist? It would have to be either inferential or non-inferential. And there look to be serious problems stand-ing in the way of either option.

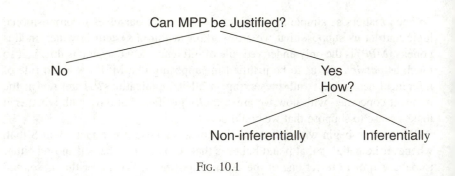

FIG. 10.1

[2] This is at least part of the moral both of Lewis Carroll's 'What the Tortoise Said to Achilles', in *Mind* 1898 and of Wittgenstein's discussion of rule-following in *Philosophical Investigations* (Oxford: Blackwell, 1958).

[3] This distinction between 'justification' and 'entitlement' is distinct from Tyler Burge's well-known distinction, but bears some resemblance to it. See his 'Content Preservation', *Philo-sophical Review* 102 (1993): 457-88.

How could our justification for MPP be non-inferential? In any ordinary sense of 'see', we cannot just *see* that it is valid. To be sure, the idea that we possess a quasi-perceptual faculty—going by the name of 'rational intuition'—the exercise of which gives us direct insight into the necessary properties of the world, has been historically influential. It would be fair to say, however, that no one has succeeded in saying what this faculty really is nor how it manages to yield the relevant knowledge. 'Intuition' seems like a name for the mystery we are addressing, rather than a solution to it.

A related thought that is often mentioned in this connection has it that we can know that MPP is truth-preserving because we cannot *conceive* or *imagine* what a counter-example to it might be.[4] But the suggestion that 'conceiving' or 'imagining' is here the name for a non-inferential capacity to detect logical, or other necessary, properties will not withstand any scrutiny. When we say that we cannot conceive a counter-example to some general claim—for example, that all bachelors are unmarried—we do not mean that we have some imagistic, non-propositional ability to assess whether such a case can be coherently described. What we mean is that a more or less elementary piece of *reasoning* shows that there cannot be any such state of affairs: if someone is a bachelor, then he is an unmarried male. If someone is an unmarried male, then he is unmarried. Therefore, any bachelor would have to be unmarried. So, there cannot be any such thing as an unmarried bachelor. Talk of 'conceiving' here is just a thin disguise for a certain familiar style of logical reasoning. This is not, of course, to condemn it. But it is to emphasize that its acceptability as an epistemology for *logic* turns on the acceptability of an inferential account more generally.

This brings us, then, to the inferential path. Here there are a number of distinct possibilities, but they would all seem to suffer from the same master difficulty: in being inferential, they would have to be *rule-circular*. If MPP is the only underived rule of inference, then any inferential argument for MPP would either have to use MPP or use some other rule whose justification depends on MPP. And many philosophers have maintained that a rule-circular justification of a rule of inference is no justification at all.

Thus, it is tempting to suppose that we can give an *a priori* justification for modus ponens on the basis of our knowledge of the truth-table for 'if, then'. Suppose that p is true and that 'if p, then q' is also true. By the truth-table for 'if, then', if p is true and if 'if p, then q' is true, then q is true. So q must be true, too.

As is clear, however, this justification for MPP must itself take at least one step in accord with MPP.

---

[4] See e.g. Henry Kyburg, 'Comments on Salmon's 'Inductive Evidence'', *American Philosophical Quarterly* 2 (1965): 274-6.

THE BAN ON RULE-CIRCULAR JUSTIFICATION

Doubt about the cogency of rule-circular justification was expressed most recently by Gilbert Harman. Harman's specific target was a recent attempt of mine to defend the notion of analyticity from Quine's famous critique and to try to show how it might be used to provide a theory of a priori knowledge, including our knowledge of fundamental logical principles.[5] In finding the inferential character of the proposed account problematic, Harman follows a substantial tradition in the philosophy of logic and the theory of knowledge of assuming that one's warrant for a principle of logic cannot consist in reasoning that employs that very principle. Since, furthermore, Harman cannot see how there might be an account of the apriority of our core logical principles that did not have to presuppose that subjects reasoned in accord with those very principles, he concludes that those principles cannot be a priori.

If, however, the core logical principles are not a priori, then neither is anything that is based on them, and so it looks as though we have to concede that nothing of much interest can be a priori after all.

By his own account, Harman's worry here derives from Quine's 'Truth by Convention'. Quine too argues that if there is to be any sort of explanation of logic's apriority, it would have to be based on something like what I have called implicit definition. He too argues that any such account would have to presuppose that subjects reasoned according to the principles of logic. And he too concludes that this renders such accounts useless and, hence, that logic's apriority cannot be vindicated. Quine goes on, in later work, to present an alternative epistemology for logic, one that portrays our warrant for it as consisting in a combination of empirical and pragmatic elements.

On the following point, I am in complete agreement with Quine and Harman. If we accept the ban on the use of a logical principle in reconstructing our a priori warrant for that very principle, we would have to conclude that there can be no such reconstruction. If so, we would have to give up on the idea that our warrant for logic can be a priori.

AN EMPIRICAL JUSTIFICATION FOR LOGIC?

What I do not see, however, is how this point can be used to motivate an alternative epistemology for logic, one that is empirical in nature. For if we are barred

---

[5] See my 'Analyticity Reconsidered', in *Nous* 1996; Harman's reply, 'Analyticity Regained?' is in the same issue. Quine's classic discussions are 'Truth by Convention' and 'Carnap and Logical Truth', both repr. in W. Quine, *The Ways of Paradox and Other Essays*, 2nd edn. (Cambridge, Mass.: Harvard University Press, 1976).

from supposing that reasoning using a given logical principle can reconstruct an a priori warrant for that very principle, are we not equally barred from supposing that it could reconstruct an *empirical* warrant for that principle? Yet would not any empirical account of our warrant for believing the core principles of logic inevitably involve attributing to us reasoning using those very principles?

To see why, let us take a look at the only reasonably worked out empirical account of logic, namely, Quine's.[6] According to this account, warrant accrues to a logical principle in the same way that it accrues to any other empirical belief, by that principle's playing an appropriate role in an overall explanatory and predictive theory that maximizes simplicity and minimizes the occurrence of recalcitrant experience. We start with a particular theory T with its underlying logic L and from T we derive, using L, a claim p. Next, suppose we undergo a string of experiences that are recalcitrant in that they incline us to assent to not-p. We need to consider how T might best be modified in order to accommodate this recalcitrance, where it is understood that one of our options is to so modify the underlying logic of T that the offending claim p is no longer derivable from it. We need to consider, that is, various ordered pairs of theory and logic— <T, L>, <T', L>, <T'', L> . . . , <T, L''>, <T, L''> . . .—picking that pair that entails the best set of observation sentences. Whatever logic ends up being so selected is the logic that is maximally justified by experience. In rough schematic outline, that is the Quinean picture.

But there is a problem with this picture if the ban on circular justifications is in place. For it is very difficult to see how the use of core logical principles, such as those of non-contradiction, modus ponens, universal instantiation, and others, is to be avoided in the meta-theory in which this comparative assessment of the various theory-logic pairs is to take place. For instances of the following forms of reasoning are presumably unavoidable in that meta-theory:

> The best set of observation sentences is the set with property F. Set O has property F. Therefore, O is best.
>
> <T*, L*> is that theory–logic pair that predicts O. O is the best set of observation sentences. Therefore, <T*, L*> predicts the best set of observations sentences.

And so forth. A little thought should reveal that a large number of the core principles of logic will have to be used to select the logic that, according to the picture under consideration, is maximally justified by experience. I do not say that it will involve the *whole* of classical logic, so it is not out of the question that such a picture may be used coherently to adjudicate *certain* disagreements about logic— for instance, whether quantum mechanics dictates rejection of the distributive

---

[6] I base my account of Quine on Crispin Wright's treatment in 'Inventing Logical Necessity', in J. Butterfield (ed.), *Language, Mind and Logic* (Cambridge: Cambridge University Press, 1984).

principles. But it is clear that it will involve a *sizeable* number of the core principles of ordinary logic. It follows, therefore, that so long as the ban on circular justification is kept in place, there is no question of using the procedure described by the Quinean picture to generate a warrant for the core principles of logic.

SCEPTICISM ABOUT LOGIC

The point here is, I think, perfectly general. It is very hard to see how there could be any sort of compelling *empirical* picture of our warrant for logic that did not rely on a very large number of the core principles of ordinary logic. Contrary to what some philosophers seem to think, then, the ban on circular justifications of logic cannot be used selectively, to knock out only a priori accounts of our warrant for logic. If it is allowed to stand, I do not see how it can be made to stop short of the very severe conclusion that we can have *no* warrant of any kind for our fundamental logical beliefs—whether of an a priori or an a posteriori nature.

If this is correct, we find ourselves on the left-hand path of our flowchart, answering 'No' to the question whether our fundamental logical beliefs can be justified.

But is this itself a conclusion we can live with? Can we coherently accept the claim that our fundamental principles of reasoning are completely unjustifiable?

Well, if it is impossible for the *claim* that MPP is truth-preserving to be justified that would seem to imply that our *use* of MPP is also unjustifiable. For how could we be entitled to reason according to a given inference rule if it is impossible for the claim that that rule is truth-preserving to be justified in the slightest?

There is a principle here, linking the epistemic status of reasoning in accord with a rule and that of a belief concerning the rule, that it will be useful to spell out:

> (LP): We can be entitled to reason in accordance with a logical rule only if the belief that that rule is truth-preserving can be justified.

Stated contrapositively:

> (LP') If it is impossible for us to be justified in believing that a certain logical rule is truth-preserving, we cannot be entitled to reason in accordance with that rule.[7]

The appeal of this linking principle is quite intuitive. If it is—logically or metaphysically—impossible for us ever to be justified in claiming that a particular

---

[7] Notice that LP states that it is necessary that our belief in MPP be justified if we are to be entitled to reason in accordance with it. It says nothing about which of these notions will be prior to the other in the order of explanation. This will become important later on.

logical truth is truth-preserving, it seems to follow that we could never be entitled to reason in accordance with it. Any plausible epistemology for logic should respect this link between our entitlement to reason according to a certain rule and the corresponding meta-claim. (More on this below.)

Now, however, we are in a position to see that saying that we cannot justify our fundamental rules of inference is extremely problematic. For if a claim to the effect that MPP is truth-preserving is not justifiable, then, the linking principle tells us, neither is our use of MPP. If, however, our use of MPP is unjustifiable, then so is anything that is based on it, and that would appear to include any belief whose justification is deductive.

In particular, since this sceptical conclusion is itself one of those claims that is based on deductive reasoning, the very thesis that our core logical principles are unjustifiable will itself come out unjustifiable, on such a view. Prima facie, this does not seem to be a stable platform on which to stand.

What are we to do? We cannot simply accept the proffered result unadulterated. If we are to accept it at all, we have to try to embed it in some larger conception that will render it stable.

The dialectical situation here is reminiscent of Kripke's famous reconstruction of Wittgenstein's discussion of rules, albeit concerning a different subject matter.[8] A powerful argument leads to a sceptical thesis that looks to be self-undermining. Is there a 'straight solution' that, by rejecting one of the assumptions that led to the sceptical conclusion, shows how it is to be avoided? Or is there, at best, a 'sceptical solution', one that can accommodate the sceptical conclusion while removing the taint of paradox that renders it unstable?

SOLUTIONS: SCEPTICAL AND STRAIGHT

As far as I can see, there are four interesting possibilities in this particular case, one sceptical and three straight. The sceptical solution would attempt to argue that it was a mistake to think of logic in a factual way to begin with, that the 'claim' that MPP is truth-preserving is not a genuine claim after all and so does not need to be justified.

As for the straight solutions, there look to be three possibilities, two non-inferential and one inferential.

On the non-inferential path, I see no prospect of developing a theory in terms of the notion of rational intuition or its ilk. But an idea that has been gaining influence recently has it that there are certain beliefs that are 'default-justified', reasonable to believe in the absence of any positive reasons that recommends

---

[8] Saul Kripke, *Wittgenstein on Rules and Private Language* (Cambridge, Mass.: Harvard University Press, 1980).

them. If there were such beliefs, and if belief in MPP were among them, this would constitute a straight solution to our sceptical problem about logic.

A further idea derives from recent work on non-factualist conceptions of normative concepts: it suggests a distinct way in which logical belief might be non-inferentially justifiable, namely, if the notion of justification were itself to be treated non-factually.

Finally, on the inferential path, there is the question whether it is irremediably true that rule-circular arguments provide no justification. Given these further options, our flowchart now looks as in Fig. 10.2.

I will begin with a discussion of the sceptical solution.

NON-FACTUALISM ABOUT LOGIC

How might it turn out to have been a mistake to think that our belief in MPP requires justification? The only possible answer would appear to be: if it were a mistake to think of it as a belief in the first place. What is in view, in other words, is an *expressivist* conception of the sentences that are used to state what we naïvely suppose are logical beliefs.

How should we formulate such a view? Here is a simple version: to say that P follows logically from Q is not to state some sort of fact about the relation between P and Q; rather, it is to express one's acceptance of a system of norms

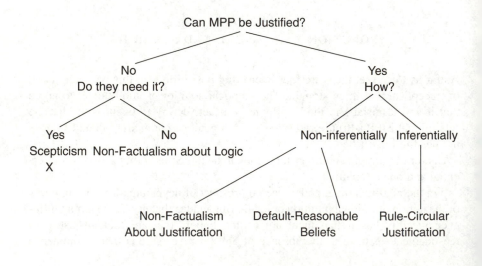

Fig. 10.2

that permits inferring P from Q. Since there are no facts about logical implication on this view, there is no need to justify one's selection of the norms. Furthermore, since in saying that a particular inference is valid, one is not actually saying anything, but only expressing one's acceptance of a system of norms that permits it, there is no question of justifying that either. It is, therefore, perfectly unproblematic that the claims of logic are not justifiable; properly understood, there was nothing to justify in the first place.

Now, naturally, this view would have to be elaborated in much greater detail before it could count as an expressivist or non-factualist *theory* of logical truth. But it seems to me that we can identify a fatal difficulty right at the start, one that obviates the need to consider any further refinements.

To see what it is, consider the sort of *conventionalist* theory of logical truth, famously discussed by Quine in 'Truth by Convention', according to which facts about logical implication are the products of convention. If we had not conventionally stipulated that this follows from that, according to this view, there would not have been any facts about what follows from what.

Against this particular *metaphysical* view of the source of logical truth, it seems to me, one of Quine's objections is decisive. For as he points out, the conventional stipulations that would have to be responsible for generating the infinity of logical truths that there are would have to be general in nature. Thus, they might take the form of saying: For all x, y, and z, if x and y stand in the modus ponens relation to z, then x and y imply z.

Now let us suppose that P, and 'If P, then Q', stand in the modus ponens relation to Q. And consider the question: do these two propositions imply Q? Well, that depends on whether it follows from the stipulated convention and the supposition, that P and 'If P, then Q' imply Q. That is, it is the question whether it follows from:

(a) P and 'If P, then Q', stand in the modus ponens relation to Q

and

(b) If P and 'If P, then Q' stand in the modus ponens relation to Q, then P and 'If P, then Q' imply Q

that

(c) P and 'If P, then Q', imply Q?

But that in turn is just the question whether it is true that if x and y stand in the modus ponens relation to z, that x and y imply z.

The problem is clear. We can not have it both that what logically follows from what is determined by what follows from certain conventions and that what follows from the conventions is determined by what logically follows from what. Facts about logical implication not accounted for by conventionalism are presupposed by the model itself.

Now, although a non-factualist expressivism about logical truth is a distinct view from a conventionalism about it, it suffers from an exactly analogous problem. The expressivist has it that to say that P follows from Q is to express one's acceptance of a system of norms that permits inferring P from Q. Once again, though, these norms of permission will have to assume a general form:

> For all x, y and z, if x and y stand in the modus ponens relation to z, then it is permissible to infer z from x and y.

Does this norm allow inferring Q from P and 'If P, then Q'? Well, the norm has it, by universal instantiation, that:

> If P and 'If P, then Q', stand in the modus ponens relation to Q, then it is permissible to infer Q from them.

If, furthermore, P and 'If P, then Q' do stand in the modus ponens relation to Q, then by modus ponens, it would follow that it is permitted to infer Q from the premises in question.

Once again, the problem is clear. We cannot coherently have it both that whether A follows from B depends on what the system of norms permits *and* that what the system of norms permits depends on whether A follows from B. Just as with conventionalism, facts about logical implication not accountable for by the non-factualism are presupposed by the model itself.

A non-factualist construal of logical implication, then, does not seem a promising strategy for blocking the paradoxical consequences of the claim that fundamental logical beliefs are incapable of being justified. If there is to be a solution to our sceptical problem, it looks as though it has to be a straight solution. I will begin with a discussion of default-reasonable beliefs.

DEFAULT-REASONABLE BELIEFS

An increasingly influential thought these days runs along the following lines: It is a mistake to suppose that a belief is unreasonable or unjustified merely because it is not supported by some observation or argument. Some beliefs are simply 'default reasonable,' reasonable in and of themselves, without any supporting justification. In particular, the fundamental logical beliefs have this feature.[9] It is reasonable to believe them, but *not* because there is some positive *ground* by virtue of which they are reasonable. So although it is true that no inference or observation supports our fundamental logical beliefs, it does not follow that they are unjustified, and so the potentially paradoxical conclusion is blocked.

I am not implacably opposed to the idea that there might be some beliefs that

---

[9] See Hartry Field's 'Apriority as an Evaluative Notion,' this volume.

are reasonable on the basis of nothing, especially if this is understood to mean simply that they are *presumptively but defeasibly justified*. It is possible that this will prove to be the best description of the epistemology of our first-person knowledge of the contents of our own minds. What I do not see is how this idea could plausibly apply to the case at hand, to the generalization that all inferences of a certain form are necessarily truth-preserving.

If a particular class of beliefs is default reasonable, then, it seems to me, there must be some *explanation* for why it is. This insistence does not contravene the root idea that, in the case of a default-reasonable belief, there is no ground that *makes* it reasonable; for it is consistent with a belief's having that status that there be a criterion by virtue of which it has that status and an explanation for why it has it. All that the insistence amounts to is that there be some principled way of saying which beliefs are default reasonable in the relevant sense and why. What I think we can't obtain, in the case under consideration, is any sort of satisfactory explanation for why belief in the validity of MPP should count as default reasonable.

One popular suggestion has it that a default-reasonable belief is any belief which, by virtue of being presupposed in any justification that a thinker might have, is neither justifiable nor refutable. But this has two implausible consequences. First, it entails that what is default reasonable has to be relativized to individual thinkers, for different thinkers may build their epistemic systems around different claims. Second, it has the consequence that some very implausible claims would come out as default reasonable for someone if they happened to be presupposed by that person's epistemic system. For example, suppose that someone takes as basic the *negation* of the law of non-contradiction; on this view, we would have to say that the negation of that law is default reasonable for him, because, by assumption, it will be neither justifiable nor refutable for that person.

A second suggestion has it that the beliefs that are default reasonable are those beliefs that a thinker finds 'self-evident'—that is, that he is disposed to find plausible simply on the basis of understanding them and without any further support or warrant. But this proposal, too, would seem to be subject to the previous two objections. Once again, it is entirely possible that two people will find very different propositions 'self-evident', and that some of those will include propositions that are intuitively highly implausible.

Nor would it help to strengthen the requirement so that it concerns those beliefs that actually *are* self-evident, as opposed to those that merely *seem* self-evident. Here the problem is that no one seems to me to have shown how this notion is to be spelled out. In particular, no one has supplied a criterion for distinguishing those propositions that are self-evident from those that—like the parallel postulate in Euclidean geometry or the proposition that life cannot be reduced to anything biological—merely seemed self-evident to many people for a very long time.

By contrast, there is one form of explanation that seems to me have some promise. There may be beliefs that are such that, having those beliefs is a condition for having one of the concepts ingredient in them. Any such belief, it seems to me could plausibly be claimed to be default reasonable. For if it really were part of the possession condition for a given concept that to possess it one had to believe a certain proposition containing it, then that would explain why belief in that proposition is at least presumptively (though defeasibly) justified. It would certainly not make sense to insist—in the way that it would with the belief that all swans are white—that one justify the proposition *before* one came to believe it.

Unfortunately for the problem that concerns us, it is not remotely plausible that anyone possessing the concept of conditional would have to have the belief that MPP is a valid rule of inference. Surely, one can have and reason with conditional without so much as having the concept of validity or of logical implication. At most what the theory of concept possession would license is that *inferring* according to MPP is part of the possession condition for conditional, not the *belief* that MPP is valid. But what we are after now is the justification for the belief.[10]

NON-FACTUALISM ABOUT JUSTIFICATION

Another thought that has also been gaining in influence recently is even more radical. It denies not merely that there always has to be a ground in virtue of which a belief has the property of being reasonable; it denies that being reasonable is a property in the first place. How are we to think about this?

We are assuming that logic is factual, so there are facts about what logically follows from what. What we are contemplating is the idea that there is *no fact of the matter* to about what it would be reasonable to believe, given a specification of the available evidence, however exactly the notion of evidence is to be understood.

---

[10] At various point in his writings, Christopher Peacocke seems to come close to suggesting that we can explain the apriority of our knowledge that, say, MPP is valid by supposing that acceptance of its validity is built into the possession conditions for conditional (his preferred example is conjunction). Thus he writes in 'Explaining the A Priori' (this volume), of a special case 'in which it is written into, or is a consequence of, the possession conditions for one or more concepts in [a] given principle that to possess those concepts, the thinker must be willing to accept the principle, by reaching it in a [given] way. This seems to be the case for acceptance of the a priori principle that from A and B, it can be inferred that A, where the way in question is accepting inferences one finds non-inferentially compelling.' This seems to imply that believing the principle 'A and B imply A' is a precondition for having the concept conjunction. If so, then it is subject to the objection specified in the text. If it does not imply that, if it is taken merely to be the claim that *inferring* accord to this rule is a precondition for having conjunction, then it falls short of explaining our entitlement to the belief itself.

Now, belief, we may all agree, constitutively aims at the truth, so that anyone who was in the business of inquiry and belief in the first place would have to subscribe to the norm that one ought to believe only what is true. Furthermore, it seems reasonable to suppose that this norm will, by itself, ground various other norms: for example, that one ought to believe that which is likely to be true and not believe that which has no chance of being true; that one ought not to believe p if some alternative proposition incompatible with p has a higher likelihood of being true; that one ought to believe p only if its likelihood of being true is high enough, given the sort of proposition it is.[11]

Plausibly, then, all of this will be common ground between believers, however their epistemic principles may otherwise differ. So what we are imagining, when we imagine that there is no fact of the matter about what it would be most reasonable to believe on the basis of a given specification of the evidence, is that there is no fact of the matter which *rules of evidence* are correct—no fact of the matter, that is, about which hypothesis a given piece of evidence confirms. To put matters crudely, but starkly: we might have one epistemic system incorporating a rule of simple induction, and another a rule of simple counter-induction, and there would be no saying that one system is more correct than the other.

But this sounds like an impossible view. If every epistemic system can be said to be as correct as any other, does not it follow that every proposition is as justifiable as any other, since every proposition can be justified relative to some evidential system or other? And is not such a gross relativism about justification not only false but self-undermining? For if every proposition is just as justifiable as any other, then that would appear to imply that for any proposition p, p and its negation are equally justifiable. In particular, it would seem that the claim that not every proposition is as justifiable as any other is just as justifiable as the claim that it is, if the claim that it is is true. And that would appear to leave us lacking a reason for believing anything in particular.

Now, this objection would have been decisive if the view that there are no facts about the correctness of evidential systems had to be accommodated in overtly relational terms. The contemplated objection assumes, in other words, that on the view in question, the predicate 'x is justified' denotes a relational property that obtains between a belief and an evidential system. That assumption, then, in conjunction with the non-factualism about evidential systems, generates the relativism that we found to be problematic. But, as is well known, and as we have just seen in the case of logic, non-factualism does not have to be elaborated in this way. Instead, it is better to try to understand it along expressivist lines.

Allan Gibbard has developed just such an expressivist theory of judgements of rationality; adapted to the present case it would yield something like the following view: When someone says 'x is a justified belief' they are not attributing any

---

[11] These and other norms are discussed in Robert Nozick, *The Nature of Rationality*, (Princeton: Princeton University Press, 1993).

sort of property to it at all, relational or otherwise; rather, they are *expressing* their acceptance of a system of norms that permits that belief in those circumstances.[12]

Does this formulation evade the self-undermining relativism just described? Well, since in saying that 'x is justified' I am not stating anything at all, but merely expressing my acceptance of a system of norms that permits that belief in those circumstances, and since, naturally, I do not accept an evidential system that permits believing just anything, I do not have to agree that every proposition is just as justifiable as any other, even if I am a non-factualist about justification. So it appears—prima facie anyway—that a Gibbard-style expressivism about justification is not subject to the relativistic worries just outlined.

That makes it worth while to ask whether it can help with the problem about logic with which we are concerned. The following thought might seem tempting. On a non-factualist view, nothing is really justified as such, for there is no such property for things either to have or to lack. Rather, talk about a belief's being justified is just a way of expressing one's acceptance of a system of norms that permits believing L. Since there is no further question about whether L is *really* justified, apart from its figuring in an epistemic system that I accept, our problem with the justifiability of logical beliefs disappears. I am entitled to say that a given logical principle is justified if I accept an epistemic system that permits it. And, naturally, I do accept an epistemic system that permits the core principles of logic.

So it can seem as if this is the answer we were looking for: a viable reconstrual of the notion of justification that refutes the claim that the core logical beliefs are unjustifiable. Unfortunately, these appearances are deceptive. Ultimately, an expressivism about justification is just as unpalatable as a relativism about it. Or so I will argue.

Let us imagine that I come across someone—call him AR—who holds a view I consider utterly unjustified: for example, that there is a spaceship trailing the comet Hale-Bopp that is going to come down and swoop him away. What can be my attitude towards such a person, given a Gibbard-style expressivism? I can express my acceptance of a system of norms that forbids that belief, all right, but that seems to leave something important out. If I tell AR that his belief that p is irrational and unjustified, I am not merely expressing my acceptance of a system of norms that forbids it; I am claiming to see something that he is not, namely that p ought not to be believed, given the available evidence. I am saying (roughly): I do not believe p; you should not either.

Gibbard tries to account for the normativity of such judgements by invoking a classic expressivist resource: the conversational demand. In saying that x is unjustified, he says, I am expressing my acceptance of a system of norms that forbids x and adding: Do so as well!

---

[12] Allan Gibbard, *Wise Choices, Apt Feelings* (Cambridge, Mass.: Harvard University Press, 1990).

In and of itself, however, this does not capture the claim that I appear to be making when I claim that I am justified and he is not, for even someone who is simply browbeating his interlocutor can issue a conversational demand. So the question is: with what *right* do I insist that someone accept my view and abandon his, on non-factualist views of justification? Could not AR insist, with equal right, that I abandon my view in favour of his? Indeed, as a non-factualist, would not I have to recognize that our claims to normative authority here are perfectly symmetrical, thereby undermining any hold I might have had on the thought that I am justified and he is not? And is not this a version of the sort of relativism expressivism was supposed to avoid?

Now, AR's belief about alien spaceships may arise in a number of different ways. He may share all my epistemic norms on the fixation of belief and he may be very good at reasoning from those norms and the available evidence to the relevant conclusions. He may simply not be aware that there is not a scintilla of evidence that there is a spaceship trailing Hale-Bopp. In that case, there is no difficulty accounting for my demand that he give up his view in favour of mine. Knowing that his problem stems simply from an ignorance of the relevant facts, I can coherently ask that he take my reasoning as proxy for his own. And he, for his part, would be entirely reasonable in taking me up on my invitation.

Then, again, AR's curious belief may derive not from his ignorance of any item of evidence but from his poor abilities at reasoning: he may be bad at moving from the epistemic norms that we share and the evidence to the appropriate conclusions. Here, again, there is no difficulty accounting for the normative authority that I claim. Given that we share the relevant norms, I can again ask him to take my reasoning as proxy for his own.

But suppose that the difference between AR's beliefs and mine stems not from such mundane sources but rather from a deep-seated difference in the fundamental epistemic norms to which we subscribe, norms for the fixation of belief that are not derived from any others. In calling his view irrational, then, I am in effect demanding that he give up *his* fundamental epistemic norms in favour of the ones that I employ. And the question I am asking is: With what right do I do this, on a non-factualist view?

As a realist, I would have no trouble explaining my attitude here. Since, as a realist, I take there to be a fact of the matter which fundamental norms are correct, and since I take myself to know what those facts are, I can easily explain why I am insisting that my interlocutor give up his norms in favour of mine. Of course, my interlocutor, convinced of the correctness of his own norms, may make a similar demand on me. If the norms are fundamental, this may well result in an impasse, a disagreement from which neither of us can be budged by argument. But it would at least make sense that there *is* a disagreement here, and it would make sense why we are issuing (potentially ineffective) conversational demands on each other. But what explanation can the non-factualist offer of these matters?

The non-factualist may reply that there is no difficulty here. After all, he will say, the rules of evidence that I accept are unconditional: they apply to someone whether or not that person is inclined to accept them.

There seem to me to be two problems with this reply, however, one with the assumption that I accept unconditional norms in the first place, the other with my insistence that someone else also accept them.

First, if a non-factualism about justification is correct, with what right do I accept epistemic norms that are unconditional, so that they apply to someone whether or not they accept them?[13] If there really are no perspective-independent facts about which epistemic norms are correct, with what right do I accept norms that apply to people whether or not they accept them? Should not an appropriate sensitivity to the fact that there is nothing that makes my norms more correct than anyone else's result in my being hesitant about accepting norms that apply to others regardless of whether they are also inclined to accept them?

Second, and putting this first problem to one side, on what basis do I insist that AR give up his unconditional norms in favour of mine? I accept a particular set of fundamental norms. He accepts another. By assumption, the norms in dispute are fundamental, so there is no neutral territory on which the disagreement can be adjudicated. Furthermore, on the non-factualist view, there are no facts about which fundamental epistemic norms are correct and which ones are not. So, on what basis do I insist that he give up his norms in favour of mine?

The expressivist thinks he can evade the clutches of a self-undermining relativism by claiming that talk about a belief's being justified expresses a state of mind rather than stating anything. But this stratagem does not long conceal the view's inevitable relativist upshot, which can now be restated in terms of the problem of normative authority. If no evidential system is more correct than any other, then I cannot coherently think that a particular belief is unjustified, no matter how crazy it may be, so long as that belief is grounded in a set of fundamental epistemic norms that permit it, no matter how crazy they may be.

To repeat: the point here is not about suasive *effectiveness*. I do not mean that the realist about justification will have an easier time persuading anyone of anything. In fact, it is quite clear that there are numerous extreme positions from which no one can be dislodged by argument, whether confronted by a realist or an expressivist (this is a point to which we will have occasion to return).

The issue is rather about having the resources with which to think certain thoughts coherently. By virtue of believing that there are objective facts about what justifies what, the realist can coherently think that a particular epistemic system is mistaken. The non-factualist, however, cannot.

In a sense, the difficulty should have been evident from the start. For the root problem is with the claim with which the expressivist about justification must begin, that there is nothing that epistemically privileges one set of epistemic principles over another. Once that thought is in place, it becomes impossible to evade

---

[13] David Velleman has emphasized this point to me.

some sort of relativist upshot. It does not matter whether the basic thought is embedded in an expressivist or a non-expressivist framework

RULE-CIRCULAR JUSTIFICATION: TWO PROBLEMS

If this is correct, then only one possibility remains: that we were too hasty in assuming that a rule-circular justification of a logical belief cannot confer genuine justification upon it. Let us, then, reopen that question. What intuitive constraint on justification does a rule-circular argument violate?

It will be useful to approach this question with another: what intuitive constraint on justification does a *grossly* circular argument violate? For it is plausible that a rule-circular argument will be problematic to the extent to which it approximates a grossly circular argument, an argument that explicitly includes among its premises that which it is attempting to prove.

There are at least two things wrong with a grossly circular argument. First, it assumes that which it is trying to prove and that, quite independently of any further consequences, seems wrong. An argument is being put forward with the intent of justifying—earning the right to believe—a certain claim. But it will only do so if it proceeds from premisses that are justified. If, however, the premiss is also the conclusion, then it is simply helping itself to the claim that the conclusion is justified, instead of earning the right to it. And this manoeuvre offends against the very idea of proving something or arguing for it. As we are prone to say, it begs the question.

A second problem is that, by allowing itself the liberty of assuming that which it is trying to prove, a grossly circular argument is able to prove absolutely anything, however intuitively unjustifiable. Let us call the first problem the problem of 'begging the question' and the second that of 'bad company'. Is a merely rule-circular justification subject to the same or analogous worries?

It is not obvious that a rule-circular argument begs the question, for what we have is an argument that is circular only in the sense that, in purporting to prove the validity of a given logical law, it must take at least one step in accordance with that law. And it is not immediately clear that we should say that an argument relies on its implicated rule of inference in the same way as we say that it relies on its premisses.[14]

---

[14] Now, it is true that there exist accounts of how an argument confers justification on a conclusion that would effectively transform a rule-circular justification into a grossly circular one. Here is one such (discussed but not endorsed by William Alston in 'Epistemic Circularity', in *Philosophy and Phenomenological Research* 47 (1986)):

(A) S is justified in believing the premisses, q.
(B) q and p are logically related in such a way that if q is true, that is a good reason for supposing that p is at least likely to be true.

Well, perhaps not in the *same* way, but it is not difficult to motivate a worry on this score. One clear way of doing so is to look at the role that a rule-circular argument might play in a dialectical context in which it is being used to silence a *sceptic*'s doubt about its conclusion.

Suppose that you doubt some claim C and I am trying to persuade you that it is true. I offer you an argument A in its support. In general, in such a context, you could question A's cogency either by questioning one of its premisses or by questioning the implicated rule of inference R. If you were to proceed by challenging R, then I would have to defend R and my only option would appear to be to try to defend my *belief* that R is truth-preserving.

Now, suppose that the context in question is the special case where C is the proposition that R is truth-preserving and my argument for C is rule-circular in that it employs R in one of its steps. Here it very much looks as if I have begged the question: I have certainly begged *your* question. You doubt MPP. I give you an argument in support of MPP that uses MPP. Alert enough to notice that fact, you question my argument by reiterating your doubts about MPP. I defend my argument by asserting that MPP is truth-preserving. In this dialectical sense, a rule-circular argument might be said to beg the question.

At a minimum, then, the sceptical context discloses that a rule-circular argument for MPP would beg a sceptic's question about MPP and would, therefore, be powerless to quell his doubts about it. In doing this, however, it reveals yet another sense in which a worry might arise about a rule-circular argument. An argument relies on a rule of inference. As the sceptical scenario highlights, one's reliance on such a rule might be questioned. But, quite apart from whether it is questioned, in what does one's entitlement to rely on that rule consist, if not in one's entitlement to the *belief* that the rule is truth-preserving? And if it does not consist in anything else, how can a rule-circular argument in support of belief in MPP confer warrant on its conclusion? In relying on a step in accord with MPP, in the course of an argument for MPP, one would be leaning on the very conclusion one is allegedly trying to prove.

Under the general heading of a worry about begging the question, then, I want to distinguish two problems: first, to say in what the entitlement to use a rule of inference consists, if not in one's justified belief that that rule is truth-preserving;

(C) S knows, or is justified in believing that the logical relation between q and p is as specified in (B).

(D) By virtue of S's inferring p from q, justification is conferred on S's belief that p.

If these were the correct requirements on an argument's conferring a justification on the belief that p, there would be an obvious conflict between them and rule-circular justifications. For (C) requires that, if S is to use an argument using modus ponens to support modus ponens, S has to know that being related by way of modus ponens is truth-preserving. But that would make the inference otiose: the knowledge arrived at is already presupposed. It is clear, however, that (C) is far too strong a requirement on inferential justification in general, and so I reject this way of accusing rule-circularity of begging the question.

second, to say how a rule-circular argument can confer warrant on its conclusion even if it is powerless to move the relevant sceptic.

What about the problem of bad company? Prima facie, anyway, there looks to be a big difference between a grossly circular argument, on the one hand, and a rule-circular argument on the other, so far as their potential to positively rationalize belief is concerned. A grossly circular argument is guaranteed to succeed, no matter what proposition it is attempting to rationalize. A similar charge could not be made against a merely rule-circular argument: the mere licence to use an inferential step in accord with modus ponens, for example, does not *in and of itself guarantee* that a given argument will succeed in demonstrating the validity of modus ponens. Appropriate permisses from which, by (as it might be) a single application of MPP, we can get the general conclusion that MPP is truth-preserving, may simply not exist. In general, it is a non-trivial fact that a given rule of inference is self-supporting in this way.

While this point is strictly correct, however, the fact is that unless constraints are placed on the acceptability of rule-circular arguments, it will nevertheless be true that we will be able to justify all manner of absurd rules of inference. We must confront the charge that unconstrained rule-circular justifications keep bad company.

Consider someone who has somehow come to adopt the unreflective practice of inferring according to Prior's introduction and elimination rules for the 'tonk' connective:

(I) A/A tonk B; (E) A tonk B/ B.

If we suppose that we are allowed to *use* inferences in accord with these rules in mounting a justification for them, then it would seem that we could justify them as follows:[15]

1. 'P tonk Q' is true iff 'P' is true tonk 'Q' is true	Meaning Postulate
2. P	Assumption
3. 'P' is true	2, T-scheme
4. 'P' is true tonk 'Q' is true	2, tonk-introduction
5. 'P tonk Q' is true	4, 1, biconditional-elimination
6. P tonk Q	5, T-scheme
7. If P, then P tonk Q	6, logic

Here line 7 expresses a canonical statement of tonk-introduction dependent just on the meaning postulate in line 1. So this template is available to explain how someone for whom inference in accordance with tonk introduction was already part of their unreflective practice could arrive at an explicit justification for it.

---

[15] The example is Crispin Wright's, drawn from his commentary on this paper at the Stirling Conference on Naturalism.

And an exactly corresponding example could be constructed to yield a 'justification' for the principle of tonk elimination.

Or consider the following example (due to Marcus Guaquinto). Let R be the rule that, for any P, P, *therefore* All snow is white. Now, we seem to be in a position to mount a justification for it along the following lines. Pick any proposition P:

1. P	Assumption
2. All snow is white	1, R
3. If P, then All snow is white	Conditional Weakening

Therefore, the inference from P to all snow is white is truth-preserving. Since this is independent of the particular proposition P that is chosen, then, for any proposition P, the inference from P to 'All snow is white' is truth-preserving.

Clearly, we cannot simply assert that rule-circular justifications are acceptable and leave it at that. The question is whether there is some intuitively plausible constraint that they should be made to satisfy that will repel the bad company they would otherwise keep while leaving in place the justificatory arguments that interest us.

I will begin by discussing the second half of the problem about begging the question.

BEGGING THE QUESTION: REASONABLE EMPLOYMENT OF A RULE

Could we be entitled to use a rule of inference without first being justified in the corresponding general claim that that rule is valid?

It seems to me that we can if a plausible—perhaps even inescapable—account of what determines the meanings of our logical constraints is true. Let me explain.

By virtue of what does 'and' mean *conjunction* and refer to a certain truth function, and 'if, then' mean *conditional* and refer to a distinct truth function? That these expressions mean what they do cannot be a primitive fact about them; there must be facts by virtue of which these semantic facts obtain.

As I see it, the most plausible—perhaps the only plausible—account has it that our constants mean what they do by virtue of their conceptual role: 'if, then' means what it does by virtue of participating in some inferences and not in others. How, exactly, is this to be understood?

The thought is that there is a particular set of inferences involving 'if, then' that are meaning-constituting for a thinker: of all the inferences that 'if, then' can and does participate in, a specific subset is responsible for fixing its meaning. Given that subset, 'if, then' means that unique logical concept, *if any*, whose semantic value makes the inferences in that subset truth-preserving. The qualification is necessary because for all that a conceptual role theory can guarantee, a specified conceptual role may fail to determine a unique, or indeed, any meaning for the constant in question.[16]

Any such approach to the meanings of the constants faces, it must be conceded, a formidable number of obstacles. First, there is the impression, much encouraged by Carnap and the middle Wittgenstein, that doctrines of implicit definition lead inexorably to irrealist conclusions, that to view a fundamental logical principle as an implicit definer is to subscribe to some sort of conventionalism or non-factualism about its truth. Second, there is the charge, levelled by Quine, that an implicit definition view of logic leads to a vicious regress, because the very logical vocabulary allegedly being defined has to be used to formulate the stipulations. Third, there is the difficulty, also urged by Quine, of saying which of the many sentences a thinker may be disposed to assert serve as implicit definers of its ingredient terms. Fourth, there is the problem, most often discussed in connection with Arthur Priori's 'tonk' example, of saying what conditions a set of implicit definers must meet if it is to define a genuinely meaningful term. Finally, there is the difficulty of showing how any such account would succeed in determining a unique logical concept.

Some of these questions have satisfactory answers.[17] Others await one. It is hard to believe, however, that they do not all have satisfactory answers because it is very hard to see what *other* type of theory could explain the meanings of our logical constants. In any event, the present essay should be seen as issuing a large IOU on the outstanding problems for a conceptual-role semantics. I am interested in what we should say about the epistemology of logic, if, as seems likely, a conceptual-role semantics provides the correct account of the meaning of the logical constants.

With that in mind, I want to propose the following principle:

(L) If M is a genuinely meaning-constituting rule for S, then S is entitled to infer according to M, independently of having supplied an explicit justification for M.

Notice that (L) does not require that S *know* that M is meaning-constituting for S

---

[16] This represents one particular way of formulating a conceptual role semantics. There are other, less truth-theoretic more purely 'use-theoretic' formulations. In this paper I cannot discuss the reasons for preferring this formulation over the others. Effectively, they have to do with the requirement that connectives like 'tonk' should turn out not to express a meaning and this seems to me to demand a truth-theoretic formulation. However, the epistemic purposes to which I wish to put a conceptual-role semantics in this paper would be unaffected by this particular issue. For an important defence of a distinct, though related, truth-theoretic version of a conceptual-role semantics, see Christopher Peacocke, *A Study of Concepts* (Cambridge, MA.: MIT Press, 1992).

[17] I have tried to give some of them in 'Analyticity Reconsidered'.

if S to be entitled to infer according to M but only that M *be* meaning-constituting for S.

Is there anything that speaks in favour of (L) independently of the fact that it helps with the problem about rule-circularity? It seems to me that there is, that (L) is intuitively plausible. If it is true that certain of our inferential dispositions fix what we mean by our logical words (in the language of thought), then it is very plausible that we should be entitled to act on those inferential dispositions prior to, and independently of, having supplied an explicit justification for the general claim that they are truth-preserving, for *without* those dispositions there is nothing about whose justification we can intelligibly raise a question about: without those dispositions we could not even *have* the general belief whose justification is supposed to be in question.

The only items that are candidates for being justified are either contentful items or certain kinds of transition between contentful items (inferences). But if it is true that there could be no contentful items unless certain dispositions are already in place, there cannot be a serious question whether those dispositions are ones to which we are entitled.[18]

Our difficulty was to find a source for our entitlement to rely on a given rule of inference, independently of having supplied a justification for the general claim that that rule is truth-preserving, so that we are able to use that reliance to supply that justification. What I am urging is that that entitlement is precisely what flows naturally from a conceptual-role account of the meanings of our logical words.

This proposal does, of course, bring to the fore the question: what makes a rule meaning-constituting? This is one of the questions that still awaits a definitive answer. My present concern, however, is just to emphasize that our problem about our entitlement to employ a rule of inference *reduces* to that problem, a problem that any conceptual-role semantics faces.

DEALING WITH BAD COMPANY

With (L) in place, we are now poised to resolve the problem of bad company. For (L) suggests the following restriction on rule-circular justifications:

> (RC) S's rule-circular argument for a rule of inference M will confer
> warrant on S's belief that M is truth-preserving, provided that M is a
> genuinely meaning-constituting rule for S.

---

[18] This line of thought provides one way of understanding Wittgenstein's remark: 'To use a word without justification does not mean to use it without right' (para. 289 of *Philosophical Investigations*). For further discussion see my 'How Are Objective Epistemic Reasons Possible?', forthcoming.

Two questions arise. First, does (RC) yield the right results as far as rule-circular justifications are concerned? Does it exclude the justification of unwanted rules? Second, can anything of an intuitive nature be said to support it?

If we apply to (RC) to our problematic examples above, it is easy to see that they are immediately ruled out. R is not meaning-constituting: it is obviously not part of the meaning of 'all' that 'All snow is white' can be inferred from any proposition. Indeed, it is because we have an independent purchase on what 'All snow is white' means that we know that R is not truth-preserving and, hence, that it would be embarrassing to endorse a theory that said otherwise.

Similarly in the case of 'tonk.' It is readily shown, by attempting to construct a truth-table for 'tonk', that its introduction and elimination rules do not determine a meaning for it'; there is no proposition expressed by sentences of the form 'A tonk B.'

In fact, it should be clear that (L) will not allow any invalid rules to be circularly justified. For if M is genuinely meaning-constituting, as (L) insists it has to be, then it has a semantic value that makes M truth-preserving.

As far as the question of the intuitive support for (RC) is concerned, that question recapitulates the case for (L). If (L) is correct, then the source of our entitlement to the use of a rule of inference is distinct from our entitlement to the corresponding belief that it is valid if the rule is meaning-constituting. Thus, it may be used to confer warrant on its conclusion.

BEGGING THE SCEPTIC'S QUESTION

It is time now to turn to the final problem I outlined for a rule-circular justification, its capacity to move the appropriate sceptic. The point at issue is prefigured in Dummett's discussion when he says that rule-circularity will be damaging only to a justificatory argument that

> is addressed to someone who genuinely doubts whether the law is valid, and is intended to persuade him that it is. . . . If, on the other hand, it is intended to satisfy the philosopher's perplexity about our entitlement to reason in accordance with such a law, it may well do so. The philosopher does not seriously doubt the validity of the law and is therefore prepared to accept an argument in accordance with it. He does not seek to be persuaded of the conclusion; what he is seeking is an *explanation* of its being true.[19]

Before inquiring into the significance of this, let us make sure that we do not underestimate all that a rule-circular justification is capable of accomplishing. First, it is not at all similar to a grossly circular argument in that it is not trivially guaranteed to succeed. For one thing, the relevant premises from which, by a

---

[19] Dummett, *Logical Basis of Metaphysics* (London: Duckworth, 1991): 202.

single application of the rule the desired conclusion is to follow, may not be available. For another, not all rules are self-supporting. Second, the rule-circular argument for MPP asks in effect that it be granted that *one* application of MPP and from that it promises to deliver the conclusion that MPP is *necessarily* truth-preserving, truth-preserving in *any possible* application. Finally, this one application will itself be one to which we are entitled if, as seems plausible, MPP is meaning-constituting.

For all that, it is nevertheless true that if we were confronted by a sceptic who *doubted* the validity of MPP in *any* of its applications, we could not use this argument to rationally persuade him. Doubting the rule, he would rightly reject this particular argument in its favour. Since, by assumption, we have no other sort of argument to offer him, it seems that we are powerless to persuade him of the rightness of our position. The question is: what is the epistemic significance of this fact?

But could not we say to him: 'Look, MPP is meaning-constituting. If you reject it, then you simply mean something different by "if, then" and therefore there is no real disagreement after all.' But if our sceptic were playing his cards right, he would deny that MPP is meaning-constituting. To persuade him otherwise we would have to offer him an argument and that argument would in turn have to use MPP. And then we would be right back where we started, faced with the question: what is the epistemological significance of the fact that we are unable to persuade the sceptic about MPP?

In the passage cited above, Dummett seems to think that its significance lies in the way in which it highlights a distinction between two distinct projects: quelling the sceptic's doubts versus *explaining* to a non-sceptic why MPP is valid.

But I do not really understand what it would be to explain *why* a given logical law is true. What could it mean except something along the lines of a conventionalism about logical truth, an account which really does aspire to explain *where* logical truth comes from? As we have seen, however, there are decisive objections to conventionalism, objections that probably generalize to any explanatory project of that form.

The question that we need to be asking, I think, is rather this: Can we say that something is a real warrant for believing that p if it cannot be used to answer a sceptic about p? Is it criterial for my having a genuine warrant for believing that p that I be able to use it to persuade someone who doubts whether p?

Well, in fact, we *are* very drawn to the idea that if I am genuinely justified in believing that p, then, in principle, I ought to be able to bring you round as well— or, at the very least, I ought to be able to take you some distance towards rational belief in p. Of course, you may not understand the warrant that I have; or, being more cautious than I, you may not assign it the same weight that I do. But, prescinding from these and similar considerations, how could I be genuinely justified in believing something and yet be totally unable to have any sway with you? As Thomas Nagel puts it in his recent book *The Last Word:* 'To reason is to think systematically in ways that anyone looking over my shoulder ought to be able to recognize as correct. It is this generality that relativists and subjectivists deny.'[20]

Notice how naturally it comes to Nagel to equate the claim that *there are* objectively valid reasons, reasons that would apply to anyone anywhere, with the *epistemic* claim that anyone exposed to them ought to be able to *recognize* them as reasons.

There is a principle behind this thought, one that we may call the 'principle of the universal accessibility of reasons'. If something is a genuine reason for believing that p, then, subject to the provisos just made, its rationalizing force ought to be accessible from any epistemic standpoint.

I think that this principle has played a very large role in our thinking about justification. It is what explains, it seems to me, why the theory of knowledge is so often centred on a refutation of *scepticism*. We take it to be criterial of our having a genuine warrant for a given proposition that we be in a position to refute a sceptic about p.

If my discussion of logic has been on the right track, however, then one of its main lessons is that this principle is false. For consider: we cannot accept the claim that we have no warrant whatsoever for the core logical principles. We cannot conceive what such a warrant could consist in (whether this be a priori or a posteriori) if not in some sort of inference using those very core logical principles. So, there must be genuine warrants that will not carry any sway with a sceptic. Answering the sceptic about modus ponens cannot be criterial for whether we are warranted in believing modus ponens.

To put this point another way: we must recognize a distinction between two different sorts of reason—suasive and *non-suasive reasons*. And we have to reconcile ourselves to the fact that in certain areas of knowledge, logic featuring prominently among them, our warrant can be at most non-suasive, powerless to quell sceptical doubts.

It seems to me that this is a conclusion that we have reason to accept entirely independently of our present concern with knowledge of logic, that there are many other compartments of knowledge in which our warrant can be at most non-suasive. One such area concerns our knowledge of the existence of other minds; another concerns our knowledge of the external world. I think that in both of these areas it is very unlikely that we will be able to provide warrants for our belief that would be usable against a determined and level-headed sceptic.

CONLUSION

It is not open to us to regard our fundamental logical beliefs as unjustifiable. And yet it is hard to see how they might be justified without the benefit of deductive

---

[20] T. Nagel, *The Last Word* (Oxford: Oxford University Press 1997): 5.

reasoning. What sort of case have we been able to make for the claim that rule-circular arguments can provide genuine justifications for their conclusions? It seems to me that the case is substantial.

First, a rule-circular argument, unlike a grossly circular one, is not trivially guaranteed to succeed. Second, by relying on a small number of applications of a particular rule, a successful rule-circular argument delivers the conclusion that that rule is necessarily truth-preserving, truth-preserving in any possible application.[21] Finally, these applications of the rule will be applications to which the thinker is entitled, provided that the rule in question is meaning-constituting.

This case is constructed on the basis of several independently plausible elements. First, that the meanings of the logical constants are determined by their conceptual roles, and that not every conceptual role determines a possible meaning. Second, that if an inferential disposition is meaning-constituting, then it is a fortiori reasonable, justifiably used without supporting argument. Third, that something can be a warrant for something even if it is powerless to bring about a determined sceptic.

Putting these elements together allows us to say that we are justified in our fundamental logical beliefs in spite of the fact that we can produce only rule-circular arguments for them. The price is that we have to admit that we cannot use this form of justification to silence sceptical doubts. It is arguable, however, that, with respect to something as basic as logic, that was never in prospect anyway.

---

[21] Can we make sense of the idea that we are relying on only *one* application of a rule of inference? We do routinely discuss whether the application of a rule should be restricted—as when we debate whether MPP should be restricted in sorites cases—and that is enough to show that we *understand* what it would mean for a rule to apply in one context but not in another.

11

Explaining the A Priori: The Programme of Moderate Rationalism

Christopher Peacocke

I. INTRODUCTION

My starting point is a question about a distinction, a distinction between different ways of coming to know that something is the case. On a traditional rationalist conception, some ways of coming to know a proposition are justificationally independent of perceptual experience, while others are not. When you come to know a logical truth by way of your having a proof of it, you may need to perceive the inscription of the proof, and you may need various perceptual capacities to appreciate that it is a proof. But the justification for your belief in the logical truth is the proof itself. Perceptual experience gives access to the proof, which provides an experience-independent justification for accepting its conclusion. By contrast, if you come to believe 'That's Mikhail Gorbachev', when you see him at the airport, what entitles you to your belief is (in part) the perceptual experience by which you recognize Gorbachev. Your perceptual experience is not a mere means which gives you access to some experience-independent entitlement to believe 'That's Gorbachev.' This classical rationalist distinction between experience-dependent and experience-independent justifications or entitlements has been controverted, and objections to it raised and (in my own view) answered. Here I

Versions of this material were presented in 1999 to a symposium at the APA meeting in Berkeley, at which I was helped by the comments of co-symposiasts Laurence BonJour and Hilary Kornblith; to a seminar at New York University; to discussion groups in Oxford; and to the Princeton Philosophy Colloquium. My thanks to Tyler Burge and Michael Dummett for discussions of Fregean issues; and to Paul Boghossian, Bill Brewer, Justin Broackes, Bill Child, Michael Dummett, Dorothy Edgington, Kit Fine, Mark Johnston, Gideon Rosen, Ian Rumfitt, Stephen Schiffer, and David Wiggins for further comments and suggestions. In the early stages of writing, I had access to the superb research facilities of the Australian National University during a memorable visit there in January 1999, and was stimulated by discussions on these issues with David Chalmers, Frank Jackson, and Philip Pettit. Time was made available for work on this paper by a Research Professorship funded by the Leverhulme Trust; once again I thank the Trust for their invaluable support.

ask to be allowed, pro tem, to take for granted that the classical distinction is intelligible; and that the class of experience-dependent, and the class of experience-independent, entitlements are both non-empty. My opening question about the distinction is then as follows: what is the relation between those ways of coming to know a given proposition which are justificationally independent of experience, and the identity of the concepts in that proposition?

Propositions that can be known in a way which is justificationally independent of experience – propositions knowable in a way which is a priori, as I will say for brevity – seem to cover a vast range of subject matters. They include theorems of logic and arithmetic; they include the Gödel-sentence for any recursively axiomatized theory whose axioms are also known independently of experience; they include principles of colour-incompatibility; perhaps they include basic moral principles; perhaps they also include whatever truths of philosophy we know. So our initial question apparently concerns all the ways of coming to know that make available knowledge in these diverse areas.

The traditional rationalist answer to the question of what makes possible an a priori way of coming to know a proposition appeals to the notions of understanding and reason. Writers in the rationalist tradition, through Leibniz, Frege, and Gödel, have in one variant or another made such an appeal. They have held the view that it is in the nature of understanding certain expressions, or grasping certain concepts, that certain ways of coming to accept propositions containing those concepts are rational, and yield knowledge of those propositions, even when those ways involve no justificational reliance on perceptual experience. There are important and interesting differences between these rationalists; but that core seems to be common to them.

When one considers particular examples, the position common to the rationalists seems intuitive. When we assess the issues pre-theoretically, it does seem – for instance – that someone who possesses the logical concept of conjunction must be willing to make inferences in accordance with its introduction and elimination rules, without any need for experiential justification, and that these rules preserve not just truth, but also knowledge. Analogous points seem to hold for some basic arithmetical transitions. Similarly, it also seems that no more than grasp of the relevant colour concepts is required for one to be in a position to appreciate the incompatibility of a surface being wholly definitely red and wholly definitely green. Arguably similar points hold for the other examples too.

What has remained quite obscure in the rationalists' position, however, is the answer it would give to a how-question, the question 'How does understanding, or concept-possession, have this epistemological power? What is it about understanding which makes certain ways of coming to accept a given proposition yield knowledge, even though the way is justificationally independent of experience?' Many rationalists – including not only figures from several centuries ago, but also Gödel and Roger Penrose – have believed in a faculty of rational intuition or rational insight, a faculty which is supposed to explain the phenomenon of a priori knowledge. It is of course quite unclear how such a faculty is meant to work, how it could even provide truths about the world, let alone knowledge. The difficulties are difficulties of principle, and I will touch on them later. But the how-question which needs an answer is equally pressing for less exotic forms of rationalism. It is equally pressing for a less exotic writer such as Laurence BonJour, in whose writings the label 'rational intuition' is used merely to pick out the phenomenon of understanding-based a priori knowledge. BonJour's view is that it is 'anything but obvious' that the rational insight employed in attaining a priori knowledge involves 'a distinct psychological faculty'. BonJour holds that the psychological faculty involved in attaining a priori knowledge 'is simply the ability to understand and think'.[1] The more sober the view of what is involved in attaining a priori knowledge, the more challenging the task of explaining how understanding has the epistemological power. The more sober rationalist has to account for the epistemological phenomena from a non-exotic theory of understanding or concept-possession.

My goal in this paper is to make some proposals about the form such explanations should take, and to suggest some instances of the form in certain recalcitrant cases. A good understanding-based explanation of the capacity for knowing things by rational intuition should also have the resources for explaining why it is a fallible capacity, as it is widely acknowledged to be even by its most enthusiastic proponents.[2] If we can get a good account of the relations between understanding and a priori knowledge, we will be able to explain why some ways of coming to know a given proposition are a priori ways. If an a priori proposition is one which can be known a priori, this approach can also help to explain why any given a priori propositions has that epistemic status.

It is no part of this approach that meaning and understanding are involved only in outright a priori entitlements. On the contrary, it seems obvious that the identity of an observational concept is relevant to the issue of why it is that a thinker's perceptual experience entitles her to make a perceptual, empirical judgement. The task is rather to say what it is about understanding that makes a priori knowledge possible; which evidently does not preclude understanding from having a role in other ways of attaining knowledge too. It is also arguable that even in these empirical cases in which understanding is relevant to the status of something as a way of coming to know, a relative notion of the a priori has application. It is a priori, given the supposition that the subject is perceiving properly, and given the occurrence of a certain kind of perceptual experience, that a corresponding observational judgement will in those circumstances be correct.

The phrase 'rational intuition' has historically been associated with some of

---

[1] *In Defence of Pure Reason* (Cambridge: Cambridge University Press, 1998): 109.
[2] Ibid., sect. 4.5, 'The Corrigibility of Rational Insight'.

the headier forms of rationalism; but the phrase itself serves as a reminder for the sober too. The occurrence of the word 'rational' in the phrase emphasizes that the process of acceptance of a priori principles is a rational one. The occurrence of 'intuition' emphasizes that in many cases, the process of rational acceptance is not, or is not exclusively, one of derivation from axioms or principles already accepted. This apparently real combination – of rational acceptance which cannot be fully characterized as derivation from axioms or rules – is theoretically challenging for any rationalist, however modest and unexotic her theory of rational intuition. What we might call the *phenomena* of rational intuition which have been cited by the most interesting rationalist writers are extensive and striking. Whatever one thinks of Gödel's quasi-perceptual treatment of knowledge of the properties of concepts, the phenomena he cites – of rational acceptance of new axioms which do not follow from those previously accepted, of the notion of proof thus not being purely syntactically characterized, to mention just two – these are genuine phenomena which any good theory of understanding and the a priori ought to explain.[3]

II. MODERATE EXPLANATORY RATIONALISM

Now we can return to our opening question about the relation between ways of coming to know that are a priori, and the identity of the concepts in the content that is known. I distinguish two radically different general types of answer to the question that we can label respectively *minimalism* about the a priori and *moderate rationalism* about the a priori.

To formulate minimalism in this area properly, we need a distinction between composite and atomic ways of coming to know. One way of coming to know a logical truth is by working out a proof of it. The proof consists of a series of transitions, each one of which involves a way of coming to know a certain kind of conclusion from a certain kind of premises. The individual transitions at each line of the fully analysed proof involve an atomic way of coming to know, something that cannot be broken down further into other ways of coming to know. When you visually identify someone as a person who attended a course you gave some years ago, that can be broken down into constituent ways of coming to know. One constituent is your taking your perceptual experience at face value; another may be, for instance, your taking some memory image as of a student in your class at face value; and a third is your transition from the appearance of the face of the

---

[3] See esp. 'Russell's mathematical logic' and 'What is Cantor's continuum problem?', both repr. in *Philosophy of Mathematics: Selected Readings*, ed. P. Benaceraff and H. Putnam (Cambridge: Cambridge University Press, 1983, 2nd edn); and the philosophical papers in *Kurt Gödel Collected Works, III: Unpublished Essays and Lectures*, ed. S. Feferman *et al*. (Oxford: Oxford University Press, 1995).

person currently perceived and that of the remembered student to the conclusion that this is one and the same person. I will leave the distinction between atomic and composite methods at this relatively intuitive level for present purposes. It does need more elaboration, but this will be enough for a formulation of the core of the minimalist's position.

Minimalism is then the thesis that when an atomic way W is an a priori way of coming to know that p, it is simply primitively constitutive of the identity of one or more concepts in p that W is an a priori way of coming to know that p, or of coming to know contents of some kind under which p falls. That p can be known a priori in way W is, according to the minimalist, written into an account of understanding in the way that it is written into being a bachelor that bachelors are men, or, perhaps, written into being a chair that chairs have backs, or written into the relation of perception that a perceived object must causally affect the perceiver. It may be unobvious, and hard to discover, what is primitively constitutive of the identity of any given concept; but when one realizes that some property is so constitutive, there is no further answer to the question 'Why does that concept have that epistemic property?' According to this minimalist position, the fact that an atomic way W is an a priori way of coming to know that p is not consequential upon anything else. The minimalist will agree that those composite ways of coming to know which are a priori ways can be explained as such by being built up from atomic ways which are ways of coming to know a priori; but for the status of atomic ways as a priori ways, there is no further explanation to be given, beyond its being primitively constitutive of the identity of the concepts in the content known that they are so a priori. Perhaps the position would be better called 'epistemic conceptual minimalism', since the position employs talk of concepts without saying that such a talk is a mere manner of speaking. There are more radical forms of minimalism. But this epistemic conceptual minimalism seems to be minimalist within the class of positions which take at face value the talk of concepts and meaning in the theory of thought and understanding. What is important about the position is not that it regards the identity of concepts as in some cases given by the conditions for knowing certain contents, but that it regards the resource of what is primitively written into the identity of a concept as already a full explanation of the relation between the a priori and the concepts featuring in the content of a priori knowledge.[4] Such a minimalism remains a rationalist position, because it entails that the status of a way of coming to know as an a priori way traces back to what is, on the minimalists' view, involved in understanding and concept-possession.

There is really a cluster of positions which can be called (conceptually) minimalist. One variant of minimalism holds that when a thinker comes to know via

---

[4] That some concepts can be individuated by the conditions for knowing certain contents containing them was after all a claim of my book *Being Known* (Oxford: Oxford University Press, 1999).

an atomic a priori way that p, the thinker judges that p because of his grasp of the concepts in p. This statement is, according to this variant of minimalism, a genuinely explanatory true statement: understanding or grasp of the concepts in question explains the rational, a priori judgement that p. But that, according to this variant minimalist, is all that there is to be said on the matter.

The moderate rationalist, in the sense in which I will use that description, disagrees with all forms of minimalism. The first component of the moderate rationalist's view is that for any a priori way of coming to know a given content, there is a substantive explanation of why it is a way of coming to know that has a priori status, an explanation which involves the nature of the concepts in the given content. The moderate rationalist intends this claim to apply both to atomic and to composite ways of coming to know. For those who hold that concepts are individuated by the conditions for possessing them, this first component of the moderate rationalist's claim unfolds into the thesis that for any a priori way of coming to know a given content, there is an explanation of why it is an a priori way which has to do with the possession conditions of the concepts in that content.

The moderate rationalist is, then, committed to the feasibility of a certain explanatory programme. The goal of her programme is to identify those features of concepts which explain why a given way of coming to know a particular content is an a priori way. If the moderate rationalist thinks that concepts are individuated in terms of the conditions for their possession, execution of that programme must involve appeals to explanatory properties of concept-possession or understanding.

I am a moderate rationalist. Farther on, I will be suggesting ways in which we might make progress in carrying through the moderate rationalist's programme. But why should we prefer moderate rationalism to either variety of minimalism? I offer two arguments.

1. We already have some theoretical conception of understanding and meaning. For some of us, understanding consists in some form of grasp of truth-conditions; for others, a notion of canonical conceptual role is said to be basic. These theoretical conceptions of understanding and meaning are never put forward as merely partial determinations of understanding. These conceptions are not ones under which meaning can be fully characterized only by doing something else as well: by specifying additionally, as a further task, which ways of coming to know certain contents involving the meaning count as a priori ways of coming to know it. Once we have a conception of how meaning or content is determined, any links it has with the a priori have to be founded in that conception of how meaning or content is determined. If the links of meaning with the a priori cannot be so founded, one would not have fully explained meaning in terms of truth-conditions, or conceptual role, or whatever is the favoured notion. If meaning is already fixed as truth-conditions, or as canonical conceptual role, or whatever else is

favoured, simply to add links with the a priori as further primitive axioms for the notion of meaning is simply to concede that meaning is not fully characterized without those extra axioms.

It may help here to consider a parallel with Dummett on the justification of deduction. Dummett insisted, rightly in my view, that deductive relations must be philosophically explicable in terms of the meaning of the logical constants involved in those relations.[5] A theory of meaning must explain why those deductive relations hold. This is a point which can be accepted by realists and anti-realists alike. The same applies to a priori ways in general, of which the deductive relations are a special case. If some principle has an a priori status, its status as such must be explicable in terms of the meaning of the expressions occurring in that principle.

There is an internal instability, a kind of unavoidable illusion, on the minimalist views. When we accept an a priori principle, it seems to be rational to do so, on the basis of our understanding of the expressions, or our grasp of the concepts, it contains. But this impression of rationality must be an illusion of one sort of another, on the minimalist view. If it were not an illusion, there would be some feature of meaning and understanding which explains a priori status. But that is precisely what the minimalist rejects. The variant minimalist who insists that grasp of concepts explains acceptance of a priori principles is not really in any better position. He has not accounted for the rationality of accepting an a priori principle.

2. This first point about meaning and understanding applies equally to the general concept of knowledge too. We have some theoretical conception of what is involved in a way of coming to accept a content being a way of coming to know it. The conception need not be reductive, of course. If there are principles connecting understanding with those ways of coming to know which are a priori ways, the connecting principles cannot have the status of primitive stipulations or axioms of the sort envisaged by any kind of minimalism. The connecting principles must have their source in the nature of knowledge, as well as in the nature of understanding, and the consequent relations between the two.

Such are the two initial, presumptive reasons in favour of developing a position which endorses the first component of a moderate rationalist's treatment of the a priori, the component which has a commitment to the possibility of explaining each case of a priori status by reference to features of understanding or concept-possession. But this first component of moderate rationalism cannot exhaust the content of any rationalism which is entitled to the label 'moderate'. For all I have said so far, an explanation of a priori status might invoke a theory of understanding which is quite extreme. A position of the kind sometimes attributed to Gödel,

---

[5] 'The Justification of Deduction', in *Truth and Other Enigmas* (London: Duckworth, 1978).

on which there is some faculty of rational intuition, allegedly analogous to perception, which puts a thinker in contact with concepts or meanings, could equally well endorse the existence of explanations which refer to the nature of meaning and understanding. In short: if the theory of understanding which proposes an explanation of the a priori status of a proposition is not itself moderate, the resulting position can hardly be a form of moderate rationalism either. So a second, obligatory, component of any rationalism which calls itself moderate must be the claim that the theory of understanding mentioned in its first component is not one which postulates causal or explanatory relations between properties of things in a third realm of concepts or meanings, and says that those relations are involved in understanding.

There is another reason of principle for wanting to include this second component. Could we attempt to explain a priori knowledge that p by some kind of causal explanation of the belief that p by the holding of the fact that p? Much of what is known a priori, including the mathematical and the logical, is arguably not of the right kind to enter causal explanations of mental states. But even in cases in which it is, there are reasons of principle for thinking that no such approach can explain the phenomenon of a priori knowledge. A priori positions hold in the actual world, however the actual world may be. That is, they hold fixedly, in the terminology of Davies and Humberstone.[6] Saying that the truth that p explains one's belief that p, and perhaps by some special causal route, fails to imply a crucial feature of the a priori, which is that p will hold whichever world is the actual world.

This objection to using causal explanation by the fact that p in the explanation of a priori knowledge that p roughly parallels the objection to using causal explanation by the fact that p in the epistemology of metaphysical necessity. Only what is actually the case – or , slightly better, only propositions whose truth is settled by what holds in the actual world – can enter causal explanations. The fact that p's holding causally explains certain other events can never be sufficient for it to be necessary that p, just as it can never be sufficient for p to hold in the actual world, however the actual world may be.

In both the a priori and the modal cases, there will of course be causal explanations of why what is believed is believed, and these explanations can be of epistemic significance. The present point is only that what makes a piece of knowledge a priori cannot be fully accounted for by causal relations to what is known; and similarly for modal knowledge. It is good to be free of any commitment to causal explanation on that specific point, for attempts to develop the epistemology of the a priori or the modal in causal terms can only encourage the view that defenders of the a priori and of necessity must be committed to unacceptably non-naturalistic conceptions. One motivation for that charge, at least, is removed if our epistemology of these two notions is not causal.

    [6] M. Davies and L. Humberstone, 'Two Notions of Necessity', *Philosophical Studies* 38 (1980): 1–30.

As I said, the Gödelian phenomena are genuine and important. Gödel is sometimes regarded as having a quasi-causal view of our relations to concepts and meanings, and if he did, he will thereby be open to the objections we have been raising. Faculties conceived by analogy with perception, far from helping to explain the possibility of rational intuition and a priori knowledge, are actually incompatible with the a priori status of the beliefs they deliver. However, nothing I have said rules out the more modest idea that there is a way of coming to know propositions which is a priori, is based on the understanding, and goes far beyond the models of understanding Gödel rightly criticized. I will return to this.

Our two-component moderate rationalist is making a highly general claim about all a priori truths, whatever their subject matter. The tasks for the moderate rationalist can be divided into four broad categories:

(a) There is an *identification task*. Identifying the way in which something comes to be known is often a hard part of the moderate rationalist's task. It is often highly plausible that there is an a priori way of coming to know a given proposition, whilst it remains obscure what exactly the way is. This is true of principles of colour incompatibility, of fundamental moral principles (if indeed they are a priori), and of some of the Gödelian phenomena. Saying that these principles are known by rational intuition cannot, for the moderate rationalist, be the end of the explanation.

(b) Once an a priori way of coming to know is identified, the moderate rationalist has then to explain why it is a way of coming to know a priori the content in question, on the basis of the nature of the concepts featuring in the content, and on the basis of their possession conditions if she conceives of concepts as individuated by their possession conditions. This is the *explanatory task*. It exists equally for the relatively a priori, as when we classify an inferential principle as a priori.

(c) The explanatory account of the a priori has also to be applicable to any a priori relation which is less than conclusive. This may include inductive principles, and principles about confirmation and probability. This is the task of *extension to non-conclusive cases*.

(d) A particular subclass of non-conclusive a priori principles of which the moderate rationalist must give an account are those stating that a subject is entitled to rely on the representational content of certain kinds of informational states in coming to make judgements. These cases include a thinker's entitlement to rely on perceptual experience in making observational judgements; on experiential memory in making certain judgements about the past; and so forth. An account of ways of coming to know that are a priori will not carry much conviction unless it can be extended to these cases too. I call this the task of *extension to reliance on informational states*.

This is a set of huge tasks; probably someone could spend a lifetime on them. Let us narrow our scope just a little, and consider the nature of the explanatory task (b) facing the moderate rationalist. From now on, I will also be considering only a moderate rationalist who holds that concepts are individuated by the conditions for possessing them (again, without any reductive presuppositions).[7] The explanatory task facing this theorist in a particular instance might concern the a priori status of a way W of coming to know some particular content containing essentially the concepts C and D. That is to say, the other contained concepts, unlike C and D, could be replaced uniformly by corresponding variables, and the universal quantification of the result could also be known a priori in way W. (I take the case in which only two concepts occur essentially, but these remarks will apply to any other number.) Our moderate rationalist's task can then be thought of as one of solving for, or discovering, a relation meeting certain conditions. The relation he has to discover we can call the *key* relation for the way W and the given a priori principle. It is a relation which holds between the following terms:

(1) the respective possession conditions for the contained concepts C and D;

(2) the semantic values of C and D; and

(3) the way W.

The key relation is one which explains why, when a thinker comes to believe the content in way W, he can know it to be true in the actual world, justificationally independently of perceptual experience.

The key relation which the moderate rationalist aims to find in any given case is one which will unlock the explanation of the a priori status of the given content. It can do so only if it is a relation between all of the elements (1) through (3). A priority is a phenomenon at the level of sense, not reference, and so on this moderate rationalist's theory must be traceable to the nature of the concepts involved. Hence element (1) must be present in the key relation, if concepts are individuated in terms of their possession conditions. If they are not so individuated, then it will be the nature of the concepts involved which forms the first element in the key relation, whatever that nature is. For element (2), we argue thus. Since, at least in the conclusive cases with which we are presently concerned, what is a priori is true, and indeed true however the actual world is, the semantic value of the concepts C and D, which contribute to the determination of the truth-value of the a priori proposition, must also be part of the explanation. Element (3), the way the thinker comes to make the judgement, when it is known a priori, must also be present, since the status of a belief as knowledge depends on how it is reached.

Finding something which is plausibly the key relation for a given way and

---

[7] That is, I will not be assuming that the conditions for possession can be given in the A(C) form of *A Study of Concepts* (Cambridge, Mass.: MIT Press, 1992). See the discussion in the later sections of my paper 'Implicit Conceptions, Understanding and Rationality', in *Philosophical Issues* 9 (1998): 45-88, ed. E. Villaneuva (Ridgeview: Atascadero, Calif.).

given principle is less challenging in one special case. That is the special case in which it is written into, or is a consequence of, the possession conditions for one or more concepts in the given principle that to possess those concepts, the thinker must be willing to accept the principle, by reaching it in that way. This seems to be the case for acceptance of the a priori principle that from A&B, it can be inferred that A, where the way in question is accepting inferences one finds non-inferentially compelling. The key relation for a special case like this is one abstracted from the following condition: that what makes something the seman-tic value of conjunction (viz. a certain function from pairs of truth-values to truth-values) is that it makes truth-preserving those inferences, like the inference from A&B to B, which are mentioned in the possession condition for conjunction, and which are made in the specified way. The key relation between the possession condition for conjunction, its semantic value, and a certain way of inferring some-thing from it is the relation stated to hold in that condition. This is a key relation that brings in all the elements (1)–(3) we just identified.

This key relation explains the a priori status of the transition from A&B to B without postulating primitive, unexplained relations between understanding and the a priori, and without postulating problematic faculties. When the semantic value of conjunction is determined in such a fashion, the transition is guaranteed to be truth-preserving. It will be truth-preserving in the actual world, however the actual world is; that is, it holds Fixedly in the sense of Davies and Humberstone. This approach also explains why the way of reaching B from A&B should yield not just acceptance, but rather knowledgeable acceptance, of the transition. This method of reaching B, by inferring it from A&B, is immediately settled as correct in the actual world, however the actual world may be, given the contribution to truth-conditions made by the concept of conjunction. This goes far beyond brute reliability. The a priori correctness of the method is immediately founded in the nature of the contribution made by conjunction to the truth-values of thoughts in which it features. If that is not sufficient for a knowledgeable transition, it is not clear that anything could be.

The ordinary, non-philosophical thinker does not of course need to know the philosophical theory of why the inference is a priori. The philosophical theory is intended to explain why the ordinary thinker is entitled to make the inference from A&B to B without any justificational reliance on perceptual experience. A philosophical theory of the a priori will at many points have to use the distinction between entitlement, and what explains or grounds the enti-tlement.[8] The distinction is needed even in these very simple cases in which the transitions are written into, or consequences of, the possession conditions for the concepts involved in the transition. We must, in brief, always distin-guish between

---

[8] For more on the distinction between justification and entitlement, see T. Burge, 'Content Preservation', *Philosophical Review* 102 (1993): 457–88.

>   (1) knowing, in a way which is a priori, that *p*

and

>   (2) knowing that it is a priori that *p*.

The ordinary thinker can know, in a way which is a priori, that *p*, without know-ing that it is a priori that *p*. The initial goal of the moderate rationalist's programme is an explanatory characterization of (1), rather than (2); though of course it can also be expected to have consequences for (2) if the programme is successfully executed.

   I mention this treatment of the very special case of ways of coming to accept principles which are written into the possession conditions for concepts in the principles in the spirit of offering an existence proof for the key relations of the sort to which the moderate rationalist is committed. In the remainder of this paper, I suggest some ways in which the moderate rationalist might attempt to carry through her programme in some more challenging cases. The more chal-lenging cases are those of a priori principles which neither are, nor follow from, those principles mentioned in the relevant possession conditions. As always, the task for the moderate rationalist is to identify the key relation.

III. CONCEPTS TIED TO THE INDIVIDUATION OF PROPERTIES: TWO CASES

I turn to some case studies. Each case involves an example of a key relation which can explain epistemic phenomena that have been described by some as involving the use of rational intuition. Each of these rather different examples also illustrates a more general phenomenon: that of a concept being tied to the individuation of the property or relation it picks out. Here properties and relations are understood as being at the level of reference, but as more finely individuated than extensions or course-of-values. The different cases illustrate the different ways in which a concept can be tied to the individuation of a property or a relation.

First case: colour concepts and their a priori relations

Consider the colours red, green, blue, and the rest that are picked out by our ordi-nary colour concepts. Here I mean the colours themselves, not concepts of them, and not expressions for them. A colour's phenomenal properties are constitutive of it in at least the following respect. Take any particular finely discriminated colour shade *s*. This can be a shade as finely discriminated as Goodman would discriminate qualia: shade *s* is identical with shade *r* only if any shade matching *s* matches *r*, and conversely.[9] Here, as in Goodman, the range of 'anything' must

---

   [9] See Goodman's criterion of identity for qualia in *The Structure of Appearance*, 3rd edn. (Dordrecht: Reidel, 1977).

be either universals, or at least something going beyond the range of actual particulars. Fix also on a given colour—red, say. Then if *s* is a shade which is clearly within the colour red, it is essentially and constitutively true of the colour red that *s* is clearly within it. (If *s* is a borderline case, that it is so is also essentially and constitutively true of the colour red.) The colour red is individuated by which shades fall within it, which fall outside it, and arguably by its pattern of borderline cases in respect of shades.

Since these phenomenal properties of the colour red are constitutive of it, they hold in all possible circumstances. It is a constraint on the genuine possibility of a world, or a world-description, that it respect the constitutive properties of objects, including colours. Hence: whichever world is the actual world, these phenomenal properties will hold of the colour red. They hold both necessarily and Fixedly. So far, these points all concern the level of reference, the level at which colours and shades themselves are located.

Now let us move to the level of concepts, sense and thought. The possession conditions for the concept *red* of the colour red are tied to these very conditions which individuate the colour red. Suppose a shade *s* is clearly a shade of red. If a thinker possesses the concept *red*, is taking his visual experience at face value, and if the experience represents an object as having shade *s*, then the thinker must be willing to judge 'That's red' of the presented object. We can relativize this to a part or region of the object; the point will still go through under such relativization. The thought 'That shade *s* [given in perception] is red' is not informative to the thinker who fully possesses the concept *red*.

Similarly, if a shade is clearly not a shade of red, the thinker must in those given circumstances be willing to judge 'That's not red.'

Next take a given shade *s* which is a shade of red and is not a shade of green. By the same reasoning again, applied both to the colour concept *red* and to the colour concept *green*, the thinker will be willing to judge, when taking perceptual experience at face value, when something is perceived as being shade *s*, 'That's red and not green.' The conditions for possessing the concepts *red* and *green* require the thinker to be willing to make this judgement; and it will be true.

It will also be relatively a priori that something with *that* shade (perceptually given) is red and not green. What I mean here by the claim of relative a priority is that the thinker's entitlement to this belief does not rely on the content of her perceptual experiences, beyond that content needed for having the relevant concepts in the first place. There is a way of thinking of a particular shade which is made available only by perceiving that shade. Such experience is necessary to have any demonstrative thoughts about that shade, including for instance such thoughts as 'That shade is or is not displayed on my colour chart', which are equally properly classified as relatively a priori. Such relatively a priori judgements contrast with 'The book with that shade is closed', which is not relatively a priori. What matters is that no further feature of the experience, beyond experience of the shade itself, is needed for the thinker's entitlement to judge, knowledgeably,

'That shade is red.' That judgement will hold whichever world is the actual world. (It will also hold necessarily.)

Now we can go for something more general. A thinker can reflect on what she can correctly judge when presented with a given shade. She can appreciate that if it is correct to judge, on the basis of perception necessary for having the demonstrative concept, something of the form 'That shade is a shade of red', it will also be correct, on the same basis, the make the corresponding judgement 'That shade is not a shade of green.' Suppose, what is also plausible, that every case in which something is red, or is not red, or is green, or is not green, could either be known to be so on the basis of perception; or else is a case in which something is counted as having one of these colour properties because it has the same physical properties which underlie the perception of colour in the perceptible cases. If a thinker can know all this, she can come to know that no perceptible shade is both a shade of red and a shade of green. Since the basis of this reflection is the relation of shades to colours which are in fact constitutive of the colours thought about, the generalization holds whichever world is the actual world. It holds fixedly that any shade which is a shade of red is not a shade of green. No particular course of perceptual experience is required to attain this knowledge: it is a priori.

This description of how such knowledge is attainable is founded in the possession conditions for the concepts *red* and *green*. Consider a concept whose possession condition is not tied to rational responses to the shades which individuate the colour to which the concept refers. For such a concept, it would not be possible for a thinker to appreciate such incompatibilities on a similar basis to that which we just outlined. Even if red is in fact the colour of the Chinese national flag, no merely understanding-based reflection could yield knowledge of the proposition that if a shade is of the same colour as that of the Chinese national flag, then it is not a shade of green. Such knowledge would have to be founded on the a posteriori, and not purely understanding-based, information that the colour of the Chinese flag is red.

What is crucial to this argument is the close relation between the way the colour is individuated, and the condition for grasping the concept *red* which refers to that colour. The relations to shades which contribute to the individuation of the colour are precisely those to which one who grasps the colour concept must be sensitive when making perceptually based judgements involving the concept. In short: the colour concept is tied to the individuation of its reference. It is only because this is so that a priori reflection on what it would be correct to judge in various circumstances can yield knowledge of colour incompatibilities.[10]

The need to invoke the tie between the colour concepts and the individuation

---

[10] I emphasize that I haven't shown that a material object has, at each point on its surface, only one colour. That would require further argument. All I have argued for is the a priori status of the proposition 'Any shade which is definitely a shade of red is not definitely a shade of green.' This would not be contradicted by the possibility of reddish-green, asserted by C. Hardin in his *Color for Philosophers: Unweaving the Rainbow* (Indianapolis: Hackett, 1988): 121–7.

of their references also seems to me to be one lesson of reflection on the early Putnam's discussion of colour incompatibilities.[11] Putnam's argument merits a paper-length discussion of its own: but to illustrate the lesson I just mentioned, I fix on the stage of his argument at which he writes 'And if it is true that no matter which shade of red and which shade of green we choose, nothing is both that shade of red and that shade of green, then it is true that 'Nothing is both red and green' even if by 'red' we mean not specific shades but broad classes of such shades' (1956: 211).

I say this by itself is not enough to explain a priori status. If the broad colour red is in fact the colour allowed by the local school for its dress code, it will equally be true that: no matter which shade of the colour allowed by the local school for its dress code and which shade of green we choose, nothing is both that shade of the colour allowed by the local school and that shade of green. But 'Nothing is both the colour allowed by the local school for its dress code and green' is not a priori. Putnam's principle needs some strengthening, some modal element, to get the stronger conclusion we need.[12] Putnam's principle is Fixedly true, and the prefixing of a 'Fixedly' operator gives the stronger premises. But then we have to ask: why are the stronger premises true? The answer I would give is that the concept *red* itself, unlike the concept *colour allowed by the local school for its dress code*, is tied to the individuation of the colour red. More specifically, this tie can be split up into several sublinks: the tie of *that shade* to a particular shade and what individuates it; the individuation of the colour in terms of its relations to the shade it includes; and the relation of the canonical broad colour concepts, *red, green*, and the rest, to the colours so individuated. So I think a fuller elaboration of this part of the early Putnam's position would need to draw on the resources I have been offering, and crucially on the notion of a concept being tied to the individuation of what it picks out.[13]

The explanation I have offered for a priori knowledge of colour incompatibilities, in being founded in the understanding-conditions for colour vocabulary, is one small step towards carrying through the moderate rationalist's programme. It

---

[11] 'Reds, Greens and Logical Analysis', *Philosophical Review* 65 (1956): 206-17, and 'Red and Green All Over Again: A Rejoinder to Arthur Pap', *Philosophical Review* 66 (1957): 100–3.

[12] There is no modal element in his formalization of his argument later in the same paper.

[13] I differ from Putnam on some other points, particularly over what counts as a rule of language. Putnam gives a postulate which he says 'formulates a feature of English usage pointed out in the informal discussion: Nothing can be classified as both a shade of red and a shade of green.' This seems to me a truth about the non-linguistic world, not one about English. Insofar as the world cannot be a certain way, that will have consequences for which English sentences cannot be true—but the source of such impossibilities seems to me to have nothing to do with language at all. In his rejoinder to Pap, Putnam says 'it seems plausible to take 'Red and Green are different colours'' as 'direct linguistic stipulation' (1957: 102). I would contest this too: what is stipulated is which colour is the reference of the respective words; and then, given these referential stipulations, it's obvious with only a little thought (but not as a matter of any linguistic stipulation) that they are distinct. This is also what one would expect if understanding of colour words involves grasp of some class of paradigms and a closeness relation.

is a small step even within the special domain of colour. The moderate rationalist will also have the ambition of explaining all the other apparently a priori principles about colour which so intrigued Wittgenstein at different stages of his life.[14]

While colour concepts have their own distinctive properties, they are far from unique in having the crucial property of being tied to the individuation of their references. This more general property can explain other examples of the a priori, in accordance with the moderate rationalist's programme, as in the next example.

Second case: arithmetical relations

Consider arithmetical relations such as 'n is the sum of m and k' and 'n is the product of m and k.' At the level of the arithmetical relation itself, what it is for a triple of natural numbers to stand in these relations is given by their standard recursive definitions. But to think of these relations in the ways just given, as the sum relation and as the product relation respectively, is to have a fundamental method of calculating sums and products for which it is immediately obvious that it respects these recursions. So, for instance: the fundamental procedure for finding the sum of 7 and 5 involves counting up 5 steps from 7; and it is immediately obvious that this procedure respects the principle that 7 plus the successor of a number n is identical with the successor of the sum of 7 with n, i.e. that it respects the recursion for addition. A person may sometimes just see, or realize without conscious reasoning, that one number is the sum of two others; but if his judgement is queried, he must fall back on methods of calculating the sum of which it is clear (without substantial arithmetical computation) that they respect the standard recursive definition of addition. These latter methods are the thinker's fundamental procedures.

Judgements about the sum of two numbers, made by counting correctly, and without other mistakes, in the way one does in ordinary arithmetical calculation, will be correct in the actual world. They will also be correct whatever the actual world is like, because they involve thinking of these relations in ways tied to their very individuation. So these ways of coming to know the sums of two numbers are a priori ways of coming to know. The position is in agreement with Kant that 7+5 = 12 is a priori (though the reasons for this classification may not be the same). The a priori knowability of arithmetical sums is founded in the nature of the possession conditions for the concepts they contain, for they are tied to the individuation of the very relations the concepts pick out. A similar argument can be given for the a priori knowability of arithmetical multiplications, in relation to methods of calculating them involving addition.

A parallel argument can also be given about the relation between the individuation of the natural numbers themselves, and canonical concepts of them, if we

---

[14] *Philosophical Remarks*, ed. R. Rhees (Oxford: Blackwell, 1975), and *Remarks on Colour* ed. G. E. M. Anscombe, trans. L. McAlister and M. Schättle (Oxford: Blackwell, 1977).

regard conditions for application as partially or wholly individuative of the natural numbers. Once again, we first consider the natural numbers themselves, rather than concepts thereof. The number 0 is individuated by the condition that for there to be 0 Fs is for there to be nothing which is F. The number 1 is individuated by the condition that for there to be 1 F is for there to be something that is F and nothing else which is F. For any natural number which is the successor $s(n)$ of some natural number n, the number $s(n)$ is individuated by its being such that for any property F, for there to be $s(n)$ Fs is (as Frege would have said) for there to be an object u such that the number of Fs other than u is n. The individuation of any number n in terms of the condition for there to be n Fs holds in the actual world, however the actual world may be. In this case, it is also necessary. This is still all at the level of reference, individuation, and metaphysics.

Then at the level of thought, to have a canonical concept c of some natural number n is to have a fundamental procedure for determining whether there are c Fs for which it is immediately obvious that the procedure respects the condition for there to be n Fs, the condition that is individuative of the number n. Counting is such a procedure. So the transition from the premises that the distinct objects x, y, and z are F, and exhaust the Fs, to the conclusion that there are 3 Fs, if the conclusion is reached by counting applied to x, y, and z, is an a priori transition. The transition is guaranteed to be true in the actual world, whichever is the actual world, because it is underwritten by what is individuative of the number 3.

This treatment of the case of numerical quantifiers can be combined with that of $7+5 = 12$. We can thereby argue that the a priori status of 'If there are 7 Fs and 5 Gs, and nothing which is both F and G, then there are 12 things which are either F or G' can also be traced back to the phenomenon of concepts being individuated by their relations to the objects, properties, and relations they pick out.

IV. OBSERVATIONS ON THE PHENOMENON OF CONCEPTS TIED TO THE INDIVIDUATION OF OBJECTS AND PROPERTIES

I have been taking it throughout this paper that the a priori status of some content is a phenomenon at the level of sense. This may make it seem as if the a priori can only have to do with how we think of objects and properties. But when we realize that sometimes senses or ways of thinking are individuated by their relations to the very nature of what they pick out, it becomes clear that a priori truth can both be a phenomenon at the level of sense, and also have something to do with the nature of the objects or properties thought about. There is no incompatibility between those two characteristics.

The characterization of what it is for a concept to be tied to the individuation of its reference may make it sound as if this approach to such cases is committed to taking the ontology at the level of reference as somehow explanatorily prior.

But that is not so. All that is needed in these philosophical explanations of certain cases of the a priori is a *link* between the concept and the individuation of the reference. That link can still exist even for a theorist who regards, say, the ontology of natural numbers or other abstract objects as some kind of projection of certain kinds of discourse, or modes of thought. That is certainly not a view I would recommend; but such a theorist would still have access to the present treatment of some cases of the a priori.

Second, I will briefly consider the relation between a principle's having an priori status because its constituent concepts are tied to the individuation of the properties and relations it picks out, and one of Frege's characterizations of apriority. In a famous passage, Frege wrote:

It then depends on finding the proof and following it back up to the fundamental truths. If on this path one comes across only general logical laws and definitions, one has an analytic truth... But if it is not possible to carry through the proof without using truths which are not of a general logical nature, but belong to a particular domain of knowledge, then the proposition is a synthetic one. For a truth to be a posteriori, it is required that its proof should not go through without appeal to facts; that is, without appeal to unprovable truths lacking generality, and which contain assertions about particular objects. If on the contrary it is possible to carry through the proof wholly from general laws, which are neither capable of proof nor in need of it, then the truth is a priori.[15]

Few would want to argue that principles of colour exclusion are analytic in Frege's sense. But are such principles a priori by the characterization suggested by this passage? Is it possible to carry through proofs of them wholly from general laws which are neither capable of proof, not in need of it?[16] As Tyler Burge remarked to me, we have to take note of Frege's differentiation between the 'general logical laws' mentioned in Frege's characterization of analyticity, and the 'general laws', not necessarily logical, mentioned in Frege's condition for

---

[15] *Foundations of Arithmetic*, sect. 3, my translation (with some improvements thanks to David Wiggins). The original reads: 'Es kommt nun darauf an, den Beweis zu finden und ihn bis auf die Urwahrheiten zurückzuverfolgen. Stösst man auf diesem Wege nur auf die allgemeinen logischen Gesetze und auf Definitionen, so hat man eine analytische Wahrheit. ... Wenn es aber nicht möglich ist, den Beweis zu führen, ohne Wahrheiten zu benutzen, welche nicht allgemein logischer Natur sind, sondern such auf besonderes Wissengebiet beziehen, so ist der Satz ein synthetischer. Damit eine Wahrheit aposteriori sei, wird verlangt, dass ihr Beweis nicht ohne Berufung auf Thatsachen auskomme; d. h. auf unbeweisbare Wahrheiten ohne Allgemeinheit, die Aussagen von bestimmten Gegenständen enthalten. Ist es dagegen möglich, den Beweis ganz aus allgemeinen Gesetzen zu führen, die selber eines Beweises weder fähig noch bedürftig sind, so ist die Wahrheit apriori.' It is true that in this passage Frege is talking only about what makes a truth of mathematics an a priori truth. But no different criterion is suggested for other kinds of a priori truth; and his sufficient condition for being a posteriori is not confined to purely mathematical subject matter.

[16] I write 'suggested by this passage', because read strictly, Frege is here offering only a sufficient condition for a truth to be a priori. He may well also have believed it to be necessary. This is a complex and philosophically interesting question in Frege scholarship which I will have to forgo here.

apriority. Our question is to be understood as concerning the latter general, and not necessarily logical, laws.

The argument I offered earlier to the conclusion that no shade is both a shade of red and a shade of green relied on two assertions which Frege would classify as 'lacking generality'. It relied on the possession condition for the concept *red* of the colour red. That possession condition is not, as far as I can tell, a consequence of completely general laws alone. The argument also relied on principles about what individuates the particular colour red. These too are specific to the colour red. There was a dependence on the possession condition for the concept *red* in explaining the rationality (and relatively a priori character) of the transition from the experience, of any given shade which is clearly a shade of red, to 'That's a shade of red'. There was dependence on the individuation of the colour red in explaining why the argument is sound however the actual world turns out to be. There seems to be no satisfactory way to elaborate the soundness and a priori availability of this argument without appealing to truths about the particular colour red and the particular concept *red* (and, of course, their interrelations, which was the point of the preceding section).

It is true that I have relied upon a general philosophical theory of the way in which a relation between a concept and the individuation of the property or object it picks out can yield knowledge which is a priori. That general theory is formulated in terms which Frege would likely count as 'general laws'. But that general theory entails only conditionals of the form: if the relation between a property or object and a concept thereof is of a certain specified kind, then there will correspondingly exist a priori truths of a certain kind. To obtain specific truths which have an a priori status from the general theory, we need information about specific concepts, properties, and objects which are of the specified kind.

It has always been part of the rationalist position that understanding is a crucial resource in explaining a priori knowledge. Moderate rationalism is no exception. On the position I have outlined in the cases of colour and natural numbers, it is specifically a concept – that is, what is possessed in having understanding – which is tied to the conditions which individuate the object, property, or relation it picks out. But reflection on the quoted passage from Frege suggests that he may have been operating with a conception which recognizes three categories, of which, he seems to have held, only the first two may contain a priori truths. (a) There are the domain-independent logical laws. Arithmetical laws will reduce to these, in the presence of suitable definitions, if logicism is correct. (b) There are general laws which are domain-specific, but which are neither capable of proof nor in need of it. Frege famously held that geometry is a priori.[17] If the condition in the displayed passage is intended as a necessary, as well as a sufficient, condition of being a priori, Frege is thereby committed to saying that the axioms of geometry fall in this second category (b) (and thereby of course

---

[17] *Grundlagen*, sects. 87, 89.

acquires many a problem). (c) There are truths which are both domain-specific and specific to certain entities within that domain. Again, if Frege is offering a necessary condition of being a priori, then such truths as are in this category (c) will not be a priori under his account.

It is this last point that will elicit dissent on the part of the moderate rationalist who recognizes the consequences of the linking of certain concepts to the individuation of the properties or objects they pick out. That phenomenon generates a priori truths specific to particular concepts concerned with elements of a specific domain. The phenomenon is incompatible with simultaneous acceptance of the categorization (a) through (c), and of restriction of the a priori to the first two subcategories.

A rationalist may very reasonably want to distinguish between wholly general domain-unspecific principles and principles specific to particular subject matters. As far as I can see, however, there is no reason of principle to think that a priori knowledge must ultimately be explicable solely in terms of such general laws. There are even some reasons for doubting the coherence of such a position. For the same means by which one explains the possibility of a priori knowledge where it is not reducible to general laws also applies to general logical principles. What individuates a particular logical concept, whether one takes it to be a set of inferential rules, or an underlying implicit conception which specifies a contribution to truth-conditions, is arguably equally tied to the individuation of (for instance) a particular truth-function. If that is right, the a priori principles concerning specific objects or concepts come under the same general explanatory umbrella as the logical ones.

I also very briefly note the pertinence of the idea of something's being tied to the individuation of a property to the Kantian conception of pure intuition as an a priori means of establishing geometrical propositions. We can use some of the apparatus of this paper to give a limited defence of Kant's conception. Suppose just for this paragraph that we do not count imagination as experience, so that acceptance of a proposition on the basis of the deliverances of pure intuition could in principle at least be an a priori way of coming to know it. Pure intuition can be conceived of as a faculty which supplies representations whose content depends only on the constitutive properties of geometric objects – properties, lines, angles, and the rest. So one way of defending a neo-Kantian position about knowledge of pure geometry would be to note that in making geometrical judgements on the basis of the deliverances of pure intuition, one is being sensitive only to the constitutive properties of geometric objects. Judgements made on the basis of a proper exercise of pure intuition are thus a priori ways of coming to know. The relation of the faculty of pure intuition to what individuates geometrical objects is an essential component of the explanation of why this is so. One could develop this position without any idealism, transcendental or otherwise, and without any commitment to the a priori applicability of Euclidean geometry. Nor is the position one which embraces what I earlier rejected, viz. causal explanations of a priori knowledge by the truths known. The reason why judgements of pure geometry based on pure intuition will hold whichever world is the actual world is not (of course) that there is causal access to the non-actual. It is rather that only the properties and relations constitutive of geometrical objects are employed by pure intuition in the first place, when that faculty is properly exercised.[18]

V. A THIRD CASE: RATIONAL INTUITION AND IMPLICIT CONCEPTIONS

Some rationalists, and most famously Gödel, have pointed to phenomena which, they have said, we need rational intuition to explain. A brief list of these Gödelian phenomena would include the following.

(A1) We can have an understanding of some notions which goes beyond the axioms (or instances of axioms) we can write down for them. This is evidenced by the fact that we can discover new axioms which do not follow from those we previously accepted.[19] A fortiori, then, we can have an understanding of some notions which goes beyond the principles we must find immediately, and non-inferentially, compelling in order to possess those notions. This consequence as formulated is of course in my terms, rather than being a report of one of Gödel's theses. It is, however, a consequence all the same.

(A2) We can attain, in ways not based on sense perception, a better explicit statement of the nature of our notions, and thereby reach new axioms, which do not follow from those we previously accepted, and which are a priori truths.[20]

(B) It is part of the task of mathematics and logic to discover such new axioms or principles. Given that task, the use of rational intuition in these disciplines is ineliminable.[21]

(C) The notion of proof cannot be formalistically characterized. The notion of 'that which provides conclusive evidence' for a proposition cannot, even within the domain of mathematics, be something purely formalistic.[22]

(D) There may be finite, non-mechanical procedures which make use of the

---

[18] I believe the position outlined here is in the spirit of the remarks about the relation between geometry and a priori intuition by B. Longuenesse, *Kant and the Capacity to Judge* (Princeton: Princeton University Press, 1998): 290–1.

[19] Some sample passages from Gödel, amongst many others: 'Some basic theorems on the foundations of mathematics and their implications' (1995) 305, 309; 'The modern development of the foundations of mathematics' (ibid.) 385. All page references to these papers come from *Kurt Gödel Collected Works, III: Unpublished Lectures and Essays*, ed. S. Feferman, J. Dawson jun., W. Goldfarb, C. Parsons, and R. Solovay (New York: Oxford University Press, 1995).

[20] Sample passage: 'The modern development' (ibid.) 383.

[21] Sample passage: 'Is mathematics syntax of language?' (ibid.) 346–7; also in *Collected Works, III*.

[22] Sample passage: 'Undecidable diophantine propositions' (ibid.) 164.

fact that 'we understand abstract terms more and more precisely as we go on using them.'[23]

(A)–(D) do not exhaust what Gödel said about rational intuition. (D) also raises the issue of whether some sound procedures lie beyond the realm of the mechanical, an issue for which a full treatment would need some other occasion. But the Gödelian phenomena (A)–(C) are already ones which a philosophical theory of understanding and the a priori must explain somehow or other, if it is not (implausibly) simply to deny their existence. Gödel employed his underdeveloped quasi-perceptual theory of rational intuition in attempting to account for these phenomena. Though we may reject Gödel's philosophical account of rational intuition, it is, as Charles Parsons says, a 'real problem . . . for a theory of reason to give a better account'.[24] For the moderate rationalist, the challenge is to explain these phenomena by reference to properties of the (non-exotic) understanding involved in possessing the concepts involved in the axioms, proofs, and procedures Gödel is discussing.

More specifically, the moderate rationalist's task is once again to find in these Gödelian instances what I earlier called the key relation between the following three items:

(1) the possession conditions for the concepts in the axioms and principles Gödel discusses;
(2) the semantic values of those concepts; and
(3) the a priori way in which these axioms and principles come to be known in the Gödelian cases.

I want to suggest that the key relation for the Gödelian phenomena involves implicit conceptions of the properties and relations mentioned in the a priori axioms and principles.[25]

An implicit conception is, amongst other things, a content-involving subpersonal state, involved in fundamental cases in the explanation of a thinker's application of a given concept or expression to something. The content of the implicit conception specifies the condition for something's falling under the concept, or for the expression to be true of an object. To possess the concept, or to understand the expression, is to have the right implicit conception for it. Since possessing the concept and understanding are notions at the personal level, an implicit conception also has a characterization at the personal level. I would maintain that the implicit conception underlying the concept 'natural number' has the content given in these three familiar clauses:

[23] K. Gödel, *Collected Works, II: Publications 1938–1974*, ed. S. Feferman *et al.* (New York: Oxford University Press, 1990), at 306.
[24] 'Platonism and Mathematical Intuition in Kurt Gödel's Thought', *Bulletin of Symbolic Logic* 1 (1995): 44–74, at 64.
[25] For more on implicit conceptions, see my 'Implicit Conceptions, Understanding and Rationality'.

(1) 0 is a natural number;
(2) the successor of a natural number is a natural number;
(3) only what can be determined to be a natural number on the basis of (1) and (2) is a natural number.

As I emphasized in earlier work, it may sometimes be hard to articulate the content of an implicit conception underlying one of one's own concepts.[26] To articulate its content may be a major achievement. The process of articulation involves reflection and unification of the cases in which one knows that the concept does apply, and of the cases in which one knows it does not. Once the content of the implicit conception is correctly articulated, a thinker may be in a position to learn new principles, involving the concept he was employing all along, and which had not previously occurred to him. In the example of the natural numbers, one such principle would be the axiom that every natural number has only finitely many predecessors.

If it is true that to possess the concept *natural number* is to possess an implicit conception with the content (1)–(2), then this is also another case of a concept tied to the individuation of the property it picks out. For it is highly plausible that the conditions (1)–(2) also specify what it is to be a natural number, specify what is constitutive of that property.

Now we can take the Gödelian phenomena, starting with the fact the understanding of some notions outruns the general principles the thinker has so far written down for it, or even the principles he must be able to articulate in order to be credited with the relevant concepts. This is the Gödelian point I summarized in (A1) and (A2). If understanding sometimes consists in having an underlying implicit conception, then it is predictable that understanding in such cases may outrun the abstract schemata for the concept that one may be able to state. An account of understanding which appeals to implicit conceptions will already be opposed to the view of mathematics as 'syntax of language' to which Gödel was so opposed, and it will cite some of the same phenomena in its grounds for opposition.[27] Already in the humble case of the concept *natural number*, we mentioned a new a priori principle. Acceptance of the principle that any natural number has only finitely many predecessors is not something primitively written into possession of the concept of a natural number, along the lines minimal theories would have to propose. The principle is rather something whose correctness can be worked out by an ordinary user of the concept, on the basis of an understanding which is characterized without reference to that principle. As Gödel would say, it is an 'unfolding' of the concept we already had prior to formulation of the principle.

This explanation in terms of implicit conceptions does not require any appeal

[26] 'Implicit Conceptions, Understanding and Rationality'.
[27] See esp. the two versions of 'Is Mathematics Syntax of Language?' in *Collected Works, III*.

to a quasi-perceptual faculty of rational intuition to account for the phenomena. It is right to reject theories of understanding which cannot accommodate the phenomena, wrong to suppose that it is only the more exotic theories of rational intuition which can explain them.

Perhaps the most salient Gödelian case, for which the capacity for rational intuition has also been frequently and famously invoked by Roger Penrose, is that of the Gödel sentence g for a given recursively axiomatized theory with sufficient expressive resources to frame that sentence.[28] Penrose's view is that we can explain our knowledge that the Gödel sentence g is true only by appeal to what he calls 'mathematical insight'; and this, he says, eludes formalistic characterization. In 1990 he wrote,

by the very way that such a Gödel proposition is constructed, we can *see*, using our insight and understand[ing—CP] about what the symbols in the formal system are supposed to mean, that the Gödel proposition is actually *true*! This tells us that the very concepts of truth, meaning and mathematical insight cannot be encapsulated within any formalist scheme.[29]

In *Shadows of the Mind*, five years later, he says that Gödel's theorem tells us 'the insights that are available to human mathematicians – indeed to anyone who can think logically with understanding and imagination – lie beyond anything that can be formalized as a set of rules. Rules can be a partial substitute for understanding, but they can never replace it entirely.'[30]

The significance of Penrose's argument, and thereby what is required to address the argument, has in my judgement been missed in the extensive discussions his argument has generated. There is a curious parallel here with the published discussions of John Lucas's partially similar views. I agree with David Lewis's remark that many of Lucas's critics have missed something important in Lucas's argument.[31] In the critics' rush to block arguments for the views which Penrose and Lucas reach, the critics have missed, and failed to address, important insights about truth and understanding which are involved in their respective cases. These oversights of many of the critics have then led Penrose and Lucas to think that their case is stronger than it really is. But let us move right to the core issue in Penrose's argument.

Suppose we accept some particular theory T, with a recursive set of axioms, and which includes first-order arithmetic. If we accept the theory, rationality requires us to accept that its axioms are true and that its inference rules are truth-preserving. So rationality requires us to accept that the theory is consistent. So far, it seems to me, this argument should be uncontroversial. Gödel gave a method of

---

[28] For a recent statement, see R. Penrose, *Shadows of the Mind: A Search for the Missing Science of Consciousness* (London: Random House, 1995).

[29] R. Penrose, 'Précis', in *Behavioural and Brain Sciences* 13 (1990): 643–705, at 648.

[30] *Shadows of the Mind*: 72.

[31] See D. Lewis, *Papers in Philosophical Logic* (Cambridge: Cambridge University Press, 1998): 166.

constructing a Gödel-sentence *g* for the theory, of which we can prove that if the theory is consistent, then *g* is not provable. This too is uncontroversial: these are theorems. So if we accept the theory, we are committed to holding that no number is the Gödel-number of a proof of *g*. By Gödel's method of construction, the sentence 'Every number is not the Gödel-number of a proof of *g*' is the sentence *g* itself. So we have just given an informal argument that, if we accept the original theory T, then it is rational to accept its Gödel sentence *g*, even though that sentence it is unprovable in T. This should still all be uncontroversial.

The controversy enters—or ought to enter—over the following issue: what is the correct account of our grasp of the meaning of universal quantification over the natural numbers, when it is such that we can appreciate the soundness of this reasoning to the truth of *g*? This is the crucial question on which discussions of Penrose's argument ought to be focused. Any treatment of Penrose's views, however convincing on other issues, will not have engaged with his argument unless it addresses the question of the nature of this understanding of such universal quantifications. Several writers have objected that nothing in Penrose's argument rules out the existence of an algorithm which correctly describes our mathematical reasoning, but which we cannot know to be such a correct description.[32] The objection is surely good; but it does not answer Penrose's question about understanding. Unless a better account of understanding is forthcoming, Penrose will go on thinking that a faculty of rational intuition involving mysterious relations to a Platonic realm is required for understanding; in any case, he will not have been given a full answer.

It seems to me that what is right in Penrose's argument is that the meaning of one or more expressions in the Gödel sentence *g* goes beyond anything wholly determined by the axioms and inference-rules of the theory T. If the meanings of all the expressions in *g* were fixed only by those axioms and inference-rules, it would be completely unexplained why *g* is true (let alone how we can know that *g* is true), since those axioms and inference-rules do not determine the correctness of *g*.

The critical question is then: what is the correct account of meaning and understanding for the expressions in *g*? I will be taking it that the important expression in this sentence for present purposes is the universal quantifier. The other expressions in the Gödel sentence are all symbols for primitive recursive functions and relations, whose meaning is plausibly fully determined by their standard recursive characterizations. We can, however, explain all three of our understanding of universal quantification, the truth of the Gödel sentence *g*, and our epistemic access to its truth under this hypothesis: that to understand the universal quantifier is to have an implicit conception with the content

[32] For a vivid statement of the objection, see H. Putnam's review of *Shadows of the Mind*, under the title 'The Best of All Possible Minds?', *New York Times*, Book Review Section, 20 Nov. 1994.

(U)   Any sentence of the form 'All Fs are φ is true' if and only if every object
           of which F is true has the property expressed by φ.

The rational thinker familiar with the proof of Gödel's theorem knows that if the
original recursively axiomatized theory T is consistent, then each of '0 is not the
Gödel number of a proof of *g*', '1 is not the Gödel-number of a proof of *g*', '2 is
not the Gödel-number of a proof of *g*', . . . is true. A thinker whose understanding of universal quantification consists in possession of an implicit conception
with the content (U) can correctly and knowledgeably move from these ω
premises to the conclusion that 'Every natural number is not the Gödel-number
of a proof of *g*' is also true. Here I am taking it that the quantification over properties is unrestricted, and includes the property of being true.[33]

That (U) is the content of the implicit conception underlying this understanding is something which shows up in the pattern of cases in which a universal
quantification is evaluated as true, and the pattern of cases in which a universal
quantification is evaluated as false. The thinker may not yet have made explicit
the content (U), though of course he may do so. It is not always necessary, in reaching knowledge based on possession of concepts underlain by an implicit conception, that the thinker himself make explicit the content of that conception (one can
know that some seen object is a chair without being able to define the concept *chair*
explicitly). The case also, incidentally, involves a second implicit conception—that
underlying the concept *natural number*, which we mentioned earlier.

This account of knowledge of the proposition expressed by the Gödel sentence
is in line with the moderate rationalist's programme. The account appeals to a
property of the understanding of universal quantification, the property it has of
consisting in possession of an implicit conception with the content (U). So on the
present treatment, we have another case in which the phenomena which have
been cited in support of rational intuition are genuine; but they do not require any
exotic form of intuition or insight for their explanation.

One could imagine Penrose objecting to this account. 'Why', he might say,
'cannot we add the axiom (U), which you certainly accept as true, to the theory
T, together with appropriate axioms for truth? When we do that, though, there will
be a new Gödel-sentence g(TU) for the expanded theory; and how are you to give
an account of truth, meaning and knowledge for that sentence g(TU)?'

Here, though, we must move very carefully. If we have a theory which includes
disquotational principles for a truth-predicate, and is also capable of referring to
all of its own expressions, we will be able to formulate the Liar Paradox, and the
theory will be inconsistent. I think that (U), with its unrestricted quantification
over genuine properties and meaningful expressions, does capture the content of
the implicit conception underlying our grasp of universal quantification. (It does

---

[33] I rely on the natural extension (to the case of properties) of R. Cartwright's important
defence of the legitimacy of such quantifications for the case of objects. See his 'Speaking of
Everything', *Nous* 28 (1994): 1–20.

so in a non-reductive fashion, of course.) But precisely because of the problem of inconsistency, it does not follow that (U) can be embedded in just any theory which also uses a truth-predicate, and includes disquotation for all the sentences formulable in the language of the theory. The inconsistency stems not from any error in (U), but from permitting ungrounded uses of the truth-predicate in combination with an unrestricted principle of disquotation. The various known ways around this obstacle, some of which impose hierarchies, do not show that there is anything wrong with (U). Nor do they show that our grasp of truth is not capturable in general principles. They do not, in my view, even show that truth is an indefinitely extensible concept or property. They show only that one needs to take care in formulating a theory which contains a truth-predicate, contains axioms governing the truth-predicate, and also contains apparatus for talking about all of its own sentences, including those containing the truth-predicate.

There is an argument that any view which tries to explain meaning proof-theoretically will have difficulty in giving a satisfactory answer to the Penrose-like question about meaning and understanding. It seems to me that the symbols for universal quantification over the natural numbers have exactly the same meaning when they occur in sentences formulable in some particular theory T, and as they occur in the Gödel sentence for T. Since the Gödel-sentence is a true universal quantification over the natural numbers which is not establishable by the methods of T, the person who accepts a proof-theoretical view of meaning must explain how such universal quantifications when they occur in sentences formulable in the language of T have the same meaning as the quantifier when it occurs in the Gödel sentence. The person who tries to explain meaning in proof-theoretic, or more generally evidential, terms may fairly say that the meanings are rather similar, though distinct. It seems to me, however, that the meanings are exactly the same.

The same challenge arises not only for proof-theoretical or evidential views. It also arises for a theorist who combines the following two theses. (1) He tries to explain the notion of natural number not modally, but has in place of clause (c) above some condition to the effect that the principle of arithmetical induction applies to the natural numbers; but (2) he does not think that one can quantify over all properties, but only over a limited totality. The theorist who holds this combination will also be vulnerable to the objection that he is forced to acknowledge only similar meanings, when there is really identity of meaning. For when the truth-predicate is added to a range of properties to which arithmetical induction can be applied, this theorist will have to say that the resulting 'new' notion of natural number and universal quantification over them is one for which new sentences can be shown to be true which could not be so shown on the old conception. But it seems to me, once again, that we ought not to say that the notion 'natural number' is ambiguous, or requires further determination.

I should also emphasize that there will be no problem for yet another theorist who follows the preceding theorist in respect (1), but does not follow him on (2).

This latest theorist prefers to explain the notion of natural number with induction written into the third clause of its characterization, but also permits the use of unrestricted quantification over properties, a range which will include the property of being true. This theorist will not suffer from any problem of ambiguity. This point also shows, incidentally, that the challenge from ambiguity to proof-theoretic views of meaning still arises, and can be answered, even if we do not use modality in the third clause of the characterization of a natural number.

The moderate rationalist will also agree with Gödel about (B), that is, that it is part of the task of mathematics or logic to discover new axioms or principles which do not follow from those we have already articulated, but which are nonetheless correct, and a priori, for the concepts we possess. We can learn, for a given subject matter, new a priori axioms which do not follow from those we already accept, and if 'rational intuition' is used to pick out the means, whatever it is, by which we attain such knowledge, then rational intuition is ineliminable in mathematics. Even in the case of axioms or axiom-schemata we already accept, their acceptability depends upon their respecting some meanings not explained in terms of acceptance of those axioms. We have to reflect and work out their correctness for the notions they contain, even if we have understood their vocabulary for many years.[34]

Gödel's third point (C), that the notion of proof cannot be purely formalistically explicated, will also be supported by the moderate rationalist. A formalistic account will not necessarily capture all the meaning-supported transitions which are sustained by the content of an implicit conception underlying a concept. (Even when a formalistic account extensionally captures them, what *makes* something a proof is its honouring of the links supported by that meaning.) Consider the ω-rule, that if F(0), F(1), F(2), are each provable in a system, then 'For all natural numbers n, F(n)' is provable. The moderate rationalist, again without any exotic claims about intuition, will say the following. Given the implicit conception underlying universal quantification, and the implicit conception underlying the notion of a natural number, the ω-rule is correct, and this is so not because it is a reasonable 'extension' of a meaning, or a further stipulation or determination of meaning, but because it is validated by the content of those two implicit

---

[34] For a suggested explanation of this phenomenon, see my 'Implicit Conceptions, Understanding and Rationality'. Gödel makes remarks which are consonant with this position, though what he says is not decisive against proof-theoretic explications of meaning. He writes 'It certainly looks as if one must *first* understand the meaning of a proposition *before* he can understand a proof of it, so that the meaning of 'all' could not be defined in terms of the meaning of 'proof'' (*Collected Works III*: 313). This is not decisive, since the proof-theoretical view can distinguish between implicit and explicit knowledge of meaning-determining rules. The proof-theoretical view may say that the prior understanding to which Gödel alludes involves only implicit, perhaps practical, knowledge of proof-theoretical role. Gödel goes on to add something more problematic for a proof-theoretical view: 'one may conjecture the truth of a universal proposition . . . and at the same time conjecture that no general proof for this fact exists' (ibid.).

conceptions underlying the concepts of natural number and universal quantification.

Another type of case in which Gödel notoriously wanted to apply his own conception of rational intuition is that of the rational acceptance of new axioms in set theory. He seems to have been optimistic that new, rationally acceptable axioms would eventually be found to decide the Continuum Hypothesis. I suspect many set theorists and philosophers of mathematics would agree with Charles Parsons's remark that 'The spectre of the concept of an arbitrary infinite set being a 'vague notion' that needs to be 'determined in a definite way' by new axioms isn't easily banished'.[35] It should not, however, be any part of the view of the moderate rationalist who implements his programme in some range of cases by appeal to implicit conceptions that the implicit conception underlying some particular concept of an abstract science should always be such as to determine the truth-value of such matters as the Continuum Hypothesis. What matters to the moderate rationalist are rather two points: (i) that there is a distinction of principle between those cases in which the underlying implicit conceptions are determinate in a given respect and those in which they are not; and (ii) the cases in which there is determinacy in a given respect can be used to explain some of the cases in which rationalists have made appeals to rational intuition. The moderate rationalist is not committed by the very nature of his position to endorsing the more optimistic estimates of which hypotheses and proposed axioms might eventually be decided by the implicit conceptions underlying set theory.

This moderate rationalist defence of a role for rational intuition may also part company at another point with Gödel if he held that the use of rational intuition in mathematics provides a kind of evidence that is unique to mathematics.[36] The idea of an implicit conception underlying a concept is entirely general, and can in principle be found in almost any domain, well beyond those of logic and mathematics. Implicit conceptions may underlie some observational concepts, some psychological concepts, some moral concepts, some political concepts, to name but a few other subject matters. Consider the following principles: for the observational concept *runs*, that when a person is running there is a moment at which both of the runner's feet are off the ground; for the psychological concept *being ashamed*, that shame about action requires identification with the person or institution whose action is in question. These principles can be informative to someone who has the concept. Explicit knowledge of them is not written into their possession conditions. Rather, they articulate one component of the implicit conception underlying grasp of the relevant concepts. Grander, though no doubt more controversial, examples could be

---

[35] 'Platonism and Mathematical Intuition in Kurt Gödels' Thought', 64.

[36] That it does so is either asserted outright, or attributed to Gödel, in R. Tieszen's excellent Critical Notice of Gödel's Collected Papers in *Mind* 107 (1998): 21932, at 230 (first sentence). If an attribution to Gödel is intended, Tieszen does not give chapter and verse.

given. In appealing to implicit conceptions to explain these phenomena of rational intuition, the moderate rationalist is assimilating rational intuition in the
Gödelian cases to something much more general than the logical and mathematical. If we can attain it, a uniform explanation for the more general phenomenon seems to me desirable.

VI. CONCLUDING REMARKS

The scope of explanations of a priori status which appeal to concepts tied to the
individuation of their references is not restricted to the cases I have so far
discussed. Consider the principle-based treatment of metaphysical necessity, for
instance, which I offered in *Being Known*. On that treatment, understanding metaphysical necessity involves having tacit knowledge of the conditions under which
a putatively possible world-description represents a genuine possibility. That is,
possession of the concept of metaphysical necessity is tied to the conditions
which make something a genuine possibility. We can use this to explain the a
priori status of certain principles of modal logic. If the thinker comes to accept
those principles by drawing on the information he tacitly knows, and that information states what it is to be a genuine possibility, those principles will be guaranteed to hold in the actual world, whichever is the actual world. The case of
metaphysical necessity also, incidentally, further illustrates the point that there
will be cases in which a full explanation of the a priori will require one to address
fundamental metaphysical issues about a domain.

   In closing, I want to emphasize that in trying to delineate the phenomenon of
concepts tied to the individuation of what they pick out, I have been concerned
with only one species of explanation of a priori knowledge. Other examples of a
priori knowledge have other kinds of explanation. It is equally the task of the
moderate rationalist to supply these other kinds of explanation too. Indeed, reflection on the treatment I offered of the arithmetical case strongly suggests that other
kinds of explanation must also exist. For that treatment presupposed the a priori
existence of arithmetical objects, properties, and relations. A different, or at least
an extended, model must be appropriate for explaining a priori knowledge of
existence in the first place.

   A second, very different, kind of case which shows the need for other kinds of
explanation is that of 'I am here'. This case is one in which, it certainly seems, all
the work in explaining why it is a priori is done in saying how the referents of the
indexicals are picked out. The explanation has almost nothing to do with the
nature of what is picked out, in strong contrast to many of the cases on which I
have been focusing in this paper. The content 'I am here' is of course not a problem for moderate rationalism, but it does show that the moderate rationalist must
acknowledge many subvarieties of explanation within the overarching conception

of the relation between concepts and ways of coming to know. I conjecture that in attempting to execute the moderate rationalist's programme over the full range of examples of the a priori, we will learn more about the many different ways in which a thinker may be related to the subject matter of her thoughts.

12

Implicit Definition and the A Priori

Bob Hale and Crispin Wright

1. INTRODUCTION

An explicit definition aims to supply a semantically equivalent[1] expression of the same syntactic type as its definiendum. Implicit definition, taken as the complement of explicit, embraces a variety of subtypes. What all have in common is the idea that we may fix the meaning of an expression by imposing some form of constraint on the use of longer expressions—typically, whole sentences—containing it. On one traditionally influential conception, this constraint is imposed by the (putatively) *free stipulation* of the truth of a certain sentence, or range of sentences,[2] embedding the definiendum and composed of otherwise previously understood vocabulary.

Our interest here is in a general and a more specific issue about the role and utility of implicit definition. The general issue is whether, and if so under what conditions, the meanings of any significant class of expressions—for instance, logical constants, basic terms of fundamental mathematical theories, or theoretical terms of empirical science—might be constituted by implicit definitions; the more specific issue is whether, if so, such definitions have a role to play in a satisfactory account of the possibility of a priori knowledge of logic and mathematics. We shall refer to the thesis that at least some important kinds of non-inferential a priori knowledge are founded in implicit definition as *the traditional connection*.

We have been much helped by reactions to earlier versions of this paper from and/or discussion of the issues with Jim Edwards, Paul Horwich, Gary Kemp, Jimmy Lenman, Fraser MacBride, Andrew McGonigal, Christopher Peacocke, Adam Rieger, Pat Shaw, and Nick Zangwill. The paper was prepared during Bob Hale's tenure of a British Academy Research Readership; he is grateful to the Academy for its generous support. Crispin Wright gratefully acknowledges the support of the Leverhulme Trust.

[1] Typically, synonymous—but depending on the purposes in hand, some weaker kind of semantic equivalence (such as co-reference) may suffice.

[2] For simplicity, we suppress this qualification in the sequel.

Affirmative answers to both the general and the specific question have found supporters throughout analytical philosophy's first century.[3] In particular, Gentzen's idea, that the meanings of the logical constants should be regarded as implicitly defined by the stipulation of the usual rules for their introduction and elimination in inferential contexts, has been accepted by much of the most important recent philosophical reflection on the epistemology of logic.[4] We ourselves have canvassed a similar, neo-Fregean, view of certain classical mathematical theories as founded on the stipulation of *abstraction principles*—principles like Hume's Principle[5] which share the form of Frege's ill-fated Basic Law V but which, unlike that principle, may reasonably be regarded as consistent.[6] However, there has also been no shortage of antagonists, recent and contemporary. The idea that the holding of certain sentences 'true by convention' might somehow provide a foundation for a priori knowledge generally has been regarded with suspicion ever since Quine's 'Truth by Convention',[7] while 'Two Dogmas of Empiricism'[8] sowed the seed for a widespread scepticism, persisting to this day, not just about analyticity and the a priori but about the very notion of meaning which Carnap and the other early friends of implicit definition thought such definitions might determine.

Quine's more general scepticism is not on our agenda here—though we record the opinion that the two principal lines of argument in 'Two Dogmas' (that the notion of analyticity resists all non-circular explanation, and anyway fails to accommodate the revisability in principle of all statements that participate in total empirical science) respectively impose a quite impossible standard for conceptual

---

[3] For a very comprehensive discussion, see J. Alberto Coffa, *The Semantic Tradition from Kant to Carnap: To the Vienna Station* (Cambridge: Cambridge University Press, 1991).

[4] For instance, it is supported, notwithstanding important differences, by each of Michael Dummett, Christopher Peacocke, and Paul Boghossian—see e.g. Dummett: *The Logical Basis of Metaphysics* (London: Duckworth, 1991); Peacocke: 'Understanding Logical Constants: A Realist's Account', *Proceedings of the British Academy* 73 (1987), *A Study of Concepts* (Cambridge, Mass.: MIT Press, 1992), 'Proof and Truth' in John Haldane and Crispin Wright (eds.), *Reality, Representation and Projection* (New York and Oxford: Oxford University Press, 1993); 'How are A Priori Truths Possible?' *European Journal of Philosophy* 1 (1993); Boghossian: 'Analyticity Reconsidered', *Noûs* 30 (1996); 'Analyticity' in Bob Hale and Crispin Wright (eds.), *A Companion to the Philosophy of Language* (Oxford: Blackwell, 1997).

[5] That is, the principle—under discussion in Frege's *Grundlagen* §§63–7, where Hume is (somewhat generously) credited with having recognized its correctness—that the number of Fs is the same as the number of Gs iff there is a one–one correlation between the Fs and the Gs.

[6] More precisely, the system got by adjoining Hume's Principle to second-order logic can be shown to be consistent relative to second-order arithmetic. See George Boolos's 'The Consistency of Frege's *Foundations of Arithmetic*' in J. Thomson (ed.), *On Being and Saying: Essays in Honor of Richard Cartwright* (Cambridge, Mass.: MIT Press 1987): 3–20, along with other works to which Boolos there makes reference, and the first appendix to George Boolos and Richard Heck, 'Die Grundlagen der Arithmetik §§82–3', in Matthias Schirn (ed.), *The Philosophy of Mathematics Today* (Oxford: Clarendon Press, 1998).

[7] Originally published in O. H. Lee (ed.), *Philosophical Essays for A. N. Whitehead* (New York: Longmans, 1936).

[8] Originally published in *Philosophical Review* 60 (1951) and subsequently reprinted in Quine's *From a Logical Point of View* (Harvard: Harvard University Press, 1953).

integrity and confuse what is analytic, or known a priori,[9] with what is indefeasi-
bly certain. However, we wholly endorse what we take to be one principal point
of 'Truth by Convention': even if conceiving of certain axioms and first principles[10] as implicit definitions may provide the means to explain how a priori
knowledge is possible of the truth of the propositions which they express, this
could not possibly be the model of *all* a priori knowledge—for it has nothing to
offer if we seek to understand our capacity for novel inference and our recognition of hitherto unratified logical consequences.

This limitation needs to be acknowledged from the start. But some recent
writers have challenged the capacity of implicit definition to sustain even the
epistemologically more modest role of underwriting local cases of the traditional
connection. Certainly, it can seem prima facie puzzling how exactly the matter
is to work. We take some sentence containing—in the simplest case—just one
hitherto unexplained expression. We stipulate that this sentence is to count as
true. The effect is somehow to bring it about that the unexplained expression
acquires a meaning of such a kind that a true thought is indeed expressed by the
sentence—a thought which we understand and moreover know to be true, without incurring any further epistemological responsibility, just in virtue of the stipulation. How does this happen? Paul Horwich, for one, has argued that it doesn't
happen: that there is no way whereby, merely by deciding that a sentence
containing some hitherto undefined expression is to count as true, we can be
assured not merely that that expression takes on a meaning but, more, that the
meaning it takes on so configures itself in tandem with our previous understanding of the remaining part of the sentence that the whole expresses a true
proposition.[11]

Horwich's scepticism is less radical than Quine's. He believes in meanings,
proposes his own account of their constitution in terms of use, and does see
implicit definition as playing a role in the determination of meanings. But—and
here's the rub—what plays this role, in his view, is our (mere) *acceptance* of the
sentences which implicitly define a given expression. This acceptance in turn may
contribute towards determining a meaning-constituting pattern of use for that
expression. But there can be no a priori likelihood, in Horwich's opinion, that it
is acceptance of a *truth*. That is a further matter, to be determined by how things
fare with the theory in which the definitions in question participate.[12]

---

[9] Quine, to the detriment of his polemic, made no distinction between these of course.

[10] By no means all, it should be noted. It would not be plausible, for instance, to see the
meanings of any expression as constituted in implicit definition if any matrix for an implicit
definition—the previously understood sentence-frame in which the definiendum is placed—
would have to contain an equivalent expression. (That will be the fate of expressions for the
conditional, on the conception of implicit definition on which we will eventually converge
below.)

[11] Cf. Paul Horwich, *Meaning* (Oxford: Clarendon Press, 1998: ch. 6, or his 'Implicit Definition, Analytic Truth and Apriori Knowledge', *Noûs* 31 (1997): 423–40.

[12] Cf. *Meaning*: 8, 143.

This view of the matter seems to incorporate one definite advantage. An apparent drawback of the idea that knowledge of implicitly definitional postulates is a priori knowledge is that it seems to leave no room for the suggestion that it is the very hypotheses of empirical scientific theory which are the prime determinants of the meanings of the theoretical terms which they contain. Horwich's position, by contrast, is designed to allow our mere acceptance of such hypotheses to fit them with a meaning-determining role, without compromise of their being hostage to subsequent empirical evidence. There is a point here to reckon with. Although considerations of space will prevent us from considering the issues to do with empirical theoretical terms in any detail, we accept it as a constraint upon any account of implicit definition designed to underwrite the traditional connection that it should somehow match this apparent advantage[13] of Horwich's account—that it should be broadly consonant with the idea that it is via their role in empirically revisable scientific theories that theoretical terms (at least partially) acquire their meaning.

Our programme in the sequel is as follows. In Section 2, we will review Horwich's objections to the traditional view of implicit definition as underwriting at least some a priori knowledge. It seems to us that the critical thrust of these objections entirely depends upon a certain model of what, if the traditional conception of implicit definition[14] is to be sustained, such definitions must accomplish—a model which we believe should be rejected. In Section 3 we shall outline a different conception of how the traditional connection had best be supposed to work and, in Section 4, begin to explore some of its ramifications for the metaphysics of meaning, specifically, for the question: when does fixing a use explain a meaning? In Section 5, we shall—all too briefly— sketch an approach whereby a conception of implicit definition which underwrites the traditional connection might also, without compromise of their empirical revisability, allow scientific theories themselves a role in determining the meanings of their distinctive vocabulary. Finally, in Section 6 we will connect that discussion with objections proposed by Hartry Field and Kit Fine[15] to our preferred view of the status of neo-Fregean abstraction principles.

---

[13] 'Apparent' because we don't think Horwich actually does secure this advantage—see Sect. 5 below.

[14] i.e. as proceeding through stipulation of the truth of some sentential context(s) of the definiendum.

[15] Hartry Field, 'Platonism for Cheap? Crispin Wright on Frege's Context Principle', *Canadian Journal of Philosophy* 14 (1984): 637–62, repr. in Field's *Realism, Mathematics and Modality* (Oxford: Blackwell, 1989): 147–70; Kit Fine, 'The Limits of Abstraction' in Matthias Schirn (ed.), *The Philosophy of Mathematics Today* (Oxford: Clarendon Press, 1998): 503–629.

2. A MISGUIDED MODEL

Horwich asks:

How exactly could it come about that our regarding a certain (perhaps conjunctive) sentence '#*f*' as *true* would provide the constituent '*f*' with a meaning, and what exactly is the meaning that '*f*' would acquire?[16]

He supplies on behalf of the view he wishes to oppose the answer that 'the decision to regard "#*f*" as true is, implicitly, a decision to give "*f*" the *meaning it would need to have* in order that "#*f*" be true'.[17] A number of problems are then, of course, immediately suggested by the reference in this answer to '*the* meaning "*f*" would need to have for "#*f*" to be true'. What ensures that there *is* any such a meaning? And what ensures that there is *just one* such meaning? For instance, the possibility cannot be discounted that, since the procedure of implicit definition assumes that the matrix '#–' already has a specific meaning, there simply is no meaning that '*f*' could take that would render '#*f*' true; '# –' might be such that no matter what meaning '*f*' had, '#*f*' would be false. One not very interesting case would be if '#_' were a conjunction one of whose conjuncts is a closed and false sentence—Horwich offers 'Snow is green and the moon is _'. A more interesting, classic example would be provided by the attempt to fix the meaning of a functional expression, intended to denote a function from properties to objects, by means of the matrix:

$$\forall F \forall G (\ldots F = \ldots G \leftrightarrow \forall x (Fx \leftrightarrow Gx))$$

from which, by applying the matrix to the predicate R defined by $Rx \leftrightarrow \exists F(x = \ldots F \wedge \neg Fx)$, we can derive Russell's contradiction: $R(\ldots R) \leftrightarrow \neg R (\ldots R)$. Here it would obviously be of no avail to attempt to stipulate that '*f*' is to mean just what it needs to mean in order to render:

$$\forall F \forall G (f(F) = f(G) \leftrightarrow \forall x (Fx \leftrightarrow Gx))$$

true.

One might quite properly say that in this and similar cases (for instance, Prior's connective 'tonk') that there *is* no meaning for '*f*' which renders '#*f*' true, because there *can* be none. But this way of expressing the matter has dangerous associations, to which Horwich succumbs. The danger is that of slipping into a picture—which will strike anyone but an extreme realist about meanings as tendentious—of implicit definition as aimed at hitting on some (unique) pre-existing meaning, as if it were akin to an attempt at *reference-fixing*. If some London policeman in the 1890s were to say, 'Let's call the perpetrator of these

---

[16] *Meaning*: 132.   [17] Ibid. 132–3 (our emphasis).

ghastly crimes, "Jack the Ripper", the success of his proposal would naturally be hostage to the truth of the assumption that there was indeed a (unique) perpetrator of the murders—that the grievously disfigured corpses were not the results of some bizarre series of accidents, for instance. Likewise when someone stipulates, 'Let "f" have whatever meaning it would need to have in order that "$\#f$" be true', the proposal is hostage to the possibility of there *being* such a meaning—a hostage that may not be redeemed in certain cases, as just noted. But the analogy obscures the point that, for any but the extreme realist, the existence of an appropriate meaning is not an antecedent fact of metaphysics, so to speak, but—(to oversimplify horribly; qualifications to follow)—a *matter of our intent*. In brief, it is a matter not of hoping that a platonic realm of meanings can put forward a denizen to satisfy the condition expressed by the stipulation but a matter merely of whether the stipulation *succeeds in avoiding certain operational drawbacks*— of which inconsistency is one (but only one) glaring example. If it so succeeds, our intention to fix a meaning by the stipulation will suffice to ensure that there *will be* a suitable meaning—there is no additional requirement of cooperation by a self-standing realm of meanings. This broad orientation is, we believe, crucial if justice is to be done to the traditional connection. We will prefigure some of the necessary detail below.

To forestall misunderstanding: we are not denying that implicit definitions have any genuine 'existence problem' to surmount. But if the problem were that of getting a guarantee that such a definition somehow successfully alighted upon a preconstituted meaning, it is utterly obscure how it might be solved—except by finding an *interpretation* of the definiendum: some paraphrase in independent semantic good standing (which would then of course make a mere detour of the implicit definition—this crucial point will recur in the sequel). The genuine issue of existence is rather whether the implicit definition serves so to direct and constrain the use of the definiendum that it can participate as an element in a successful communicative practice. This broadly Wittgensteinian orientation is, of course, barely a first step towards understanding how implicit definition should work. But it is curious that Horwich, who officially proposes a 'use theory' of meaning, should sustain objections to the traditional connection which seem to presuppose something quite at odds with Wittgenstein.

It is similar with what Horwich calls 'the uniqueness problem'. Again, the stipulation above for 'Jack the Ripper' is hostage to the existence of a *single* perpetrator of the crimes; if they were the work of a team, or a number of copy-cats, or coincidence, the stipulation fails to fix a referent. Likewise according to Horwich's view[18] when we say that 'f' is to have the meaning it needs to have for

---

[18] That is, according to the view Horwich takes of what has to be the case, if the traditional conception of implicit definition as proceeding through stipulation of the truth of some sentential context(s) is to be upheld—we are not, of course, speaking his own 'use-theoretic' view: the view about how implicit definition works which Horwich himself espouses and sets against the traditional conception. Our subsequent use, throughout this section, of 'Horwich's model of

'$\#f$' to be true, we presuppose not only that there is at least one meaning such that if 'f' has that meaning, '$\#f$' is true, but that there is *at most* one such meaning. One who proffers an implicit definition seeks to single out that unique meaning whose interpolation, so to speak, into the incomplete thought expressed by '$\#$–' results in a true proposition. If things go well, there will be one and only one such item in the realm of meanings. But things may not go well—there may either be no item in the realm of meanings which can combine with the meaning of '$\#$–' to give a true proposition, or there may be more than one. The uniqueness problem is then conceived as the problem of somehow getting an assurance against the latter eventuality. It is not easy to see where such assurance might come from.

This sense of the problem seems again to be largely inspired by a combination of platonist imagery and a misconceived analogy between implicit definition and reference-fixing. As with the 'existence problem', we do not dispute that there is also a *potentially* genuine issue near by—one detachable from Horwich's model. This issue, of course, is that of *indeterminacy* and it challenges not just implicit definition, as traditionally viewed, but all forms of definition and concept-fixing. A good explanation of the meaning of an expression must place real but satisfiable constraints on the explanandum. An attempted definition may thus be flawed by overconstraint—unsatisfiability—or by *underconstraint*; for instance—to take the limiting case—if '$\#$–' is such that '$\#f$' is *bound to be true*, whatever 'f' means. An implicit definition would fail in this way, if we inadvertently chose for '$\#$–' something which was, in fact, a valid schema—in that case, the attempted definition would abort because it would place no restriction, beyond that implicit in the syntactic type of 'f', on what that expression could mean. But less dramatic degrees of failure in the same dimension are obviously possible; a definition may impose some but insufficient constraint on the use, or interpretation, of the definiendum. (Consider for instance the stipulation, 'Some plane figures are f'.)

We shall return to the issue of sufficiency of constraint in Section 4, but two brief observations are in order now. First, there is no absolute level of determinacy, independent of our purposes and the particular context, to which explanations of meaning must attain, if they are to be adequate. What should count as *insufficient* constraint on a definiendum is relative to the context and purposes of the definition. It is no objection to an implicit definition that it fails to discriminate among various more specific interpretations of its definiendum, if context and purposes do not demand finer discrimination. Second, no more determinacy can reasonably be demanded of meanings purportedly fixed by implicit definition than belongs to meanings in general. Any suggestion that a special 'uniqueness

---

implicit definition', 'the conception of implicit definition with which Horwich is working', and cognate phrases should likewise be understood as making reference to his interpretation of the presuppositions of the view he is attacking, not his positive view. In our view, the opposition Horwich sets up between the traditional conception of implicit definition as proceeding through stipulation and a conception of it as working by fixing a pattern of use for the definiendum is a false one.

problem' attends implicit definition, as traditionally viewed, accordingly owes an argument that some special and pernicious sort of indeterminacy afflicts the attempt to fix meanings by implicit definition—something unmatched by other modes whereby meanings are learned, including the most basic and informal instruction we each receive in our mother tongues. Such an argument, therefore, must not merely consist in the application to implicit definitions of considerations which are easily adapted to the cause of a more general meaning-scepticism. No such specific case has, to the best of our knowledge, ever been made.

The existence and uniqueness problems are two of four objections which Horwich lodges against the traditional account. The others are what he calls the 'possession problem' and the 'explanation problem' respectively. He writes:

Even if there exists one and only one meaning '*f* [*sic*] to have for '#*f*' to be true, can we be sure that '*f* comes to possess it? And supposing it does come to possess it, what would explain how this happens?[19]

With only marginally less brevity, he 'elaborates' the possession problem thus:

In general, if you want to give a particular object a particular property, it will not be enough to say 'Let it have that property': rather (or, in addition), you have to do something. You can't make a wall red just by saying 'Let it be red'—you have to paint it. Well, this point applies to meaning properties too. You cannot give a word a certain meaning by declaring, however earnestly or passionately, that it has that meaning. Something more must be done.[20]

Since these are meant to be new and additional problems, we can assume the case is one for which existence and uniqueness are resolved; a case where we somehow have assured ourselves that the expression, 'that (unique) meaning which suffices for "#*f*" to express a truth', does have a unique, determinate referent. The alleged further difficulties would then seem to have to do with exactly how it may be brought about by stipulation that '*f* takes on *that* item as its meaning—or with explaining how the trick was pulled if it does. But why should either point give rise to any difficulty?

We suggest not merely that there is no such further difficulty but that to suppose otherwise is actually inconsistent with the 'reference-fixing' model of implicit definition in force in Horwich's critique of the traditional conception of such definition as proceeding through stipulations of truth. Consider again the stipulation of our imaginary Victorian detective for 'Jack the Ripper'. If there are no problems about existence or uniqueness—if the crimes in question are indeed the work of a single killer—how could the stipulation fail? (We need not bother with the irrelevant possibility that it fails to be taken up by others). What residual issues could there be about what makes it the case that 'Jack the Ripper' has the referent it does, or about what explains the connection between the name and the referent? By hypothesis, that referent is the unique object satisfying the reference-

---

[19] *Meaning*: 134.   [20] Ibid. 134–5.

fixing condition that was agreed on for the name. What further problem can there possibly be?

Well actually, there *is* a further problem for the reference-fixing model—though it is not clearly identified in Horwich's discussion. Grant that the detective's stipulation fixes a referent for 'Jack the Ripper'. Still, he is no nearer knowing *who the Ripper is*. But then the stipulation of '#*f*' as true, conceived as working in the way Horwich supposes it must work if the traditional view is to be viable, could indeed fix a *referent* for the expression, 'that (unique) meaning which'—assuming that '#–' retains its prior meaning—'suffices for '#*f*' to express a truth', without making it clear *what meaning that is*. So someone who *perfectly understood the stipulation* might yet not achieve an understanding of '*f*'. And that is to all intents and purposes for the implicit definition to fail—for in that case it merely *fixes* a meaning without explaining it. The real residual problem for a proponent of Horwich's model of implicit definition is thus not, as he supposes, to explain the connection which the stipulation establishes between '*f*' and its meaning—that is no more problematic than in the case of 'Jack the Ripper'—but rather to make out the capacity of implicit definitions genuinely to *explain* meanings, to impart understanding. We might call this the *understanding* problem.

It is a critical problem—on the conception of implicit definition with which Horwich is working. For think what would be required to resolve it in a particular case. In order to identify the referent of 'Jack the Ripper', explained as indicated, an agent will have to determine who committed the crimes in question, that is, will have to bring the perpetrator under some canonically identifying concept: 'the fifth from the left in that line-up', for instance, or 'the Prince of Wales'. By analogy, in order to arrive at an understanding of the meaning of '*f*', explained by its implicit definition as conceived by Horwich, a thinker will have to bring the referent of 'that (unique) meaning which suffices for "#*f*" to express a truth' under some canonically identifying concept: that is, identify it as the referent of some expression whose own meaning in turn somehow serves to disclose what meaning it is. But that is tantamount to the demand that successful, implicit definition requires a recipient to have—or to have access to—*independent* resources sufficient for an *explicit* definition of the definiendum. Yet it was all along an absolutely crucial point about implicit definitions, as traditionally conceived, that they were to serve in cases—fundamental mathematical and logical concepts, and scientific-theoretical terms—where no resources for (non-circular) explicit definition were available. Horwich's model is thus implicitly in tension with this absolutely crucial point. We take that to be a decisive objection to it.

In summary: suppose that the matrix '#–' is already understood and that '#*f*' is laid down as an implicit definition of '*f*'. In Horwich's view, the definitional purport of this performance—on the traditional conception he opposes—is best captured by modelling it on the resolution: '*f*' is to have that (unique) meaning which suffices for '#*f*' to express a truth.[21] Horwich uses this picture of the matter to generate four general difficulties for what he regards as the traditional view of implicit definition, and for its capacity to contribute towards the explanation of non-inferential a priori knowledge. Two of these problems—existence and uniqueness—do indeed arise on the model in question, and we contend that their solution—in the form in which they so arise—is to reject that model. The remaining pair—possession and explanation—are, we have suggested, spurious even on the terms of the model. However there is a further genuine problem which arises on the model—the 'understanding' problem—whose solution will once again be, we contend, to give up the model itself.

These conclusions are wholly negative. The discredited model has it that implicit definition is a kind of reference-fixing, whose candidate referents in any particular case compose a population of predeterminate meanings. The questions must arise: if that model is askew, then with what should it be opposed—what is the right way of conceiving of the workings of a successful implicit definition—and can the traditional connection with a priori knowledge still be vindicated? One clear desideratum to have emerged is that a satisfying account of explanation via implicit definition must leave room for the capacity of such explanations to *invent* meanings, to bring us to a competence with concepts which we previously simply did not possess and for which we have no other means of expression save by the terms implicitly defined. Since a satisfying account of how else a successful implicit definition might achieve that effect must presuppose a proper characterization of the effect—our coming to a genuine understanding of the definiendum by way of grasp of a novel concept—the issue raised by the first question is, potentially, a very large one, demanding no less than an account of when it is correct to regard an expression as genuinely possessing a meaning in the first place. While that is, naturally, too large an issue for the present discussion, it is possible to outline at least some of the constraints which it seems clear that a good implicit definition, viewed as introducing a novel concept, should observe. That will be a task for Section 4. First we need to consider afresh the question how, in general terms, the traditional connection between non-inferential a priori knowledge and implicit definition should be conceived as working.

3. THE TRADITIONAL CONNECTION

How, just by stipulating that a certain sentence, '#*f*', is true—where '#–' is already understood, and '*f*' is a hitherto contentless expression determined only to be of some specific syntactic category apt for a well-formed completion of '#–'

---

[21] Where this in turn is construed platonistically, along the lines suggested by the reference-fixing model.

—is it supposed to be possible to arrive at an a priori justified belief that $\#f$? Well, the route seems relatively clear *provided* two points are granted: first that a stipulation of the truth of the particular '$\#f$' is so much as properly possible—that the truth of that sentence is indeed something which we can settle at will; and second that the stipulation somehow determines a meaning for 'f'. If both provisos are good, it will follow that the meaning bestowed on 'f' by the stipulation cannot be anything other than one which, in conjunction with the antecedent meaning of the matrix, '$\#-$', results in the truth of the sentence in question. For it is the very stipulative *truth* of the sentence which determines what meaning 'f' acquires. Moreover, if the stipulation has the effect that 'f' and hence '$\#f$' are fully *understood*—because we now understand not merely the matrix but the definiendum, and the significance of their syntactic combination—then nothing will stand in the way of an intelligent disquotation: the knowledge that '$\#f$' is true will extend to knowledge that $\#f$. In other words: to know both that a meaning is indeed determined by an implicit definition, and what meaning it is, ought to suffice for a priori knowledge of the proposition thereby expressed.[22]

Everything thus depends on the two provisos noted: that it is—at least sometimes—possible to bring it about that an antecedently partially understood sentence is true just by stipulating that it is to be so, without further explanatory or epistemic obligation, and that in at least the best such cases, the result is something which does indeed *fully explain* a meaning for the definiendum. Both provisos are clearly substantial. We consider them in turn.

For all we have so far said, '$\#-$' can be *any* previously understood matrix and 'f' *any* expression of a nominated kind which is syntactically appropriate to generate a well-formed sentence if appropriately introduced into '$\#-$'. As stressed

[22] This model of how a stipulation that a given partially understood sentence is true may eventuate in a priori knowledge of a proposition expressed by it is offered as a piece of reconstructive epistemology, not a psychological hypothesis. As a parallel, consider the situation when someone with a certain item of knowledge is inclined to accept certain of its—perhaps not wholly obvious—consequences seemingly spontaneously, without being able to reconstruct an explicit derivation of them. Even if the most he can offer by way of explicit justification is quite lame, we should not scruple to regard these consequential beliefs of his as knowledge just on that account: it should be enough if it is plausible that his general intelligence is somehow sensitive to the obtaining, or not, of the relevant consequence relations and if a fully explicit account of them is available in principle. Likewise, the actual phenomenology of a priori knowledge of first principles to which the proposed model applies might bear little relation to the explicit detail of the model, involving no more than immersion in a practice in which the implicitly definitional sentences are unswervingly accepted and the dawning of simultaneous impressions of comprehension of the definiendum and of the evident correctness of those sentences. It would nonetheless be appropriate to regard this as involving a priori knowledge, justifiable along the lines illustrated by the model, provided the practice of unswerving acceptance of the sentences in question was best construed as effectively stipulative and, so conceived, the stipulations in question satisfied such additional constraints on successful implicit definition as a full working-out of the model will involve. (In recently fashionable terminology, this is to suggest that the model reconstructs an *entitlement* to knowledge, rather than a justification which ordinarily competent thinkers would need to be able to offer in order to count as knowledgeable.)

above, not every such pair serves the construction of a sentence which we are at liberty, consistently with our prior understanding of '#–', merely to stipulate to be true. Trivially, '#–' may be such that no well-formed completion of it by something of the syntactic type of '*f*' can express a truth (it may be a contradictory predicate, for example, and '*f*' a term). More interestingly, the syntactic type of '*f*' may demand that the truth of '#*f*' carries some existential or referential implication which cannot be vouchsafed just by a stipulation—let '*f*' be 'Jack the Ripper', for instance, and let '#–' be '– is the perpetrator of this series of killings'. To attempt to lay it down a priori that the sentence, 'Jack the Ripper is the perpetrator of this series of killings', is to express a truth would be merely presumptuous—for we could have no a priori entitlement to the presupposition that 'the perpetrator of this series of killings' refers at all. The properly modest stipulation would rather be that 'If anyone singly perpetrated these killings, it was Jack the Ripper' (read so that its gist is just that of 'We hereby dub the perpetrator, if any, of all these killings: Jack the Ripper.')[23]

Let us call *arrogant* any stipulation of a sentence, '#*f*', whose truth, such is the antecedent meaning of '#–' and the syntactic type of '*f*', cannot justifiably be affirmed without collateral (a posteriori) epistemic work. The traditional connection, then, between implicit definition and the a priori requires that at least some stipulations not be arrogant. How can we circumscribe the arrogant ones so as to hive off a remainder which are safe for cost-free stipulation?

A natural way of trying to capture the moral of the Ripper example would be to say that like any purported definition, implicit definition can only bestow *sense*, not reference: we may, if we please, decide to confer a meaning of a certain kind on a term, but we cannot just by a decision confer a *reference* on a term—for that, we need in addition that a cooperative world puts forward an appropriate referent. However given any semantic framework which, like Frege's, extends the notion of reference or semantic value—*Bedeutung*—to other kinds of expression besides singular terms, this cannot be a happy way of putting the point. If we determined, for instance, that 'lupina' was to mean the same as 'female wolf',

---

[23] 'Jack the Ripper', so introduced, would qualify as what Gareth Evans called a Descriptive Name (compare his own 'Julius' and 'Deep Throat'—for which see *The Varieties of Reference* (Oxford: Oxford University Press, 1982): 31–2, 35–8, 47–51, 60–1). In Evans's view—and in contrast with the descriptions by which they are introduced—such names combine the feature of rigid designation (Evans would have preferred simply 'designation') with—like those descriptions and unlike what he calls Russellian names—the possession of a sense that can survive failure to refer. A theorist who regards this combination of properties as in tension will be unhappy with the suggestion that the Jack the Ripper stipulation can be saved from presumption by conditionalization—unless, of course, 'Jack the Ripper' is conceived as a mere shorthand for its reference-fixing description. But we here assume the broad correctness of Evans's view of such names. It is implausible to suppose that, in the event that nobody murdered the women in question, the intelligent consideration of sentences embedding 'Jack the Ripper' so introduced would involve the mere illusion of thought; but the modal properties of thoughts embedding the name are such that it is equally implausible to think of it as a shorthand description.

then that would suffice for the sentence 'A female wolf is a lupina' to express a truth. And in order for that to be so, according to any broadly Fregean semantic framework, the common noun, 'lupina' would have to have acquired a *Bedeutung* as well as a sense. So a stipulative decision—in this case an explicit definition— *can* after all confer reference, as well as sense. That the meaning of '#–' and the syntactic type of '*f*' are such that the truth of '*#f*' would demand that '*f*' has a *Bedeutung* need not of itself require that the stipulation of that sentence as true would be arrogant.

What this reflects is the, plausibily, different relationship in which sense stands to reference in the respective cases of singular terms on the one hand and other kinds of expression—predicates, relations, quantifiers, and functional expressions—on the other. In the case of the former, fixing a meaning must involve establishing a condition on the identity of the referent if any; but (as in the case of definite descriptions and abbreviations of them) establishing such a condition may *fall short of* establishing an actual reference, or it may (as arguably with most proper names and demonstratives) *presuppose* successfully establishing a reference. In neither scenario can one permissibly just stipulate as true any sentence whose truth would require that the term in question refers. But with incomplete expressions, the suggestion may be, the matter stands differently: here to establish a meaning is to establish a *Bedeutung* too—there is no question of our attaching a clear satisfaction-condition to a predicate, for instance (or a clear condition on the identity of the value of the function denoted by an operator for a given argument)—yet somehow failing to supply such expressions with a *Bedeutung*. But nor, in the case of such incomplete expressions, is the sufficiency of sense for possession of a *Bedeutung* to be compared to the situation with most proper names, where meaning is conferred *via* establishing a referent. Rather— whatever *Bedeutung* is held to consist in for such expressions—one automatically confers a *Bedeutung* upon them by settling their meaning (contrast the situation with Russellian names where one confers a meaning—sense—upon them by settling their *Bedeutung*).

It would take us too far afield to review this disanalogy properly. But even if we grant that it is correct, what does it tell us about the demarcation of arrogance? Clearly it will not suffice for the stipulation of '*#f*' to avoid arrogance that neither '*f*' nor '#–' be a singular term. There are many counter-examples: for instance, a set of legitimate stipulations serving to explain the satisfaction-conditions of a hitherto undefined predicate would become arrogant if merely enlarged by the additional stipulation that something falls under that predicate. On the other hand, we had the example, not withstanding its embedded occurrence of the singular term 'Jack the Ripper', of the arguably perfectly legitimate stipulation:

If anyone singly perpetrated all these killings, it was Jack the Ripper.

Here the crucial point—what makes the stipulation acceptable—has to do not with any special relationship between sense and reference characteristic of expressions other than singular terms—for the example precisely concerns a singular term—but with the fact that the stipulation is *conditional* in such a way that no commitment to successful reference on the part of the definiendum is entrained.

One attractive general suggestion[24] would be that all *any* definition—implicit or otherwise—can legitimately (non-arrogantly) do is to fix necessary and sufficient conditions on the identity of the *Bedeutung*, if any, of its definiendum: to determine how it has to be with an entity of the appropriate kind if it is to be the *Bedeutung* of the defined expression. That much may then suffice or not suffice, depending on the syntactic type of that expression, for the existence of such a *Bedeutung*. What specific constraints this suggestion would impose on the implicit definition of predicates, functional expressions, quantifiers, and so on will naturally turn on how one conceives of the *Bedeutungen* of such expressions. But one would expect that a stipulation of *satisfaction-conditions* would be the general pattern—one would stipulate what it would take for an object to satisfy the predicate in question, or for a concept to satisfy the quantifier in question, or for an object to satisfy any definite description formed by completing the functional expression by a term standing for an entity in the relevant range of arguments. All of these stipulations could be given in the form of conditionals. So since a non-arrogant stipulation of the condition on the identity of the referent of a singular term will likewise naturally assume a conditional shape—as witness the Ripper example—our working suggestion is going to be that, in order to avoid arrogance in implicit definition, and irrespective of the syntactic type of definiendum involved, it will in general be sufficient to restrict attention to sentences which are appropriately *conditional*.

Schematically, let $S(f)$ be a sentence (or type of sentence) embedding one or more occurrences of the definiendum 'f'. Outright, categorical stipulation of the truth of $S(f)$ may well be arrogant.[25] There will, however, be no arrogance in what we shall call the *introductory stipulation* that the truth of some other sentence or sentences (of specified type(s)), S_I, is to suffice for that of $S(f)$. Further—provided that our stipulations taken as a whole are conservative, in a sense shortly to be explained[26]—there will, likewise, be no arrogance in the *eliminative stipulation* that the truth of $S(f)$ is to be itself sufficient for that of a certain other sentence or sentences (of specified type(s)), S_E. Equivalently, we may—subject to the same proviso—non-arrogantly stipulate the truth of *introductory* and/or *eliminative conditionals*, $S_I \rightarrow S(f)$ and $S(f) \rightarrow S_E$.[27] A simple example is provided

---

[24] We are here indebted to Christopher Peacocke.

[25] It *need* not be arrogant, since $S(f)$ may be already conditional in form, or equivalent to a conditional.

[26] See the opening paragraphs of Sect. 4, below.

[27] In the special case $S_I = S_E$, implicit definition of f may assume the form of a biconditional stipulation—as with implicit definition of the direction-operator by stipulation of the Direction equivalence: 'The direction of line a = the direction of line b ↔ lines a and b are parallel.'

by the obvious introductory and eliminative stipulations for material conjunction—that the truth of *A* together with the truth of *B* is to suffice for that of '*A* and
B', and that the truth of '*A* and *B*' is to suffice for that of *A*, and likewise for that
of *B*.[28]

Now to the second proviso demanded by the traditional connection: that the
stipulation somehow determine a meaning for its hitherto undefined constituent.
The crucial point here is the correct reading of 'determine'. One lesson of our
consideration of Horwich's discussion, most especially of the 'understanding'
problem which emerged, was that the success of an implicit definition cannot
consist merely in its *indirect* specification of a suitable meaning for its definiendum. The process of stipulation must somehow be conceived not merely as fixing
the truth of the stipulatum but as *conveying* a meaning perfectly adapted to ensur-
ing *both* that '*f*' so contributes to the meaning of '#*f*' that that sentence comes to
express a truth *and* that we understand what meaning that is. Here 'conveying' a
meaning cannot merely involve: making it obvious how the definiendum is to be
interpreted—where interpretation is a matter of translation into some independently accessible vocabulary. If that were all that was possible, then when '*g*' was
such an interpretation of the definiendum, the proposition expressed by '#*f*' could
be as well expressed by '#*g*', and the recognition of the adequacy of the translation would presumably depend on *antecedent* knowledge of the truth of the latter.
So absolutely no connection would have been made between the stipulative introduction of '*f*' and the possibility of a priori knowledge of that proposition. It
follows that if such a connection can indeed be made, then the implicit definition
of '*f*' must convey its meaning not in the sense of making it obvious and
inescapable how to interpret it—how to locate its meaning among those expressible in an independently available vocabulary—but in the sense of explaining that
meaning to someone who has no other means of expressing it and is, in that sense,
so far innocent of the conceptual resource which the implicit definition affords.

The traditional connection thus demands that a good implicit definition can
invent a meaning—that it is at the service of a *first-time construction* of a meaning, one which may but need not be accessible in other ways—where to invent a
meaning, we suggest,[29] can only be to bring it about that some expression has a
novel but intelligible pattern of use, perhaps unmatched by any expression either
already available in the language or explicitly definable by means of such. To
invent a meaning, so conceived, is to fashion a concept: it is to be compared to
making a mould and then fixing a certain shape-concept by stipulating that its

---

[28] The introductory conditional in this case may be taken as either '*A* → (*B* → (*A* and *B*))'
or '*B* → (*A* → (*A* and *B*))' assuming permutation of nested antecedents of conditionals; there
will be two eliminative conditional schemas: '(*A* and *B*) → *A*' and '(*A* and *B*) → *B*'. Note that
each of *A* and *B* may contain occurrences of 'and', although they will not do so in the basic
cases; the example illustrates why it would be wrong to require S_I and S_E to be free of occurrences of *f*.

[29] The suggestion is, of course, entirely in the spirit of Horwich's own official view.

instances comprise just those objects which fit the mould (or are of the same shape as something which does). There is a sense in which the shape—the bare possibility of matter so configured—existed all along. We did not create *that* possibility. But we did create a concept of that shape (whether or not we also fixed the meaning of a word to be associated with it). It would make no sense for someone who followed the performance to doubt that there is any such shape— we displayed the shape in fixing the concept of it. In rough analogy, we must so conceive implicit definition that—in the best case—it makes no sense to doubt that there is a meaning taken on by the defined expression, not because the meaning in question allows of independent specification but because it has somehow been *fully explained* in the very process that creates it. Such an explanation can only consist in the fact that the implicit definition determines—or plays a part in a more general framework which determines—a pattern of use which is *fully intelligible without further interpretation*.[30]

Under what conditions would an explanatory stipulation achieve that end? Our approach in what follows will be piecemeal: to list a range of pitfalls—a range of specific ways in which an attempted stipulation of use might fail to fix anything which intuitively amounted to a novel meaning. Our underlying suggestion will be, of course, that an implicit definition which avoids these pitfalls will indeed have what it takes to instantiate 'the best case' of use-fixing, and thereby to sustain the traditional connection with non-inferential a priori knowledge. But we will not attempt to prove the sufficiency of our proposals; our project here is merely to outline a conception of implicit definition which retains the idea that it works through stipulation of the truth of suitable sentential contexts and (thus) has a chance of sustaining the traditional connection.

4. KNOWING A USE AND UNDERSTANDING A MEANING

When does a definition—of any kind—so fix a use that it genuinely explains a meaning?

The first requirement is, evidently, that of *consistency*. The inconsistency in Frege's Basic Law V, for instance, has the effect—assuming an underlying logic which, like classical or intuitionist logic, sustains *ex falso quodlibet*—that no particular use of the terms it introduces can be stably defended as correct (except in a sense of 'correct' which allows both an assertion and its denial to be correct). No doubt it would be too brisk to insist that any such inconsistent stipulation must fail *altogether* to fix a meaning. For instance, the explicit definition of a predicate, '*f*', as follows:

---

[30] The preceding reflections apply to implicit definition what we take to be the principal point of the Delphic-seeming remark at *Investigations* §201: 'What this shows is that there is a way of grasping a rule which is *not* an *interpretation*, but which is exhibited in what we call "obeying the rule" and "going against it" in actual cases.'

x is $f =_{df}$ x is not true of itself[31]

works fine right up to the point where '*f*' is taken to lie within the range of 'x'. And because a similar move is required in order to elicit Russell's paradox from Basic Law V, it's tempting to say that the stipulation of that axiom can work as a *partial* explication of the notion of set, or extension of a concept, which must then however be further modified if a stable characterization is to eventuate. However, the point remains that a prime requirement on any coherent determination of the use of an expression, so on any implicit definition in particular, is consistency. An inconsistent stipulation cannot determine a coherent pattern of use, even if it somehow provides a glimpse of a coherent partial reconstruction of itself; and such stipulations cannot, of course, assist with the project of explaining non-inferential a priori knowledge (since that must require that we know the *truth* of the sentence which gives the definition!).

The traditional connection requires that we avoid arrogance. A good implicit definition has to be something which we can freely stipulate as true, without any additional epistemological obligation. This demands that, in the best case, such a purported definition must be not merely consistent but *conservative*: it must not introduce fresh commitments which (i) are expressible in the language as it was prior to the introduction of its definiendum and which (ii) concern the previously recognized ontology of concepts, objects, and functions, etc., whatever in detail they may be.[32] For if it does so, then an entitlement to accept it must await the

---

[31] This is of course the so-called *heterological* paradox.

[32] Note the thrust of clause (ii). It is our view that a stipulation *may* have consequences which can be expressed in the antecedent language, and to which there need have been no previous commitment, without compromise of its legitimacy *provided* the truth of these consequences makes no demands on the previously recognized ontology. If we omitted clause (ii), characterizing conservativeness purely in terms of innocence of novel consequences expressible in the antecedent language, then Hume's Principle, for instance, would be non-conservative. For it entails that the domain of objects is infinite—a claim which can be expressed purely in terms of the antecedent logical vocabulary which the Principle utilizes and to which there might well have been no commitment before. But the presence of clause (ii) restores the prospect of the conservativeness of the Principle, since its entailment of the infinity of the domain makes no demands on the previously recognized ontology, whatever it may have been, but is sustained by the objects—numbers—to which the Principle introduces means of reference.

Note also that the relevant notion of commitment here need not be proof-theoretic—it should be enough to exonerate an implicit definition from the charge of non-conservativeness if any fresh commitments it discloses are fresh only in the sense that they were not deducible using previously recognized machinery, but are indeed semantic consequences of previous theory. (However that fact will of course have to be recognized *somehow* if we are to be entitled to stipulate the definition.)

There are a number of subtleties that need exploring here. A more rigorous characterization of the kind of conservativeness which, we believe, is relevant to the case of abstraction principles may be found in C. Wright, 'On the Philosophical Significance of Frege's Theorem' in Richard G. Heck, Jr. (ed.), *Language, Thought, and Logic: Essays in Honour of Michael Dummett* (Oxford: Oxford University Press, 1997) and 'Is Hume's Principle Analytic?', *Notre Dame Journal of Formal Logic* 40:1 (1999).

ratification of those commitments and thus cannot be purely stipulative. Consider for instance the stipulation, 'The Moon is f',[33] viewed as an attempt implicitly to define a predicate 'f'. *One* thing wrong with it is its non-conservativeness: its truth demands that the Moon exists, and so it can be known only if it is known that the Moon exists. But the kind of stipulation which is to be at the service of an account of knowledge a priori must be innocent of such collateral non-a-priori commitments. Notice, however, that this requirement is imposed by the traditional connection, rather than our leading issue in this section: the demands of genuine definition. Non-conservativeness need not, in and of itself, amount to a shortcoming in the ability of an implicit definition to fix a meaning for its definiendum. If 'The Moon is f' comes short in that respect too, it does not come relevantly shorter than the presumably conservative 'If the Moon exists, then it is f'—compare 'If anyone singly perpetrated all these killings, it was Jack the Ripper' and 'Jack the Ripper is the perpetrator of this series of killings': the latter is non-conservative, but its definitional purport is exactly that of the former, and presumably quite sufficient.

A natural suggestion is that 'If the Moon exists, then it is f' leaves open too wide a latitude of interpretation for 'f'—it could mean e.g. any of 'orbits the Earth', 'is broadly spherical', 'is largely composed of rock', 'is a satellite of some planet', and so on. But it would be dangerous to insist that a term is properly defined only if it resists alternative interpretation, since Quine and others have contrived to open a standing concern about the extent to which such resistance is shown by the vast majority of (by ordinary criteria, perfectly well-understood) expressions of natural language. A better diagnosis of the shortcomings of the example sees them as having less to do with the scope it leaves us in interpreting 'f' in ways consistent with the stipulation than with how little that stipulation tells us about the truth-conditions of *other* kinds of context which, such is the syntax of 'f', a good definition of it should put us in position comprehendingly to construct. What are the truth-conditions of 'Saturn is f', 'This cricket ball is f', or 'That bust of Sophocles is f'? No basis has been provided for an identification of the truth-conditions of these claims, let alone for a determination of their truth-values.

This kind of shortcoming is closely connected with what Gareth Evans called the *Generality Constraint*. In Evans's view,[34] a subject can be credited with grasp of any particular thought only if creditable with a grasp of each thought in a relevant *local holism*. For instance, a thinker who grasps the thought, 'a is F', must likewise grasp each thought of the form, 'b is F', where 'b' is any singular term which he understands and which stands for something of which 'F' is signifi-

---

[33] Suggested by the more complicated example—'Snow is green and the moon is f'—which Horwich uses (*Meaning*: 133) to illustrate his 'existence problem'. Horwich's example is, of course, equally objectionable on grounds of non-conservativeness.

[34] See *The Varieties of Reference*: 100–5.

cantly predicable; and likewise he must grasp any thought of the form '*a* is *G*', where '*G*' expresses any property significantly predicable of items of the kind to which the referent of '*a*' belongs. The principle is plausible enough—though, taken at the level of thoughts, it has metaphysical resonances which are missing from the corresponding principle governing sentence-understanding. And the latter principle, for its part, is surely incontrovertible. For sub-sentential under-standing is essentially implicitly *general*: to grasp the meaning of any sub-sentential expression is implicitly to grasp its contribution to the meaning of any sentence in which it can significantly figure. Accordingly one must, in grasp-ing the meaning of any sub-sentential expression, '*f*', thereby grasp the meaning of any significant sentence, '#*f*', whose matrix '#–' one already understands. It is merely a special case of this that one who understands a term, '*a*', should under-stand each significant predication on '*a*' of any predicate already understood by him; or that one who understands a predicate, '*F*', should understand any signif-icant sentence in which it is applied to a term, '*a*', which he understands. It is a platitude that to understand any sentence is to understand the meanings of its constituents and the significance of the way in which they are put together. Since the latter items of understanding are essentially general, it follows that to under-stand any sentence is to understand that range of significant sentences which can be derived from it by permutation of understood constituents.

The point, then, applies not just to the constituents—terms and predicates—of expressions of singular thought on which Evans was focusing, but to expressions of every syntactic type (and—when the Generality Constraint is conceived, as by Evans, as applying directly to thoughts as such—to the conceptual abilities appro-priately corresponding to an understanding of such expressions). The bearing on successful implicit definition is clear. If the stipulation of '#*f*' really is to fix the meaning of '*f*', then it must succeed in explaining a pattern of use for that expres-sion which complies with the Generality Constraint: that is to say, the implicit definition must put a recipient in a position to understand any well-formed sentence, '. . .*f*. . .', whose matrix, '. . . — . . .', is intelligible to him. This require-ment may indeed be relaxed to allow cases where the implicit definition does not achieve this effect single-handedly, as it were, but forms an integral part of an explanatory complex whose overall effect complies with the Generality Constraint. But if a stipulation of '#*f*' falls short of fixing the meaning of an appropriately general range of contexts even when allied to other explanatory moves, then—even allowing that we may nevertheless have fixed the use of a wide class of sentence types involving '*f*'—a recipient will naturally feel that she does not really associate a meaning of '*f*', even though competent in the practice in which its use is a part, as far as it goes.

'*Any* well-formed sentence, ". . . *f*. . .", whose matrix, '. . . — ". . .", is intel-ligible to him'? There are plenty of examples of well-formed sentences contain-ing only perfectly well-understood constituents which nevertheless make no (literal) sense. The significant application of a predicate, for instance, is often restricted to one particular category of object, and one might well suspect that virtually all expressions have a limited *range of significance*—a limited range of sentential matrices in which it so much as makes sense to introduce them—so that the proper demand imposed by the Generality Constraint on the definition of an expression is only that it bestow understanding of any sentence resulting from combining the definiendum with an understood matrix encompassed in its range of significance. While it is right to regard it as a condition for the success of an implicit definition of an expression of any syntactic type that it bestow a sufficiently general mastery of the definiendum, it will thus be a substantive question in any particular case how general 'sufficiently general' is. Manifestly, however, wherever the line is drawn, 'If the Moon exists, then it is *f*' falls short.

As remarked, an implicit definition may be only part of the apparatus whereby the meaning of a term is fixed. Sometimes the remaining apparatus will itself consist in further implicit definitions. A further requirement which it seems should be imposed in such a case is, to put it very loosely, that various ingredient definitions pull in the same direction so that we do not have a situation where some members of the network of implicit definitions make a mystery of the others. The most familiar examples of violation of this constraint are cases where the inference rules which are stipulated for a logical connective are in *disharmony*. One possible disharmonious scenario is where the consequences which are stipulated to be permissibly inferable from premisses containing the connective in question do not allow of independent justification by reference to the type of ground which has been stipulated as sufficient in turn to justify premisses of that type; that is, most simply, a scenario where the *elimination* rule(s) for the target connective allow(s) the derivation from a premiss in which it is the main connective of conclusions which cannot independently be inferred from anything stipulated via the *introduction* rule(s), to be logically sufficient for such a premiss. In such a case, however, the use in tandem of the introduction and elimination rules will be non-conservative. The need for an additional constraint of harmony, over and above conservativeness, arises from the obverse scenario: that where, in the simplest case, the strongest conclusion permissibly inferable by an application of the elimination rule(s) is *weaker* than can independently be inferred from the type of premiss stipulated as sufficient by the introduction rule(s)—when intuitively, *more* ought to be inferable from a premiss of the relevant kind than the elimination rule allows.

Suppose for example we introduce a quantifier, '%', in first-order arithmetic whose introduction rule coincides with that for the universal quantifier, but whose elimination rule:

$$\frac{\Gamma \vdash \%xAx}{\Gamma \vdash At}$$

is so restricted that 't' is required to have an *even number* as its referent. The effect then is that whereas, by the introduction rule, it will be necessary in order to establish '%xAx' on a given set of premisses, to show that they suffice for an arbitrary number to be A, the permissible conclusion from '%xAx' so established will be restricted to instantiations to even numbers. This pairing of rules for the quantifier '%' is conservative (so consistent) and seems in no way deficient in point of Generality.[35] Yet it would be natural to say that they nevertheless fail to determine any meaning for '%'. For if the introduction rule is justified, it can only be because grounds for each instance of 'Ax' are necessary before one can justify '%xAx'. And in that case it's unintelligible why the range of consequences which may permissibly be elicited from '%xAx' is explicitly restricted to *even* numbers.[36]

Such a schizoid pairing of the introduction and elimination rules for a connective provides a relatively simple and clear example of disharmony. But the point is quite general. Any satisfactory explanation of the use of a term must include provision both for the justification of statements featuring that term and for the use of such statements in the justification of others which don't. If it does not do that, it will be possible to find fault with it on grounds of Generality. But if provision is indeed supplied for both kinds of use, then there has to be a pitfall to be avoided of the kind just illustrated.

To summarize, then, the principal points of this and the preceding section:

(i) Implicit definition can underwrite (non-inferential) a priori knowledge only if it serves not merely to constrain the meaning of the definiendum in the way envisaged by the Horwichian, reference-fixing model, but to *explain* that meaning in such a way that it can be grasped by someone who antecedently lacks (the resources to define) the concept which the definiendum thereby comes to express.

(ii) Our suggestion is that this achievement may be secured provided that the definition creates a pattern of use in such a way that appropriate constraints of (at least) Conservativeness (and hence consistency), Generality, and Harmony are all satisfied.

(iii) It cannot in general be a requirement on successful implicit definition that it puts us in position—as we feel—*successfully to interpret* the definiendum; interpretation must perforce draw on independently given conceptual resources and, as we have stressed, it is integral to the interest of the notion of implicit definition that it be possible to think of some concepts as given by such means and

---

[35] Since uses as both premises and conclusions have been provided for every type of sentence of the form '%xAx' where 'Ax' is any arithmetical open sentence; thus no less Generality has been achieved than we have for 'All numbers . . .' or 'Some number . . .'.

[36] Similar examples are given by Christopher Peacocke in his 'Proof and Truth' (cited in n. 4, see 167–8)—where he considers the possibility of a quantifier Qx . . . x . . . stipulated to have the same introduction rule as the usual existential quantifier, but no elimination rule at all (or, in a variant on the example, a restricted version of the usual elimination rule, allowing only conclusions shorter than some pre-assigned finite length)—and, more recently, in his chapter on the Philosophy of Language in A. Grayling (ed.), *Philosophy 2* (Oxford: Oxford University Press, 1998) where he considers (at 98–100) a connective *vel* having the same introduction rules as truth-functional disjunction, but a version of the elimination rule which permits only atomic conclusions.

no other. The proper intelligibility of an implicit definition has to consist not in its interpretability but in the type of constraints it imposes on the use of the definiendum.

(iv) Perhaps additions will need to be made to the constraints just reviewed before we will have something sufficient for the full intelligibility of the defined term. But we see no reason for pessimism that such a complete set of constraints can be given. In that case we shall have a framework of conditions such that any implicit definition which meets them will have two features: first, anyone who understands the syntactic type of the definiendum and the matrices with which it is configured in the sentences stipulated to be true, will be put in position to understand those sentences—to grasp the thoughts which they express—by their very stipulation; second, it will be integral to the meaning thereby determined that these sentences are indeed true—for the pattern of use which they demand, and which is in turn essential to the meaning successfully bestowed on the definiendum, is precisely a function of their being stipulated to be so. So a thinker who is party to the stipulative acceptance of a satisfactory implicit definition is in a position to recognize both that the sentences involved are true—precisely because stipulated to be so—and what they say. That will be to have non-empirical knowledge of the truth of the thoughts expressed.

5. THE IMPLICIT DEFINITION OF SCIENTIFIC-THEORETICAL TERMS

In the light of the foregoing, the idea that scientific theoretical terms are implicitly defined by (some proper subset of) the hypotheses of the theories in which they occur is in difficulty on two different counts. First, it is in immediate tension with the requirement of conservativeness in implicit definitions; scientific theories would be of little interest to us if they did not, in conjunction with certain observational data, provide the resources for the prediction of *new* observational consequences—consequences expressed in language innocent of the terms which they putatively define—which were not deducible before. Second, as noted at the beginning, space must be provided for a theory allegedly implicitly defining a term or range of terms, to be *disconfirmed* (i.e. shown to be probably false) by independently accumulated evidence. Yet if the meaning conferred by implicit definition on a term is always a meaning it acquires by stipulation of the truth of a sentence or sentences in which it is a constituent, any such provision is pre-empted. For in that case, there should be no explaining how subsequently gathered evidence might show the defining theory to be *false*—since that would be, *per impossibile*, a situation inconsistent with its retention of its meaning. We cannot—without lapsing into obvious incoherence—simultaneously hold that 'f' has the meaning conferred on it by the stipulation that '#f' true, but that, so understood, '#f' has turned out to be false.

These difficulties do not show that the standard account—that implicit definition proceeds through stipulation of the truth of certain sentences—must be abandoned altogether, or even that it cannot be retained, in essentials, for the scientific case.[37] All that strictly follows from them is that, whatever the correct account of the idea that scientific terms may derive their meanings from their theoretical role, it cannot be right to conceive of implicit definition in scientific contexts as working through the stipulation (or acceptance) of the relevant theory *itself*— outright, unqualified stipulation of the truth (or acceptance) of the theory straightforwardly forecloses on the possibility of empirical disconfirmation. But this consequence can be accommodated by agreeing that the vehicle of implicit definition, in the scientific case, is *not* the scientific theory itself, but must rather be some *other* sentence so related to the theory that its stipulation or acceptance as true on the one hand suffices to confer meaning on the theoretical term to be defined but, on the other, remains uncompromised by recognition, a posteriori, of evidence telling against the theory. Schematically, what is stipulated as true (or firmly accepted) is not the theory T as such, but some sentence $\phi(T)$ which can remain in force through any empirical vicissitudes T may undergo. Our question should thus be: what, for given theory T, might plausibly serve as $\phi(T)$—the stipulative vehicle of the implicit definition?

Well, one natural suggestion—encouraged by a well-known tradition of theorizing about the manner in which theoretical scientific terms acquire meaning[38]— would appeal to the idea that we may view a scientific theory, embedding one or more novel theoretical terms, as comprising two components: one encapsulating the distinctive empirical content of the theory without deployment of the novel theoretical vocabulary, the other serving to fix the meaning(s) of the theoretical term(s) we seek to introduce. The theory's total empirically falsifiable content is, roughly, that there exist entities of a certain kind, viz. entities satisfying (a schematic formulation of) the (basic) claims of the theory. This can be expressed by the theory's *Ramsey sentence*, i.e. roughly, an existential generalization obtainable from the original formulation of the theory employing the new theoretical terms by replacing each occurrence of each new term by a distinct free variable of appropriate type, and closing the resulting open sentence by prefixing the

---

[37] Both difficulties feed on features—non-conservativeness and empirical falsifiability— special to the scientific case. Thus even if—as we do not accept—those difficulties enforce rejection of the standard account for that case, they do not straightforwardly generalize to other areas—centrally, logic and mathematics—in which implicit definition is practised. It would, accordingly, remain a perfectly viable option to uphold a mixed account, preserving the traditional connection for those latter cases in which it is plausible that our knowledge is a priori, whilst conceding that the standard account requires modification or replacement to accommodate implicit definition of scientific theoretical terms.

[38] The tradition includes Bertrand Russell, *The Analysis of Matter*; F. P. Ramsey, 'Theories' in his *The Foundations of Mathematics and Other Logical Essays* (London: Routledge & Kegan Paul, 1931); Rudolph Carnap, *Der logische Aufbau der Welt* (Berlin: Weltkreis, 1928); and David Lewis, 'How to Define Theoretical Terms', *Journal of Philosophy* 67 (1970): 427–46.

requisite number of existential quantifiers. Thus if, focusing for simplicity on the case where a single new theoretical term, 'f', is introduced, the undifferentiated formulation of the theory is '#f', then its empirical content is exhaustively captured by its Ramsey sentence, '$\exists x(\#x)$', where the new variable 'x' replaces 'f' throughout '#f'. The new term 'f' can then be introduced, by means of what is sometimes called the *Carnap conditional*:[39] '$\exists x(\#x) \rightarrow \#f$', as denoting whatever (if anything) satisfies '#–' (on the intended interpretation of the old vocabulary from which it is constructed). This conditional expresses, in effect, a convention for the use of the new term 'f'. Being wholly void of empirical content, it *can* be stipulated, or held true a priori, without prejudice to the empirical disconfirmability of the theory proper.[40]

---

[39] It is called the Carnap conditional by Horwich. In the paper cited in the preceding note, David Lewis calls it the Carnap sentence.

[40] Horwich observes (*Meaning*: 135–6) that a proponent of the traditional conception of implicit definition might try to deal with his 'possession problem'—specifically, with the objection that stipulating a theory formulation '#f' as true improperly forecloses on the possibility of empirical disconfirmation—by invoking this strategy. As against this, he claims, first, that the requisite existential generalizations 'are of dubious coherence insofar as they invoke quantification into predicate positions'; and, second, that if one regards Carnap conditionals as the proper vehicle of implicit definition of *scientific* terms, 'it would seem natural to suppose that *all* implicit definitions have something like this form, including those of arithmetical, geometrical and logical terms', with the result that fundamental logical principles, for example, could not be known a priori through their being used implicitly to define the logical constants. Obviously the crucial issue, as far as Horwich's second claim goes, is whether there is any compelling reason to think that implicitly definitional stipulation must *always* assume the form of a Carnap conditional (or something not relevantly different). Only if so will the traditional connection be subverted. So far as we can see, however, Horwich gives no actual argument to the purpose. His appeal to the naturalness of his supposition leaves us completely unimpressed—since there are clearly key features of the scientific case which do not straightforwardly carry over to logic and arithmetic (unless one is *already* persuaded of the correctness of Quine's global empiricism). For further discussion bearing on this issue, see Sect. 6 below. Horwich's first claim seems to us to manifest a degree of ambivalence about the Ramsey+Carnap strategy which he can ill-afford. Notwithstanding the impression to the contrary conveyed by his claim (ibid. 138) that shifting from the standard model of implicit definition to a use-theoretic account simply sidesteps the difficulties he raises for the former, exactly the same need to make provision for empirical disconfirmation arises on a use-theoretic account as on the standard model. Merely taking the meaning for 'f' implicitly specified by embedding it in a scientific theory '#f' as 'the meaning constituted by *regarding* "#f" as true'—rather than 'the meaning "f" would need to have in order that "#f" *be true*'—makes no essential difference. On the use-theoretic account, our meaning what we do by 'f' is constituted by our basic acceptance of '#f'. Accordingly, we *cannot* reject '#f' and still mean the same thing by 'f'. Any break with the basic regularity—which consists in accepting '#f' as true—would involve either changing 'f's meaning or rendering it meaningless. Hence the use-theoretic account can no more accommodate rejecting '#f' as false than can the unreconstructed truth-theoretic account. It makes no difference that the former speaks of a regularity of *accepting* '#f' rather than a *stipulation of the truth* of '#f' (as on the former); clearly what causes the problem is the fact that 'f's meaning is supposed to be constituted by accepting '#f'— whether this results from a stipulation or not makes absolutely no difference. It is quite unclear how a proponent of Horwich's use-theoretic account is to solve the problem without invoking the Ramsey+Carnap strategy—so Horwich had better hope his misgivings about the requisite second-order existential generalizations can be assuaged.

This proposal promises an agreeably neat and simple solution to the problem of squaring a uniform account of the workings of implicit definition with the demands of empirical scientific theory. We may allow in general that a sentence or range of sentences '#f' will serve as an *indirect* implicit definition of 'f' provided there is a uniformly recoverable sentence '$\phi(\#f)$' associated with '#f', which may be viewed as an implicit definition in the standard stipulational sense. In the scientific case, the resulting proposal is, we may always take this sentence to be the corresponding Carnap conditional, regarding the theory itself as an indirect implicit definition of its distinctive vocabulary. Stipulating the truth of such a conditional is clearly neutral with respect to the epistemological status of the associated scientific theory, which can remain—just as it should—a posteriori and subject to empirical disconfirmation. Moreover it is clear just how such empirical disconfirmation can run without interference with the stipulation which, on this account, fixes the meaning of 'f'—briefly, evidence running counter to the theory is precisely evidence against the theory's Ramsey sentence ('$\exists x(\#x)$'), i.e. evidence that tends to confirm its negation '$\neg\exists x(\#x)$', and thus in turn, via the logically true contrapositive of the Carnap conditional, confirms the denial of '#f'. Finally there is no a priori reason why a Carnap conditional should not be conservative and, indeed, satisfy all the constraints on implicit definition reviewed earlier and necessary for the viability of the standard account.

It is certainly well beyond the scope of this paper to review this proposal in any detail. We have dwelt upon it briefly only because the manœuvre is quite well known. What is evident is that Carnap conditionals are not the only kind of conditional sentence by means of which the meaning of new theoretical terms might be thought implicitly to be determined. For instance, a theorist at work during the early stages of subatomic physics, asked what he meant by 'electron', might say: 'Well, I don't *know* that there are any such things as electrons, but if there are such things, this much, at least, is true of them [here he states some bundle of claims which he takes to be true of electrons, if there are such things].' That is, he might explain (or partially explain) what he means by 'electron', not by giving us the Carnap conditional: 'If there are any things satisfying such and such laws, then electrons do', but by means of a kind of converse of it: 'If there are electrons, they satisfy such and such laws.' More generally and formally, we might view implicit definition of a theoretical term 'f' as proceeding through the stipulation, not of the Carnap conditional: '$\exists x(\#x) \to \#f$', but rather through that of a conditional of the type: '$\forall x(x = f \to \#x)$'. This could be called the *converse-Carnap* proposal.

As the reader will observe, this alternative would lack none of the mentioned advantages of the proposal utilizing Carnap conditionals. And there are probably further possible approaches, all serving to scotch the idea, looming large in Horwich's discussion,[41] that the traditional conception of implicit definition just

---

[41] See esp. *Meaning*: 135–7.

confronts an impasse when it comes to recovering the notion that theoretical terms receive their meanings from the theories in which they feature. The general perspective invited, to summarize, is this. Let *T* be any (empirical or non-empirical) theory containing a term, '*f*', expressing some distinctive concept of the theory, and let '#*f*' express some selection of basic claims or principles of *T* in whose formulation '*f*' is employed—as it might be, the conjunction of axioms of some logical or mathematical theory, or some of the fundamental claims of some empirical scientific theory. Then the view that meaning is given to '*f*' by its role in *T*—that it is implicitly defined thereby—may in all cases proceed by way of the thought that we in effect stipulate as true some appropriately related sentence 'φ(#*f*)'. How precisely 'φ(#*f*)' is related to '#*f*' will then depend on the discipline to which '*f*'-talk is to be added, and perhaps on details of the particular case. In some—non-empirical—cases, 'φ(#*f*)' may just be '#*f*' itself. In scientific contexts—and others, if such there be, where it is not open to us to stipulate the truth of '#*f*' itself—it will be some other sentence, such as a Carnap conditional, or a 'converse-Carnap' conditional, or some other type of context embedding '#*f*' which is, by contrast, available for outright stipulation.

This is merely a direction. Much more work would be needed before one could be confident what if any particular form of stipulation might best serve as a suitable vehicle for implicit definition in scientific contexts quite generally. The following section will assume no more than that the prospects of an account along such lines are to be taken seriously.

6. ABSTRACTION PRINCIPLES

As indicated in our opening remarks, we believe that Fregean abstraction principles—roughly, principles of the general shape:

$$\forall\alpha\forall\beta \,(§\alpha = §\beta \leftrightarrow \alpha \approx \beta)$$

—stipulating that it is to be necessary and sufficient for the truth of identities featuring §-terms that their arguments α and β stand in the equivalence relation, ≈, may legitimately be viewed as implicitly defining the term-forming operator '§' and thereby a sortal concept covering the referents of the terms it enables us to form. In particular, we hold that the sense of the numerical operator 'Nx . . . x . . .' may be adequately explained by stipulating the truth of Hume's Principle, i.e. the generalized equivalence:

$$\forall F\forall G(NxFx = NxGx \leftrightarrow \exists R(\forall x(Fx \rightarrow \exists!y(Gy \wedge Rxy) \wedge (\forall y(Gy \rightarrow \exists!x(Fx \wedge Rxy)))).$$

If this view of the epistemological status of Hume's Principle can be sustained, then in view of its now well-known entailment in second-order logic of the

Dedekind–Peano axioms for arithmetic,[42] there is every prospect of a vindication of a kind of *neo-logicism*, at least as far as elementary arithmetic goes.[43]

The Dedekind–Peano axioms are only satisfiable in infinite domains. In 'Platonism for Cheap? Crispin Wright on Frege's Context Principle',[44] Hartry Field—convinced that no combination of logic plus acceptable explanation of concepts could have existential import—contended that Hume's Principle cannot be any sort of conceptual truth, suggesting that the closest one could legitimately come to it would be a conditionalized version:

(HP*) If numbers exist, then $\forall F \forall G(NxFx = NxGx \leftrightarrow F \ 1\text{-}1 \ G)$.[45]

This, he allows, is—or can be—a conceptual truth; but, of course, it does not entail the existence of numbers and is utterly useless for the neo-logicist's purposes.

The suggestion that one should replace Hume's Principle by such a conditionalization of it would seem to confront an immediate difficulty stressed by one of us in previous work.[46] How are we to understand the antecedent condition? In rejecting Hume's Principle as known a priori, Field holds that the obtaining of a one–one correlation between a pair of concepts cannot be regarded as *tout court* sufficient for the truth of the corresponding numerical identity. So, since that was an integral part of the proposed implicit definition of the concept of number, his position begs some other account of that concept. Otherwise there would seem to be no space for an intelligible doubt about the existence of numbers (there being no concept in terms of which the doubt might be framed). More specifically, if we take it that the hypothesis that numbers exist may be rendered as '$\exists F \exists x \ x = NyFy$', then in order to understand the condition under which Field is

---

[42] See Crispin Wright, *Frege's Conception of Numbers as Objects* (Aberdeen: Aberdeen University Press, 1983): 158–69; also the appendix to George Boolos, 'The Standard of Equality of Numbers' in G. Boolos (ed.), *Meaning and Method: Essays in Honor of Hilary Putnam* (Cambridge: Cambridge University Press, 1990): 261–77. The result—now usually called Frege's Theorem—is first explicitly noted in Charles Parsons, 'Frege's Theory of Number' in Max Black (ed.), *Philosophy in America* (London: Allen & Unwin, 1964): 180–203.

[43] Not, of course, logicism in its most exacting sense—roughly, definition of all arithmetic primitives in purely logical terms in such a way as to facilitate transcription of each theorem of arithmetic into a theorem of logic. What is in prospect, rather, is a vindication of the claim that the fundamental laws of arithmetic are provable on the basis of second-order logic supplemented only with a principle which, though not an explicit definition, may be accepted as an implicit definition, proceeding in terms of concepts of second-order logic—and hence as an explanation—of the general notion of (identity of) cardinal number. See *Frege's Conception of Numbers as Objects*, §§xvii, xviii, esp. 153–4, and 'The Philosophical Significance of Frege's Theorem', Sect. I.

[44] See 167–70 of the reprint of this paper in Field's 1989 collection.

[45] This is not Field's formulation, but differences are merely notational. Cf. Field (1989: 169).

[46] See Crispin Wright: *Frege's Conception of Numbers as Objects*: 148–52 and 'Why Numbers can Believably Be: A Reply to Hartry Field', *Revue Internationale de Philosophie* 42 (167): 425–73, see Sect. V.

prepared to allow that Hume's Principle holds, we must already understand the numerical operator. But it was the stipulation—unconditionally—of Hume's Principle, which was supposed to explain that operator. That explanation has lapsed; but Field has put nothing else in its place.

Our reflections towards the end of the preceding section may seem to put Field in a strong position to reply to this objection. Consider the system consisting of Hume's Principle and second-order logic as a 'theory', in a sense inviting its comparison to empirical scientific theories, whose capacity to introduce theoretical concepts by implicit definition is uncompromised by the fact that they may turn out to be false. Think of this theory as *indirectly* implicitly defining the concept of cardinal number. Think of the real vehicle of this definition as being not Hume's Principle but the corresponding inverse-Carnap conditional:

$$(\text{HP**}) \quad \forall F \forall G \forall u \forall v ((u = NxFx \wedge v = NxGx) \rightarrow (u = v \leftrightarrow F\ 1\text{-}1\ G)).$$

Then the complaint that Field has put nothing in place of Hume's Principle to enable us to construe the condition on which he regards it as a priori legitimate to affirm Hume's Principle is met head-on. Hume's Principle is still the key to the explanation of the concept of number—albeit indirectly. But the real explanation is given by the stipulation of HP**—a principle which stands fruitful comparison with the inverse-Carnap conditionals which we suggested might plausibly serve as the vehicles of the implicit definition of scientific theoretical terms, and which there is no reason to doubt meets all the conditions on legitimate implicit definition earlier discussed—or at least all those which Hume's Principle itself meets—while avoiding its objectionably abstract ontology. HP**, Field may say, tells us what numbers are in just the way that the inverse-Carnap conditional for any (other) scientific theory tells us what the theoretical entities it distinctively postulates are—by saying what (fundamental) law(s) they must satisfy, if they exist. That there are numbers is itself no conceptual or definitional truth—it is, rather, the content of a theory (in essence, the Ramsified version of Hume's Principle: $\exists \eta \forall F \forall G (\eta F = \eta G \leftrightarrow F\ 1\text{-}1\ G)$ which may perfectly well be—and in Field's view is—false.[47]

There is this much merit in the proposal: *if* there is good reason to insist that an implicit definition of the numerical operator should proceed, not through an outright stipulation of Hume's Principle, but through something more tentative, then it would seem that one appropriate shape for the stipulation is an

---

[47] This idea—or something closely akin to it—seems to be what Kit Fine has in mind when he suggests, in his 'The Limits of Abstraction', that Field can explain number using Hume's Principle whilst denying the existence of numbers 'by treating Hume's Law as an explanation of a variable number operator. The existence of numbers may then intelligibly be denied'—Fine claims—'since the denial simply amounts to the claim that there is no operator that conforms to the Law. If we regard Hume's Law as part of a "scientific" theory, then this response is equivalent to a Ramsey-style treatment of theoretical terms' (cf. 'The Limits of Abstraction': 524, fn. 10).

'inverse-Carnap' conditional of the kind suggested. The question is whether there is any such reason.

Can the comparison with the empirical scientific case provide one? Conditionalization is there called for in order to keep open the possibility of empirical disconfirmation. Fixing the meaning of 'f' by stipulating the truth of the whole conditional '$\forall x(x = f \rightarrow \#x)$' leaves room for acknowledgement that the antecedent (more precisely, its existential generalization '$\exists x\, x = f$') might turn out false—grounds to think it false being provided by empirical disconfirmation of the consequent (more precisely, of the theory's Ramsey sentence '$\exists x(\#x)$'). Could an insistence that the numerical operator be implicitly defined, not by laying down Hume's Principle itself, but by HP**, be provided with an entirely analogous motivation?—by the need somehow to allow for the possibility that there might turn out to be no numbers?

Well, *how* might that turn out to be so? The suggested parallel with the scientific case would seem to require that such reason take the form of *disconfirmation* of Hume's Principle. But this looks hopeless. If, as it seems reasonable to suppose, Hume's Principle is (relevantly) conservative, straightforward empirical disconfirmation in not in prospect (since it will have no proper empirical consequences). How else might it fare badly?—might we somehow detect a misfit between its right- and left-hand sides in some particular case? That would have to involve 'observing' *either* that, whilst there was indeed a one–one correspondence between the instances of some concepts F and G, the number of Fs was distinct from the number of Gs, *or* that, whilst the number of Fs is indeed the number of Gs, there is no one–one correspondence. But to make either 'observation', we would require an independent criterion by which the identity or otherwise of the number of Fs with the number of Gs could be determined—precisely what we lack, if the meaning of the numerical operator is fixed only by the suggested stipulation of HP**.

It does not, of course, follow that there cannot be other reasons to insist upon a more cautious, conditionalized form of stipulation. We have accepted that if a stipulation is to serve as the basis of an item of a priori knowledge, in accordance with the traditional connection, then it must avoid arrogance. The stipulation of the relevant sentence as true ought not to require reference for any of its ingredient terms in any way that cannot be ensured just by their possessing a sense. If, then, an outright stipulation of Hume's Principle would involve arrogance, that would—or at least might—provide an independent reason for insisting that any acceptable explanation of the numerical operator should proceed, instead, through a conditionalized version of the principle.

'At least might'? We here leave open the question whether—at least in certain types of context (like axiomatic set-theory maybe)—arrogant stipulation might be acceptable after all. For even if not, it will follow that a conditionalized version of Hume's Principle, like HP**, is the strongest legitimate stipulation in its neighbourhood only if Hume's Principle itself is indeed arrogant. And if it suffices for the avoidance of arrogance that the import of a stipulation may be parsed, as suggested earlier, into introductory and/or eliminative components, all conditional in form, prescribing which true statements free of occurrences of the defined vocabulary are to be respectively necessary and/or sufficient for true statements variously embedding it, then it is a sheer mistake to think that Hume's Principle is arrogant. The principle does not just assert the existence of numbers as 'Jack the Ripper is the perpetrator of this series of killings' asserts the existence of the Ripper. What it does—if all goes well—is to fix the truth-conditions of identities involving canonical numerical terms as those of corresponding statements of one–one correlation among concepts (compare the schematic stipulation: '*a* is the single perpetrator of these killings if and only if *a* is Jack the Ripper'). So it seems quite misdirected to complain that in stipulating the truth of the principle, we are somehow illicitly attempting simply to stipulate numbers into existence. The effect of the envisaged stipulation is, rather, to ensure that it is sufficient (as well as necessary) for the truth of identities linking numerical terms (and so for the existence of referents for those terms) that corresponding statements of one–one correlation hold true.[48] In this it is merely a paradigm instance of what we have suggested is the prototypical form of a legitimate implicit definition: its effect is that one kind of context free of the definiendum— a statement of one–one correlation between suitable concepts—is stipulated as sufficient for the truth of one kind of context embedding the definiendum: that identifying the numbers belonging to those respective concepts. That is its introductory component. And conversely, the latter type of context is stipulated as sufficient for the former. That is the principle's eliminative component. All thus seems squarely in keeping with the constraint that in order to avoid arrogance, legitimate implicit definitions must have an essentially conditional character. If the additional conditionalization in HP** is proposed in the interests of avoiding arrogance, it thus merely involves a condition too many.

This point will bear some emphasis. It derives entirely from a purely structural feature common to all Fregean abstractions. Whenever the meaning of a functional expression '§' is fixed by means of an abstraction principle '$\forall\alpha\forall\beta(\S(\alpha) = \S(\beta) \leftrightarrow \alpha \approx \beta)$', what is stipulated as true is always a (universally quantified) *biconditional*, so that what is done is to fix the truth-*conditions* for identities linking §-terms. The truth-*value* of instances of the abstraction's left-hand side is never itself a matter of direct stipulation—if any identities of the form '$\S(\alpha) = \S(\beta)$' are true, that is always the product of two factors: their truth-conditions, as

---

[48] It is, of course, true—and essential to the case for number-theoretic logicism—that the truth of certain instances of the right-hand side of Hume's Principle is a matter of logic. In particular, it is vital that the existence of a one–one correlation of the non-self-identicals with themselves should be—as it is—a theorem of second-order logic. More generally, if F is any finitely instantiated sortal concept, then, as a matter of logic alone, the identity relation correlates F's instances one–one with themselves, so that, applying Hume's Principle, we have it that NxFx = NxFx, whence $\exists y \ y = NxFx$.

given by the stipulation, together with the independently constituted and, in the best case, independently ascertainable truth of corresponding instances of the abstraction's right-hand side. The existence of referents for §-terms is therefore never part of what is stipulated—and implicit definition through Fregean abstraction is accordingly never arrogant *per se*.

It is sometimes complained that introduction of (terms for) abstract objects by Fregean abstraction somehow makes their existence a matter of mere linguistic convention, internal to language in a way which sacrifices objectivity or mind-independence.[49] The inappropriateness of this charge may be appreciated by contrasting explanation of terms by Fregean abstraction with more questionable forms of implicit definition which, if sanctioned, really would make the existence of their referents a matter of stipulation. We might, for instance, essay to fix the meanings of the primitive terms of arithmetic—'0', 'natural number', and 'successor'—by simply laying down the Dedekind–Peano axioms directly. Or we might fix the meaning of the sole non-logical primitive term of set theory—'ε'—by stipulating the truth of some suitable collection of set-theoretic axioms, such as those of Zermelo–Fraenkel. In either case, the stipulation of the axioms would directly call for the existence of an appropriately large range of objects—infinitely many finite cardinal numbers in the former case, and (prescinding from Löwenheim–Skolem problems) a much larger collection of sets in the latter—and would therefore be arrogant. Whether that must constitute a decisive objection to them is, again, not a question we shall take a view on here. However it is answered, it appears to us that the relative modesty of an explanation of *cardinal number* via Hume's Principle puts it at a definite advantage over any purported implicit definition which proceeds through arrogant axiomatic stipulation.

This is, to be sure, a point of some delicacy, to which it is easy to be tempted into misguided objection. For instance, it may be charged that since Hume's Principle has only infinite models, the stipulation that the principle is true can stand in no significant contrast with a direct stipulation of the Peano axioms—that there is no 'relative modesty', really. In both cases a stipulation is made which cannot hold good unless the domain of its first-order quantifiers is infinite, and in neither case would any antecedent justification be offered for this presupposition.[50] So what's the difference?

Well, anyone disposed to lodge this objection should ask themselves: how in principle might the infinity of the series of natural numbers *ever* be recognized? Of course there's the option of simply denying that it can be—of simply denying that the widespread belief that there are infinitely many natural numbers is anything more than a fiction, or groundless assumption. But anyone sympathetic

---

[49] See, e.g. Michael Dummett, *Frege Philosophy of Language* (London: Duckworth, 1973): 498 ff.

[50] Michael Dummett lodges essentially this objection in his original *Encyclopaedia of Philosophy* article on Frege, at 236. See Paul Edwards (ed.), *Encyclopaedia of Philosophy* (New York: Macmillan, 1965): vol. iii, 225-37.

to the opposing thought, viz. that the infinity of the natural numbers—and indeed the truth of the Dedekind–Peano axioms—is part of our most basic knowledge, should be receptive to the idea that it is *inferential* knowledge, grounded ultimately in deeper principles of some kind determining the nature of cardinal number. For the only alternative which takes it seriously—the idea that the truth of the usual axioms is somehow apprehended primitively and *immediately*—is not only epistemologically utterly unilluminating but flies in the face of the historical fact that the grasp and practice of the theory of the finite cardinals did not originate with the Dedekind–Peano axiomatization but antedated and informed it.

Very simply: if the question is raised, how do we know that the natural numbers constitute an infinite series of which the Dedekind–Peano axioms hold good, the available answers would seem to be, crudely, of just three broad kinds: that we don't actually know any such thing—it's a fiction or a groundless stipulation; or that we just do, primitively and immediately, know it; or that we know it in a manner informed by deeper principles of some sort. Our proposal is an answer of the third kind: the infinity of the number series may known by knowing that it follows from the constitutive principle for the identity of cardinal numbers. It does not compromise the insight of this answer if the 'deeper principle' is itself stipulative, and it does not make the infinity of the number series a matter of sheer stipulation in its own right. To think otherwise is to overlook the essentially conditional character of the original stipulation. It is also and independently to make a mistake akin to that of someone who supposes that, because the rules of chess have an ultimately stipulative character, we might as well just have stipulated directly that it is impossible to mate with just bishop and king.

In sum: the stipulation that the Peano axioms are true would be a stipulation that there is an infinite population of objects behaving as they require. We are urging, by contrast, that the stipulation of Hume's Principle should be seen first and foremost as a meaning-conferring stipulation—one providing for the introduction and elimination of contexts of numerical identity—of which it is a relatively un-immediate, interesting, and welcome consequence that there is a population of objects of which the Peano axioms are true. But there is another objection to this way of looking at the matter, a little subtler than that just considered. This is that, although Hume's Principle seems to fit squarely with the pattern of non-arrogant stipulation which we suggested suffices for an implicit definition to be safe, it bears a disanalogy to other examples of the same pattern—one which effectively brings out that it does not suffice, in order for a stipulation to be unarrogant in the intuitive sense intended, that it break down into conditional, introductory and eliminative components after the fashion described. Compare any instance of the introductory component of Hume's Principle:

$$F \ 1\text{-}1 \ G \to NxFx = NxGx$$

with, once again, the presumably quite innocent introductory stipulation for 'Jack the Ripper':

If any single person perpetrated all these crimes, Jack the Ripper did.

Then the salient difference is simply this: that whereas the truth of the introductory content—the antecedent—in the Ripper stipulation implicates exactly the ontology implicated by the consequent, viz. the existence of a human being who is responsible for the crimes in question, the introductory context in an instance of Hume's Principle is *ontologically leaner* than the consequent; for it does not, whereas the consequent does imply the existence of a referent for the terms, 'NxFx' and 'NxGx'. So, an objector may contend, all the emphasis upon the conditionality of Hume's Principle, and other abstraction principles, is really a charade. There may be a difference between merely *directly* stipulating that certain objects exist on the one hand and, on the other, stipulating that, in order for certain contexts which require their existence to be true, it is to suffice that certain other contexts are to be true which don't!—but it is surely a difference of no philosophical significance whatever.

This would be a sharp objection if it did not misrepresent the situation. The misrepresentation consists in the suggestion that the introductory contexts in Hume's Principle are innocent of commitment to an ontology of numbers. For that precisely overlooks the fact that, as we've expressed the matter elsewhere,[51] the stipulation of Hume's Principle, and other abstraction principles, is tantamount to a resolution to *reconceive* the subject matter of their introductory components in a fashion determined by the overall syntax of and antecedently understood components in the type of identity statement introduced. The objection takes it that in stipulating an abstraction principle is to hold—for instance, that for directions:

$$Da = Db \leftrightarrow a \mathbin{/\mkern-5mu/} b,$$

—we would somehow be attempting to make it the case that contexts concerning just lines and their relations which are *wholly innocent* of the distinctive ontology of the left-hand sides—directions—are nevertheless both necessary and sufficient for the truth of statements which are *not* so innocent. That, of course, would not even be a *possible* stipulation. It would not be possible even if we somehow possessed a collateral assurance that every line had a direction. (For if that assurance did not extend to the point that these 'directions' were identified and distinguished in the manner described by the abstraction, we could not *make* that so just by stipulating it; and if the assurance *did* extend to that point, then the 'stipulation' would be altogether pre-empted and otiose—for the abstraction would hold good without it.) The response which we are proposing, then, is that in order to understand how an abstraction principle *can* be a proper object of stipulation, it is precisely necessary to receive it as so determining the *concept* of the objects to

[51] Wright, 'On the Philosophical Significance of Frege's Theorem', Sect. 1; Hale, '*Grundlagen* §64', *Proceedings of the Aristotelian Society* 1996–7: 243–61 and 'Arithmetic Reflection without Intuition', *Aristotelian Society*, Suppl. Vol. 73: 75–98.

which it serves to introduce means of reference that its introductory—right-hand side—contexts would precisely *not* be innocent of commitment to those objects. Directions, for instance, are precisely to be conceived as entities of such a kind that it is conceptually sufficient for a pair of lines to share their direction that they be parallel. That is the whole point of Frege's own initial metaphorical gloss, that in an abstraction principle we 'carve up' a single content in a new way.[52] The objection is good only if this way of looking at the matter is illicit. But the neo-logicist contention is precisely that it is not illicit—that it is, indeed, the key to an understanding of a great deal of our thought and talk about abstracta.

We are under no illusions but that this matter will stand much more critical discussion. Our aim in this concluding section has been merely to outline a case that if the traditional connection between implicit definition and non-inferential a priori knowledge can indeed be sustained along the lines offered earlier, then the prospects are also good for applying that idea so as to achieve viable neo-Fregean foundations for arithmetic, and indeed for more extended classical mathematical theories.[53]

---

[52] Frege, *Die Grundlagen der Arithmetik* (Breslau: Wilhelm Koebner, 1884): §64.

[53] For work towards the formulation of a suitable abstractionist basis for classical analysis, see Bob Hale, 'Reals by Abstraction', *Philosophia Mathematica* (3) vol 8, 2000.

13

Representation, Scepticism, and the
A Priori

Frank Jackson

Here is a familiar philosophical profile: a naturalist in the sense of holding that science gives us the best picture of what our world is like; a realist about scientific entities and everyday objects; against scepticism; against the analytic–synthetic distinction and the a priori with an exemption for the logical truths and their kin; and against conceptual analysis. I think that this is an unhappy package. One reason is that implementing the anti–sceptical part of the package requires conceptual analysis. In my view, you cannot properly address the question of when the naturalist part of the package (which I broadly accept) does, and when it does not, warrant scepticism about the existence of, for example, phlogiston, tables and chairs, moral value, abhorrence of vacua, vital forces, and the prepositional attitudes, without doing conceptual analysis. I have argued this in a little detail elsewhere.[1]

In this paper I focus on another reason for holding that the package is an unhappy one. I argue that those naturalists who are against scepticism and who accept that logical truths are a priori should accept that the class of a priori truths greatly outruns the logical truths; in particular, they should accept that there are many sentences that are a priori in the sense that, given the logical truths, understanding them is in principle enough to reveal that they are true. I will argue that it is hard to be against *both* scepticism and the a priori. I hope that this will encourage some to abandon their hostility to the a priori. I will be sorry if I turn out to have made converts to scepticism. I will say nothing about how one might argue that the logical truths (and their kin, by which I mean mathematics etc.) are a priori. I am seeking to establish the conditional claim that if you allow that the logical truths and their kin are a priori, then, on pain of scepticism, you should accept a whole class of a priori truths.

I have already used two highly contested terms, namely 'understanding' and 'a

I am indebted to many discussions and especially to one of the editors who saved me from a blunder in Section 2.

[1] Frank Jackson, *From Metaphysics to Ethics: A Defence of Conceptual Analysis* (Oxford: Clarendon Press, 1998).

priori'. So I make a start by explaining what I will mean in this paper by those terms. We will then see why anyone against scepticism should accept that there are more a priori sentences than the logical truths. I conclude by considering some possible objections.

1. REPRESENTATION, MEANING, UNDERSTANDING

We give putative information about how things are by means of sentences. English sentences, for example, are part of a highly sophisticated system of representation that enables one understander of English to transfer to other understanders of English, in considerable detail and complexity, what they believe and know about our world. A moment's reflection on what happens when we read history books, travel guides, and physics texts makes this obvious. But we could not give putative information about how things are unless we associate various sentences with various ways things might be. Just as the use of flags to give information—about diseases on ships, deaths of famous people, the end of a race, and so on—requires known associations between flags, on the one hand, and diseases, deaths, race–endings, and so on, on the other, so giving information by means of English sentences requires known associations between various sentences and various ways things might be.

It is an open question how these associations come into being. Perhaps we first establish connections between, on the one hand, words and, on the other hand, things and properties, and use rules of combination to build up to associations between sentences and ways things might be. Or perhaps we first establish connections between sentences, including one–word sentences, and ways things might be. Then, by virtue of the fact that we must be able to see structure in the way sentences connect with ways things might be—otherwise sentences could not constitute, as they manifestly do, part of an open–ended, powerful system of representation—we identify or abstract out the contribution of certain parts of these sentences, certain words, to the representational contents of the wholes they make up. This then allows us to link the words to things and properties.

Equally, it is an open question exactly how we should understand the talk of 'connections' or 'associations', and an open question how we should understand the talk of 'ways things might be'. All that I am claiming to be settled and obvious is, first, that English sentences (to focus on the language this paper is written in) are part of a system of representation that serves to represent how things are; second, that this requires what we are calling 'associations' between sentences and the items we are calling 'ways things might be' or 'how things might be', which are typically not sentences; and, third, that although there are problems in elucidating these various notions, we all have to accept the basic picture outlined.

It is a folk theory. It is not something devised by philosophers, although philosophers make it explicit and, very properly, debate various views about how to elucidate the key notions.

It is a folk theory because everyone who understands English knows why hearing the sentence 'There is a tiger right behind you' makes a typical English speaker very nervous; and they know it has nothing especially to do with the sentence itself, but, rather, has to do with *what* they *associate* the sentence with. Again, if I give the sentence 'There is a circle on the board behind me' to a competent speaker of English and ask them to draw on the board a figure that corresponds to how the sentence represents things as being, they will know perfectly well what is required, and whether they are able to fulfil the task depends simply on whether they can find a piece of chalk, how good they are at drawing, and the like. And these are not isolated examples. We should not let the philosophical problems attendant on spelling out the various notions needed when we theorize about the representational nature of language, and English in particular, blind us to the plain facts concerning this representational nature. Accordingly, I will talk freely in what follows of sentences being associated with a way things might be, and, equally, of how a sentence represents things as being. The question of how to analyse these notions will not be important for what follows.[2]

I can now say what I mean by 'meaning' in this paper. The meaning of a sentence is how it represents things as being. Accordingly, to grasp the meaning of a sentence is to know how it represents things as being. For example, those people who know what would be required to make the sentence 'There is a circle on the board behind me' true, who know how it represents things as being, know what the sentence means; they grasp its meaning, in the sense that these terms are being given here.

This is, in part, a stipulation. Although this meaning of 'meaning'—the representational meaning, as we will sometimes call it—is one thing people have often meant by 'meaning', it is obviously not the only thing people have meant, and have properly meant, by the term. Those philosophers who say that the meaning of a sentence is how it is used, or that the meaning of a sentence is the totality of the inferences in which the sentence figures, or perhaps some proper subset of that totality, are not denying (I trust) that (most) sentences represent how things are. They are addressing the separate question of how a sentence gets to have the representational meaning that it does. Thus, one attractive account of how a sentence gets its representational meaning is via the way it is *used* to give how speakers take things to be; another approach sees the totality, or

[2] Though, for the record, I think, following John Locke, *An Essay Concerning Human Understanding* (1690), H. P. Grice 'Meaning', *Philosophical Review*, 66 (1957): 377–88, and David Lewis *Convention* (Cambridge, Mass.: Harvard University Press, 1969), that, roughly, a sentence is associated with a certain way things might be if it is the conventionally adopted way of expressing the belief that things are that way.

perhaps some proper subset thereof, of the set of inferences the sentence stands in, as settling, or as an important factor in settling, representational meaning Or perhaps these philosophers, or some of them, have in mind some other topic altogether that might go under the title of 'meaning'. The key point for us is that there is no competition with what we mean by 'meaning' here, *unless* these theories are being offered as ways of denying that sentences represent how things are. And, to borrow from *Yes Minister*, that is too courageous for me.

Also, I should emphasize that our stipulation does not require that we regard the representational meaning of, for example, 'This is an equilateral triangle' and 'This is an equiangular triangle' as one and the same. Some hold, influenced most likely by the possible–worlds treatment of content by David Lewis and Robert Stalnaker, that the way sentences represent things as being is capturable in terms of the possible worlds at which the sentences are true.[3] They hold that the representational meaning of 'This is an equilateral triangle' and 'This is an equiangular triangle' is the same, but, for all we say here, you could insist on a more fine–grained approach which treats how the two sentences represent things as being as different.

Speaking for myself, I cannot see a principled way of implementing the more fine–grained strategy without, in one way or other, giving the sentences themselves an individuative role in settling the nature of how they represent things as being. And this seems bad to me. We want how a sentence represents things as being to be distinct from the sentence itself, in much the way we want the point represented by Cartesian or polar co–ordinates to be distinct from the co–ordinates themselves. Also, many, myself included, want 'X is an equilateral triangle iff X is an equiangular triangle' to come out a priori, despite its not being transparently true. And, as will become clear, the argument for the a priori I will be offering only delivers that answer if the two component sentences have the same representational meaning. But, be all this as it may, all we will require from the notion of representational meaning is that it can be thought of in a set–theoretic way. To represent is to make a division among entities of some kind or other—possible worlds, sets of sentences, combinations of things and properties, structured universals or concepts, fictions, or whatever— into those which are in accord with how things are being represented as being, and those which are not. When there are two airlines flying out of a city, what you want on your way to the airport is some sign that *divides* the one you are booked on from the other one. In slogan form: no division, no representation. But, for our purposes here, we will not need to inquire closely into what entities the division is among.

---

[3] David Lewis, *On the Plurality of Worlds* (Oxford: Blackwell, 1986); Robert Stalnaker, *Inquiry* (Cambridge, Mass.: MIT Press, 1984).

2. A PRIORI SENTENCES, UNDERSTANDING, AND TRUTH

There are, of course, many ways of defining what it is to be a priori on the market, and many entities that are said to be the putative bearers of this property: beliefs, propositions, and sentences, most notably. My concern here will be with *sentences*, and by an a priori (true) sentence I will mean one such that understanding it is sufficient for being able to see that it is true. But what is it to understand a sentence? And how might we connect understanding and truth? The answers to these questions in this section will tell us how it is possible for there to be a priori true sentences. The next section will be concerned with why we should believe that this possibility is realized.

If sentences serve to represent how things are, if they are associated with ways things might be, one good thing to mean by understanding a sentence is grasping how it represents things as being, or its representational meaning, as we are calling it. And if we think of understanding in this way, we can make the connection with truth by first making the connection between truth and representation via the following representation schema:

(R)   S is true iff things are the way S represents them as being.

But to represent is to divide into that which accords with the representation and that which does not, and to say that the way things are (in full detail—the kind that no sentence or mind can capture) lies in the 'accord' part. So, for things to be as S represents them is for the way things are to be included in the way S represents things as being. Hence, we get

(R*)   S is true iff the way S represents things as being includes the way they are.

How does the representation schema, in either form, connect with the more famous truth schema? The latter drops out as a corollary of the former, as the following argument shows:

(i)   'Snow is white' represents things as being a certain way. [From the representational nature of language]

(ii)   'Snow is white' is true iff things are/are included in the way it represents them as being. [Applying (R)/(R*) to 'Snow is white']

(iii)   'Snow is white' is true iff things are the way it represents them as being. [From (i) and (ii)]

(iv)   'Snow is white' is true iff snow is white. [From (i) and (iii)].

We can now connect understanding a sentence with truth; more particularly, we can say how understanding (along with the logical truths) might deliver the result that some understood sentence is true. If to understand S is to grasp the way it represents things as being, and if S is true iff the way it represents things as being includes the way they are, whenever it is a logical truth that the way S represents things as being includes the way they are, understanding alone will deliver truth, and we will have an a priori true sentence.

It follows that in order to show that there are a priori true sentences, we need to show that we really do grasp the representational meanings of certain sentences, in particular, ones for which it is a logical truth that these meanings include the way things are. One task is to show how it might be that there are a priori sentences in some language. This section's main burden has been to give definitions of and tease out interconnections between the notions of representation, representational meaning, understanding, and truth, that explain how there might be a priori sentences in some sense of 'a priori' that is close enough to traditional conceptions to justify the title of this paper. A second task is to argue that it is true for some actual language—English, as it might be—that we understand its sentences in the required sense. This is the business of the next section.

3. WHY OPPONENTS OF SCEPTICISM SHOULD ACCEPT THE A PRIORI

Opponents of scepticism think we know that there are electrons, who won the last elections in Britain, that Newtonian theory is false, that the Bengal tiger is under threat—and they are right. We do know these things. But we know these things through the testimony of others. Very few of us have carried out the crucial experiments that establish the existence of electrons. We know that they exist because someone else told us. And the same goes for the other examples. Indeed, it is hardly news that a great deal of what we know depends in one way or another on accepting the testimony of others.

But what happens when we accept the testimony of others? No magical transfer of information from one head to another takes place. Rather, we are confronted by various sentences, sometimes as inscriptions in books, sometimes as displays on screens, and sometimes as sound patterns in the air, and these confrontations effect the needed transfer. But what we learn is not merely various things about inscriptions, displays, and sounds; we learn about tigers, electrons, and elections (and, typically, what we learn about the inscriptions etc. *per se* is rather fragmentary and quickly forgotten). Therefore, it must be the case that we grasp how the sentences we come across represent things as being. When I learn that the Bengal tiger is under threat, I do so by hearing or seeing sentences which represent it as under threat. Moreover, I know they represent it as under threat. For if they represent the Bengal tiger as under threat but I do not know this, I will not learn that it is under threat—looking at petrol gauges only tells you how much petrol is left in the tank if you know what the various pointer positions represent. In short, our knowledge of the world depends very heavily on grasping the representational meanings of the sentences produced by the members of our language community. Accordingly, to the extent—the considerable extent, we anti–sceptics insist—that we have knowledge of our world, we must know the representational meanings of lots of the sentences we come across.

It is a short step now to the existence of a priori sentences. Anti–scepticism tells us that we often grasp representational meanings. Let 'P' and 'Q' be two sentences whose representational meanings we grasp and which are such that the representational meaning of the first is a subset of the representational meaning of the second; that is, how 'P' represents things as being is included in how 'Q' represents things as being. Then it is a logical truth that the way things are is either not included in the way 'P' represents things or is included in the way 'Q' represents things. Hence, a grasp of representational meanings alone, that is, understanding plus nothing more than logical truths, entails that 'not–P or Q' is true, and so, by the elucidations of the previous section, 'not–P or Q' is a priori true.

A similar argument can be made in terms of the representational properties of words to show, for example, that some sentences of the form 'Every A is a B' are a priori. Anti–sceptics must allow that we can learn about the distribution of properties in the world by confronting certain predicates and common nouns in certain combinations. How else did most of us learn that proximity to high levels of radioactivity goes along with illness? But if how 'A' represents any object as being is included in how 'B' represents it as being, then this fact about representational meanings is the very fact that anything which is as 'A' represents it as being is as 'B' represents it as being. And, from the representation schema plus the definition of understanding, we get that 'Every A is a B' is true, and so that it is a priori true. Similar arguments apply to other cases.

It might be asked whether we might not grasp the representational meanings of 'P' and 'Q', or of 'A' and 'B', in the case where the representational meaning of the first of each pair is included in the second of each pair, and yet it be impossible, from our grasp of these meanings, to see that the relevant inclusion relations hold. In this case, it might be suggested, 'Not–P or Q' and 'All A and B' would fail to be a priori. However, it would be a strange sort of grasping if it did not in principle reveal the inclusion relations. Think of what we would say of someone who insisted that they knew where London was and where England was, but no amount of reflection on what they knew could reveal that London was in England. However, if someone insists that we might grasp representational meanings, really grasp them, and yet not be able in principle to see their relations of identity, inclusion, exclusion, and overlap, we could conduct the argument given above in terms of the need for a *full* grasp of representational meanings, where full grasp means a grasp that does deliver the relations. The information about how things are that comes from testimony comes in a huge number of gobbets via sentences and words that issue from the mouths, computers, and pens of the many different people we hear and read. These gobbets would not be much use to us if we could not tell when one overlapped with another, or included it, or excluded it. So we must have a full grasp in the defined sense, on very many occasions, of the representational meanings of the words and sentences we come across. Otherwise, we could not put the pieces together aright. My inclination is to argue that a grasp is automatically a full grasp in the defined sense. But if this is wrong, we need an extra step in the argument for the existence of a priori sentences, a step which notes that if we are to escape scepticism, we must often have a full grasp of the representational meanings of the many sentences we come across.

The simplicity of my argument for the a priori arouses the suspicions of many—naturally enough. 'It can't be that easy! And, anyway, what of the famous arguments against the a priori?' The rest of this paper is concerned with a few of the many objections that might be raised.

4. DICTIONARIES AND ENCYCLOPEDIAS

One slogan often used by Quineans against the analytic–synthetic distinction is that there is no distinction between dictionaries and encyclopedias. Is there a problem here for our argument for the a priori? The Quinean claim is that we cannot distinguish what is *known* about Ks from what is *definitive* of Ks. Is the property of typically having stripes true by definition of tigers, or is it merely something that we know for certain sure is true of tigers? Is being an animal true by definition of cats or merely something we know for certain sure is true of cats? The thought is that there is no answer to questions like these, and (maybe) that even if there were an answer, who could care what it was.

No doubt often there is no answer to this kind of question. But to say that there cannot be, or never is, is a profoundly sceptical view of our capacities. Philosophers talk and write about possibilities that we all know will never be realized. So do science–fiction writers and their readers. So do writers and readers of chess problems. So do people who answer questions about what they would do if they won the pools ten times in a row. We are able to pick out in thought, and place on the table for discussion using language, *extremely* unlikely situations, situations we know for certain sure will never arise. But whenever we use language to discuss a situation where a K is such–and–such, when such–and–such is something no K will ever possibly be, and everyone knows this, we, of necessity, rely on a distinction between how the term 'K' represents something as being, what is definitive of being a K, and some feature F we know for absolute certain every K has. For we are considering a K that is *not* F. When we think or write about the *extremely* unlikely, we rely on our ability to identify the subject of our thought and talk by separating out what identifies it from what is certainly true but not definitive of it. Or consider discussions of blockhead or swampman in the philosophy of mind. It is common ground in these discussions that there is absolutely no chance whatever of there being a blockhead or a swampman, and yet we have no trouble identifying the subject of our discussions. Even someone like Daniel Dennett, who thinks these cases show nothing, knows *what* he thinks shows nothing.[4] Unless we embrace scepticism concerning our ability to think and talk about these cases, we must allow that we can distinguish in thought and talk between what picks out some subject of thought and talk, and what is certainly true of that subject.

5. THEORIES AS THE UNIT OF SIGNIFICANCE

The rejection of the a priori, especially when stated as the rejection of the analytic–synthetic distinction, is often linked to a radical holism about meaning according to which the units of significance are whole theories. We cannot sensibly talk of the meanings of individual words and sentences, only of whole theories, for, runs the view, words and sentences do not have meaning independently of the theories in which they appear.

The trouble with this objection is its vagueness. In order for meaning holism to be an objection to the existence of a priori sentences, we need a version of meaning holism which, first, might possibly be true, and, second, which would, if true, undermine the case given above for the existence of a priori sentences. I know of no version which meets these two constraints at the same time.

If by holism is meant the view that you cannot know how someone is representing things to be when they produce a sentence unless you know what they believe about everything, their total theory, holism would indeed entail that there are no a priori sentences. We never know everything about what someone else believes, so this form of holism would mean that we do not have the grasp of representational meanings our argument relied on. However, we clearly often do know what people are telling us about how things are, even though there is much about their views we are ignorant of. Directions to the airport, election results, and news of breakthroughs in medicine are given to us by people who have *lots* of beliefs we know nothing about, but we know perfectly well how they are representing things as being to us. Otherwise we could not know how to use someone's directions to get to the airport, could not know who won the election from the words uttered on the news, and could not sensibly celebrate the latest advance in cancer treatment after reading a press report.

If by holism is meant the view that you cannot know *exactly* how someone is

---

[4] See e.g. Daniel Dennett, *Consciousness Explained* (Boston: Little, Brown & Co., 1991, App. A).

representing things to be when they produce a sentence unless you know what they believe about everything, their total theory, holism would, in my view, still be a view we should reject. But we don't need to for the purposes of this paper. A sensible version of this doctrine must allow that we have a pretty good idea of how people are representing things to be despite substantial ignorance about what they believe in general. That is how we get to the airport, know who won the election, and know what we are celebrating. And this is enough to give us a priori sentences by the argument of this paper. It does not matter if we cannot say precisely what division others are making in how things might be, a view which is anyway plausible in lots of cases; what matters is simply that we know enough to be confident that certain ways things might be fall on the 'in accord' side of the division they are marking, and certain others fall on the 'not in accord' side. The fact that there are 'don't knows' and vague cases where there is no answer does not matter. Perhaps the point is clearest if we take the example of 'not–P or Q', and think of the ways 'P' and 'Q' represent matters as regions in logical space. The point is that the 'P' region plus a penumbra representing ignorance and vagueness can be known to be completely inside the 'Q' region minus its penumbra of ignorance and vagueness. Or take a real–life example. Many are pretty shaky on the relationships between the British Isles, Britain, England, Ireland, Northern Ireland, Scotland, Wales, and the United Kingdom. But they know lots of inclusion relations for sure: they know, for example, that Wales is included in the United Kingdom, and Britain is included in the British Isles. The key point here is the familiar one that a good deal of ignorance and indeterminacy about the boundaries of two regions is consistent with knowing that one is inside the other, or that they exclude each other, or that they overlap.[5]

6. WATER AND H_2O

It might be thought that what we have learned from Saul Kripke about the necessary a posteriori makes serious trouble for our defence of the existence of a priori sentences.[6] We have learned, the objection might run, that 'There is water' is true in a possible world iff 'There is H_2O' is. This implies that they have the very same representational meaning. Further, we understand the sentences. It follows, the objection might run, that I must allow that we grasp that meaning. But then, arguing as I did above, we should, in principle, be able to see that, for example, 'There is water iff there is H_2O' is true from this grasp of that meaning. But everyone agrees that this sentence is not a priori.

---

[5] For more on this, see David Chalmers *The Conscious Mind* (New York: Oxford University Press, 1996).

[6] Saul Kripke, *Naming and Necessity* (Oxford: Blackwell, 1980).

One possible reply points out that, although to represent is to make a division among entities, these entities must be individuated in a more fine–grained manner than are possible worlds. However, as indicated earlier, I am sympathetic to approaches to representational meaning in terms of sets of possible worlds, because I cannot see any principled way of going more fine–grained without blurring the distinction between the vehicles of representation, in this case, certain sentences, and how things are being represented as being.[7] In consequence, I prefer a quite different response to the objection.

This response argues that the set of worlds that gives the representational meaning of 'There is water' is a different set from that which gives the representational meaning of 'There is H_2O', despite the fact that they are true in just the same worlds. And it does this for an independently powerful reason. When we use the sentence 'There is water' to make a claim about how things are, we are making a claim about how things *actually* are. To give putative information about how things are is to give putative information about how they actually are (which is not to say that we can't and don't sometimes give information about how things would have been *had . . .*). This means that if we wish to capture the representational content of 'There is water' in terms of possible worlds, in the sense which connects most closely to the information about how things are that we use the sentence to transmit, the possible worlds that are in accord with the sentence in the required sense are those which satisfy the following conditions: if this is how things actually are, the sentence is true. In other words, the partition the sentence effects *qua* vehicle of representation is not between the worlds where it is true and those where it is false, but between the worlds such that if they are actual, the sentence is true, and those such that if they are actual, the sentence is false. So, when we think about how to capture the representational meaning of 'There is water', we need to think about the worlds such that if they are actual, then 'There is water' is true. But if (*if*) Twin Earth is the actual world, if the way things actually are is that it is XYZ which is the clear, potable liquid that fills the ocean, acquaintance with which led us to coin the word 'water' (and the corresponding words in other languages) and there is no H_2O present at all, that sentence is true. True, if, as we well know, the actual world has H_2O playing the 'water' role, then the sentence 'There is water' is false at Twin Earth; it is irrelevant that XYZ exists in Twin Earth and plays the 'water' role there. But if we make the supposition that the way things actually are has XYZ playing the 'water' role, that is to suppose

---

[7] It might well be asked why I neglect the option of going more fine–grained by identifying representational meanings as constructions out of properties and things. The idea would be that the construction for, say, 'A is an equilateral triangle' would differ from that for 'A is an equiangular triangle', by virtue of the difference between being equilateral and being equiangular. My reason is that I cannot see how to make plausible a notion of property which distinguishes being equilateral from being equiangular without reference to the distinction between the predicates 'is equilateral' and 'is equiangular', which would violate the principle of keeping vehicle and content distinct.

in effect that it 'turned out' that water is XYZ; which is why the sentence is true at Twin Earth under the supposition that Twin Earth is the actual world.

In sum, the representational meaning of 'There is water' is that there is stuff playing the 'water' role. Or, to put the matter in the terms of Kripke, the representational meaning of 'There is water' is given by the reference fixers for 'water'.[8] Thus, the possible worlds approach to representational meaning allows the representational meaning of 'There is water' to be different from the representational meaning of 'There is H_2O.' However, whatever you think of the way just sketched of how a possible worlds approach might capture the representational meaning of 'There is water' and distinguish it from that of 'There is H_2O', it is clear that the sentences *do* differ in how they serve to represent things as being. Any objection that starts from the claim that they are alike in representational meaning starts from somewhere false. At most, we have here a problem for possible–worlds treatments of representational meaning.

7. HAVE I ASSUMED WHAT WAS TO BE SHOWN?

A short paper arguing for something as controversial and encumbered as the existence of a priori sentences necessarily makes any arguable assumptions. I beg many questions in this paper. But it might be objected that I all but beg *the* question. In treating representing in terms of making a division among entities, I in effect admit almost from the beginning a notion of necessity: to be necessary is simply to be true throughout all the entities among which the division is made.

I plead guilty to presuming a notion of necessity. I cannot see how anyone who holds that sentences represent—something I regard as undeniable—can avoid doing so. And I think this for the reason given in the objection: to represent *is* to make a division, so we get immediately a notion of necessity as truth throughout the entities being divided. However, to presume necessity is not to presume a priority. The key, and essentially very simple, argument of this paper is that if we are to get information from testimony, as we manifestly do, sentences must have representational meanings, *and* we must, on many occasions, grasp them. Scepticism about meaning to the extent that it is, or implies, scepticism about representational meaning and our grasp on many occasions of it, is a highly contagious doctrine. It spreads the scepticism far and wide.

---

[8] Kripke, *Naming and Necessity*. Or, to put the point in still other words, the representational meaning of 'There is water' is the A intension of the sentence in the terminology of Frank Jackson, *From Metaphysics to Ethics: A Defence of Conceptual Analysis*, and is the diagonal proposition in the terminology of Robert Stalnaker, 'Assertion', in P. Cole (ed.), *Syntax and Semantics*, ix (New York: Academic Press, 1978): 315–32, though I suspect he would not approve of this use of his notion. See also David Chalmers, *The Conscious Mind*.

8. CODA

I have said nothing about how one might argue that the truths of logic and their kin are a priori (other than that I would be presuming that they are a priori in order to argue that anyone who grants that they are should grant that many more sentences are a priori). I have been asked (by one of the editors, as it happens) whether I am also setting aside the question of the a priori status of sentences like 'I am here.' My answer is that the approach to the a priori via what it is to understand how things are being said to be when various bits of language are being used in communication does explain why 'I am here' is a priori.

'I am here' is only a priori true in certain contexts. If I point to a spot on a map and say 'I am here', what I say may well be false. If I 'throw' my voice so that the sound comes from the far side of the room, what I say will be false. The circumstances in which 'I am here' is a priori are those in which the conventions of the language and the context are such that 'here' picks out the location of the producer of the sentence (not where the speaker is pointing to or where the sound is coming from). An example is when you say the sentence *sotto voce* to yourself. Moreover, the role of the word 'I' in such a sentence is to pick out the producer of the sentence. So what is involved in understanding the representational meanings (which requires, of course, a grasp of the role of context) of the words 'here' and 'I' in the sentence tells us that it is true iff the location of the producer of the sentence is identical with the location of the producer of the sentence. We have, that is, a case where grasp of representational meanings plus logical truths delivers truth.

14

The Status of Logic

Stewart Shapiro

I confess at the outset that I have no new insights to bring on the general nature of a priori knowledge. This paper concerns the nature of knowledge (or warranted assertions) on matters of logic. What is the status of statements like 'that argument is valid' and 'you have just committed a fallacy because it is possible for your premisses to be true and your conclusion false'?

On standard conceptions, a proposition is a priori if it can be known independently of experience. As Simon Blackburn puts it, a proposition is known a priori if the knowledge is not based on any 'experience with the specific course of events of the actual world'.[1] Experience may be needed to grasp the relevant concepts, but beyond that no particular experience is necessary. There is much fun to be had in spelling this out, but I will resist and leave things at this basic level.

Some philosophers assume that an a priori warrant cannot be undermined, and so a priori knowledge is incorrigible. Philip Kitcher, for example, argues that mathematics is not a priori by showing that mathematical knowledge is fallible.[2] Some of Kitcher's critics challenge this transition, suggesting that there can be defeasible, a priori knowledge. Fallibility is one thing and apriority is another. A proposition may be a priori knowable even if (in some sense) it can be undermined *empirically*. I presume that a proposition that *is* undermined (empirically or otherwise) is not known, and so is not known a priori.

The view that a priori knowledge is infallible derives moral support from the widely held view that there is no synthetic a priori knowledge. If 'analytic' comes to 'true by definition' or 'true in virtue of the language', then the primary, or the

Much of this paper was developed when I led the Monday Seminar at the University of St Andrews during the autumn 1998 term. Special thanks to Crispin Wright, John Skorupski, Peter Clark, and Sven Rosenkranz. I am indebted to my colleague Neil Tennant, Jill Dieterle, and Michael Resnik for a fruitful correspondence on this project. I especially appreciate the spirit of collegiality. Thanks also to the editors Christopher Peacocke and Paul Boghossian for encouraging me and providing helpful direction.

[1] S. Blackburn, *The Oxford Dictionary of Philosophy* (Oxford: Oxford University Press, 1994): 21.

[2] P. Kitcher, *The Nature of Mathematical Knowledge* (New York: Oxford University Press, 1983).

only, source of a priori knowledge is knowledge of the correct use of language. How can we—the community of language users—be wrong about that?

I presume that everyone agrees that there can be legitimate uncertainty about whether a long proof is correct, and that the uncertainty can be attenuated with the (empirical) information that others have checked the proof. We are never *really* certain of long mathematical proofs, are we? There have been cases of incorrect proofs that were accepted by the mathematical community over a long period of time, before the fallacy was uncovered. Perhaps the thesis should be that if a proposition is a priori, then it has a warrant that can be broken down into pieces, each of which is infallible because it is a definition or some other immediate or trivial consequence of how language works.

There is no need to decide here whether there are a priori warrants that cannot be broken down into infallible pieces. The typical cases, where the warrant can be broken down, broach the subject of this paper. Many of the small steps in extended warrants are mediated by logical rules of inference. If the very logic is not a priori, then there go virtually all of the paradigm cases of supposed a priori knowledge.

Gottlob Frege took the basis of a priori knowledge to lie in the 'ultimate ground upon which rests the justification for holding [a proposition] to be true'.[3] In mathematics, at least,

[t]he problem becomes . . . that of finding the proof of the proposition, and of following it up right back to the primitive truths. If, in carrying out this process, we come only on general logical laws and on definitions, then the truth is an analytic one . . . For a truth to be *a posteriori*, it must be impossible to construct a proof of it without including an appeal to facts, i.e. to truths which cannot be proved and are not general . . . But if, on the contrary, its proof can be derived exclusively from general laws, which themselves neither need nor admit of proof, then the truth is a priori.

Frege's whole approach presupposes that logic itself is a priori. If experience infects the very inferences we use in mathematical proof, then Frege's orientation collapses.

The received view of logic is that it is analytic—and thus a priori—*par excellence*. But, of course, the received view is not the universal view. In his celebrated 'Two dogmas of empiricism', W. V. O. Quine argued that there are no analytic (or synthetic) truths.[4] The concern of the present article, and the present volume, is not with analyticity as such, but with a priori knowledge. To put it mildly, Quine's unrelenting empiricism suggests a strong distaste for the a priori. Nevertheless, some of Quine's later work may allow that logic, or part of logic, might be analytic and a priori in some sense commensurate with the traditional understanding of the terms.

---

[3] G. Frege, *Die Grundlagen der Arithmetik* (Breslau: Kobener, 1884); *The Foundations of Arithmetic*, tr. by J. Austin, 2nd edn. (New York: Harper, 1960): §3.
[4] W. V. O. Quine, 'Two dogmas of empiricism', *Philosophical Review* 60 (1951): 20–43.

Recently, Michael Resnik revived the original Quinean position and argued that logic is not a priori.[5] Resnik's main contention is that logic is not 'cognitive'. He argues that there is no 'fact to the matter' whether a given sentence is logically true or whether a given inference is valid. Statements of logical truth, validity, and the like do not state facts. I presume that it follows from Resnik's view that there is no logical knowledge, and if there is no logical knowledge then there is no a priori logical knowledge. That is, if there is no fact that a sentence of the form $A \vee B$ follows from B, then one cannot know that this inference holds, and so on cannot know this inference a priori.

I argue below (Section 5) that logic is *objective* if anything is. If logic is objective, then it is cognitive, against Resnik. The converse does not hold, however. A discourse may be subjective or culture-relative (and so not objective) but still invoke facts—albeit subjective or culture-relative facts. Many of the arguments below apply equally against views that logic is non-cognitive, subjective, and culture-relative.

The view that judgements of logical truth and logical validity are not objective has another influential advocate on the other side of the Atlantic. In his 'Inventing logical necessity', Crispin Wright argued that statements of logical necessity, such as a claim that a given proof must turn out a certain way, are not apt for objective truth or falsity.[6] This issue is bolstered by one of the most extensive treatments of objectivity in recent years, Wright's *Truth and Objectivity*.[7]

Wright's 1986 paper suggests an important distinction. Let Φ be a sentence whose status as a logical truth is up for discussion. For example, Φ might be an instance of $\Psi \rightarrow (\Psi \vee \chi)$. Person A, representing the bulk of humanity, holds that Φ is logically true. Another person B agrees that Φ is true, and he agrees that he cannot imagine things otherwise, and yet B doubts the modal claim that Φ is logically true. He suggests that his inability to conceive of $\neg\Phi$ may just be a quirk of his psychology, and need not entail anything about the modal status of Φ. Person B is Wright's *Cautious Man*.

Call this a *status dispute*, or for emphasis, a *mere* status dispute. Resnik agrees that a sentence in the form $\Psi \rightarrow (\Psi \vee \chi)$ is true—perhaps objectively so—but claims that there is no further metaphysical fact that the sentence is logically true. So Resnik sides with the Cautious Man.

Contrast the dispute between Person A and the Cautious Man with another. Consider an instance of excluded middle, $\Psi \vee \neg\Psi$, where Ψ is as yet undecided. A classical logician accepts $\Psi \vee \neg\Psi$ as a logical truth, and so as a truth, while the

---

[5] M. Resnik, 'Ought there to be but one logic?', in B. J. Copeland (ed.), *Logic and Reality: Essays on the Legacy of Arthur Prior* (Oxford: Oxford University Press, 1996): 489–517; and *Mathematics as a Science of Patterns* (Oxford: Oxford University Press, 1997): §8.3.

[6] C. Wright, 'Inventing logical necessity', in J. Butterfield (ed.), *Language, Mind and Logic* (Cambridge: Cambridge University Press, 1986): 187–209.

[7] C. Wright, *Truth and Objectivity* (Cambridge, Mass.: Harvard University Press, 1992).

intuitionist demurs from $\Psi \vee \neg \Psi$, even as a plain truth (let alone as a logical truth). Or consider an inference, such as $\neg \neg \Psi \vdash \Psi$. The classical logician says that the inference is valid while the intuitionist says that it is invalid. Call this an *extension dispute*, since our principals disagree on the extension of logic.

Other instances of the extension dispute concern quantum logic and the various paraconsistent and relevance logics. Resnik argues that these extension disputes are also non-cognitive. He claims that there is no fact to the matter whether the classical logician or the intuitionist, relevance logician, etc. is correct. I consider both the status dispute and the extension dispute below, but it prevents confusion to have the distinction in mind.

1. THE (WORLDWIDE) WEB OF BELIEF

Quine's metaphor is suggestive. He argues that at any given time, the sum total of our beliefs constitutes a seamless web. Each 'node' (belief) has innumerable links to other nodes in the web. Experience impinges on the web only at the 'periphery', through irritations on our nerve endings—observation. New observations bring about changes inside the web, via the innumerable links between the nodes, until some sort of equilibrium is achieved. The single goal of the scientific-philosophical enterprise is to organize the system of beliefs in order to account for experience and predict future observations.

I presume that many of the links between the nodes of the web are logical. For example, suppose we had a belief of the form 'If P and Q then R', and then some experience arrives that get us to deny R. Then we ought to deny the conjunction of P and Q, and perhaps matters elsewhere in the web might then lead us to deny Q, heading us toward equilibrium.

So one would think that for Quine, logic is the study of how belief and disbelief (are supposed to) move through the web of belief in response to other beliefs and disbeliefs. This would accord with the traditional orientation of logic as the study of consequence and consistency, with these notions now pressed into a pragmatic role. We would thus expect a study of how consequence and consistency, so construed, differ from their previous conceptions as, say, the laws of the laws of thought. What becomes of the longstanding view that logic is analytic and a priori? It is thus ironic that virtually the whole of Quine's *Philosophy of Logic* focuses on logical *truth*.[8] In the preface, we find: 'I would say that logic is the systematic study of the logical truths' (p. vii), and the book goes on to present a view concerning what is special about the logical truths.

Thus Quine has logic focusing on certain nodes *in* the web of belief. What is

---

[8] W. V. O. Quine, *Philosophy of Logic*, 2nd edn. (Englewood Cliffs, NJ: Prentice-Hall, 1986).

so interesting about these nodes in the web? Individual logical truths are among the least interesting and least important parts of logical theory. Why should one bother figuring out what is distinctive about this particular class of sentences, especially in light of the thesis that the web is seamless? What matters, or should matter, is the status of the ways that we move around the web. What matters is *inference.*[9]

To be sure, it is tempting to focus the present inquiry on the notion of logical truth, since the traditional notions of objectivity, analyticity, and apriority were themselves designed to apply to individual propositions or sentences. To get beyond this, we have to extend the traditional notions and ask what it is for an *inference* to be objective, or analytic, or a priori.

In 'Two dogmas', Quine explicitly states that rules of inference are also nodes in the web: 'Re-evaluation of some statements ... entails re-evaluation of others, because of their logical interconnections—*the logical laws being in turn further statements in the web*' (emphasis mine). This is not correct as it stands. The overall status of logical inferences does not come down to the status of logical truths, or of any other sentence. One moral of Lewis Carroll's 'What the tortoise said to Achilles' is that a link between sentences and inferences cannot be taken for granted.

A more or less standard manoeuvre is to point to an equivalence between logical truth and logical inference. An inference from a sentence Φ to a sentence Ψ is valid if and only if the sentence 'if Φ then Ψ' is logically true. More generally, an inference from $\Phi_1 \ldots \Phi_n$ to Ψ is valid if and only if the sentence 'if Φ_1 and $\ldots \Phi_n$ then Ψ' is logically true. Let us call these *transfer principles*, since they represent an equivalence between inference and logical truth.

Notice, first, that this simple account, or reduction, of logical inference presupposes that inference is compact. Suppose, for example, that we were allowed to infer a conclusion from an infinite number of premises, where the conclusion does not follow from any finite subset of the premises. An instance of this would be the ω-rule for arithmetic: from $\Phi(0), \Phi(1), \ldots, \Phi(n), \ldots$ infer $\forall x \Phi(x)$. I am not arguing (here) that logic is not compact, nor that the ω-rule is logically valid. The point is that if the transfer principles give a complete account or reduction of logical consequence, then infinitary inferences are ruled out from the start—a priori. There is no place for them, since they are not equivalent to sentences. On what basis can our Quinean preclude infinitary inferences? In some cases, it is quite possible for us finite humans to realize that the premises of an instance of the ω-rule, for example, all hold. We can apply the rule, even in practice. Is it an a priori or analytic truth that inference is compact, or are there some empirical grounds to be brought for this conclusion? What sorts of grounds? In any case, the decision to focus on logical truth is not just a practical one. It has consequences for logical consequence, or main concern.

---

[9] For a very similar point, see G. Priest, 'Two dogmas of Quineanism', *Philosophical Quarterly* 29 (1979): 289–301.

Notice that there are common logical systems in which the transfer principles fail, along with the deduction theorem. In some modal logics, for example, an inference $\Phi \vdash \Box\Phi$ is valid (via the rule of necessitation), but $\Phi \rightarrow \Box\Phi$ is not a thesis. Quine himself is ambivalent (at best) concerning modal logic, but the point is general. Does our Quinean reject logics without a deduction theorem out of hand—on a priori grounds?

What is the status of the transfer principles themselves? Can we contemplate changing them in response to recalcitrant empirical data? What would a web look like without them? A gut reaction would be that the transfer principles are *analytic*, substantially based on the meaning of conjunction and the conditional. The left-to-right direction flows from the standard elimination rules for conjunction and the material conditional, and the right-to-left direction recapitulates the standard introduction rules (or the deduction theorem). If one holds that the transfer principles are themselves analytic or somehow based on meaning, then there seems to be at least one principle that is not subject to empirical refutation, and the door to the a priori is open—*pace* the radical rejection of such notions. If the transfer principles are immune from empirical refutation, then why not other inferences, such as the introduction and elimination rules for the other logical terminology or, more boldly, the axioms and rules for the natural numbers, such as the aforementioned ω-rule?

The alternative would be to maintain the staunch rejection of the a priori and hold that the transfer principles are indeed as corrigible and a posteriori as any other part of the web is. That is, our Quinean envisions the possibility that an unfortunate string of observations might get us to revise the transfer principles. If she insists on this possibility, then she cannot rest content with a treatment of logical truth and owes us an account of logical inference, or inference generally, that does not go via the transfer principles—not to mention an account of how the transfer principles would themselves be revised.

The complaint here is similar, if not identical, to one lodged in Wright's 'Inventing logical necessity'. Since nothing is outside the web of belief, the Quinean would have it that the identification of the correct logic is part of the web. In particular, logic itself is subject to modification the way anything in the web is. Suppose someone is considering a change in logic, because less drastic measures are not working. Presumably the troubled theorist would follow the model for any change in the web. He would replace the old logic with the new one and see how it comes out. That is, the theorist would examine the consequences of the change in logic for the proposed new web of belief. Consequences? Which logic do we use to assess the consequences of different logics? Is there a correct logic for that, and is this super-logic also just a bunch of nodes in the current web? Regress threatens. Is the super-logic analytic, a priori, or incorrigible?

Wright invites us to consider a sentence of the form: 'Sentence Φ follows from sentences Γ in logic L.' He argues that even for the Quinean, correct sentences like these are a priori and so outside the web of belief—any web of belief. Wright concludes that there is at least a weak logic that regulates changes in the web due to alterations of logic. We use the weak extra-web logic to assess the *consequences* of a change in logic. If this extra-web logic takes something like a standard form of being a calculus on a formal language, we can speculate on its details. It probably does not go much beyond the transfer principles above, or the standard introduction and elimination rules for conjunction and the material conditional. But still at least *something* is a priori.

2. QUINE ON LOGICAL TRUTH AND CONSEQUENCE

Quine's *Philosophy of Logic* proposes a distinctive account of logical truth and, derivatively, an account of logical consequence. He proposes that a sentence Φ is logically true if Φ is true and remains true under any uniform substitutions of its non-logical terminology. For example, the sentence 'if it is raining, then if it is cold, then it is raining' is logically true because every substitution instance of 'if S_1, then if S_2, then S_1' is true. A straightforward extension of this would be that a sentence Φ follows logically from a set of sentences Γ just in case there is no uniform substitution instance of the non-logical terminology that makes every member of Γ true and Φ false. Call this the *substitutional* account of logical truth and consequence. It is a nice, clean account. The only notions involved are substitution (grammar) and truth. Quine might claim that no modal or semantic matters soil the definition, but P. F. Strawson shows how the requisite notion of substitution depends on analyticity.[10] That need not detain us here. We have other fish to fry.

Quine shows that *if* we (1) restrict the logical vocabulary to the truth-functional connectives and first-order quantifiers and variables, (2) insist that the symbol for identity is non-logical, and (3) include a theory of the natural numbers (in the web), *then* his substitutional notion of logical truth (and consequence) coincides with the standard proof-theoretic and model-theoretic one.[11] Quine's notion of logical consequence is compact because first-order logic is complete.

---

[10] P. F. Strawson, 'Propositions, concepts and logical truths', *Philosophical Quarterly* 7 (1957): 15–25.

[11] The connection between Quine's substitutional definition and the standard model-theoretic and proof-theoretic conceptions depends on a delicate balance in Quine's logical system. We can set aside his rejection of higher-order logic (condition (1)). If Quine included the identity symbol as a *logical* primitive (against condition (2)), his substitutional definition of logical truth would diverge in extension from the standard conceptions. The sentence $\exists x \exists y (\neg(x=y))$ would come out logically true on Quine's definition, since it is true and has no non-logical terms (and so nothing to substitute). But that sentence is not logically true on standard conceptions, since it is false in models whose domain has a single element. From the other side, consider a sentence in the form [$[\forall x \forall y \forall z ((Rxy \ \& \ Ryz) \rightarrow Rxz) \ \& \ \forall x \exists y Rxy] \rightarrow \exists x Rxx]$, whose only non-logical item is a binary predicate R. If the universe is finite, then such a sentence would come

Quine points out that if a sentence is logically true (in one of the aforementioned senses), then either it is *obvious* or it can be seen to follow from obvious truths by a sequence of obvious steps. This, he thinks, is as close as we need to come to the traditional notion of apriority. The potential obviousness of logical truths explains why our ancestors were led to believe that logical truth is analytic and a priori. The ancient beliefs are (or were) understandable, but mistaken.

The theorems linking the Quinean substitutional notion of logical truth with the more standard notions have some unsettling consequences. In particular, if a sentence Φ is logically true in Quine's austere sense, then Φ is satisfied by all models. Assume that any group of sentences reporting observations—or, better, observations we are going to take seriously—is satisfiable. Given completeness, this just comes to the consistency of the reports that we intend to take seriously. It follows that logical truth is *demonstrably* independent of observation. That is, under this assumption, we *prove* that a logical truth is true no matter what observations we may have.

There is a further epistemic conclusion to draw. The foregoing result entails that his logic is complete. That is, if a sentence is a logical truth in Quine's austere sense, then its truth can be determined in a standard deductive system. Deductions are not observations. So by Quine's own lights, each logical truth is *knowable a priori*. Our ancestors were not mistaken after all; logic is a priori. The indicated theorems show that the notion of logicality that Quine commends applies only to sentences true and knowable independently of experience.[12]

The meta-theory used to establish these results about Quinean logical truth is a weak set theory, a small chunk of mathematics. A Quinean would surely retort that this meta-theory has the same epistemological background as the rest of the web. That is, the weak meta-theory is established via its utility in science, as a vehicle to organize experience. The Quinean insists that the weak meta-theory is itself empirical and so are its theorems concerning the logical truths. So we have a well-established empirical theory tell us that a certain bunch of sentences and inferences are a priori.

Let's try to be clear about the sense of apriority in play here, and the role of empirical observation. Let Φ be a logical truth and let Π be a derivation of Φ in a standard deductive system. Then Π is a warrant for Φ. Since the derivation itself

---

out logically true on Quine's substitutional definition, but it is not a first-order logical truth, since the sentence is false on the natural numbers, with Rxy interpreted as $x<y$. Quine's insistence that the web include number theory (condition (3)) ensures that the universe is infinite, and so sentences like this one do not come out logically true.

[12] Quine insists on completeness in any case. See e.g. his arguments against higher-order logic. Notice that *if* we construe the axioms and basic inferences of a deductive system as constituting the meaning of the logical terminology, then it follows from the results that Quine cites that logical truths are analytic—true solely in virtue of meaning (assuming that logical consequence preserves analyticity). But, of course, this is a big 'if'. The present concern is with priority.

does not depend on any particular observations, Π is an a priori warrant and so Φ is a priori. Suppose, however, that one asks further questions concerning what makes derivations like Π legitimate warrants. What is it that makes such derivations reliable? Why are we warranted in believing the results of logical derivations? One can give the soundness proof at this point, but then someone will ask a question about the reliability of the meta-theory used to prove soundness. At some point during this sequence of 'meta-questions', the Quinean waxes holistic and refers to the role of the meta-theory in the web of belief.

In sum, then, we have that each logical truth Φ has an a priori warrant, but in justifying the warranting process, we *ultimately* appeal to observation via roles in the web of belief. Say that such a proposition (or inference) is *locally a priori*. This is not enough 'apriority' for some traditional philosophers (such as Frege). Let us say that a proposition is *fundamentally a priori* if it is a priori all the way up (or down). That is, a proposition is fundamentally a priori if it has an a priori warrant, and the reliability (or legitimacy) of this warrant is a priori, and the reliability of that is a priori, etc.—with the process continuing until we come on something that needs no warrant.[13] The notion of fundamental apriority is of a piece with traditional foundationalism. As a holist, the Quinean holds that nothing is fundamentally a priori. Ultimately everything is justified by its place in the web. Notice, however, that for Quine the naturalist, the only epistemic standards are those implicit in normal scientific practice. The scientist is rarely—if ever—concerned with ultimate justification. Normally, justification is more local. Suppose someone is not sure whether a given proposition Φ is logically true, or whether it is true at all. This doubt is alleviated by giving a derivation of Φ in a standard deductive system. It would be perverse for anyone to attempt to answer the doubt about Φ by elaborating the entire web of belief and showing the role of Φ in that (even if this were possible without presupposing the logic). As a naturalist, Quine takes scientific justifications at face value, without looking for extra-scientific justification for any sentence. As far as I know, scientists and mathematicians never justify logical truths in terms of their role in the web. As we have seen, there are a priori warrants at the local level, the level where justification usually takes place.

---

[13] A proposition can be fundamentally a priori and still fallible, and even subject to empirical refutation. Fundamental apriority turns on the nature of the warrant, not its strength. So the present distinction between local and fundamental apriority is orthogonal to the distinction between corrigible and incorrigible knowledge. I am indebted to Crispin Wright and John Skorupski here, although I do not think they agree with the way I put things. John Skorupski points out that the arch-empiricist John Stuart Mill agreed that basic intuition and inference is reliable, but the *realiability* of intuition and inference is itself an empirical matter. That is, Mill held that *continued observation* confirms that intuition and inference lead to truths. So for Mill, logic and intuition are locally but not fundamentally a priori. See J. Skorupski, *John Stuart Mill* (London: Routledge, 1989): ch. 5; and 'Mill on language and logic', in J. Skorupski (ed.), *The Cambridge Companion to Mill* (Cambridge: Cambridge University Press, 1998): 35–56.

The situation here is ironic. Everyone agrees that the truth of any true sentence is due to both how language works and the way the world is. The staunch holist holds that those two components cannot be separated. Every legitimate belief is held only because of the role it plays in the web of belief. But now we see that it follows from certain parts of the web—namely the aforementioned weak set-theoretic meta-theory—that a certain chunk of the web is immune from empirical confirmation and refutation. So the web has seams after all.

To take stock, we see first that by Quine's own lights, something in the neighbourhood of the transfer principles is *fundamentally* a priori. The rest of Quine's logic is at least locally a priori.

None of this undermines the key thrust of Quine's thinking. The main target of his early work was not the very notion of analytic or a priori truth, but the role of the analytic and the a priori in previous philosophy, mainly logical positivism. In a retrospective moment, Quine wrote:[14]

I now perceive that the philosophically important question about analyticity and the linguistic doctrine of logical truth is not how to explicate them; it is the question rather of their relevance to epistemology. The second dogma of empiricsm, to the effect that each empirically meaningful sentence has an empirical content of its own, was cited in 'Two Dogmas' merely as encouraging false confidence in the notion of analyticity; but now I would say further that the second dogma creates a need for analyticity as a key notion of epistimology, and that the need lapses when we heed Duhem and set the second dogma aside.

For, given the second dogma, analyticity is needed to account for the meaningfulness of logical and mathematical truths, which are clearly devoid of empirical content. But when we drop the second dogma and see logic and mathematics rather as meshing with physics and other sciences for the joint implication of empirical consequences, the question of limiting empirical content to some sentences at the expense of others no longer arises.

Notice Quine's reference to 'implication' here. Our present topic concerns the status of that. The 'implication' here is probably not much more than the transfer principles.

Quine concludes that the 'notion of analyticity . . . just subsides into the humbler domain where its supporting intuitions hold sway: the domain of language learning and empirical semantics' (*ibid.* 208). On the present analysis, the apriority of logical truth subsides into set theory.

For Quine's teacher and opponent, Rudolf Carnap, analytic truths characterize 'framework principles'.[15] That is, analytic truths describe a linguistic framework, giving the grammar and rules of inference for operating within the framework. Once a framework is adopted, and one is working within the framework, the

[14] W. V. O. Quine, 'Reply to Geoffrey Hellman', in *The Philosophy of W. V. Quine*, ed. by L. E. Hahn and P. A. Schilpp (La Salle, Ill.: Open Court, 1986): 206–8; the quoted passage is on 207.

[15] See e.g. R. Carnap, 'Empiricism, semantics, and ontology', *Revue Internationale de Philosophie* 4 (1950): 20–40; repr. in P. Benacerraf and H. Putnam, *Philosophy of Mathematics*, 2nd edn. (Cambridge: Cambridge University Press, 1983): 241–57.

framework principles are necessary truths. They determine what it is to be working in the framework. By definition, if one violates them, one is not working in the framework. From this internal perspective, the framework principles are knowable a priori. One who is working within the framework can justify an utterance or an inference by claiming that it is analytic, constitutive of the game she is playing. Analytic truths have a one-stop justification. However, for Carnap the decision to adopt a given framework is a contingent, pragmatic affair. We decide which frameworks to work in based on our needs. One of these needs is to organize experience and make predictions. From *outside* the framework, its analytic truths are conventions which we may or may not decide to adopt, on pragmatic grounds.

Against this picture, Quine argued that the criteria we use to adopt a theoretical scientific hypothesis—*within* a scientific linquistic framework—are the same as the criteria Carnap says we use to adopt a framework, namely closeness of fit with the data, simplicity, expressive power, etc. In other words, the pragmatism of framework adoption applies *within* the scientific enterprise. There is no difference in kind between adopting a scientific framework and working within one. Quine thus rejected the difference between the internal and external perspectives. All we have is the single web of belief, and there is no place to stand outside of it. There simply is no room for a privileged class of framework-regulatory statements that we decide to adopt *before* confronting the world of experience.[16]

I argued above that this is not quite correct. Something in the neighbourhood of the transfer principles is fundamentally a priori. However, those principles are far too weak to cover the needs of the logical positivists. The foregoing considerations do not yield the fundamental apriority of even first-order logic, let alone all of mathematics.

What of the locally a priori principles? The present considerations indicate that the Quinean web does indeed have a class of truths and inferences that are immune from empirical verification and refutation. In a sense, the logical truths and inferences are like Carnap's framework principles, since the logical inferences determine how we are to move around the web. But these locally a priori principles are *not* external to the web. On the picture sketched here, the local apriority of the logical truths and inferences is a highly theoretical matter, decided within the web on the basis of a weak set theory. This is a long cry from the analytic truths of logical positivism.

In the above retrospective passage, Quine claims that when we give up on the second dogma, the *need* for a notion of analyticity lapses. This raises a challenge to the defender of such notions to delineate an interesting use for them (assuming we do not need the notions for a positivistic programme). Here, at least, we see a use for apriority in characterizing the relationship between a theory and its consequences, both on a fundamental level and locally.[17]

---

[16] I am indebted here to conversations with Penelope Maddy.
[17] I am indebted to Crispin Wright here.

3. REFLECTIVE EQUILIBRIUM

Resnik endorses the original Quinean doctrine that logic is not a priori:

Many contemporary philosophers of mathematics believe that mathematical proofs are the bastions of a priori mathematical knowledge, because they lead us to logical truths. Specifically, we learn from them that it is logically true that if the proof's axioms are true (or true in a structure) then so is its conclusion. Because these conditional statements are logically true, they are supposed to be insulated from empirically motivated revision . . . I . . . argue against this supposition. (*Mathematics as a Science of Patterns* 155–6)

So Resnik holds that logical truths are subject to empirically motivated revision. Again, we need to sort out several senses of this statement.

To provide a framework for his claim, Resnik presents a methodology for logic, an adaption of the programme of 'wide reflective equilibrium' formulated by Nelson Goodman and used by John Rawls for an account of justice.[18] Resnik states that wide reflective equilibrium is the 'method logicians use when constructing systems for codifying correct reasoning or notions of logical necessity or possibility' (*ibid.* 159). I do not know if this is intended as an empirical claim that can be confirmed or rejected by studying logic texts, the work notes of active logicians, interviews with them, etc. Or is it a normative claim that logicians ought to work this way? Let us take Resnik's methodological statement as something like a rational reconstruction of the study of logic, without going further into what this comes to.

Resnik's 'Logic, normative or descriptive?' contains a more detailed sketch of the methodology,[19] but we can be content with the briefer description in the 1997 book:

One starts with one's own intuitions concerning logical correctness (or logical necessity). These usually take the form of a set of test cases: arguments that one accepts or rejects, statements that one takes to be logically necessary, inconsistent, or equivalent . . . One then tries to build a logical theory whose pronouncements accord with one's initial considered judgements. It is unlikely that initial attempts will produce an exact fit between the theory and the 'data' . . . Sometimes . . . one will yield one's logical intuitions to powerful or elegant systematic considerations. In short, 'theory' will lead one to reject the 'data'. Moreover, in deciding what must give, not only should one consider the merits of the logical theory *per se* . . . but one should also consider how the theory and one's intuitions cohere with one's other beliefs and commitments, including philosophical ones. When the theory rejects no example one is determined to preserve and countenances none one is

---

[18] Nelson Goodman, 'The new riddle of induction', in *Fact, Fiction and Forecast* (Cambridge, Mass.: Harvard University Press, 1955): 59–83; J. Rawls, *A Theory of Justice* (Cambridge, Mass.: Harvard University Press, 1971).

[19] M. Resnik, 'Logic, normative or descriptive? The ethics of belief or a branch of psychology', *Philosophy of Science* 52 (1985): 221–38; see also Resnik, 'Ought there to be but one logic'.

determined to reject, then the theory and its terminal set of considered judgements are in
. . . *wide reflective equilibrium.* (Ibid. 159)

Unlike Quine, Resnik thus gives explicit and direct attention to logical consequence as well as logical truth, and other notions like consistency and logical
equivalence. The theorist's 'intuitions' about these things are up for grabs in the
process of attaining reflective equilibrium.

With this methodological account as background, Resnik goes on to argue that
logic is not a priori and that logical truth is not necessary truth. He also claims
that logic is not cognitive, in the sense that there are no 'facts to the matter'
concerning whether a given argument is valid, a given theory consistent, etc.
Nevertheless, Resnik maintains that there is (or ought to be) only one logic.
Suppose, for example, that classical logic is the outcome of the methodology
(which is presumably Resnik's own view). So long as the theorist remains in
reflective equilibrium, there is no room for any other logic, such as intuitionistic
logic, relevance logic, paraconsistent logic, or quantum logic.

Here I examine each of Resnik's theses, and challenge most of them. Let us
start with the claim that logic is not a priori. Resnik agrees that in proving a theorem 'we do come to know the conditional truth that the axioms hold only if the
theorem does' and that current methodology has us 'insulate' that truth 'from
empirical refutation' (ibid. 171). He concedes that in normal scientific practice, it

is essential that we have such a practice and truths that we treat this way. For theory development and testing must take place against a backdrop of principles and rules for generating consequences and commitments. What we call our logic is what we take as fixed in
testing and developing our theories . . . [I]n using logic this way, we place it outside the
circuit by which we test our beliefs, and thereby allow no experience to confirm or refute
logical truths. So in this sense—of being outside the circuit through which we test our
other beliefs against experience—logic is a priori. Consequently, so is our knowledge that
a theorem follows from the axioms if that knowledge has its source in logical deduction.

This is consonant with the above claim that logic is at least *locally* a priori.
However, Resnik's conclusion seems to conflict with his thesis that logical
matters are not cognitive, or at least it does if we accept the platitude that knowledge of *P* entails the (factual) truth of *P*. If we can *know* (a priori) that a conclusion follows from its premises, then it is a fact that the conclusion follows.
Perhaps I am picking a nit here. Resnik could retort that we can have (a priori)
knowledge of the non-cognitive stance projected by claims of correct inference or
he could withdraw the knowledge claim or else claim that it is only a priori
knowledge of the corresponding conditional statement, not knowledge of what
follows from what.

The above process of attaining reflective equilibrium is modelled on the
Quinean picture of normal scientific practice. However, during the logician's
quest for equilibrium, the logical principles are presumably *not* held fixed. In that
case, logical principles are the ones that are being studied, and modifications to

logic 'tested'. Resnik is correct that 'theory development and testing must take place against a backdrop of principles and rules for generating consequences and commitments' and that what 'we call our logic is what we take as fixed in testing and developing our theories.' So what is the 'logic' that we hold as fixed during the *logician's* quest?

There are several locutions in the above passage that explicitly invoke the logic one is to *use* while groping for reflective equilibrium. Resnik says that the logician tries to 'build a logic whose pronouncements *accord* with [her] initial considered judgements', and the logician constantly checks if an intuition '*coheres with*' her other beliefs and commitments. The theory determines when the 'data' and the 'theory' are in conflict. What is the logic for this? Presumably, at each point in the process, the theorist is to *use* the logic accepted at that point. The logician is on the ship of Neurath, building that very ship. She uses the logic she is developing in order to modify that very logic.

The aforementioned point from Wright's 'Inventing logical necessity' (Section 1 above) against Quine surfaces here. Suppose that a logician has an intuition that a certain argument *A* is invalid, and wants to see if this intuition coheres with her evolving logical theory *T*. Sadly, she finds out that the invalidity conflicts with *T*. Consider the sentence:

(*) The theory *T* is not in accord with the invalidity of the Argument *A*,

presumably accepted by the theorist. We are told that *any* sentence is up for revision. Can our logician maintain both *T* and the invalidity of *A* by rejecting (*)? That is, can our logician just reject the inference *from T to* the validity of *A*? Regress threatens.

Resnik reports that Quine does allow a change in logic in order to block an unwanted inference: 'when we revise logic to save a hypothesis in the face of conflicting experience, we effectively refuse to acknowledge the "fateful implication" as such' (*Mathematics as a Science of Patterns*: 117). The issue here is whether we can accept the logical theory *T* by refusing the inference from *T* to the validity of the argument *A*.

As far as I can see, Resnik, or any other Quinean, has only two options. One is to bite the bullet and maintain that the logician is free to reject sentences like (*), and thereby block the unwanted inferences. This allows someone to attain reflective equilibrium very easily. He can just refuse any inference that a pet argument is valid, when his intuitions tell him the argument is invalid (and vice versa). If we point out that this refusal conflicts with some principles, or the very theory, that he explicitly accepts, he will simply refuse *that* inference—much like Lewis Carroll's tortoise.[20]

---

[20] Recall Resnik's definition: 'When the theory rejects no example one is determined to preserve and countenances none one is determined to reject, then the theory and its terminal set of considered judgements are in . . . *wide reflective equilibrium*.' Our logician's 'theory' indeed

I am sure we all know people who occasionally refuse inconvenient inferences, as well as refusing the inference that they are being inconsistent. They also refuse to acknowledge that they are giving the word 'inconsistent' a new meaning. I presume that no right-thinking person (Quinean or otherwise) can recommend this sort of reasoning (if we can call it that)—despite its reflective equilibrium (and apparent popularity). On the present option, the Quinean only has pragmatic grounds for refusing to recommend this 'theory'. The 'theory' seems to be useless. But it is hard to spell even this out without a shared logic.

The other option for our Quinean is to follow the previous sections (and Wright) and concede that at least some principles are *fundamentally* a priori, and not up for revision. Examples might include the aforementioned transfer principles and some sentences in the form (*). This is to admit that something is outside the process of reflective equilibrium and so not up for revision, even during the process of attaining reflective equilibrium. We have reached another variation of the above theme concerning the web of belief. An advocate of this second strategy might go on to point out how weak the fundamentally a priori principles are, as an attempt at damage control.

Let us move on to the rest of our logician's logic. Once reflective equilibrium is attained, the logic takes up its role in testing ordinary scientific hypotheses and theories. Resnik argues that our full logic enjoys only a 'weak sense' of apriority: 'it delineates a set of truths we have *for now* marked off as immune to refutation on the grounds that they are a convenient way to define the parameters through which confirmation and refutation take place' (ibid. 173, emphasis mine). He claims that logical consequence 'is not a priori in another sense, that is, of being immune to revision'. The argument is reminiscent of Quine's orientation to the web of belief, focused especially on the logical parts. Resnik writes:

[W]e might find that certain developments in science and mathematics generate tensions in our system of beliefs so disquieting and so difficult to resolve that we begin to look at the framework that links the system together and to experience. Thus we might find it rational to revise our logic or its limits—to alter our inferential norms, that is—and in so doing change what we count as logical truths and implications. (Ibid. 172)

In other words, some developments in science might knock us out of the reflective equilibrium we had achieved concerning logic, and we may resolve the dilemma with a change in logic. Notice that Resnik's claim here is consistent with the existence of a core of logic that is fundamentally a priori, and unchangeable. The strongest conclusion is that *some* logical principles can be revised.

Quantum logic, had it proved successful, would have been a case in point. We would have changed our logic due to developments elsewhere in the web of belief. Of course, quantum logic was not successful, but Resnik's claim is a modal one. Some part of our current logic *might* get undermined and so is not

rejects no example he is determined to preserve, nor does it countenance one he is determined to reject.

'immune from revision'. However, even if Resnik is correct about this modal claim, the proper conclusion is that our current logic is not wholly incorrigible. We face the prospect that we might have to change some parts of it. This does not undermine the thesis that our current logic—all of it—is a priori. As noted at the beginning of this paper, fallibility is one thing and apriority is another. An inference, say, is a priori if we know, or can know, its validity independently of sensory experience. If the indicated knowledge here has to be infallible, then perhaps nothing is a priori (following Kitcher, *Nature of Mathematical Knowledge*), but why should we adopt such an austere conception of a priori knowledge? As noted above, we know from our current theories, themselves well established in the web of belief, that logical inference is independent of experience. That should be good enough, and must be good enough for a Quinean like Resnik, since the web is the only knowledge we have. The fact (if it is a fact) that we 'might' have to change the logic in the web one day does not, by itself, defeat the thesis that logic is at least locally a priori.

What is troubling about the envisioned logic revision is that the change might be motivated by *sensory* experience. The ominous spectre of something like quantum logic is that it would be an *empirical* development, not a lot different from the advent of non-Euclidean geometry in physics, which undermined the Kantian thesis that Euclidean geometry is synthetic a priori. A posteriori we learned that the best account of the geometry of space is non-Euclidean. But that is history. Here we speculate about what the future *might* bring for logic. If something like quantum logic were to be proposed and empirical data got us to change to that logic, then we would correctly hold that at least parts of our current logic are not a priori. Indeed, we would hold that some principles of our current logic are not known at all, let alone known a priori. Looking back to our (current) state of ignorant bliss, we would say that we were mistaken in our quaint claim that the parts of classical logic that conflict with the new empirical logic are knowable a priori. But unless this empirical logic revision actually happens, it seems to me that we are still justified in the claim that logic—our logic—is independent of sensory experience, since as noted above, our best theories entail that it is. The extra fact that our philosophical theories (the web of belief and all) indicate that we may have to change the logic does not undermine the pronouncements of the scientific theories themselves.

Resnik or another Quinean might argue that our current logic is not a priori, since the methodology of wide reflective equilibrium allows empirical matters to infect judgements of logicality. But the fact that (in principle) empirical matters *could have* infected our judgements, as we groped towards the present reflective equilibrium, does not undermine the apriority of logic. To show that logic is a posteriori, one must show that empirical matters have in fact infected our own judgements about logicality. If no empirical matters were involved in those judgements, then logical truth and validity are independent of empirical experience and so a priori.

Of course, to settle on what counts as *infecting* our judgements we have to have settled on a logic, but this is the predicament of the logician trying for reflective equilibrium, working on the ship of Neurath (in two senses of 'on'). At any stage, she must use the logic she has developed that far.

We must examine the modal notions involved here. Indeed, the very notion of 'revisability' is modal. In what sense is it 'possible' for us to adopt a different logic in light of recalcitrant data, or in any other light for that matter? Consider two of Resnik's views:

(1) Empirical matters could have affected at least some of our judgements of what is logical.

(2) Since reflective equilibrium is holistic, two different logicians could come to different outcomes, both following the process correctly.

What is the sense of 'could have' in these statements? With (1) we envision something like quantum logic succeeding. With (2) we envision a rival logician making different choices in the trade-off between 'theory', the data of considered judgements, background philosophical views, etc., and then coming to a different logic from ours. For example, it is not hard to imagine an intuitionist or an advocate of relevant or paraconsistent logic being in reflective equilibrium.

The problem, however, is that Resnik is left with no room for this modal notion of 'could have'. Is it a *logical* possibility we envision? If so, the only logic we have at our disposal is our own. From that perspective, the paraconsistent logician contradicts himself, and so what he came up with is not a logical possibility.[21] From a classical perspective, the intuitionist and relevance logicians fail to acknowledge some logical truths and valid inferences. The classical logician simply cannot say that it is logically possible for double-negation elimination to be invalid—not while remaining a classical logician.

Resnik or another Quinean may be using a more everyday modality in the revisability thesis. We 'could have' adopted a different logic in the sense that we could have adopted different rules for the *words* 'or', 'for all', etc. However, no defender of analyticity or apriority ever denied that. Surely, the word 'or', for example, could have meant something other than it does. It could have had the meaning that 'and' has. This would not amount to a change in the logic, would it? At most, one can conclude that classical logic does not apply to a language unless it has certain logical particles.[22]

This broaches the problem of 'shared content'. Advocates of classical logic and advocates of intuitionistic logic invariably speak past each other, since each assigns different meanings to the logical terminology. Quine's inextricability thesis is that there is no 'fact of the matter' whether a given word has changed

---

[21] The paraconsistent logician contradicts himself from any perspective (including his own).

[22] See N. Tennant, 'Conventional necessity and the contingency of deduction', *Dialectica* 41 (1987): 79–95.

meaning, say, in the transition from classical to intuitionistic logic. If so, it is hard to make out a substantial thesis of revisability, a thesis that a defender of analyticity and the a priori will deny.

This is a troubling matter. Quineans want to say that it is possible for us to revise our logic (in a non-trivial sense), and I think we have some idea what they mean. On an intuitive level, the thesis that things could have turned out differently for the logician sounds plausible enough. The problem is that this thesis invokes a notion of modality that is prior to, outside of, or independent of the whole process of reflective equilibrium. Such a free-standing, prior modality is anathema to the Quinean. She claims that nothing is outside the web. There is no room in the framework for the relevant 'possibility'.

For his part, Quine demurs from any talk of modality:

We should be within our rights in holding that no formulation of any part of science is definitive so long as it remains couched in idioms of . . . modality Such good uses as the modalities are ever put to can probably be served in ways that are clearer and already known. (Quine, *Philosophy of Logic*: 33–4)

One 'good use' of modality is to state the thesis of logic revisability, but it is hard to make our a 'clearer and already known' way to do this.

Resnik acknowledges something like this predicament. At first, he says that a system of beliefs, logical theories, and considered judgements is in reflective equilibrium if 'it is coherent by the lights of its own logical theory' (*Mathematics as a Science of Patterns*: 160). This seems to presuppose that there is a notion of 'system *S* is coherent by the lights of logic *L*', like the aforementioned sentence (*). Resnik here envisions a binary relation between systems and logics. This relation seems to be transcendent, prior to, or independent of any particular logic. The very notion of reflective equilibrium is formulated in terms of 'conflict' and 'accordance', and these are logical notions. Which logic?

Resnik then writes:

Since in determining reflective equilibrium one uses the logic contained in one's own evolving logical theory, one might think that a theory may be in reflective equilibrium from its own internal point of view and not so from the point of view of another theory. I hesitate to draw this conclusion, since I wonder whether one could make sense of a rival logical theory while remaining true to one's own. Reflective equilibrium may be a notion that is immanent to a logic rather than transcendent.

To adapt what Quine says about truth, a notion is 'immanent to a logic' if it just applies within that logic, and a notion is transcendent if it applies to lots of logics at once. Resnik maintains that reflective equilibrium is immanent. But the definition of reflective equilibrium does not mention a specific logic. It is a *relation* that *logics*, systems of belief, etc. may or may not enjoy. Resnik speaks of *the* method of reflective equilibrium, which seems to indicate that there is a single notion that applies to all logics. Moreover, as we have seen, the definition itself invokes logical notions like coherence and conflict and, on Resnik's view, those notions have no meaning except in the logic one has adopted.

The foregoing considerations show that on Resnik's view, an advocate of one logic $L1$ cannot even recognize that an advocate of another logic $L2$ is in reflective equilibrium *even from the point of view of L2*. In trying to evaluate $L2$ our advocate of $L1$ must use $L1$, since it is the only logic she has. From her perspective, $L2$ is incoherent or incomplete and certainly not in reflective equilibrium.

4. FACTS

Resnik defines *logical realism* to be

[T]he doctrine that statements attributing logical properties or relationships, such as ' "0 = 0" is logically true' or ' "0 = 0" does not imply "0 = 1" ', are true or false independently of our holding them to be true, our psychology, our linguistic and inferential conventions, or other facts about human beings. (*Mathematics as a Science of Patterns*: 162)

He then argues against logical realism and provides a sketch of a non-cognitivist account of logic to take its place. Resnik thus denies that there are 'facts to the matter' concerning logical truth and logical consequence.

To continue the dialectic, we have to put aside one of the foregoing conclusions, and assume that there is a coherent and useful modality, according to which a logician can concede that the process of reflective equilibrium *could have* turned out otherwise, and so we could have adopted another logic. For the sake of an example, let us assume that a classical logician and an intuitionist have each found reflective equilibrium.

Resnik argues that in this case,

[W] have no reason for thinking that one logic rather than another has captured the pre-systematic notions of logical necessity and logical correctness. But this raises an epistemological problem for logical realism. To borrow from Benacerraf's criticism of mathematical realism, if logical necessity is a metaphysical property of sentences or propositions, then we have no grounds for thinking that we can always know when it applies. (Ibid. 162)

The argument seems to be that the classical logician has no grounds for thinking that the intuitionist is wrong since both of them have followed the methodology of reflective equilibrium correctly (each by his or her own lights). Paul Benacerraf famously argues that someone who believes in the independent existence of mathematical objects has a serious—unsurmountable—epistemological problem.[23] If numbers, for example, are abstract, eternal, acausal, etc., then how on earth can humans come to know anything about them? Here Resnik's argument is that if there are objective, mind-independent facts concerning, say, logical

---

[23] P. Benacerraf, 'Mathematical truth', *Journal of Philosophy* 70 (1973): 661–79; repr. in Benacerraf and Putnam, *Philosophy of Mathematics*: 403–20.

consequence, then how can we learn what they are, especially in light of the claim that methodology of reflective equilibrium may not yield a unique logic?

Benacerraf's other blockbuster article argues that numbers are not set-theoretic objects because there is no (objective) ground to prefer the von Neumann finite ordinals over the Zermelo numerals.[24] Here the argument is that there is no objective ground to prefer one logic over the other.

In arguing for 'intolerance' of rival logics, Resnik writes

but for a whim I would be in the shoes of one of my rivals. But I am not in their shoes. To convert to one of their theories I must give up intuition X or principle Y. Why should I do that when my theory is working so well now? From the present point of view, I made the right choices—by luck or whim perhaps—but that makes them no less right. (Ibid.)

On Resnik's view, the choices he made to get into reflective equilibrium are 'right' just because he is in reflective equilibrium. Resnik suggests that there was 'luck' and 'whim' involved in getting into reflective equilibrium. Since luck and whim need not track the facts, the logical realist has no reason to think that she has hit upon the one true logic in her march towards reflective equilibrium. She should admit that, for all she knows, her opponent may be the one who is right, or neither of them hit on the correct logic. According to logical realism, one can be in reflective equilibrium and still be wrong. Resnik finds it more congenial to drop the logical realism.

Resnik's rejection of logical realism is premature. Compare Quine's thesis of the underdetermination of theory by data with the situation of two rival logicians each in reflective equilibrium. Quine famously argues that there can be two scientific theories that each fit the 'data' of sense experience and yet are different from each other. Given Quine's account of the methodology of the empirical sciences, there would be no telling which theory is right. An advocate of one of the rival theories should admit that 'but for luck or whim', he might be an advocate of the other. And so the *scientific* realist has a similar dilemma to the logical realist. Famously, Quine does not conclude that there is something wrong with scientific realism, and retreat to the conclusion that, to paraphrase Resnik, statements attributing scientific properties or relationships are not 'true or false independently of our holding them to be true, our psychology, our linguistic and inferential conventions, or other facts about human beings'.

According to Quine, the underdetermination of theory by data is ubiquitous, holding for vast areas of inquiry. If the possibility of rival theories both in the relevant kind of equilibrium is sufficient to rule out realism, then *no* area of discourse can enjoy a realist interpretation. Of course, Resnik is not out to defend a global irrealism. He maintains a realist orientation to mathematics and, presumably, also for ordinary scientific discourse.

---

[24] P. Benacerraf, 'What numbers could not be', *Philosophical Review* 74 (1965): 47–73; repr. in Benacerraf and Putnam, *Philosophy of Mathematics*: 272–94.

It must be conceded that even if the 'underdetermination' phenomenon (when it occurs) does not undermine the objectivity of a discourse, it does present an awkward epistemology—for both science and logic. When there is (or might be) underdetermination, a realist cannot rule out the existence of unknowable truths.[25] In the case of logic and science generally, one can follow the prescribed, or best, methodology perfectly and still come out wrong. To modify a Quinean metaphor, if two theorists each find themselves in the relevant sort of reflective equilibrium, then the truth is inscrutable, or, perhaps better, truth is inscrutable so long as they remain in reflective equilibrium (i.e. so long as neither of them manages to dislodge the other from reflective equilibrium).

To maintain that logic is non-cognitive and science is objective, Resnik must find some difference between the method of wide reflective equilibrium in logic and the relevant scientific or mathematical methodology, or whatever it is that leads to the (alleged) underdetermination of theory by data in science. One possibility is to point out that to obtain wide reflective equilibrium in logic, we sometimes have to reject the 'data' of inferences that we intuitively hold to be correct, or statements we hold to be logical truths. Resnik cites the paradox of implication as an example. Our initial intuitions might have us reject an inference from a contradiction to an arbitrary conclusion, but this 'datum' gets corrected by classical theory (unless of course one is a relevance logician and finds a different reflective equilibrium).

This much does not distinguish logical from scientific methodology. I presume that for Quine and Resnik, the scientific 'data' consist of observations. Students of scientific methodology often point out that sometimes scientists will reject data that do not accord with theory, sometimes with an explicit assumption that something must have been done incorrectly.[26]

Another way to separate logical methodology from scientific methodology would be to claim that in logic the 'data' are themselves non-cognitive. Idealism aside, the prevailing opinion is that in a scientific context, laboratory or field observations track an objective world and scientific theories are attempts to organize and predict the future of this objective world. A follower of Resnik might

---

[25] For an anti-realist who holds that all truths are knowable, the underdetermination of theory by data would confirm the rejection of bivalence, and the demurral at excluded middle. I am indebted to Neil Tennant here. See Tennant's *The Taming of the True* (Oxford: Oxford University Press, 1997) for a sustained global anti-realism. Incidentally, colleagues and students often express surprise and wonder at Resnik's combination of realism for mathematics and science and non-cognitivism for logic. Resnik himself (*Mathematics as a Science of Patterns*: 165n.) reports a similar reaction.

[26] Personal anecdote: When taking science labs my first and second year in college, I would often (more than not) have my reports rejected simply because I could not get my data to agree with theory. Of course, I am not claiming that I did the experiments correctly. Quite the contrary. I am as sure as my instructors were that I botched them simply because the results did not accord with theory. I deserved the marks I got (except when I fudged the data). The point here is that in science as well as in logic, the 'data' are not incorrigible and are subject to correction by theory.

claim that with logic, the 'data' of intuitive judgements of correct inference and the like do not track anything objective, and so our logical theories are not out to organize objective data. It is an irrealist endeavour from the start.

One might retort that this manœuvre begs the question against the logical realist. Who says that our intuitions do not (fallibly) track objectively correct inference patterns? The debate would then focus on the status of the nature of observations in the case of science and our pre-theoretic logical intuitions in the case of logic. Resnik might point out that rival scientists can usually get each other to agree on observation reports (at least when doing Kuhnian 'normal science') by carefully manipulating the equipment. In contrast, rival logicians notoriously do not and cannot come to agree on the disputed 'intuitions'. Is this to say that there is no such thing as Kuhnian 'normal logic'? Notice, however, that once the debate takes this focus, any claims about the nature of wide reflective equilibrium, such as whether it delivers a unique theory, are irrelevant. What matters are pre-reflective intuitions, the matter upon which reflective equilibrium operates.

Moreover, even if the logical irrealist wins this preliminary skirmish, he will lose the war. Suppose that we concede for the sake of argument that our pre-reflective intuitions are not cognitive, and so do not track an objective realm. This does not alter the fact that the central role of logic is not explicable solely in terms of 'our linguistic and inferential conventions'. A common slogan is that logical consequence is *truth-preserving*. The relevant feature here is that consequence must preserve *objective* truth, since logic is applicable in areas which are up for realist construal, such as science. Logical consequence must answer to, and preserve, objective truth. That's the point of logic. So logic is not completely dependent on just our conventions (again, see Tennant, 'Conventional necessity').

Suppose, for example, that a community adopted a tonk-like connective.[27] Then their consequence relation would be faulty, on objective grounds, simply because it fails to preserve truth. To be sure, if the members of that community had a minimal amount of intelligence, they would soon realize that they are not in wide reflective equilibrium. The *reason* they are not in reflective equilibrium is simply that they are allowed to deduce objective falsehoods from objective truths.

Robert Brandom comes to a similar conclusion:[28]

Even if, to begin with, attention is restricted to inferential proprierties, it is clear that not just any notion of correctness of inference will do as a rendering of the sort of content we take our claims and beliefs to have. A semantically correct notion of correct inference must . . . fund the idea of *objective* truth conditions and so of *objectively* correct inferences. Such proprieties of . . . inference outrun actual attitudes of taking or treating judgements and inferences as correct. They are determined by how things actually are, independently

[27] See A. N. Prior 'The runabout inference ticket', *Analysis* 21 (1960): 38–9.

[28] R. Brandom, *Making It Explicit: Reasoning, Representing, and Discursive Commitment* (Cambridge, Mass.: Harvard University Press, 1994): 137.

of how they are taken to be. Our cognitive attitudes must ultimately answer to these attitude-transcendent facts.

This means that although the inferentialist order of explanation may start with inferences that are correct in the sense that they are accepted in the practice of a community, it cannot end there. It must somehow move beyond this sense of correctness if it is to reach a notion of propositional conceptual content recognizable as that expressed by our ordinary empirical claims and possessed by our ordinary empirical beliefs.

In present terms, a lot of objectivity must be built into logical consequence if reflective equilibrium is to be obtained. Logic is objective if anything is.

A third possibility for separating logic from science would be to claim that the methodology for logic is *wide* reflective equilibrium while the marching orders for science and other objective disciplines are only to achieve narrow reflective equilibrium. Recall that in Resnik's account of logic, 'in deciding what must give, not only should one consider the merits of the logical theory *per se* . . . but one should also consider how the theory and one's intuitions cohere with one's other beliefs and commitments, including philosophical ones' (*Mathematics as a Science of Patterns*: 159). Presumably in achieving narrower reflective equilibrium, one would only consider the merits of the theory vis-à-vis the 'data', and ignore 'other beliefs and commitments' along the way. Indeed, for a naturalist, if one's best scientific theory does not cohere with philosophical commitments, then the latter have to go.

This distinction could allow Resnik to accord objectivity to science and withhold that honour from logic, but only if the 'other beliefs and commitments' *actually used* in achieving wide reflective equilibrium in logic are themselves non-cognitive (or non-objective) matters.[29] That is, to pursue the distinction in this manner, the non-cognitivist must show exactly which 'beliefs and other commitments' were in fact used in achieving wide reflective equilibrium, and then show that some of these beliefs and other commitments are non-cognitive.

Perhaps a non-cognitivist holds that his logic is supported by a philosophy of language, and that this philosophy played a role in coming to wide reflective equilibrium. So the status of the logic might turn on the status of the philosophy of language. If the philosophy is itself non-cognitive, then, perhaps, so is the resulting logic. At this juncture, perhaps an opponent can ask for details concerning this philosophy of language (or other beliefs and commitments), how exactly it played a role in the non-cognitivist's choice of logic, and why the philosophy (etc.) is itself non-cognitive. Otherwise, the question is begged.

Surely, *semantic* matters affect the choice of logic. The validity of an inference turns on the meanings of some of the words used in it. Our non-cognitivist might agree with Quine that matters like semantics are not cognitive, citing the indeterminacy of translation and the attack on analyticity. If semantic matters infect the

---

[29] To bring up an earlier matter, the present ploy also presupposes that one can make sense of 'cohere' independent of the logic arrived at in the end.

choice of logic, then logic is not cognitive either. QED. On the other hand, Quine's views on semantics are very controversial, and perhaps it would be wise not to let the status of logic turn on them. Someone who holds that logic is cognitive might then be inclined to reject the Quinean themes (as an attempt at philosophical reflective equilibrium).

Moreover, Quine himself is ambivalent on the semantic status of the logical connectives. In later work, he suggests that if a radical translator has a native denying (or refusing assent to) a logical truth, then we have strong evidence that we have mistranslated. The problem is that if we interpret a native as denying or refusing assent to a logical truth, then we have attributed a deep incoherence to him. Better to think we have made an error in translating than to attribute deep incoherence. This would suggest that at least the logical terminology has fixed (objective?) meanings, and perhaps Quine's overall views on the status of semantics do not force the conclusion that logic is not cognitive.

As far as I know, Resnik does not provide other direct arguments in favour of his logical non-cognitivism. The bulk of his treatment consists of showing how some putative arguments and intuitions in support of logical realism can be accommodated on some irrealist alternatives. The relevance of these considerations depends on where the burden of proof lies. If logical irrealism is the default, then all Resnik has to do is refute arguments for realism. But where does the burden lie?

Resnik's 'Ought there to be but one logic?' provides a lucid account of various positions one can take on the status of logic, such as relativism, realism, conventionalism, and psychologism. That article and the 1997 book (§8.3) contain a very brief sketch his own non-cognitivist account, which is a Blackburn-style projectivism.[30] The idea is that free-standing, or categorical, statements of, say, consistency or of what follows from what do not serve to state facts. Rather,

> they play a signaling role in our inferential practice. In calling someone's remark 'contradictory', for example, we are not describing it as, say, . . . false in all possible worlds. Rather, we manifest that we expect it to be treated in a certain way. Among other things, we show that we are confident that our audience can see this for themselves, that the person uttering the remark should retract or qualify it, and, perhaps, that we will regard those who persist in failing to see our point as intellectually incompetent . . . Categorical judgements of consistency, implication, and equivalence play a similar role in our inferential practice by policing transitions between statements and commitments to groups of statements. (*Mathematics as a Science of Patterns*: 168)

In other words, free-standing statements in matters of logic serve to manifest a certain stance (or stances) toward the sentences in question.

Projectivisms have notorious problems in handling statements that are not

---

[30] See S. Blackburn, *Spreading the Word* (Oxford: Oxford University Press, 1984).

free-standing but are embedded in complex contexts like conditionals.[31] Resnik cites a few examples, including 'any theory implying a falsehood is itself false' and 'Frege's earlier views on meaning do not contradict his later ones.' He concedes that such statements 'have truth-values', presumably objective truth-values. The tension is resolved with the claim that once a sentence in matters of logic is embedded in a richer statement, it no longer serves to manifest a stance. The complex statement does state a fact. The embedded statement is interpreted as 'tacitly referring to the norms that govern (or ought to govern) our inferential practices'. So the above two examples get 'rendered' as 'any theory from which we may infer a falsehood is false itself' and 'Frege's earlier views on meaning do not prohibit one from asserting his later ones'. Since these norms are not independent of our minds and practices, at least the spirit of irrealism is maintained.

Perhaps Resnik's overall argument is thus an inference to the best explanation. His sketched account is put forward as a philosophical explanation of inferential practice, attitudes, etc., which then competes with other explanations, such as realism, relativism, etc. If this is the strategy in place, then we need an account of what makes an explanation better (or best), so that a neutral reader can come to some reasoned view of the matter. Perhaps future work will provide this overall context.

5. TRUTH AND OBJECTIVITY

To move the dialogue forward, I propose to invoke the criteria developed in one of the most sustained and thorough treatments of objectivity, Wright's *Truth and Objectivity*. Recall that Resnik defines logical realism to be 'the doctrine that statements attributing logical properties or relationships . . . are true or false independently of our holding them to be true, our psychology, our linguistic and inferential conventions, or other facts about human beings' (*Mathematics as a Science of Patterns*: 162). This much seems consonant with the notion or notions of realism developed in Wright's book.

Truth and Objectivity begins by articulating a 'minimalist' notion of truth, which does not presuppose a realist interpretation. A non-cognitivist in ethics, for example, might maintain that murder is wrong, and so she can assert that it is *true that* murder is wrong, in the minimal sense of 'truth'. I will go along, since it is convenient to use a neutral notion in order to state the various criteria and theses. In what follows, I do not intend a locution in the form '*S* is true' to entail that *S* is objective or that *S* is cognitive. A reader who does not like this can substitute

---

[31] For a compelling account of the problem, see Bob Hale, 'Can there be a logic of attitudes', in John Haldane and Crispin Wright (eds.), *Reality, Representation and Projection* (New York: Oxford University Press, 1993): 337–63.

something like '*S* is correct' or '*S* is merely correct' for '*S* is true' in most of what follows.

The conclusion of this section is that for each of Wright's criteria, either logic comes out objective, or the criterion is useless in this context since logic must be exempted from it. The end result is to further the foregoing thesis that if any area of discourse is objective, then logic is objective as well.

5.1 Epistemic constraint

We have invoked one of Wright's criteria already, in the discussion of the under-determination of theory by data (Section 4). A discourse is *epistemically constrained* if it is not possible for there to be unknowable truths in the discourse, or to be precise, if the possibility of unknowable truths can be ruled out a priori. An objective or cognitive discourse may or may not be epistemically constrained. However, Wright argues that if a discourse is *not* epistemically constrained, then an irrealist interpretation for it cannot get off the ground. So epistemic constraint is necessary for irrealism, and the failure of epistemic constraint is sufficient for realism. This much seems correct. I do not see how the various irrealisms, and especially Resnik's non-cognitivism, can be squared with the possibility of unknowable truths. This criterion seems to fit what Resnik says as well. In holding logic to be non-cognitive, he denies that statements in logic are true or false independently of our holding them to be true, our psychology, our linguistic, and inferential conventions, etc. So on Resnik's view, if, say, Φ follows from Γ, then humans should have the wherewithal to detect that Φ follows from Γ. There can be no logical truths or inferences that lie beyond our ability to be warranted in asserting them as logical truths or inferences.

The previous section showed that *if* one is a realist about logic, and *if* reflective equilibrium is the methodology for logic, and *if* there can be two rival logicians both in wide reflective equilibrium, then logical inference (etc.) is *not* epistemically constrained. The antecedents of this conditional allow that two logicians may follow the methodology correctly (each of his own lights) and yet at least one of them is wrong. There are truths about logic that one of them cannot know (so long as his reflective equilibrium is maintained).

But of course this explicitly begs the question in favour of realism, through the first antecedent. Without assuming realism or irrealism, is logic epistemically constrained? Arguably, classical first-order formal logical consequence is epistemically constrained, due to the completeness theorem. If a sentence Φ follows from a set Γ, then in principle, this can be learned through a deduction. So if first-order logical consequence is the only matter up for discussion, then the door to an irrealism is open. The criterion of epistemic constraint does not help here.

What of first-order consistency? If a set Γ of sentences is inconsistent, then it is possible to deduce a contradiction from Γ, but if Γ is consistent, there may be no way to detect this. Church's theorem is that the set of consistent sentences is not recursively enumerable. Given classical logic (in the meta-theory), for any sentence Φ, either Φ is consistent or Φ is inconsistent. If we make the mechanistic assumption that human epistemic abilities (concerning consistency) are captured in a single formal deductive system or Turing machine, then consistency is not epistemically constrained. There are consistent sentences that cannot be known (as a result of a mechanical procedure) to be consistent. So under the mechanistic assumption, one must be a realist about classical first-order consistency.

Second-order logic is inherently incomplete in the sense that there is no formal deductive system whose consequences exactly coincide with second-order consequence.[32] If we continue the mechanistic assumption that human epistemic abilities are captured in a single formal deductive system or Turing machine, then second-order logical consequence is not epistemically constrained. So if second-order logic and mechanism reign, then there are logical truths that cannot be known to be logical truths.

Even without the mechanistic assumption, the expressive resources of second-order languages are formidable. Suppose, for example, that Φ is a sentence of second-order real analysis. There is a categorical axiomatization Γ of real analysis, and so Φ is true of the real numbers if and only if Φ is a second-order consequence of Γ. So if second-order logic is epistemically constrained, then so is real analysis. The same goes for just about every other mathematical theory short of higher set theory. On the score of epistemic constraint, second-order logic and most of mathematics stand or fall together.

Suppose that second-order logic is epistemically *un*constrained, and suppose that a logician has adopted second-order logic (as in my *Foundations without Foundationalism*) and is in reflective equilibrium. Then following Wright's main criterion and Resnik's definition, this logician (me) will be a realist about logic. As a sort of converse, if second-order logic is epistemically unconstrained, then a theorist like Resnik who maintains logical non-cognitivism would presumably reject second-order logic (as logic) since it conflicts with his *philosophical* views concerning logic.[33] In sum, nobody who holds that second-order logic is epistemically unconstrained, and that second-order logic is logic, and who is a logical non-cognitivist can be in wide reflective equilibrium.

In any case, Resnik insists that he is not concerned with *formal* notions like first-order and second-order logical consequence. He concedes that those are parts of mathematics and so fully objective (since he holds that mathematics is objective). The issues here concern the basic notions of validity and consequence for *natural language*. The relationship between the formal notions and their infor-

---

[32] See S. Shapiro, *Foundations without Foundationalism: A Case for Second-Order Logic* (Oxford: Oxford University Press, 1991): ch. 4.

[33] Resnik himself does reject second-order logic. See his 'Second-order logic still wild', *Journal of Philosophy* 85 (1988): 75–87.

mal counterparts is not so clear. What does it mean to say that the underlying logic of mathematics is first-order or second-order? Rather than settle that troubling matter, let us assume for the sake of argument that logic is epistemically constrained, and move on to Wright's more specific criteria for objectivity: width of cosmological role, the Euthyphro contrast, and Cognitive Command.

5.2 Wide cosmological role

The idea here is that a discourse is apt for a realist construal if statements in that discourse figure in explanations provided within a wide range of discourses, including those well beyond the discourse in question. To take a mundane example, Wright points out that the wetness of some rocks can explain 'my perceiving, and hence believing, that the rocks are wet', 'a small . . . child's interest in his hands after he has touched the rocks', 'my slipping and falling', and 'the abundance of lichen growing on them' (*Truth and Objectivity*: 197). So statements about rock wetness figure in explanations concerning perception, belief, the interests of children, the human abilities to negotiate terrain, and lichen growth.

Officially, Wright defines a subject matter to have wide cosmological role 'just in case mention of the states of affairs of which it consists can feature in at least some kinds of explanation of contingencies which are not of that sort—explanations whose possibility is not guaranteed merely by the minimal truth aptitude of the associated discourse' (ibid. 198). Statements about rock wetness thus have wide cosmological role and, of course, a realist interpretation of this discourse is most natural. Wright argues that moral discourse fails to have wide cosmological role. Moral 'states of affairs' do not figure in explanations of non-moral matters.

Despite the word 'cosmological' in the title, Wright is anxious to add that the explanations involved do not have to be causal. Otherwise, only science-like discourses that traffic in causality would even have a chance of passing the test.[34] Of course, the philosophical literature on explanation is long, deep, and troubling, and I hope we do not need a definitive resolution of that matter here. Intuitively, to explain something is to give a reason for it. According to Webster's *Twentieth Century Unabridged Dictionary*, to explain is to 'make plain, clear, or intelligible; to clear of obscurity'. I take it that, normally, a successful explanation should be objective, or at least factually true—especially if the thing to be explained is itself an objective or factual matter. How can someone clear away obscurity or make some thing intelligible by merely manifesting a stance, or exhibiting some other non-cognitive attitude?

What of logic? It seems to me that in present terms, logic has the *widest* cosmological role of all. Just about any complex explanation of anything is going

---

[34] For an illuminating account of explanation in mathematics, and mathematical explanations of physical phenomena, see M. Steiner, 'Mathematical explanation and scientific knowledge', *Nous* 12 (1978): 17–28; and 'Mathematical explanation', *Philosophical Studies* 34 (1980): 135–52.

to involve claims of logical consequence. We explain the tides and the orbit of the moon by *deducing* the relevant data from gravitational theory (and initial conditions). We explain the divergence of species by deduction from principles of biology (and specific hypotheses about mutations, population splittings, etc.). We explain trends in the stock market, global warming, etc. in like manner. It is no accident that logic is said to be completely general. On the official definition of cosmological role, nothing is wider than logic.

A non-cognitivist about logic might concede that the aforementioned explanations involve deductions, but argue that matters of logical consequence do not themselves figure in the explanations. Suppose that someone is curious about a phenomenon Φ, and assume that Φ is itself an objective matter. A normal explanation of Φ might have the following form: 'Look, the background theory is Γ and the initial conditions are I; Φ is a *logical consequence* of Γ&I.' According to the reply considered here, the last sentence is not part of the explanation, but is rather a shorthand for a specific deduction Π of Φ from Γ and I (plus some mathematics perhaps). The non-cognitivist might claim that the *status* of Π as a *logical* deduction, is not relevant to—or part of—the explanation. However, the deduction succeeds *as an explanation* (of Φ) only if the inferences invoked in Π are truth-preserving. That is, the inferences must preserve *objective* truth. If the inferences used in Π do no more than 'play a signalling role in our inferential practice', then there is no *explanation* of (the objective truth of) Φ. We cannot clear away obscurity and make phenomena intelligible via inference unless those inferences preserve truth.

Nevertheless, given the lack of consensus over what an explanation is, it is perhaps open for someone to exempt logic from the criteria of wide cosmological role. The idea is that logical matters do not figure in the explanations, but rather logic concerns the *framework* for generating explanations. Notice, however, that this manœuvre runs against the spirit of the holism advocated by Quineans like Resnik. Like Carnap's conception of analyticity, the present manœuvre presupposes that we can distinguish framework matters from substantial explanatory matters, and that the framework principles lie outside the web of belief. Moreover, the manœuvre exempts logic from the very question of cosmological role and thus weakens the very sense we can attach to the question of whether logical consequence (etc.) is objective and cognitive.

5.3 The Euthyphro contrast

Let us move on to Wright's second tool, the Euthyphro contrast. By definition, in any discourse that satisfies epistemic constraint, 'truth' and 'best opinion' coincide in extension. The situation would be similar to the dialectic in Plato's *Euthyphro*. At first, Socrates did not contest Euthyphro's claim that an act is pious if and only if it is pleasing to the gods. The debate centred on which of these is the chicken and which the egg. Euthyphro contended that there is no more to piety than what the gods want. Socrates argued that (at best) the gods have the ability to *detect* piety. The contrast between Socrates and Euthyphro would remain if the gods were replaced with more human agents acting under ideal conditions and even if the opinions of these human agents were infallible. Socrates' view here is that piety is objective. As far as it goes, Euthyphro's view is consistent with piety being subjective or otherwise relative, in which case the opinion of the gods is what *constitutes* piety. Euthyphro's view is also consistent with a non-cognitivism about piety, in which case there are no piety-facts at all (objective or otherwise). The appendix to chapter 3 of Wright's *Truth and Objectivity* lays out constraints on a Euthyphro contrast for discourses concerning colour, shape, morality, modality, etc.[35] Here we turn to logic.

Let us say that a human agent is acting under optimal conditions for logic if she is in wide reflective equilibrium and does not make errors due to lack of attention and the like. For the sake of discussion, let us agree on the following (material) biconditional:

> An argument is valid if and only if an ideal agent acting under optimal conditions judges it to be valid.

Does the agent's verdict *detect* validity, as Socrates might contend? Does the verdict *constitute* validity, as a logical subjectivist or relativist might hold? Or does the verdict serve to manifest a non-cognitive stance towards the argument (e.g. signalling its role in inferential practice) as Resnik contends? The issue is whether the methodology of wide reflective equilibrium is a very good (fallible or infallible) method for *figuring out* whether a given argument is valid, or whether there is no more to validity than the end result of the process?

Notice, first, that most of the criteria and nuances that Wright develops in order to articulate the Euthyphro contrast deploy the notion of logical consequence explicitly. This suggests that either logic comes out on the objective side automatically or we make the aforementioned unQuinean move of exempting logic from the whole contrast. Once again, logic would concern the framework for determining what counts as objective. If this latter course is adopted then there is no sense to the very question of which side of the Euthypro contrast logic falls on. The general issue of the objectivity of logic is further undermined since we have lost one of the tools for determining the contrast.

However, a point from the previous subsection applies here. The fact that logical consequence preserves objective truth allows for some objectivity. Suppose that we are dealing with an area of discourse, like physics or Carnap's Thing language, that is agreed to be objective. If an ideal subject under optimal condi-

---

[35] I am reminded of a joke involving three baseball umpires. The first says, 'there's balls and there's strikes and I call 'em as I see 'em.' The second says, 'there's balls and there's strikes and I call 'em as they are.' The third says, 'there's balls and there's strikes, but they ain't nothing till I call 'em.' The first and second umpire go with Socrates, the first taking himself to be fallible and the second infallible. The third umpire goes with Euthyphro.

tions determines that an inference is valid, then she has detected that the inference preserves objective truth. No fiat and no non-cognitive stance can *make* an inference truth-preserving. So that much goes toward Socrates' construal of the contrast. This is consonant with Resnik's concession that if Φ follows from a sentence Ψ, then the conditional 'if Ψ then Φ' is objectively true. Does it now follow that we have to accord objectivity to the inference?

There may still be room for Euthyphro-type reading concerning the status of some inferences. Suppose, for example, that someone is considering the moves that relevant logicians refuse. Two logicians can agree that the irrelevant inferences preserve truth, in the sense that they never lead from true premises to false conclusions, without agreeing on the status of the inference.[36] The classical logician declares the inference to be valid, while the relevance logician demurs. That is, they disagree on the *status* of an inference agreed to be truth-preserving. So far, we have no argument that a pronouncement either for classical logic or relevance logic would count as detecting the facts, constituting them, or manifesting a stance. A logical realist would say that the logicians are attempting to detect the correct logic, while the subjectivist, non-cognitivist, and relativist would say otherwise. On this narrow range, we seem to have reached a stand-off.

5.4 Cognitive Command

Wright's third criterion, *Cognitive Command*, is an attempt to further articulate Socrates' side of the Euthyphro contrast. Suppose that a given area of discourse functions to describe some mind-independent reality. It follows that if two speakers disagree about something in that area of discourse, then at least one of them has *misrepresented* reality, and so is guilty of some cognitive shortcoming. For example, if two people disagree over whether there is one car or two in the garage, then at least one of the people has a cognitive shortcoming. She did not look carefully enough, or her memory is faulty, etc. On the other hand, if a discourse does not serve to describe a mind-independent realm, then disagreements need not involve cognitive shortcoming on the part of either party. To take one of Wright's favourite examples, two people can disagree about what is funny without either of them having any cognitive shortcoming. One of them may have a warped sense of humor, but nothing wrong with her cognitive faculties. A non-cognitivist about ethics might say the same about moral discourse. Wright writes that

A discourse exhibits Cognitive Command if and only if it is a priori that differences of opinion arising within it can be satisfactorily explained only in terms of 'divergent input', that is, the disputants working on the basis of different information (and hence guilty of ignorance or error . . .), of 'unsuitable conditions' (resulting in inattention or distraction

---

[36] The situation would be more complicated if the relevance logician claimed that the inference involves a conditional with relevance built into its meaning.

and so in inferential error, or oversight of data, and so on), or 'malfunction' (for example, prejudicial assessment of data . . . or dogma, or failings in other categories already listed). (*Truth and Objectivity*: 92)

So again, what of logic? This case looks particularly straightforward (but looks can be deceiving). Suppose that two people disagree about the validity of a certain inference, such as double negation elimination. Suppose also that each of them is in wide reflective equilibrium. Then (by definition) each of them will accuse the other of *inferential error*. After all, inference is the very thing they disagree on. And inferential error is one of the explicit items listed as a 'cognitive shortcoming'. So each of them will (justifiably) hold that the other has a cognitive shortcoming. Thus, logic exhibits Cognitive Command. QED. This is close to an analytic truth, or so it appears.

Clearly, this little argument begs the question against the non-cognitivist, since Wright explicitly includes 'inferential error' as one of the ways to attribute a *cognitive* shortcoming. By way of analogy, it would not do to argue that ethics is objective by formulating a version of Cognitive Command that includes 'errors in value judgement' as a cognitive shortcoming.[37]

Elsewhere, Wright qualifies the Cognitive Command constraint, noting that two people can disagree about whether someone is bald without either of them exhibiting a cognitive shortcoming (ibid. 144). In this case, the disagreement turns on the vagueness of baldness and not on any failing in either of them (except perhaps in sensitivity to the feelings of hair-challenged folks). Wright lists some other exceptions, writing that a discourse exerts Cognitive Command just in case it

is a priori that differences of opinion formulated within the discourse, unless excusable as a result of vagueness in a disputed statement, or in the standards of acceptability, or variation in personal evidence thresholds, so to speak, will involve something which may properly be described as a cognitive shortcoming.

A philosopher might propose adding logic to this list of exceptions. That is, differences of opinion 'excusable as a result of different logics' might not qualify as a cognitive shortcoming.

The idea behind this manœuvre is that the criterion of Cognitive Command can be applied only against the background of a shared logic—with respect to which inferential errors can be judged. The explicit inclusion of 'inferential error' in the original list of cognitive shortcomings would be restricted to errors within one's own logic. This would be consonant with Resnik's suggestion that wide reflective equilibrium is an 'immanent' notion, limited to one logic at a time.

This proposal is similar to the above moves to exempt logic from the consideration of wide cosmological role and the Euthyphro contrast. The effect of the proposal is not to support non-cognitivism about logic (with or without begging

---

[37] Thanks to Jill Dieterle, Christopher Peacocke, and Neil Tennant here.

the question). Rather, the proposal removes logic from the arena in which Cognitive Command operates. Logic is declared to be part of the framework for determining whether Cognitive Command holds, rather than subject to the constraint. The proposal thus weakens the very sense we can attach to the question of whether logic is cognitive.[38]

However, there is a related matter that does tell, at least in part, in favour of the objectivity of logic. Given how pervasive logic is, disagreements about logic are likely to result in disagreements elsewhere. An advocate of classical logic, for example, will disagree with an intuitionist about the intermediate-value theorem, since the latter theorem has a classical but not an intuitionistic proof.[39] That is, the logicians will disagree about real numbers and functions on real numbers. If the two logicians agree that space-time is continuous, then their disagreement about logic (and so the intermediate-value theorem) will result in a disagreement about space-time.

Another of Wright's notions comes to the fore here. Returning to comedy, he argues that 'differences of opinion about what is funny need not ramify into differences of opinion about anything else.' Then comes a definition:

Say that one discourse *disputationally supervenes* on another just in case the rational intelligibility of differences of opinion expressible in the former will depend on the existence of differences expressible in the latter. (ibid. 155)

On the next page, Wright glosses this as follows: 'rationally sustaining a disagreement about' the former subject 'would necessitate differences of opinion' in the latter. Wright then argues that discourse about comedy is 'disputationally pure' in the sense that it does not disputationally supervene on anything else. The foregoing considerations show that logic disputationally supervenes on mathematics and, if space-time is continuous, on physics. Given the widely held view that logic is universally applicable, then logic disputationally supervenes on just about everything.

---

[38] The present section has the same flavour as Paul Boghossian's 'The status of content' (*Philosophical Review* 99 (1990): 157–84), an extended argument that if any areas of discourse are cognitive—if the cognitive–non-cognitive boundary is not trivial—then matters of semantic content are cognitive as well. Here the further question of objectivity is broached, with similar results. Robert Kraut ('Robust deflationism', *Philosophical Review* 102 (1993): 247–63) and Wright (*Truth and Objectivity*: 231–6) argue that Boghossian's conclusion can be avoided if one maintains that the distinction between areas of discourse that are cognitive and those that are not cognitive is itself a non-cognitive matter. According to the rescue in question, an assertion that a given discourse is cognitive (or not) is itself a non-cognitive matter. That move is not available here, since the above matters of epistemic constraint, wide cosmological role, the Euthyphro contrast, and Cognitive Command are independent of the status of claims of whether a discourse is cognitive. The foregoing unQuinean way to avoid the conclusion that logic is cognitive is to claim that logic is part of the very framework for determining whether a discourse is cognitive. This is to exempt logic from the very question of being cognitive or non-cognitive.

[39] The intermediate-value theorem is that if f is a continuous function from the real numbers to the real numbers such that for some $a<b$, $fa<0$ and $fb>0$, then there is a number c such that $a<c<b$ and $fc = 0$.

This bears on the present issue. Suppose that someone is a realist about mathematics (following Resnik for example), and agrees that mathematics exhibits Cognitive Command. Then the difference in logic results in a difference concerning objective facts, and this latter difference requires a cognitive shortcoming on at least one of the parties—a difference not excusable as a difference in some non-cognitive stance maintained by one of the parties. Similarly, if physics is objective (and space-time is continuous) then a difference in logic results in a difference in physics and so the difference in logic requires a cognitive shortcoming somewhere. In general, if a discourse *A* disputationally supervenes on a discourse *B*, then if *B* exhibits Cognitive Command, then so does *A*.

One rescue for the logical irrealist would be to maintain that logic does not disputationally supervene on *any* objective discourse (or any discourse that exhibits Cognitive Command). This would require the advocate of classical logic and the intuitionist to agree that mathematics is not cognitive, and neither is the theory of space-time (if the mathematical theory of continuity applies to space-time). Indeed, the two logicians would have to agree that both of their logics hold for *any* objective discourse, and their dispute concerning logic would be limited to non-cognitive domains. Something similar would hold for advocates of relevance logic, paraconsistent logic, etc.[40] The non-cognitivist about logic must maintain that there is no disputational supervenience between logic (in wide reflective equilibrium) and any objective area. I leave it to the reader to determine whether the field of non-cognitivism has narrowed too far to make the view exciting.

---

[40] The present conclusion is congenial with the views of at least some intuitionists. Brouwer and Heyting agreed that classical logic holds for finite domains, but fails once we broach the infinite. Much of their philosophical writing suggests that mathematical objects are mind-dependent (perhaps in a Kantian sense), and so perhaps mathematics is not objective. If all objective discourses have finite domains, then the classical–intuitionistic logic dispute does not supervene on any objective discourse. I do not know if this orientation is palatable to a more contemporary intuitionist (and global anti-realist) like Dummett or Tennant.

15

Transcendental Philosophy and A Priori Knowledge: A Neo-Kantian Perspective

Michael Friedman

In the Introduction to the *Critique of Pure Reason* Kant formulates what he calls 'the general problem of pure reason', namely 'How are synthetic a priori judgements possible?' Kant explains that this general problem involves two more specific questions about particular a priori sciences: 'How is pure mathematics possible ?' and 'How is pure natural science possible?'—where the first concerns, above all, the possibility of Euclidean geometry, and the second concerns the possibility of fundamental laws of Newtonian mechanics such as conservation of mass, inertia, and the equality of action and reaction.[1] Moreover, with this formulation of the general problem of pure reason Kant has also, at the same time, articulated the peculiar task of what he calls 'transcendental philosophy', in which the subject matter of philosophy is clearly and sharply delimited from that of the natural and mathematical sciences themselves—including, in particular, those elements of a priori knowledge present in these latter sciences:

[N]ot every a priori cognition should be called transcendental, but only that through which we cognize that and how certain representations (intuitions or concepts) are applied wholly a priori, or are possible (that is, [through which we cognize] the possibility or the a priori employment of the cognition). Therefore, neither space nor any a priori geometrical determination thereof is a transcendental representation, but what can alone be called transcendental is the cognition that these representations are not at all of empirical origin, and the possibility that they can nevertheless relate a priori to objects of experience. (A56/B80)

---

[1] This 'general problem of pure reason', along with its two more specific sub-problems, is formulated in §VI of the Introduction at B19–24. Sections V and VI, which culminate in the three questions 'How is pure mathematics possible?', 'How is pure natural science possible?', and 'How is metaphysics as a science possible?', are added to the second (1787) edition of the *Critique* and clearly follow the structure of the 1783 *Prolegomena to Any Future Metaphysics*, which was intended to clarify the first (1781) edition. This way of framing the general problem of pure reason also clearly reflects the increasing emphasis on the question of pure natural science found in the 1786 *Metaphysical Foundations of Natural Science*. For an extended discussion of Kant's theory of pure natural science and its relation to Newtonian physics see my *Kant and the Exact Sciences* (Cambridge Mass.: Harvard University Press, 1992): esp. chs. 3 and 4. Here, and in what follows, references to the *Critique of Pure Reason* are given by pagination of the first (A) and/or second (B) editions (translations are my own).

I term all cognition transcendental which occupies itself in general, not so much with objects, but rather with our mode of cognition of objects, in so far as this is supposed to be possible a priori. (B25)

Precisely by taking the a priori elements of scientific knowledge to be its distinctive object, transcendental philosophy thereby becomes a meta-discipline, as it were, whose characteristic task is to investigate the nature and conditions of possibility of first-level scientific knowledge.

In the current state of the sciences, however, we no longer believe that Kant's specific examples of synthetic a priori knowledge are even true, much less that they are a priori and necessarily true. For the Einsteinian revolution in physics has resulted in both an essentially non-Newtonian conception of space, time, and motion, in which the Newtonian laws of mechanics are no longer universally valid, and the application to nature of a non-Euclidean geometry of variable curvature, wherein bodies affected only by gravitation follow straightest possible paths or geodesics. And this has led to a situation, in turn, in which we are no longer convinced that there are any real examples of scientific a priori knowledge at all. If Euclidean geometry, at one time the very model of rational or a priori knowledge of nature, can be empirically revised, so the argument goes, then everything is in principle empirically revisable. Our reasons for adopting one or another system of geometry or mechanics (or, indeed, of mathematics more generally or of logic) are at bottom of the very same kind as the purely empirical considerations that support any other part of our total theory of nature. But then, if there are in fact no genuine examples of a priori knowledge, Kant's idea of a characteristically 'transcendental' task for philosophy must also be given up. Philosophy no longer has a distinctive 'general problem of pure reason' with which to occupy itself, and it then becomes tempting to view philosophy, too, as simply one more part—perhaps a peculiarly abstract and general part—of our total natural-scientific theory of the world.

This kind of strongly holistic picture of knowledge, in which both scientific convictions formerly taken to be a priori and philosophy as a discipline are now viewed simply as additional components (albeit peculiarly abstract and general ones) in our total empirical theory of the world, is of course most closely identified with the work of W. V. Quine. Our system of knowledge, in Quine's well-known figure, should be viewed as a vast web of interconnected beliefs on which experience or sensory input impinges only along the periphery. When faced with a 'recalcitrant experience' standing in conflict with our system of beliefs we then have a choice of where to make revisions. These can be made relatively close to the periphery of the system (in which case we make a change in a relatively low-level part of natural science), but they can also—when the conflict is particularly acute and persistent, for example—affect the most abstract and general parts of science, including even the truths of logic and mathematics, lying at the centre of our system of beliefs. To be sure, such high-level beliefs at the centre of our system are relatively entrenched, in that we are relatively reluctant to revise them or to give them up (as we once were in the case of Euclidean geometry, for example). Nevertheless, and this is the crucial point, absolutely none of our beliefs is forever 'immune to revision' in light of experience:

The totality of our so-called knowledge or beliefs, from the most casual matters of geography and history to the profoundest laws of atomic physics or even of pure mathematics and logic, is a man-made fabric which impinges on experience only along the edges. Or, to change the figure, total science is like a field of force whose boundary conditions are experience. A conflict with experience at the periphery occasions readjustments in the interior of the field. . . . But the total field is so underdetermined by its boundary conditions, experience, that there is much latitude of choice as to what statements to re-evaluate in the light of any single contrary experience. . . .

If this view is right . . . it becomes folly to seek a boundary between synthetic statements, which hold contingently on experience, and analytic statements, which hold come what may. Any statement can be held true come what may, if we make drastic enough adjustments elsewhere in the system. Even a statement very close to the periphery can be held true in the face of recalcitrant experience by pleading hallucination or by amending certain statements of the kind called logical laws. Conversely, by the same token, no statement is immune to revision. Revision even of the logical law of the excluded middle has been proposed as a means of simplifying quantum mechanics; and what difference is there in principle between such a shift and the shift whereby Kepler superseded Ptolemy, or Einstein Newton, or Darwin Aristotle?[2]

As the last sentence makes clear, examples of revolutionary transitions in our scientific knowledge, and, in particular, that of the Einsteinian revolution in geometry and mechanics, constitute a very important part of the motivations for this view.

Yet it is important to see that such a strongly anti-apriorist conception of scientific knowledge was by no means prevalent during the late nineteenth and early twentieth centuries—during the very period, that is, when the great revolutions in geometry and mechanics we now associate with the work of Einstein were actually taking place. If we begin with the key figures in the philosophy of non-Euclidean geometry, for example, whereas it is certainly true that Hermann von Helmholtz viewed the choice between Euclidean and non-Euclidean geometries as an empirical one, he also suggested that the more general structure of space common to both Euclidean and non-Euclidean systems (that of constant curvature or what Helmholtz called 'free mobility') was a necessary presupposition of all spatial measurement and thus a 'transcendental' form of our spatial intuition in the sense of Kant. And, partly on this basis, Henri Poincaré went even further. Although no particular geometry—neither Euclidean nor non-Euclidean—is an a priori

---

[2] From the first two paragraphs of §6—entitled 'Empiricism without the dogmas'—of Quine's 'Two dogmas of empiricism', *Philosophical Review* 60 (1951): 20–43; the passage occurs on pp. 42–3 of the reprinting of this paper in *From a Logical Point of View* (Cambridge Mass.: Harvard University Press, 1953).

condition of our spatial intuition, it does not follow that the choice between them, as Helmholtz thought, is an empirical one. For there remains an irreducible gulf between our crude and approximate sensory experience and our precise mathematical descriptions of nature. Establishing one or another system of geometry, Poincaré argued, therefore requires a free choice, a *convention* of our own—based, in the end, on the greater mathematical simplicity of the Euclidean system.[3]

Nor was such a strongly anti-apriorist conception of scientific knowledge adopted by the first scientific thinkers enthusiastically to embrace Einstein's new theory. These thinkers, the logical empiricists, of course rejected the synthetic a priori in Kant's original form. They rejected the idea of absolutely fixed and unrevisable a priori principles built, once and for all, into our fundamental cognitive capacities. In place of an holistic empiricism, however, they instead adopted a radically new conception of the a priori. Perhaps the clearest articulation of the logical empiricists's new view was provided by Hans Reichenbach in his first book, *The Theory of Relativity and A Priori Knowledge*, published in 1920.[4] Reichenbach distinguishes two meanings of the Kantian a priori: necessary and unrevisable, fixed for all time, on the one hand, and 'constitutive of the concept of the object of [scientific] knowledge', on the other. Reichenbach argues, on this basis, that the great lesson of the theory of relativity is that the former meaning must be dropped while the latter must be retained. Relativity theory involves a priori constitutive principles as necessary presuppositions of its properly empirical claims, just as much as did Newtonian physics, but these principles have essentially changed in the transition from the later theory to the former: whereas Euclidean geometry is indeed constitutively a priori in the context of Newtonian physics, for example, only *infinitesimally* Euclidean geometry is constitutively a priori in the context of general relativity. What we end up with, in this tradition, is thus a relativized and dynamical conception of a priori mathematical-physical principles, which change and develop along with the development of the mathematical and physical sciences themselves, but which nevertheless retain the characteristically Kantian constitutive function of making the empirical natural knowledge thereby structured and framed by such principles first possible.[5]

---

[3] For extended discussion of Helmholtz and Poincaré—including their relationships to both Kant and the logical empiricists—see my 'Poincaré's conventionalism and the logical positivists', ch. 4 of my *Reconsidering Logical Positivism* (Cambridge: Cambridge University Press, 1999); 'Helmholtz's *Zeichentheorie* and Schlick's *Allgemeine Erkenntnislehre*', *Philosophical Topics* 5 (1997); 'Geometry, construction, and intuition in Kant and his successors', in G. Scher and R. Tieszen (eds.), *Between Logic and Intuition: Essays in Honor of Charles Parsons* (Cambridge: Cambridge University Press, 2000).

[4] H. Reichenbach, *Relativitätstheorie und Erkenntnis Apriori* (Berlin: Springer, 1920); trans. as *The Theory of Relativity and A Priori Knowledge* (Berkeley and Los Angeles: University of California Press, 1965). The distinction between the two meanings of the Kantian a priori described in the next sentence occurs in ch. 5, entitled 'Two meanings of the a priori and Kant's implicit presupposition'.

[5] For a discussion of Kant's characteristic conception of the constitutive function of a priori

Rudolf Carnap's philosophy of formal languages or linguistic frameworks, first developed in his *Logical Syntax of Language* in 1934 and then reemphasized, in the context of later debates with Quine, in his paper 'Empiricism, semantics, and ontology', published in 1950, was the most mature expression of the logical empiricist's new view.[6] All standards of 'correctness', 'validity', and 'truth', according to Carnap, are relative to the logical rules definitive of one or another formal language or linguistic framework. The rules of classical logic and mathematics, for example, are definitive of certain logical calculi or linguistic frameworks, while the rules of intuitionistic logic and mathematics (wherein the law of excluded middle is no longer universally valid) are definitive of others. Since standards of 'validity' and 'correctness' are thus relative to the choice of linguistic framework, it makes no sense to ask whether any such choice of framework is itself 'valid' or 'correct'. For the logical rules relative to which alone these notions can be well defined are not yet in place. Such rules are *constitutive* of the concepts of 'validity' and 'correctness'—relative to one or another choice of linguistic framework, of course—and are in this sense a priori rather than empirical.

This Carnapian philosophy of linguistic frameworks rests on two closely related distinctions. The first is the distinction between formal or *analytic* sentences of a given framework and empirical or *synthetic* sentences—or, as Carnap puts it in *Logical Syntax*, between *logical rules* ('L-rules') of a linguistic framework and *physical rules* ('P-rules'). The L-rules include laws of logic and mathematics (and may also, at least in spaces of constant curvature, include laws of physical geometry), whereas the P-rules include empirical laws standardly so-called such as Maxwell's equations of electromagnetism. In this way, Carnap's distinction between L-rules and P-rules closely parallels Reichenbach's distinction, developed in his 1920 book, between 'axioms of coordination' (constitutive

principles see G. De Pierris, 'The constitutive a priori', *Canadian Journal of Philosophy*, Suppl. Vol. 18 (1993): 179–214.

[6] R. Carnap, *Logische Syntax der Sprache* (Vienna: Springer, 1934), trans. as *The Logical Syntax of Language* (London: Kegan Paul, 1937); 'Empiricism, semantics, and ontology', *Revue international de philosophie* 11 (1950): 20–40, repr. in *Meaning and Necessity*, 2nd edn. (Chicago and London: University of Chicago Press, 1956). It is in 'Empiricism, semantics, and ontology' where Carnap first explicitly introduces the notion of linguistic framework and the accompanying distinction between internal and external questions. Footnote 5 (*Meaning and Necessity*: 215) refers to Quine's 1948 'On what there is' and remarks that 'Quine does not acknowledge the distinction [between internal and external questions] because according to his general conception there are no sharp boundary lines between logical and factual truth, between questions of meaning and questions of fact, between the acceptance of a language structure and the acceptance of an assertion formulated in the language.' It is clear, then, that the analyticity debate—which originated in discussions at Harvard in the years 1939–41 involving Carnap, Quine, and Alfred Tarski—constitutes the philosophical background for this divergence. For discussion of the analyticity debate see the Introduction to R. Creath (ed.), *Dear Carnap, Dear Van: The Quine–Carnap Correspondence and Related Work* (Berkeley and Los Angeles: University of California Press, 1990).

principles) and 'axioms of connection' (properly empirical laws).[7] Carnap's differentiation between logical and physical rules (analytic and synthetic sentences) then induces a second fundamental distinction between *internal* and *external* questions. Internal questions are decided within an already adopted framework, in accordance with the logical rules of the framework in question. External questions, by contrast, concern precisely the question of which linguistic framework—and therefore which logical rules—to adopt in the first place. And since no logical rules are as yet in place, external questions, unlike internal questions, are not strictly speaking rationally decidable. Such questions can only be decided conventionally on the basis of broadly pragmatic considerations of convenience or suitability for one or another purpose. An overriding desire for security against the possibility of contradiction, for example, may prompt the choice of the weaker rules of intuitionistic logic and mathematics, whereas an interest in ease of physical application may prompt the choice of the stronger rules of classical logic and mathematics.

Now it was precisely this Carnapian philosophy of linguistic frameworks that formed the background and foil for Quine's articulation of a radically opposed form of epistemological holism according to which no fundamental distinction between a priori and a posteriori, logical and factual, analytic and synthetic can in fact be drawn. As we have seen, it was in Quine's 1951 paper 'Two dogmas of empiricism', where his challenge to the analytic–synthetic distinction was first made widely known, that the holistic figure of knowledge as a vast web of interconnected beliefs also first appeared. But it is important to see here that it is Quine's attack on the analytic–synthetic distinction, and not simply the idea that no belief whatsoever is forever immune to revision, that is basic to Quine's new form of holism. For Carnap's philosophy of linguistic frameworks is wholly predicated on the idea that logical or analytic principles, just as much as empirical or synthetic principles, can be revised in the progress of empirical science.[8] Indeed, as we have seen, Reichenbach's initial formulation of this new view of constitutive a priori principles was developed precisely to accommodate the revolutionary changes in the geometrical and mechanical framework of physical theory wrought by Einstein's development of the theory of relativity. The difference between Quine and Carnap is rather that the latter persists in drawing a sharp distinction between changes of language or linguistic framework, in which

---

[7] For discussion of the relationship between Carnap's philosophy of linguistic frameworks and Reichenbach's 1920 book see my 'Geometry, convention, and the relativized a priori', ch. 3 of my *Reconsidering Logical Positivism* (n. 3 above).

[8] Carnap explicitly embraces this much of epistemological holism (based on the ideas of Poincaré and Pierre Duhem) in §82 of *Logical Syntax*. Quine is therefore extremely misleading when he (in the above-cited passage from §6 of 'Two dogmas') simply equates analyticity with unrevisability. He is similarly misleading in §5 when he asserts that the 'dogma of reductionism' (i.e. the denial of Duhemian holism) is 'at root identical' with the dogma of analyticity (*Logical Point of View*: 41).

constitutive principles definitive of the very notions of 'validity' and 'correctness' are revised, and changes in ordinary empirical statements formulated against the background of such an already-present constitutive framework. And this distinction, for Carnap, ultimately rests on the difference between analytic statements depending solely on the meanings of the relevant terms and synthetic statements expressing contentful assertions about the empirical world.

Quine's attack on the analytic–synthetic distinction—and thus on Carnap's particular version of the distinction between a priori and empirical principles—is now widely accepted, and I have no desire to defend Carnap's particular way of articulating this distinction here. I do want to question, however, whether Quinean epistemological holism is really our only option, and whether, in particular, it in fact represents our best way of coming to terms with the revolutionary changes in the historical development of the sciences that are now often taken to support it.

Quinean holism pictures our total system of science as a vast web or conjunction of beliefs which face the 'tribunal of experience' as a corporate body. Quine grants that some beliefs, such as those of logic and arithmetic, are relatively central, whereas others, such as those of biology, say, are relatively peripheral. But this means only that the former beliefs are less likely to be revised in case of a 'recalcitrant experience' at the periphery, whereas the latter are more likely to be revised:

Suppose an experiment has yielded a result contrary to a theory currently held in some natural science. The theory comprises a whole bundle of conjoint hypotheses, or is resoluble into such a bundle. The most that the experiment shows is that at least one of these hypotheses is false; it does not show which. It is only the theory as a whole, and not any of the hypotheses, that admits of evidence or counter-evidence in observation and experiment.

And how wide is a theory? No part of science is quite isolated from the rest. Parts as disparate as you please may be expected to share laws of logic and arithmetic, anyway, and to share various common-sense generalities about bodies in motion. Legalistically, one could claim that evidence counts always for or against the total system, however loose-knit, of science. Evidence against the system is not evidence against any one sentence rather than another, but can be acted on rather by any of various adjustments.

Thus suppose from a combined dozen of our theoretical beliefs a scientist derives a prediction in molecular biology, and the prediction fails. He is apt to scrutinize for possible revision only the half-dozen beliefs that belonged to molecular biology rather than tamper with the more general half-dozen having to do with logic and arithmetic and the gross behavior of bodies. This is a reasonable strategy—a maxim of minimum mutilation. But an effect of it is that the portion of theory to which the discovered failure of prediction is relevant seems narrower than it otherwise might.[9]

Strictly speaking, then, empirical evidence—either for or against—spreads over

[9] W. V. Quine, *Philosophy of Logic*, Englewood, NJ: Prentice-Hall, 1970: 5, 7.

all the elements of the vast conjunction that is our total system of science, wherein all elements whatsoever equally face the 'tribunal of experience'. And it is in this precise sense, for Quine, that all beliefs whatsoever, including those of logic and mathematics (and, for that matter, of philosophy), are equally empirical.

But can this beguiling form of epistemological holism really do justice to the revolutionary developments within both mathematics and natural science that have led up to it? Let us first consider the Newtonian revolution that produced the beginnings of mathematical physics as we know it—the very revolution, as we have seen, that Kant's conception of synthetic a priori knowledge was originally intended to address. In constructing his mathematical physics Newton created, virtually simultaneously, three revolutionary advances: a new form of mathematics, the calculus, for dealing with infinite limiting processes and instantaneous rates of change; new conceptions of force and quantity of matter encapsulated in his three laws of motion; and a new universal law of nature, the law of universal gravitation. Each of these three advances was revolutionary in itself, and all were introduced by Newton in the context of the same scientific problem: that of developing a single mathematical theory of motion capable of giving a unified account of both terrestrial and celestial phenomena. Since all three advances were thus inspired, in the end, by the same empirical problem, and since they together amounted to the first known solution to this problem, Quine's holistic picture appears so far correct. All elements in this particular system of scientific knowledge—mathematics, mechanics, gravitational physics—appear equally to face the 'tribunal of experience' together.

Nevertheless, there are fundamental asymmetries in the way in which the different elements of this Newtonian synthesis actually function. To begin with the relationship between mathematics and mechanics, Newton's second law of motion says that force equals mass times acceleration, where acceleration is the instantaneous rate of change of velocity (itself the instantaneous rate of change of position). So without the mathematics of the calculus this second law of motion could not even be formulated or written down, let alone function to describe empirical phenomena. The combination of calculus plus the laws of motion is not happily viewed, therefore, as a conjunction of propositions symmetrically contributing to a single total result: the mathematical part of Newton's theory rather supplies elements of the language or conceptual framework, we might say, within which the rest of the theory is then formulated. And an analogous (if also more subtle) point holds with respect to the relationship between Newton's mechanics and gravitational physics. The law of universal gravitation says that there is a force of attraction, directly proportional to the product of the two masses and inversely proportional to the square of the distance between them, between any two pieces of matter in the universe—which therefore experience accelerations towards one another in accordance with this same law. But relative to what frame of reference are the accelerations in question defined? Since these accelerations are, by hypothesis, universal, no particular materials body can be taken as actually at rest in this frame, and thus the motions in question are not motions relative to any particular material body. Newton himself understood these motions as defined relative to absolute space, but we now understand them as defined relative to an arbitrary *inertial frame*—where an inertial frame of reference is simply one in which the Newtonian laws of motion actually hold (the centre of mass frame of the solar system, for example, is a very close approximation to such a frame). It follows that without the Newtonian laws of motion Newton's theory of gravitation would not even make empirical sense, let alone give a correct account of the empirical phenomena: in the absence of these laws we would simply have no idea what the relevant frame of reference might be in relation to which the universal accelerations due to gravity are defined.[10] Once again, Newton's mechanics and gravitational physics are not happily viewed as symmetrically functioning elements of a larger conjunction: the former is rather a necessary part of the language or conceptual framework within which alone the latter makes empirical sense.

Now the Newtonian theory of gravitation has of course been superseded by Einstein's general theory of relativity, and one might naturally expect Quine's holistic picture of knowledge to describe this latter theory much more accurately. General relativity, like Newtonian theory, can be seen as the outcome of three revolutionary advances: the development of a new field of mathematics, tensor calculus or the general theory of manifolds, by Bernhard Riemann in the late nineteenth century; Einstein's principle of equivalence, which identifies gravitational effects with the inertial effects formerly associated with Newton's laws of motion; and Einstein's equations for the gravitational field, which describe how the curvature of space-time is modified by the presence of matter and energy so as to direct gravitationally affected bodies along straightest possible paths or geodesics. Once again, each of these three advances was revolutionary in itself, and all three were marshalled together by Einstein to solve a single empirical problem: that of developing a new description of gravitation consistent with the special theory of relativity (which is itself incompatible with the instantaneous action at a distance characteristic of Newtonian theory) and also capable, it was hoped, of solving well-known anomalies in Newtonian theory such as that involving the perihelion of Mercury. And the three advances together, as marshalled and synthesized by Einstein, in fact succeeded in solving this empirical problem for the first time.

---

[10] I have argued in *Kant and the Exact Sciences* (n. 1 above) that Kant's theory of pure natural science is based on an analogous analysis of the relationship between the Newtonian laws of motion and the law of universal gravitation. The difference is that Kant does not have the concept of inertial frame and instead views the Newtonian laws of motion (together with other fundamental principles Kant takes to be a priori) as defining a convergent sequence of ever-better approximations to a single privileged frame (a counterpart of absolute space) at rest at the centre of gravity of all matter.

It does not follow, however, that the combination of mathematical theory of manifolds, geodesic law of motion, and field equations of gravitation can be happily viewed as a symmetrically functioning conjunction, such that each element then equally faces the 'tribunal of experience' when confronted with the anomaly in the perihelion of Mercury, for example. To begin again with the relationship between mathematics and mechanics, the principle of equivalence depicts the space-time trajectories of bodies affected only by gravitation as geodesics in a variably curved space-time geometry, just as the Newtonian laws of motion, when viewed from this same space-time perspective, depict the trajectories of bodies affected by no forces at all as geodesics in a flat space-time geometry. But the whole notion of a variably curved geometry itself only makes sense in the context of the revolutionary new theory of manifolds recently created by Riemann. In the context of the mathematics available in the seventeenth and eighteenth centuries, by contrast, the idea of a variably curved space-time geometry could not even be formulated or written down, let alone function to describe empirical phenomena. And, once again, a closely analogous (but also more subtle) point holds for the relationship between mechanics and gravitational physics. Einstein's field equations describe the variation in curvature of space-time geometry as a function of the distribution of matter and energy. Such a variably curved space-time structure would have no empirical meaning or application, however, if we had not first singled out some empirical phenomena as counterparts of its fundamental geometrical notions—here the notion of geodesic or straightest possible path. The principle of equivalence does precisely this, however, and without this principle the intricate space-time geometry described by Einstein's field equation would not even be empirically false, but rather an empty mathematical formalism with no empirical application at all.[11] Just as in the case of Newtonian gravitation theory, therefore, the three advances together comprising Einstein's revolutionary theory should not be viewed as symmetrically functioning elements of a larger conjunction: the first two function rather as necessary parts of the language or conceptual framework within which alone the third makes both mathematical and empirical sense.

It will not do, in either of our two examples, to view what I am calling the constitutively a priori parts of our scientific theories as simply relatively fixed or entrenched elements of science in the sense of Quine, as particularly well-established beliefs which is a reasonable scientific conservatism takes to be relatively difficult to revise. When Newton formulated his theory of gravitation, for example, the mathematics of the calculus was still quite controversial—to such an

---

[11] For an analysis of the principle of equivalence along these lines, including illuminating comparisons with Reichenbach's conception of the need for 'coordinating definitions' in physical geometry, see R. DiSalle, 'Spacetime theory as physical geometry', *Erkenntnis* 42 (1995): 317–37.

extent, in fact, that Newton disguised his use of it in the *Principia* in favour of traditional synthetic geometry. Nor were Newton's three laws of motion any better entrenched, at the time, than the law of universal gravitation.[12] Similarly, in the case of Einstein's general theory of relativity, neither the mathematical theory of manifolds nor the principle of equivalence was a well-entrenched part of main-stream mathematics or mathematical physics; and this is one of the central reasons, in fact, that Einstein's theory is so profoundly revolutionary. More gener-ally, then, since we are dealing with deep conceptual revolutions in both mathe-matics and mathematical physics in both cases, entrenchment and relative resistance to revision are not appropriate distinguishing features at all. What char-acterizes the distinguished elements of our theories is rather their special *consti-tutive function*: the function of making the precise mathematical formulation and empirical application of the theories in question first possible. In this sense, the relativized and dynamical conception of the a priori developed by the logical empiricists appears to describe these conceptual revolutions far better than does Quinean holism. This is not at all surprising, in the end, for this new conception of the constitutive a priori was inspired, above all, by just these conceptual revo-lutions.

It is no wonder, then, that in Thomas Kuhn's theory of the nature and charac-ter of scientific revolutions we find an informal counterpart of the relativized conception of constitutive a priori principles first developed by the logical empiricists. For Kuhn's central distinction between change of paradigm or revo-lutionary science, on the one side, and normal science, on the other, closely parallels the Carnapian distinction between change of language or linguistic framework and rule-governed operations carried out within such a framework. Just as, for Carnap, the logical rules of a linguistic framework are constitutive of the notion of 'correctness' or 'validity' relative to this framework, so a particu-lar paradigm governing a given episode of normal science, for Kuhn, yields generally-agreed-upon (although perhaps only tacit) rules constitutive of what counts as a 'valid' or 'correct' solution to a problem within this episode of normal science. Just as, for Carnap, external questions concerning which linguistic framework to adopt are not similarly governed by logical rules, but rather require a much less definite appeal to conventional and/or pragmatic considerations, so changes of paradigm in revolutionary science, for Kuhn, do

---

[12] Newton himself portrays the laws of motion as already familiar and accepted, as natural generalizations of the work of such predecessors as Galileo and Huygens. In one sense, this is perfectly correct—and, indeed, the laws of motion are perhaps most illuminatingly viewed as generalizations of the conservation of momentum principle contained in the the laws of impact, extended to include continuously acting forces on the model of Galileo's treatment of uniform acceleration. However, the way Newton actually deploys these laws—especially the third law, the equality of action and reaction—essentially involves an application to action-at-a-distance forces which, as such, would be entirely unacceptable from the point of view of the then domi-nant mechanical philosophy. In this sense, Newton's laws of motion constitute a quite radical *transformation* of the previous tradition.

not proceed in accordance with generally-agreed-upon rules as in normal science, but rather require something more akin to a conversion experience.[13]

Indeed, towards the end of his career, Kuhn himself drew this parallel between his theory of scientific revolutions and the relativized conception of a priori constitutive principles explicitly:

Though it is a more articulated source of constitutive categories, my structured lexicon [= Kuhn's late version of 'paradigm'] resembles Kant's a priori when the latter is taken in its second, relativized sense. Both are constitutive of *possible experience* of the world, but neither dictates what that experience must be. Rather, they are constitutive of the infinite range of possible experiences that might conceivably occur in the actual world to which they give access. Which of these conceivable experiences occurs in that actual world is something that must be learned, both from everyday experience and from the more systematic and refined experience that characterizes scientific practice. They are both stern teachers, firmly resisting the promulgation of beliefs unsuited to the form of life the lexicon permits. What results from respectful attention to them is knowledge of nature, and the criteria that serve to evaluate contributions to that knowledge are, correspondingly, epistemic. The fact that experience within another form of life—another time, place, or culture—might have constituted knowledge differently is irrelevant to its status as knowledge.[14]

Thus, although Quine may very well be right that Carnap has failed to give a precise logical characterization of what I am here calling constitutive principles, there is also nonetheless no doubt, I suggest, that careful attention to the actual historical development of science, and, in particular, to the very conceptual revolutions that have in fact led to our current philosophical predicament, shows that relativized a priori principles of just the kind Carnap was aiming at are central to our scientific theories.

But this close parallel between the relativized yet still constitutive a priori and Kuhn's theory of scientific revolutions implies (as the last sentence of our passage from Kuhn suggests) that the former gives rise to the same problems and questions concerning the ultimate rationality of the scientific enterprise that are all too familiar in the post-Kuhnian literature in history, sociology, and philosophy of science. In particular, since there appear to be no generally-agreed-upon

---

[13] It is similarly no wonder, therefore, that Carnap, in his capacity as editor of the volume of the *International Encyclopedia of Unified Science* in which *The Structure of Scientific Revolutions* first appeared in 1962, wrote to Kuhn with warm enthusiasm about the then projected work. Carnap's two letters to Kuhn (12 April 1960 and 28 April 1962) are reproduced, and discussed, in G. Reisch, 'Did Kuhn kill logical empiricsm?' *Philosophy of Science* 58 (1991): 264–77. A particularly striking passage occurs in the first letter, where Carnap writes: 'I am myself very much interested in the problems which you intend to deal with, even though my knowledge of the history of science is rather fragmentary. Among many other items I liked your emphasis on the new conceptual frameworks which are proposed in revolutions in science, and, on their basis, the posing of new questions, not only answers to old problems.'

[14] T. Kuhn, 'Afterwards', in P. Horwich (ed.), *World Changes: Thomas Kuhn and the Nature of Science* (Cambridge, Mass.: MIT Press, 1993): 331–2.

constitutive principles governing the transition to a revolutionary new scientific paradigm or conceptual framework, there would seem to be no sense left in which such a transition can still be viewed as rational, as based on good reasons. And it is for precisely this reason, of course, that Carnap views what he calls external questions as conventional as opposed to rational, and Kuhn likens paradigm shifts rather to conversion experiences. In order fully to vindicate the relativized or constitutive a priori, then, we need to articulate an *inter*-paradigm or *inter*-framework notion of rationality not confined to the constitutive principles of any single given paradigm or conceptual framework. And it is precisely here, I now want to suggest, that we therefore need to move beyond both Carnap and Kuhn, by describing a fundamentally new function for what Kant called transcendental philosophy.

Let us first remind ourselves that, despite the fact that we radically change our constitutive principles in the revolutionary transition from one conceptual framework to another, there is still an important element of *convergence* in the very same revolutionary process of conceptual change. Special relativistic mechanics approaches classical mechanics in the limit as the velocity of light goes to infinity; variably curved Riemannian geometry approaches flat Euclidean geometry as the regions under consideration become infinitely small; Einstein's general relativistic field equations of gravitation approach the Newtonian equations for gravitation as, once again, the velocity of light goes to infinity. Indeed, even in the transition from Aristotelian terrestrial and celestial mechanics to classical terrestrial and celestial mechanics we find a similar relationship. From an observer fixed on the surface of the earth we can construct a system of lines of sight directed towards the heavenly bodies; this system is spherical, isomorphic to the celestial sphere of ancient astronomy, and the motions of the heavenly bodies therein are indeed described, to a very good approximation, by the geocentric system favoured by Aristotle. Moreover, in the sublunary region close to the surface of the earth, where the earth is by far the principal gravitating body, heavy bodies do follow straight paths directed towards the centre of the earth, again to an extremely good approximation. In all three revolutionary transitions, therefore, key elements of the preceding paradigm are preserved as approximate special cases in the succeeding paradigm.

This type of convergence between successive paradigms allows us to define a *retrospective* notion of inter-framework rationality based on the constitutive principles of the later conceptual framework: since the constitutive principles of the earlier framework are contained in those of the later as an approximate special case, the constitutive principles of the later framework are thus fully contained in the earlier framework (as infinitesimally Euclidean geometry is contained in Euclidean geometry, for example). But this does not yet give us a *prospective* notion of inter-framework rationality accessible from the point of view of the earlier framework. Nevertheless, such a prospective notion begins to emerge as well when we observe that, in addition to containing the constitutive principles of

the older framework as an approximate special case, the concepts and principles
of the revolutionary new constitutive framework also evolve continuously, as it
were, by a series of natural transformations of the old concepts and principles.

The Aristotelian constitutive framework, for example, is based on Euclidean
geometry, a background conception of a hierarchically and teleologically organized universe, and conceptions of natural place and natural motion appropriate
to this universe. Thus, in the terrestrial realm heavy bodies naturally move in
straight lines towards their natural place at the centre of the universe, and in the
celestial realm the heavenly bodies naturally move uniformly in circles around
this centre. The conceptual framework of classical physics then retains Euclidean
geometry, but eliminates the hierarchically and teleologically organized universe
together with the accompanying conceptions of natural place. We thereby obtain
an infinite, homogeneous, and isotropic universe in which all bodies naturally
move uniformly along straight lines to infinity. But how did we arrive at this
conception? An essential intermediate stage was Galileo's celebrated treatment of
free fall and projectile motion. For, although Galileo indeed discards the hierarchically and teleologically organized Aristotelian universe, he retains—or better,
transforms—key elements of the Aristotelian conception of natural motion.
Galileo's analysis is based on a combination of what he calls naturally acceler-
ated motion directed towards the centre of the earth and uniform or equable
motion directed horizontally. Unlike our modern conception of rectilinear inertial
motion, however, this Galilean counterpart is uniformly *circular*—traversing
points equidistant from the centre at constant speed. But, in relatively small
regions near the earth's surface, this circular motion is quite indistinguishable
from rectilinear motion, and Galileo can thus treat it as rectilinear to an extremely
good approximation. And it is in precisely this way, therefore, that the modern
conception of natural (inertial) motion is actually continuous with the preceding
Aristotelian conception of natural motion.

An analogous (if also more complex) point can be made concerning the transition from Newtonian mechanics and gravitation theory, through special relativity, to general relativity. The key move in general relativity, as we have seen, is to
replace the law of inertia—which, from the space-time perspective inaugurated
by special relativity, depicts the trajectories of force-free bodies as geodesics in a
flat space-time geometry—with the principle of equivalence, according to which
bodies affected only by gravitation follow geodesics in a variably curved space-
time geometry. How did Einstein actually make this revolutionary move, which
represents the first actual application of a non-Euclidean geometry to nature?
Einstein's innovation grows naturally out of the nineteenth-century tradition in
the foundations of geometry, as Einstein interprets this tradition in the context of
the new non-Newtonian mechanics of special relativity. The key transition to a
non-Euclidean geometry of variable curvature in fact results from applying the
Lorentz contraction arising in special relativity to the geometry of a rotating disk,
as Einstein simultaneously delicately positions himself within the debate on the

foundations of geometry between Helmholtz and Poincaré. In particular, whereas Einstein had earlier made crucial use of Poincaré's idea of convention in motivating the transition, on the basis of mathematical simplicity, from Newtonian space-time to what we currently call Minkowski space-time, now, in the case of the rotating disk, Einstein rather follows Helmholtz in taking the behaviour of rigid measuring rods to furnish us with an empirical determination of the underlying geometry—in this case, a non-Euclidean geometry.[15]

In each of our revolutionary transitions fundamentally philosophical ideas, belonging to what we might call epistemological meta-paradigms or meta-frameworks, play a crucial role in motivating and sustaining the transition to a new first-level or scientific paradigm. Such epistemological meta-frameworks guide the all-important process of conceptual transformation and help us, in particular, to articulate what we now mean, during a given revolutionary transition, by a natural, reasonable, or responsible conceptual transformation. By interacting productively with both older philosophical meta-frameworks and new developments taking place within the sciences themselves, a new epistemological meta-framework thereby makes available a prospective notion (accessible even in the pre-revolutionary conceptual situation) of inter-framework or inter-paradigm rationality.

In the transition from Aristotelian–Scholastic natural philosophy to classical mathematical physics, for example, at the same time that Galileo was subjecting the Aristotelian conception of natural motion to a deep (yet continuous) conceptual transformation, it was necessary to eliminate the hierarchical and teleological elements of the Aristotelian conceptual framework in favour of an exclusively mathematical and geometrical point of view—which was encapsulated, for the mechanical natural philosophy of the time, in the distinction between primary and secondary qualities. Euclidean geometry, as an exemplar of rational inquiry, was of course already a part of the Aristotelian framework, and the problem then was, accordingly, to emphasize this part at the expense of the hylomorphic and teleological conceptual scheme characteristic of Aristotelian metaphysics. This task, however, required a parallel reorganization of the wider concepts of Aristotelian

[15] Einstein's creation of the special theory of relativity in 1905 proceeds by giving the Lorentz transformations—already familiar in turn-of-the-century electrodynamics in the work of H. A. Lorentz and Poincaré—a radically new conceptual interpretation (as defining what we now conceive as the geometry of Minkowski space-time). Here Einstein makes crucial use of Poincaré's conventionalist perspective on geometry (now applied, as it were, to the geometry of space-time) in *Science and Hypothesis*—which Einstein was intensively reading at the time (see A. Miller, *Albert Einstein's Special Theory of Relativity* (Reading: Addison-Wesley, 1981): esp. ch. 2, 'Einstein's philosophic viewpoint in 1905'). Einstein explains how the creation of the general theory in 1915 then required a fundamental reconsideration of Poincaré's conventionalism in 'Geometrie und Erfahrung', *Sitzungsberichte der Preussische Akademie der Wissenschaft* 5 (1921): 123–30, trans. as 'Geometry and experience' in G. Jeffrey and W. Perrett (eds.), *Sidelights on Relativity* (London: Methuen, 1923). For an extended discussion of this example see my 'Geometry as a branch of physics: background and context for Einstein's Geometry and Experience', to appear in a Festschrift for Howard Stein, ed. D. Malament.

metaphysics (concepts of substance, force, space, time, matter, mind, creation, divinity), and it fell to the philosophy of Descartes to undertake such a reorganization—a philosophy which in turn interacted productively with recent scientific advances such as Copernican astronomy, new results in geometrical optics, and Descartes' own initial formulation of the law of rectilinear inertia.[16] Similarly, in the transition from classical mechanics to relativity theory, at the same time that Einstein was subjecting the classical conceptions of space, time, and motion to a deep (yet continuous) conceptual transformation, philosophical debate on the foundations of geometry between Helmholtz and Poincaré, in which empiricist and conventionalist interpretations of that science opposed one another against the ever-present backdrop of the Kantian philosophy, played a central role—and, in turn, was itself carried out in response to mathematical advances in the foundations of geometry made throughout the nineteenth century.

So what we see here, I finally want to suggest, is that the enterprise Kant called transcendental philosophy—the project of investigating and philosophically contextualizing the most basic constitutive principles defining the fundamental spatio-temporal framework of empirical natural science—plays an indispensable orienting role with respect to conceptual revolutions within the sciences precisely by generating new epistemological meta-frameworks capable of bridging, and thus guiding, the revolutionary transitions to a new scientific framework. Transcendental philosophy in this sense thereby makes available prospective notions of inter-framework rationality in the light of which radically new constitutive principles can then appear as rational—as Descartes' appropriation and transformation of the concepts of Aristotelian–Scholastic metaphysics made the new mechanical natural philosophy a reasonable option, for example, or Einstein's appropriation and transformation of the earlier epistemological reflections of Poincaré and Helmholtz did the same for relativity theory.

In place of the Quinean figure of an holistically conceived web of belief, wherein both knowledge traditionally understood as a priori and philosophy as a discipline are supposed to be wholly absorbed into empirical natural science, I am therefore proposing an alternative picture of a thoroughly dynamical yet nonetheless differentiated system of knowledge that can be analysed, for present purposes, into three main components or levels. At the base level, as it were, are the concepts and principles of empirical natural science properly so-called: empirical laws of nature, such as the Newtonian law of gravitation or Einstein's equations for the gravitational field, which squarely and precisely face the

---

[16] Newton's transformation of the mechanical philosophy (n. 12 above) similarly involved deep metaphysical disagreements (mediated, in part, by Cambridge neo-Platonism) with Descartes—concerning, once again, such concepts as substance, force, space, time, matter, mind, creation, divinity. Metaphysical disagreements among partisans of the first-level paradigm of the mechanical philosophy (involving Descates, Gassendi, Hobbes, Spinoza, and Leibniz, for example) also form part of the necessary 'meta-background', as it were, for Newton's radical transformation of that paradigm.

'tribunal of experience' via a rigorous process of empirical testing. At the next or second level are the constitutively a priori principles that define the fundamental spatio-temporal framework within which alone the rigorous formulation and empirical testing of first- or base-level principles is then possible. These relativized a priori principles constitute what Kuhn calls paradigms: relatively stable sets of rules of the game, as it were, that make possible the problem solving activities of normal science—including, in particular, the rigorous formulation and testing of properly empirical laws. In periods of deep conceptual revolution it is precisely these constitutively a priori principles which are then subject to change—under intense pressure, no doubt, from new empirical findings and especially anomalies. It does not follow, however, that such second-level constitutive principles are empirical in the same sense as are the first-level principles. On the contrary, since here, by hypothesis, a generally-agreed-upon background framework is necessarily missing, no straightforward process of empirical testing, in periods of deep conceptual revolution, is then possible. And it is precisely here, in fact, that our third level, that of philosophical meta-paradigms or meta-frameworks, plays an indispensable role, by serving as a source of guidance or orientation in motivating and sustaining the transition from one paradigm or conceptual framework to another.

None of these three levels is fixed and unrevisable, and the distinctions I am drawing have nothing to do, in particular, with differing degrees of certainty or epistemic security. Indeed, the whole point of the present conception of relativized and dynamical a priori principles is to accommodate the profound conceptual revolutions that have repeatedly shaken our knowledge of nature to its very foundations. It is precisely this revolutionary experience, in fact, that has revealed that our knowledge *has* foundations in the present sense: subject-defining or constitutive paradigms whose revision entails a genuine expansion of our space of intellectual possibilities, to such an extent, in periods of radical conceptual revolution, that a straightforward appeal to empirical evidence is then no longer directly relevant. And it is at this point, moreover, that philosophy plays its own distinctive role, not so much in justifying or securing a new paradigm where empirical evidence cannot yet do so, but rather in guiding the articulation of the new space of possibilities and making the serious consideration of the new paradigm a rational and responsible option. The various levels in our total evolving and interacting system of beliefs are thus not distinguished by differing degrees of epistemic security at all—neither by differing degrees of centrality and entrenchment in the sense of Quine nor by differing degrees of certainty in the more traditional sense—but rather by their radically different, yet mutually complementary contributions to the total ongoing dialectic of human knowledge.

16

Externalism and Armchair Knowledge

Martin Davies

[I]f you could know a priori that you are in a given mental state, and your being in that state conceptually or logically implies the existence of external objects, then you could know a priori that the external world exists. Since you obviously *can't* know a priori that the external world exists, you also can't know a priori that you are in the mental state in question.[1]

Let us call someone who combines an externalist view of mental content with a doctrine of privileged self-knowledge a *compatibilist*. . . . [I]f compatibilism were true, we would be in a position to know certain facts about the world a priori, facts that no one can reasonably believe are knowable a priori.[2]

1. KYLIE'S PUZZLE

On summer afternoons in Canberra, the baking sun reflects off Lake Burley Griffin, and the water shimmers. Up behind the university, in the botanical gardens, a

Versions of this material were presented at a conference on externalism and self-knowledge held at the University of Bristol in February 1999 and in a symposium with Brian McLaughlin and Brian Loar at the Pacific Division meeting of the American Philosophical Association held in Berkeley in April 1999. I learned much from those occasions and from a seminar with Jessica Brown and Michael McKinsey held in Oxford during the spring of 1999. Comments by Mark Greenberg on what I once thought of as a penultimate version of the paper were extremely useful and a period as a Visiting Fellow in the Research School of Social Sciences, Australian National University, provided the opportunity for a complete overhaul of the text. In Canberra, I was helped by discussions with members of the Philosophy Program and other visitors including especially Helen Beebee, Frank Jackson, and Michael Martin. Audiences at the University of Western Australia and the University of Melbourne and in the Faculties at ANU helped me to clarify both substance and presentation. I am also grateful to Antonia Barke, Paul Boghossian, Bill Brewer, Kirk Ludwig, Christopher Peacocke, Paul Pietroski, Sarah Sawyer, Stephen Schiffer, Ernest Sosa, and Tom Stoneham for comments and conversations. This paper continues some of the themes of and, I hope, improves on 'Externalism, architecturalism, and epistemic warrant' (1998). It certainly inherits some of the debts of that earlier paper, especially a debt to Crispin Wright's British Academy lecture, 'Facts and certainty' (1985). In his 'Cogency and question-begging: Some reflections on McKinsey's paradox and Putnam's proof' (2000), Wright defends a position that is similar to the one that I adopt here though there are differences in detail and in explicit motivation. A systematic comparison of the two approaches must wait for another occasion.

[1] McKinsey (1991: 16).   [2] Boghossian (1997: 161).

cascading stream of water helps to maintain the humidity of the rainforest gully. These are just a couple of Kylie's thoughts on the subject of water, her water thoughts. Amongst Kylie's many other thoughts that involve the concept of water are these: that there is water in the lake, that trees die without water, that water is a liquid, and, of course, that water is wet. When Kylie thinks consciously, in a way that occupies her attention, she is able to know what it is that she is thinking.[3] This is true for thoughts about water, as for any other thoughts. So when Kylie thinks consciously that water is wet, she knows, even as she thinks, that she is thinking that water is wet.

Kylie is a student of philosophy. She has studied many arguments that purport to show that, in order to think that water shimmers, or cascades, or is wet, in order to think any water thoughts at all, a thinker must be in some way familiar with water. In Kylie's estimation, it is a complex and delicate question whether these arguments are compelling. But her present judgement is that, in order for someone to think, say, that water is wet, that thinker must be, or at least must have been, in an environment that contains some samples of water.

As she ponders, consciously, the wetness of water, Kylie notes that she is thinking that water is wet. She also judges, on the basis of her philosophical reflections, that if she is thinking that water is wet then she must be, or have been, embedded in an environment that contains samples of water. From these two premisses, she draws the obvious inference: she herself is, or has been, in a watery environment. There is nothing counter-intuitive or even surprising about this conclusion. She is in Canberra, in the university; in one direction there is the water in the lake, in another direction there is the water in the gully, and there are many other samples of water all around.

There is a puzzle looming here, but just considering the premisses and conclusion of Kylie's argument does not bring it out. The argument is obviously valid and she is no less certain about the conclusion than she is about the conjunction of the premisses. The puzzle that is looming is not about validity or about certainty but about knowledge. In particular, it is about ways of gaining knowledge.

When Kylie thinks, consciously, that water is wet, she knows that this is what she is thinking; and she knows it in a special first-personal way. This is Kylie's first piece of knowledge. When philosophical theorizing goes well, careful evaluation of arguments yields knowledge of true principles. So if Kylie is right in her philosophical reflections on water thoughts, then she has a second piece of knowledge. She knows that if she is thinking that water is wet then she is, or has been, in an environment containing samples of water. It then seems a trivial matter to achieve a third piece of knowledge. For these first two pieces of knowledge appear to offer Kylie a very short route to knowledge that she herself is, or has been, in a watery environment. It is here that the puzzle arises.

---

[3] For discussion of the way in which conscious thought occupies attention, and of 'consciously based self-ascriptions', see Peacocke (1998; 1999: ch. 5).

What is puzzling is not simply the idea that Kylie knows that there is water in her environment. In the last few days, she has taken showers, drunk lots of mineral water, and walked around the lake and down through the rainforest gully; so of course Kylie knows that there is water in her environment. What is puzzling is, rather, the apparent availability of a particular route to this knowledge. This route goes via Kylie's knowledge about what she is thinking and her knowledge about the conditions that any thinker must meet in order to think water thoughts. The methods that are involved in gaining these two pieces of knowledge are, first, the special first-personal way of knowing what one is thinking and, second, philosophical theorizing. But it strikes Kylie as counter-intuitive that the use of just these methods should deliver knowledge that there is water in her environment.

One way of dramatizing Kylie's puzzle is this. Sitting in her armchair, Kylie may think that water is wet. If she does so, then she can know immediately that this is what she is thinking. Sitting in her armchair, Kylie may consider and evaluate philosophical arguments. If she does this well, then she may end up knowing that if she is thinking that water is wet then she is, or has been, in an environment containing samples of water. Sitting in her armchair, Kylie can draw the obvious conclusion. Yet it is counter-intuitive that this exercise in armchair reflection should be a way of knowing that she is, or has been, in a watery environment.

As it happens, Kylie already knows that there is water in her Canberra environment. So, if armchair reflection provides a route to knowledge of this same environmental fact, then what it offers to Kylie is additional warrant for something that she already knows by the familiar methods of observation and investigation. It offers resources that she might use to confirm that there is water in her environment should a doubt arise. That is already strange enough to be the core of a puzzle. But the puzzle may appear to be even more acute. For if, as things are, armchair reflection can provide this additional epistemic warrant, then it seems that it could, in principle, have provided her with a way of learning about her relationship with water *for the first time*.[4]

2. RESPONDING TO THE PUZZLE

Kylie's puzzle is this. An argument that seems palpably valid has two premisses:

---

[4] Kylie's puzzle can be dramatized as a problem of armchair knowledge. But her sense of puzzlement is not the product of absolute and non-negotiable convictions about what is, and what is not, knowable from the armchair. She accepts that she may have to allow that more things can be known from the armchair than she had initially expected. But it seems to Kylie that, even against the background of a more generous view of the possibilities of armchair knowledge, it would still be implausible that this *particular* armchair route could lead to this piece of knowledge about her environment.

Water(1) I am thinking that water is wet.

Water(2) If I am thinking that water is wet then I am (or have been) embedded in an environment that contains samples of water.

Therefore:

Water(3) I am (or have been) embedded in an environment that contains samples of water.

One premisse seems to be knowable in the special first-personal way; the other seems to be knowable by philosophical theorizing. But the conclusion is not intuitively something that we would expect to be able to know just by combining self-knowledge with philosophical theorizing in this way.

Suppose we allow that self-knowledge is a kind of a priori knowledge and also that philosophical theorizing yields a priori knowledge. Then we can say that what is puzzling is that both premisses of the argument should be knowable a priori when the conclusion is something that should not, intuitively, be knowable a priori. In the quotations at the beginning of the paper, Michael McKinsey (1991) and Paul Boghossian (1997) pose puzzles like Kylie's in terms of a priori knowledge and, in Section 7, we shall consider those puzzles and Kylie's in the light of a distinction between two notions of a priori knowledge. But we do not need to make use of any particular conception of a priori knowledge in order to introduce Kylie's puzzle.

Someone might respond to the puzzle by recommending that we simply embrace what initially seems so counter-intuitive; namely that self-knowledge and philosophical theorizing can together provide a route to knowledge that there is water in the environment. This bold strategy is what Sarah Sawyer proposes: 'introspection becomes a viable method of acquiring knowledge of our environment' (1998: 532). Sawyer then adds a consideration that is intended to make this strategy more plausible: '[I]t must be recognised that introspection will yield knowledge *only* of those empirical facts that the subject could already have come to know via empirical means' (ibid.). However, this was already taken into account in Kylie's puzzle. Kylie not only could have come to know that there was water in her environment 'via empirical means'; we assumed that she did already know this by the familiar empirical methods. What is puzzling is that the use of those armchair methods should offer additional warrant or provide confirmation in case of doubt.

Bill Brewer (1999) responds to Kylie's puzzle by advancing a claim that is somewhat similar to the consideration that Sawyer puts forward. According to Brewer's account of what is involved in having the concept of water, when Kylie thinks that water is wet it must already be the case that she 'is in a position to express non-inferential knowledge [about water]' (1999: 267). What this amounts to is this:

[E]ither . . . [she] currently has non-inferential reason of some kind to believe something about [water], or . . . [she] has retained knowledge based upon such a reason in memory. (Ibid.)

Putting the point crudely we can say that, on Brewer's account, if Kylie is in a position to think any water thoughts at all then she already knows some things about water. So, as Brewer continues:

[She] is already in a position to arrive at the knowledge that there is (or was) [water] in [her] environment if only [she] turns [her] mind to the matter. Therefore this argument [the argument in Kylie's puzzle] cannot possibly constitute a problematic non-empirical *source* of new empirical knowledge: if its premises are simply true, then the subject already has the wherewithal to arrive at knowledge of its conclusion. (Ibid.)

If Brewer is right about this, then it is wrong to cast Kylie's puzzle in terms of armchair reflection providing her with a way of learning about her relationship with water *for the first time*.[5] But the core of the puzzle remains. For it is strange to allow that Kylie's armchair reflections should provide her with a warrant or justification for believing that there is water in her environment. This is counter-intuitive even if we accept that the warrant or justification that would be provided is one for which Kylie would have no need unless doubt arose.

Suppose that a subject believes the premises of a palpably valid argument to be true on the basis of certain considerations and as a result also believes that the conclusion is true. Consider what typically happens if such a subject comes to doubt the truth of the conclusion. Doubting the truth of the conclusion, she also doubts the truth of the conjunction of the premises, and may attach that doubt to one of the premises in particular. But then, by replaying the considerations that led her to accept the premises in the first place, she may be able to rule out certain alternatives to the truth of the premises and so resolve her doubt about them and also her doubt about the conclusion. Typically, the subject's justification for believing the premises offers resources that can be used to resolve a doubt about the truth of the conclusion. But in Kylie's case it is counter-intuitive, quite apart from questions of first knowledge, that she could rationally resolve a doubt about the existence of water in her environment by replaying her armchair reflections.[6]

The bullet-biting strategy recommended by Sawyer does not appeal and the additional considerations put forward by her and by Brewer are not adequate to solve the puzzle. Diana Raffman (1998) responds in a different way, charging that arguments that threaten to generate puzzles like Kylie's face a trilemma. Either the truth of the first premiss cannot be known in the special first-personal way or the truth of the second premiss cannot be known by philosophical theorizing alone or else the argument equivocates on what is involved in thinking that water

---

[5] See again the apparently more acute version of the puzzle mentioned at the end of the last section.

[6] I am grateful to Michael Martin for stressing the need to connect justification for believing with resolution of doubt.

is wet. The worry that the notion of thinking that water is wet might be given a thin construal in the first premiss and a thicker construal in the second premiss is genuine;[7] but it is open to us simply to stipulate that there is to be no equivocation. Given that stipulation, Raffman's charge becomes the claim that not both of the premisses can be known in the prescribed way; that is, in the special first-personal way (first premiss) or by philosophical theorizing (second premiss).

This is, indeed, a very natural response to Kylie's puzzle. The puzzle shows, it may be said, that we cannot consistently combine a certain claim about self-knowledge with a certain claim about philosophical theories relating to water thoughts.[8] But, in this paper, I shall be arguing that there is another way of responding to Kylie's puzzle. To this end, we can consider a kind of worst-case scenario that might arise with respect to Kylie's specific puzzle or another of the same form. In this scenario, the bullet-biting strategy is inapplicable: it really is problematic to allow that the conclusion of the argument could be known by combining self-knowledge and philosophical theorizing. In addition, the premisses are both true, and they can be known in the special first-personal way and by philosophical theorizing respectively. The premisses can be known in those particular armchair ways and, since there is to be no equivocation, the argument is palpably valid. Can we maintain that it *still* does not follow that those armchair methods provide a route to knowledge of the conclusion?

3. EXTERNALISM, SELF-KNOWLEDGE, AND THE THREAT OF *REDUCTIO*

The conditional premiss, Water(2), that figures in Kylie's puzzle is an instance of a general principle:

---

[7] According to some theories, the concept of water is descriptive in character so that thinking that water is wet is thinking something along the lines of: 'The chemical kind that exists in my actual environment and which falls from clouds, flows in rivers, is drinkable, colourless, odourless, etc. is wet'. (For a defence of description theories, see Jackson (1998). Davies and Humberstone (1980) pointed out that much of what Putnam (1975) says would come out as correct on this construal of natural kind terms.) Given this construal of thinking that water is wet, the force of Raffman's charge is clear. In putting forward Kylie's puzzle about water thoughts, we assume that there is some other way to conceive of thinking that water is wet. Provisionally, we suppose that the thought that water is wet is about water in somewhat the same way that so-called recognition-based thoughts are about their objects (Evans 1982; Brown 1998). This is not to deny that there are chemical kinds that Kylie can think about even though she has had no causal engagement with samples and could not reliably recognize a sample if one were presented. Nor do we deny that there are chemical kinds that Kylie can think about even though there are no samples in her environment (Burge 1982).

[8] This, in effect, is the response of McKinsey (1991) and Boghossian (1997); see again the quotations at the beginning of this paper. Wright (2000: sect. 6) offers considerations against this response.

($\forall$x) (If x is thinking that water is wet, then x is (or has been) embedded in an environment that contains samples of water).

I call the claim that this universally quantified conditional holds, not just as things actually are but as a matter of necessity (WaterDep), an *externalist dependence thesis*.

In general, *externalism* about some mental property, M, is the thesis that whether a person has M depends, not only on conditions inside the person's skin, but also on the person's environment and the way that the person is embedded in that environment. Expressed in terms of possible worlds, externalism about M says that there are two possible worlds w_1 and w_2, differing in environmental conditions, such that an individual, *a*, has M in w_1 but a duplicate individual, *b*, lacks M in w_2. This is a thesis about the existence of Twin Earth examples for M.[9]

If we are given the truth of the externalist dependence thesis, WaterDep, then it is a relatively straightforward matter to construct a Twin Earth example for the property of thinking that water is wet. But it is far from easy to move in the opposite direction from the existence of a Twin Earth example to the truth of any externalist dependence thesis as specific as WaterDep.[10] Kylie's puzzle arises if externalist philosophical theorizing leads, not just to Twin Earth externalism about water thoughts, but to an externalist dependence thesis about water thoughts.

3.1. Two problems for externalism and self-knowledge

Kylie's puzzle arises from the combination of two ideas. The first, as we have just noted, is that philosophical theorizing leads to externalist dependence theses; in particular, to a dependence thesis about the property of thinking that water is wet. The second idea is that we have a special first-personal way of knowing what we are thinking. When we know in that special way what we are thinking, our knowledge does not depend for its status as knowledge on any empirical investigation of our environment or of our way of being embedded in it.[11]

Kylie's puzzle points to a seemingly counter-intuitive consequence of self-

---

[9] Elsewhere, I have distinguished *modal* externalist theses like this one from *constitutive* modal theses (Davies, 1991, 1992, 1993, 1996, 1998).

[10] See Gallois and O'Leary-Hawthorne (1996) and compare Wright (2000: sect. 3). This view about the difficulty of moving from the existence of Twin Earth examples to a specific externalist dependence thesis seems to stand in contrast with a remark by Boghossian (1997: 163): '[A Twin Earth] thought experiment motivates externalism only by motivating a specific form of dependence of mental contents on external facts.'

[11] First-personal knowledge is subject to a thesis of *privileged access* along the lines that Brian McLaughlin and Michael Tye formulate in their discussion of these issues (1998: 286): 'It is conceptually necessary that if we are able to exercise our actual normal capacity to have beliefs about our occurrent thoughts, then if we are able to occurrently think that p, we are able to know that we are thinking that p without our knowledge being justificatorily based on empirical investigation of our environment.'

knowledge given an externalist dependence thesis. But there is another, and more familiar, way of developing the idea that there is some tension between the truth of externalist dependence theses and the possibility of self-knowledge. How can I achieve a special kind of knowledge about what I am thinking, knowledge that is not justificatorily based on empirical investigation of my environment, when my thinking what I am in fact thinking depends on my environment? We can call this the *achievement problem* for self-knowledge given externalism to distinguish it from the *consequence problem* for self-knowledge given externalism which is the problem posed by Kylie's puzzle.

Approaches to the achievement problem typically make some use of the fact that, when I think that I am thinking that water is wet, I deploy in thought the very same concepts of water and of being wet that are involved in my thinking that water is wet. So an externalist dependence thesis that is true for my first-order thinking that water is wet will be no less true for my second-order thinking that I am thinking that water is wet. Because the content of my second-order thought embeds the content of my first-order thought, my second-order thinking shares the dependence on the environment that is characteristic of my first-order think-ing.[12] Of course, this fact about embedding does not by itself explain how it is that my second-order judgement that I am thinking that water is wet amounts to knowledge. We still need a general account of how authoritative self-knowledge is possible.[13] But, according to these approaches to the achievement problem, the fact about embedding can be used to show that there is no *special* problem for the achievement of self-knowledge in the fact that my first-order thinking is subject to an externalist dependence thesis.

An account of how self-knowledge is possible has to show how a second-order judgement that I am thinking that water is wet can be knowledge, when the judge-ment is made on the basis of my (conscious, first-order) thinking that water is wet. In part, this account will be the same as applies to cases in which no externalist dependence thesis is true for the first-order thinking. The worry is that there is an additional problem to be solved when an externalist dependence thesis does hold. But because of the point about embedding, the philosophical argument that supports the externalist dependence thesis for the first-order thinking will show something else as well. It will show, quite independently of the epistemic status of my second-order judgement, that I can frame that second-order thought only if I am embedded in an environment that contains samples of water. So, at the very start-ing point for an assessment of the epistemic status of the second-order judgement, it is already guaranteed that I meet the externalist conditions for the first-order thinking.[14] Thus, the truth of an externalist dependence thesis for the first-order thinking poses no special problem for the achievement of self-knowledge.

<hr/>

[12] Burge (1988), Heil (1988), Peacocke (1999: ch. 5).
[13] Burge (1996, 1998), Peacocke (1996, 1998, 1999).
[14] For a critical assessment of Heil's (1988) use of the point about embedding, see Brueck-ner (1990). For further discussion, see Falvey and Owens (1994) and Brueckner (1994).

3.2. *The threat of* reductio

Let us agree that these familiar approaches are successful in dealing with the achievement problem for self-knowledge given externalism. It is essential to that success that, in order to arrive at knowledge that I am thinking that water is wet, I do not need to know anything of externalist philosophical theorizing and I do not need to know that the conditions required by an externalist dependence thesis actually obtain.[15] But to the extent that the truth of an externalist dependence thesis is no bar to the achievement of self-knowledge, the consequence problem becomes pressing. When she thinks, consciously, that water is wet, Kylie knows that this is what she is thinking; and the status of her knowledge as knowledge does not depend on any empirical investigation of her environment. Then she engages in some philosophical theorizing and comes to know that if she is thinking that water is wet then certain conditions must obtain. She draws the obvious consequence that those conditions do indeed obtain. Yet, as Tyler Burge says, 'To know that such conditions obtain, one must rely on empirical methods' (1988: 654). This is precisely Kylie's puzzle.

Paul Boghossian presents the consequence problem as a *reductio ad absurdum* of the combination of externalism and self-knowledge. (See the second quotation at the beginning of this paper.) In his presentation, externalism is 'the view that what concepts our thoughts involve may depend not only on facts that are internal to us, but on facts about our environment' (1997: 161). The claim about self-knowledge is 'that we are able to know, without the benefit of empirical investigation, what our thoughts are in our own case' (ibid.). The conclusion for *reductio* is that, if both these claims were true, then 'we would be in a position to know certain facts about the world a priori, facts that no one can reasonably believe are knowable a priori' (ibid. 161–2). According to Boghossian, one or the other claim has to be rejected.

My aim is to show how both claims can be maintained. Some specific externalist dependence theses are true and can be known by engaging in philosophical theorizing. We can know what we are thinking without this knowledge being justificatorily based on investigation of our environment. Yet those armchair reflections that yield knowledge of an externalist dependence thesis and of what I am thinking do not provide a route to knowledge of facts about the world which 'no one can reasonably believe are knowable a priori'.[16]

---

[15] There is a complication here if we accept Brewer's (1999) claim that anyone who is in a position to think that water is wet will inevitably know many things about water (see above Sect. 2). However, even then it remains the case that the self-knowledge is not justificatorily dependent on that empirical knowledge about water.

[16] Boghossian notes the possibility of a response to the threat of *reductio* along the lines that I propose but is sceptical about its prospects (1997: 175): 'I have to say that I would be very surprised if there turned out to be any such cases [where a priori warrant for the premises of an argument is not transmitted to the entailed conclusion] that survived scrutiny.' However, I have an ally in Wright (2000) whose response to the threat of *reductio* is similar to mine.

4. CLOSURE OF KNOWLEDGE AND TRANSMISSION OF WARRANT

Whether it is genuinely possible to respond to Kylie's puzzle in the way that I am proposing is related to the question whether knowledge is closed under known entailment. If someone knows the premisses of an argument and knows that a particular conclusion follows from those premisses, does it follow that the person knows, or is at least in a position to know, that conclusion?

Fred Dretske (1970) allows that a father who takes his son to visit the zoo may know that the animal in the pen in front of them is a zebra even without gathering any evidence to rule out the alternative possibility that it is a cleverly disguised mule. Dretske presents the example as a case in which the father knows both:

Zebra(1) The animal in the pen is a zebra.

and:

Zebra(2) If the animal in the pen is a zebra, then it is not a cleverly disguised mule.

yet does not know:

Zebra(3) The animal in the pen is not a cleverly disguised mule.

Even more famously, Robert Nozick (1981) presents an analysis of knowledge on which any one of us can know many truths about the external world that are plainly incompatible with a radical sceptical hypothesis, even though we cannot know that the sceptical hypothesis about the external world is itself false.

If knowledge is not closed under known entailment, then it can happen that a thinker has justifications or warrants for believing the premisses of a valid argument but has no epistemically adequate justification or warrant for believing the conclusion. If that is so, then the justifications or warrants for believing the premisses do not themselves add up to a justification or warrant for believing the conclusion. In such a case, we shall say that those justifications or warrants are not *transmitted* from premisses to conclusion.[17]

Where knowledge is not closed, warrant is not transmitted. But the converse is not guaranteed to hold. In a particular case where justification or warrant is not

---

[17] In an earlier paper (Davies, 1998), I spoke of *transfer* of warrant. Wright's term 'transmission' seems preferable. He says (Wright 2000) that 'a particular warrant, w, transmits across a valid argument just in case the argument is cogent when w is the warrant for its premisses.' And: 'A cogent argument is one whereby someone could be moved to rational conviction of the truth of its conclusion.' As Wright stresses, transmission or non-transmission of warrant is not a property of an argument in itself. It may be that one possible warrant for the premisses is transmitted to the conclusion while another possible warrant is not. My only reservation about Wright's way of introducing the idea of transmission of warrant is that he ties it quite closely to the idea of first knowledge. (See again the discussion of Brewer (1999) in Sect. 2 above.)

transmitted from the premisses of a valid argument to its conclusion, it could still be that anyone who knew the premisses would also know, or be in a position to know, that the conclusion is true. It might be, for example, that anyone who knew the premisses on the basis of a warrant that did not transmit to the conclusion would inevitably have some other warrant for the conclusion. Or, alternatively, it might be that, although warrant does not transmit from premisses to conclusion, it is possible to have knowledge of the conclusion without any justification or warrant at all, but with a different kind of entitlement. It may not be obvious how either of these ways of having closure of knowledge without transmission of warrant would apply to Dretske's zebra example.[18] But the transmission question and the closure question are still distinct and there is room for the possibility that a failure of transmission need not be inevitably accompanied by a breach of closure.[19] What is crucial to our strategy for responding to Kylie's puzzle is the idea of there being some limitations on transmission of justification or warrant.

In fact, we have already allowed that Brewer (1999) may be right to claim that if Kylie is in a position to think any water thoughts at all, then she is already in a position to know that there is water in her environment. We said that it is still counter-intuitive to allow that Kylie's armchair reflections provide her with an additional justification or warrant for believing that there is water in her environment or with resources that she might use to confirm that there is water in her environment should a doubt arise. So we need to provide a motivation for limiting transmission of warrant even in cases where there is no breach of closure.

Our response to Kylie's puzzle is developed in two stages. The aim of the first stage is to uncover a plausible principle for limiting the transmission of observational warrant from premisses to conclusion in cases like Dretske's and Nozick's examples. It is also intended that this first principle should apply to Moore's (1959) putative anti-sceptical argument since, intuitively, an everyday observational warrant for believing that here is a hand and here is another does not amount to a justification for denying radical scepticism (Section 6). Moore's argument is naturally described as question-begging, and we shall defend the idea that failure of transmission of epistemic warrant is the analogue, within the thought of a single subject, of the dialectical phenomenon of begging the question (Section 5).[20]

---

[18] On Gail Stine's (1976) contextualist account of knowledge, Dretske's zebra example would be a case of closure of knowledge without transmission of warrant. Wright (2000: sect. 7) argues that the zebra case and others of Dretske's examples are indeed failures of transmission rather than of closure.

[19] This distinction has often been missed in the literature on epistemic closure but one writer who has consistently emphasized it is Wright. For a clear statement of the distinction see e.g. his (1985: 438, n. 1).

[20] Wright (1985) argues that Moore's putative 'Proof of an external world' founders on a failure of transmission of warrant. Something like the connection that I shall make between begging the question and failure of transmission of warrant is presumably implicit in the title of Wright (2000) though he does not elaborate on the notion of question begging.

In Dretske's and Nozick's examples, and in Moore's argument, it is not the case that both premisses are known by armchair reflection. So, even if the first stage of our response were to be completed successfully, it would be open to someone to insist that while empirical warrants are not always transmitted, still there can be no failure of transmission for armchair warrants (or for a priori warrants). The aim of the second stage of our response is to transpose the principle for limiting the transmission of observational warrant into a principle for limiting the transmission of the particular kinds of armchair justification that figure in Kylie's puzzle (Section 8). However, we also need to examine an important ancestor of Kylie's puzzle that is found in the work of Michael McKinsey (1991), since it is far from obvious that our strategy for responding to Kylie's puzzle would apply to the *reductio* argument that McKinsey presents (Section 7).

5. BEGGING THE QUESTION AND TRANSMISSION OF WARRANT

Suppose that someone suspects that the animal in the pen is a cleverly disguised mule and that a speaker attempts to convince this suspicious hearer of the truth of Zebra(3) by advancing the argument in Dretske's example. Even in the absence of any further details about the case, there is a quite strong intuition that the speaker is begging the question. If we imagine a speaker who advances Moore's argument in an attempt to convince a sceptic of the existence of the external world, then the intuition of question-begging is even stronger. However, in order to know what to make of these intuitions, we need an account of what it is to beg the question. Once we have an account, we can ask how this dialectical phenomenon is related to questions about transmission of epistemic warrant in the thinking of a single subject.[21]

5.1. Begging the question

In an important discussion of begging the question on which we shall rely heavily, Frank Jackson (1987: 107) argues that: 'The utility of valid argumentation . . . in convincing audiences of conclusions lies in the evidence implicitly offered for borrowing by the presentation and selection of premises.' By advancing an argument, rather than flatly asserting the conclusion, the speaker invites the hearer to borrow his evidence; and by his choice of premisses the speaker provides some information about what the nature and structure of this evidence is.

---

[21] I am grateful to Helen Beebee for raising the question about the relationship between begging the question and transmission of warrant, and for helping me to get clear about my answer to it.

Because advancing an argument with a particular choice of premisses indicates what kind of evidence is available for borrowing, it is possible for a speaker to engage in what Jackson calls 'misleading advertising' (ibid. 108). But in order to isolate 'begging the question proper', Jackson asks us to consider examples in which an argument is advanced and the advertising of evidence for borrowing is not misleading. What is important for begging the question is the particular way in which evidence that is available for borrowing supports the premisses of the argument. The issues are particularly clear if set out in terms of a Bayesian account of the confirmation of hypotheses by evidence.

So long as we ignore the existence of background assumptions, we can say that evidence E supports hypothesis H if the probability of H given E, Pr(H/E), is greater than the prior probability of H, Pr(H). Once background assumptions are in play, E supports H relative to background assumptions B if the probability of H given E plus the background assumptions B, Pr(H/(E&B)), is greater than the prior probability of H given B alone, Pr(H/B). It can happen that E supports H relative to background assumptions B_1 but not relative to background assumptions B_2. So, in particular, it may happen that E supports H relative to a speaker's background assumptions but not relative to the background assumptions of a hearer.

Suppose, then, that a speaker propounds an argument to a hearer who needs to be convinced of the argument's conclusion C. Suppose, too, that A is among the argument's premisses. By advancing the argument, the speaker advertises that he has evidence of a certain kind for A. We are supposing that this advertisement is not misleading. So the evidence offered for borrowing is available and does indeed support A *relative to the speaker's background assumptions*. But it does not follow that the evidence supports A relative to the hearer's background assumptions. In fact, the hearer's doubt about C may virtually guarantee that the speaker's offered evidence does not support A relative to the hearer's background assumptions and, in that case, advancing the argument will be ineffectual. It will not provide the hearer with any grounds for accepting the conclusion C because the offered evidence will not provide the hearer with any grounds for accepting the premiss A.[22]

In summary, then, it may be that:

> [A] given argument to a given conclusion is such that anyone – or anyone sane – who doubted the conclusion would have background beliefs relative to which the evidence for the premisses would be no evidence. (Ibid. 111)

---

[22] In the simplest case, the conclusion C is entailed by the premiss A and C is itself one of the speaker's background assumptions B. Since this is not to be a case of misleading advertising, the offered evidence, E, supports the premiss A relative to the speaker's background assumptions; so Pr(A/E&B) > Pr(A/B). Also, since A entails C, Pr(C/E&B) ≥ Pr(A/E&B). But it does not follow that the speaker's evidence, E, provides support for the conclusion C even relative to the speaker's own background assumptions. For those assumptions include C and so Pr(C/E&B) = Pr(C/B) = Pr(C/C) = 1.

Of this kind of case, Jackson says: 'Such an argument could be of no use in convincing doubters, and is properly said to beg the question' (ibid. 112).

5.2. *Justification and the resolution of doubt*

Now that we have an account of begging the question, we can turn to the relation between this dialectical phenomenon and the transmission of epistemic warrant from premisses to conclusion. To this end, we shall borrow and adapt an example from Crispin Wright.[23] It has the evidential structure of begging the question proper, but now within the thought of a single subject. Acceptance of the background assumptions that are required if the subject's own evidence for the premisses is to be evidence cannot be rationally combined with doubt about the conclusion.

At the MCG,[24] I see what seems to be an Australian Rules football match in progress, and one of the players kicks the ball between the tall central uprights. The crowd roars, the goal umpire makes a sign with his hands and then waves two flags. Ordinarily, this would count as overwhelming evidence that a goal had been scored. So I would have a warrant for believing the first premiss of the following obviously valid argument:

> Goal(1) A goal has been scored.
> Goal(2) If a goal has been scored, then a football match is in progress.

Therefore:

> Goal(3) A football match is in progress.

But there are imaginable background beliefs relative to which the apparent evidence for that premiss would be no evidence.

If I believe that what I am watching is the seventeenth take for a scene in a movie, then the ball sailing between the uprights, the roaring crowd, and the two flags do nothing to confirm the hypothesis that a goal has genuinely been scored. Even if I believe that it is an open question whether there is a football match or a movie scene or some other elaborate pretence before my eyes, then, for me, the evidence does not support the claim that a goal has really been scored. Relative to these background beliefs, the trajectory of the ball and the behaviour of the players, the umpires, and the crowd do not amount to evidence that supports Goal(1).

However, the mere possibility of such background beliefs does not show that advancing the argument would be begging the question as Jackson defines that notion. For it is not true that anyone sane who doubted the conclusion, Goal(3),

---

[23] See Wright (1985: 436) and, in much more detail, Wright (2000: sect. 2).
[24] The Melbourne Cricket Ground is used for Australian Rules football several times each weekend during the winter.

would have background beliefs relative to which the offered evidence for the premiss Goal(1) would be no evidence.[25] In order to generate a clear case of begging the question we can make one of two changes to the example. We can modify the setting of the example so that anyone sane who doubted Goal(3) in that setting would believe that they were watching a movie scene. We could do this by making the movie scene possibility especially salient. Alternatively, and more simply, we can adjust the argument itself so that the conclusion actually speaks of the movie scene possibility:

> Goal(1) A goal has been scored.
> Goal(2′) If a goal has been scored, then a football match is in progress and this is not just a movie scene.

Therefore:

> Goal(3′) This is not just a movie scene.

Advancing this argument and advertising the availability of the evidence of the ball, the crowd, and the flags in support of the premiss Goal(1) could be of no use in convincing a hearer who doubted Goal(3′). It really would be begging the question. And if I were to doubt whether this was a real match or just a movie scene, then reviewing that evidence in an attempt to resolve my own doubt would be no less futile.

Beginning in a state of doubt and appreciating the futility of relying on the evidence of ball, crowd, and flags for a resolution of that doubt, I might seek out an answer to the question whether it is a football match or a movie scene that I am watching. Suppose that I gather independent evidence that it is, after all, a genuine match. Given this background information, I do have a justification or warrant for believing that a goal has been scored; and intuitively this warrant is provided by the evidence of ball, crowd, and flags. But, Crispin Wright (2000: 142–3) says, '[I]t would be absurd to regard that warrant as transmissible across the entailment to [Goal(3)]. You don't get any *additional* reason for thinking that a game is in progress by having the warrant for [Goal(1)]'.

It seems to me that Wright is correct to say that there is a failure of transmission of warrant here, although it is clearer if we consider the argument in which the conclusion explicitly mentions the movie scene possibility. There is a background assumption that is required if my evidence for Goal(1) is to count as evidence. But acceptance of this background assumption cannot be rationally combined with doubt about Goal(3′). So the particular evidential justification that

---

[25] Someone arriving at the MCG at 2.15 p.m. on a winter Saturday might doubt that a football match is in progress because he believes that the day's fixture is an evening rather than an afternoon match. Or perhaps he believes that it is an afternoon match but that there are still several minutes to go before the start. Entering the stand with this belief he sees one of the players kick the ball between the goalposts and he hears the crowd roar. He realizes that a goal has been scored and that the match is already in progress. (Afternoon matches start at 2.10 p.m.)

I have for believing Goal(1) does not provide me with a resource that can be used to settle a doubt about Goal(3ʹ). If I came to doubt the independent evidence that I had gathered and so started to wonder whether, after all, I was just watching a movie scene, the evidence of ball, crowd, and flags would be of no help to me in resolving that doubt.

5.3. Transmission of warrant in the absence of doubt

On a Saturday during the football season there is no serious prospect that the MCG would be used as a film set. As I sit in the stand, it does not occur to me to doubt that it is a genuine match that I am watching. Against the background of my assumption (my not doubting) that a football match is in progress, the trajectory of the ball and the behaviour of the players, the umpires, and the crowd add up to a very good justification or warrant for believing that a goal has been scored. In addition, a small amount of conceptual analysis provides me with a compelling justification for believing the conditional premiss, Goal(2ʹ), since it is only in the context of a genuine match that a goal can be scored. Does my observation of the ball, the crowd, and the flags, combined with my elementary piece of conceptual analysis, add up to a justification or warrant for believing that a football match, rather than a movie scene, is in progress?

It was in these terms that we introduced the idea of transmission of epistemic warrant (Section 4). But someone might suggest that, if the idea of transmission is understood in these terms, then warrant is indeed transmitted in the case that we have just described. Since I believe the premisses of a palpably valid argument, I am surely justified in believing the conclusion as well; indeed, it would be irrational for me not to do so. This suggestion about transmission of epistemic warrant has to be rejected. The crucial question is not whether I am right to believe that a football match is in progress, nor even whether I have some epistemic warrant for believing it. The question is whether the epistemic warrants that I have for believing the premisses add up to an epistemically adequate warrant for the conclusion.

Against the background of the assumption that a genuine Australian Rules football match is in progress, the evidence of ball, crowd, and flags counts in favour of the hypothesis that a goal has been scored and against a host of alternative hypotheses. For example, the evidence counts against the hypothesis that only a behind has been scored,[26] and against the hypothesis that the ball has been kicked out of bounds. In short, the evidence rules out various ways in which the hypothesis that a goal has been scored could have been false, and it is for this reason that the evidence provides a resource for resolving doubt. It is also by ruling out alternatives that the evidence confers knowledge. This is how evidence

---

[26] A behind is scored if the ball is kicked between the shorter outer uprights but not between the tall central uprights.

constitutes an *epistemic* warrant. But the evidence of ball, crowd, and flags does not count in favour of the hypothesis that a football match rather than a movie scene is in progress and against alternative hypotheses. The evidence, even taken together with the considerations that support the conditional premiss, does nothing to rule out the most obviously salient alternative hypothesis, namely that it is a movie scene that I am watching. That evidence would be of no help in resolving doubt and it does not confer knowledge. My epistemic warrants for the premisses do not add up to an epistemic warrant for the conclusion.

In fact, there are two ways of conceiving my justificatory situation when, on a winter Saturday at the MCG, the movie scene possibility is utterly ignored. On one account, what I see of ball, crowd, and flags constitutes my justification for believing that a goal has been scored. The background assumption that a football match, rather than a movie scene, is in progress is one that I am entitled to make, without justification, in the circumstances of being at the MCG on a Saturday afternoon during the football season. It is a substantive philosophical question what the nature of this entitlement would be. But one defining mark of the entitlement is that the dependence of my evidential justification on that unjustified assumption does not prevent my knowing that a goal has been scored. On the other account, my justification for believing that a goal has been scored properly consists in what I see of ball, crowd, and flags *together with* some justification for the background assumption that it is a football match, and not a movie scene, that is in progress. On both accounts, the evidence of ball, crowd, and flags contributes to an epistemic warrant for Goal(1) but contributes nothing to an epistemic warrant for Goal(3′).

6. MOORE'S ARGUMENT AND A LIMITATION PRINCIPLE

Failure of transmission of epistemic warrant is the analogue, within the thought of a single subject, of the dialectical phenomenon of begging the question.[27] We said at the end of Section 4 that Moore's argument:

> Moore(1)   Here is one hand and here is another.
> Moore(2)   If here is one hand and here is another, then an external world exists.

Therefore:

> Moore(3)   An external world exists.

---

[27] In a case of begging the question, the hearer is provided with no grounds for accepting either the premiss or the conclusion. Helen Beebee has raised the point that this makes it difficult to see how there can be an analogy with failure of transmission of warrant since, from the hearer's point of view, there is no warrant to transmit. The response to this worry is that we need to focus on the situation of the speaker, rather than the hearer, in a case of begging the question.

is naturally described as question-begging and, unsurprisingly, Jackson classifies it as a case of question-begging proper. Anyone sane who doubted the conclusion, Moore(3), would have background beliefs relative to which the perceptual evidence for Moore(1) that is offered for borrowing would be no evidence.[28] Acceptance of the background assumptions that are required if the offered evidence for Moore(1) is to be evidence cannot be rationally combined with doubt about Moore(3). So, if I were beset by sceptical doubt, then attempting to resolve that doubt by reviewing the perceptual evidence for Moore(1) would be a futile exercise.

In ordinary circumstances, it does not occur to me to doubt that there is an external world. Against the background of my assumption (my not doubting) that there is an external world, my perceptual experience adds up to a very good justification for believing Moore(1). An analysis of the concepts of hand and of external world provides me with a justification for believing the second premiss, Moore(2). But the obvious parallel with the case of a goal being scored shows that my observation of two hands, combined with my modest piece of conceptual analysis, does not add up to an epistemic warrant for the conclusion that an external world exists.

As we continue with the parallel, there seem to be two ways of conceiving the everyday justificatory situation. On one account, the background assumption that there is an external world is one that I am entitled to make without justification.[29] The role of this unjustified assumption in the justification of everyday beliefs like the belief that here is a hand and here is another does not prevent those beliefs from being knowledge.[30] On the other account, a proper justification for my belief that here is a hand and here is another would have to include a justification of the background assumption that there is an external world. The decision between these accounts is not a trivial matter; large issues in epistemology turn on it.[31] But both accounts agree that the epistemic warrant for Moore(1) that is furnished by perceptual experience is not transmitted to Moore(3).

---

[28] See Jackson (1987: 113). Commenting on Moore's argument, Wright says (1985: 437): 'Once the hypothesis is seriously entertained that it is as likely as not, for all I know, that there is no material world as ordinarily conceived, my experience will lose all tendency to corroborate the particular propositions about the material world which I normally take to be certain.'

[29] In essence, this is the proposal that Wright (1985) canvasses though it is there set in the context of the suggestion that propositions like Moore(3) are not 'fact-stating'.

[30] It is consistent with the first way of conceiving the everyday justificatory situation to say that the background assumption is itself known without justification. In that case, we would have closure of knowledge without transmission of warrant.

[31] Because it is not clear where a justification of the background assumption could come from, the second way of conceiving the everyday justificatory situation tends in the direction of scepticism.

6.1. Completing the first stage of the plan

The aim of the first stage of the two-stage plan announced at the end of Section 4 was to uncover a principle for limiting the transmission of observational warrant from premises to conclusion in cases such as Moore's argument as well as Dretske's and Nozick's examples. In an earlier paper (1998), I suggested a limitation on transmission of epistemic warrant along the following lines:

> *First Limitation Principle (first version):*
> Epistemic warrant cannot be transmitted from the premises of a valid argument to its conclusion if, for one of the premises, the truth of the conclusion is a precondition of our warrant for that premiss counting as a warrant.

The motivation for this principle was straightforward. Our reflections on examples such as Moore's argument are supposed to be captured by the idea that the truth of Moore(3) is a 'precondition' for our observational warrant for Moore(1) to count as a warrant. But this initial formulation of the principle is problematic, not least because it involves the unexplained notion of a precondition.[32] If the notion is interpreted so that a precondition is simply a necessary condition, then the First Limitation Principle is certainly open to counter-examples. For example, Bill Brewer (this volume; see also 1999) points out that, on that interpretation of the notion of precondition, the principle has the consequence that warrant can never be transmitted to a necessary truth—a result that is disastrous for logic and mathematics. In addition, on that interpretation the principle has the somewhat counter-intuitive consequence that warrant could never be transmitted to the proposition that I have a warrant for something or that someone has a warrant for something.

Our discussion of begging the question suggests a better way of codifying the idea behind the First Limitation Principle:

> *First Limitation Principle (revised version):*
> Epistemic warrant cannot be transmitted from the premisses of a valid argument to its conclusion if, for one of the premisses, the warrant for that premiss counts as a warrant only against the background of certain assumptions and acceptance of those assumptions cannot be rationally combined with doubt about the truth of the conclusion.

Where the original version speaks (in effect) of the conclusion C's being a necessary condition for the warrant to count as a warrant, the revised version says, instead, that doubt about C cannot be rationally combined with acceptance of certain background assumptions. There are two features of this revised version that promise to make it less open to counter-examples than the original version.

---

[32] This worry about the notion of precondition is explicit in Davies (1998: 352) and is echoed by Wright (2000).

One is the introduction of the notion of *rational combination*; the other is the introduction of an explicit mention of *background assumptions*.[33]

First, the original version's use of the notion of a necessary condition has the result that if the principle blocks transmission of warrant to C, then it also blocks transmission of warrant to any proposition that is entailed by C and, in particular, to any logical truth. But the notion of rational combination is to be interpreted in such a way that it will often be possible for a thinker rationally to combine acceptance of one proposition, A, with doubt about another proposition, B, even though A entails B. We shall say that a thinker *cannot* rationally combine acceptance of A with doubt about B only when doubt about B *immediately* constitutes a reason for not accepting A. With the notion of rational combination interpreted in this way, it may be that acceptance of A cannot be combined with doubt about B, but can be rationally combined with doubt about some proposition that is entailed by B. It may also be that acceptance of various propositions can be rationally combined with doubt about a proposition that is, in fact, necessarily true, or even a priori necessarily true.[34]

A version of the principle incorporating just this first improvement would be as follows:

> Epistemic warrant cannot be transmitted from the premisses of a valid argument to its conclusion if, for one of the premisses, doubt about the truth of the conclusion cannot be rationally combined with acceptance that the warrant for that premiss counts as a warrant.

But it is plausible that one cannot rationally combine acceptance that a particular warrant counts as a warrant for a certain premiss with doubt about whether one has, or whether anyone has, a warrant for anything. So this version would still have the consequence that epistemic warrant could never be transmitted to the proposition that I have a warrant for something or that someone has a warrant for something. To the extent that this is genuinely a counter-intuitive consequence, the problem lies in the fact that the half-improved version of the principle does not yet say anything about background assumptions.

The second attractive feature of the revised version that is motivated by our discussion of begging the question is that it is explicit that there is a role for back-

---

[33] Wright's proposed account (2000: sect. 2) of examples in which there is a failure of transmission for what he calls 'information-dependent' warrants already incorporates, in effect, at least the second of these two features. In fact, the importance of the role of background assumptions should have been clear from Wright (1985; see e.g. 436) but it was not reflected in the original version of the First Limitation Principle (Davies 1998: 351.)

[34] This still leaves it open that there may be a proposition, B, such that doubt about B cannot be rationally combined with acceptance of any propositions. The revised version of the First Limitation Principle, as presently formulated, has the consequence that epistemic warrant cannot be transmitted to such a proposition. Similarly, any argument advanced in support of such a proposition would be *vacuously* question-begging. We shall not pursue here the question whether the vacuous case should be ruled out.

ground assumptions to play. It may be that evidence E supports a hypothesis H only relative to certain background assumptions. But we do not need to include amongst those assumptions the very proposition that E supports H. It may be that my justification for believing the premiss of an argument is constituted by certain evidence and that my justification counts as a justification only against the background of certain assumptions. But it does not follow that the proposition that my evidence counts as a warrant must itself be included amongst those background assumptions. Nor does it follow that acceptance of those background assumptions cannot be rationally combined with doubt about whether anyone has a warrant for anything.

There can be no doubt that even this revised version of the First Limitation Principle will face counter-examples and will require further modifications. This is not the place to pursue the matter at any length, but we can very briefly indicate two ways in which the principle could be improved further.

First, although the principle talks about background assumptions there is still some unclarity about the way in which these assumptions have to be accepted. At a couple of points we have spoken of not doubting as an alternative to explicitly assuming and, in fact, absence of doubt seems to be the way in which background assumptions usually figure in our justificatory practices. Further work on the First Limitation Principle should lead to a clearer specification of the role of background assumptions in the justification of beliefs.

Second, it would be natural to interpret the principle as indicating that there is some unique set of background assumptions relative to which a warrant for some proposition A counts as a warrant. But this indication of uniqueness does not seem quite right. We begin, perhaps, with a default set of assumptions; we do not doubt that certain possible circumstances do not obtain. If any one of these circumstances were to obtain, then our putative warrant for A would not, after all, be a warrant. Also, if we were to doubt that these circumstances do not obtain— if we were seriously to consider that these circumstances might obtain—then we would no longer be justified in believing A. These circumstances are defeaters of our warrant. But the defeaters may themselves be defeated and warrant may be restored. So our warrant may count as a warrant relative to a set of background assumptions that is different from the default set. Further work should incorporate the notion of defeaters and defeaters of defeaters (and so on) into the First Limitation Principle.[35]

Even without these further improvements, the principle seems to give a reasonable account of the failure of transmission of observational warrant in Moore's argument, in Dretske's and Nozick's examples, and in the case of my

---

[35] I am grateful to Michael Martin for discussion of the issues raised in these last two paragraphs. The indication of uniqueness that is present in the First Limitation Principle (revised version) is not a feature of Jackson's (1987) account of begging the question, so it is not obvious that the envisaged refinements would involve any departure from the idea of a close connection between begging the question and failures of transmission of warrant.

seeing a goal being scored. To the extent that this principle enjoys a measure of plausibility, we can allow that the first stage of the two-stage plan that was announced at the end of Section 4 is complete.

6.2. Problems for the second stage of the plan

The second stage of the plan was to transpose the principle that limits the transmission of observational warrant into a principle for limiting the transmission of the particular kinds of armchair justification that figure in Kylie's puzzle. But this now looks problematic. The motivation for the First Limitation Principle comes from examples in which entertaining a doubt undermines or defeats a warrant that is constituted by observational evidence. The warrant is undermined because acceptance of certain (default) background assumptions cannot be rationally combined with the doubt. But it is far from clear how this idea could be applied in the case of Kylie's puzzle.

The first problem is that neither self-knowledge nor the kind of knowledge that comes from philosophical theorizing seems to be based on observational evidence. In response to this first problem it might be said that the notion of observational evidence figures in the examples that motivate the revised version of the First Limitation Principle but does not figure in the principle itself. All that is really required for a successful transposition is that there should be background assumptions for self-knowledge or for philosophical reasoning. But although this response is correct, it highlights two further problems.

The second problem is that it is not at all obvious what the (default) background assumptions for self-knowledge or for philosophical theorizing are. The third problem is that it is even less obvious that acceptance of those assumptions, whatever they may be, cannot be rationally combined with doubt about whether I am embedded in an environment that contains samples of water.[36]

However, despite these problems for the second stage of the announced plan, I shall, in the final section of the paper, propose a principle that limits the transmission of armchair (or a priori) warrant. Before that, we need to consider an important ancestor of Kylie's puzzle.

7. MCKINSEY'S ORIGINAL RECIPE

Michael McKinsey (1991) presented a *reductio* argument that has been widely regarded as establishing a model for puzzles like Kylie's. Brian McLaughlin and

---

[36] Because of these striking differences between Moore's argument and Kylie's puzzle, some philosophers have proposed that an argument rather like the one in Kylie's puzzle can be used effectively against a sceptic about the external world even though Moore's argument cannot. See e.g. Warfield (1998).

Michael Tye speak of 'McKinsey's recipe for trying to show that [a] version of externalism is incompatible with privileged access' and describe the recipe as follows:

[F]ind some E such that (1) E cannot be known a priori . . . yet (2) the version of externalism implies that it is a conceptual truth that if one is thinking that p, then E. According to McKinsey, if such an E can be found, it can be successfully argued that *either* one cannot know a priori that one is currently thinking that p *or* it is not a conceptual truth that if one is thinking that p, then E, from which it may be inferred that the version of externalism is incompatible with privileged access. (1998: 290)

They continue: 'McKinsey's recipe is, we believe, a perfectly fine one.'

In the passage quoted at the beginning of this paper, McKinsey does not offer any explicit defence of the truth of the conditional statement about a priori knowledge (1991: 16): '[I]f you could know a priori that you are in a given mental state, and your being in that state conceptually or logically implies the existence of external objects, then you could know a priori that the external world exists.' He merely asserts (ibid.): 'It's just that simple.' So from that passage alone it is not clear whether McKinsey has in mind what we have called the achievement problem for self-knowledge given externalism, or the consequence problem, or some other problem. But elsewhere in his paper he spells out the argument for *reductio* in terms of a thinker being able to deduce E from premises that are knowable a priori, and so being able to know E a priori as well. It is for this reason that I regard McKinsey's *reductio* argument as being an ancestor of Kylie's puzzle.

If we are to carry through the second stage of our announced plan for responding to Kylie's puzzle, then we must defend the idea that even armchair or a priori warrants may depend on empirical background assumptions. But at just this point a distinctive feature of McKinsey's original presentation of his recipe becomes important. McKinsey (1991: 9) says that a priori knowledge is 'knowledge obtained independently of empirical investigation', but he makes a significant addition when he talks about the character of self-knowledge:

[W]e can in principle find out about these states in ourselves 'just by thinking', without launching an empirical investigation *or making any assumptions about the external physical world*. (Ibid; emphasis added)

Let us say that *strict* a priori knowledge is knowledge that is not justificatorily based on empirical investigation and *also involves no empirical assumptions*.[37] The lesson that McKinsey draws from his *reductio* argument is this. If thinking that p is conceptually or logically dependent on environmental conditions (about which I could not have strict a priori knowledge), then I cannot have strict a priori knowledge that I am thinking that p. So we cannot know about our own external-

---

[37] It is not clear that there could be any motivation for ruling out empirical assumptions about the external physical world while allowing empirical assumptions about, for example, the workings of my brain.

ist mental states without either launching an empirical investigation or making some assumptions about the external physical world.

We have already noted that there are two ways of conceiving the justificatory situation when background assumptions are in play. On one account, what we ordinarily take to be the justification really does constitute the justification for believing the proposition in question, and we are entitled to make the background assumptions without justification. On the other account, the justification for believing the proposition in question properly consists of what we would ordinarily take to be the justification together with a justification for the background assumptions. There are also two ways of conceiving the significance of the lesson that McKinsey draws from his *reductio* argument.

On the first account, the status of my self-knowledge as knowledge would not depend on my having a justification for the empirical assumptions that I made. Instead, I would have an entitlement to make some empirical assumptions without justification. On this account, the lesson that McKinsey draws about strict a priori knowledge would be consistent with our knowledge about our own externalist mental states being a priori in the weaker sense of being not justificatorily based on empirical investigation.

On the second account, the status of my self-knowledge as knowledge would depend in part on my having a justification for any empirical assumption that I made and this justification would presumably have to involve empirical investigation. Thus, any dependence on empirical background assumptions would already be enough to ensure that self-knowledge does not even meet the standard of being not justificatorily based on empirical investigation. So, on this account, there is no significant difference between a priori knowledge as initially defined and strict a priori knowledge.

It is clear from a later paper (McKinsey, forthcoming) that McKinsey himself favours the second account of the justificatory situation when background assumptions are in play. He explicitly argues that there is no relevant difference between 'knowledge that has certain empirical presuppositions' and 'knowledge that is directly based on empirical investigation'. This, of course, is why, in the original paper, he moves without comment from the apparently less strict notion of a priori knowledge to the strict one.

We cannot expect there to be any limitation on the transmission of strict a priori warrant in McKinsey's sense. So suppose, for a moment, that I could know strictly a priori that I am thinking that water is wet, and could know strictly a priori that if I am thinking that water is wet then environmental condition E holds. We have no reason to deny that the strict a priori warrant for those premises could be transmitted to the conclusion that condition E holds. But, as McKinsey points out and as we must surely agree, it is absurd to suppose I could know strictly a priori that E holds. McKinsey's *reductio* argument is compelling when it is cast in terms of strict a priori knowledge as he defines that notion. On that construal, McKinsey's recipe is indeed 'a perfectly fine one'.

Someone who accepts the a priori truth of externalist dependence theses and who wants to maintain the idea of authoritative self-knowledge must insist on a distinction between strict a priori knowledge and knowledge that is a priori in the weaker sense of being not justificatorily based on empirical investigation. As we have seen, making this distinction involves allowing for the idea of epistemic entitlement without justification.

With the distinction in place, it is possible to respond to McKinsey's *reductio* argument by allowing that self-knowledge is not strictly a priori but maintaining that it is, nevertheless, not justificatorily based on empirical investigation.[38] In fact, for reasons that have nothing to do with externalism, it is implausible that our knowledge of our own mental states is strictly a priori in McKinsey's sense. For example, Christopher Peacocke considers a range of ways in which the causal processes that underlie our normal ability to make knowledgeable self-ascriptions of mental states can go wrong. Some of these ways are associated with symptoms of schizophrenia; others are more science-fictional. The upshot is that there can be dissociations between a conscious thought's being initiated by a subject and a conscious thought's being experienced as self-initiated. Peacocke concludes:

There is then a reliance, in everyday conscious self-ascriptions, on these dissociations not actually obtaining. The ordinary self-ascriber is entitled to such presuppositions. . . . [A]lthough there are many deep respects in which self-knowledge cannot be assimilated to perceptual knowledge, there is, even in consciously based self-ascription, reliance on a network of causal relations whose obtaining is by no means necessary. (1999: 244–5)

But even if we can offer an adequate response to McKinsey's *reductio* argument as he originally presented it, the argument remains important because its pattern can be repeated for a more relaxed notion of a priori knowledge than the one that McKinsey himself favours. This is what Boghossian's *reductio* argument shows[39] and, of course, Kylie's puzzle can be cast in terms of a priori knowledge as well. Kylie knows a priori (in a way that is not justificatorily based on empirical investigation) that she is thinking that water is wet. She also knows a priori that if she is thinking that water is wet then she is embedded in an environment that contains samples of water. But it is counter-intuitive that the use of just these a priori methods should provide Kylie with knowledge that there is water in her environment.

---

[38] It would seem that something like this thought is pivotal to Wright's (2000: sect. 7) argument that McKinsey's *reductio* argument falls foul of a failure of transmission of warrant. However, the details of Wright's diagnosis are, at least on the surface, quite different from the resolution that I propose. I hope to return in future work to a comparison and evaluation of the two accounts. See also McLaughlin (2000) which appeared while the present paper was in press.

[39] See also Brown (1995).

8. A SECOND LIMITATION PRINCIPLE AND THE RESOLUTION OF KYLIE'S PUZZLE

At the end of Section 6, we noted some problems for the idea of adapting the First Limitation Principle to block the transmission of epistemic warrant in Kylie's puzzle. After our consideration of McKinsey's original recipe in Section 7, we know that there must be background assumptions for self-knowledge that we are entitled to make without justification. But this does not yet tell us how to move from the First Limitation Principle to something that will resolve Kylie's puzzle.

In the earlier paper (Davies 1998) that I have already mentioned, I proposed a second principle that was intended to apply to puzzle cases like Kylie's:

> *Second Limitation Principle (first version):*
> Epistemic warrant cannot be transmitted from the premises of a valid argu-
> ment to its conclusion if, for one of the premises, the truth of the conclu-
> sion is a precondition of the knower even being able to believe that premiss.

The idea behind this principle was clear. In the case of Moore's argument or Dretske's example, if the conclusion were false, then our putative warrant for the first premiss would not, after all, be a warrant, though that premiss would (let us allow for the purposes of this discussion) still be something that we could enter-tain. In the case of Kylie's puzzle, if the conclusion were false then, according to the externalist philosophical theorizing that supports the second premiss, I could not think that water is wet. What is more, I could not think any thought in which the concept of water is deployed and so, in particular, I could not even think that I am thinking that water is wet.[40] So, if the conclusion were false then I could not believe or even entertain the first premiss. The Second Limitation Principle simply makes this relationship between conclusion and premiss the triggering condition for failure of transmission of warrant and so is guaranteed to have the desired result. Unfortunately, however, the Second Limitation Principle, in that early version, appears both desperately *ad hoc* and open to counter-examples.

The Second Limitation Principle makes use of the notion of a precondition and so faces all the problems associated with that notion. In addition, the principle has the somewhat counter-intuitive consequence that warrant could never be trans-mitted to the proposition that I am able to believe something or that someone is able to believe something.[41] These worries about counter-examples are serious. But what is more important is to provide a principle that not only offers a resolu-tion of Kylie's puzzle but also draws on some of the motivation for the revised version of the First Limitation Principle, so avoiding the charge of being *ad hoc*.

---

[40] Here we make use of 'the fact about embedding' that was important for work on the achievement problem for self-knowledge given externalism.

[41] This counter-intuitive consequence is explicit in Davies (1998: 354) and is also mentioned by Wright (2000).

If we could achieve that much then discussion of counter-examples could be left for another occasion.

But we face serious problems. It is not at all obvious what the background assumptions for self-knowledge or for philosophical theorizing are, and it is even less obvious that acceptance of those assumptions cannot be rationally combined with doubt about whether I am embedded in an environment that contains samples of water. These problems are addressed in the next two subsections.

8.1. Towards a motivated principle

As we saw in Section 7, Peacocke argues that in the case of self-knowledge, as in the case of perceptual knowledge, there is 'reliance on a network of causal relations whose obtaining is by no means necessary' (1999: 245). But I want to focus on an even more basic background assumption, not only for self-knowledge, but for any kind of justification or warrant.[42] For any proposition, A, if there were no such proposition as A, if there were no such thing to think, to entertain, to believe, to doubt, to confirm, or to disconfirm as the proposition A, then there could be no question of anything justifying my believing A. So a putative warrant for A counts as a warrant only against the background of the assumption that there is such a proposition as the proposition A.

If we incorporate just this idea into the Second Limitation Principle, then the result is as follows:

> Epistemic warrant cannot be transmitted from the premises of a valid argument to its conclusion if, for one of the premises, the truth of the conclusion is a precondition of there being any such proposition for the knower to think as that premiss.

But now, in order to move the principle closer to the revised version of the First Limitation Principle and closer to the notion of begging the question, we need to make a second change. Instead of talking about preconditions or necessary conditions, the principle should speak of rationally combining doubt about the conclusion with acceptance of what we have now identified as a background assumption:

> Epistemic warrant cannot be transmitted from the premises of a valid argument to its conclusion if, for one of the premises, acceptance of the assumption that there is such a proposition for the knower to think as that premiss cannot be rationally combined with doubt about the truth of the conclusion.

---

[42] Even when we have improved limitation principles available (see the next subsection) it does not appear to be possible to resolve Kylie's puzzle by appealing only to the background assumptions that Peacocke mentions.

The principle that we have arrived at seems to be well motivated rather than *ad hoc*. In fact, there is only one difference between this principle and the revised version of the First Limitation Principle. Where the first principle speaks of the warrant for a premiss counting as a warrant only against the background of certain assumptions, the principle that we have just formulated speaks of the specific assumption that there is such a proposition as that premiss We might, perhaps, allow that calling into question the assumption that there is such a proposition as the premiss to be believed is simply a very radical way of undermining our justification for believing that premiss. If we were to allow that, then the principle that we have arrived at could be regarded as a consequence of the revised version of the First Limitation Principle.

Unfortunately, however, the principle that we have arrived at is not adequate to resolve Kylie's puzzle. The reason is that it is clearly possible rationally to combine doubt about the truth of the conclusion (Water(3)) that there are samples of water in my environment with acceptance that there is such a thing for me to think as the premiss (Water(1)) that I am thinking that water is wet. Many philosophers who do not endorse externalist arguments would be prepared to combine that doubt with that acceptance. Certainly, doubt about Water(3) does not immediately constitute a reason for not accepting that there is such a thing for me to think as Water(1).

8.2. The final step

There is one more step that we need to take if we are to resolve Kylie's puzzle. We need to take full account of the fact that the argument that gives rise to Kylie's puzzle has more than one premiss. Return, for a moment, to the dialectical phenomenon of begging the question. When a speaker advances an argument with several premisses, he implicitly offers the hearer evidence for, or more generally considerations in favour of, each of the premisses. It seems to be a legitimate extension of what Jackson actually says (1987: 111) to suggest the following. Advancing a multi-premiss argument will be begging the question if anyone sane who doubted the conclusion *and accepted the evidence offered in support of all but one of the premisses* would have background beliefs relative to which the evidence offered in support of *the remaining premiss* would be no evidence. For that would be enough to guarantee that the argument (ibid. 112) 'could be of no use in convincing doubters'.

It might be that (as in the original definition) anyone sane who doubted the conclusion would, whether or not they accepted the evidence offered in support of the other premisses, have background beliefs relative to which the evidence offered in support of one of the premisses would be no evidence. In such a case, the question-begging nature of the argument is likely to be obvious. But suppose that what is offered in support of one of the premisses is a complex and subtle piece of philosophical theory. Then it might not be obvious what assumptions could sanely be combined with acceptance of that philosophical theory and doubt about the conclusion of the argument.

The revised version of the First Limitation Principle was motivated by the idea that failure of transmission of warrant is the analogue, within the thought of a single subject, of begging the question. So we should expect the First Limitation Principle to incorporate the extension to multi-premiss question begging thus:

> *First Limitation Principle (multi-premiss version):*
> Epistemic warrant cannot be transmitted from the premisses of a valid argument to its conclusion if, for one of the premisses, the warrant for that premiss counts as a warrant only against the background of certain assumptions and acceptance (i) of those assumptions and (ii) of the warrants for the other premisses cannot be rationally combined with doubt about the truth of the conclusion.

Then we can incorporate the same extension into the improvement on the Second Limitation Principle that we have already arrived at:

> *Second Limitation Principle (multi-premiss version):*
> Epistemic warrant cannot be transmitted from the premisses of a valid argument to its conclusion if, for one of the premisses, acceptance (i) of the assumption that there is such a proposition for the knower to think as that premiss and (ii) of the warrants for the other premisses cannot be rationally combined with doubt about the truth of the conclusion.

The second of these principles is far from being *ad hoc* since it is certainly closely related to the first and can perhaps even be regarded as a consequence of it. Furthermore, it promises to block transmission of warrant from the premisses to the conclusion of the argument in Kylie's puzzle.

The puzzle arises because of the threat that Kylie's warrant for Water(1) and her warrant for Water(2) should jointly constitute a warrant for Water(3). Her warrant for Water(2) is a piece of philosophical theory that shows, in effect, that if there is to be such a thing for me to think as that water is wet, then there must be samples of water in my environment. That same theory would equally have the consequence that if there is to be such a thing for me to think as that I think that water is wet, then, likewise, there must be samples of water in my environment. So acceptance of the assumption that there is such a proposition for me to think as Water(1) and acceptance of the warrant for Water(2) cannot be rationally combined with doubt about the truth of Water(3).[43] The multi-premiss version of the Second Limitation Principle is triggered and our resolution of Kylie's puzzle is, at last, complete.

---

[43] We have already agreed that doubt about the truth of Water(3) can be rationally combined with acceptance of the assumption that there is such a proposition for me to think as Water(1). But there are still two ways in which the Second Limitation Principle (multi-premiss version)

References

Boghossian, P. A. (1997), What the externalist can know a priori. *Proceedings of the Aristotelian Society* 97: 161–75. repr. in C. Wright, B. C. Smith, and C. Macdonald (eds.), *Knowing Our Own Minds* (Oxford: Oxford University Press): 271–84.

Brewer, B. (1999), *Perception and Reason* (Oxford: Oxford University Press).

Brown, J. (1995), The incompatibility of anti-individualism and privileged access. *Analysis* 55: 149–56.

—— (1998), Natural kind terms and recognitional capacities. *Mind* 107: 275–303.

Brueckner, A. (1990), Scepticism about knowledge of content. *Mind* 99: 447–51.

—— (1994), Knowledge of content and knowledge of the world. *Philosophical Review* 103: 327–43.

Burge, T. (1979), Individualism and the mental, in P. A. French, T. E. Uehling, and H. K. Wettstein (eds.), *Midwest Studies in Philosophy,* iv: *Studies in Metaphysics* (Minneapolis: University of Minnesota Press): 73–121.

—— (1982), Other bodies, in A. Woodfield (ed.*), Thought and Object: Essays on Intentionality* (Oxford: Oxford University Press): 97–120.

—— (1988), Individualism and self-knowledge. *Journal of Philosophy* 85: 649–63.

—— (1996), Our entitlement to self-knowledge. *Proceedings of the Aristotelian Society* 96: 91–116.

—— (1998), Reason and the first person, in C. Wright, B. C. Smith, and C. Macdonald (eds.), *Knowing Our Own Minds* (Oxford: Oxford University Press): 243–70.

Davies, M. (1991), Individualism and perceptual content. *Mind* 100: 461–84.

—— (1992), Perceptual content and local supervenience. *Proceedings of the Aristotelian Society* 92: 21–45.

—— (1993), Aims and claims of externalist arguments, in E. Villanueva (ed.), *Philosophical Issues,* iv: *Naturalism and Normativity* (Atascadero, Calif.: Ridgeview Publishing Co.): 227–49.

—— (1996), Externalism and experience, in A. Clark, J. Ezquerro, and J. M. Larrazabal (eds.), *Philosophy and Cognitive Science: Categories, Consciousness and Reasoning* (Dordrecht: Kluwer Academic Publishers): 1–33. repr. in N. Block, O. Flanagan, and G. Güzeldere (eds.), *The Nature of Consciousness: Philosophical Debates* (Cambridge, Mass.: MIT Press, 1997): 309–28.

—— (1998), Externalism, architecturalism, and epistemic warrant, in C. Wright, B. C. Smith, and C. Macdonald (eds.), *Knowing Our Own Minds* (Oxford: Oxford University Press): 321–61.

—— and Humberstone, L. (1980), Two notions of necessity. *Philosophical Studies* 38: 1–30.

Dretske, F. (1970), Epistemic operators. *Journal of Philosophy* 67: 1007–23.

Evans, G. (1982), *The Varieties of Reference* (Oxford: Oxford University Press).

could be triggered. It could be that doubt about the truth of Water(3) cannot be rationally combined with acceptance of the warrant for the conditional premiss Water(2). Or it could be that, while that combination is rationally possible, that pair of doubt and acceptance cannot rationally be further combined with acceptance that there is such a proposition for me to think as Water(1). Further consideration needs to be given to the first of these possibilities.

Falvey, K., and Owens, J. (1994), Externalism, self-knowledge, and skepticism. *Philosophical Review* 103: 107–37.

Gallois, A., and O'Leary-Hawthorne, J. (1996), Externalism and scepticism. *Philosophical Studies* 81: 1–16.

Heil, J. (1988), Privileged access. *Mind* 97: 238–51.

Jackson, F. C. (1987), *Conditionals* (Oxford: Blackwell).

—— (1998), Reference and description revisited, in J. E. Tomberlin (ed.), *Philosophical Perspectives 12: Language, Mind, and Ontology* (Oxford: Blackwell): 201–18.

McKinsey, M. (1991), Anti-Individualism and privileged access. *Analysis* 51: 9–16.

—— (forthcoming), Forms of externalism and privileged access.

McLaughlin, B. P (2000), Self-knowledge, externalism, and skepticism. *Proceedings of the Aristotelian Society Supplementary Volume* 74: 93–117.

—— and Tye, M. (1998), Externalism, Twin Earth, and self-knowledge, in C. Wright, B. C. Smith, and C. Macdonald (eds.), *Knowing Our Own Minds* (Oxford: Oxford University Press): 285–320.

Moore, G. E. (1959), Proof of an external world, in *Philosophical Papers* (London: Allen & Unwin): 127–50.

Nozick, R. (1981), *Philosophical Explanations* (Oxford: Oxford University Press).

Peacocke, C. (1996), Entitlement, self-knowledge and conceptual redeployment. *Proceedings of the Aristotelian Society* 96: 117–58.

—— (1998), Conscious attitudes, attention, and self-knowledge, in C. Wright, B.C. Smith, and C. Macdonald (eds.), *Knowing Our Own Minds* (Oxford: Oxford University Press): 63–98.

—— (1999), *Being Known* (Oxford: Oxford University Press).

Putnam, H. (1975), The meaning of 'meaning', in *Mind, Language and Reality* (Cambridge: Cambridge University Press): 215–71.

Raffman, D. (1998), First-person authority and the internal reality of beliefs, in C. Wright, B. C. Smith, and C. Macdonald (eds.), *Knowing Our Own Minds* (Oxford: Oxford University Press): 363–9.

Sawyer, S. (1998), Privileged access to the world. *Australasian Journal of Philosophy* 76: 523–33.

Stine, G. C. (1976), Skepticism, relevant alternatives, and deductive closure. *Philosophical Studies* 29: 249–61.

Warfield, T. A. (1998), A priori knowledge of the world: Knowing the world by knowing our minds. *Philosophical Studies* 92: 127–47.

Wright, C. (1985), Facts and certainty. *Proceedings of the British Academy* 71: 429–72.

—— (2000), Cogency and question-begging: Some reflections on McKinsey's paradox and Putnam's proof, in *Philosophical Issues* 10 (published as a supplement to Noûs): 140–63.

17

Externalism and A Priori Knowledge of Empricial Facts

Bill Brewer

I want to discuss the possibility of combining a so-called 'externalist' theory of empirical content, on which the contents of a person's beliefs are determined in part by the nature of his extra-bodily environmental embedding, with a plausible account of self-knowledge, in particular, of a person's knowledge of the contents of his own beliefs. A difficulty for this combination is thought to be that it leads to the availability of a kind of non-empirical, a priori knowledge about the mind-independent physical world which is intuitively intolerable.[1] The inference which is held to create this difficulty can be put like this.

(E1) I believe that *p*.

(E2) If *x* believes that *p*, then *x*'s environmental embedding is thus-and-so.

Therefore:

(E3) My environmental embedding is thus-and-so.

An example of this purportedly problematic inference might be the following.

(w1) I believe that water is wet.

(w2) If *x* believes that water is wet, then *x*'s environment contains (or did contain) water.

Therefore:

(w3) My environment contains (or did contain) water.

This paper inherits many acknowledgements from Brewer (1999), and has acquired its own too. I should like to thank the following for their very helpful comments on earlier versions of this material: John Campbell, David Charles, Bill Child, Martin Davies, Naomi Eilan, Jennifer Hornsby, Brian McLaughlin, Mike Martin, Christopher Peacocke, Johannes Roessler, Helen Steward, Tom Stoneham, Rowland Stout, Ralph Walker, and Tim Williamson.

[1] The particular formulation of the issue which I address here is due to Martin Davies (1997). Indeed, my thoughts in this area were initially stimulated by the opportunity to give a reply to an earlier version of his paper at a meeting of the European Society for Philosophy and Psychology in Barcelona during the summer of 1996. Paul Boghossian also presses the issue as a challenge to content externalism of the kind defined in the text below (1989, 1997).

Note that the truth of the consequent of (w2) requires that x's environment contains (or did contain) *water*, rather than any kind of 'twin-water', which is like water in all superficial respects but happens to have a different chemical composition—that is, it requires that x's environment contains (or did contain) *this stuff* (H_2O) as opposed to *that stuff* (XYZ) (Putnam 1975). This is precisely the force of the relevant form of content externalism. So the conclusion states that my environment contains *water*, as opposed to twin-water. This is a contingent matter of empirical fact, though. Hence the prospect of my knowing it a priori, or without any kind of empirical investigation, certainly raises a prima-facie problem.

I

The proponent of this line of objection to combining an adequate account of self-knowledge with content externalism argues as follows. First, any adequate account of a person's knowledge of the contents of his own beliefs entails that his knowledge of instances of (E1) is *non-empirical*: neither its acquisition nor its status as knowledge necessarily involves any specific empirical investigation. Second, content externalism entails that instances of (E2) can be derived from non-empirical philosophical reflection upon the necessary conditions upon determinate empirical belief possession. Third, therefore, the truth of content externalism—in the presence of an adequate account of self-knowledge—enables a person knowledgeably to derive instances of (E3), on the basis of the argument above, without any empirical investigation whatsoever. Fourth, such non-empirical knowledge of empirical facts is intuitively intolerable. Therefore, fifth, content externalism is incompatible with any adequate account of a person's knowledge of the contents of his own beliefs. The reaction which is implicitly recommended by advocates of this argument, of course, is to reject content externalism. Like many others, though—e.g. Putnam (1975); Burge (1979, 1986); Evans (1982); Pettit and McDowell (1986); McGinn (1989); Davies (1991, 1992); Peacocke (1993)—I explicitly endorse a version of this very view (1999). On my account, a person's possession of certain demonstrative beliefs about particular mind-independent things and their properties essentially depends upon his standing in certain perceptual–attentional relations *with those very things*; and since I regard such perceptual demonstrative beliefs as the indispensable core of his system of empirical belief as a whole, and as the foundations, in a certain sense, of all of his empirical knowledge, my commitment to content externalism runs very deep.[2] So what alternative do I propose to the recommended reaction of rejecting it?

There are obviously a number of possibilities. The one which I shall eventually propose and defend is to reject the very first move of the objection set out

---

[2] These commitments are defended in Brewer (1999).

above: I deny that a person's knowledge of the contents of his own beliefs is non-empirical in any way in which it really would follow that he could thereby acquire intolerably non-empirical knowledge of the contingent facts about his own environmental embedding. Before developing this claim, I want briefly to survey the alternatives. First, it might be possible to argue that the content externalist is not committed to the a priori knowability of *specific instances* of (E2). Although he is committed by definition to the conceptual necessity of the claim that concepts of certain types are externally individuated, in a way which entails the possibility of establishing that claim by non-empirical reflection upon the necessary conditions upon determinate empirical belief possession, he may nevertheless deny that the question of which particular concepts instantiate these types can be settled without empirical investigation.[3] Second, it might also be possible to deny the third move above, according to which the truth of content externalism—in the presence of an adequate account of self-knowledge—enables a person *knowledgeably* to derive instances of (E3) without any empirical investigation. This is Martin Davies' response (1997), which I shall consider in some detail shortly. There are two further responses, which I shall simply mention and set aside without argument as, in my view, extremely unpromising. The first of these would be to insist, in extreme rationalist spirit, that there is no difficulty whatsoever in the idea of wholly non-empirical knowledge of empirical matters of fact. Against this, I just take it for granted that a person's acquisition of *new* empirical knowledge, about the *contingent* nature of his environmental embedding, without any perceptual or other empirical investigation whatsoever, by pure reflection, is unacceptable.[4] The second unpromising response would be to claim that a person's self-ascriptions of beliefs are not, contrary to appearances, genuinely truth-evaluable statements, but rather non-truth-evaluable avowals of some kind (Wittgenstein 1958: 190–2; 1980, §§ 470–504; Malcolm 1991). Thus, they are incapable of constituting the premises of an argument, as they are supposed to do in (E1) above, the first premiss of the argument which is in turn supposed to cause trouble for content externalism. Against this, I simply deny it. Whatever their logical and epistemological peculiarities, self-ascriptions of beliefs are statements about a person, to the effect that he is in a certain condition, namely that of believing that p, say. They are determined as true or false by whether or not the subject is in exactly the same condition as determines the truth or falsity of the corresponding other-ascriptions: 'he believes that p', say, said of the subject of the self-ascription by someone else. Such self-ascriptions, like their corresponding other-ascriptions, are true if and only if the person in question—that is, the subject making the self-ascription, who is the object of the corresponding other-ascription—has the belief in question—in this case, that p.

---

[3] Christopher Peacocke urged me to take account of this possibility in correspondence.

[4] There are important issues here concerning the possibility of exploiting content externalism to present a transcendental argument against various forms of scepticism, which I must leave to one side for present purposes. See my (forthcoming) for a full discussion.

II

Let me return, then, to the two more plausible alternatives identified above to my own preferred strategy for establishing the compatibility of self-knowledge and content externalism in the face of the present line of objection to this combination. The first of these denies that specific instances of (E2) are knowable a priori, whilst granting that content externalism itself is a priori true, by arguing that it is a matter of empirical investigation to *which* actual concepts this externalism applies. For the standard externalist examples are natural-kind concepts. Yet knowledge that any given concept is a genuine natural-kind concept requires knowledgeably ruling out the following two ways in which putative reference to natural kinds might fail, which is surely an empirical matter. First, what appears to be reference to a natural kind may fail to be so because the characteristic theoretical role associated with the putative kind in question is not in fact played by anything at all. 'Phlogiston' provides a familiar actual case of this type. There just is no kind of stuff which is released into the surrounding medium quickly by burning and slowly by rusting, and so on. These processes involve instead the absorption of oxygen from the atmosphere. So there is no such thing as phlogiston. Apparent reference to a natural kind by the use of that term is merely illusory, and therefore certainly not susceptible to externalist treatment. Call this *the possibility of emptiness* with respect to a given putative natural-kind term. Second, the range of items to which a term is correctly applied may turn out to be quite heterogeneous at the relevant level of theoretical description involved in the discrimination and unification of natural kinds. 'Jade' provides a familiar actual example of this phenomenon; for it is correctly used of two quite different substances: jadeite, which is a silicate of sodium and aluminium; and nephrite, which is a silicate of lime and magnesia. In principle, cases of this general kind could clearly turn out to be far more wildly heterogeneous, sufficiently so to make quite implausible any attempt to think in terms of a single unified natural kind with a number of sub-varieties, as it may be correct to think that some water is H_2O and some is D_2O, although both are sub-varieties of the single natural kind, water, and not of the natural kind, twin-water (XYZ). In the more extreme cases, again, what appears to be a natural kind term turns out, on empirical investigation, not to be so. Call this *the possibility of heterogeneity*.

Thus, it may be claimed, knowledge of any particular instance of (E2) depends upon knowledge that the relevant component concept of the content that *p* is a *genuine* natural-kind concept, which in turn depends upon the *empirical* knowledge required to rule out the possibilities of emptiness and heterogeneity with respect to the term expressing that concept. So the argument from (E1) and (E2) to (E3) does not, after all, threaten to provide an untenable, because wholly non-empirical, source of any specific piece of empirical knowledge.

I think that the content externalist should not be overly impressed by this apparent resolution of the tension between his position and the possibility of a plausible account of self-knowledge. The way in which parallel issues arise in connection with perceptual demonstrative reference to particular mind-indepen-dent objects helps to bring out why. Consider, for example, the following instance of the argument (E1), (E2) ⊢ (E3).

> (d1) I believe that that ball will go into the pocket.
> (d2) If x believes that that ball will go into the pocket, then x's environ-ment contains that ball.

therefore:

> (d3) My environment contains that ball.

Of course, there is no threat that such an argument should constitute an unten-ably non-empirical source of empirical knowledge—that a particular ball exists in his environment—if the subject's attempted demonstrative reference fails. And there are at least the following two ways in which this might come about. First, there may be no ball at all, or anything else for that matter, at the place in his envi-ronment where the subject takes there to be one: that is to say, he may be subject to some kind of hallucination. Second, his thinking may fail to be responsive to the behaviour of a single ball, as he fails, for example, to keep track of the move-ment of a single red ball after a very strong break in a game of snooker. In the absence of any such defeating abnormality, though, the argument is perfectly sound; and neither his successful demonstrative reference to the particular ball in question, nor his knowledge of the particular instance of (E2)—that is, his knowl-edge of (d2) above—depends upon his having carried out any prior, or indepen-dent, empirical investigation to rule out all the possible sources of hallucination, unnoticed substitution of one ball by another, failure of attentional tracking, and so on.

Similarly, I contend, in the case of reference to natural kinds. According to the most natural development of the externalist position, understanding of natural kind terms is, in the most basic cases, acquired by some kind of demonstrative identification of the kind in question, as *'that stuff'*, on the basis, either of percep-tion of its instances, or of testimony as to their distinguishing perceptible features, characteristic behaviour, normal function or whatever—or, more likely, on the basis of some combination of these. The possibilities of emptiness and hetero-geneity with respect to putative natural kind terms therefore arise as follows. In the first case, the theoretically supported perceptual and/or testimonial *appear-ance* of an underlying kind is entirely hallucinatory. In the second case, the attempted demonstrative identification fails sufficiently to keep track of any *single* kind. Either way, the relevant instance of the argument (E1), (E2) ⊢ (E3) is therefore harmless to the content-externalist. Nevertheless, in the normal case, when the demonstrative identification crucial to the subject's understanding of the term in question makes successful reference to a genuine natural kind, neither this, nor his knowledge of the corresponding specific instance of (E2), depends upon the subject's having carried out any prior, or independent, empirical investigation to rule out all the possible sources of such error due to emptiness or heterogeneity. Thus, the relevant instance of (E1), (E2) ⊢ (E3) is back in contention as a threat to content externalism, in conjunction with which it appears to provide an untenably non-empirical source of empirical knowledge. In any case, the present attempt to avoid this difficulty for combining content externalism with a plausible account of self-knowledge is unsuccessful.

The second prima-facie promising alternative to my own account of how content externalism and self-knowledge are correctly to be combined is to appeal to Davies's (1997) claim that, regardless of the validity of the argument from (E1) and (E2) to (E3), of a person's knowledge of instances of its two premisses, and, indeed, of his knowledge of the validity of the relevant form of argument itself, knowledge of instances of its conclusion *cannot* be acquired by these means. For this would be in contravention of the following Limitation Principle.

> (LP) Epistemic warrant cannot be transferred from A to B, even given an a priori known entailment from A to B, if the truth of proposition B is a precondition of the knower being able to believe the proposition A.

The only motivation which he offers for this principle is that it is supposed to save him from precisely the present difficulty with reconciling self-knowledge and externalism; and it looks a little bit like the following principle which he reads into Wittgenstein's *On Certainty* (1975):

> (WP) Epistemic warrant cannot be transferred from A to B, even given an a priori known entailment from A to B, if the truth of proposition B is a precondition of the warrant for A counting as a warrant.

I think that neither is what Wittgenstein has in mind. More importantly, neither is remotely plausible in my view: (LP) even less so than (WP). Two kinds of counter-example to (LP) come immediately to mind. First, consider the following inference.

> (M1) r_1 and r_2 are real numbers.
> (M2) The product of any two real numbers is a real number.

Therefore:

> (M3) $r_1 r_2$ is a real number.

Its conclusion is a necessary truth, which is therefore, presumably, a precondition of anything possible. Hence it is certainly a precondition of a person's believing the premisses (M1) and (M2). So it follows from (LP) that epistemic warrant cannot be transferred from (M1) and (M2) to (M3). Generalizing the case, (LP) has the consequence that inferential knowledge of any necessary truth is impossible, which certainly places logic, mathematics, and, on many conceptions, philosophy, in a very poor position epistemologically speaking. Something must have gone badly wrong with (LP).

Second, there are clearly certain empirical preconditions upon the actual thought of humans. Suppose that '*Ax*' is some such condition, for any human thinker, *x*. Now, it is surely possible for a person, *b*, to acquire inferential knowledge that *Ab*, on the basis of her observation of various scientific instruments along with her knowledge of the significance of their readings, say. Yet the truth of *Ab* is a precondition of her being able to think, and so believe, anything. Hence, trivially, it is a precondition of her being able to believe the premisses of this inference. So (LP) entails that no such knowledge is possible. Again, this is clearly unacceptable. Thus, it seems to me that appeal to (LP) is a wildly implausible and quite *ad hoc* avoidance tactic in the present context.

III

The key to my own strategy for reconciling self-knowledge with content externalism lies in the idea that true content-externalist requirements are a consequence of the following version of Russell's Principle of Acquaintance (1917: 159), which I shall call (A).

> (A) A person's capacity to make determinate reference to certain objects and kinds in belief depends upon his *having demonstratively based knowledge* about them.

This is what makes it the case that his possession of such beliefs depends upon his being embedded in an environment actually containing the objects and kinds in question. What does this acquaintance condition amount to, though? Well, a person has demonstratively based knowledge about a given object or kind if and only if, either, he has knowledge expressible using demonstrative reference to that object or kind, or, he had such knowledge, some of which is retained, perhaps linguistically categorized and no longer demonstratively expressible, in memory.

Establishing this principle (A) obviously requires extended argument, of which I can only give a brief sketch here.[5] The crucial claim is that externalist relations are necessarily *reason-giving* relations, constituting a source of demonstratively expressible knowledge; where by this I mean reason-giving *from the subject's point of view*, rather than from the perspective of some external theorist. Let me explain why I endorse this.

The externalist holds that certain empirical beliefs have their contents determined in part by the subject's relations with particular things in his environment,

---

[5] The argument is developed in detail, given extended illustration, and defended against putative counter-examples in ch. 3 of Brewer (1999).

the causal relations, for example, in which he stands to such things—to that object, say, or (instances of) that natural kind—when he is perceiving them, being informed about them by others, remembering them, and so on. Call these his *causal-perceptual relations* with the external worldly things in question. These causal-perceptual relations contribute essentially to the determination of objective truth-conditions for the relevant empirical beliefs about such things, which is what makes them genuinely beliefs *about* mind-independent reality, beliefs, that is to say, about just *that object*, say, or *that natural kind*. Now, suppose that these content-determining causal-perceptual relations are *not* reason-giving relations. It follows that for any pair of empirical contents, *x* and *y*, a person's causal-perceptual relations with the things in the world around him give him no more reason to believe that *x* than to believe that *y*, and vice versa. Consider, then, a person, *S*, who believes that *p*, where this is supposed to be an empirical belief, with externalistically determined content, about how things are in the mind-independent world around him. Since his causal-perceptual relations with certain such things play an *essential* role in the determination of the contents of his empirical beliefs, on the externalist's account, there is a range of alternative such beliefs—beliefs which he might have had instead—whose difference in content with his actual belief that *p* would have been due *entirely* to his standing in the relevant content-determining causal-perceptual relations with different mind-independent things. Suppose that the belief that *q* is one of these.

So, the situation is this. *S* actually believes that *p*, because his actual environmental embedding determines this, as opposed to *q*, as the empirical content of his belief, through its causal-perceptual impact upon him. He does not believe that *q*. Had his environmental embedding been appropriately different, though, his position would have been precisely the reverse: he would have believed that *q*, and not believed that *p*. Yet, by hypothesis, the relevant content-determining causal-perceptual relations in which he stands to the actual things in the world around him are not reason-giving relations. So these give him no more reason to believe that *p* than to believe that *q*. Thus, he has, *and could have*, no reason whatsoever to believe that *p* rather than that *q*, or vice versa. For, recall, nothing *other than* his causal-perceptual relations with certain things in the world around him decides between the two contents—this is how *q* was introduced. Which of the two beliefs he actually has is due entirely to the contents of the environment in which he finds himself. Any supposed difference between believing that *p* and believing that *q* is therefore *nothing to him*; for there *could be* no reason *for him* to decide between them. So he does not really *understand* them *as alternatives*. Believing that *p* and believing that *q* are identical for him. Hence the supposedly content-determining role of *S*'s environmental embedding is empty. For there is nothing more, or less, to the content of a belief than the way the subject takes the world to be. Thus, if the proposed causal-perceptual relations in which a person stands to certain mind-independent things are not reason-giving relations, then they contribute *nothing* to the determination of specific worldly truth-conditions for his empirical beliefs about such things. In other words, the content-determining relations between a person and certain things in the world around him which are posited by the content-externalist are necessarily reason-giving relations.

The argument here can obviously be generalized in two ways. First, the content *q* might be replaced throughout with any other content from the relevant range of alternatives to *p*, whose differentiation from *p* is likewise supposed to be due *entirely* to the subject's standing in the relevant content-determining relations with different possible, but non-actual, external environments. Second, *S*'s initial belief that *p* might be replaced by any other empirical belief, of any other person, whose content is supposed to be partially determined in externalist fashion by the subject's causal-perceptual relations with mind-independent things. The result of these generalizations is this. However the putative content-determining causal-perceptual relations are conceived, insofar as these are supposed not to be reason-giving relations, they contribute nothing to the determination of specific worldly truth-conditions for the empirical beliefs in question. Thus, only reason-giving causal-perceptual relations with the external environment could possibly serve the content-determining role required by the content-externalist.

The form of this argument is that of what Peacocke calls 'the *switching* tactic' (1988: 475 ff).[6] A more familiar historical paradigm is provided by Strawson's (1959: ch. 3; 1966: pt. III, sect. II, esp. 168 ff; and 1974) reading of Kant's (1929: A341/B399 ff) argument against Descartes' (1986: 107 ff) substance dualism. According to this Kantian argument, substance dualism entails the coherence of a distinction between qualitative and numerical identity for immaterial souls; yet the dualist's own conception of such things, as exhaustively characterized by what is infallibly given to their own subjective point of view, denies her the resources to give any genuine content to the idea of two qualitatively identical but numerically distinct souls. So, the substance dualist depends upon a distinction—between qualitative and numerical identity for immaterial souls—which she is, by her own lights, incapable of making. Thus, the position is internally inconsistent.

Similarly, here, we are to consider a theorist who insists that the non-reason-giving causal-perceptual relations in which a person's stands to certain objects or kinds in his worldly environment are essential to the determination of specific contents for his empirical beliefs. Such a theorist is therefore committed to the existence of pairs of beliefs with genuinely distinct contents, the distinction between which is entirely due to their subjects' standing in the relevant causal-perceptual relations with different possible objects or kinds. Given his own conception of the nature of these content-determining relations, though, as *non-reason-giving* relations, this entails an overall conception of belief content which countenances the following situation. A person believes that *p*, and does not

---

[6] So-called, I presume, because the tactic is to object to a theory on the grounds that it is in principle incapable of giving any significance to switches which are by that theory's own lights crucial.

believe that q, even though he has, and could have, no more reason to believe that p than to believe that q and vice versa, that is, no reason to believe that p as opposed to believing that q or vice versa. It follows from this that the theorist in question is committed to a conception of belief content which is more discriminating than the subject's own understanding of the contents of his beliefs. For the theorist is obliged to distinguish p and q, even in the face of the fact that they are absolutely on a par as far as the subject's actual or possible reasons for, or against, endorsing them in belief are concerned. In other words, he is obliged to distinguish between these contents even though it is necessarily irrational for the subject, given full under-standing of both of them, ever, even in principle, to take different attitudes towards them, that is, as Evans puts it (1982: 19), by accepting (rejecting) one while reject-ing (accepting), or being agnostic about, the other. Thus, the purported distinction between p and q outstrips anything which is involved in the subject's understand-ing of these contents. This is surely unacceptable by anybody's standards. For the content of a belief is precisely, no more and no less than, the way the subject takes things to be. Hence the position under consideration is incoherent. It entails a distinction which, by its own lights, it is incapable of making.

So, if a person's causal-perceptual relations with mind-independent objects and kinds are to contribute essentially to the determination of the empirical contents of his beliefs, then his standing in these relations must provide the subject with reasons for such beliefs: beliefs, that is to say, about just *that object*, or *that kind*. These content-determining causal-perceptual relations therefore constitute a source of demonstratively expressible knowledge about these objects and kinds: the very objects and kinds which are the semantic values of the rele-vant externalist concepts. Hence the source of externalist conditions upon deter-minate empirical belief possession is indeed my version of Russell's Principle of Acquaintance, (A) above. The requirement upon possession of empirical beliefs with certain contents that the subject should be in an environment actually containing certain things is derived from the fact that his possession of such beliefs depends upon his actually standing in certain basic reason-giving relations with such things.

Furthermore, I think that considerations from a rather different area lend addi-tional support to (A). Recall, first, Evans's comments about a person's use of the proper name 'Louis' in the course of his discussion of the causal theory of names (1985a):

A group of people are having a conversation in a pub, about a certain Louis of whom S has never heard before. S becomes interested and asks: 'What did Louis do then?' There seems to be no question but that S denotes a particular man and asks about him. Or on some subsequent occasion S may use the name to offer a new thought to one of the participants: 'Louis was quite right to do that.' Again he clearly denotes whoever was the subject of the conversation in the pub. This is difficult to reconcile with the Description Theory [on which there is supposed to be associated with each name as used by a group of speakers who believe and intend that they are using the name with the same denotation a description or set of descriptions cullable from their beliefs which an item has to satisfy to be the bearer of that name] since the scraps of information which he picked up during the conversation might involve some distortion and fit someone else much better. Of course he has the description 'the man they were talking about' but the theory has no explanation for the impossibility of its being outweighed.

The Causal Theory [on which it is sufficient for someone to denote x on a particular occasion with a name, that this use of the name on that occasion be a causal consequence of his exposure to other speakers using the expression to denote x] can secure the right answer in such a case but I think deeper reflection will reveal that it too involves a refusal to recognize the [Wittgensteinian] insight about contextual definition [that for an item to be the object of some psychological state of yours may be simply for you to be placed in a context which relates you to that thing]. . . . For the theory has the following consequence: that at any future time, no matter how remote or forgotten the conversation, no matter how alien the subject matter and confused the speaker, S will denote one particular Frenchman—perhaps Louis XIII—so long as there is a causal connection between his use at that time and the long distant conversation. (1985a: 6–7)

Evans has two important points here: first, that possession of a uniquely identifying definite description is unnecessary for successful singular reference; second, that the mere existence of a causal chain of 'reference-preserving' links back to the object in question, as these are conceived, for example, by Kripke (1980) and other proponents of the so-called 'causal theory of reference', is insufficient. Our intuitions about the 'Louis' case surely confirm both of these points. My hypothesis is that these intuitions are organized precisely by the existence of *epistemic* constraints upon genuine reference, that is, reference with real understanding on the subject's part. What makes S's context in the pub conversation sufficient for him to denote Louis XIII in this way, say, is that he is there, at that time and in the context of that conversation, in possession of some demonstratively based *knowledge* about that man. His grasp of what is being said by those around him, and his understanding engagement in the discussion generally, provide him with knowledge expressible using demonstrative reference to the person in question.[7] Equally, I contend, what denies his later uses of any such significance, in the circumstances which Evans describes, is that he then no longer retains anything of this knowledge in memory.

---

[7] I realize that I have said nothing about how exactly testimony might provide such direct demonstrative *knowledge* about the objects of discussion in certain circumstances. I believe that it does; and I would expect the correct account of this possibility to emerge from an investigation into the way in which what might be called *testimonial demonstratives*—as, for example, when S says '*that man* was a villain' in the context of Evans's case of the pub conversation about Louis XIII—succeed in referring to particular persisting mind-independent objects. This would be very much in accord with the way in which I argue elsewhere that an account can be derived of the way in which perceptual experiences provide non-inferential *reasons* for empirical beliefs from reflection upon perceptual demonstrative *reference* to mind-independent things (1999: esp. ch. 6). The key moves of this latter derivation are set out very briefly below. See Evans (1982: chs. 5 and 9); Fricker (1987); Coady (1992); and McDowell (1994) for important work on the epistemology of testimony.

I am reasonably confident that this line of argument can be generalized. Here all that I can offer is a brief sketch of how this might be done. Assume that there is some genuine illumination to be had about the relation of reference—both to particular objects and to natural kinds—holding between certain referring expressions, as they are used in a given linguistic community, and the things which they denote, through reflection upon the practice of the radical interpreter in formulating a truth-theory for the language in which such expressions occur (see Davidson (1984: esp. essays 3, 9, 10, 11, 14, 15, and 16); Evans and McDowell (1976: intro); McDowell (1977, 1978)). As McDowell often insists (e.g. 1977, 1978), thinking in this way enables one to give a perfectly adequate account of the relations between thinkers and things which are required if the former are to refer to the latter in thought and talk, whilst resisting any supposed need reductively to formulate this account in terms of certain specific types of causal relations, or relations of any other kind, conceivable quite independently of their role in the intelligible engagement of a rational agent with the world around him. He puts the point like this:

> It is not true that we condemn a truth-theory to floating in a void, if we reject the alleged obligation to fasten it directly to the causal realities of language-use by way of its axioms [that is, to give a reductive causal theory of reference]. On my account, those truth-theories that can serve as theories of sense are already anchored to the facts of language-use at the level of their theorems: the anchoring being effected by the requirement that assignments of truth-conditions are to be usable in specifications of content of intelligible speech-acts. Since the theorems must be derivable within the theory, the requirement bears indirectly on the theory's deductive apparatus, including assignments of denotation; and the deductive apparatus needs no attachment to the extra-theoretical facts over and above what that affords. Thus we can acquire such understanding as we need of the deductive apparatus (in particular, of the denoting relation) by reversing the order of the theory's deductive direction, starting from our understanding of the requirement of serviceability in interpretation imposed on its consequences. We grasp what it is for a name to denote something by grasping the role played by the statement that it does in derivations of acceptable assignments of truth-conditions to sentences—assignments, that is, which would pull their weight in making sense of speakers of the language that we are concerned with. (1977: 183–4)

So, the idea is that the relations between a person, in his use of a referring expression, and the thing to which he refers in using it, in virtue of which the expression does indeed refer to that thing, are precisely those relations which compel an ideal radical interpreter, in her attempts to make best overall sense of what he says and does, to regard him as talking about that thing in using the expression in question. Furthermore, my contention is that this process of making sense of what people are thinking and talking about is constrained precisely by considerations of what they have *knowledge* about, most importantly, what it is about which they are provided with demonstratively expressible knowledge by the way in which their attention is focused upon the world in perception, testimony, memory, and so on. That is, I claim that the relevant process of radical interpretation is governed by the question which things in the world around them the subjects to be interpreted have demonstratively based *knowledge* about, given the relations in which they stand to such things in using the linguistic expressions which they use in the ways in which they do. In other words, there are, amongst the factors determining the interpreter's assignment of a particular object, or natural kind, as the reference of a given referring expression in use in a certain linguistic community, significant *epistemic* constraints of precisely the kind which my reading of Russell's Principle of Acquaintance, (A) above, demands. The sort of engagement between the language-users and the particular object or kind in question which is required if this assignment is really to make best sense of what they say and do is precisely that involved in their acquiring *knowledge* about just *that object*, or *that kind*, and retaining this to some extent in memory, in the circumstances of their use of the expression. This is my principle (A): direct reference is possible only to objects and kinds about which a person has demonstratively based knowledge. Put another way, the claim is that a person succeeds in singling out a determinate particular or kind in thought, in each of the wide variety of modes of reference by which this is possible, only in virtue of his standing in certain relations with that object or kind which provide him with demonstratively based knowledge about it. These *epistemic* constraints upon reference are what, in McDowell's terms, anchor the correct semantic theory for a given language to the actual facts of its use.

In the context of a certain attractive conception of the relation between the sense and reference of expressions referring to particular objects and natural kinds (see Frege 1993), along the lines proposed by Evans (1982: 20 ff; 1985*b*: esp. 301 ff), this thesis provides a new way of articulating the idea that sense constitutes a 'mode of *presentation*' of reference. Evans's idea is that the sense of a given expression is to be elucidated, and distinguished from the sense of any other expression with the same reference, by giving an explanation of what it is that makes it the case that a person using the term in question is thinking deter-minately about the particular object or kind which serves as its reference rather than about any other thing, what it is about his thinking, therefore, which makes *that object*, or *that kind*, its concern. My present contention is that whatever the correct account here is, it must suffice for the subject's possession of demonstra-tively based knowledge about that thing. Conjoining the two ideas leads to the suggestion that the sense of a referring expression is such that grasping it consti-tutes a capacity for the acquisition and retention of such knowledge about its reference. This, I think, gives substance to the metaphor of the sense of a refer-ring expression as a *mode of presentation* of its reference; and understanding a referring expression therefore involves *acquaintance* with its reference in just this sense.

What remains to be shown, then, is exactly how this basis for content exter-nalism, in the Russellian thesis (A), undermines its purported incompatibility with any adequate account of self-knowledge.

Suppose that a person's belief that *p* comprises an externalist concept *C*. The putatively problematic inference would then be this.

> (e1) I believe that *p*.
> (e2) If *x* believes that *p*, then *x*'s environment contains (or did contain) *C*.

Therefore:

> (e3) My environment contains (or did contain) *C*.

On my view, as I say, the externalist requirement upon possession of the concept *C* derives from the fact that its semantic value is necessarily a natural kind, say, about which any person who has the concept has demonstratively based knowledge, where what this amounts to is either that he has knowledge expressible using demonstrative reference to that kind—e.g. 'that is water in the glass over there', or 'that water looks refreshing'—or that he had such knowledge, some of which is retained, perhaps linguistically categorized and no longer demonstratively expressible, in memory—e.g. 'cool water is refreshing to drink', or 'the water in Hinksey pool was very cold'. Now, if the inference set out above is to be an unwarrantedly non-empirical source of knowledge, then its premises must at least be true. The truth of (e1) depends upon the subject's grasp of the content '*p*', though, which in turn depends upon his possession of the concept *C*. From (A), he therefore has demonstratively based knowledge about *C*, along the lines suggested above on the basis of perfectly unproblematic perception, testimony, or whatever. Hence he is already in a position to arrive at the knowledge that there is (or was) *C* in his environment if only he turns his mind to the matter. Therefore this argument cannot possibly constitute a problematic non-empirical *source* of new empirical knowledge: if its premises are simply true, then the subject already has the wherewithal to arrive at knowledge of its conclusion.

Exactly the same applies, I contend, with respect to the following line of argument.

> (e1)   I believe that *p*.
> (e2*) If *x* believes that *p*, then *x* has (or has had) causal-perceptual relations with *C*.

therefore:

> (e3*) I have (or have had) causal-perceptual relations with *C*.

Possession of the demonstratively based knowledge about *C* which is necessary for the truth of (e1) is itself sufficient for the subject unproblematically to arrive at knowledge of (e3*). What is required for the possibility of (e1) already requires the obtaining of relations between the subject and *C* which provide a source of knowledge of (e3*).

So far so good; but what about the following argument?

(e1)   I believe that *p*.

(e2**) If *x* believes that *p*, then *x* has demonstratively based knowledge about *C*.

therefore:

(e3**) I have demonstratively based knowledge about *C*.

Again, I think that a structurally similar point applies. For the causal-perceptual relations between the subject and *C* which are required for the truth of (e1) are necessarily reason-giving *for the subject*. For otherwise they induce unacceptable distinctions in content which are, *from his point of view*, without a difference. These reason-giving relations, then, are not merely sufficient for the subject's acquisition of demonstratively based knowledge about *C*. They also put him in a position to recognize this knowledge as such. That is to say, the required encounters with *C*, in perception, or through the testimony of others, say, in making demonstratively based knowledge available, themselves enable him to recognize his position as one of epistemic openness to *C*.[8]

Put slightly differently, the claim in each case is that the proponent of the relevant line of objection to externalism wrongly neglects the empirical-epistemic constraints upon concept possession which essentially enter into a person's knowledge of (e1) through their application simply to its truth. This already presupposes his standing in an *epistemic* relation—Russell's *acquaintance*, as it were—with samples of *C*. It is the first move in the objector's reasoning above, then, that any adequate account of a person's knowledge of the contents of his own beliefs entails that this is *wholly non-empirical*, which is to be rejected. For this self-knowledge requires his grasp of the contents of the beliefs in question, his possession of whose component concepts in turn depends upon his empirical-epistemic relations with their semantic values. Thus, content externalism of this kind is perfectly compatible with an adequate account of a person's knowledge of the contents of his own beliefs.

The key idea behind this reconciliation, to repeat, is that determinate concept possession is an *epistemic* skill. It is a matter of a person's being in relations with the relevant worldly semantic values which provide him with demonstratively based knowledge about such things. This is the source of the externalist requirements upon concept possession. That is to say, the world-involving causal-perceptual relations between a person and certain things in the world around him which are essential to his possession of concepts with those things as their determinate semantic values are precisely the *reason-giving* content-determining relations which undermine the purported difficulty with which I began for combining content externalism with a plausible account of self-knowledge.

---

[8] This is how I think that the content-externalist is able to register what is correct about epistemic internalism. It is clearly a contentious claim, though, of which a full defence is impossible here. See Section IV below for a sketch, and Brewer (1999: esp. ch. 6), for the details.

IV

Having avoided the problematic possibility of non-empirical knowledge of empirical matters of fact in this way, I should confess that, on my own account, the way in which the Russellian requirement (A) is met in the most basic cases yields a significant parallel between perceptual demonstrative knowledge and a priori knowledge on a certain traditional conception of the latter. This parallel, though, I contend, is perfectly harmless. I shall end by saying something which I hope may help to make this somewhat ironic outcome intelligible.[9]

Consider a case in which a person refers demonstratively to a particular mind-independent object on the basis of his perception of it. His successful reference to a persisting *mind-independent* thing depends upon more than there happening to be such a thing at the end of his pointing finger when he thinks 'that is *F*', say. He must have some appreciation of the fact that his thought is the joint upshot of the way that thing is and his meeting some further, independent enabling conditions upon recognizing this—being in the right place, looking in the right direction, with sufficient illumination and so on. For it is precisely his grasp of the possibility that these further, independent conditions might fail to obtain which enables him to make sense of the possibility that that very thing might have been just as it is without his recognizing it; and this, in turn, is essential to his understanding of the demonstrative by which he identifies the relevant object *as making reference to a mind-independent thing* whose existence is quite independent of his awareness of it.

The subject's appreciation of this joint dependence then constitutes, in my view, his grasp of the particular perceptual demonstrative thought which he has— 'that is F'—as his openness to the way things objectively are in the world around him. Thus, his understanding of that thought, as the thought which it is about the way a particular mind-independent thing is, is sufficient for his appreciation of its revealing to him the way that thing is out there. Hence his grasp of the empirical content in question—that is F—is sufficient to provide him with an epistemic right to endorse that very content in belief. Although this right is defeasible, in the sense that he may take himself to have it in cases in which he has not—when, for some reason, an apparent episode of perceptual demonstrative thought is not a case of the facts being displayed to him in experience—it is nevertheless adequate to constitute certain perceptual demonstrative beliefs as knowledge in cases in which he has. Thus, as I shall explain, perceptual demonstrative knowledge meets at least *a* conception of a priori knowledge, although it absolutely does not meet another equally traditional conception of the a priori which is often not distinguished from the first.

---

[9] What I say here will mainly be unargued assertion, meant as elucidation rather than proof. The details of the account are spelt out in Brewer (1999), where it is also defended at length against a number of pressing objections (see esp. chs. 6 and 7).

The characterization of a priori knowledge is of course a highly controversial matter in itself, but one familiar idea is that contents are knowable a priori if, perhaps only in certain favourable circumstances and for appropriate subjects, understanding them is sufficient for knowledge of their truth. In this sense, certain perceptual demonstrative contents are on my view knowable a priori, or at least they are a priori reasonable. For a person's grasp of their reference to mind-independent spatial particulars in his environment, essential to his understanding those contents as the contents which they are, provides him with a reason to endorse them in belief: they are presented to him as his epistemic access to the objective facts about such things. Having pointed up this analogy with the a priori, though, it is important to realize at the same time that such contents are about as far from being a priori as they possibly could be on another familiar conception of what this involves. For it is clearly false that their epistemic status is in any way independent of experience. Perceptual experiences are *precisely* what provide the subject's reasons for believing those contents. The initial oddity of this cross-categorization of such perceptual demonstrative beliefs by two perfectly familiar criteria of a priority is immediately resolved by recognizing that the perceptual experiences which provide reasons for them are essential to understanding them. This is how it is that a person's understanding of them can be sufficient for their positive epistemic status, even though this epistemic status is essentially experiential in source.

References

Boghossian, P. (1989), 'Content and Self-Knowledge', *Philosophical Topics* 17: 5–26.

—— (1997), 'What the Externalist Can Know A Priori', *Proceedings of the Aristotelian Society* 97, 161–75.

Brewer, B. (1999), *Perception and Reason* (Oxford: Oxford University Press).

—— (forthcoming), 'Self-Knowledge and Externalism'.

Burge, T. (1979), 'Individualism and the Mental', in French *et al.* (eds.), *Midwest Studies in Philosophy* 4: 73–121.

—— (1986), 'Individualism and Psychology', *Philosophical Review* 95: 3–45.

Coady, C. A. J. (1992), *Testimony* (Oxford: Oxford University Press).

Davidson, D. (1984), *Inquiries into Truth and Interpretation* (Oxford: Oxford University Press).

Davies, M. (1991), 'Individualism and Perceptual Content', *Mind*, 100: 461–84.

—— (1992), 'Perceptual Content and Local Supervenience', *Proceedings of the Aristotelian Society* 92: 21–45.

—— (1997), 'Externalism, Architecturalism and Epistemic Warrant', in C. MacDonald, B. Smith, and C. Wright (eds.), *Knowing Our Own Minds* (Oxford: Oxford University Press).

Descartes, R. (1986), *Meditations on First Philosophy*, tr. J. Cottingham (Cambridge: Cambridge University Press).

Evans, G. (1982), *The Varieties of Reference* (Oxford: Oxford University Press).

Evans, G. (1985*a*), 'The Causal Theory of Names', in his *Collected Papers* (Oxford: Oxford University Press).

—— (1985*b*), 'Understanding Demonstratives', in his *Collected Papers* (Oxford: Oxford University Press).

—— and McDowell, J. (eds.) (1976), *Truth and Meaning* (Oxford: Oxford University Press).

Frege, G. (1993), 'On Sense and Reference', in A. Moore (ed.), *Meaning and Reference* (Oxford: Oxford University Press).

Fricker. E. (1987), 'The Epistemology of Testimony', *Proceedings of the Aristotelian Society,* Suppl. Vol. 61: 57–83.

Kant, I. (1929), *Critique of Pure Reason*, tr. N. Kemp Smith (London: Macmillan).

Kripke, S. (1980), *Naming and Necessity* (Oxford: Blackwell).

McDowell, J. (1977), 'On the Sense and Reference of a Proper Name', *Mind* 86: 159–85.

—— (1978), 'Physicalism and Primitive Denotation: Field on Tarski', *Erkenntnis* 13: 131–52.

—— (1994), 'Knowledge by Hearsay', in B. K. Matilal and A. Chakrabarti (eds.), *Knowing from Words* (Amsterdam: Kluwer).

McGinn, C. (1989), *Mental Content* (Oxford: Blackwell).

Malcolm, N. (1991), 'I Believe that p', in E. LePore and R. Van Gulick (eds.), *John Searle and his Critics* (Oxford: Blackwell).

Peacocke, C. (1988), 'The Limits of Intelligibility: A Post-Verificationist Proposal', *Philosophical Review* 97: 463–96.

—— (1993), 'Externalist Explanation', *Proceedings of the Aristotelian Society* 93: 203–30.

Pettit, P., and McDowell, J. (eds.) (1986), *Subject, Thought and Context* (Oxford: Oxford University Press).

Putnam, H. (1975), 'The Meaning of "Meaning"', in his *Mind, Language and Reality* (Cambridge: Cambridge University Press).

Russell, B. (1917), 'Knowledge by Acquaintance and Knowledge by Description', in his *Mysticism and Logic* (London: Allen and Unwin).

Strawson, P. F. (1959), *Individuals* (London: Methuen).

—— (1966), *The Bounds of Sense* (London: Methuen).

—— (1974), 'Self, Mind and Body', in his *Freedom and Resentment and Other Essays* (London: Methuen).

Wittgenstein, L. (1958), *Philosophical Investigations*, tr. G. E. M. Anscombe (Oxford: Blackwell).

—— (1975), *On Certainty*, ed. G. E. M. Anscombe and G. H. von Wright, tr. D. Paul and G. E. M. Anscombe (Oxford: Blackwell).

—— (1980), *Remarks on the Philosophy of Psychology*, i, ed. G. E. M. Anscombe and G. H. von Wright, tr. G. E. M. Anscombe (Oxford: Blackwell).

18

The Psychophysical Nexus

Thomas Nagel

1. THE MIND-BODY PROBLEM AFTER KRIPKE

This essay will explore an approach to the mind–body problem that is distinct both from dualism and from the sort of conceptual reduction of the mental to the physical that proceeds via a functionalist analysis of mental concepts. The essential element of the approach is that it takes the subjective phenomenological features of conscious experience to be perfectly real and not reducible to anything else–but nevertheless holds that their systematic relations to neurophysiology are not contingent but necessary.

A great deal of effort and ingenuity has been put into the reductionist programme, usually in the form of a functionalist theory, and there have been serious attempts in recent years to accommodate within a functionalist framework consciousness and phenomenological qualia in particular.[1] The effort has produced results that reveal a good deal that is true about the relations between consciousness and behaviour, but not an account of what consciousness is. The reason for this failure is unsurprising and always the same. However complete an account may be of the functional role of the perception of the colour red in the explanation of behaviour, for example, such an account taken by itself will have nothing to say about the specific subjective quality of the visual experience, without which it would not be a conscious experience at all.

If the intrinsic character of conscious experience remains stubbornly beyond the reach of contextual, relational, functional accounts, an alternative strategy seems called for. The exploration of such an alternative should be of interest even

Some portions of this essay derive from 'Conceiving the Impossible and the Mind-Body Problem', *Philosophy* 73 (1998): 337–52. I am grateful to audiences at the Townsend lectures in Berkeley and at the Kripke symposium in Haifa for a number of valuable criticisms.

[1] See e.g. Sydney Shoemaker, 'Self-Knowledge and "inner sense", Lecture III: The phenomenal character of experience', in *The First-person Perspective and Other Essays* (Cambridge University Press, 1996). I will use the term 'functionalism' throughout this essay in an unsophisticated way, to refer to theories that identify mental states by their typical causal roles in the production of behaviour—also called their 'functional' roles. I shall leave aside the version of functionalism that identifies mental states with computational states.

to those who remain convinced that functionalism is the right path to follow, since philosophical positions can be evaluated only by comparison with the competition. The alternative I wish to explore can be thought of as a response to the challenge issued by Saul Kripke at the end of *Naming and Necessity*:

That the usual moves and analogies are not available to solve the problems of the identity theorist is, of course, no proof that no moves are available. . . . I suspect, however, that the present considerations tell heavily against the usual forms of materialism. Materialism, I think, must hold that a physical description of the world is a *complete* description of it, that any mental facts are 'ontologically dependent' on physical facts in the straightforward sense of following from them by necessity. No identity theorist seems to me to have made a convincing argument against the intuitive view that this is not the case.[2]

Kripke's view of functionalism and causal behaviourism is the same as mine: that the inadequacy of these analyses of the mental is self-evident. He does not absolutely rule out a form of materialism that is not based on such reductionist analyses, but he says that it has to defend the very strong claim that mental phenomena are strictly necessary consequences of the operation of the brain—and that the defence of this claim lies under the heavy burden of overcoming the prima-facie modal argument that consciousness and brain states are only contingently related, since it *seems* perfectly conceivable about any brain state that it should exist exactly as it is, physically, without any accompanying consciousness. The intuitive credibility of this argument, which descends from Descartes' argument for dualism, is considerable. It certainly seems at first blush that we have a clear and distinct enough grasp on both phenomenological consciousness and physical brain processes to see that there can be no necessary connection between them.

That is the position that I hope to challenge. It seems to me that post-Kripke, the most promising line of attack on the mind-body problem is to see whether any sense can be made of the idea that mental processes might be physical processes necessarily but not analytically. I would not, however, try to defend the claim that 'a physical description of the world is a *complete* description of it', so my position should probably not be described as a form of materialism. It is certainly not a form of physicalism. But there may be other forms of non-contingent psychophysical identity. That is my point.

Because I am going to be talking about different kinds of necessity and contingency throughout the argument, I should say something at the outset about my assumptions, which will not be universally shared. The set of ideas about necessity and contingency with which I shall be working derives largely from Kripke. This means that the semantic category of analytic or conceptual truths, the epistemological category of a priori truths, and the metaphysical category of necessary truths do not coincide—nor do their complements: synthetic, a posteriori, and contingent truths.

---

[2] Saul Kripke, *Naming and Necessity* (Harvard University Press, 1980): 155.

I believe that there are conceptual truths, and that they are discoverable a priori, through reflection by a possessor of the relevant concepts—usually with the help of thought experiments—on the conditions of their application. Often the process of discovery will be difficult, and the results controversial. Conceptual truths may or may not be necessary truths. In particular, conceptual truths about how the reference of a term is fixed may identify contingent properties of the referent, though these are knowable a priori to a possessor of the concept.

Not everything discoverable a priori is a conceptual truth—for example the calculation of the logical or mathematical consequences that follow from a set of theoretical premises is a priori, but not, I would say, conceptual. And while some conceptual truths are necessary, not all necessary truths are conceptual. This applies not only to mathematical or theoretical propositions discoverable by a priori reasoning, but also, as Kripke showed, to certain identity statements that cannot be known a priori, such as the identity of heat with molecular motion or that of water with H_2O.

The relations among these different types of truths are intricate. In the case of the relation between water and H_2O, for example, as I shall explain more fully later, the following appears to hold. First, there are some conceptual truths about water—its usual manifest physical properties under the conditions that prevail in our world. These are the properties by which we fix the reference of the term 'water', and they are knowable a priori. Most of them are contingent properties of water, because they depend on other things as well, but some of them may be necessary if they follow from the intrinsic nature of water alone. Second, there are theoretical truths, derivable from principles of chemistry and physics, about the macroscopic properties, under those same conditions, of the compound H_2O. These are necessary consequences of premises which are partly necessary (the nature of hydrogen and oxygen) and partly contingent. Third, there is the a posteriori conclusion, from evidence that the manifest properties of the water with which we are acquainted are best explained in this way, that water is in fact nothing but H_2O. This is a necessary truth, though discovered a posteriori, because *if* it is true, then any other substance with the same manifest properties which did not consist of H_2O would not be water. And this last conditional clause, following 'because', is a conceptual truth, discoverable by reflection on what we would say if . . .

In the context with which we shall be concerned here, the mind-body problem, functionalism is the claim that it is a conceptual truth that any creature is conscious, and is the subject of various mental states, if and only if it satisfies certain purely structural conditions of the causal organization of its behaviour and interaction with the environment—whatever may be the material in which that organization is physically (or non-physically) realized. As I have said, I do not believe that this is a conceptual truth because I do not believe that the conceptual implication from functional organization to consciousness holds.

I don't doubt that all the appropriately behaved and functionally organized creatures around us are conscious, but that is something we know on the basis of evidence, not on the basis of conceptual analysis. It may even be in fact impossible for a creature to function in these ways without consciousness; but if so, it is not a conceptual impossibility but some other kind. The functional organization of purely physical behaviour, without more, is not enough to entail that the organism or system has subjective conscious experience, with experiential qualities. I make this claim particularly about sensations and the other qualities of sentience, rather than about higher-order intentional states like belief or desire—though I am inclined to think that they too require at least the capacity for sentience. My rejection of functionalism is based on the conviction that the subjective qualitative character of experience—what it is like for its subject—is not included or entailed by any amount of behavioural organization, and that it is a conceptually necessary condition of conscious states that they have some such character.

On the other hand, I will argue later that there is a conceptual connection between consciousness and behavioural or functional organization, but in the opposite direction. I deny the functionalist biconditional because of the falsity of one of its conjuncts, but I think a weak version of the opposite conjunct is true. I believe it is a conceptual truth about the visual experience of colours, for example, that it enables a physically intact human being to discriminate coloured objects by sight, and that this will usually show up in his behaviour in the appropriate circumstances, provided that he meets other psychological and physical conditions. This is a conceptual truth about colour vision analogous to the conceptual truths about the manifest properties of water in our world: in both cases the manifestations are contingent properties of the thing itself, dependent on surrounding circumstances. Functional organization is not a conceptually sufficient condition for mental states, but it is part of our concept of mental states that they in fact occupy something like the roles in relation to behaviour that functionalists have insisted upon. Such roles permit us to fix the reference of mental terms. But they are, at least in general, contingent rather than necessary properties of the conscious mental states that occupy them.

Finally, and this is the main point, while it is obviously not conceptually necessary that conscious mental states are tied to specific neurophysiological states, I contend that there are such connections and that they hold necessarily. They are not conceptual, and they are not discoverable a priori, but they are not contingent. They belong, in other words, to the category of a posteriori necessary truths. To explain how, and to characterize the type of necessity that could hold in such a case, is the problem.

Kripke showed that if the psychophysical identity theory is to be a hypothesis analogous to other empirical reductions or theoretical identifications in science, like the identification of heat with molecular motion or fire with oxidation, it cannot be a contingent proposition. It must be necessarily true if true at all, since a theoretical identity statement tells us what something is, not just what happens to be true of it. In the vocabulary introduced by Kripke, the terms of such an identity are both rigid designators, and they apply or fail to apply to the same things in all possible worlds.

Kripke observes that there is an appearance of contingency even in the standard cases of theoretical identity. The identification of heat with molecular motion is not analytic, and it cannot be known a priori. It may seem that we can easily conceive of a situation in which there is heat without molecular motion, or molecular motion without heat. But Kripke points out that this is a subtle mistake. When one thinks one is imagining heat without molecular motion, one is really imagining the feeling of heat being produced by something other than molecular motion. But that would not be heat—it would merely be a situation epistemically indistinguishable from the perception of heat. 'Heat', being a rigid designator, refers to the actual physical phenomenon that is in fact responsible for all the manifestations on the basis of which we apply the concept in the world as it is. The term refers to that physical phenomenon and to no other, even in imagined situations where something else is responsible for similar appearances and sensations. This is so because the appearances and sensations of heat are not themselves heat, and can be imagined to exist without it.

Kripke then points out that a similar strategy will not work to dissipate the appearance of contingency in the case of the relation between sensations and brain processes. If I seem to be able to imagine the taste of chocolate in the absence of its associated brain process, or the brain process unaccompanied by any such experience, we cannot say that this is merely to imagine the *appearance* of the experience without the experience, or vice versa. There is, in this case, no way of separating the thing itself from the way it appears to us, as there is in the case of heat. We identify experiences not by their contingent effects on us, but by their intrinsic phenomenological qualities. So if they are really identical with physical processes in the brain, the vivid appearance that we can clearly conceive of the qualities without the brain processes, and vice versa, must be shown to be erroneous in some other way.

My hope is to show that this can be done, without abandoning a commitment to the reality of the phenomenological content of conscious experience. If the appearance of contingency in the mind-body relation can be shown to be illusory, or if it can be shown how it might be illusory, then the modal argument against some sort of identification will no longer present an immovable obstacle to the empirical hypothesis that mental processes are brain processes.

The hypothesis would resemble familiar theoretical identities, like that between heat and molecular motion, in some respects but not in others. It would be non-analytic, discoverable only a posteriori, and necessarily true if true. But of course it could not be established by discovering the underlying physical cause of the *appearance* of conscious experience, on analogy with the underlying physical cause of the appearance of heat—since in the case of experience, the appearance is the thing itself and not merely its effect on us.

Clearly this would require something radical. We cannot at present see how the relation between consciousness and brain processes might be necessary. The logical gap between subjective consciousness and neurophysiology seems unbridgeable, however close may be the contingent correlations between them. To see the importance of this gap, consider how the necessary connection is established in other cases.

To show that water is H_2O or that heat is molecular motion, it is necessary to show that the chemical or physical equivalence can account fully and exhaustively for everything that is included in the ordinary pre-scientific concepts of water and heat—the manifest properties on the basis of which we apply those concepts. Not only must the scientific account explain causally all the external effects of water or heat, such as their effects on our senses. It must also account in a more intimate manner for their familiar intrinsic properties, revealing the true basis of those properties by showing that they are *entailed* by the scientific description. Thus, the density of water, its passage from solid to liquid to gas at certain temperatures, its capacity to enter into chemical reactions or to appear as a chemical product, its transparency, viscosity, electrical conductivity, and so forth, must all be accounted for in a particularly strong way by its chemical analysis as H_2O, together with whatever laws govern the behaviour of such a compound. In brief, the essential intrinsic properties of water on the macro-level must be entailed by the hypothesis that it consists of molecules of H_2O, together with the background conditions that prevail in our world. Otherwise it will not be possible to say that water is *constituted* of H_2O and nothing else.[3]

This 'upward entailment' is a necessary condition of any successful scientific reduction in regard to the physical world. It is the a priori element in a posteriori

---

[3] A qualification is necessary here, because the relation between the physics of H_2O and the macroscopic properties of water is probabilistic. It is, I am assured by those who know more about these matters than I, physically possible for H_2O to be a solid at room temperature, though extremely unlikely. That means that if water is H_2O, it is possible for water to be a solid at room temperature. And similar things can apparently be said about the other manifest properties of water by means of which the reference of the term is fixed. Yet I think these esoteric facts do not remove the element of necessity in the relation between the properties of H_2O and the macroscopic properties conceptually implied by our concept of water. Those macroscopic, manifest properties are not really inconsistent with an interpretation under which they are merely probabilistic, provided the probabilities are so astronomically high that their failure is for all practical purposes impossible, and it would never be rational to believe that it had occurred. It is enough if the physics of H_2O entails that the probability of water having these properties under normal background conditions is so close to 1 as makes no experiential difference. Let me take this qualification as understood in what follows.

Let me add that even if there are laws governing the behaviour of molecules in large numbers that are genuinely higher-order and not merely the statistical consequences of the probabilistic or deterministic laws governing the individual particles—holistic laws, so to speak—it still does not affect the point. Facts about the macroscopic properties of a substance like water, or an event like a thunderstorm, would still be *constitutively* entailed by the facts about the behaviour of the microscopic or submicroscopic constituents—whatever kinds of laws might be required to account for this behaviour.

necessary theoretical identities, because without it we cannot maintain the a posteriori 'downward' identification that allows us to say that 'Water is H_2O' is an empirical but necessary truth. We begin with an ordinary concept of a natural kind or natural phenomenon. This concept—*heat* or *water*—refers to the actual examples to which we apply it, and with which we are in some kind of direct or indirect contact through our occupation of the world. To establish that those examples are in fact identical with something not directly manifest to perception but describable only by atomic theory, we must show that the pre-scientifically familiar intrinsic features of heat and water are nothing but the gross manifestations of the properties of these physico-chemical constituents—that the liquidity of water, for example, consists simply of a certain type of movement of its molecules with respect to one another. If the properties of the substance that we refer to by the term 'water' can be exhaustively accounted for by such a micro-analysis, and if experiment confirms that this is in fact the situation that obtains, then that tells us what water really is.

The result is a posteriori because it requires not only the demonstration that H_2O *could* account for the phenomena, but empirical confirmation that this and not something else is what *actually* underlies the manifest properties of the substance we refer to as water. That would come from experimental confirmation of previously unobserved implications of the hypothesis, and disconfirmation of the implications of alternative hypotheses, e.g. that water is an element. Thus it is not a conceptual reduction. Nevertheless it is a necessary identity because our concept of water refers to the actual water around us, whatever it is, and not to just any substance superficially resembling water. If there could be something with the familiar manifest properties of water which was not H_2O, it would not be water. But to reach this conclusion, we must see that the behaviour of H_2O provides a true and complete account, with nothing left out—a strict entailment— of the features that are conceptually essential to water, and that this account is in fact true of the water around us.

It is this 'upward entailment' that is so difficult to imagine in the case of the corresponding psychophysical hypothesis, and that is the nub of the mind-body problem. We understand the entailment of liquidity of water by the behaviour of molecules through geometry, or more simply the micro–macro or part–whole relation. Something analogous is true of every physical reduction, even though the spatio-temporal framework can be very complicated and hard to grasp intuitively. But nothing like this will help us with the mind-body case, because we are not dealing here merely with larger and smaller grids. We are dealing with a gap of a totally different order, between the objective spatio-temporal order of the physical world and the subjective phenomenological order of experience. And here it seems clear *in advance* that no amount of physical information about the spatio-temporal order will entail anything of a subjective, phenomenological character. However much our purely physical concepts may change in the course of further theoretical development, they will all have been introduced to explain features of the objective spatio-temporal order, and will not have implications of this totally different logical type.

But without an upward entailment of some kind, we will not have a proper reduction, since in any proposed reduction of the mental to the physical, something will have been left out by the reductive account, something essential to the phenomenon being reduced. Unless this obstacle can be overcome, it will be impossible to claim that the relation between sensations and brain processes is analogous to the relation between heat and molecular motion—a necessary but a posteriori identity. Yet I believe that is the region in which the truth probably lies. The evident massive and detailed dependence of what happens in the mind on what happens in the brain provides in my opinion strong evidence that the relation is not contingent but necessary. It cannot take the form of a reduction of the mental to the physical, but I believe it may be necessary all the same. The task is to try to understand how that might be the case.[4]

II. SUBJECTIVITY AND THE CONCEPTUAL IRREDUCIBILITY OF CONSCIOUSNESS

The source of the problem—what seems to put such a solution out of reach—is the lack of any intelligible internal relation between consciousness and its physiological basis. The apparent conceivability of what in current philosophical jargon is known as a 'zombie'—i.e. an exact physiological and behavioural replica of a living human being that nevertheless has no consciousness—may not show that such a thing is possible, but it does show something about our concepts of mind and body. It shows that those concepts in their present form are not logically connected in such a way that the content of the idea of consciousness is exhausted by a physical or behavioural-functional specification.

But the rejection of conceptual reduction is only the beginning of the story. The problem is to look for an alternative account of the evidently very close relation between consciousness and the brain which does not in any way accord a diminished reality to the immediate phenomenological qualities of conscious experience. Because of the causal role of mental events in the physical world, and their association with specific organic structures and processes, Cartesian dualism is implausible. Physicalism, in the sense of a complete conceptual reduction of the mental to the physical, is not a possibility, since it in effect eliminates what is distinctive and undeniable about the mental. Ostensibly weaker forms of physicalism seem always to collapse into behaviouristic reductionism.

---

[4] My position is very like that of Colin McGinn, but without his pessimism. See *The Problem of Consciousness* (Blackwell, 1991). What I have to say here is also a development of a suggestion in *The View From Nowhere* (Oxford University Press, 1986): 51–3.

For that reason I have occasionally been drawn to some kind of property dualism; but like substance dualism, it seems just to be giving a name to a mystery, and not to explain anything. Simply to say that mental events are physical events with additional, non-physical properties is to force disparate concepts together without thereby making the link even potentially intelligible. It suggests pure emergence, which explains nothing. But I believe these dead ends are not exhaustive, and that starting from our present concepts of mind and body, another approach is possible.

When we try to reason about the possible relations between things, we have to rely on our conceptual grasp of them. The more adequate the grasp, the more reliable our reasoning will be. Sometimes a familiar concept clearly allows for the possibility that what it designates should also have features not implied by the concept itself—often features very different in kind from those directly implied by the concept. Thus ordinary pre-scientific concepts of kinds of substances, such as water or gold or blood, are in themselves silent with regard to the microscopic composition of those substances but nevertheless open to the scientific discovery, often by very indirect means, of such facts about their true nature. If a concept refers to something that takes up room in the spatio-temporal world, it provides a handle for all kinds of empirical discoveries about the inner constitution of that thing.

On the other hand, sometimes a familiar concept clearly excludes the possibility that what it designates has certain features: for example we do not need a scientific investigation to be certain that the number 379 does not have parents. There are various other things that we can come to know about the number 379 only by mathematical or empirical investigation, such as what its factors are, or whether it is greater than the population of Chugwater, Wyoming, but we know that it does not have parents just by knowing that it is a number. If someone rebuked us for being closed-minded, because we can't predict in advance what future scientific research might turn up about the biological origins of numbers, he would not be offering a serious ground for doubt.

The case of mental processes and the brain is intermediate between these two. Descartes thought it was closer to the second category, and that we could tell just by thinking about it that the human mind was not an extended material thing and that no extended material thing could be a thinking subject. But this is, to put it mildly, not nearly as self-evident as that a number cannot have parents. What does seem true is that the concept of a mind, or of a mental event or process, fails to plainly leave space for the possibility that what it designates should turn out also to be a physical thing or event or process, as the result of closer scientific investigation—in the way that the concept of blood leaves space for discoveries about its composition. The trouble is that mental concepts don't obviously pick out things or processes that take up room in the spatio-temporal world to begin with. If they did, we could just get hold of some of those things and take them apart or look at them under a microscope. But there is a prior problem about how those concepts might refer to anything that could be subjected to such investigation: they don't give us the comfortable initial handle on the occupants of the familiar spatio-temporal world that pre-scientific physical substance concepts do.[5]

Nevertheless it is overconfident to conclude, from one's inability to imagine how mental phenomena might turn out to have physical properties, that the possibility can be ruled out in advance. We have to ask ourselves whether there is more behind the Cartesian intuition than mere lack of knowledge, resulting in lack of imagination.[6] Of course it is not enough merely to say, 'You may be mistaking your own inability to imagine something for its inconceivability.' Though one should be open to the possibility of withdrawing a judgement of inconceivability if offered a reason to think it might be mistaken, there does have to *be* a reason, or at least some kind of story about how this illusion of inconceivability might have arisen.

If mental events really have physical properties, an explanation is needed of why they seem to offer so little purchase for the attribution of those properties. Still, the kind of incomprehensibility here is completely different from that of numbers having parents. Mental events, unlike numbers, can be roughly located in space and time, and are causally related to physical events, in both directions. The causal facts are strong evidence that mental events have physical properties, if only we could make sense of the idea.[7]

Consider another case where the pre-scientific concept did not obviously allow for the possibility of physical composition or structure—the case of sound. Before the discovery that sounds are waves in air or another medium, the ordinary concept permitted sounds to be roughly located, and to have properties like loudness, pitch, and duration. The concept of a sound was that of an objective phenomenon that could be heard by different people, or that could exist unheard. But it would have been very obscure what could be meant by ascribing to a sound a precise spatial shape and size, or an internal, perhaps microscopic, physical structure. Someone who proposed that sounds have physical parts, without offering any theory to explain this, would not have said anything understandable. One might say that in advance of the development of a physical theory of sound, the hypothesis that sounds have a physical microstructure would not have a clear meaning.

Nevertheless, at one remove, the possibility of such a development is evidently not excluded by the concept of sound. Sounds were known to have certain physical causes, to be blocked by certain kinds of obstacles, and to be perceptible by hearing. This was already a substantial amount of causal information, and it

---

[5] See Colin McGinn, 'Consciousness and Space', *Journal of Consciousness Studies* 2 (1995): 220–30.

[6] This is the objection that Arnauld made to Descartes, in the fourth set of objections to the *Meditations*.

[7] Compare Donald Davidson, 'Mental Events', in his *Essays on Actions and Events* (Oxford University Press, 1980).

opened the way to the discovery of a physically describable phenomenon that could be identified with sound because it had just those causes and effects—particularly once further features of sound, like variations of loudness and pitch, could also be accounted for in terms of its precise physical character. Yet it is important that *in advance,* the idea that a sound has a physical microsructure would have had no clear meaning. One would not have known how to go about imagining such a thing, any more than one could have imagined a sound having weight. It would have been easy to mistake this lack of clear allowance for the possibility *in* the concept for a positive exclusion of the possibility *by* the concept.

The analogy with the case of mental phenomena should be clear. They too occupy causal roles, and it has been one of the strongest arguments for some kind of physicalism that those roles may prove upon investigation to be occupied by organic processes. Yet the problem here is much more serious, for an obvious reason: identifying sounds with waves in the air does not require that we ascribe phenomenological qualities and subjectivity to anything physical, because those are features of the perception of sound, not of sound itself. By contrast, the identification of mental events with physical events requires the unification of these two types of properties in a single thing, and that remains resistant to understanding. The causal argument for identification may make us believe that it is true, but it doesn't help us to understand it, and in my view, we really shouldn't believe it unless we can understand it.

The problem here, as with the other issue of purely conceptual reduction, lies in the distinctive first-person/third-person character of mental concepts, which is the grammatical manifestation of the subjectivity of mental phenomena. Though not all conscious beings possess language, our attribution of conscious states to languageless creatures implies that these states are of the kind that in the human case we pick out only through these distinctive concepts, concepts which the subject applies in his own case without observation of his body.

They are not pure first-person concepts: to try to detach their first-person application from the third person results in philosophical illusions. For example, from the purely first-person standpoint it seems intelligible that the subject of my present consciousness might have been created five minutes go and all my memories, personality, etc. transferred from a previous subject in this same body to the newly created one, without any outwardly or inwardly perceptible sign—without any other physical or psychological change. If the pure first-person idea of 'I' defined an individual, that would make sense, but it seems reasonably clear that the real idea of 'I' has lost its moorings in this philosophical thought experiment. The point goes back to Kant, who argued that the subjective identity of the consciousness of myself at different times does not establish the objective identity of a subject or soul.[8]

That is not to say that I understand just how the first person and the third form

---

[8] See *Critique of Pure Reason*, A 363–4: the Paralogisms of Pure Reason.

two logically inseparable aspects of a single concept—only *that* they do. This applies to all conscious mental states and events, and their properties. They are subjective, not in the sense that they are the subjects of a purely first-person vocabulary, but in the sense that they can be accurately described only by concepts in which non-observational first-person and observational third-person attributions are systematically connected. Such states are modifications of the point of view of an individual subject.

The problem, then, is how something that is an aspect or element of an individual's subjective point of view could also be a physiologically describable event in the brain—the kind of thing which, considered under that description, involves no point of view and no distinctively immediate first-person attribution at all. I believe that as a matter of fact you can't have one without the other, and furthermore that the powerful intuition that it is conceivable that an intact and normally functioning physical human organism could be a completely unconscious zombie is an illusion—due to the limitations of our understanding. Nevertheless those limitations are real. We do not at present possess the conceptual equipment to understand how subjective and physical features could both be essential aspects of a single entity or process. Kant expresses roughly the same point in terms of his apparatus of phenomena and noumena:

If I understand by soul a thinking being in itself, the question whether or not it is the same in kind as matter—matter not being a thing in itself, but merely a species of representation in us—is by its very terms illegitimate. For it is obvious that a thing in itself is of a different nature from the determinations which constitute only its state.

If on the other hand, we compare the thinking 'I' not with matter but with the intelligible that lies at the basis of the outer appearance which we call matter, we have no knowledge whatsoever of the intelligible, and therefore are in no position to say that the soul is in any inward respect different from it.[9]

What I want to propose, however, is that these conceptual limitations might be overcome—that there is not a perfect fit at every stage of our conceptual development between conceptual truths and necessary truths, and that this is the most probable interpretation of the present situation with respect to mind and brain: the dependence of mind on brain is not conceptually transparent but it is necessary nonetheless.

III. NECESSARY TRUTH AND CONCEPTUAL CREATIVITY

The greatest scientific progress occurs through conceptual change which permits empirically observed order that initially appears contingent to be understood at a

---

[9] *Critique of Pure Reason*, A 360. McGinn, too, remarks on the similarity of Kant's view to his own. See *The Problem of Consciousness*: 81–2.

deeper level as necessary, in the sense of being entailed by the true nature of the phenomena. Something like this must have happened at the birth of mathematics, but it is a pervasive aspect of physical science. This is the domain in which I think it is appropriate to speak of natural, as opposed to conceptual, necessity.

To take a simple and familiar example: it was observable to anyone before the advent of modern chemistry that a fire will go out quickly if enclosed in a small airtight space. Given the pre-scientific concepts of air and fire, this was not a conceptual truth, and there would have been no way, on purely conceptual grounds, to discover that it was anything other than a strict but contingent correlation. However, its very strictness should have suggested that it was not really contingent, but could be accounted for as a logical consequence of the true nature of fire and air, neither of which is fully revealed in the pre-scientific concepts.

This phenomenon is itself one of the evidentiary grounds for identifying fire with rapid oxidation, and air with a mixture of gases of which oxygen is one. Those identifications in turn reveal it to be a necessary truth that the enclosed fire will go out. The very process of oxidation that constitutes the fire eventually binds all the free oxygen in the airtight container, thus entailing its own termination. Once we develop the concepts of atomistic chemistry and physics that enable us to see what fire and air really are, we understand that it is not really conceivable that a fire should continue to burn in a small airtight space, even though our pre-scientific concepts did not make this evident.

The consequence is that conceivability arguments for the contingency of a correlation or the distinctness of differently described phenomena depend for their reliability on the adequacy of the concepts being employed. If those concepts do not adequately grasp the nature of the things to which they refer, they may yield deceptive appearances of contingency and non-identity.

The mind–brain case seems a natural candidate for such treatment because what happens in consciousness is pretty clearly supervenient on what happens physically in the brain. In the present state of our conceptions of consciousness and neurophysiology, this strict dependence is a brute fact and completely mysterious. But pure, unexplained supervenience is never a solution to a problem but a sign that there is something fundamental we don't know. If the physical necessitates the mental, there must be some answer to the question *how* it does so. An obviously systematic connection that remains unintelligible to us calls out for a theory.[10]

From the conceptual irreducibility of the mental to the physical, together with the empirical evidence of a connection between the mental and the physical so strong that it must be necessary, we can conclude that our mental concepts, or our physical concepts, or both, fail to capture something about the nature of the

[10] A similar position is endorsed by Galen Strawson in *Mental Reality* (MIT Press, 1994): 81–4, and by Allin Cottrell in '*Tertium datur*? Reflections on Owen Flanagan's *Consciousness Reconsidered*', *Philosophical Psychology* 8 (1995).

phenomena to which they refer, however accurate they may be as far as they go. The conceptual development that would be needed to reveal the underlying necessary connection is of a radical and scientifically unprecedented kind, because these two types of concepts as they now stand are not already open to the possibility that what they refer to should have a true nature of the other type. Ordinary physical concepts, like that of fire, are candidly incomplete in what they reveal about the inner constitution of the manifest process or phenomenon to which they refer: they are open to the possibility that it should have a microstructural analysis of the kind that it in fact proves to have. But nothing in the ordinary concepts of either consciousness or the brain leaves space for the possibility that they should have inner constitutions that would close the logical gap between them. Physical phenomena can be analysed into their physical constituents, with the aid of scientific experimentation, and mental phenomena can perhaps be analysed into their mental constituents, at least in some cases, but these two paths of analysis do not meet. The apparent conceivability of each of the correlated items without the other cannot be defused without something much more radical than the type of reduction that we are familiar with in the physical sciences.

That poses the general question of how we can attempt to develop conceptions that reflect the actual necessary connections and are therefore reliable tools for reasoning, and what determines whether there is hope of developing such concepts for a domain where we do not yet have them. After all, humans did not always have logical, geometrical, and arithmetical concepts, but had to develop them. Yet we cannot will a new conceptual framework into existence. It has to result from trying to think, in light of the evidence, about the subject we want to understand, and devising concepts that do better justice to it than the ones we have.

So how might we proceed in this case? While I am not going to follow them, it should be noted that there are precedents for this revisionist project. The idea that the physical description of the brain leaves out its mental essence and that we need to reform our concepts accordingly is not new. A version of it is found in Spinoza and it is at the heart of Bertrand Russell's neutral monism, expounded in *The Analysis of Matter*, *An Outline of Philosophy*, and other writings. He holds that physics in general describes only a causal structure of events, leaving the intrinsic nature of its elements unspecified, and that our only knowledge of that intrinsic nature is in respect to certain physical events in our own brains, of which we are aware as percepts. He also holds that physics contains nothing incompatible with the possibility that all physical events, in brains or not, have an intrinsic nature of the same general type—though their specific qualities would presumably vary greatly. Here is what he says:

There is no theoretical reason why a light-wave should not consist of groups of occurrences, each containing a member more or less analogous to a minute part of a visual percept. We cannot perceive a light-wave, since the interposition of an eye and brain stops it. We know, therefore, only its abstract mathematical properties. Such properties may belong to groups composed of any kind of material. To assert that the material *must* be very different from percepts is to assume that we know a great deal more than we do in fact know of the intrinsic character of physical events. If there is any advantage in supposing that the light-wave, the process in the eye, and the process in the optic nerve, contain events qualitatively continuous with the final visual percept, nothing that we know of the physical world can be used to disprove the supposition.[11]

Russell holds that both minds and bodies are logical constructions out of events. When I see the moon, my percept of the moon is one of an immense set of events, radiating out in all directions from the place where the moon is located, out of which the moon as physical object is a logical construction. The same percept also belongs to the psychologically connected set of events which constitute my mind, or mental life. And it also belongs to the set of events, centred in my skull but radiating out from there in all directions, out of which my brain as a physical object is a logical construction. (A physiologist's percept of my brain would also belong to this set, as well as to the sets constituting his mind and his brain.)

This means that the type of identification of a sensation with a brain process that Russell advocates amounts to the possibility of locating the sensation in a certain kind of causal structure—for example as the terminus of a sequence of events starting from the moon, and the origin of a sequence of events ending with the physiologist's observation of my brain. The import of describing it as a physical event is essentially relational. Its phenomenological quality is intrinsic in a way that its physical character is not.

This is a rich and interesting view, but it seems to me to solve the mind-body problem at excessive cost, by denying that physical properties are intrinsic. I believe that both mental and physical properties are intrinsic, and that this leaves an identity theory with the problem of how to understand the internal and necessary relation between them. The theory also leaves untouched the problem of relating the subjectivity of the mental to its physical character. Russell did have something to say about this—identifying subjectivity with dependence on the specific character of the individual's brain—but I don't think it is sufficient.

Russell's view that the intrinsic nature of physical brain processes is mental would certainly explain why the apparent conceivability of a zombie was an illusion, but it seems to me not to account for the necessity of the mind-body relation in the right way. I am sympathetic to the project of reducing both the physical and the mental to a common element, but this is too much like reducing the physical to the mental.

---

[11] *The Analysis of Matter* (London: Allen & Unwin, 1927): 263–4. For an excellent discussion and defence of Russell's and similar views, see Michael Lockwood, *Mind, Brain and the Quantum* (Blackwell, 1989): ch. 10. See also Grover Maxwell, 'Rigid Designators and Mind-Brain Identity', in C. Wade Savage (ed.), *Minnesota Studies in the Philosophy of Science* IX (University of Minnesota Press, 1978). Maxwell argues that it is physical rather than mental concepts that are topic-neutral, and that there is nothing to prevent their referring non-rigidly to what mental concept designate rigidly.

More recent forms of reductionism are unsatisfactory in other ways. Even if we interpret the physicalist-functionalist movement in philosophy of mind as a form of conceptual revisionism rather than analysis of what our ordinary concepts already contain, I believe it has failed because it is too conservative: it has tried to reinterpret mental concepts so as to make them tractable parts of the framework of physical science. What is needed is a search for something more unfamiliar, something which starts from the conceptual unintelligibility, in its present form, of the subjective–objective link. The enterprise is one of imagining possibilities: identity theorists like Smart, Armstrong, and Lewis tried to explain how the identity of mental with physical states could be a contingent truth; I am interested in how some sort of mind–brain identity might be a necessary truth.

That would require not only the imagination of concepts that might capture the connection, but also some account of how our existing concepts would have to be related to these and to one another. We must imagine something that falls under both our mental concepts and the physiological concepts used to describe the brain, not accidentally but necessarily.

IV. MENTAL REFERENCE

We first have to interpret the third-person and first-person conditions of reference to mental states as inextricably connected in a single concept, but in a rather special way. I have insisted that mental concepts are not exhausted by the behavioural or functional conditions that provide the grounds for their application to others. Functionalism does not provide sufficient conditions for the mental. However in the other, 'outward', direction there does seem to be a conceptual connection between conscious mental states and the behavioural or other interactions of the organism with its environment. This is a consequence of the inseparable first-person/third-person character of mental concepts. To put it roughly, functional states aren't necessarily mental states, but it is a conceptual truth that our mental states actually occupy certain functional roles.

Imaginability and thought experiments are essential in establishing conceptual connections—or their absence. Those methods have to be used with care, but the pitfalls are not so serious here as when they are used to test for non-conceptual necessary connections—as in the case of consciousness and the brain. We can discover the presence or absence of a conceptual connection a priori because all the necessary data are contained in the concepts we are thinking with: we just have to extract those data and see what they reveal.

Sometimes, as in the case of functional characteristics of consciousness, the conceptual connection may be somewhat hidden from view. But I believe we can know a priori both (a) that specific conscious states typically occupy certain functional roles, and (b) that those functional roles do not, as a matter of conceptual necessity, entail those specific conscious states. For the latter conclusion, we only have to imagine a being whose colour vision, for example, is functionally equivalent to ours but is based on a completely different neurophysiology. This may not in fact be possible, but there is no reason to believe either that it is *conceptually* excluded, or that if it were possible, such a being would have the same colour phenomenology as we do.

My main interest is in the further proposition that mental states are related to certain *neurophysiological* states by an equivalence relation that is necessary but not conceptual. But these other claims about the conceptual relation between phenomenology and behaviour are an essential part of the picture. The aim is to connect phenomenology, physiology, and behaviour in a single nexus.

I am denying two familiar types of functionalist view:

> (1) Non-rigid functionalism: Mental concepts refer contingently to whatever inner states happen as a matter of fact to occupy certain functional roles. It is analytically true that to be a mental state of a given kind is simply to occupy a certain functional role, but it is contingently true of any particular inner state that it is a mental state of that kind. Empirical science reveals that mental concepts non-rigidly designate states that are in fact essentially physiological.[12]
>
> (2) Rigid functionalism: Mental concepts refer to functional states themselves—to the state of being in a state with a certain functional role. It is both analytically and necessarily true of a given mental state that it manifests itself in certain relations to behaviour and to other mental states. Mental states are not identified with their physiological basis.[13]

The first view is unacceptable both because it analyses mental concepts reductively and because it makes it a contingent fact that a mental state is the mental state it is. The second is unacceptable because it analyses mental concepts reductively and implies that they don't refer to inner states of the organism.

Consider next the following alternative:

> (3) Reference-fixing functionalism: The reference of our mental concepts to inner states is fixed by the contingent functional roles of those states, but the concepts apply rigidly to the occupants of those roles. It is neither necessarily true of a given mental state, nor analytically equivalent to its being the mental state it is, that it occupy a certain functional role, but that is how we in fact pick it out. Mental concepts rigidly designate states that are essentially physiological or phenomenological, or both.[14]

---

[12] See David Lewis, 'Psychophysical and Theoretical Identifications', *Australasian Journal of Philosophy* 50 (1972): 249–58.

[13] See Hilary Putnam, 'The Nature of Mental States', in his *Mind, Language and Reality: Philosophical Papers, II* (Cambridge University Press, 1975).

[14] This interesting option, which I had never heard before, was suggested to me by an NYU

This seems to me close to the truth, but it leaves out the fact that the reference of mental terms for conscious states is fixed not only by their functional role but by their immediate phenomenological quality—an intrinsic and essential property. Something must relate these two reference-fixers, one necessary and one contingent, and I believe it can be done by the following proposal:

> (4) Though mental concepts cannot be analysed functionally, functional roles are needed to fix the reference of mental terms, because of the inextricable first-person/third-person character of mental concepts. It is a *conceptual* but *contingent* truth that each mental state plays its characteristic functional role in relation to behaviour. It is a *conceptual* and *necessary* truth that each conscious mental state has the phenomenological properties that it has. And it is a *non-conceptual* but *necessary* truth that each conscious mental state has the physiological properties that it has.

This seems to me to do justice to the 'internal' character of the relation between phenomenology and behaviour. Phenomenological facts have to be in principle, though not infallibly, introspectively accessible. If two simultaneous colour impressions, or two sound impressions in close succession, are the same or different, I ought in general to be able to tell—just because they are both mine—and this discriminatory capacity will have behavioural consequences under suitable conditions. Similarly, if a sensation is very unpleasant, I will want to avoid it, and if I am not paralysed this will also have behavioural consequences. Although phenomenological features cannot be analysed behaviourally or functionally, their relation to their typical functional role in the production of behaviour is, in the outward direction, an a priori conceptual truth.

This is the conception of the relation between mental states and behaviour—conceptual but non-reductionist—that is suggested to me by Wittgenstein's anti-private-language argument, even though it is almost certainly not Wittgenstein's conception. If each phenomenal property were in principle detectable only introspectively, there could be no concepts for such properties, for the concepts could not be governed by rules that distinguished between their correct and incorrect application. Therefore our phenomenal concepts must actually work differently, picking out properties that are detectable from both the first-person and the third-person perspective. And this seems phenomenologically accurate, so long as it is not turned into a behaviourist or essentially third-person causal-role analysis of mental concepts. Pain, colour impressions, and so forth are intrinsic properties of the conscious subject, which we can identify only in virtue of their relations to other mental properties and to causal conditions and behavioural manifestations.

To state Wittgenstein's point: in order to name a sensation that I notice, I must

---

undergraduate, James Swoyer. A theory of similar form, but offered in the service of physicalism, is defended by Michael E. Levin in *Metaphysics and the Mind-Body Problem* (Oxford: Clarendon Press, 1979): 113–25.

have the concept of the same (type of) sensation—of its feeling the same to me—and this must be the idea of something that can hold objectively, so that if I give the name 'S' to the type of sensation I am having now, that baptism sets up a rule which determines whether any particular future application of the term by me to another event will be correct or incorrect. It either will be the same—i.e. will feel the same phenomenally—or it will not. That I am correctly remembering the meaning of the term must be an objective fact independent of my actual sincere application of the term, or else the term wouldn't carry any meaning. So I must be relying on my mastery of a concept of phenomenal similarity to which my personal usage conforms over time—a concept whose applicability to me is independent of my application of it to myself, in a way that underwrites the objective meaning of my own personal application of it.

Concepts can be objective in more than one way, but phenomenological concepts seem in fact to secure their objectivity through an internal connection to behaviour and circumstances. That is how we establish that someone else has the concept of sensation, and that is how an individual knows that he himself has mastered a phenomenological concept—by confirmation from others who can observe that he uses it correctly. It is also how we tell that we ourselves or someone else have forgotten what a phenomenological term means, and have misapplied it. The concept that we apply introspectively to ourselves is the same concept that others apply to us—and we to others—observationally.

To have the concept of pain a person must apply it to his own sensation in the circumstances that enable others to apply it to him. This conjunction is the only way to identify the concept. The third-person conditions are not sufficient, but they are (conceptually) necessary. Someone doesn't have the phenomenological concept of pain unless he can apply it introspectively in accordance with certain standard circumstantial and behavioural conditions. These include its tendency to signal damage and to provoke avoidance in an otherwise intact organism.

As Kripke says, the reference of the word 'pain' is fixed by an essential property of the referent, its immediate phenomenological quality—but the possibility of such reference-fixing depends on the systematic relation between immediate phenomenological quality and dispositions to behaviour, given the right conditions. The phenomenological quality is real, and not reducible to a functional state, but there is no independent way to identify it, except through first-person access whose objectivity is secured by its conformity to third-person criteria.

The reference of a phenomenological term is fixed, then, by its immediate phenomenological quality, whose identification depends on its functional role. A given functional role might be occupied by different phenomenological qualities in different organisms—and conceivably there could be a system in which the same functional role was not occupied by a conscious experience at all. And my hypothesis is that when a functional role helps to fix the reference of a sensation term, the term refers to something whose immediate phenomenological quality and physiological basis are both essential properties of it, properties without which it could not exist.

This is parallel to the case of water. There could be a watery liquid ('behaviourally' indistinguishable from water) that wasn't the compound H_2O and therefore wasn't water; but in the world as it is, the essential gross properties of water are entailed by its being H_2O, and that is what water is. Similarly, it is conceivable that there could be a state functionally equivalent to pain in a mechanism with a completely different internal constitution, but if it were both physically and phenomenologically different, it would not be the same sensation. But in us, the behaviour that helps to fix the reference of 'pain' is produced by a state whose phenomenological and physiological properties are both essential, and that is what pain is.

So the proposal is that mental states would have a dual essence—phenomenological and physiological—but we still don't understand how this could be, since our modal intuitions go against it. In particular, we still have to deal with the apparent conceivability of an exact chemical-physiological-functional replica of a conscious human being that nevertheless has no subjective phenomenological 'interior' at all—a zombie, in current jargon. This is an illusion, according to the above proposal, but it still has to be dissolved. The task of defending a necessary connection between the physical and the phenomenological requires some account of how a connection that is in fact internal remains stubbornly external from the point of view of our understanding.

Colin McGinn gives a similar description of the situation in his essay, 'The Hidden Structure of Consciousness', though he puts it in terms of the distinction between the 'surface' of consciousness and its true nature, inaccessible to us either by introspection or by external observation:

My position is that the hidden structure of consciousness contains the machinery to lock consciousness firmly onto the physical world of brain and behaviour and environment, but that the surface of consciousness encourages us to believe that these links are merely contingent. When you cannot perceive (or conceive) necessary links you are apt to think there are not any, especially when you have racked your brains trying to discover them. This is a mistake, but a natural one. Cognitive closure with respect to necessary links is misinterpreted as contingency in those links.[15]

By 'the surface of consciousness' I take him to mean the way it appears from the first-person standpoint—whether we are experiencing our own or imagining someone else's. This seems to be both something we have a very clear grasp of and something logically quite unconnected with the physical workings of the brain, even though there are obviously causal connections. McGinn holds that both these appearances are illusory in a way we are prevented from seeing because we cannot get beneath the surface of consciousness.

---

[15] In *The Problem of Consciousness* (Blackwell, 1991): 106–7, n. 23.

V. WHAT'S WRONG WITH THE CONCEIVABILITY ARGUMENT

Though I believe McGinn is right about our present situation, I think we can advance beyond it once we acknowledge that our immediate first-person grasp on the phenomenology may be logically incomplete. But is that a real possibility? Perhaps our concepts of consciousness and the brain, while not containing full information about these two types of thing, are still adequate to allow us to know a priori that no necessary relation between them can be discovered no matter how much more we learn about their deeper constitutions. Perhaps the difference in type is such as to set limits on the paths along which fuller knowledge of the nature of these things can develop.

This is what seems forced on us by the clarity with which we appear to be able to conceive absolutely any physiological process existing unaccompanied by conscious experience. The vivid imaginability of zombie, resembling a conscious being only in its physical constitution, seems not to depend in any way on the details of that constitution. That is because conceiving that the system has no consciousness is completely independent of conceiving anything about its physical character. The latter is a conception of it from the outside, so to speak, as a spatio-temporal structure, whereas the former is a conception of it from the subjective point of view, as having no subjective 'inside' at all. The two types of conception are so completely unrelated that the first seems incapable of ruling out the second: all I have to do is imagine the physical system from the outside, and then imagine it from the inside—as not having any inside in the experiential sense. That is, I project my own point of view into the zombie, and imagine that there is nothing of that kind going on behind its eyes at all. What could be more clearly independent than these two conceptions?[16]

But it is just the radical difference between these modes of conceiving that may undermine the result. I want now to argue not directly for the necessary connection between mind and brain, but rather for the position that even if there were such a necessary connection, it would still appear through this kind of conceivability argument that there was not. The process of juxtaposing these two very different kinds of conception is inherently misleading.

In testing philosophical hypotheses by thought experiments, one should be wary of intuitions based on the first-person perspective, since they can easily create illusions of conceivability.[17] The zombie thought experiment clearly depends on the first-person perspective, because although it is an intuition about

---

[16] This argument has recently been given much prominence by David Chalmers; see *The Conscious Mind* (Oxford University Press, 1996). It was thinking about Chalmer's book that stimulated me to write the present essay. And while we come to very different conclusions, there is a great deal in his book with which I agree.

[17] See Sydney Shoemaker, 'The First-Person Perspective', in *The First-Person Perspective and Other Essays* (Cambridge University Press, 1996).

a being other than oneself, it depends on taking up that being's point of view in imagination—or rather, finding that it has no point of view that one can take up. In this case the very disparity between the two forms of conception that gives rise to the strong intuition of conceivability should make us suspicious. The absence of any conceptual connection when phenomena are grasped by such disparate concepts may conceal a deeper necessary connection that is not yet conceptual because not accessible to us by means of our present forms of thought.

I still think we can rely on such thought experiments to refute the most common types of *conceptual* reductionism. Even if there is some kind of entailment of the mental by the physical-functional, it is not analytic or definitional: there is no hidden conceptual contradiction in the description of a zombie—even if in reality a zombie is logically impossible. Our mental concepts do not, for example, exclude the possibility that mental states are states of an immaterial soul, and that there could be a fully functioning physical replica of a human body without a soul. As I have said, this does not rule out a conceptual link in the other direction—from the mental to the behavioural—on account of the public criteria for the application of mental concepts, which go with their distinctive first-person/third-person character. But while third-person criteria are necessary for the operation of mental concepts, they are not sufficient. In any case, those criteria are functional rather than physiological, and what I am talking about here is the relation between mental states and the brain, not between mental states and behaviour. Here there is no conceptual connection, and this tempts us to think that their separation is conceivable.

Let me try to say what is wrong with conceivability arguments against the necessity of the mind–brain relation. The following things seem prima facie conceivable which are pretty certainly impossible in a very strong sense, namely:

> (1) a living, behaving, physiologically and functionally perfect human organism that is nevertheless completely lacking in consciousness, i.e. a zombie;
> (2) a conscious subject with an inner mental life just like ours that behaves and looks just like a human being but has electronic circuitry instead of brains.

To repeat, I believe the apparent conceivability of these things reveals something about our present concepts but not about what is really possible. Analytic psychophysical reductionism is false, but there is independent reason to believe that these are not logical possibilities, and if so, our concepts are missing something. They don't lead to contradiction—it's not as bad as that—but they fail to reveal a logical impossibility.

Contrast these thought experiments with the a priori inconceivability of a number having parents. The latter involves a straightforward clash between concepts, not merely a disparity. No number could enter into the kind of biological relation with a predecessor that is a necessary condition of being a child of offspring. In that case we see a contradiction between the conditions of numberhood and the conditions of being the child of anything or anyone. In the relation of consciousness to the physical world, by contrast, our concepts fail to reveal a necessary connection, and we are tempted to conclude to the absence of any such connection. Our intuition is of a logical compatibility, not a logical incompatibility. We conceive the body from outside and the mind from inside, and see no internal connection, only an external one of correlation or perhaps causation. But in spite of the vividness of the intuition, I believe that it reflects our conceptual limitations rather than the truth. The difference between the modes of conception is so great that there is every reason to suspect that we would be unable to see an internal necessary connection even if there were one.

Conceivability and inconceivability are the main evidence we have for possibility and necessity, but they can be misleading, and conceivability that depends on the relation between first- and third-person reference is particularly treacherous terrain. The first-person view of our experiential states may reveal something that is not just contingently related to their physical basis, despite appearances. It may be that the physical description of the brain states associated with consciousness is an incomplete account of their essence—that it is merely the outside view of what we recognize from within as conscious experience. If anything like that is true, then our present conceptions of mind and body are radically inadequate to the reality, and do not provide us with adequate tools for a priori reasoning about them.

Suppose I try to think about all these relations with respect to the taste of the cigar I am now smoking. What I must do first is to regard the experience as a state of myself of whose subjective qualities I am immediately aware, which also has certain publicly observable functional relations to stimuli and discriminatory capacities. There is already a natural illusion of conceptual independence with respect to these latter relations, because they are concealed in my introspective identification of the experience—but this introspective identification is itself one of those mental acts that cannot be completely separated from its functional connections (for example the capacity to distinguish this taste from that of a cigarette). Recognizing this, I can see that the Cartesian thought-experiment of imagining myself having this experience without ever having had a body at all is an unreliable guide to what might really be the case. It depends on the concealment of the necessary conditions of reference of the phenomenological concept that I am employing to think about the experience. That is the point I take from Wittgenstein.

But now what of the relation between the experience and its physiological basis? Here I seem to be able to imagine either myself or someone else tasting exactly this flavour of cigar—and its having all the usual functional connections as well—although my brain or the other person's brain is in a completely different physiological state from the one it is actually in. Indeed it seems imaginable, though unlikely, that when I offer a friendly cigar to an exotic visitor from outer space who has a completely different physiology, it should taste the same to him. But here too the imagination is a poor guide to possibility, because it relies on an assumption of the completeness of the manifest conditions of reference of the concept (now taken to include functional as well phenomenological conditions).

The first thing to acknowledge is that if there were a necessary connection between the phenomenology and the physiology of tasting a cigar, it would not be evident a priori on the basis of the ordinary concept of that experience, since the possession of that concept involves no awareness of anything about the brain. It isn't just that, like the behavioural connections, the relation to the brain is *hidden from view* in my first-person use of the concept: the relation is completely absent from the concept, and cannot be retrieved by philosophical analysis. Nevertheless, if there is such a relation, having the full concept (including the first-person aspect) would require having a brain, indeed a brain with exactly the right physiological characteristics, and the brain would be directly involved in the act of imagination—though its involvement would be completely outside the range of my awareness in employing the concept. To imagine a mental state from the inside would be what I have elsewhere called an act of *sympathetic* imagination—putting myself in a conscious state *resembling* the thing imagined—and it would be impossible to do this without putting my brain in corresponding physical state.[18]

This shows that I cannot rely on the apparent imaginability of the separation of phenomenology and physiology to establish the contingency of the relation, since I can know in advance that this act of imagination would seem subjectively the same whether the relation was contingent or necessary. If the relation is necessary, then I have not really succeeded in imagining the phenomenology without the physiology. The imagination here is essentially ostensive, and I cannot point to one without pointing to the other.

If the relation is necessary, then someone is mistaken if he says, concentrating on his present sensation of tasting a cigar, 'I can conceive of *this* experience existing while my brain is in a very different state.' He is mistaken because he is actually referring, by 'this experience', to something that is at the same time a specific brain state. And *if* the relation is necessary, then someone is also mistaken who says, 'I can conceive of the brain state that is in fact the physical condition of my tasting the cigar as existing without any such sensation existing.' He is mistaken because he is actually referring, by 'the brain state . . .', to something that is at the same time the experience. He does not really succeed in detaching the one from the other in imagination, because he cannot demonstratively pick out either of them separately—even though the lack of visible connection between the two ways of picking out the same thing conceals this from him.

This does not show that the relation is necessary, but it does show that the

---

[18] See 'What Is It Like to Be a Bat?' (*Philosophical Review*, 1974; repr. in *Mortal Questions*, Cambridge University Press, 1979): n. 11. This was an earlier response to the modal argument against materialism. See also Christopher Hill, 'Imaginability, Conceivability, Possibility and the Mind-Body Problem', *Philosophical Studies* 87 (1995): 61–85.

familiar subjective thought experiment doesn't prove that the relation is contingent. It would come out the same way whether the relation was necessary or contingent.

VI. A NEW CONCEPT

How am I to form the conception that the relation might actually be necessary—as opposed to merely acknowledging that I can't discover a priori that it isn't? I have to think that these two ways of referring—by the phenomenological concept and the physiological concept—pick out a single referent, in each case rigidly, but that the logical link cannot be discovered by inspecting the concepts directly: rather it goes only through their common necessary link to the referent itself.

The idea would have to be, then, that there is a single event to which I can refer in two ways, both of them via concepts that apply to it non-contingently. One is the mental concept that I am able to acquire in both first- and third-person applications because I am a subject of this state, which has the special character of consciousness and introspective accessibility—the state of tasting a cigar. The other is a (so far unspecified) physiological concept that describes the relevant physical state of the brain. To admit the possibility of a necessary connection here, we would have to recognize that the mental concept as it now operates has nothing to say about the physiological conditions for its own operation, and then open up the concept to amplification by leaving a place for such a condition—a place that can be filled only a posteriori, by a theory of the actual type of event that admits these two types of access, internal and external, from within and from without. But this description of the task tells us nothing about how to carry it out.

What will be the point of view, so to speak, of such a theory? If we could arrive at it, it would render transparent the relation between mental and physical, not directly, but through the transparency of their common relation to something that is not merely either of them. Neither the mental nor the physical point of view will do for this purpose. The mental will not do because it simply leaves out the physiology, and has no room for it. The physical will not do because while it includes the behavioural and functional manifestations of the mental, this doesn't enable it, in view of the falsity of conceptual reductionism, to reach to the mental concepts themselves. The right point of view would be one which, contrary to present conceptual possibilities, included both subjectivity and spatio-temporal structure from the outset, all its descriptions implying both these things at once, so that it would describe inner states and their functional relations to behaviour and to one another from the phenomenological inside and the physiological outside simultaneously—not in parallel. The mental and physiological concepts and their reference to this same inner phenomenon would then be seen as secondary and each partial in its grasp of the phenomenon: each would be seen as referring to something that extends beyond its grounds of application.

Such a viewpoint cannot be constructed by the mere conjunction of the mental and the physical. It must be something genuinely new, otherwise it will not possess the necessary unity. It would have to be a new theoretical construction, realist in intention, and contextually defined as part of a theory that explained both the familiarly observable phenomenological and the physiological characteristics of these inner events. Its character would be determined by what it was introduced to explain—like the electromagnetic field, gravity, the atomic nucleus, or any other theoretical postulate. This could only be done with a truly general theory, containing real laws and not just dispositional definitions, otherwise the theoretical entity would not have independent reality.

If strict correlations are observed between a phenomenological and a physiological variable, the hypothesis would be not that the physiological state causes the phenomenological, but that there is a third term that entails both of them, but that is not defined as the mere conjunction of the other two. It would have to be a third type of variable, whose relation to the other two was not causal but constitutive. This third term should not leave anything out. It would have to be an X such that X's being a sensation and X's being a brain state both follow from the nature of X itself, independent of its relation to anything else.

Even though no transparent *and direct* explanatory connection is possible between the physiological and the phenomenological, but only an empirically established extensional correlation, we may hope and ought to try as part of a scientific theory of mind to form a third conception that does have direct transparently necessary connections with both the mental and the physical, and through which their actual necessary connection with one another can therefore become transparent to us. Such a conception will have to be created; we won't just find it lying around. A utopian dream, certainly: but all the great reductive successes in the history of science have depended on theoretical concepts, not natural ones—concepts whose whole justification is that they permit us to give reductive explanations.

But there is another objection—that such extravagance is unnecessary. Why wouldn't a theory be sufficient that systematically linked mental phenomena to their physical conditions without introducing any concepts of a new type? That is the approach favoured by John Searle, who maintains that a purely empirical theory would enable us to see that mental states are higher-order *physical* states of the brain, caused by lower-order physiological states to which they are not reducible.[19] Searle, too, wants to avoid dualism without resorting to functionalist reductionism, but I don't think his way of doing it succeeds. The problem is that so long as the mental states remain characteristically subjective and radically emergent, there is no basis for describing them as physical, or physically constituted.

[19] See *The Rediscovery of the Mind* (MIT Press, 1992).

This is not just a verbal point. The mental–physical distinction cannot be abolished by fiat. I agree with Searle that the correct approach to the mind–body problem must be essentially biological, not functional or computational. But his proposal is still, as I understand it, too dualistic: in relating the physiological and the mental as cause and effect, it does not explain how each is literally impossible without the other. A causal theory of radically emergent higher-order properties would not show how mind arises from matter by necessity. That is the price of sticking with our existing mental and physical concepts.

The inadequacy of those concepts is revealed by their incapacity to display a necessary connection that obviously must exist. Only new concepts that turn the connection into a conceptual one can claim to grasp the phenomena in their basic nature.

Clearly not just any concept that we can create, which has both mental and physical implications, would reveal a necessary connection between the two. In some cases, we will only have created a conjunctive concept, relative to which the two categories are analytically, but not necessarily, connected. For example, even if Cartesian dualism were true, we could introduce the concept of a human being as the combination of a body and soul. In that case there would be one thing, a human being, whose existence entails both mental and physical characteristics, but that would not mean that one can't exist without the other, any more than the concept of a ham sandwich shows that bread can't exist without ham.

What is the difference between these purely conjunctive, analytic connections, and the more metaphysically robust type of concept that reveals true necessity? Physical science is full of examples of the latter. The clearest are found in the atomic theory of matter. The hypothesis that familiar substances are composed of invisibly small particles, whose motion is responsible for the observable manifestations of temperature and pressure, made it possible to see that the positive correlation between changes in temperature and pressure of a gas at constant volume was not a contingent but a necessary connection. Likewise the chemical analysis of air, and of fire as rapid oxidation, reveals it to be a necessary truth that a fire will go out if enclosed in a small airtight space. The postulation of electromagnetic fields, similarly, made it possible to see many previously mysterious correlations, such as the capacity of a moving magnet to induce an electric current, as necessary consequences of the nature of the component phenomena— though in this case the new concept requires a greater leap from pre-scientific intuition than the direct analogy with the familiar part–whole relation that yields atomism.

One of the things that is true in these cases is that the 'single' postulated underlying phenomenon explains the manifestations of each of the superficially distinct phenomena in a way that makes it impossible to separate the explanation of the one from the explanation of the other. The very same atomic (or molecular) agitation that accounts for increased pressure against the walls of the container accounts for increased temperature of the gas within. The process of oxidation that constitutes the fire eventually binds all the free oxygen in the airtight container, thus entailing its own termination. So the new account of the correlated phenomena makes their separability no longer conceivable.[20]

In addition, the postulated underlying basis explains more things than it was introduced to explain. Atomic theory was the avenue to the endless developments of chemistry; the theory of electromagnetism led vastly beyond the curious phenomena of lodestones and electrostatic charge from which it began. It is clear that such postulates cannot be analysed in terms of the manifestations on the basis of which they were introduced, since they imply so much more that is not implied by those manifestations themselves. For all these reasons, the unification accomplished by such concept formation is not merely verbal, or conjunctive. It is the genuine discovery that things that appeared distinct and only contingently correlated are in fact, in virtue of their true nature, necessarily connected.

So the discovery of a genuinely unifying, rather than conjunctive, basis for the relation between mind and body would require the postulation of something that accounted for them both in terms of the same activity, or properties, or structure, or whatever. And its reality would be confirmed if it could also account for things other than those it had been postulated to explain or their direct implications— other, previously unremarked psychophysical correlations, for example. That would require more than an inference from observed correlations to psychophysical laws that in turn predict further correlations. It would mean finding something that entailed such laws as the logically necessary consequence of its essential nature.

It is a real question whether there is something already present in our current concepts of mental and physical—some unbridgeable gulf—that precludes their both being accounted for in the requisite unified way by a common basis. The atomistic method, of accounting for a property of the whole by explaining all its physical manifestations in terms of the activities of the parts, is not sufficient here, because there is more to be explained than the observable physical manifestations of mental processes

Merely adding phenomenological qualities to brain states as an extra property is not enough, since it would imply that the same brain state might exist without that property. It has to follow from what these states really *are* that they have both these types of properties. If we are going to take reduction in physics and chemistry as our logical model, we have to recognize, as was explained earlier, that the necessary identity of water with H_2O or fire with oxidation or heat with molecular motion depends on another necessary connection. It requires that the manifest properties by which we pre-scientifically identify water or fire or heat must be explained without residue, and in their essential respects strictly entailed, by the reducing account. This upward entailment—that all the distinguishing marks of

---

[20] Given the character of modern physics, all these necessities have to understood probabilistically. See n. 3 above.

heat are in fact exhaustively explained by molecular motion—is essential for the validity of the downward entailment—that heat is identical with molecular motion and cannot exist without it. The only way we can discover that heat *is* molecular motion—so that if something felt the same to us but was not molecular motion it would not be heat—is to discover that in our world the actual complete account of the features by which we identify heat pre-theoretically is given in terms of molecular motion, and that this account is complete in the sense that it entails what is essential in those features.

In the mind-body case, there is no direct entailment in either direction between the phenomenological and the physiological, and at present we don't have the concept of a third type of state or process that would entail both the phenomenological and the physiological features of an experiential episode like tasting chocolate. But that is what would be required to warrant the conclusion that tasting chocolate had this physiological character necessarily, or vice versa. Only if we discovered such an actual common basis would be able to say that a zombie is impossible, as water that is H_2O is impossible, or fire that is not oxidation.

If we did discover such a thing, it would perhaps still be conceivable that something should look outwardly like a living human being with a functioning brain but not have consciousness. But such a system would have to be constituted out of different material, and would therefore not, despite appearances, be a physical duplicate of a human body, merely lacking consciousness. On the supposition that in us, the psychophysical connection is necessary, the brain of such a creature could not be made of what our brains are made of, and would be similar only in its external appearance—just as there might be a different colourless, odourless, tasteless liquid that was not H_2O and therefore not water.[21]

---

[21] This leaves us with a further question. Suppose we did discover such a common basis. Would there not then be an analogue, for the zombie case, of the possibility of another liquid that resembles water in its manifest qualities, but that is not water because it is not H_2O? Can we imagine something like that with respect to consciousness and the brain?

The question has two parts. First, even if our conscious states were in fact brain states couldn't we imagine a different physical system that to external observation resembled a human being in all behavioural and physiological and chemical respects, but consisted of intrinsically different material that lacked consciousness? Second, couldn't we imagine a different conscious subject with experience that subjectively resembled human pain, but that was not pain because it was not a brain state but, say, a state of an immaterial soul?

I believe that in both of these cases, unlike the water case, there is no reason to think that we have imagined any possibility at all. Even if such alternative systems were possible, our use of our own imagination of the presence or absence of subjective experience could give us no evidence of it. If the connection between our minds and our brains is indeed necessary, then our imagination provides no way of peeling off the experience from its physical embodiment, or vice versa. We have no way of conceiving of the presence or absence of the purely mental features of experience by themselves. By contrast, we do have a way of conceiving of the presence or absence of the perceptual appearances of water by themselves, since those appearances involve a relation to something else, namely the perceiver.

VII. UNDER MIND

I have described these conditions for the existence of a necessary connection between phenomenology and physiology very abstractly. They do not yet offer any suggestion of what kind of concept might entail both, and thus reveal their common foundation. It would have to be the concept of something that in its essence has, and cannot fail to have, both a subjective inside and a physical outside.

Let me at last, after this very long wind-up, offer a more specific but entirely speculative conjecture. I suggest that we take the macroscopic relation between mental processes and their behavioural manifestations, which I have said is conceptual but not necessary, as a rough model for a deeper psychophysical connection that *is* necessary—pushing embodiment inward, so to speak. The gross and manifest relations between consciousness and behaviour would thus be reinterpreted as a rough indicator of something much tighter in the interior of the brain, that can be discovered only by scientific inference, and that explains the manifest relations in virtue of its usual links to the rest of the body. Perhaps, for example, the reason for the relation between pain and avoidance at the level of the organism is that at a deeper physiological level, the state that generates the appropriate observable behaviour in an intact organism by the mediation of nerves, muscles, and tendons is an essentially subjective state of the brain with an *unmediated, non-contingent* 'behavioural expression' of its own.

We have to consider whether this pushing down of the relation between mind and its behavioural manifestations makes sense–whether there could be a tighter version of this relation below the level of the whole organism. Well, to begin with the first level down, these relations should certainly be reflected in some form in the case of a separated but still operating brain—the classic imaginary 'brain in a vat'—deprived of its body but still receiving inputs and producing outputs, and functioning internally otherwise like an embodied brain. Its mental states (I assume it would have mental states) would bear a relation to its purely electronic inputs and outputs analogous to those of a normal person to perceptual inputs and behavioural outputs—but without the contingency due to dependence on the usual external connections.

The next question is whether the same is true of half brains. In the case of individuals with brain damage, or those with split brains, each functioning cerebral hemisphere seems to interact with the brain stem in a way that expresses behaviourally the somewhat reduced conscious activity associated with the partial brain. I believe the remarkable split-brain results have a philosophical significance that has not been sufficiently appreciated.[22] They show that both the brain and the mind are in some sense composed of parts, and that those parts are simultaneously physical

---

[22] I have discussed those results in 'Brain Bisection and the Unity of Consciousness', (*Synthese*, 1971; repr. in *Mortal Questions*, Cambridge University Press, 1979).

and mental systems, which can to some extent preserve their dual nature when separated. In an intact brain, the two halves do not lead distinct conscious lives: they support a single consciousness. But the fact that each of them can support a distinct consciousness when separated seems to show that the normal unified consciousness is composed of mental parts embodied in the physical parts. These parts are 'mental' in a derivative but nonetheless real sense.

If this phenomenon of composition can be seen to exist at the gross level of bisection, it makes sense to conjecture that it may be carried further, and that some form of more limited psychophysical unity may exist in smaller or more specialized subparts of the system, which in ordinary circumstances combine to form a conscious being of the familiar kind, but may also in some cases be capable of existing and functioning separately. The strategy would be to try to push down into the interior of the brain the supposition of states loosely resembling ordinary mental states in that they combine constituents of subjective mental character (in an extended sense) with behavioural or functional manifestations—with the difference that here the 'behaviour' would be internal to the brain, rather than being mediated by links to the body—an intrinsic, non-contingent feature of the state rather than a relation to something outside of it.

Such hypothetical subparts of consciousness would not be subjectively imaginable to us. They would be subjective only in the sense that they are inherently capable of combining to constitute full states of consciousness in an intact organism, even though they have no independent consciousness when they are so combined, and may or may not have independent consciousness when they occur separately. The compositional character of consciousness is evident not only from bisected brains but from the description of people with the sort of brain damage that causes behaviourally spectacular and subjectively alien mental changes. Certain cases of agnosia are like this, as when a person can pick a pen out of a group of objects if asked to do so, but can't say, if shown a pen, what it is, and can't show how it is used—though he can when he touches it. This is due to some cut between the visual, tactile, and speech centres, and it isn't really imaginable from the inside to those who don't suffer from it.[23]

A theory of the basis of the mental–physical link might begin from the component analysis suggested by the deconnection syndromes. Some such pushing down of the link to a level lower than that of the person is necessary to get beyond brute emergence or supervenience. Even if crude spatial divisions are only part of the story, they might be a beginning. More global but functionally specialized psychophysical subsystems might follow. The conceptual point is that both the mind and the brain may be composed of the same subsystems, which are essentially both physical and mental, and some variants of which are to be found in other conscious organisms as well.

---

[23] See Norman Geschwind, 'Disconnexion Syndromes in Animals and Man', *Brain* 88 (1965) for extensive discussion of such disorders.

The idea of a third type of phenomenon which is the real nature of these processes is easier to grasp if one thinks of the mental aspect as irreducibly real but not subjectively imaginable from an ordinary complete human viewpoint. It must be conceived by inference from what can be observed—inference precisely to what is needed to explain those observations. Since such constituents would be inferred to explain simultaneously both the physiological and the phenomenological data, they would not be classifiable in the old style either as physical or as mental. We would have to regard their physical combinations, which we could observe both behaviourally and physiologically, as providing only a partial view of them.

The reason to seek such a compositional theory is that it seems one possible way and perhaps the only way to give content to the idea of a necessary connection between the physiological and the mental. Though I'm not sure of the status of this assumption, it seems clear to me that any necessary connection must be a matter of detail, and not just global. The necessary connection between two things as complex as a creature's total mental state and its total physiological state must be a consequence of something more fundamental and systematic. We can't form the conception of a necessary connection in such a case just by stipulating that they are both essential features of a single state. The inseparability must be the logical consequence of something simpler to avoid being a mere constant conjunction that provides evidence of necessity without revealing it. Necessity requires reduction, because in order to see the necessity we have to trace it down to a level where the explanatory properties are simply the defining characteristics of certain basic constituents of the world.

Our ordinary sensation concepts paint these states with a broad brush. We all know that in our own case there is much more detail, both phenomenological and physiological, than we can describe in ordinary language. The systematic though imprecise relation at the level of the organism between mind and behaviour is captured by ordinary mental concepts, but it is only the rough and macroscopic manifestation of objective lawlike conditions that must lie much deeper. And the detailed macroscopic relation between mind and brain is necessary, though it appears contingent, because it is the consequence of the non-contingent physiological manifestations of component states at a submental level.

This hypothesis invites several questions. First, would the states I am imagining at the basic level really be unified, rather than raising again the question of the relation between their mental and physical aspects? Second, can we really make sense of the idea of each mind being composed of submental parts? Third, what is the relation between the physicality of these submental processes and the account of what happens in the brain in terms of physics and chemistry alone?

The first question requires us to distinguish a manifestation of a property that is truly essential, revealing an internal, non-contingent relation, from one that is due to a merely contingent, external relation.

All our working concepts require that there be some form of generally available access to what they refer to, and that means that any concept of a type of process or substance, or of a property, mental or physical, will refer to something that is systematically connected to other things, allowing different people from their different points of view to get a handle on it. This is the grain of truth in verificationism. It is true whether the property is liquidity or heat or painfulness. There are no natural kinds without systematic connections to other natural kinds.[24] All properties that we can think about have to be embedded in a web of connections, and I suspect that this is even true of properties we can't think about, because it is part of our general concept of a property.

Sometimes the properties that permit us to make contact with a natural kind are external, contingent properties. This, I have said, is true of the ordinary behavioural manifestations of mental states that permit us to have public mental concepts. It is also true of the manifest properties by which we fix the reference of many other natural kind terms. But the closer we get to the thing itself, the more unmediated will be its manifestations, its effects, and its relations to certain other things. Eventually we arrive at effects that are directly entailed by the essential properties of the natural kind itself. The mass and charge of a proton, for example, without which it would not be a proton, have strict consequences for its relations to other particles, similarly specified. Even in describing radically counterfactual situations we have to suppose these essential relations preserved in order to be sure we are talking about the same property or thing.

Let us look more closely at the familiar physical case. The manifest properties of ordinary physical objects—their shape, size, weight, colour, and texture, for example—already have necessary consequences for their interactions with other things whose properties are specified with sufficient precision. The properties are not reducible to these external relations, but the consequences are not merely contingent. An object simply would not weigh one pound if it did not affect a scale in the appropriate way, in the absence of countervailing forces. But all these necessary connections at the gross level have implications for the type of analysis at the level of physical theory that can reveal more fully the intrinsic nature of such an object. An analysis in terms of microscopic components, however strange and sophisticated its form, must in some way preserve these necessary external relations of the properties of the manifest object. The properties of the parts may be different—a crude mechanistic atomism, while a natural presocratic speculation, has proved too simple—but they must have their own necessary consequences for interaction with other things, of a kind that in combination will imply the relational properties of the larger entity which they compose. However far we get from the manifest world of perception and common sense, that link must not

---

[24] This position is much more fully and precisely expressed and defended by Sydney Shoemaker in his remarkable paper, 'Causality and Properties', in *Identity, Cause and Mind: Philosophical Essays* (Cambridge University Press, 1984), with which I agree entirely. He also points out that it is a consequence of the view, fully worked out, that causal necessity is a species of logical necessity.

be broken. The properties of quarks and their relations explain the properties of atoms and their relations, which in turn explain the properties of molecules and their relations, which in turn explain the properties of more familiar substances and processes and their relations.

Something similar is needed if our starting point is not the manifest world of inanimate physical objects, but the world of conscious creatures. In a case like thirst, for example, the subjective quality and the functional role are already internally connected in the ordinary concept. It is the concept of a phenomenological state that has physical manifestations. The details remain unspecified; the full intrinsic character of the state has to be discovered. But the ordinary concept already contains, in rough form, an idea of the kind of state it is—just as an ordinary substance concept like water already contains, in rough form, an idea of the kind of thing it is, setting the possible paths to further detailed discovery of its true nature, which have led to the development of physics and chemistry.

The analogue of a presocratic speculation of psychic atoms that are just like animals, only smaller, is not even a starter in this case, because we don't have ready a coherent idea of larger conscious subjects being composed of smaller ones—as we did have the perfectly clear geometrical idea of larger physical objects or processes being composed of smaller ones. But the more abstract idea of a form of analysis of conscious organisms whose elements will preserve in stricter form the relation between mental reality and behaviour should constrain and guide the development of any reductive theory in this domain. There must be some kind of strict inner–outer link at more basic levels that can account for the far looser and more complicated inner–outer link at the level of the organism. And of course the idea would have to include a completely new theory of composition—of mental parts and wholes.

My conjecture is that the relation between conscious states and behaviour, roughly captured in the way ordinary mental concepts function, is a manifest but superficial and contingent version of the truth, that truth being that the active brain is the scene of a system of subpersonal processes which combine to constitute both its total behavioural and its phenomenological character, and each of which is itself a version of a 'mental-behavioural' relation that is not contingent but necessary because it is not mediated by anything.

This differs from traditional functionalism, coupled with an account of the physiological realization of functional states, in that the 'realization' here envisioned is to be not merely physiological, but in some sense mental all the way down—something that accounts for the phenomenology as well. The combination of these postulated processes would entail at more complex levels not only the observable behaviour and functional organization but the conscious mental life conceptually related but not reducible to it. We are looking for a realization not just of functional states but of mental states in the full sense, and that means the realization cannot be merely physiological. The reductive basis must preserve, in broad terms, the logical character of the mental processes being reduced. That is just as true here as it is in reductions of purely physical substances, processes, or forces.

So I suggest that the problem of adequate unity in the inferred explanatory concept—the problem of how it can avoid being a mere conjunction of the phenomenological and the physiological—can be addressed by seeing it as a purification of the ordinary concept of mind, with the sources of contingency in the mental–behavioural connection gradually removed as we close in on the thing itself. States of this kind, if they exist, could be identified only by theoretical inference; they would not be definable as the conjunction of independently identifiable mental and physical components.

I said there were three questions about the proposal. The second was how we could conceive of a single mind resulting from the combination of subpersonal components. On that issue, we have very few data to go on, only the split-brain cases. Further experiments to investigate the results of combining parts of different conscious nervous systems would be criminal if carried out on human subjects—the only kind who would be able to tell us about the experiential results. (There's a piece of science fiction for you.) But the contents of an animal mind are complex enough so that the idea of composition seems a fairly natural one—though who knows what kinds of 'parts' the combinable components might be. We certainly can't expect them in general to be anatomically separable. The now common habit of thinking in terms of mental modules is a crude beginning, but it might lead somewhere, and might join naturally with the creation of concepts of the sort I am suggesting, which entail both physiology and phenomenology. The real conceptual problems would come in trying to describe elements or factors of subjectivity too basic to be found as identifiable parts of conscious experience. I will not try to say more about compositionality at this point.

The third question was about the relation between explanation employing such concepts and such a theory on the one hand, and traditional, purely physical explanation on the other. The idea is that such a theory would explain both the phenomenology and the physiology by reference to a more fundamental level at which their internal relation to one another was revealed. But wouldn't that require that there be no account of the physical interactions of a conscious organism with its environment, and of its internal physical operation, in terms of the laws of physics and chemistry alone? Whether or not such an account is possible, the denial of its possibility would certainly seem too strong a claim to want to harness to any hypothesis of the kind I am suggesting.

My quick response to this question is that there is no reason to think that the explanations referring to this psychophysical level need conflict with purely physical explanations of the purely physical features of the same phenomena, any more than explanations in terms of physics have to conflict with explanations in terms of chemistry. If there is a type of description which entails both the mental and the physical, it can be used to explain more than what a purely physical theory can explain, but it should also leave intact those explanations that need to refer only to the physical. If there are special problems here, they have to do with the compatibility between psychological and physical explanations of action, and freedom of the will. Those problems are serious, but they are not, I think, made any more serious by a proposal of this kind, whereby the relation between the mental and the psychological is necessary rather than contingent. Indeed, such a proposal would probably dispose of one problem, that of double causation, since it would imply that at a deeper level the distinction between mental and physical causes disappears.

VIII. UNIVERSAL MIND

All this is speculation of the most extravagant kind, but not for that reason imper-missible. Armchair proto-science as the philosophical formulation of possibilities is an indispensable precondition of empirical science, and with regard to the mind-body problem we are not exactly awash in viable possibilities.[25] I have described in abstract terms the logical character of a different theory and different concepts. Their creation, if possible at all, would have to be based on empirical research and theoretical invention. But one feature such a theory should have that is of the first importance is a universality that extends to all species of conscious life, and is not limited to the human. That just seems to me to be common sense about how the world works. The mind-brain relation in us must be an example of something quite general, and any account of it must be part of a more general theory. That concep-tion ought to govern us even if we have to start with humans and creatures very like them in gathering evidence on which to base such a theory.

This has an important consequence for the basic theoretical terms it will employ, the terms which entail both the phenomenological and the physiological descriptions of inner states. They must be understood to imply that experiences have a subjective character, without necessarily allowing the theorist to fully understand the specific subjective character of the experiences in question—since those experiences may be of a type that he himself cannot undergo or imagine, and of which he cannot therefore acquire the full first- and third-person mental concepts. The terms will therefore have to rely, in their full generality, a good deal on what I have elsewhere[26] called 'objective phenomenology'—structural features like quality spaces that can be understood and described as aspects of a type of subjective point of view without being fully subjectively imaginable except by those who can share that point of view.

---

[25] See 'Philosophical Naturalism', Michael Friedman's presidential address to the Central Division of the American Philosophical Association, *Proceedings and Addresses of the Ameri-can Philosophical Association*, 71(2) (1997) 7–21.

[26] In 'What Is It Like to Be a Bat?'

If such a theory is ever developed, the reason for believing in the reality of what it postulates, like the reason for believing in the reality of any other theoretical entities, will be inference to the best explanation. The relation between phenomenology and physiology demands an explanation; no explanation of sufficient transparency can be constructed within the circle of current mental and physical concepts themselves; so an explanation must be sought which introduces new concepts and gives us knowledge of real things we didn't know about before. We hypothesize that there are things having the character necessary to provide an adequate explanation of the data, and their real existence is better confirmed the wider the range of data the hypothesis can account for. But they must be hypothesized as an explanation of the mental and the physical data taken together, for there will be no reason to infer them from physiological and behavioural data alone. As Jeffrey Gray observes,

The reason the problem posed by consciousness seems so acute, at least to non-functionalists, is the following: nothing that we know so far about behaviour, physiology, the evolution of either behaviour or physiology, or the possibilities of constructing automata to carry out complex forms of behaviour is such that the hypothesis of consciousness would arise if it did not occur in addition as a datum in our own experience; nor, having arisen, does it provide a useful explanation of the phenomena observed in those domains.[27]

The most radical thing about this conjecture is the idea that there is something more fundamental than the physical—something that explains both the physical and the mental. How can the physical be explained by anything but the physical? And don't we have ample evidence that all that needs to be postulated to get ever-deeper explanations of physical phenomena is just more physics? However, I am not proposing that we look for a theory that would displace or conflict with physical explanation of the ordinary sort—any more than it would conflict with ordinary psychological explanation of actions or mental events. Clearly the processes and entities postulated by such a theory would have to conform to physical law. It's just that there would be more to them than that. What reveals itself to external observation as the physiological operation of the brain, in conformity with physical law, would be seen to be something of which the physical characteristics were one manifestation and the mental characteristics another—one being the manifestation to outer sense and the other the manifestation to inner sense, to adapt Kant's terminology.

This leaves open the question of the level and type of organization at which the stuff becomes not just dead matter but actually conscious: its mental potentialities might be completely inert in all but very special circumstances. Still, it would have to explain the mental where it appears, and in a way that also explains the systematic connections between the mental and the physical and the coexistence

---

[27] Jeffrey A. Gray, 'The contents of consciousness: A neuropsychological conjecture', *Behavioral and Brain Sciences* 18 (1995): 660.

of mental and physical explanations, as in the case of thought and action. And this conception would, if it were correct, provide a fuller account of the intrinsic nature of the brain than either a phenomenological or a physiological description, or the conjunction of the two.

To describe the logical characteristics of such a theory is not to produce it. That would require the postulation of specific theoretical structures defined in terms of the laws governing their physical and mental implications, experimentally testable and based on sufficiently precise knowledge of the extensional correlations between physical and mental phenomena. The path into such a theory would presumably involve the discovery of systematic structural similarities between physiological and phenomenological processes, leading eventually to the idea of a single structure that is both, and it would have to be based on vastly more empirical information than we have now.

Previous efforts at reduction have been too external and in a sense too conservative. We need a conceptual creation that makes conceivable what at present is inconceivable, so it won't be possible to imagine such a theory properly before it is produced. But it won't be possible even to look for an answer unless we have an incomplete conception of it in advance, as a goal. That requires the willingness to contemplate the idea of a single natural phenomenon that is in itself, and necessarily, both subjectively mental and objectively physical.

It would have to be graspable by us, and therefore would have to be formulated in terms of a model that we could work with, to accommodate psychophysical data that we do not yet have. But it would not be simply an extension of our existing ideas of mind and matter, because those ideas do not contain within themselves the possibility of a development though which they 'meet'. I have suggested one possible form of an approach that would permit such convergence.

No such development will permit us to transcend the division between subjective and objective standpoints. The aim is rather to integrate them all the way to the bottom of our world view, in such a way that neither is subordinate to other. This means that what Bernard Williams calls the 'absolute' conception of reality[28] will not be a physical conception, but something richer that entails both the physical and the mental. To the extent that we could arrive at it, it would describe subjective experience in terms that imply its subjectivity without necessarily relying on our capacity to undergo or fully imagine experiences of that type. That means that our grasp of such an absolute conception will inevitably be incomplete. Still, it would include more than a purely physical description of reality.

Whatever unification of subjective points of view and complex physical structures may be achieved, each of us will still be himself, and will conceive of other perspectives by means of sympathetic imagination as far as that can reach, and by extrapolation from imagination beyond that. The difference between the inside and the outside view will not disappear. For each of us, the site and origin of his

[28] Bernard Williams, *Descartes* (Penguin Books, 1978).

conception of the world as a unified physical-phenomenological system will always be the particular creature that he himself is, and therefore the conception will have a centred shape that is at variance with its centreless content. But that need not prevent us from developing that content in a way that captures the evident unity of what in our own case we can experience both from within and from without.

Index